KU-543-770

Philosophies of Social Science

THE CLASSIC AND CONTEMPORARY READINGS

Edited by Gerard Delanty and Piet Strydom

Open University Press
Maidenhead · Philadelphia

Open University Press
McGraw-Hill Education
McGraw-Hill House
Shoppenhangers Road
Maidenhead
Berkshire
England
SL6 2QL

email: enquiries@openup.co.uk
world wide web: www.openup.co.uk

and

325 Chestnut Street
Philadelphia, PA 19106, USA

First published 2003

Copyright © Gerard Delanty and Piet Strydom 2003

All rights reserved. Except for the quotation of short passages for the purposes of criticism and review, no part of this publication may be reproduced, stored in a retrieval system, or transmitted, in any form or by any means, electronic, mechanical, photocopying, recording or otherwise, without the prior permission of the publisher or a licence from the Copyright Licensing Agency Limited. Details of such licences (for reprographic reproduction) may be obtained from the Copyright Licensing Agency Ltd of 90 Tottenham Court Road, London, W1P 0LP.

A catalogue record of this book is available from the British Library

ISBN 0 335 20884 3 (pb) 0 335 20885 1 (hb)

The Library of Congress data for this book has been applied for from the Library of Congress

Typeset by RefineCatch Limited, Bungay, Suffolk
Printed in Great Britain by Biddles Ltd, *www.biddles.co.uk*

Contents

Preface and acknowledgements

The aim of this reader is to attempt to map out systematically the field of the philosophy of social science as viewed from the perspective of the early twenty-first century. It contains key extracts from the classic and contemporary works dealing with questions of epistemology, methodology and knowledge in social science raised in the course of the twentieth century. The field has undergone drastic transformation, especially during the second half of the twentieth century, and as a consequence a range of approaches are competing with one another today, none of which can claim to be the leader. We are convinced, however, that the way in which the selected texts in this book are brought together indicates the broad direction in which the field is currently moving.

The book is the outcome of collaboration between two social scientists, more specifically sociologists, both of whom have a long-standing shared interest in the philosophy of social science. Practical and pedagogical considerations served as the initial motivation for the collection of the readings. None of the relatively few available anthologies succeed in covering the diversity and range of issues and currents that we regard as necessary for the purposes of teaching courses on the philosophy and methodology of social science in the twenty-first century. On the one hand, therefore, this reader can be regarded as a volume complementing Gerard Delanty's *Social Science: Beyond Constructivism and Realism* (1997) by providing the necessary textual backup for the arguments developed there. On the other hand, however, the present volume also pursues some of the major currents and developments further than was possible in that book. This is particularly true of the rejuvenated cognitive current in the social sciences in which Piet Strydom has been interested for some time. In so far as it goes beyond its companion volume, the present book involves more than just an exercise in fulfilling practical and pedagogical needs. It was also undertaken out of friendship and the furthering of our own closely related and overlapping concerns. However, we avoided imposing these concerns of ours too strongly on the selection of the texts in order to encourage discussion through the presentation of contrasting positions and allow glimpses of the complexity of the issues.

As in editing any collection of readings, we have had to be selective. The readings chosen have been taken for their classic status and for being representative of major developments in the philosophy of social science. The approach that has been adopted is largely historical and thematic in that the selected readings illustrate the emergence and transformation of the philosophy of social science in the twentieth century around major debates. Four organizing principles have shaped the volume, namely: major authors, key works, thematic concerns and historical narrative.

The readings have also been selected with a view to being representative of the major schools of thought, including American and European trends as well as approaches that are often excluded from the mainstream traditions.

The readings are mostly short extracts from larger works and are therefore to be read in the light of their incompleteness. We have avoided unnecessary editing, but in many cases some work had to be done to make the readings presentable. Breaks in the text are indicated by dots. Footnotes and references have in most cases been eliminated. The interested reader is advised to use these extracts as an initial entry to the works and not as a substitute for the complete work. The guide to further reading (see p. 468) gives an overview of just some of the relevant literature available. We have confined this to general texts. The extensive introduction to each part will, we hope, provide the reader with the necessary background on the readings and authors as well as on the thematic rationale.

All readings, with the exception of those by Jon Elster, Ian Hacking and Steve Fuller in Part 6, have been previously published. In addition to these authors, we are grateful to the large number of other authors and publishers for granting permission to republish parts of their publications. The details of permissions and rights are listed on the first page of each extract as a footnote, where the source of the extract is also identified.

Every effort has been made to find the owners of copyright of material published in this volume. In some cases this has been impossible. The editors and publishers would be pleased to hear from any copyright owners we have been unable to trace.

The editors are grateful for advice from many sources, especially from four advisers consulted by the publishers at the initial stage, and Justin Vaughan and Miriam Selwyn at Open University Press. They would also like to express their thanks to Jonathan Ingoldby, for his careful copy-editing, and to William Outhwaite and Steve Seidman for reading an earlier version of the typescript. The editors alone bear responsibility for any errors in this book.

Gerard Delanty
and Piet Strydom

INTRODUCTION
What is the philosophy of social science?

Philosophy and social science

The subject domain of the philosophy of the social sciences is a broad one and one that is not easily defined in either philosophical or social scientific terms. Strictly speaking, it is a branch of the discipline of philosophy, and in that sense comparable to political philosophy, social philosophy or the philosophy of science. But philosophy, especially in so far as its reaches into social and political concerns, enters uncertain territory and it is doubtful that the philosophy of social science can exist exclusively as a rigorously philosophical endeavour, and a branch of pure philosophy. This is more true today than in the past. Many of the traditional concerns of philosophy have been taken over by the social sciences and, in the view of many, sociology is the inheritor of philosophy. On the other hand, it is hard to see how philosophy could be completely incorporated by the social sciences. The question of the relation of the philosophy of social science to the actual practice of social science generally, is therefore, a contested one and will in all probability continue to be debated.

For our purpose, the philosophy of social science is a reflexive activity. Reflexivity in this sense is an activity of a different order than the actual practice of social science itself. But since there are degrees of reflexivity, it is important to clarify the different usages. We find three broad conceptions of philosophy of social science, each embodying a different degree of reflexivity, with the first having the weakest commitment to reflexivity and the third the strongest:

1   According to one model, reflection on scientific activity can be conceived as a second order activity which specifies how science ought to be done. This is a prescriptive activity that offers an essentially normative vision of how social science should be conducted. In this view, the philosophy of social science is a secondary activity for which philosophers are responsible. For the proponents of this stance, the philosophy of social science is not different from the philosophy of science, of which it is a sub-area. The legislative role philosophy plays in this conception of the philosophy of social science roughly mirrors the broader subordination of the social sciences to the natural sciences. Thus, many of the leading

proponents of this traditional kind of philosophy of social science were positivists, generally of the hypothetico-deductive (Popper) or deductive-nomological (Hempel) school of thought and, moreover, were primarily philosophers of science. There were some exceptions. A famous one was Peter Winch, who wrote a highly influential work on the philosophy of social science arguing that it is only philosophers who could give social science a normative direction, which for him required a departure from the natural sciences. Despite this difference, we can say that many philosophers of social science in the first half of the twentieth century saw themselves as directing social science from the discipline of philosophy, which could serve as a mirror of truth. The kind of reflexivity implicit in this way of thinking was thus closer to reflection than the more transformative and critical notion of reflexivity that has surfaced today.

2   A second position emerged *within* social science as a reaction to the first prescriptive or legislative model. It has generally been associated with the hermeneutical tradition but is perhaps more explicit in the critical tradition. Since Max Weber, many leading social scientists advocated a specifically *social* science epistemology, seeing the philosophy of social science as something that goes on within social science and for which philosophers are not responsible. For example, Norbert Elias and Pierre Bourdieu, to mention just two notable names, always resisted the role of philosophers in epistemological and methodological debates specific to social science. Thus, for many 'philosophers' of social science, social science does not need to look to philosophers to achieve reflexivity and to reflect on the practice of social science. Indeed, many famous social scientists – for instance, Alfred Schutz – were social philosophers but whose ideas were derivative of developments specific to social science. In this tradition, the reflexivity of social science is to be attributed to the fact that social science is closer to its object of research than are the experimental and natural sciences and, moreover, the philosophy of social science is now a practice associated with social theorists who reflect on social science from within the social science disciplines. The resistance to pure philosophy goes back to Marx's famous statement of the 'end of philosophy' and the coming of a more engaged relation of knowledge to practice. Despite the differences from the first model, in this second one philosophical reflection on social science is essentially epistemological – that is, concerned with the nature and status of scientific knowledge.

3   According to another model, which is closely related to the second model but which we believe is the more influential one today, the practice of social science and philosophical reflection are not separate activities occupying different levels but are rather intrinsically connected with one another. This new understanding developed in the wake of the demise of positivism, especially in conjunction with Thomas Kuhn's paradigm theory, which led many to ignore the division between the philosophy of science and the social scientific study of science, such as the history and sociology of science. It is further reinforced by the recent decline in disciplinarity. In this view, the social scientist – the sociologist, the historian, the anthropologist – is not simply a practitioner of a scientific discipline, but is at the same time also a philosopher of social science. In this case, there is less resistance

to philosophy than in the second model, for philosophy has lost its prescriptive or legislating role. The social scientist is indeed aware of the normative and justificatory aspects of social science, but always sees them in relation to the cognitive practices and processes constituting the social sciences in the first place. Also, in this third position there is an awareness that reflexivity is a much wider process than in the second, where it was limited to science. In this view, the philosophy of social science is a reflective discourse on the practice of social science, but one that is neither prescriptive-legislative nor proclaims a specific philosophy of *social science*. Thus, much of the concern of the philosophy of social science today is not purely epistemological but relates to wider issues relating to cognition and knowledge.

In the three kinds of reflexivity and hence philosophy of social science outlined above there is a clearly discernable trend away from philosophers and towards social scientists practicing the philosophy of social science. We also detect within this a move away from epistemology in the philosophy of social science to the question of knowledge and the cognitive practices, structures and processes in which it is generated, structured, transmitted and applied. The role of philosophy in social science responds to the circumstance that the social scientist does not simply engage in doing or practicing his or her discipline, but at the same time also thinks about or reflects upon how the process unfolds and is structured and that this thinking has an influence on the conduct of research and the way in which it is embedded in its larger social context. Of central importance to such thinking are the general criteria of acceptability implied in social scientific or sociological judgement and in its potential employment in the organization of society. According to which criteria do we proceed in doing our work, and according to which criteria do we evaluate our own contributions as well as those of others? Which criteria are recognized by the international scientific community to which we belong? Unavoidably today, and hence equally important, however, are also such questions as: According to which criteria is the relation of social science to practice evaluated? Which criteria are recognized in the public sphere as applicable to social science and at the same time as serving the public interest? For the focus is no longer simply on science, including social science, but more broadly on the role that it plays in the creation and shaping of a common world through joint action and interaction.

Some preliminary conceptual analysis

Having obtained a preliminary grasp of its contemporary sense, it will be useful to begin with some conceptual analysis of the key terms that generally define the domain of the philosophy of social science. In the most general terms, the philosophy of social science concerns the principles regulating the search for and acquisition of knowledge (in this case, social scientific knowledge) about reality (in this case, social reality) through a series of intersubjectively accessible and justifiable methodical steps. In so far as it is a matter of a principled yet productive process unfolding in a step-like manner, the philosophy of social science involves what is called 'methodology'. Secondly, in so far as the product of this process, namely social scientific knowledge, is a species of knowledge, the philosophy of social science overlaps with the more general philosophical discipline traditionally called 'epistemology'. Finally, in so far as the knowledge produced in the course of this process is about reality, the philosophy of social science touches on yet another basic philosophical discipline, what is traditionally called 'ontology.' Let us briefly consider each of these key terms in turn.

What is methodology?

The word 'methodology' derives from the Greek *methodos*, meaning 'way towards or procedure for the attainment of a goal' – for instance, the acquisition of knowledge – and *logos*, meaning 'theory'; thus: 'theory of the way in which knowledge is acquired'. Corresponding to the German form *Wissenschaftstheorie* or *Wissenschaftslehre*, methodology is in English sometimes referred to as 'the theory of science' or, more often, 'the philosophy of science'. Most frequently, however, due to the influence of positivism, we come across the use of the more reductive 'scientific method'.

These various forms suggest that methodology is a generic term covering the specific approach of each of the sciences, irrespective of the category (for instance, natural, human or social) to which they belong. The fact that methodology since the late nineteenth century has been regarded as related to logic accounts for the fact that it is sometimes called 'the logic of science'. And since science in the twentieth century increasingly became understood as essentially a matter of research, the expression 'logic of research' is also used instead of methodology. In the final analysis, however, methodology refers to the systematic investigation of the various rational and procedural principles and processes which guide scientific inquiry. In the case of a special scientific discipline, say sociology, it more specifically concerns the structure and procedures of the discipline.

In the case of social science, for instance, methodology is an investigation of the assumptions upon which we proceed as regards the following:

- the nature and scope of its field of study;
- the relation of the social scientist (or subject of knowledge) to reality;
- how this relation unfolds in the process of the development of knowledge;
- the type of statements made regarding reality;
- its philosophical assumptions; and finally
- its relation to other disciplines or types of knowledge.

What is epistemology?

The word 'epistemology' derives from the Greek *episteme*, meaning 'knowledge', and *logos*, meaning 'theory'; thus: 'the theory of knowledge'. The concept made its first appearance in its German form, *Erkenntnistheorie*, having been introduced in the Kantian tradition in 1789. The English form 'epistemology' made its entry in 1854, and by the 1860s it had gained general currency, thus ousting its competitor term 'gnosiology'. Epistemology, strictly speaking, refers to a fundamental branch of philosophy that investigates the possibility, limits, origin, structure, methods and validity (or truth) of knowledge.

As such, epistemology embraces problems like the following:

- The possibility of knowledge: given dogmatism and scepticism, is genuine knowledge achievable at all – for instance, by way of controlled doubt or scepticism?
- The limits of knowledge: where does the line run between the knowable and the unknowable?
- The origin or source of knowledge: reason, the senses or experience of some other kind?
- The problem of the *a priori*: what are the presuppositions of knowledge – for instance, innate ideas, the perspectival situatedness of the body, or the validity basis of language or communication?
- The methodological problem: rationalism/deduction, empiricism/induction, pragmatism/abduction, phenomenology/intuition of essence or critique/unmasking hidden forces?
- Different types of knowledge: observational/perceptual, descriptive, inferential, introspective, reflective?
- The structure of the knowledge situation: what is the relation between the subjective and objective components of the knowledge situation, and what, if anything, mediates the relation?
- The problem of truth: intrinsic, correspondence, coherence, or consensus theory?

As regards the concept of knowledge, more specifically, it should be noted that since Plato philosophers have debated about the nature of knowledge and whether there was a distinction between knowledge (*logos*) and opinion (*doxa*). The entire classical and modernist tradition assumed a basic distinction between knowledge and opinion. The linguistic or pragmatic turn, the appearance of poststructuralism and the rise of a discursive understanding of knowledge, reinforced by the appearance of postmodernism, have called this separation into question. Today, accordingly, we need a more differentiated view of knowledge as taking distinct forms, such as:

- self-knowledge;
- tacit, common-sense or taken-for-granted forms of knowledge;
- local or everyday knowledge;
- wisdom;
- science.

Within science itself, there are also different forms of knowledge, such as:

- inductive knowledge (empirical knowledge/knowledge of facts/information);
- deductive knowledge (rationalism/mathematical knowledge/logical reasoning);

- pragmatic knowledge (knowledge as action/knowing 'how'/action-oriented; knowledge);
- instrumental knowledge (utilitarian knowledge/task-oriented knowledge);
- transcendental knowledge (knowledge of conditions or limits);
- reflective knowledge (transformative and critical knowledge).

What is ontology?

The word 'ontology' derives from the Greek *on* meaning 'being' and *logos* meaning 'theory'; thus: 'the theory of being as being', which means the theory of the nature of what is or the theory of the nature of reality. In relation to scientific inquiry, ontology concerns the nature and knowledge of social reality.

In the social sciences assumptions are made and arguments developed as regards the nature of social reality or the aspect of reality that is most important for the attainment of knowledge. Is social reality:

- a common-sense physical or perceptual entity, a thing, a social fact that can be observed (positivism, Durkheim)?
- A phenomenal or mental entity (neo-positivism, constructivism)?
- A changeable historical-cultural configuration identifiable only in relation to values and requiring a degree of interpretation (Weber)?
- A set of relations hidden behind a veil that needs to be removed first and thus requiring a critical stance (Marx)?
- A discourse that can be understood only from a point within it (Foucault)?

As far as key terms or basic concepts such as 'the philosophy of social science', 'methodology', 'epistemology', 'knowledge', 'ontology', 'reality' and so forth are concerned, the reader should be warned that for various reasons an unequivocal circumscription is unattainable. One of these reasons is language, and another is history.

Language

In the recent past, problems such as 'patriarchy' and 'eurocentrism' have attracted much attention, but a still more basic related problem in the social sciences, one that has been with us since their beginnings centuries ago, is that of language. The core of the problem is the parochialism of separate and isolated linguistic worlds that accounts for our inability or failure to grasp the full range of meaning of concepts. While many, if not most, basic concepts are affected, this is particularly true of the central concepts we are concerned with here. The result is that many concepts in social science are fundamentally contested. Although a concept belongs to a common or shared universe of discourse, the participants not only interpret the concept differently but they actively disagree and contest each other's interpretations, claims and decisions. This contestation even extends to the very meaning of 'science', 'methodology' and 'philosophy of science', including 'the philosophy of social science'. In the case of all these concepts, different linguistic worlds and, therefore, linguistic or national traditions make themselves strongly yet largely inconspicuously felt. For example:

- The word and concept 'science':
    - the English 'science', which has the narrow meaning of 'Science' (with an emphasis on the capital letter);
    - the French 'science' and the Italian 'scienza'; and
    - the German 'Wissenschaft' – all Continental concepts with a broader meaning.
- The concept 'methodology':
    - the unity of science or scientific method, and the reduction of epistemology and methodology to method, which have long been prevalent in the English-speaking, (especially the Anglo-American) world;
    - dualism, which for has long been a characteristic Continental (particularly German) phenomenon;
    - tripartite division of knowledge – a newer (originally Continental) idea;
    - interdisciplinarity – a post-Second World War idea which has begun to take on new meaning in recent decades.
- The title of the philosophical or reflective discipline concerned with the study of science:
    - 'philosophy of science', the Anglo-American title, emphasizing the logical rather than the psychological, sociocultural and historical dimension;
    - Wisenschaftstheorie, or Wissenschaftslehre (e.g. Weber), the German title, emphasizing the logical but in particular the historical and cultural dimension and the cognitive constitution of the object of knowledge;
    - Épistémologie (e.g. Bachelard, Bourdieu, Foucault), the French title, emphasizing the historical dimension and the cognitive constitution of the object of knowledge.

History

Besides the problem of language, there is also a second problem: the problem of history. It concerns the fact that no concept is purely formal or analytical, but has a history and is continually under pressure to undergo change. Towards the end of the nineteenth century, Nietzsche, for instance, made this point very strongly. It demands that we remain aware of the modulation and reformulation that concepts undergo in relation to the transformation of the problems they are meant to deal with. This brings us to the next major point.

Contemporary interpretative difficulties: the post-positivist decentring of epistemology and methodology

The central concepts in the philosophy of social science, indeed, the whole range of key concepts in the general area of science, have undergone a significant change of meaning since the 1970s – including 'epistemology' and 'methodology' as well as 'philosophy of science'.

Epistemology

From the historical and conceptual information given above, it is obvious that epistemology is a modern invention. It was identified and became established in the late eighteenth and the nineteenth centuries. This circumstance, to be sure, is the source of a certain difficulty when it comes to speaking about twentieth-century reflections on knowledge from the perspective of the twenty-first century. The situation as it has unfolded in our own time entails a questioning and rejection of some of the most central and characteristic assumptions informing epistemology. Indeed, the dominant modern view that epistemology possesses a certain priority, that a certain prescriptive or legislative force emanates from it in the pursuit of knowledge (Descartes, Locke and Kant: epistemology as 'legislator'), has itself been under vehement attack in recent decades (e.g. from postmodernism, feminism, radical hermeneutics – e.g. Richard Rorty, – etc.). Although the concern with knowledge has by no means disappeared and indeed is unlikely to do so, doubt nevertheless arises as to whether the concept of epistemology in its traditional sense can be said any longer to be adequate under contemporary conditions. In this respect, we can note the transformation or overcoming (socialization – e.g. Habermas, or naturalization – e.g. Fuller) of 'epistemology'. In some sense or another, this involved a shift from Cartesian (i.e. dualism and total description) and Newtonian (i.e. stable time-reversible systems) assumptions to a holistic and intersubjective world addressed in the public sphere.

Methodology

We can also detect a remarkable decentring of 'methodology'. There is a discernible shift from the normative sense of a set of obligatory rules to the process of science in which a variety of cognitive practices, paradigms and processes play a role. Feyerabend's slogan 'everything goes' gives graphic expression to this relativization of methodology.

Philosophy of science

The 'philosophy of science' can no longer be regarded as purely logical, but has to be seen in relation to the history of science and the (social and human) sciences of science, including psychology, sociology and rhetoric. This major transformation provides the background against which arose such developments as Kuhn's concern with paradigms, Lakatos' 'research programmes', Foucault's discourses, Knorr-Cetina's 'constructivism', de Mey's 'cognitive paradigm', Fuller's 'social epistemology' and many others.

Explanation, interpretation, and critique

Regularly recurring key concepts in the philosophy of social science, such as explanation, interpretation and critique, also exhibit a similar shift in meaning that is expressed in a remarkable proliferation of interpretations:

- *explanation:* for example, neopositivist hypothetico-deductive (Popper) or deductive-nomological (Hempel), cultural-historical causal (Weber), realist (Harré, Bhaskar), rational (Elster);
- *interpretation:* for example, symbolic (Freud, Weber), explanatory (Weber), hermeneutic (Gadamer), critical hermeneutic (Habermas, Apel), thick description (Geertz), standpoint (Smith), reflexive (Garfinkel);
- *critique:* for example, transcendental (Kant), ideology (Marx, Horkheimer, Adorno, Marcuse, Habermas), social (Bourdieu, Eder) cognitive (Strydom), pragmatic (Boltanski).

In order to fully appreciate the current situation, including the changes in meaning mentioned above, a brief sketch of the major epistemic shifts in the twentieth century is ventured below. This will serve as a reference point for locating the different approaches in the dialectical development of the philosophy of social science in this volume.

Major epistemic shifts in the twentieth century

By 'epistemic shift' is meant a fundamental change in ways of thinking about science and knowledge more generally. There were four major epistemic shifts in the twentieth century which in their various ways led not only to the demise of positivism and the assumptions of the classical tradition, but also to the elaboration of new approaches which often involved the recontextualization and reconstitution of preceding assumptions. This dialectical development of the philosophy of social science can be summarized as the logical turn, the linguistic turn, the historical-cultural turn and finally the knowledge (cognitive or epistemological) turn. These developments, several of which have been co-terminal, can be seen as confirmation of the crisis of the possibility of grounding social science on epistemic foundations. Whereas initially the attempt had been made to ground science on a single unit such as facts, the emphasis was first shifted towards the structural properties of objects as captured by language. But the fact that language possesses a pragmatic dimension over and above syntax and semantics, drove the search for grounding to focus on the context of science which it was the task of history, sociology, anthropology and psychology to clarify. The inherent diffuseness and ambiguity of context, however, finally demanded that the question of the structuring of knowledge in the non-linear and dynamic process of its production be squarely confronted.

The first shift beyond the horizons of the nineteenth century was an incomplete one in that it retained that century's concern with the search for a firm foundation for knowledge, but ultimately brought about a far-reaching intellectual and epistemic revolution. In the logical positivism of the Vienna Circle, a new kind of positivism characterized by deductive reasoning overthrew the pre-eminence of empiricism and inductive inquiry that had become the orthodoxy in the natural and the social sciences. The significance of this development was the recognition that knowledge cannot be grounded in reality.

The second shift was the linguistic one which emerged partly out of the logical turn but had an independent origin in much older traditions. Within Anglo-American analytical philosophy this was marked by a shift from the correspondence theory of truth to conventionalism (Ayer) and towards ontological relativism (Quine). In the later philosophy of Wittgenstein, the search for a firm foundation for knowledge in reality became even more implausible. Not only reality, but the very categories of science and of knowledge more generally began to be seen as shaped in and by language – not only by its syntactic and semantic but also its pragmatic dimension. This is true too of the American pragmatic tradition of Peirce and Morris. Science ceases to be a representation of reality, and anti-foundational thinking becomes more and more influential.

The third epistemic shift emerged in the second half of the twentieth century and was marked by an extension of the linguistic turn into a full historical-cultural revolution which radically contextualized science. Science became seen as a historically and socially shaped cultural artifact and with this for the first time a conflict within the culture of science ensued. If scientific knowledge is embedded in language and if language is a historical, social and cultural product, the conflict within cultural practices and models becomes extended to science. The pre-eminent example of this is the work of Thomas Kuhn on the conflict of paradigms. Although it was never Kuhn's intention, the inevitable result of this development was the gradual descent of science into relativism. This was reinforced by the contextualization of science. Examples of the relativistic turn are feminist standpoint epistemology, Foucault and various kinds of radical hermeneutics (Rorty), constructivism and postmodernism.

The fourth epistemic shift accompanied the historical-cultural shift but was more characteristic of the later twentieth century. It was an attempt to deal with the problem of the inherent ambiguity of context and can be characterized as the turn towards knowledge in the discourses of the human and social sciences. In this further shift, knowledge recovers from the full implications of the historical-cultural turn with the recognition that knowledge is formed in a continuous but interrupted historical development of cognitive forms carried by research programmes, traditions and scientific communities. Knowledge is less about knowing reality than about emergent forms of the real and a reflexive relation to the world in which reality is shaped by cognitive practices, structures and processes. Examples of this epistemic shift are Apel and Habermas' 'transcendental pragmatics', different forms of realism and cognitivism, and Fuller's 'social epistemology'.

The readings we have selected illustrate these epistemic shifts. They are divided into six parts. Part 1 covers the broad framework of positivism, its decline and the emergence of post-empiricism. Beginning with some major examples of positivism and neo-positivism in social science, the following readings illustrate the gradual demise of positivism, particularly under the influence of the logical turn but also the gradually unfolding linguistic turn. In Part 1 the broader debate about positivism in science and is outlined, but the focus is the 'internal' decline of positivism within the philosophy of the natural sciences, since other social scientific attacks against positivism are reserved for subsequent parts.

Part 2 covers the interpretative tradition where the philosophy of social science developed to a significant degree under the influence of the linguistic turn, but in particular the contextual and the cognitive turns. The emphasis is on the explanation versus understanding controversy that began with Wilhelm Dilthey in 1883 and still determined discussions in the early twentieth century. Other readings document the phenomenological approach of Alfred Schutz and mid-century debates about interpretation, such as those associated with Gadamer and Winch. Another group of readings (Ricoeur, Habermas) deal with the idea of a critical hermeneutics. The final group of readings covers the emergence of a distinctive cognitive and reflexive approach in social science that developed in the wake of the earlier phenomenological and hermeneutic philosophies and the emerging cognitive sciences, which is represented by Aaron Cicourel, Harold Garfinkel and Erving Goffman, who all advocated in different ways the need for social science to address common-sense forms of knowledge.

Part 3 concerns the critical tradition that goes back to Kant, Hegel and Marx. The major twentieth-century representatives of this approach are the critical theorists of the Frankfurt School, especially Horkheimer, Adorno and other critical theorists such as Marcuse and later Habermas, Apel and Wellmer. While the early critical theorists had been strong critics of positivism and the predominance of logic in the philosophy of the social sciences, their successors were acutely aware of the linguistic and the contextual turns as well as the resultant relativistic consequences which they sought to counter. The principal aim of Part 3 is to illustrate the idea of social science as a form of critique.

Part 4 presents readings on the largely American tradition of pragmatism that developed out of the writings of Charles Sanders Pierce. He anticipated the linguistic turn, particularly its later phase which Morris interpreted in terms of pragmatics and Apel more radically in terms of transcendental pragmatics. The aim of the readings is first of all to illustrate the distinctively American conception of science as a form of action, but they seek also to draw attention to the interaction between pragmatism and European traditions which was stimulated by the epistemic shifts of the late twentieth century.

Part 5 contains readings that illustrate the revolution in thought that occurred in France from the 1950s to the 1970s and which is generally associated with the poststructuralist movement that emerged in reaction to the work of the Claude Lévi-Strauss. Over a number of decades, this revolution fed on several of the above-mentioned epistemic shifts, such as the linguistic turn, the contextual turn and the knowledge turn. In fact, it illustrates the co-terminal and even coeval nature of these shifts. The selected readings concentrate on what can be called the structuralist controversy. The major representatives of this movement are Derrida and Foucault, one the one side, and Pierre Bourdieu on the other.

The final section, Part 6, deals with the last two decades of the twentieth century in which new controversies (such as constructivism versus realism) and new directions have emerged around, for instance, reflexivity, standpoint, rational choice and cognitivism. The readings in this part at times still reflect attempts to deal with problems that had been thrown up by the third epistemic shift as it broadened the focus to include the context of science. More interesting and important, however, are the new avenues opened up by the fourth and currently most significant and topical epistemic shift.

PART 1

Positivism, its dissolution and the emergence of post-empiricism

Introduction: a general outline

[handwritten margin notes: "belief/practice", "authorized/accepted"]

In accordance with the narrative line encapsulated by the above title, the selections in this part have been made with a threefold goal in mind. First, the fact that positivism attained the status of an orthodoxy in social science in the first half of the twentieth century demands that a number of canonical statements which make clear what positivism stands for in social science be presented. Readings 1 to 7 have been selected to serve this purpose. However, considering that it was liberalized and transformed through both internal development (i.e. within positivism) and external criticism (from anti-positivist traditions), it is, secondly, necessary to trace the gradual dissolution of positivism. Readings 8 to 11 capture the process of the reassessment and transformation which had positivism in its grip and in the late 1930s took a drastic turn. Finally, the remaining readings – i.e. 12–14 – document the emergence of post-empiricism in the 1960s and 1970s and its eventual displacement of positivism. Whereas the account in this part draws largely on internal developments, external criticisms of positivism are presented in some detail in later parts – particularly in Part 2 on the interpretative turn and Part 3 on critical social science, but also in parts 4 and 5 which deal with pragmatism and structuralism respectively.

[handwritten margin note: "experiential"]

To create a context within which to understand the different representatives of positivism and to appreciate both what they have in common and the connections between them, to begin with it is necessary to indicate what the word 'positivism' is generally taken to mean. Particularly since the beginning of the modern period, positivist ideas have enjoyed a relatively widespread acceptance in the western world, particularly in Britain, France and the USA. Historically, at least six complexes of ideas can be extrapolated as being the basic suppositions or tenets of positivism, a brief review of which should be helpful in developing an understanding of the doctrine.

- *Unified science:* based on a series of assumptions – i.e. that the universe is a causally ordered, homogeneous, one-layer world, that there is a basic unity to human experience and that we are therefore able to gain knowledge of reality and indeed construct a knowledge system about it. It is claimed that it is possible to produce a unified scientific language for all scientific disciplines, which effectively means that all the different scientific disciplines, including the social sciences, can be reduced to physics – a claim that in its extreme form takes on the character of an ideology, namely scientism.

- *Empiricism:* an anti-metaphysical doctrine stressing the experiential basis of all knowledge which takes one of two possible forms – i.e. either phenomenalism, in which case the emphasis is on the immediate experience of phenomenal or mental entities in the form of observables or sense data; or physicalism (or naturalism), in which case the emphasis is on perceptual or physical entities or common-sense things and events that can be intersubjectively verified by recourse to empirical evidence.

- *Objectivism:* on the basis of the separation of the subject and object of knowledge, the purely theoretical attitude of the uninvolved observer is adopted so that the focus is exclusively on the object, typically accompanied by the claim that there is no such thing as the subject or substantial self.

- *Value freedom:* based on the assumption of the necessity of upholding a logical separation of facts and values or descriptive and normative statements, the demand is made that science should proceed in a neutral manner, free from all infection by personal, ethical, moral, social or cultural values, with the scientist actively desisting from deriving 'ought from is' or 'values from facts'.

- *Instrumentalism:* an orientation towards the manipulation of the world rather than understanding it and, closely related, an instrumental view of theory as consisting of nothing but observations and being nothing more than a tool of prediction.

- *Technicism:* the tendency to value techniques or methods more than results or the development of knowledge, even to the point of essentializing the former.

The relatively long history of positivist ideas in western thinking and the widespread acceptance of some of them account, at least partially, for the fact that positivism attained the status of an orthodoxy in the philosophy of social science. What complicates matters considerably, however, is that there is not just one but in fact at least two distinct forms of positivism. The second, twentieth-century form has been called 'neo-positivism' to distinguish it from the older, preceding form of positivism which had been in its heyday in nineteenth-century France (August Comte, 1798–1857) and Britain (John Stuart Mill, 1806–73) in particular, but also in Germany (Ernst Mach, 1838–1916). During the twentieth century, many a social scientist conflated these two forms of positivism and thus drew the criticism upon themselves of typically being 20 to 30 years behind the times. By contrast, it should be emphasized that the distinction between old and neo-positivism is crucial for an understanding of the development of the positivist philosophy of social science in the nineteenth century.

The eighteenth-century Scottish Enlightenment author David Hume (1711–76) is generally regarded as the founder of positivism, but it was Comte who, leaning on Saint-Simon, actually coined the term 'positive philosophy' in the nineteenth century. Hume's legacy was the question whether certain knowledge based on individual facts was possible, but contrary to his pronounced (albeit not always intentional) scepticism, his nineteenth-century successors regarded scientific knowledge, the sole form of certain knowledge, not only as the paradigm of all valid knowledge but even as the solution to collective problems facing humankind. This was the case with Comte in particular who represented what has been called 'systematic positivism'. Closely related to the latter was the so-called 'critical positivism' of Mill and Mach which shifted the emphasis from philosophy as a synthetic harmonization of the results of science with the advancement of society to the sameness of the methods for the acquisition of valid knowledge in all spheres of inquiry. The characteristic feature of this older positivism, however, was that it adopted the positively given or the empirical as its supreme value. This means that it focused on existence, reality or nature, or to put it still differently, on things, events or facts as such. Depending on how experience was defined, the positively given or the empirical dimension was understood either in phenomenalist or in physicalist terms, and sometimes even collapsed into a metaphysical naturalism. In general it was an approach that strongly emphasized induction, which can be defined as presuppositionless inquiry by which theory is arrived at from the observation of facts. It is in this respect that twentieth-century neo-positivism differs sharply from its predecessor. As its alternative names – i.e. 'logical positivism' or 'logical empiricism' – suggest, the positively given or the empirical was no longer total, as earlier. An additional dimension, the logical, was introduced and came to play a significant role in neo-positivism, which took a strongly anti-inductive stance, favouring instead deductive logic (the application of theory to the concrete case).

Neo-positivism was originated by a group of philosophers called the Vienna Circle who reacted to the predominance of German idealism in particular and metaphysical doctrines in general. Their own doctrine, variously referred to as 'logical positivism' or 'logical empiricism', came into its own in the early 1920s around Moritz Schlick (1882–1936) and was carried forward by such group members as Rudolf Carnap, Herbert Feigl, Philipp Frank, Kurt Gödel, Victor Kraft, Otto Neurath, Friedrich Waismann and others. Through the travels of Ludwig Wittgenstein (1889–1951) and Alfred Ayer, there was a relation of mutual influence between Vienna and Cambridge, and due to the emigration of various Vienna Circle group members as a result of Hitler's rise to power, neo-positivism later spread also to the USA.

Neo-positivism looked to Mach, a physicist and professor of philosophy in Vienna, as one of its precursors and went on to draw heavily on Russell and Whitehead's *Principia Mathematica* as a major resource and example. Starting from a neutral monism according to which reality or the universe was a one-layer world consisting of basic entities in the form of experiences, impressions or 'sensa', these authors made a clear distinction between the logical and the empirical dimensions. Whereas they regarded the former as the form of knowledge represented by the language of science, the latter concerned experience as the basis of the knowledge we have of the world. Besides the above authors, however, neo-positivism depended in particular on the early Wittgenstein, especially in so far as its objectivism and empiricism was not merely a continuation of nineteenth-century positivism. Breaking with the older positivist thing-event-fact model, Wittgenstein presented the first radical and therefore influential neo-positivistic thing-event-fact-language model. Rather that being concerned with things, events, facts or nature as such, he shifted the focus to the language in which things, events or facts are captured. But since everyday language was vague and misleading, his concern was with scientific language, the one intersubjective language of science. His aim was to discover the logic of language, the true logical structure of all the sentences of the language of science. A basic assumption here was that there was an isomorphic or mapping relation between this ideal language and reality. If scientific language is suitably constructed it could, through its logical structure, capture the very logical form of the world. It was further assumed that the capacity of language to depict the world was such that it made the thinking human subject superfluous, which implied that only the sentences of the natural sciences were meaningful or intersubjectively verifiable.

Wittgenstein thus provided the neo-positivists with a starting point for their objectivist programme of unified science, which included a programme of the reduction of the social sciences to so-called 'behavioural sciences'. According to them, social sciences such as sociology were not genuine sciences due to their use of intentional sentences and therefore would gain respectability only if they patterned themselves upon the model of the natural sciences. In fact, the neo-positivists did not really develop a philosophy of the social sciences as such, but since they believed that what they discovered in respect of the natural sciences should be universally applicable to everything worthy of the title 'science', they simply extended their philosophy of science to the social sciences. To the detriment of their own disciplines, social scientists in the English-speaking world in particular for a considerable period during the twentieth century sympathetically embraced the recommendation to seek scientific respectability by subjecting themselves to positivism. Some kept up with developments in neo-positivism and as it dissolved were thus able to gradually emancipate themselves from this debilitating recommendation. Tragically, however, a large number of credulous social scientists, never appreciating the difference between old and neo-positivism, not only continued to operate with an old form of naïve positivism, but also sought to emulate a long out of date model of the natural sciences.

After its emergence in the early 1920s, neo-positivism underwent a gradual process of internal development which from one point of view appears as liberalization and from another as dissolution. In keeping with the fact that the analytic philosophy of language had been the dominant approach in the first part of the twentieth century and thus provided a widely accepted framework for philosophy, the change in the neo-positivist philosophy of science paralleled its philosophy of language. Whereas analytic philosophy successively passed through 'logical atomism', 'logical positivism' and 'ordinary language analysis', a shift of emphasis occurred in the philosophy of science from 'syntactics' – in the sense of logical form – via 'semantics' – in the sense of frameworks of meaning – to 'pragmatics' – in the sense of the use of language. It is during the second phase of analytic philosophy in particular that the neo-positivist – variously called the 'logical positivist', 'logical empiricist' or 'empirical-analytical' – philosophy of science enjoyed its most elaborate formulation and reached its peak.

In the first phase, exemplified by various Vienna Circle group members inspired by Wittgenstein such as Carnap and Neurath, the emphasis was on the one logical form of the language of science by which alone the logical form of the world could be extracted and captured. Under the pressure of the so-called problem of 'empirical significance', however, this strict demand to formulate the ideal language of unified science was abandoned in the second phase in favour of the requirement that scientific statements must be intersubjectively verifiable. Karl Popper (1902–94), in a certain sense a reluctant member of the Vienna Circle, played an important role here by means of his theory of falsification as well as his recognition that theories structure the observation of reality – what meanwhile has come to be called 'the thesis of theory-ladenness of observation'. This change meant that a shift occurred from logical form or syntactics to semantics, or the meaning of scientific language in so far as it refers to objects and from induction to a general preference for deduction. The concern with the semantic or meaningful conceptual framework of science was central to the work of Carnap, who drew on the seminal contribution of Alfred Tarski. Closely related to this liberalization was, for instance, Carl Hempel's (1905–97) attempts to transform the problem of causality into the problem of explanation and to show that the explication of a scientific law requires contextual over and above formal criteria and that empirical significance resides not in concepts and sentences but in whole postulational or theoretical systems.

By the third phase, however, it had become apparent that it was not enough to embed logical relations in the content or meaning of concepts, sentences and postulational systems. It was realized that, beyond the construction of semantic or meaningful frameworks, the semantic dimension itself presupposed the pragmatic dimension of the established use – or rather uses – of language by the various sciences as they have developed historically. Carnap only reluctantly accepted Charles Morris' idea, derived from American pragmatism, of the pragmatic dimension alongside syntactics and semantics. The introduction of the element of choice into science, which earlier softened the sharp distinction between the logical and the empirical, now took on the character of a much stronger conventionalism which decisively blurred the distinction. Eventually, Carnap himself embraced the idea of a multitude of possible syntactic-semantic systems or linguistic frameworks among which the scientists had to choose according to external criteria. Both Hempel and Quine revived the conventionalism of the French philosopher of science Pierre Duhem (1861–1916), with Quine for instance arguing that it is impossible to falsify a hypothesis because it is always possible to modify the language or the system of postulation involved. On the basis of lectures that Wittgenstein started giving in Cambridge in 1932 in which he, in self-criticism and partial repudiation of his earlier work, focused on the empirical pluralism of self-consistent and self-justifying language games, British analytic philosophy embarked on the analysis of the plethora of uses made of ordinary, everyday language. The internal criticism and revision inaugurated by such philosophers as Popper, Morris, the later Wittgenstein and Quine opened the way for what can be regarded as the gradual dissolution of positivism from the late 1930s onwards and its displacement by post-empiricism. The break with the positivist or empiricist conception of science became fully apparent with Stephen Toulmin and especially Thomas Kuhn's account of the development of scientific knowledge in terms of shifting frameworks of understanding or paradigms rather than the testing, confirmation or falsification of hypotheses. In a similar post-empiricist vein, Imre Lakatos stressed the role of research programmes in the growth of knowledge, while Paul Feyerabend more radically argued that inductive and deductive logic and also the methodology of hypothesis testing are irrelevant to the development of scientific knowledge.

The selected texts

Against the above background, it is now possible to locate each of the following selected texts within the narrative framework of positivism, its decline and the emergence of post-empiricism.

Positivism

Let us begin with readings 1 to 7 which clarify what positivism in social science entails.

Emile Durkheim (1858–1917), a representative of the older positivism, understood himself as a follower of Comte who, in his opinion, had not been positivist enough due to the fact that he remained attached to the metaphysical concept of progress. In the selection below, he puts forward his so-called *chosism*, his positivistic doctrine of social facts as things or externally constraining realities that require to be studied objectively from the outside. The text demonstrates how the positivistic assumption of the positive as being the ready to hand, immediately and factually given, could be social-scientifically interpreted: 'A social fact is every way of acting, fixed or not, capable of exercising on the individual an external constraint; or again, every way of acting which is general throughout a given society, while at the same time existing in its own right independent of its individual manifestations'. Historically, Durkheim's approach has proved very influential in the positivist or empiricist social sciences, with some sociologists curiously remaining under its spell perhaps even to this day.

Otto Neurath (1882–1945), a Marxist sociologist and scientific socialist, was a member of the Vienna Circle and editor of the official neo-positivist journal *Einheitswissenschaft* which was in the late 1930s succeeded by the *International Encyclopedia of Unified Science*. In the selected text, he puts forward all the characteristic arguments of the neo-positivist philosophy of science with reference to authors such as Russell and Wittgenstein. What distinguishes neo-positivism from the older positivism, according to him, is the 'method of logical analysis' and hence the focus on the language of science. The latter is an ideal language, a 'neutral system of formulae' or a 'total system of concepts' which differs sharply from historical languages. It is characterized by the reduction through logical analysis of the meaning of sentences to the simplest statements about something empirical. Scientific knowledge thus derives from experience which in turn rests on what is immediately given. From this point of view, metaphysics and apriorism are rejected since both lack the necessary basis in the experience of positively given empirical objects and states of affairs. The goal that logical empiricism projects for scientific effort is the attainment of 'unified science', which Neurath – quite ironically does not consider might itself be metaphysical – interprets as the uniting of all people by means of a language articulating their common knowledge.

Carl Hempel (1905–97), a member of the Berlin group supporting the Vienna

Circle who emigrated to the USA in 1937, is considered one of the masters of the logical positivist or logical-empiricist philosophy of science. While his work exhibits many signs of the liberalization of neo-positivism in its second phase, he nevertheless upheld the basic tenets of positivism in his writings on scientific explanation and the structure of scientific theory. In the selected text, he proceeds from the assumption of unified science to argue that there is no 'essential methodological difference' between the natural and the social sciences. If there is a difference between the two fields, it can be attributed to the fact that the social sciences are underdeveloped and therefore do not yet live up to the level reached by the natural sciences. Not only do the social sciences lack a 'general theory' and hence a basis for appraisal, but they also neglect to give whatever theory they have adequate 'empirical interpretation' by specifying relevant 'behavioural regularities'. As a result of thus proceeding in 'intuitive terms', the social sciences are incapable of fulfilling the 'explanatory and predictive' task characteristic of empirical science. It is interesting to note that Hempel's piece is an explicit response to social scientists whom he regards as opponents in need of being silenced. Among them are those who attach 'misleading connotations' to ideal type constructs and their use in the social sciences, such as Max Weber, Alfred Schutz and other representatives of the interpretative tradition. In his view, they are inconsistent and mistaken not only because they regard ideal types as playing a role in 'understanding' – i.e. Weber's so-called *Verstehen* – as distinct from explanation and therefore as having nothing to do with behavioural regularities and hypothesis testing, but also, and in particular, because they insist that the social sciences have a distinctive methodology of their own.

Ernst Nagel (1901–85), a Czechoslovakian residing in the USA since age 10, was one of the first American philosophers to sympathize with the Vienna Circle. Like Hempel, he represents an orthodox logical-empiricist position, clearly expressed in the selected text, which played an influential role in leading many an American and English-speaking practitioner to adopt the positivist view of empirical social science. On the basis of the assumption that there is no appreciable difference between 'social inquiry' and 'natural science', in the text he for the most part laments the fact that the social sciences have not yet registered any progress towards approximating 'genuine science' which disposes over 'a body of general laws' or 'an empirically warranted theory', allowing both explanation and prediction, and indeed are not likely to do so in the foreseeable future. The most promising direction for the social sciences to take, according to him, is to adopt an objectivist approach which screens out intentional or meaningful action in favour of observable behavioural regularities, to draw 'generalizations' from such empirical observations, for these purposes to make use of 'techniques of quantitative analysis', and finally to pursue social science as an administrative or 'social policy' science.

Karl Popper (1902–94) was an 'insider' critic of the Vienna Circle whose sharp analyses played an important role in changing the direction of the neo-positivist philosophy of science during its second phase. Although he wrote extensively on the philosophy of the social sciences, his most important work – and arguably the most influential book on human knowledge written in the twentieth century – *The Logic of*

Scientific Discovery (1934) concerned the philosophy of science and advocated a general approach to epistemology. It was the principal reference point for all of his thinking, the aim of which was to demarcate knowledge from opinion, science from non-science. Being concerned with the growth of knowledge, he moved against those who instead pursued the establishment of certain knowledge once and for all or the ideal of eternal knowledge. This stance is reflected in the text below, from the opening chapter of *The Logic of Scientific Discovery* where he objects to Schlick and Waismann, but his fundamental disagreement was with the emphasis on inductive logic that emerged in the shift from the Vienna Circle's original epistemological concern with the nature of knowledge to their new concern with confirmation – i.e. how a hypothesis is confirmed by evidence. While Popper makes multiple references to Reichenbach in the selected text, Carnap (in the next reading) was actually the one to whom neo-positivism owed the laying of the foundations of inductive logic. In the text, Popper vehemently rejects inductive logic in favour of what he calls 'deductivism' or 'the theory of the deductive method of [empirical] testing' of a hypothesis. According to his argument, which he believes is also a solution to the long-standing scandal of philosophy known as 'Hume's problem', it is utterly impossible to verify a hypothesis or theory yet it is quite possible to falsify or refute it. For instance, although no number of observations of white swans allows us logically to derive the universal statement 'All swans are white', one single observation of a black swan allows us logically to assert that 'Not all swans are white'. While this epistemological position means that the development of scientific knowledge proceeds by falsification through the use of empirical method rather than verification of the meaning of a sentence, Popper also offers some broad methodological injunctions: first, a hypothesis should be subjected to the severest test possible, for the more severe the test it is able to withstand, the more it is corroborated; and second, if it is to play a role in the growth of knowledge, as it should, a theory or a knowledge system should consist of bold or daring hypotheses that are highly falsifiable in principle. Unfortunately, as was apparent from Popper's later writings on social science, most of social science would not be able to pass this test.

Rudolf Carnap (1891–1970), who led the progressive wing of the Vienna Circle and went to the USA in 1936, played a leading role in revising various of its basic assumptions. In the selected text, he draws on criticisms of the principle of verifiability originally stemming from Wittgenstein and defended in the first phase of neo-positivism in order to develop a theory of the confirmation of hypotheses and theories or, rather, sentences belonging to the language of science. While conceding Popper's objection that absolute verification is impossible, he nevertheless continues to defend inductive logic, under the title of 'the theory of confirmation and testing', as being central to science. As against Schlick, he argues that verifiability or confirmability is not merely a matter of 'logical possibility' but rather a process of testing and confirming or disconfirming a sentence by observation. The fact that confirmation can never be achieved completely and fully, however, compels him to introduce a 'conventional component' into the process. In keeping with the available options, the scientist has to make a choice and decide accordingly what is acceptable as a 'practically sufficient certainty'. It is his willingness to face this problem that allowed Carnap to recast the task of the scientist from the earlier neo-positivist notion of building theory by generalizing observed regularities to the later notion of the construction of a logical-semantic framework which cannot simply be reduced to the observable and is therefore only partially empirically meaningful.

Talcott Parsons (1902–79) was a leading twentieth-century functionalist sociologist who nevertheless cast his work in a neo-positivist, logical positivist, logical empiricist or empirical analytical mould. In the text below, Parsons discusses what he regards as fundamental methodological problems, yet without making explicit the basis of his position. Fortunately, his stance, as well as where it fits into the neo-positivist philosophy of science, are readily apparent. On the one hand, Parsons launches a sustained frontal attack against 'a very common methodological position in the social sciences' – what he calls 'empiricism'. This is an old positivist view according to which science consists of the observation and accumulation of facts, devoid of any theory whatsoever, and the subsequent allowing of facts to speak for themselves. On the other hand, however, he conducts a much less visible criticism of first phase neo-positivism. This becomes tentatively apparent from his objections to the syntactic notion of scientific theory as a 'dependent variable' determined by the facts alone – i.e. as 'a body of logically interrelated "general concepts" of empirical reference'. But this more covert attack is confirmed by the particular standpoint from which he undertakes it. Parsons writes against the background of the second phase of the neo-positivist philosophy of science in which Popper conducted a serious campaign against the Vienna Circle's initial position and Carnap revised and developed it further. In fact, a number of Parsons' arguments become comprehensible only against this foil: first, he stresses the 'progress' or 'development' of scientific knowledge as against a concern with certain or eternal knowledge, just like Popper does; second, he regards theory as an interpreted, logically closed system or framework of propositions, comparable to Carnap's notion of a logical-semantic framework; third, he conceives of theory in various respects like Popper, namely that theory from the outset structures our observation and is something that we 'deliberately' or boldly pursue rather than passively acquire; and finally, he gives much attention to the 'verification' of theory which, through the contributions of Carnap and Popper, had become a central problem of the neo-positivist philosophy of science during the second phase of its development in the 1930s.

The dissolution of positivism

Let us now turn to readings 8 to 11 which give evidence of the radical redirection and even dissolution of positivism.

Alfred Ayer (1910–89), a Professor of Logic at Oxford, was principally instrumental in introducing the ideas of the Vienna Circle into British philosophy. In the 1930s he still forcefully applied the logic of confirmation in the form of his so-called 'deducibility criterion' to metaphysical, theological and moral claims which go beyond experience. By 1940, however, as the selected text attests, he recognized it as overly restrictive and felt himself compelled to admit that an appeal to sense data is not conclusive in proving assertions about the physical world. In the text, he emphasizes instead that the empirical significance of a sentence depends on the way in which it is used.

Willard van Orman Quine (1908–2000), the best-known American logician, astonished his neo-positivist contemporaries when in the late 1940s and early 1950s he launched a devastating attack against some of the basic tenets of logical empiricism – what in the selected text he calls 'two dogmas of empiricism'. The first is the fundamental distinction between incorrigible logical or analytical and corrigible empirical or synthetic propositions and the second is reductionism, or the assumption that every scientific statement can be led back to immediate experience. Underpinning his attack is what became known as the 'Duhem-Quine thesis', according to which scientific theories are underdetermined by empirical data. On the one hand, this thesis means that the evidence is never sufficient either to corroborate or refute a theory, with the implication that the theoretical system as a whole – in what is known as 'the holistic turn' – enjoys a certain priority. On the other hand, however, the fact that every proposition belongs to the theoretical system as a whole warns us that no proposition is ever protected against modification by experience. Quine mentions the case of a scientific revolution, what he calls 'a shift' from one theoretical system to another system, such as for instance from Ptolemy to Kepler or from Newton to Einstein. An interesting implication of his attack against positivism on which he elaborates in the text could also be noted. Whereas neo-positivists sought to demarcate science sharply from metaphysics, Quine argues that 'Science is a continuation of common-sense', which means that our ordinary everyday assumptions about reality can and do play a role in science.

Ludwig Wittgenstein (1889–1951), having initially provided the basis for neo-positivism, in the early 1930s started a process of the virtual reversal of his position which found its final expression in his posthumously published *Philosophical Investigations* (1953) of which the text below is an excerpt. At the core of the thinking of the later Wittgenstein is the concept of 'language game' which he introduces in the text below (paragraph 7). Here he gives up his earlier insistence on the importance of the logical form of language in favour of the proposal that we consider the concrete unity of the use of language as it is interwoven with a particular form of life and a certain way of seeing the world or, rather, the plurality of such language games which he suggests should be compared (paragraph 130) with one another on the basis of their 'family resemblances' (paragraph 67). In so far as he stresses a use theory of meaning (paragraphs 9, 29) – i.e. that the meaning of a sentence can only be understood with reference to the use of language according to the 'rules' (paragraphs 82–5, 198–9, 201–2, 206, 217–18, 224–5) of the given form of life – Wittgenstein approximates the pragmatic turn in neo-positivism represented for instance by Morris. Yet far from conceiving the connection between language and practice in terms of human activity and the employment of signs, as Morris does, he assumes a prior consensus or 'agreement' (paragraphs 224, 240–2) among the participants which they have acquired through upbringing, learning or 'training' (paragraphs 9, 206). By contrast with the attempt to discover an ideal language – as in the first phase of neo-positivism

– or constructing a formal language – as in its second phase – therefore, Wittgenstein here recommends that we focus on the order immanent in natural language. Language games should be analysed from the inside, as it were, by obtaining a 'perspicuous representation' or by 'seeing connexions' (paragraph 122), so that meanings could be grasped in terms of the interwovenness of the rules of the language game, the form of life, the rule following behaviour of the participants and, if necessary, the learning or training they underwent. That this radical reformulation of his position meant the dissolution of positivism is apparent from the fact that the later Wittgenstein's pragmatic or sociolinguistic turn directed attention away from the language of the natural sciences to a subject matter which is the topic of the social sciences.

Post-empiricism

Finally, we come to readings 12 to 14 which document the conclusive breakdown of positivism with the emergence of post-empiricism.

Stephen Toulmin (1922–), an Anglo-American historian and philosopher of science, was the first to conduct an inquiry into a crucial aspect of science to which authors like Wittgenstein and Quine drew attention and which was later captured by Kuhn's concept of 'paradigm'. Wittgenstein wrote, for instance, that 'new types of language, new language games, as we may say, come into existence, and others become obsolete and get forgotten. (We get a rough picture of this from the changes in mathematics.)'. In keeping with his so-called 'holistic turn' according to which the 'unit of empirical significance is science as a whole', Quine in turn referred to radical revisions of theoretical systems such as 'the shift whereby Kepler superseded Ptolemy, or Einstein Newton, or Darwin Aristotle'. Proceeding from the assumption that 'Science is . . . a slice of life', Toulmin in the selected text speaks of 'rational patterns of connections' by means of which scientists 'make sense of the flux of events' or, more emphatically, of 'ideals of natural order'. These patterns or ideals consist of 'preformed concepts' or 'prior theoretical considerations' which structure the scientist's approach to reality from the outset and throughout. He also remarks on the peculiar status of these patterns of connections. On the one hand, 'they change and develop . . . with history' and therefore must be something 'empirical' in the broad sense, yet on the other we 'cannot confront them directly with the results of observation and experiment'since they are conditions making scientific work possible. The recognition of this component of science and its dual status does not merely mark the break with positivism but is characteristic of post-empiricism.

Thomas Kuhn (1922–94), an American historian of science making use of sociological and social psychological in addition to epistemological ideas, published a landmark book which was responsible for bringing the break with the positivist or empiricist conception of science as well as the emergence of post-empiricism to full and general awareness. The central concept of this work, *The Structure of Scientific Revolutions* (1962), is that of 'paradigm' in the sense of the shifting or historically changing framework of understanding and commitment forming the basis of the practice of science. The selected text is an excerpt from this famous book.

Exposing the textbook image of science as consisting of methods, observations, facts, laws and theories and scientific development as a piecemeal process of 'accumulation' or 'accretion', Kuhn here effectively rejects the unhistorical and idealizing approach of positivism to science. Far from proceeding by 'confirmation and falsification', as for instance Carnap and Popper respectively held, and far from being a matter of 'individual inventions and discoveries' and a 'cumulative process', as textbooks generally suggest, science is based on a 'set of commitments', indeed an 'arbitrary element', accepted by the scientific community at a given time. Such a paradigm makes possible 'normal science' in so far as it not only allows 'attempts to force nature into conceptual boxes', but also calls forth defensive strategies such as the suppression of 'fundamental novelties' or 'anomalies' which stubbornly refuse to be aligned with or accommodated in the established framework of understanding. Under these conditions, scientific development involving controversies, the redefinition of problems and standards, the transformation of the scientific imagination and the reconstitution of the world in which scientific work is done, proceeds by competition over fundamental novelties and anomalies which can no longer be ignored by normal science. As Kuhn sees it: 'Competition between segments of the scientific community is the only historical process that ever actually results in the rejection of one previously accepted theory and the adoption of another'. When such an event occurs, normal science is transcended and we enter one of those extraordinary situations referred to as 'scientific revolutions' in which 'tradition-shattering' competition gives rise to 'a new set of commitments, a new basis for the practice of science'. Considering the actual situations in which knowledge is gained, accepted and assimilated, Kuhn comes to the conclusion that a whole series of basic distinctions, from which the neo-positivist philosophy of science has proceeded, become untenable. This applies, above all, to the most fundamental positivist distinction, enshrined in the very name 'logical empiricism', as is clear from what could be regarded as Kuhn's post-empiricist motto: 'Scientific fact and theory are not categorically separable'.

Imre Lakatos (1922–74) (and in the following text, Paul Feyerabend) exhibits the characteristic features of post-empiricism. Instead of projecting an ideal image of science and pursuing a model of eternal knowledge, Lakatos focuses on the development of knowledge. For this reason, he turns against the ahistorical approach to science in order to regard it as an ongoing enterprise or human activity. In turn, this leads him, along with Feyerabend, to jettison the positivistic emphasis on methods in favour of being task oriented. Reminding one of Kuhn's 'extended conception of the nature of scientific revolutions', Lakatos in the selected text rejects the view of science as the testing, confirmation or falsification of hypotheses due the fact that it assumes 'instant rationality' and 'instant learning', while in fact 'rationality works much slower than most people tend to think'. Far from being characterized by 'crucial experiments' in terms of 'isolated theories', therefore, science should be construed as consisting of 'research programmes' which possess 'heuristic power' and work over a more or less long timespan. Indeed, science is 'a battleground of research programmes'. Although thus ascribing to Kuhn's proposal to account for the development of knowledge in terms of competition, Lakatos regards his notion of 'paradigms' as being too social psychological and therefore prefers the more normative concept of research programmes instead.

Paul Feyerabend (1924–94), although initially having made contributions to the logical empiricist philosophy of science, for instance on explanation, later took to the extreme the historical view of the development of knowledge in the context of science as a task-oriented process carried by messy human activities. Some regard him as having thereby declared science impossible, yet he at most holds that it might in the end turn out that empirical science is a chimera. The radical 'anarchist' position that he puts forward in the selected text was preceded by criticism of what he called the 'empiricistic' metaphysics of logical empiricism and its precursors. As against a belief of many social scientists which led them to adhere to positivism, Feyerabend earlier also demonstrated that the logical empiricist philosophy of science actually does not at all fit physics, the supposed model discipline. In the text below, he argues against the positivist fixation on method and the underlying narrow model of scientific rationality in order to highlight the anarchic – that is, messy, untidy, cluttered and jumbled – nature of the process of the development and acquisition of scientific knowledge. Since he thinks it is clear from the historical record that factors of all sorts – training, interests, forces, propaganda, indoctrination, playful activity, vague urges, unreasonable beliefs, silly cosmology, but also the voice of reason, argumentation and reasoning – enter the process and in some way or another contribute to the development of knowledge, Feyerabend insists that the idea of a 'fixed [scientific] method' is an impoverishment. According to him, only one principle can be defended under all circumstances: the principle of 'anything goes'.

1

EMILE DURKHEIM
What is a social fact?* (1895)

Before inquiring into the method suited to the study of social facts, it is important to know which facts are commonly called 'social.' This information is all the more necessary since the designation 'social' is used with little precision. It is currently employed for practically all phenomena generally diffused within society, however small their social interest. But on that basis, there are, as it were, no human events that may not be called social. Each individual drinks, sleeps, eats, reasons; and it is to society's interest that these functions be exercised in an orderly manner. If, then, all these facts are counted as 'social' facts, sociology would have no subject matter exclusively its own, and its domain would be confused with that of biology and psychology.

But in reality there is in every society a certain group of phenomena which may be differentiated from those studied by the other natural sciences. When I fulfil my obligations as brother, husband, or citizen, when I execute my contracts, I perform duties which are defined, externally to myself and my acts, in law and in custom. Even if they conform to my own sentiments and I feel their reality subjectively, such reality is still objective, for I did not create them; I merely inherited them through my education. How many times it happens, moreover, that we are ignorant of the details of the obligations incumbent upon us, and that in order to acquaint ourselves with them we must consult the law and its authorized interpreters! Similarly, the church-member finds the beliefs and practices of his religious life ready-made at birth; their existence prior to his own implies their existence outside of himself. The system of signs I use to express my thought, the system of currency I employ to pay my debts, the instruments of credit I utilize in my commercial relations, the practices followed in my profession, etc., function independently of my own use of them. And these statements can be repeated for each member of society. Here, then, are ways of acting, thinking, and

* Reprinted with the permission of The Free Press, a Division of Simon & Schuster, Inc. from *The Rules of the Sociological Method*, Eighth edition by Emile Durkheim, translated by Sarah A. Solvay and John H. Mueller. Edited by George E.G. Catlin. Copyright © 1938 by George E.G. Catlin. Copyright © renewed 1966 by Sarah A. Solvay, John H. Mueller and George E.G. Catlin, pp. 1–5, 10–13.

feeling that present the noteworthy property of existing outside the individual consciousness.

These types of conduct or thought are not only external to the individual but are, moreover, endowed with coercive power, by virtue of which they impose themselves upon him, independent of his individual will. Of course, when I fully consent and conform to them, this constraint is felt only slightly, if at all, and is therefore unnecessary. But it is, nonetheless, an intrinsic characteristic of these facts, the proof thereof being that it asserts itself as soon as I attempt to resist it. If I attempt to violate the law, it reacts against me so as to prevent my act before its accomplishment, or to nullify my violation by restoring the damage, if it is accomplished and reparable, or to make me expiate it if it cannot be compensated for otherwise.

In the case of purely moral maxims; the public conscience exercises a check on every act which offends it by means of the surveillance it exercises over the conduct of citizens, and the appropriate penalties at its disposal. In many cases the constraint is less violent, but nevertheless it always exists. If I do not submit to the conventions of society, if in my dress I do not conform to the customs observed in my country and in my class, the ridicule I provoke, the social isolation in which I am kept, produce, although in an attenuated form, the same effects as a punishment in the strict sense of the word. The constraint is nonetheless efficacious for being indirect. I am not obliged to speak French with my fellow-countrymen nor to use the legal currency, but I cannot possibly do otherwise. If I tried to escape this necessity, my attempt would fail miserably. As an industrialist, I am free to apply the technical methods of former centuries; but by doing so, I should invite certain ruin. Even when I free myself from these rules and violate them successfully, I am always compelled to struggle with them. When finally overcome, they make their constraining power sufficiently felt by the resistance they offer. The enterprises of all innovators, including successful ones, come up against resistance of this kind.

Here, then, is a category of facts with very distinctive characteristics: it consists of ways of acting, thinking, and feeling, external to the individual, and endowed with a power of coercion, by reason of which they control him. These ways of thinking could not be confused with biological phenomena, since they consist of representations and of actions; nor with psychological phenomena, which exist only in the individual consciousness and through it. They constitute, thus, a new variety of phenomena; and it is to them exclusively that the term 'social' ought to be applied. And this term fits them quite well, for it is clear that, since their source is not in the individual, their substratum can be no other than society, either the political society as a whole or some one of the partial groups it includes, such as religious denominations, political, literary, and occupational associations, etc. On the other hand, this term 'social' applies to them exclusively, for it has a distinct meaning only if it designates exclusively the phenomena which are not included in any of the categories of facts that have already been established and classified. These ways of thinking and acting therefore constitute the proper domain of sociology. It is true that, when we define them with this word 'constraint,' we risk shocking the zealous partisans of absolute individualism. For those who profess the complete autonomy of the individual, man's dignity is diminished whenever he is made to feel that he is not completely self-determinant. It is generally accepted today, however, that most of our ideas and our tendencies are not developed by ourselves but come to us from without. How can they become a part of us except by imposing themselves upon us? This is the whole meaning of our definition. And it is generally accepted, moreover, that social constraint is not necessarily incompatible with the individual personality.

Since the examples that we have just cited (legal and moral regulations, religious faiths, financial systems, etc.) all consist of established beliefs and practices, one might be led to believe that social facts exist only where there is some social organization. But there are other facts without such crystallized form which have the same objectivity and the same ascendency over the individual. These are called 'social currents.' Thus the great movements of enthusiasm, indignation, and pity in a crowd do not originate in any one of the particular individual consciousnesses. They come to each one of us from without and can carry us away in spite of ourselves. Of course, it may happen that, in abandoning myself to them unreservedly, I do not feel the pressure they exert upon me. But it is revealed as soon as I try to resist them. Let an individual attempt to oppose one of these collective manifestations, and the emotions that he denies will turn against him. Now, if this power of external coercion asserts itself so clearly in cases of resistance, it must exist also in the first-mentioned cases, although we are unconscious of it. We are then victims of the illusion of having ourselves created that which actually forced itself from without. If the complacency with which we permit ourselves to be carried along conceals the pressure undergone, nevertheless it does not abolish it. Thus, air is no less heavy because we do not detect its weight. So, even if we ourselves have spontaneously contributed to the production of the common emotion, the impression we have received differs markedly from that which we would have experienced if we had been alone. Also, once the crowd has dispersed, that is, once these social influences have ceased to act upon us and we are alone again, the emotions which have passed through the mind appear strange to us, and we no longer recognize them as ours. We realize that these feelings have been impressed upon us to a much greater extent than they were created by us. It may even happen that they horrify us, so much were they contrary to our nature. Thus, a group of individuals, most of whom are perfectly inoffensive, may, when gathered in a crowd, be drawn into acts of atrocity. And what we say of these transitory outbursts applies similarly to those more permanent currents of opinion on religious, political, literary, or artistic matters which are constantly being formed around us, whether in society as a whole or in more limited circles . . .

We thus arrive at the point where we can formulate and delimit in a precise way the domain of sociology. It comprises only a limited group of phenomena. A social fact is to be recognized by the power of external coercion which it exercises or is capable of exercising over individuals, and the presence of this power may be recognized in its turn either by the existence of some specific sanction or by the resistance offered against every individual effort that tends to violate it. One can, however, define it also by its diffusion within the group, provided that, in conformity with our previous remarks, one takes care to add as a second and essential characteristic that its own existence is independent of the individual forms it assumes in its diffusion. This last criterion is perhaps, in certain cases, easier to apply than the preceding one. In fact, the constraint is easy to ascertain when it expresses itself externally by some direct reaction of society, as is the case in law, morals, beliefs, customs, and even fashions.

But when it is only indirect, like the constraint which an economic organization exercises, it cannot always be so easily detected. Generality combined with externality may, then, be easier to establish. Moreover, this second definition is but another form of the first; for if a mode of behavior whose existence is external to individual consciousnesses becomes general, this can only be brought about by its being imposed upon them.

But these several phenomena present the same characteristic by which we defined the others. These 'ways of existing' are imposed on the individual precisely in the same fashion as the 'ways of acting' of which we have spoken. Indeed, when we wish to know how a society is divided politically, of what these divisions themselves are composed, and how complete is the fusion existing between them, we shall not achieve our purpose by physical inspection and by geographical observations; for these phenomena are social, even when they have some basis in physical nature. It is only by a study of public law that a comprehension of this organization is possible, for it is this law that determines the organization, as it equally determines our domestic and civil relations. This political organization is, then, no less obligatory than the social facts mentioned above. If the population crowds into our cities instead of scattering into the country, this is due to a trend of public opinion, a collective drive that imposes this concentration upon the individuals. We can no more choose the style of our houses than of our clothing – at least, both are equally obligatory. The channels of communication prescribe the direction of internal migrations and commerce, etc., and even their extent. Consequently, at the very most, it should be necessary to add to the list of phenomena which we have enumerated as presenting the distinctive criterion of a social fact only one additional category, 'ways of existing'; and, as this enumeration was not meant to be rigorously exhaustive, the addition would not be absolutely necessary.

Such an addition is perhaps not necessary, for these 'ways of existing' are only crystallized 'ways of acting.' The political structure of a society is merely the way in which its component segments have become accustomed to live with one another. If their relations are traditionally intimate, the segments tend to fuse with one another, or, in the contrary case, to retain their identity. The type of habitation imposed upon us is merely the way in which our contemporaries and our ancestors have been accustomed to construct their houses. The methods of communication are merely the channels which the regular currents of commerce and migrations have dug, by flowing in the same direction. To be sure, if the phenomena of a structural character alone presented this permanence, one might believe that they constituted a distinct species. A legal regulation is an arrangement no less permanent than a type of architecture, and yet the regulation is a 'physiological' fact. A simple moral maxim is assuredly somewhat more malleable, but it is much more rigid than a simple professional custom or a fashion. There is thus a whole series of degrees without a break in continuity between the facts of the most articulated structure and those free currents of social life which are not yet definitely molded. The differences between them are, therefore, only differences in the degree of consolidation they present. Both are simply life, more or less crystallized. No doubt, it may be of some advantage to reserve the term 'morphological' for those social facts which concern the social substratum, but only on condition of not overlooking the fact that they are of the same nature as the others.

Our definition will then include the whole relevant range of facts if we say: A social fact is every way of acting, fixed or not, capable of exercising on the individual an external constraint; or again, every way of acting which is general throughout a given society, while at the same time existing in its own right independent of its individual manifestations.

2

OTTO NEURATH
The scientific world conception* (1929)

The scientific world conception is characterised not so much by theses of its own, but rather by its basic attitude, its points of view and direction of research. The goal ahead is unified science. The endeavour is to link and harmonise the achievements of individual investigators in their various fields of science. From this aim follows the emphasis on collective efforts, and also the emphasis on what can be grasped intersubjectively; from this springs the search for a neutral system of formulae, for a symbolism freed from the slag of historical languages; and also the search for a total system of concepts. Neatness and clarity are striven for, and dark distances and unfathomable depths rejected. In science there are no 'depths'; there is surface everywhere: all experience forms a complex network, which cannot always be surveyed and can often be grasped only in parts. Everything is accessible to man; and man is the measure of all things. Here is an affinity with the Sophists, not with the Platonists; with the Epicureans, not with the Pythagoreans; with all those who stand for earthly being and the here and now. The scientific world-conception knows no unsolvable riddle. Clarification of the traditional philosophical problems leads us partly to unmask them as pseudo-problems, and partly to transform them into empirical problems and thereby subject them to the judgment of experimental science. The task of philosophical work lies in this clarification of problems and assertions, not in the propounding of special 'philosophical' pronouncements. The method of this clarification is that of logical analysis; of it, Russell *says* (*Our Knowledge of the External World*, p. 4) that it 'has gradually crept into philosophy through the critical scrutiny of mathematics . . . It represents, I believe, the same kind of advance as was introduced into physics by Galileo: the substitution of piecemeal, detailed and verifiable results for large untested generalities recommended only by a certain appeal to imagination.'

It is the method of logical analysis that essentially distinguishes recent empiricism and positivism from the earlier version that was more biological-psychological in its orientation. If someone asserts 'there is a God', 'the primary basis of the world is the

* From Otto Neurath *Empiricism and Sociology Sociology: The Life and Work of Otto Neurath*, Dordrecht: Reidel, 1973, pp. 305–310. Edited and translated from the German by Paul Foulkes and Marie Neurath. Reproduced by permission from Kluwer Academic Publishers.

unconscious', 'there is an entelechy which is the leading principle in the living organism', we do not say to him: 'what you say is false'; but we ask him: 'what do you mean by these statements?' Then it appears that there is a sharp boundary between two kinds of statements. To one belong statements as they are made by empirical science; their meaning can be determined by logical analysis or, more precisely, through reduction to the simplest statements about the empirically given. The other statements, to which belong those cited above, reveal themselves as empty of meaning if one takes them in the way that metaphysicians intend. One can, of course, often re-interpret them as empirical statements; but then they lose the content of feeling which is usually essential to the metaphysician. The metaphysician and the theologian believe, thereby misunderstanding themselves, that their statements say something, or that they denote a state of affairs. Analysis, however, shows that these statements say nothing but merely express a certain mood and spirit. To express such feelings for life can be a significant task. But the proper medium for doing so is art, for instance lyric poetry or music. It is dangerous to choose the linguistic garb of a theory instead: a theoretical content is simulated where none exists. If a metaphysician or theologian wants to retain the usual medium of language, then he must himself realise and bring out clearly that he is giving not description but expression, not theory or communication of knowledge, but poetry or myth. If a mystic asserts that he has experiences that lie above and beyond all concepts, one cannot deny this. But the mystic cannot talk about it, for talking implies capture by concepts and reduction to scientifically classifiable states of affairs.

The scientific world-conception rejects metaphysical philosophy. But how can we explain the wrong paths of metaphysics? This question may be posed from several points of view: psychological, sociological and logical. Research in a psychological direction is still in its early stages; the beginnings of more penetrating explanation may perhaps be seen in the investigations of Freudian psychoanalysis. The state of sociological investigation is similar; we may mention the theory of the 'ideological superstructure'; here the field remains open to worthwhile further research.

More advanced is the clarification of the logical origins of metaphysical aberration, especially through the works of Russell and Wittgenstein. In metaphysical theory, and even in the very form of the questions, there are two basic logical mistakes: too narrow a tie to the form of traditional languages and a confusion about the logical achievement of thought. Ordinary language for instance uses the same part of speech, the substantive, for things ('apple') as well as as for qualities ('hardness'), relations ('friendship'), and processes ('sleep'); therefore it misleads one into a thing-like conception of functional concepts (hypostasis, substantialisation). One can quote countless similar examples of linguistic misleading, that have been equally fatal to philosophers.

The second basic error of metaphysics consists in the notion that thinking can either lead to knowledge out of its own resources without using any empirical material, or at least arrive at new contents by an inference from given states of affair. Logical investigation, however, leads to the result that all thought and inference consists of nothing but a transition from statements to other statements that contain nothing that was not already in the former (tautological transformation). It is therefore not possible to develop a metaphysic from 'pure thought'.

In such a way logical analysis overcomes not only metaphysics in the proper, classical sense of the word, especially scholastic metaphysics and that of the systems of German idealism, but also the hidden metaphysics of Kantian and modern apriorism. The scientific world-conception knows no unconditionally valid knowledge derived from pure reason, no 'synthetic judgments a priori' of the kind that lie at the basis of Kantian epistemology and even more of all pre- and post-Kantian ontology and metaphysics. The judgments of arithmetic, geometry, and certain fundamental principles of physics, that Kant took as examples of a priori knowledge will be discussed later. It is precisely in the rejection of the possibility of synthetic knowledge a priori that the basic thesis of modern empiricism lies. The scientific world-conception knows only empirical statements about things of all kinds, and analytic statements of logic and mathematics.

In rejecting overt metaphysics and the concealed variety of apriorism, all adherents of the scientific world-conception are at one. Beyond this, the Vienna Circle maintain the view that the statements of (critical) realism and idealism about the reality or non-reality of the external world and other minds are of a metaphysical character, because they are open to the same objections as are the statements of the old metaphysics: they are meaningless, because [they are] unverifiable and without content. For us, something is 'real' through being incorporated into the total structure of experience.

Intuition, which is especially emphasised by metaphysicians as a source of knowledge, is not rejected as such by the scientific world-conception. However, rational justification has to pursue all intuitive knowledge step by step. The seeker is allowed any method; but what has been found must stand up to testing. The view which attributes to intuition a superior and more penetrating power of knowing, capable of leading beyond the contents of sense experience and not to be confined by the shackles of conceptual thought – this view is rejected.

We have characterised the scientific world-conception essentially by two features. First it is empiricist and positivist: there is knowledge only from experience, which rests on what is immediately given. This sets the limits for the content of legitimate science. Second, the scientific world-conception is marked by application of a certain method, namely logical analysis. The aim of scientific effort is to reach the goal, unified science, by applying logical analysis to the empirical material. Since the meaning of every statement of science must be statable by reduction to a statement about the given, likewise the meaning of any concept, whatever branch of science it may belong to, must be statable by step-wise reduction to other concepts, down to the concepts of the lowest level which refer directly to the given. If such an analysis were carried through for all concepts, they would thus be ordered into a reductive system, a 'constitutive system'. Investigations towards such a constitutive system, the 'constitutive theory', thus form the framework within which logical analysis is applied by the scientific world-conception. Such investigations show very soon that traditional Aristotelian scholastic logic is quite inadequate for this purpose. Only modern symbolic logic ('logistic') succeeds in gaining the required precision of concept definitions and of statements, and in formalising the intuitive process of inference of ordinary thought, that is to bring it into a rigorous automatically controlled form by means of a symbolic mechanism. Investigations into constitutive theory show that the lowest layers of the constitutive system contain concepts of the experience and qualities of the individual psyche; in the layer above are physical objects; from these are constituted other minds and lastly the objects of social science. The arrangement of the concepts of the various branches of science into the constitutive system can already be discerned in outline today, but much remains to be done in detail. With the proof of the possibility and the outline of the shape of the total system of concepts, the relation of all statements to the given and with it the general structure of unified science become recognisable too.

A scientific description can contain only the structure (form of order) of objects, not their 'essence'. What unites men in language are structural formulae; in them the content of the common knowledge of men presents itself. Subjectively experienced qualities – redness, pleasure – are as such only experiences, not knowledge; physical optics admits only what is in principle understandable by a blind man too.

3

CARL G. HEMPEL
Concept and theory in social science* (1952)

But is it not true, after all, that in physics as well, there are theories, such as those of ideal gases, of perfectly elastic impact, of the mathematical pendulum, of the statistical aspects of a game played with perfect dice, etc., which are not held to be invalidated by the fact that they possess no precise exemplification in the empirical world? And could not ideal types claim the same status as the central concepts of those 'idealized' theories? Those concepts refer to physical systems satisfying certain extreme conditions which cannot be fully, but only approximately, met by concrete empirical phenomena. Their scientific significance lies, I think, in the following points: (a) The laws governing the behavior of the ideal physical systems are deducible from more comprehensive theoretical principles, which are well confirmed by empirical evidence; the deduction usually takes the form of assigning certain extreme values to some of the parameters of the comprehensive theory. Thus, e.g., the laws for an ideal gas are obtainable from more inclusive principles of the kinetic theory of gases by 'assuming' that the volumes of the gas molecules vanish and that there are no forces of attraction among the molecules – i.e., by setting the appropriate parameters equal to zero. (b) The extreme conditions characterizing the 'ideal' case can at least be approximated empirically, and whenever this is the case in a concrete instance, the ideal laws in question are empirically confirmed. Thus, e.g., the Boyle-Charles law for ideal gases is rather closely satisfied by a large variety of gases within wide, specifiable ranges of pressure and temperature (for a fixed mass of gas), and it is for this reason that the law can be significantly invoked for explanatory purposes.

The preceding analysis suggests the following observations on the 'ideal' and the empirical aspects of ideal-type concepts in the social sciences:

(i) 'Ideal' constructs have the character not of concepts in the narrower sense, but of theoretical systems. The introduction of such a construct into a theoretical context requires, therefore, not definition by genus and differentia, but the specification of a

* From 'Problems of Concept and Theory Formation in the Social Sciences' by Carl Hempel in *Science, Language, and Human Rights*, pp. 80–84, by The American Philosophical Association. Copyright © 1952 University of Pennsylvania Press. Reprinted with permission.

set of characteristics (such as pressure, temperature, and volume in the case of an ideal gas) and of a set of general hypotheses connecting those characteristics.

(ii) An idealized concept P does not, therefore, function in hypotheses of the simple form 'If P then Q.' Thus, e.g., the hypothesis 'If a substance is an ideal gas then it satisfies Boyle's law,' which is of that form, is an analytic statement entailed by the definition of an ideal gas; it cannot serve explanatory purposes. Rather, the hypotheses characterizing the concept of ideal gas connect certain quantitative characteristics of a gas, and when they are applied to concrete physical systems, they make specific empirical predictions. Thus, to put the point in a somewhat oversimplified form, what enters into physical theory is not the concept of ideal gas at all, but rather the concepts representing the various characteristics dealt with in the theory of ideal gases; only they are mentioned in the principles of thermodynamics.

(iii) In the natural sciences at least, a set of hypotheses is considered as characterizing an ideal system only if they represent what might be called theoretical, rather than intuitive, idealizations; i.e., if they are obtainable, within the framework of a given theory, as special cases of more inclusive principles. Thus, e.g., the formula for the mathematical pendulum as empirically discovered by Galileo did not constitute a theoretical idealization until after the establishment of more comprehensive hypotheses which (a) have independent empirical confirmation, (b) entail the pendulum formula as a special case, (c) enable us to judge the degree of idealization involved in the latter by giving an account of additional factors which are relevant for the motion of a physical pendulum, but whose influence is fairly small in the case of those physical systems to which the formula is customarily applied.

No theory, of course, however inclusive, can claim to give a completely accurate account of any class of empirical phenomena; it is always possible that even a very comprehensive and well-confirmed theory may be improved in the future by the inclusion of further parameters and appropriate laws: the most comprehensive theory of today may be but a systematic idealization within the broader theoretical framework of tomorrow.

Among the ideal-type concepts of social theory, those used in analytical economics approximate most closely the status of idealizations in natural science: the concepts of perfectly free competition, of monopoly, of economically rational behavior on the part of an individual or a firm, etc., all represent schemata for the interpretation of certain aspects of human behavior and involve the idealizing assumption that non-economic factors of the sort that do in fact influence human actions may be neglected for the purposes at hand. In the context of rigorous theory construction, those ideal constructs are given a precise meaning in the form of hypotheses which 'postulate' specified mathematical connections between certain economic variables; frequently, such postulates characterize the ideal type of behavior as maximizing a given function of those variables (say, profit).

In two important respects, however, idealizations in economics seem to me to differ from those of the natural sciences: first of all, they are intuitive rather than theoretical idealizations in the sense that the corresponding 'postulates' are not deduced, as special cases, from a broader theory which covers also the nonrational and noneconomic factors affecting human conduct. No suitable more general theory is available at present, and thus there is no theoretical basis for an appraisal of the idealization involved in applying the economic constructs to concrete situations. This takes us to the second point of difference: the class of concrete behavioral phenomena for which the 'idealized' principles of economic theory are meant to constitute at least approximately correct generalizations is not always clearly specified. This of course hampers the significant explanatory use of those principles: an ideal theoretical system, as indeed any theoretical system at all, can assume the status of an explanatory and predictive apparatus only if its area of application has been specified; in other words, if its constituent concepts have been given an empirical interpretation which, directly or at least mediately, links them to observable phenomena. Thus, e.g., the area of application for the theory of ideal gases might be indicated, roughly speaking, by interpreting the theoretical parameters 'P,' 'V,' 'T' in terms of the 'operationally defined' magnitudes of pressure, volume, and temperature of gases at moderate or low pressures and at moderate or high temperatures. Similarly, the empirical applicability of the principles of an ideal economic system requires an interpretation in empirical terms which does not render those principles analytic; hence the interpretation must not amount to the statement that the propositions of the theory hold in all cases of economically rational behavior – that would be simply a tautology; rather, it has to characterize, by criteria logically independent of the theory, those kinds of individual or group behavior to which the theory is claimed to be applicable. In reference to these, it has then to attach a reasonably definite 'operational meaning' to the theoretical parameters, such as 'money,' 'price,' 'cost,' 'profit,' 'utility,' etc. In this fashion, the propositions of the theory acquire empirical import: they become capable of test and thus susceptible to disconfirmation – and this is an essential characteristic of all potential explanatory systems.

The results of the preceding comparison between the ideal constructs of economics with those of physics should not be considered, however, as indicating an essential methodological difference between the two fields. For in regard to the first of our two points of comparison, it need only be remembered that much effort in sociological theorizing at present is directed toward the development of a comprehensive theory of social action, relatively to which the ideal constructs of economics, in so far as they permit of empirical application, might then have the status of theoretical rather than intuitive idealizations. And quite apart from the attainability of that ambitious goal, it is clear that an interpretation is required for any theoretical system which is to have empirical import – in the social no less than in the natural sciences.

The ideal types invoked in other fields of social science lack the clarity and precision of the constructions used in theoretical economics. The behavioral regularities which are meant to define a given ideal type are usually stated only in more or less intuitive terms, and the parameters they are meant to connect are not explicitly specified; finally, there is no clear indication of the area of empirical applicability and consequent testability claimed for the typological system. In fact, the demand for such testability is often rejected in a sweeping manner which, I think, the preceding discussion has shown to be inconsistent with the claim that ideal types provide an understanding of certain empirical phenomena.

If the analysis here outlined is essentially sound, then surely ideal types can serve their purpose only if they are introduced as interpreted theoretical systems, i.e., by (a) specifying a list of characteristics with which the theory is to deal, (b) formulating a set of hypotheses in terms of those characteristics, (c) giving those characteristics an empirical interpretation, which assigns to the theory a specific domain of application, and (d), as a long-range objective, incorporating the theoretical system, as a 'special case,' into a more comprehensive theory. To what extent these objectives can be attained cannot be decided by logical analysis; but it would be self-deception to believe that any conceptual procedure essentially lacking in the first three respects can give theoretical understanding in any field of scientific inquiry. And to the extent that the program here outlined can actually be carried through, the use of 'ideal types' is at best an unimportant terminological aspect, rather than a distinctive methodological characteristic, of the social sciences: the method of ideal types becomes indistinguishable from the methods used by other scientific disciplines in the formation and application of explanatory concepts and theories.

In sum, then, the various uses of type concepts in psychology and the social sciences, when freed from certain misleading connotations, prove to be of exactly the same character as the methods of classification, ordering, measurement, empirical correlation, and finally theory formation used in the natural sciences. In leading to this result, the analysis of typological procedures exhibits, in a characteristic example, the methodological unity of empirical science.

4

ERNST NAGEL
Methodological problems of the social sciences* (1961)

The study of human society and human behavior molded by social institutions has been cultivated for about as long as has the investigation of physical and biological phenomena. However, much of the 'social theory' that has emerged from such study, in the past as well as the present, is social and moral philosophy rather than social science, and is made up in large measure of general reflections on the 'nature of man,' justifications or critiques of various social institutions, or outlines of stages in the progress or decay of civilizations. Although discussions of this type often contain penetrating insights into the functions of various social institutions in the human economy, they rarely pretend to be based on systematic surveys of detailed empirical data concerning the actual operation of societies. If such data are mentioned at all, their function is for the most part anecdotal, serving to illustrate rather than to test critically some general conclusion. Despite the long history of active interest in social phenomena, the experimental production and methodical collection of evidence for assessing beliefs about them are of relatively recent origin.

But in any event, in no area of social inquiry has a body of general laws been established, comparable with outstanding theories in the natural sciences in scope of explanatory power or in capacity to yield precise and reliable predictions. It is of course true that, under the inspiration of the impressive theoretical achievements of natural science, comprehensive systems of 'social physics' have been repeatedly constructed, purporting to account for the entire gamut of diverse institutional structures and changes that have appeared throughout human history. However, these ambitious constructions are the products of doubtfully adequate notions of what constitutes sound scientific procedure, and, though some of them continue to have adherents, none of them stands up under careful scrutiny.† Most competent students

---

* From Ernst Nagel *The Structure of Science*, London, Routledge & Kegan Paul, 1961, pp. 447–449. Reproduced with permission.
† Many of these systems are 'single factor' or 'key cause' theories. They identify some one 'variable' – such as geographic environment, biological endowment, economic organization, or religious belief, to mention but a few – in terms of which the institutional arrangements and the development of societies are to be understood.

today do not believe that an empirically warranted theory, able to explain in terms of a single set of integrated assumptions the full variety of social phenomena, is likely to be achieved in the foreseeable future. Many social scientists are of the opinion, moreover, that the time is not yet ripe even for theories designed to explain systematically only quite limited ranges of social phenomena. Indeed, when such theoretical constructions with a restricted scope have been attempted, as in economics or on a smaller scale in the study of social mobility, their empirical worth is widely regarded as a still unsettled question. To a considerable extent, the problems investigated in many current centers of empirical social research are admittedly concerned with problems of moderate and often unimpressive dimensions.

It is also generally acknowledged that in the social sciences there is nothing quite like the almost complete unanimity commonly found among competent workers in the natural sciences as to what are matters of established fact, what are the reasonably satisfactory explanations (if any) for the assumed facts, and what are some of the valid procedures in sound inquiry. Disagreement on such questions undoubtedly occurs in the natural sciences as well. But it is usually found at the advancing frontiers of knowledge; and, except in areas of research that impinge intimately upon moral or religious commitments, such disagreement is generally resolved with reasonable dispatch when additional evidence is obtained or when improved techniques of analysis are developed. In contrast, the social sciences often produce the impression that they are a battleground for interminably warring schools of thought, and that even subject matter which has been under intensive and prolonged study remains at the unsettled periphery of research. At any rate, it is a matter of public record that social scientists continue to be divided on central issues in the logic of social inquiry which are implicit in the questions mentioned above. In particular, there is a long-standing divergence in professed scientific aims between those who view the explanatory systems and logical methods of the natural sciences as models to be emulated in social research, and those who think it is fundamentally inappropriate for the social sciences to seek explanatory theories that employ 'abstract' distinctions remote from familiar experience and that require publicly accessible (or 'intersubjectively' valid) supporting evidence.

In short, the social sciences today possess no wide-ranging systems of explanations judged as adequate by a majority of professionally competent students, and they are characterized by serious disagreements on methodological as well as substantive questions. In consequence, the propriety of designating any extant branch of social inquiry as a 'real science' has been repeatedly challenged – commonly on the ground that, although such inquiries have contributed large quantities of frequently reliable information about social matters, these contributions are primarily descriptive studies of special social facts in certain historically situated human groups, and supply no strictly universal laws about social phenomena. It would not be profitable to discuss at any length an issue framed in this manner, particularly since the requirements for being a genuine science tacitly assumed in most of the challenges lead to the unenlightening result that apparently none but a few branches of physical inquiry merit the honorific designation. In any event, it will suffice for present purposes to note that, although descriptive studies of localized social fact mark much social research, this statement does not adequately summarize its achievements. For inquiries into human behavior have also made evident (with the increasing aid, in recent years, of rapidly developing techniques of quantitative analysis) some of the relations of dependence between components in various social processes; and those inquiries have thereby supplied more or less firmly grounded generalized assumptions for explaining many features of social life, as well as for constructing frequently effective social policies. To be sure, the laws or generalizations concerning social phenomena made available by current social inquiry are far more restricted in scope of application, are formulated far less precisely, and are acceptable as factually sound only if understood to be hedged in by a far larger number of tacit qualifications and exceptions, than are most of the commonly cited laws of the physical sciences. In these respects, however, the generalizations of social inquiry do not appear to differ radically from generalizations currently advanced in domains usually regarded as unquestionably respectable subdivisions of natural science – for example, in the study of turbulence phenomena and in embryology.

The important task, surely, is to achieve some clarity in fundamental methodological issues and the structure of explanation in the social sciences, rather than to award or withhold honorific titles . . .

5

KARL POPPER
The problem of induction* (1934)

According to a widely accepted view – to be opposed in this book – the empirical sciences can be characterized by the fact that they use 'inductive methods', as they are called. According to this view, the logic of scientific discovery would be identical with inductive logic, i.e. with the logical analysis of these inductive methods.

It is usual to call an inference 'inductive' if it passes from singular statements (sometimes also called 'particular' statements), such as accounts of the results of observations or experiments, to universal statements, such as hypotheses or theories.

Now it is far from obvious, from a logical point of view, that we are justified in inferring universal statements from singular ones, no matter how numerous; for any conclusion drawn in this way may always turn out to be false: no matter how many instances of white swans we may have observed, this does not justify the conclusion that all swans are white.

The question whether inductive inferences are justified, or under what conditions, is known as the problem of induction.

The problem of induction may also be formulated as the question of the validity or the truth of universal statements which are based on experience, such as the hypotheses and theoretical systems of the empirical sciences. For many people believe that the truth of these universal statements is 'known by experience'; yet it is clear that an account of an experience – of an observation or the result of an experiment – can in the first place be only a singular statement and not a universal one. Accordingly, people who say of a universal statement that we know its truth from experience usually mean that the truth of this universal statement can somehow be reduced to the truth of singular ones, and that these singular ones are known by experience to be true; which amounts to saying that the universal statement is based on inductive inference. Thus to ask whether there are natural laws known to be true appears to be only another way of asking whether inductive inferences are logically justified.

Yet if we want to find a way of justifying inductive inferences, we must first of all

---

* Sections 1 & 6 of Chapter 1 of *The Logic of Scientific Discovery* reprinted by permission of the estate of Sir Karl Popper. First published by Hutchinson 1959, by Routledge since 1992. © Karl R. Popper.

try to establish a principle of induction. A principle of induction would be a statement with the help of which we could put inductive inferences into a logically acceptable form. In the eyes of the upholders of inductive logic, a principle of induction is of supreme importance for scientific method: '. . . this principle', says Reichenbach, 'determines the truth of scientific theories. To eliminate it from science would mean nothing less than to deprive science of the power to decide the truth or falsity of its theories. Without it, clearly, science would no longer have the right to distinguish its theories from the fanciful and arbitrary creations of the poet's mind'.

Now this principle of induction cannot be a purely logical truth like a tautology or an analytic statement. Indeed, if there were such a thing as a purely logical principle of induction, there would be no problem of induction; for in this case, all inductive inferences would have to be regarded as purely logical or tautological transformations, just like inferences in deductive logic. Thus the principle of induction must be a synthetic statement; that is, a statement whose negation is not self-contradictory but logically possible. So the question arises why such a principle should be accepted at all, and how we can justify its acceptance on rational grounds.

Some who believe in inductive logic are anxious to point out, with Reichenbach, that 'the principle of induction is unreservedly accepted by the whole of science and that no man can seriously doubt this principle in everyday life either'. Yet even supposing this were the case – for after all, 'the whole of science' might err – I should still contend that a principle of induction is superfluous, and that it must lead to logical inconsistencies.

That inconsistencies may easily arise in connection with the principle of induction should have been clear from the work of Hume; also, that they can be avoided, if at all, only with difficulty. For the principle of induction must be a universal statement in its turn. Thus if we try to regard its truth as known from experience, then the very same problems which occasioned its introduction will arise all over again. To justify it, we should have to employ inductive inferences; and to justify these we should have to assume an inductive principle of a higher order; and so on. Thus the attempt to base the principle of induction on experience breaks down, since it must lead to an infinite regress.

Kant tried to force his way out of this difficulty by taking the principle of induction (which he formulated as the 'principle of universal causation') to be 'a priori valid'. But I do not think that his ingenious attempt to provide an a priori justification for synthetic statements was successful.

My own view is that the various difficulties of inductive logic here sketched are insurmountable. So also, I fear, are those inherent in the doctrine, so widely current today, that inductive inference, although not 'strictly valid', can attain some degree of 'reliability' or of 'probability'. According to this doctrine, inductive inferences are 'probable inferences'. 'We have described', says Reichenbach, 'the principle of induction as the means whereby science decides upon truth. To be more exact, we should say that it serves to decide upon probability. For it is not given to science to reach either truth or falsity . . . but scientific statements can only attain continuous degrees of probability whose unattainable upper and lower limits are truth and falsity'.

At this stage I can disregard the fact that the believers in inductive logic entertain an idea of probability that I shall later reject as highly unsuitable for their own purposes. I can do so because the difficulties mentioned are not even touched by an appeal to probability. For if a certain degree of probability is to be assigned to statements based on inductive inference, then this will have to be justified by invoking a new principle of induction, appropriately modified. And this new principle in its turn will have to be justified, and so on. Nothing is gained, moreover, if the principle of induction, in its turn, is taken not as 'true' but only as 'probable'. In short, like every other form of inductive logic, the logic of probable inference, or 'probability logic', leads either to an infinite regress, or to the doctrine of apriorism.

The theory to be developed in the following pages stands directly opposed to all attempts to operate with the ideas of inductive logic. It might be described as the theory of the deductive method of testing, or as the view that a hypothesis can only be empirically tested – and only after it has been advanced.

Before I can elaborate this view (which might be called 'deductivism', in contrast to 'inductivism'), I must first make clear the distinction between the psychology of knowledge which deals with empirical facts, and the logic of knowledge which is concerned only with logical relations. For the belief in inductive logic is largely due to a confusion of psychological problems with epistemological ones. It may be worth noticing, by the way, that this confusion spells trouble not only for the logic of knowledge but for its psychology as well.

Falsifiability as a criterion of demarcation

The criterion of demarcation inherent in inductive logic – that is, the positivistic dogma of meaning – is equivalent to the requirement that all the statements of empirical science (or all 'meaningful' statements) must be capable of being finally decided, with respect to their truth and falsity; we shall say that they must be 'conclusively decidable'. This means that their form must be such that to verify them and to falsify them must both be logically possible. Thus Schlick says: '. . . a genuine statement must be capable of conclusive verification'; and Waismann says still more clearly: 'If there is no possible way to determine whether a statement is true then that statement has no meaning whatsoever. For the meaning of a statement is the method of its verification'.

Now in my view there is no such thing as induction. Thus inference to theories, from singular statements which are 'verified by experience' (whatever that may mean), is logically inadmissible. Theories are, therefore, never empirically verifiable. If we wish to avoid the positivist's mistake of eliminating, by our criterion of demarcation, the theoretical systems of natural science, then we must choose a criterion which allows us to admit to the domain of empirical science even statements which cannot be verified.

But I shall certainly admit a system as empirical or scientific only if it is capable of being tested by experience. These considerations suggest that not the verifiability but the falsifiability of a system is to be taken as a criterion of demarcation. In other words: I shall not require of a scientific system that it shall be capable of being singled out, once and for all, in a positive sense; but I shall require that its logical form shall be such that it can be singled out, by means of empirical tests, in a negative sense: it must be possible for an empirical scientific system to be refuted by experience.

(Thus the statement, 'It will rain or not rain here tomorrow' will not be regarded as empirical, simply because it cannot be refuted; whereas the statement, 'It will rain here tomorrow' will be regarded as empirical.)

Various objections might be raised against the criterion of demarcation here proposed. In the first place, it may well seem somewhat wrong-headed to suggest that science, which is supposed to give us positive information, should be characterized as satisfying a negative requirement such as refutability. However, I shall show, in sections 31 to 46, that this objection has little weight, since the amount of positive information about the world which is conveyed by a scientific statement is the greater the more likely it is to clash, because of its logical character, with possible singular statements. (Not for nothing do we call the laws of nature 'laws': the more they prohibit the more they say.)

Again, the attempt might be made to turn against me my own criticism of the inductivist criterion of demarcation; for it might seem that objections can be raised against falsifiability as a criterion of demarcation similar to those which I myself raised against verifiability.

This attack would not disturb me. My proposal is based upon an asymmetry between verifiability and falsifiability; an asymmetry which results from the logical form of universal statements. For these are never derivable from singular statements, but can be contradicted by singular statements. Consequently it is possible by means of purely deductive inferences (with the help of the *modus tollens* of classical logic) to argue from the truth of singular statements to the falsity of universal statements. Such an argument to the falsity of universal statements is the only strictly deductive kind of inference that proceeds, as it were, in the 'inductive direction'; that is, from singular to universal statements.

A third objection may seem more serious. It might be said that even if the asymmetry is admitted, it is still impossible, for various reasons, that any theoretical system should ever be conclusively falsified. For it is always possible to find some way of evading falsification, for example by introducing ad hoc an auxiliary hypothesis, or by changing ad hoc a definition. It is even possible without logical inconsistency to adopt the position of simply refusing to acknowledge any falsifying experience whatsoever. Admittedly, scientists do not usually proceed in this way, but logically such procedure is possible; and this fact, it might be claimed, makes the logical value of my proposed criterion of demarcation dubious, to say the least.

I must admit the justice of this criticism; but I need not therefore withdraw my proposal to adopt falsifiability as a criterion of demarcation. For I am going to propose (in sections 20 f.) that the empirical method shall be characterized as a method that excludes precisely those ways of evading falsification which, as my imaginary critic rightly insists, are logically possible. According to my proposal, what characterizes the empirical method is its manner of exposing to falsification, in every conceivable way, the system to be tested. Its aim is not to save the lives of untenable systems but, on the contrary, to select the one which is by comparison the fittest, by exposing them all to the fiercest struggle for survival.

The proposed criterion of demarcation also leads us to a solution of Hume's problem of induction – of the problem of the validity of natural laws. The root of this problem is the apparent contradiction between what may be called 'the fundamental thesis of empiricism' – the thesis that experience alone can decide upon the truth or falsity of scientific statements – and Hume's realization of the inadmissibility of inductive arguments. This contradiction arises only if it is assumed that all empirical scientific statements must be 'conclusively decidable', i.e. that their verification and their falsification must both in principle be possible. If we renounce this requirement and admit as empirical also statements which are decidable in one sense only – unilaterally decidable and, more especially, falsiflable – and which may be tested by systematic attempts to falsify them, the contradiction disappears: the method of falsification presupposes no inductive inference, but only the tautological transformations of deductive logic whose validity is not in dispute.

6

RUDOLPH CARNAP
Confirmation, testing and meaning* (1936)

Two chief problems of the theory of knowledge are the question of meaning and the question of verification. The first question asks under what conditions a sentence has meaning, in the sense of cognitive, factual meaning. The second one asks how we get to know something, how we can find out whether a given sentence is true or false. The second question presupposes the first one. Obviously we must understand a sentence, i.e. we must know its meaning, before we can try to find out whether it is true or not. But, from the point of view of empiricism, there is a still closer connection between the two problems. In a certain sense, there is only one answer to the two questions. If we knew what it would be for a given sentence to be found true then we would know what its meaning is. And if for two sentences the conditions under which we would have to take them as true are the same, then they have the same meaning. Thus the meaning of a sentence is in a certain sense identical with the way we determine its truth or falsehood; and a sentence has meaning only if such a determination is possible.

If by verification is meant a definitive and final establishment of truth, then no (synthetic) sentence is ever verifiable, as we shall see. We can only confirm a sentence more and more. Therefore we shall speak of the problem of confirmation rather than of the problem of verification. We distinguish the testing of a sentence from its confirmation, thereby understanding a procedure – e.g. the carrying out of certain experiments – which leads to a confirmation in some degree either of the sentence itself or of its negation. We shall call a sentence testable if we know such a method of testing for it; and we call it confirmable if we know under what conditions the sentence would be confirmed. As we shall see, a sentence may be confirmable without being testable; e.g. if we know that our observation of such and such a course of events would confirm the sentence, and such and such a different course would confirm its negation without knowing how to set up either this or that observation . . .

The connection between meaning and confirmation has sometimes been

* From 'Testability and Meaning', *Philosophy of Science*, 3(4), 1936, pp. 442–427. Reprinted with permission of the University of Chicago Press.

formulated by the thesis that a sentence is meaningful if and only if it is verifiable, and that its meaning is the method of its verification. The historical merit of this thesis was that it called attention to the close connection between the meaning of a sentence and the way it is confirmed. This formulation thereby helped, on the one hand, to analyze the factual content of scientific sentences, and, on the other hand, to show that the sentences of trans-empirical metaphysics have no cognitive meaning. But from our present point of view, this formulation, although acceptable as a first approximation, is not quite correct. By its oversimplification, it led to a too narrow restriction of scientific language, excluding not only metaphysical sentences but also certain scientific sentences having factual meaning. Our present task could therefore be formulated as that of a modification of the requirement of verifiability. It is a question of a modification, not of an entire rejection of that requirement. For among empiricists there seems to be full agreement that at least some more or less close relation exists between the meaning of a sentence and the way in which we may come to a verification or at least a confirmation of it.

The requirement of verifiability was first stated by Wittgenstein, and its meaning and consequences were exhibited in the earlier publications of our Vienna Circle; it is still held by the more conservative wing of this Circle. The thesis needs both explanation and modification. What is meant by 'verifiability' must be said more clearly. And then the thesis must be modified and transformed in a certain direction.

Objections from various sides have been raised against the requirement mentioned not only by anti-empiricist metaphysicians but also by some empiricists, e.g. by Reichenbach, Popper, Lewis, Nagel, and Stace. I believe that these criticisms are right in several respects; but on the other hand, their formulations must also be modified. The theory of confirmation and testing which will be explained in the following chapters is certainly far from being an entirely satisfactory solution. However, by more exact formulation of the problem, it seems to me, we are led to a greater convergence with the views of the authors mentioned and with related views of other empiricist authors and groups. The points of agreement and of still existing differences will be evident from the following explanations.

A first attempt at a more detailed explanation of the thesis of verifiability has been made by Schlick in his reply to Lewis' criticisms. Since 'verifiability' means 'possibility of verification' we have to answer two questions: 1) what is meant in this connection by 'possibility'? and 2) what is meant by 'verification'? Schlick – in his explanation of 'verifiability' – answers the first question, but not the second one. In his answer to the question: what is meant by 'verifiability of a sentence S', he substitutes the fact described by S for the process of verifying S. Thus he thinks e.g. that the sentence S1: 'Rivers flow up-hill,' is verifiable, because it is logically possible that rivers flow up-hill. I agree with him that this fact is logically possible and that the sentence S1 mentioned above is verifiable – or, rather, confirmable, as we prefer to say for reasons to be explained soon. But I think his reasoning which leads to this result is not quite correct. S1 is confirmable, not because of the logical possibility of the fact described in S1, but because of the physical possibility of the process of confirmation; it is possible to test and to confirm S1 (or its negation) by observations of rivers with the help of survey instruments.

Except for some slight differences, e.g. the mentioned one, I am on the whole in agreement with the views of Schlick explained in his paper. I agree with his clarification of some misunderstandings concerning positivism and so-called methodological solipsism. When I used the last term in previous publications I wished to indicate by it nothing more than the simple fact, that everybody in testing any sentence empirically cannot do otherwise than refer finally to his own observations; he cannot use the results of other people's observations unless he has become acquainted with them by his own observations, e.g. by hearing or reading the other man's report. No scientist, as far as I know, denies this rather trivial fact. Since, however, the term 'methodological solipsism' – in spite of all explanations and warnings – is so often misunderstood, I shall prefer not to use it any longer. As to the fact intended, there is, I think, no disagreement among empiricists; the apparent differences are due only to the unfortunate term. A similar remark is perhaps true concerning the term 'autopsychic basis' (*'eigenpsychische Basis'*) . . .

If verification is understood as a complete and definitive establishment of truth then a universal sentence, e.g. a so-called law of physics or biology, can never be verified, a fact which has often been remarked. Even if each single instance of the law were supposed to be verifiable, the number of instances to which the law refers – e.g. the space-time-points – is infinite and therefore can never be exhausted by our observations which are always finite in number. We cannot verify the law, but we can test it by testing its single instances, i.e. the particular sentences which we derive from the law and from other sentences established previously. If in the continued series of such testing experiments no negative instance is found but the number of positive instances increases then our confidence in the law will grow step by step. Thus, instead of verification, we may speak here of gradually increasing confirmation of the law.

Now a little reflection will lead us to the result that there is no fundamental difference between a universal sentence and a particular sentence with regard to verifiability but only a difference in degree. Take for instance the following sentence: 'There is a white sheet of paper on this table.' In order to ascertain whether this thing is paper, we may make a set of simple observations and then, if there still remains some doubt, we may make some physical and chemical experiments. Here as well as in the case of the law, we try to examine sentences which we infer from the sentence in question. These inferred sentences are predictions about future observations. The number of such predictions which we can derive from the sentence given is infinite; and therefore the sentence can never be completely verified. To be sure, in many cases we reach a practically sufficient certainty after a small number of positive instances, and then we stop experimenting. But there is always the theoretical possibility of continuing the series of test-observations. Therefore here also no complete verification is possible but only a process of gradually increasing confirmation. We may, if we wish, call a sentence disconfirmed in a certain degree if its negation is confirmed in that degree.

The impossibility of absolute verification has been pointed out and explained in detail by Popper. In this point our present views are, it seems to me, in full accordance with Lewis and Nagel. Suppose a sentence S is given, some test-observations for it have been made, and S is confirmed by them in a certain degree. Then it is a matter of practical decision whether we will consider that degree as high enough for our acceptance of S, or as low enough for our rejection of S, or as intermediate between these so that we neither accept nor reject S until further evidence will be available. Although our decision is based upon the observations made so far, nevertheless it is not uniquely determined by them. There is no general rule to determine our decision. Thus the acceptance and the rejection of a (synthetic) sentence always contains a conventional component. That does not mean that the decision – or, in other words, the question of truth and verification – is conventional. For, in addition to the conventional component there is always the non-conventional component – we may call it, the objective one – consisting in the observations which have been made. And it must certainly be admitted that in very many cases this objective component is present to such an overwhelming extent that the conventional component practically vanishes. For such a simple sentence as, e.g. 'There is a white thing on this table' the degree of confirmation, after a few observations have been made, will be so high that we practically cannot help accepting the sentence. But even in this case there remains still the theoretical possibility of denying the sentence. Thus even here it is a matter of decision or convention.

The view that no absolute verification but only gradual confirmation is possible, is sometimes formulated in this way: every sentence is a probability-sentence; e.g. by Reichenbach and Lewis. But it seems advisable to separate the two assertions. Most empiricists today will perhaps agree with the first thesis, but the second is still a matter of dispute. It presupposes the thesis that the degree of confirmation of a hypothesis can be interpreted as the degree of probability in the strict sense which this concept has in the calculus of probability, i.e. as the limit of relative frequency. Reichenbach holds this thesis. But so far he has not worked out such an interpretation in detail, and today it is still questionable whether it can be carried out at all. Popper has explained the difficulties of such a frequency interpretation of the degree of confirmation; the chief difficulty lies in how we are to determine for a given hypothesis the series of 'related' hypotheses to which the concept of frequency is to apply. It seems to me that at present it is not yet clear whether the concept of degree of confirmation can be defined satisfactorily as a quantitative concept, i.e. a magnitude having numerical values. Perhaps it is preferable to define it as a merely topological concept, i.e. by defining only the relations: 'S1 has the same (or, a higher) degree of confirmation than S2 respectively,' but in such a way that most of the pairs of sentences will be incomparable. We will use the concept in this way – without however defining it – only in our informal considerations which serve merely as a preparation for exact definitions of other terms. We shall later on define the concepts of complete and incomplete reducibility of confirmation as syntactical concepts, and those of complete and incomplete confirmability as descriptive concepts.

7

TALCOTT PARSONS
Theory and empirical fact* (1937)

In the following discussion some fundamental methodological propositions will be laid down without any attempt to give them a critical foundation. It will, however, turn out that the question of the status of these views will form one main element of the subject matter of the whole study. Their soundness is to be judged not in terms of the arguments brought forward in their defense in the present introductory discussion but in terms of the way they fit into the structure of the study as a whole and its outcome. There is, more often implicit than explicit, a deep-rooted view that the progress of scientific knowledge consists essentially in the cumulative piling up of 'discoveries' of 'fact.' Knowledge is held to be an entirely quantitative affair. The one important thing is to have observed what had not been observed before. Theory, according to this view, would consist only in generalization from known facts, in the sense of what general statements the known body of fact would justify. Development of theory would consist entirely in the process of modification of these general statements to take account of new discoveries of fact. Above all, the process of discovery of fact is held to be essentially independent of the existing body of 'theory,' to be the result of some such impulse as 'idle curiosity.'

It is evident that such terms as 'fact,' are much in need of definition. This will come later. At the present juncture against the view just roughly sketched may be set another, namely, that scientific 'theory' – most generally defined as a body of logically interrelated 'general concepts' of empirical reference – is not only a dependent but an independent variable in the development of science. It goes without saying that a theory to be sound must fit the facts but it does not follow that the facts alone, discovered independently of theory, determine what the theory is to be, nor that theory is not a factor in determining what facts will be discovered, what is to be the direction of interest of scientific investigation.

Not only is theory an independent variable in the development of science, but the body of theory in a given field at a given time constitutes to a greater or less degree an

* Reprinted with the permission of The Free Press, a division of Simon & Shuster, Inc, from *The Structure of Social Action* by Talcott Parsons. Copyright © 1964 by the Free Press. Copyright © renewed 1977 by Talcott Parsons, pp. 6–14.

integrated 'system.' That is, the general propositions (which may be, as will be seen later, of different kinds) which constitute a body of theory have mutual logical relations to each other. Not, of course, that all the rest are deducible from any one – that would confine theory to the one proposition – but in the sense that any substantive change in the statement of one important proposition of the system has logical consequences for the statement of the others. Another way of putting this is to say that any system of theory has a determinate logical structure.

Now obviously the propositions of the system have reference to matters of empirical fact; if they did not, they could have no claim to be called scientific. Indeed, if the term fact is properly interpreted it may be said that a theoretical proposition, if it has a place in science at all, is either itself a statement of fact or a statement of a mode of relations between facts. It follows that any *important* change in our knowledge of fact in the field in question must of itself change the statement of at least one of the propositions of the theoretical system and, through the logical consequences of this change, that of other propositions to a greater or lesser degree. This is to say, the structure of the theoretical system is changed. All this seems to be in accord with the empiricist methodology sketched above.

But, in the first place, it will be noted that the word 'important' used above was italicized. What does an important change in our knowledge of fact mean in this context? Not that the new facts are vaguely 'interesting,' that they satisfy 'idle curiosity,' or that they demonstrate the goodness of God. But the scientific importance of a change in knowledge of fact consists precisely in its having consequences for a system of theory. A scientifically unimportant discovery is one which, however true and however interesting for other reasons, has no consequences for a system of theory with which scientists in that field are concerned. Conversely, even the most trivial observation from any other point of view – a very small deviation of the observed from the calculated position of a star, for instance – may be not only important but of revolutionary importance, if its logical consequences for the structure of theory are far-reaching. It is probably safe to say that all the changes of factual knowledge which have led to relativity theory, resulting in a very great theoretical development, are completely trivial from any point of view except their relevance to the structure of a theoretical system. They have not, for instance, affected in any way the practice of engineering or navigation.

This matter of the importance of facts is, however, only one part of the picture. A theoretical system does not merely state facts which have been observed and their logically deducible relations to other facts which have also been observed. In so far as such a theory is empirically correct it will also tell us what empirical facts it should be possible to observe in a given set of circumstances. It is the most elementary rule of scientific integrity that the formulator of a theoretical proposition must take into account all the relevant known facts accessible to him. The process of verification, fundamental to science, does not consist merely in reconsideration of this applicability to known facts by others than the original formulator of the theory, and then simply waiting for new facts to turn up. It consists in deliberately investigating phenomena with the expectations derived from the theory in mind and seeing whether or not the facts actually found agree with these expectations.

This investigation is one of situations which have been studied either never at all before or not with these particular theoretical problems in mind. Where possible the situations to be investigated are experimentally produced and controlled. But this is a matter of practical technique, not of logic. In so far as the expectations from the theory agree with the facts found, making allowance for 'errors of observation,' etc., the theory is 'verified.' But the significance of the process of verification is by no means confined to this. If this does not happen, as is often so, either the facts may be found to disagree with the theoretical expectations, or other facts may be found which have no place in the theoretical system. Either result necessitates critical reconsideration of the system itself. There is, then, a reciprocal process: direction, by the expectations derived from a system of theory, toward fields of factual investigation, then reaction of the results of this investigation on the theory.

Finally, verification in this sense is not the only important relation of a theoretical system to the direction of empirical investigation. Not only are specific theoretical propositions which have been directly formulated with definite matters of fact in view subject to verification. But further, a theoretical system built up upon observations of fact will be found, as its implications are progressively worked out, to have logical consequences for fields of fact with which its original formulators were not directly concerned. If certain things in one field are true, then other things in another, related field must also be true. These implications also are subject to verification, which in this case takes the form of finding out what are the facts in this field. The results of this investigation may have the same kind of reaction on the theoretical system itself.

Thus, in general, in the first instance, the direction of interest in empirical fact will be canalized by the logical structure of the theoretical system. The importance of certain problems concerning the facts will be inherent in the structure of the system. Empirical interest will be in the facts so far as they are relevant to the solution of these problems. Theory not only formulates what we know but also tells us what we want to know, that is, the questions to which an answer is needed. Moreover, the structure of a theoretical system tells us what alternatives are open in the possible answers to a given question. If observed facts of undoubted accuracy will not fit any of the alternatives it leaves open, the system itself is in need of reconstruction.

A further point is of importance in the present connection. Not only do theoretical propositions stand in logical interrelations to each other so that they may be said to constitute 'systems' but it is in the nature of the case that theoretical systems should attempt to become 'logically closed.' That is, a system starts with a group of interrelated propositions which involve reference to empirical observations within the logical framework of the propositions in question. Each of these propositions has logical implications. The system becomes logically closed when each of the logical implications which can be derived from any one proposition within the system finds its statement in another proposition in the same system. It may be repeated that this does not mean that all the other propositions must be logically derivable from any one – on the contrary, if this were true scientific theory would be sheer tautology.

The simplest way to see the meaning of the concept of a closed system in this sense is to consider the example of a system of simultaneous equations. Such a system is determinate, i.e., closed, when there are as many independent equations as there are independent variables. If there are four equations and only three variables, and no one of the equations is derivable from the others by algebraic manipulation then there is another variable missing. Put in general logical terms: the propositions stated in the four equations logically involve an assumption which is not stated in the definitions of the three variables.

The importance of this is clear. If the explicit propositions of a system do not constitute a logically closed system in this sense it may be inferred that the arguments invoked rest for their logical cogency on one or more unstated assumptions. It is one of the prime functions of logical criticism of theoretical systems to apply this criterion and, if gaps are found, to uncover the implicit assumptions. But though all theory tends to develop logically closed systems in this sense it is dangerous to confuse this with the 'empirical' closure of a system. To this issue, that of 'empiricism,' it will be necessary often to return.

The implications of these considerations justify the statement that all empirically verifiable knowledge – even the common-sense knowledge of everyday life – involves implicitly, if not explicitly, systematic theory in this sense. The importance of this statement lies in the fact that certain persons who write on social subjects vehemently deny it. They say they state merely facts and let them 'speak for themselves.' But the fact a person denies that he is theorizing is no reason for taking him at his word and failing to investigate what implicit theory is involved in his statements. This is important since 'empiricism' in this sense has been a very common methodological position in the social sciences.

From all this it follows what the general character of the problem of the development of a body of scientific knowledge is, in so far as it depends on elements internal to science itself. It is that of increasing knowledge of empirical fact, intimately combined with changing interpretations of this body of fact – hence changing general statements about it – and, not least, a changing structure of the theoretical system. Special emphasis should be laid on this intimate interrelation of general statements about empirical fact with the logical elements and structure of theoretical systems.

In one of its main aspects the present study may be regarded as an attempt to verify empirically this view of the nature of science and its development in the social field. It takes the form of the thesis that intimately associated with the revolution in empirical interpretations of society sketched above there has in fact occurred an equally radical change in the structure of theoretical systems. The hypothesis may be put forward, to be tested by the subsequent investigation, that this development has been in large part a matter of the reciprocal interaction of new factual insights and knowledge on the one hand with changes in the theoretical system on the other. Neither is the 'cause' of the other. Both are in a state of close mutual interdependence.

8

A.J. AYER
The characterization of sense-data* (1940)

...I have already shown that if a 'language' is to be capable of being used as a language, that is to say, for the purpose of communication, it must also be character-ized by non-formal rules, which connect some of its symbols, not with other symbols, but with observable states of affairs. What is not necessary, however, is that a symbol, the use of which is determined by such a non-formal rule, should have any further connexion with what it symbolizes beyond that which is constituted by the existence of the rule ... A symbol may or may not share a common quality with which it symbolizes. There is no ground whatsoever for saying that it must.

I believe that this mistake about the nature of meaning is reflected in the ordinary formulation of 'the correspondence theory of truth'. For when we are told that a sentence expresses a true proposition if and only if it is used in such a way that it corresponds to a fact, we are inclined to interpret the word 'correspondence' literally, as implying some sort of resemblance, and then we find ourselves confronted with such questions as, What do sentences which express false propositions resemble? and How is it that sentences, which express what we have every reason for supposing to be true propositions, do not appear in any way to resemble the relevant facts? – and to these questions we are unable to give any satisfactory answer. But such problems do not arise, once it is made clear that the word 'correspondence', if it is to be used at all in this connexion, must not be understood literally. To say that I am using the sen-tence 'there is a match-box on my table' to correspond to the fact that there is a match-box on my table, or to express a proposition which corresponds to this fact, is to say no more than that I am using the words 'there is a match-box on my table' to mean that there is a match-box on my table, and there is a match-box on my table. But how do I discover that there is a match-box on my table? How is it to be determined that any empirical proposition does, in this sense, correspond to a fact? The answer is that, in the last resort, it is always to be determined by actual observation. I say 'in the last resort' because it is necessary here to draw a distinction between propositions the

* From *The Foundations of Empirical Knowledge*, Macmillan, 1940, pp. 107–110. Reproduced with the permission of Palgrave.

truth of which are determined directly by observation, and those that are verified indirectly. One's ground for believing a given proposition is often, in the first instance, the truth of a second proposition which is evidence for it; and one's ground for believing the second proposition may, in its turn, be the truth of a third; but this series cannot be prolonged indefinitely. In the end it must include at least one proposition that is believed, not merely on the ground that it is supported by other propositions, but in virtue of what is actually observed. For, as I have already shown, we are not entitled to regard a set of propositions as true merely because they support one another. In order that we should have reason to accept any of them, it is necessary that at least one of their number should be directly verified by observation of an empirical fact.

Is it now possible for us to delimit the class of propositions that are capable of being directly verified? The only means that I can see of doing this is to say that a proposition is capable of being directly verified when it is expressed by a sentence the meaning of which is determined by a non-formal rule. But the consequence of this is that the question, whether a given proposition is or is not capable of being directly verified, does not admit of a straightforward answer. We must say that it depends upon the language in which the proposition is expressed. If, for example, we have agreed to use the sense-datum language, we shall have to say that propositions like 'this is a match-box' or 'this is a pencil' are not directly verifiable. For we must hold that the meaning of sentences which express such propositions is to be determined by reference to sentences which designate sense-data, and that it is only when a sentence explicitly designates a sense-data that its meaning is determined by reference to fact. On the other hand, when we are teaching English to a child, we imply that propositions about material things can be directly verified. For we do not then explain the meaning of sentences like 'this is a match-box' or 'this is a pencil' in terms of sentences which designate sense-data. We indicate it ostensively. But whereas the meaning of a sentence which refers to a sense-datum is precisely determined by the rule that correlates it with the sense-datum in question, such precision is not attainable in the case of a sentence which refers to a material thing. For the proposition which such a sentence expresses differs from a proposition about a sense-datum in that there are no observable facts that constitute both a necessary and sufficient condition of its truth.

9

W.V.O. QUINE
Two dogmas of empiricism* (1951)

Modern empiricism has been conditioned in large part by two dogmas. One is a belief in some fundamental cleavage between truths which are analytic, or grounded in meanings independently of matters of fact, and truths which are synthetic, or grounded in fact. The other dogma is reductionism: the belief that each meaningful statement is equivalent to some logical construct upon terms which refer to immediate experience. Both dogmas, I shall argue, are ill founded. One effect of abandoning them is, as we shall see, a blurring of the supposed boundary between speculative metaphysics and natural science. Another effect is a shift toward pragmatism . . .

Kant's cleavage between analytic and synthetic truths was foreshadowed in Hume's distinction between relations of ideas and matters of fact, and in Leibniz's distinction between truths of reason and truths of fact. Leibniz spoke of the truths of reason as true in all possible worlds. Picturesqueness aside, this is to say that the truths of reason are those which could not possibly be false. In the same vein we hear analytic statements defined as statements whose denials are self-contradictory. But this definition has small explanatory value; for the notion of self-contradictoriness, in the quite broad sense needed for this definition of analyticity, stands in exactly the same need of clarification as does the notion of analyticity itself. The two notions are the two sides of a single dubious coin . . .

Carnap seems to have appreciated this point afterward; for in his later writings he abandoned all notion of the translatability of statements about the physical world into statements about immediate experience. Reductionism in its radical form has long since ceased to figure in Carnap's philosophy.

But the dogma of reductionism has, in a subtler and more tenuous form, continued to influence the thought of empiricists. The notion lingers that to each statement, or each synthetic statement, there is associated a unique range of possible sensory events such that the occurrence of any of them would add to the likelihood of truth of the statement, and that there is associated also another unique range of

* From 'Two Dogmas of Empiricism', *Philosophical Review* 60, 1951, pp. 20, 338–343. Copyright 1951 Cornell University. Reproduced with permission of the publisher.

possible sensory events whose occurrence would detract from that likelihood. This notion is of course implicit in the verification theory of meaning.

The dogma of reductionism survives in the supposition that each statement, taken in isolation from its fellows, can admit of confirmation or infirmation at all. My countersuggestion, issuing essentially from Carnap's doctrine of the physical world in the *Aufbau*, is that our statements about the external world face the tribunal of sense experience not individually but only as a corporate body.

The dogma of reductionism, even in its attenuated form, is intimately connected with the other dogma: that there is a cleavage between the analytic and the synthetic. We have found ourselves led, indeed, from the latter problem to the former through the verification theory of meaning. More directly, the one dogma clearly supports the other in this way: as long as it is taken to be significant in general to speak of the confirmation and infirmation of a statement, it seems significant to speak also of a limiting kind of statement which is vacuously confirmed, *ipso facto*, come what may; and such a statement is analytic.

The two dogmas are, indeed, at root identical. We lately reflected that in general the truth of statements does obviously depend both upon language and upon extra-linguistic fact; and we noted that this obvious circumstance carries in its train, not logically but all too naturally, a feeling that the truth of a statement is somehow analyzable into a linguistic component and a factual component. The factual component must, if we are empiricists, boil down to a range of confirmatory experiences. In the extreme case where the linguistic component is all that matters, a true statement is analytic. But I hope we are now impressed with how stubbornly the distinction between analytic and synthetic has resisted any straightforward drawing. I am impressed also, apart from prefabricated examples of black and white balls in an urn, with how baffling the problem has always been of arriving at any explicit theory of the empirical confirmation of a synthetic statement. My present suggestion is that it is nonsense, and the root of much nonsense, to speak of a linguistic component and a factual component in the truth of any individual statement. Taken collectively, science has its double dependence upon language and experience; but this duality is not significantly traceable into the statements of science taken one by one.

Russell's concept of definition in use was, as remarked, an advance over the impossible term-by-term empiricism of Locke and Hume. The statement, rather than the term, came with Russell to be recognized as the unit accountable to an empiricist critique. But what I am now urging is that even in taking the statement as unit we have drawn our grid too finely. The unit of empirical significance is the whole of science.

᚛ The totality of our so-called knowledge or beliefs, from the most casual matters of geography and history to the profoundest laws of atomic physics or even of pure mathematics and logic, is a man-made fabric which impinges on experience only along the edges. Or, to change the figure, total science is like a field of force whose boundary conditions are experience. A conflict with experience at the periphery occasions readjustments in the interior of the field. Truth values have to be redistributed over some of our statements. Re-evaluation of some statements entails re-evaluation of others, because of their logical interconnections – the logical laws being in turn simply certain further statements of the system, certain further elements of the field. Having re-evaluated one statement we must re-evaluate some others, whether they be statements logically connected with the first or whether they be the statements of logical connections themselves. But the total field is so undetermined by its boundary conditions, experience, that there is much latitude of choice as to what statements to re-evaluate in the light of any single contrary experience. No particular experiences are linked with any particular statements in the interior of the field, except indirectly through considerations of equilibrium affecting the field as a whole. ⊃

If this view is right, it is misleading to speak of the empirical content of an individual statement – especially if it be a statement at all remote from the experiential periphery of the field. Furthermore it becomes folly to seek a boundary between synthetic statements, which hold contingently on experience, and analytic statements which hold come what may. Any statement can be held true come what may, if we make drastic enough adjustments elsewhere in the system. Even a statement very close to the periphery can be held true in the face of recalcitrant experience by pleading hallucination or by amending certain statements of the kind called logical laws. Conversely, by the same token, no statement is immune to revision. Revision even of the logical law of the excluded middle has been proposed as a means of simplifying quantum mechanics; and what difference is there in principle between such a shift and the shift whereby Kepler superseded Ptolemy, or Einstein Newton, or Darwin Aristotle?

For vividness I have been speaking in terms of varying distances from a sensory periphery. Let me try now to clarify this notion without metaphor. Certain statements, though about physical objects and not sense experience, seem peculiarly germane to sense experience – and in a selective way: some statements to some experiences, others to others. Such statements, especially germane to particular experiences, I picture as near the periphery. But in this relation of 'germaneness' I envisage nothing more than a loose association reflecting the relative likelihood, in practice, of our choosing one statement rather than another for revision in the event of recalcitrant experience. For example, we can imagine recalcitrant experiences to which we would surely be inclined to accommodate our system by re-evaluating just the statement that there are brick houses on Elm Street, together with related statements on the same topic. We can imagine other recalcitrant experiences to which we would be inclined to accommodate our system by re-evaluating just the statement that there are no centaurs, along with kindred statements. A recalcitrant experience can, I have already urged, be accommodated by any of various alternative re-evaluations in various alternative quarters of the total system; but, in the cases which we are now imagining, our natural tendency to disturb the total system as little as possible would lead us to focus our revisions upon these specific statements concerning brick houses or centaurs. These statements are felt, therefore, to have a sharper empirical reference than highly theoretical statements of physics or logic or ontology. The latter statements may be thought of as relatively centrally located within the total network, meaning merely that little preferential connection with any particular sense data obtrudes itself.

As an empiricist I continue to think of the conceptual scheme of science as a tool, ultimately, for predicting future experience in the light of past experience. Physical objects are conceptually imported into the situation as convenient intermediaries – not by definition in terms of experience, but simply as irreducible posits comparable, epistemologically, to the gods of Homer. Let me interject that for my part I do, *qua* lay physicist, believe in physical objects and not in Homer's gods; and I consider it a scientific error to believe otherwise. But in point of epistemological footing the physical objects and the gods differ only in degree and not in kind. Both sorts of entities enter our conception only as cultural posits. The myth of physical objects is epistemologically superior to most in that it has proved more efficacious than other myths as a device for working a manageable structure into the flux of experience.

Imagine, for the sake of analogy, that we are given the rational numbers. We develop an algebraic theory for reasoning about them, but we find it inconveniently complex, because certain functions such as square root lack values for some arguments. Then it is discovered that the rules of our algebra can be much simplified by conceptually augmenting our ontology with some mythical entities, to be called irrational numbers. All we continue to be really interested in, first and last, are rational numbers; but we find that we can commonly get from one law about rational numbers to another much more quickly and simply by pretending that the irrational numbers are there too. I think this a fair account of the introduction of irrational numbers and other extensions of the number system. The fact that the mythical status of irrational numbers eventually gave way to the Dedekind-Russell version of them as certain infinite classes of ratios is irrelevant to my analogy. That version is impossible anyway as long as reality is limited to the rational numbers and not extended to classes of them.

Now I suggest that experience is analogous to the rational numbers and that the physical objects, in analogy to the irrational numbers, are posits which serve merely to simplify our treatment of experience. The physical objects are no more reducible to experience than the irrational numbers to rational numbers, but their incorporation into the theory enables us to get more easily from one statement about experience to another.

The salient differences between the positing of physical objects and the positing of irrational numbers are, I think, just two. First, the factor of simplification is more overwhelming in the case of physical objects than in the numerical case. Second, the positing of physical objects is far more archaic, being indeed coeval, I expect, with language itself. For language is social and so depends for its development upon intersubjective reference.

Positing does not stop with macroscopic physical objects. Objects at the atomic level and beyond are posited to make the laws of macroscopic objects, and ultimately the laws of experience, simpler and more manageable; and we need not expect or demand full definition of atomic and subatomic entities in terms of macroscopic ones, any more than definition of macroscopic things in terms of sense data. Science is a continuation of common sense, and it continues the common-sense expedient of swelling ontology to simplify theory.

Physical objects, small and large, are not the only posits. Forces are another example; and indeed we are told nowadays that the boundary between energy and matter is obsolete. Moreover, the abstract entities which are the substance of mathematics – ultimately classes and classes of classes and so on up – are another posit in the same spirit. Epistemologically these are myths on the same footing with physical objects and gods, neither better nor worse except for differences in the degree to which they expedite our dealings with sense experiences.

The overall algebra of rational and irrational numbers is underdetermined by the algebra of rational numbers, but is smoother and more convenient; and it includes the algebra of rational numbers as a jagged or gerrymandered part. Total science, mathematical and natural and human, is similarly but more extremely underdetermined by experience. The edge of the system must be kept squared with experience; the rest, with all its elaborate myths or fictions, has as its objective the simplicity of laws.

Ontological questions, under this view, are on a par with questions of natural science. Consider the question whether to countenance classes as entities. This, as I have argued elsewhere, is the question whether to quantify with respect to variables which take classes as values. Now Carnap has maintained that this is a question not of matters of fact but of choosing a convenient language form, a convenient conceptual scheme or framework for science. With this I agree, but only on the proviso that the same be conceded regarding scientific hypotheses generally. Carnap has recognized that he is able to preserve a double standard for ontological questions and scientific hypotheses only by assuming an absolute distinction between the analytic and the synthetic; and I need not say again that this is a distinction which I reject.

Some issues do, I grant, seem more a question of convenient conceptual scheme and others more a question of brute fact. The issue over there being classes seems more a question of convenient conceptual scheme; the issue over there being centaurs, or brick houses on Elm Street, seems more a question of fact. But I have been urging that this difference is only one of degree, and that it turns upon our vaguely pragmatic inclination to adjust one strand of the fabric of science rather than another in accommodating some particular recalcitrant experience. Conservatism figures in such choices, and so does the quest for simplicity.

Carnap, Lewis, and others take a pragmatic stand on the question of choosing between language forms, scientific frameworks; but their pragmatism leaves off at the imagined boundary between the analytic and the synthetic. In repudiating such a boundary I espouse a more thorough pragmatism. Each man is given a scientific heritage plus a continuing barrage of sensory stimulation; and the considerations which guide him in warping his scientific heritage to fit his continuing sensory promptings are, where rational, pragmatic.

10

LUDWIG WITTGENSTEIN
Language games and meaning* (1953)

2. That philosophical concept of meaning has its place in a primitive idea of the way language functions. But one can also say that it is the idea of a language more primitive than ours. Let us imagine a language for which the description given by Augustine is right. The language is meant to serve for communication between a builder A and an assistant B. A is building with building-stones: there are blocks, pillars, slabs and beams. B has to pass the stones, and that in the order in which A needs them. For this purpose they use a language consisting of the words 'block', 'pillar', 'slab', 'beam'. A calls them out; B brings the stone which he has learnt to bring at such-and-such a call. Conceive this as a complete primitive language.

7. In the practice of the use of language one party calls out the words, the other acts on them. In instruction in the language the following process will occur: the learner names the objects; that is, he utters the word when the teacher points to the stone. And there will be this still simpler exercise: the pupil repeats the words after the teacher, both of these being processes resembling language.

We can also think of the whole process of using words . . . as one of those games by means of which children learn their native language. I will call these games 'language-games' and will sometimes speak of a primitive language as a language-game.

And the processes of naming the stones and of repeating words after someone might also be called language-games. Think of much of the use of words in games like ring-a-ring-a-roses.

I shall also call the whole, consisting of language and the actions into which it is woven, the 'language-game'.

8. Let us now look at an expansion of language. Besides the four words 'block', 'pillar', etc., let it contain a series of words . . . (it can be the series of letters of the alphabet); further, let there be two words, which may as well be 'there' and 'this'

* From *Philosophical Investigations*, Basil Blackwell, 1968. First published in 1953. Reproduced with the permission of Blackwell Publishers.

(because this roughly indicates their purpose), that are used in connexion with a pointing gesture; and finally a number of colour samples. A gives an order like: 'd slab there'. At the same time he shows the assistant a colour sample, and when he says 'there' he points to a place on the building site. From the stock of slabs B takes one for each letter of the alphabet up to 'd', of the same colour as the sample, and brings them to the place indicated by A. On other occasions A gives the order 'this there'. At 'this' he points to a building stone. And so on.

9. When a child learns this language, it has to learn the series of 'numerals' a, b, c, . . . by heart. And it has to learn their use. Will this training include ostensive teaching of the words? Well, people will, for example, point to slabs and count: 'a, b, c, slabs'. Something more like the ostensive teaching of the words 'block', 'pillar', etc. would be the ostensive teaching of numerals that serve not to count but to refer to groups of objects that can be taken in at a glance. Children do learn the use of the first five or six cardinal numerals in this way.

Are 'there' and 'this' also taught ostensively? Imagine how one might perhaps teach their use. One will point to places and things – but in this case the pointing occurs in the use of the words too and not merely in learning the use.

17. It will be possible to say: In language (8) we have different kinds of word. For the functions of the word 'slab' and the word 'block' are more alike than those of 'slab' and 'd'. But how we group words into kinds will depend on the aim of the classification, and on our own inclination. Think of the different points of view from which one can classify tools or chess-men.

19. It is easy to imagine a language consisting only of orders and reports in battle. Or a language consisting only of questions and expressions for answering yes and no. And innumerable others . . .

23. But how many kinds of sentence are there? Say assertion, question, and command? There are countless kinds: countless different kinds of use of what we call 'symbols', 'words', 'sentences'. And this multiplicity is not something fixed, given once for all; but new types of language, new language-games, as we may say, come into existence, and others become obsolete and get forgotten. (We can get a rough picture of this from the changes in mathematics.) . . .

27. 'We name things and then we can talk about them: can refer to them in talk.' As if what we did next were given with the mere act of naming. As if there were only one thing called 'talking about a thing'. Whereas in fact we do the most various things with our sentences. Think of exclamations alone, with their completely different functions.

Water!
Away!
Ow!
Help!

Fine!

No!

Are you inclined still to call these words 'names of objects'?

In languages (2) and (8) there was no such thing as asking something's name. This, with its correlate, ostensive definition, is, we might say, a language-game on its own. That is really to say: we are brought up, trained, to ask: 'What is that called?' – upon which the name is given. And there is also a language-game of inventing a name for something, and hence of saying, 'This is . . .' and then using the new name.

28. Now one can ostensively define a proper name, the name of a colour, the name of a material, a numeral, the name of a point of the compass and so on. The definition of the number two, 'That is called "two" ' – pointing to two nuts – is perfectly exact. But how can two be defined like that? The person one gives the definition to doesn't know what one wants to call 'two'; he will suppose that 'two' is the name given to this group of nuts! He may suppose this; but perhaps he does not. He might make the opposite mistake; when I want to assign a name to this group of nuts, he might understand it as a numeral. And he might equally well take the name of a person, of which I give an ostensive definition, as that of a colour, of a race, or even of a point of the compass. That is to say: an ostensive definition can be variously interpreted in every case.

29. Perhaps you say: two can only be ostensively defined in this way: 'This number is called "two" '. For the word 'number' here shows what place in language, in grammar, we assign to the word. But this means that the word 'number' must be explained before the ostensive definition can be understood. The word 'number' in the definition does indeed show this place; does show the post at which we station the word. And we can prevent misunderstandings by saying: 'This colour is called so-and-so', 'This length is called so-and-so', and so on. That is to say: misunderstandings are sometimes averted in this way. But is there only one way of taking the word 'colour' or 'length'? Well, they just need defining. Defining, then, by means of other words! And what about the last definition in this chain? (Do not say: 'There isn't a "last" definition'. That is just as if you chose to say: 'There isn't a last house in this road; one can always build an additional one'.) Whether the word 'number' is necessary in the ostensive definition depends on whether without it the other person takes the definition otherwise than I wish. And that will depend on the circumstances under which it is given, and on the person I give it to.

And how he 'takes' the definition is seen in the use that he makes of the word defined.

40. Let us first discuss this point of the argument: that a word has no meaning if nothing corresponds to it. It is important to note that the word 'meaning' is being used illicitly if it is used to signify the thing that 'corresponds' to the word. That is to confound the meaning of a name with the bearer of the name. When Mr. N.N. dies one says that the bearer of the name dies, not that the meaning dies. And it would be nonsensical to say that, for if the name ceased to have meaning it would make no sense to say 'Mr. N.N. is dead'.

65. . . . Instead of producing something common to all that we call language, I am saying that these phenomena have no one thing in common which makes us use the same word for all, but that they are related to one another in many different ways. And it is because of this relationship, or these relationships, that we call them all 'language'. I will try to explain this.

66. Consider for example the proceedings that we call 'games'. I mean board-games, card-games, ball-games, Olympic games, and so on. What is common to them all? Don't say: 'There must be something common, or they would not be called "games" ' but look and see whether there is anything common to all. For if you look at them you will not see something that is common to all, but similarities, relationships, and a whole series of them at that. To repeat: don't think, but look! Look for example at board-games, with their multifarious relationships. Now pass to card-games; here you find many correspondences with the first group, but many common features drop out, and others appear. When we pass next to ball-games, much that is common is retained, but much is lost. Are they all 'amusing'? Compare chess with noughts and crosses. Or is there always winning and losing, or competition between players? Think of patience. In ball-games there is winning and losing; but when a child throws his ball at the wall and catches it again, this feature has disappeared . . .

67. I can think of no better expression to characterize these similarities than 'family resemblances'; for the various resemblances between members of a family: build, features, colour of eyes, gait, temperament, etc. etc. overlap and criss-cross in the same way. And I shall say: 'games' form a family . . .

75. What does it mean to know what a game is? What does it mean, to know it and not be able to say it? Is this knowledge somehow equivalent to an unformulated definition? So that if it were formulated I should be able to recognize it as the expression of my knowledge? Isn't my knowledge, my concept of a game, completely expressed in the explanations that I could give? That is, in my describing examples of various kinds of game; showing how all sorts of other games can be constructed on the analogy of these; saying that I should scarcely include this or this among games; and so on.

76. If someone were to draw a sharp boundary I could not acknowledge it as the one that I too always wanted to draw, or had drawn in my mind. For I did not want to draw one at all. His concept can then be said to be not the same as mine, but akin to it. The kinship is that of two pictures, one of which consists of colour patches with vague contours, and the other of patches similarly shaped and distributed, but with clear contours. The kinship is just as undeniable as the difference.

82. What do I call 'the rule by which he proceeds'? The hypothesis that satisfactorily describes his use of words, which we observe; or the rule which he looks up when he uses signs; or the one which he gives us in reply if we ask him what his rule is? But what if observation does not enable us to see any clear rule, and the question brings none to light? For he did indeed give me a definition when I asked him what he

understood by 'N', but he was prepared to withdraw and alter it. So how am I to determine the rule according to which he is playing? He does not know it himself. Or, to ask a better question: What meaning is the expression 'the rule by which he proceeds' supposed to have left to it here?

83. Doesn't the analogy between language and games throw light here? We can easily imagine people amusing themselves in a field by playing with a ball so as to start various existing games, but playing many without finishing them and in between throwing the ball aimlessly into the air, chasing one another with the ball and bombarding one another for a joke and so on. And now someone says: The whole time they are playing a ball-game and following definite rules at every throw.

And is there not also the case where we play and make up the rules as we go along? And there is even one where we alter them as we go along.

84. I said that the application of a word is not everywhere bounded by rules. But what does a game look like that is everywhere bounded by rules? Whose rules never let a doubt creep in, but stop up all the cracks where it might? Can't we imagine a rule determining the application of a rule, and a doubt which it removes and so on?

But that is not to say that we are in doubt because it is possible for us to imagine a doubt. I can easily imagine someone always doubting before he opened his front door whether an abyss did not yawn behind it, and making sure about it before he went through the door (and he might on some occasion prove to be right) – but that does not make me doubt in the same case.

85. A rule stands there like a sign-post. Does the sign-post leave no doubt open about the way I have to go? Does it show which direction I am to take when I have passed it; whether along the road or the footpath or cross-country? But where is it said which way I am to follow it; whether in the direction of its finger or (e.g.) in the opposite one? And if there were, not a single sign-post, but a chain of adjacent ones or of chalk marks on the ground – is there only one way of interpreting them? So I can say, the sign-post does after all leave no room for doubt. Or rather: it sometimes leaves room for doubt and sometimes not. And now this is no longer a philosophical proposition, but an empirical one.

122. A main source of our failure to understand is that we do not command a clear view of the use of our words. Our grammar is lacking in this sort of perspicuity. A perspicuous representation produces just that understanding which consists in 'seeing connexions'. Hence the importance of finding and inventing intermediate cases.

The concept of a perspicuous representation is of fundamental significance for us. It earmarks the form of account we give, the way we look at things. (Is this a 'Weltanschauung'?)

130. Our clear and simple language-games are not preparatory studies for a future regularization of language – as it were first approximations, ignoring friction and air-resistance. The language-games are rather set up as objects of comparison which are

meant to throw light on the facts of our language by way not only of similarities, but also of dissimilarities.

198. 'But how can a rule show me what I have to do at this point? Whatever I do is, on some interpretation, in accord with the rule.' That is not what we ought to say, but rather: any interpretation still hangs in the air along with what it interprets, and cannot give it any support. Interpretations by themselves do not determine meaning.

'Then can whatever I do be brought into accord with the rule?' Let me ask this: what has the expression of a rule – say a sign-post – got to do with my actions? What sort of connexion is there here? Well, perhaps this one: I have been trained to react to this sign in a particular way, and now I do so react to it.

But that is only to give a causal connexion; to tell how it has come about that we now go by the sign-post; not what this going-by-the-sign really consists in. On the contrary; I have further indicated that a person goes by a sign-post only in so far as there exists a regular use of sign-posts, a custom.

199. Is what we call 'obeying a rule' something that it would be possible for only one man to do, and to do only once in his life? This is of course a note on the grammar of the expression 'to obey a rule'.

It is not possible that there should have been only one occasion on which someone obeyed a rule. It is not possible that there should have been only one occasion on which a report was made, an order given or understood; and so on. To obey a rule, to make a report, to give an order, to play a game of chess, are customs (uses, institutions).

To understand a sentence means to understand a language. To understand a language means to be master of a technique.

201. . . . What this shows is that there is a way of grasping a rule which is not an interpretation, but which is exhibited in what we call 'obeying the rule' and 'going against it' in actual cases. Hence there is an inclination to say: every action according to the rule is an interpretation. But we ought to restrict the term 'interpretation' to the substitution of one expression of the rule for another.

202. And hence also 'obeying a rule' is a practice. And to think one is obeying a rule is not to obey a rule. Hence it is not possible to obey a rule 'privately': otherwise thinking one was obeying a rule would be the same thing as obeying it.

203. Language is a labyrinth of paths. You approach from one side and know your way about; you approach the same place from another side and no longer know your way about.

204. As things are I can, for example, invent a game that is never played by anyone. But would the following be possible too: mankind has never played any games; once, however, someone invented a game – which no one ever played?

205. 'But it is just the queer thing about intention, about the mental process, that the

existence of a custom, of a technique, is not necessary to it. That, for example, it is imaginable that two people should play chess in a world in which otherwise no games existed; and even that they should begin a game of chess – and then be interrupted.'

But isn't chess defined by its rules? And how are these rules present in the mind of the person who is intending to play chess?

206. Following a rule is analogous to obeying an order. We are trained to do so; we react to an order in a particular way. But what if one person reacts in one way and another in another to the order and the training? Which one is right?

Suppose you came as an explorer into an unknown country with a language quite strange to you. In what circumstances would you say that the people there gave orders, understood them, obeyed them, rebelled against them, and so on?

The common behaviour of mankind is the system of reference by means of which we interpret an unknown language.

217. 'How am I able to obey a rule?' If this is not a question about causes, then it is about the justification for my following the rule in the way I do.

If I have exhausted the justifications I have reached bedrock, and my spade is turned. Then I am inclined to say: 'This is simply what I do.' . . .

218. Whence comes the idea that the beginning of a series is a visible section of rails invisibly laid to infinity? Well, we might imagine rails instead of a rule. And infinitely long rails correspond to the unlimited application of a rule.

224. The word 'agreement' and the word 'rule' are related to one another, they are cousins. If I teach anyone the use of the one word, he learns the use of the other with it.

225. The use of the word rule' and the use of the word 'same' are interwoven. (As are the use of 'proposition' and the use of 'true'.)

240. Disputes do not break out (among mathematicians, say) over the question whether a rule has been obeyed or not. People don't come to blows over it, for example. That is part of the framework on which the working of our language is based (for example, in giving descriptions).

241. 'So you are saying that human agreement decides what is true and what is false?' It is what human beings say that is true and false; and they agree in the language they use. That is not agreement in opinions but in the form of life.

242. If language is to be a means of communication there must be agreement not only in definitions but also (queer as this may sound) in judgments. This seems to abolish logic, but does not do so. It is one thing to describe methods of measurement, and another to obtain and state results of measurement. But what we call 'measuring' is partly determined by a certain constancy in results of measurement.

243. A human being can encourage himself, give himself orders, obey, blame and

punish himself; he can ask himself a question and answer it. We could even imagine human beings who spoke only in monologue; who accompanied their activities by talking to themselves . . . But could we also imagine a language in which a person could write down or give vocal expression to his inner experiences – his feelings, moods, and the rest – for his private use? Well, can't we do so in our ordinary language? But that is not what I mean. The individual words of this language are to refer to what can only be known to the person speaking; to his immediate private sensations. So another person cannot understand the language.

11

STEPHEN TOULMIN
The evolution of scientific ideas* (1961)

Science is not an intellectual computing-machine: it is a slice of life. We set out on our enquiry into the aims of science, hoping to do two things: first, to define in a life-like way the common intellectual tasks on which scientists are engaged, and the types of explanation their theories are intended to provide; and secondly, to pose the problem, how we are to tell good theories from bad, and better ideas, hypotheses, or explanations from worse ones.

We began by scrutinizing one popular answer to these questions: the 'predictivist' account. It soon became clear that this account would not do all we wanted. Scientists are concerned with 'forecasting-techniques' only incidentally; and any more satisfactory sense of 'prediction' takes for granted the idea of explanation, rather than defining it. The central aims of science are, rather, concerned with a search for understanding – a desire to make the course of Nature not just predictable but intelligible – and this has meant looking for rational patterns of connections in terms of which we can make sense of the flux of events. So we have placed in the centre of our enquiry two questions: 'What patterns of thought and reasoning give scientific understanding?', and: 'What factors determine which of two rival theories or explanations yields greater understanding?'

The first question brought us up against the basic conceptions or 'ideals of natural order', which settle what a scientist regards as 'self-explanatory' or 'natural'. At any stage in the evolution of science, I argued, certain forms of explanation present themselves to men as being entirely intelligible – e.g. the standard, though different, types of motion accepted as self-explanatory by Aristotle, Galileo, and Newton, and also such ideas as that of a 'pure substance' or a 'typical life-cycle'. The scientist may start with half a dozen different ideal structures or processes, yet in one way or another he must put them to work if he is to make the course of Nature intelligible. For the logician, these explanatory ideals pose a particular problem. On the one hand, they change and develop, as time goes on, in the light of discovery and experience: so

* From *Foresight and Understanding: An Inquiry into the Aims of Science* by Stephen Toulmin, Greenwoood Press, 1961, pp. 99–101. Reproduced with permission of Indiana University Press.

they must be classed as 'empirical', in a broad enough sense of the term. On the other hand, one cannot confront them directly with the results of observation and experiment. They have to prove their worth over a longer term, in a way which still needs analysing. Though changing with history, they are also – for the individual scientist – 'preconceived' notions: thought out beforehand, and applied only subsequently to particular scientific problems.

Yet, if one speaks of these conceptions as preconceived, a distinction must be made, for they are 'preconceived' in a perfectly innocent sense of the word. Scientists are rightly suspicious of 'preconceived ideas' and pride themselves on coming to Nature in a spirit of objectivity. If a man enters the observatory or laboratory with preconceived ideas about what he will find, this (scientists feel) will prejudice his investigation. If he has already made up his mind (say) that pigs can fly, that will disqualified him as an observer: he will go around the world looking for evidence to support his prior belief, and may end by hailing some porker leaping off the roof of his sty as proof of his contention. So far, the scientists are undoubtedly in the right: when it comes to interrogating Nature, in the laboratory or in the field, we must leave her to answer for herself – and answer without any prompting.

That, however, is not the point at which our 'ideals of natural order' come in. Their influence is felt earlier. For, though Nature must of course be left to answer to our interrogations for herself, it is always we who frame the questions. And the questions we ask inevitably depend on prior theoretical considerations. We are here concerned, not with prejudiced belief, but rather with preformed concepts; and, to understand the logic of science, we must recognize that 'preconceptions' of this kind are both inevitable and proper – if suitably tentative and subject to reshaping in the light of our experience. If we fail to recognize the conceptions for what they are, we shall not appreciate the true character of our scientific ideas, nor the intellectual problems which faced our predecessors, through whose labours our own ideas were gradually formed.

12

THOMAS KUHN
A role for history* (1962)

History, if viewed as a repository for more than anecdote or chronology, could produce a decisive transformation in the image of science by which we are now possessed. That image has previously been drawn, even by scientists themselves, mainly from the study of finished scientific achievements as these are recorded in the classics and, more recently, in the textbooks from which each new scientific generation learns to practice its trade. Inevitably, however, the aim of such books is persuasive and pedagogic; a concept of science drawn from them is no more likely to fit the enterprise that produced them than an image of a national culture drawn from a tourist brochure or a language text. This essay attempts to show that we have been misled by them in fundamental ways. Its aim is a sketch of the quite different concept of science that can emerge from the historical record of the research activity itself.

Even from history, however, that new concept will not be forthcoming if historical data continue to be sought and scrutinized mainly to answer questions posed by the unhistorical stereotype drawn from science texts. Those texts have, for example, often seemed to imply that the content of science is uniquely exemplified by the observations, laws, and theories described in their pages. Almost as regularly, the same books have been read as saying that scientific methods are simply the ones illustrated by the manipulative techniques used in gathering textbook data, together with the logical operations employed when relating those data to the textbook's theoretical generalizations. The result has been a concept of science with profound implications about its nature and development. If science is the constellation of facts, theories, and methods collected in current texts, then scientists are the men who, successfully or not, have striven to contribute one or another element to that particular constellation. Scientific development becomes the piecemeal process by which these items have been added, singly and in combination, to the ever growing stockpile that constitutes scientific technique and knowledge. And history of science becomes the discipline that chronicles both these successive increments and the obstacles that

* From *The Structure of Scientific Revolutions*, 2nd edition by Thomas Kuhn, University of Chicago Press, 1972, pp. 1–9. Reproduced by permission of University of Chicago Press.

have inhibited their accumulation. Concerned with scientific development, the historian then appears to have two main tasks. On the one hand, he must determine by what man and at what point in time each contemporary scientific fact, law, and theory was discovered or invented. On the other, he must describe and explain the congeries of error, myth, and superstition that have inhibited the more rapid accumulation of the constituents of the modern science text. Much research has been directed to these ends, and some still is.

In recent years, however, a few historians of science have been finding it more and more difficult to fulfill the functions that the concept of development-by-accumulation assigns to them. As chroniclers of an incremental process, they discover that additional research makes it harder, not easier, to answer questions like: When was oxygen discovered? Who first conceived of energy conservation? Increasingly, a few of them suspect that these are simply the wrong sorts of questions to ask. Perhaps science does not develop by the accumulation of individual discoveries and inventions. Simultaneously, these same historians confront growing difficulties in distinguishing the 'scientific' component of past observation and belief from what their predecessors had readily labeled 'error' and 'superstition.' The more carefully they study, say, Aristotelian dynamics, phlogistic chemistry, or caloric thermodynamics, the more certain they feel that those once current views of nature were, as a whole, neither less scientific nor more the product of human idiosyncrasy than those current today. If these out-of-date beliefs are to be called myths, then myths can be produced by the same sorts of methods and held for the same sorts of reasons that now lead to scientific knowledge. If, on the other hand, they are to be called science, then science has included bodies of belief quite incompatible with the ones we hold today. Given these alternatives, the historian must choose the latter. Out-of-date theories are not in principle unscientific because they have been discarded. That choice, however, makes it difficult to see scientific development as a process of accretion. The same historical research that displays the difficulties in isolating individual inventions and discoveries gives ground for profound doubts about the cumulative process through which these individual contributions to science were thought to have been compounded.

The result of all these doubts and difficulties is a historiographic revolution in the study of science, though one that is still in its early stages. Gradually, and often without entirely realizing they are doing so, historians of science have begun to ask new sorts of questions and to trace different, and often less than cumulative, developmental lines for the sciences. Rather than seeking the permanent contributions of an older science to our present vantage, they attempt to display the historical integrity of that science in its own time. They ask, for example, not about the relation of Galileo's views to those of modern science, but rather about the relationship between his views and those of his group, i.e., his teachers, contemporaries, and immediate successors in the sciences. Furthermore, they insist upon studying the opinions of that group and other similar ones from the viewpoint – usually very different from that of modern science – that gives those opinions the maximum internal coherence and the closest possible fit to nature. Seen through the works that result, works perhaps best exemplified in the writings of Alexandre Koyré, science does not seem altogether the same enterprise as the one discussed by writers in the older historiographic tradition.

By implication, at least, these historical studies suggest the possibility of a new image of science. This essay aims to delineate that image by making explicit some of the new historiography's implications.

What aspects of science will emerge to prominence in the course of this effort? First, at least in order of presentation, is the insufficiency of methodological directives, by themselves, to dictate a unique substantive conclusion to many sorts of scientific questions. Instructed to examine electrical or chemical phenomena, the man who is ignorant of these fields but who knows what it is to be scientific may legitimately reach any one of a number of incompatible conclusions. Among those legitimate possibilities, the particular conclusions he does arrive at are probably determined by his prior experience in other fields, by the accidents of his investigation, and by his own individual makeup. What beliefs about the stars, for example, does he bring to the study of chemistry or electricity? Which of the many conceivable experiments relevant to the new field does he elect to perform first? And what aspects of the complex phenomenon that then results strike him as particularly relevant to an elucidation of the nature of chemical change or of electrical affinity? For the individual, at least, and sometimes for the scientific community as well, answers to questions like these are often essential determinants of scientific development. We shall note, for example, in Section II that the early developmental stages of most sciences have been characterized by continual competition between a number of distinct views of nature, each partially derived from, and all roughly compatible with, the dictates of scientific observation and method. What differentiated these various schools was not one or another failure of method – they were all 'scientific' – but what we shall come to call their incommensurable ways of seeing the world and of practicing science in it. Observation and experience can and must drastically restrict the range of admissible scientific belief, else there would be no science. But they cannot alone determine a particular body of such belief. An apparently arbitrary element, compounded of personal and historical accident, is always a formative ingredient of the beliefs espoused by a given scientific community at a given time.

That element of arbitrariness does not, however, indicate that any scientific group could practice its trade without some set of received beliefs. Nor does it make less consequential the particular constellation to which the group, at a given time, is in fact committed. Effective research scarcely begins before a scientific community thinks it has acquired firm answers to questions like the following: What are the fundamental entities of which the universe is composed? How do these interact with each other and with the senses? What questions may legitimately be asked about such entities and what techniques employed in seeking solutions? At least in the mature sciences, answers (or full substitutes for answers) to questions like these are firmly embedded in the educational initiation that prepares and licenses the student for professional practice. Because that education is both rigorous and rigid, these answers come to exert a deep hold on the scientific mind. That they can do so does much to account both for the peculiar efficiency of the normal research activity and for the direction in which it proceeds at any given time. When examining normal science in Sections III, IV, and V, we shall want finally to describe that research as a strenuous and devoted attempt to force nature into the conceptual boxes supplied by professional education. Simultaneously, we shall wonder whether research could proceed without such boxes, whatever the element of arbitrariness in their historic origins and, occasionally, in their subsequent development.

Yet that element of arbitrariness is present, and it too has an important effect on scientific development, one which will be examined in detail in Sections VI, VII, and VIII. Normal science, the activity in which most scientists inevitably spend almost all their time, is predicated on the assumption that the scientific community knows what the world is like. Much of the success of the enterprise derives from the community's willingness to defend that assumption, if necessary at considerable cost. Normal science, for example, often suppresses fundamental novelties because they are necessarily subversive of its basic commitments. Nevertheless, so long as those commitments retain an element of the arbitrary, the very nature of normal research ensures that novelty shall not be suppressed for very long. Sometimes a normal problem, one that ought to be solvable by known rules and procedures, resists the reiterated onslaught of the ablest members of the group within whose competence it falls. On other occasions a piece of equipment designed and constructed for the purpose of normal research fails to perform in the anticipated manner, revealing an anomaly that cannot, despite repeated effort, be aligned with professional expectation. In these and other ways besides, normal science repeatedly goes astray. And when it does – when, that is, the profession can no longer evade anomalies that subvert the existing tradition of scientific practice – then begin the extraordinary investigations that lead the profession at last to a new set of commitments, a new basis for the practice of science. The extraordinary episodes in which that shift of professional commitments occurs are the ones known in this essay as scientific revolutions. They are the tradition-shattering complements to the tradition-bound activity of normal science. The most obvious examples of scientific revolutions are those famous episodes in scientific development that have often been labeled revolutions before. Therefore, in Sections IX and X, where the nature of scientific revolutions is first directly scrutinized, we shall deal repeatedly with the major turning points in scientific development associated with the names of Copernicus, Newton, Lavoisier, and Einstein. More clearly than most other episodes in the history of at least the physical sciences, these display what all scientific revolutions are about. Each of them necessitated the community's rejection of one time-honored scientific theory in favor of another incompatible with it. Each produced a consequent shift in the problems available for scientific scrutiny and in the standards by which the profession determined what should count as an admissible problem or as a legitimate problem-solution. And each transformed the scientific imagination in ways that we shall ultimately need to describe as a transformation of the world within which scientific work was done. Such changes, together with the controversies that almost always accompany them, are the defining characteristics of scientific revolutions.

These characteristics emerge with particular clarity from a study of, say, the Newtonian or the chemical revolution. It is, however, a fundamental thesis of this essay that they can also be retrieved from the study of many other episodes that were not so obviously revolutionary. For the far smaller professional group affected by them, Maxwell's equations were as revolutionary as Einstein's, and they were resisted accordingly. The invention of other new theories regularly, and appropriately, evokes the same response from some of the specialists on whose area of special competence they impinge. For these men the new theory implies a change in the rules governing the prior practice of normal science. Inevitably, therefore, it reflects upon much scientific work they have already successfully completed. That is why a new theory, however special its range of application, is seldom or never just an increment to what is already known. Its assimilation requires the reconstruction of prior theory and the re-evaluation of prior fact, an intrinsically revolutionary process that is seldom completed by a single man and never overnight. No wonder historians have had difficulty in dating precisely this extended process that their vocabulary impels them to view as an isolated event.

Nor are new inventions of theory the only scientific events that have revolutionary impact upon the specialists in whose domain they occur. The commitments that govern normal science specify not only what sorts of entities the universe does contain, but also, by implication, those that it does not. It follows, though the point will require extended discussion, that a discovery like that of oxygen or X-rays does not simply add one more item to the population of the scientist's world. Ultimately it has that effect, but not until the professional community has re-evaluated traditional experimental procedures, altered its conception of entities with which it has long been familiar, and, in the process, shifted the network of theory through which it deals with the world. Scientific fact and theory are not categorically separable, except perhaps within a single tradition of normal-scientific practice. That is why the unexpected discovery is not simply factual in its import and why the scientist's world is qualitatively transformed as well as quantitatively enriched by fundamental novelties of either fact or theory.

This extended conception of the nature of scientific revolutions is the one delineated in the pages that follow. Admittedly the extension strains customary usage. Nevertheless, I shall continue to speak even of discoveries as revolutionary, because it is just the possibility of relating their structure to that of, say, the Copernican revolution that makes the extended conception seem to me so important. The preceding discussion indicates how the complementary notions of normal science and of scientific revolutions will be developed in the nine sections immediately to follow. The rest of the essay attempts to dispose of three remaining central questions. Section XI, by discussing the textbook tradition, considers why scientific revolutions have previously been so difficult to see. Section XII describes the revolutionary competition between the proponents of the old normal-scientific tradition and the adherents of the new one. It thus considers the process that should somehow, in a theory of scientific inquiry, replace the confirmation or falsification procedures made familiar by our usual image of science. Competition between segments of the scientific community is the only historical process that ever actually results in the rejection of one previously accepted theory or in the adoption of another. Finally, Section XIII will ask how development through revolutions can be compatible with the apparently unique character of scientific progress. For that question, however, this essay will provide no more than the main outlines of an answer, one which depends upon characteristics of the scientific community that require much additional exploration and study.

Undoubtedly, some readers will already have wondered whether historical study can possibly effect the sort of conceptual transformation aimed at here. An entire arsenal of dichotomies is available to suggest that it cannot properly do so. History, we too often say, is a purely descriptive discipline. The theses suggested above are, however, often interpretive and sometimes normative. Again, many of my generalizations are about the sociology or social psychology of scientists; yet at least a few of my conclusions belong traditionally to logic or epistemology. In the preceding paragraph I may even seem to have violated the very influential contemporary distinction between 'the context of discovery' and 'the context of justification.' Can anything more than profound confusion be indicated by this admixture of diverse fields and concerns?

Having been weaned intellectually on these distinctions and others like them, I could scarcely be more aware of their import and force. For many years I took them to be about the nature of knowledge, and I still suppose that, appropriately recast, they have something important to tell us. Yet my attempts to apply them, even *grosso modo*, to the actual situations in which knowledge is gained, accepted, and assimilated have made them seem extraordinarily problematic. Rather than being elementary logical or methodological distinctions, which would thus be prior to the analysis of scientific knowledge, they now seem integral parts of a traditional set of substantive answers to the very questions upon which they have been deployed. That circularity does not at all invalidate them. But it does make them parts of a theory and, by doing so, subjects them to the same scrutiny regularly applied to theories in other fields. If they are to have more than pure abstraction as their content, then that content must be discovered by observing them in application to the data they are meant to elucidate. How could history of science fail to be a source of phenomena to which theories about knowledge may legitimately be asked to apply?

13

IMRE LAKATOS
Falsification and the methodology of scientific research programmes* (1970)

There are no such things as crucial experiments, at least not if these are meant to be experiments which can instantly overthrow a research programme. In fact, when one research programme suffers defeat and is superseded by another one, we may – with long hindsight – call an experiment crucial if it turns out to have provided a spectacular corroborating instance for the victorious programme and a failure for the defeated one (in the sense that it was never 'explained progressively' – or, briefly, 'explained' – within the defeated programme). But scientists, of course, do not always judge heuristic situations correctly. A rash scientist may claim that his experiment defeated a programme, and parts of the scientific community may even, rashly, accept his claim. But if a scientist in the 'defeated' camp puts forward a few years later a scientific explanation of the allegedly 'crucial experiment' within (or consistent with) the allegedly defeated programme, the honorific title may be withdrawn and the 'crucial experiment' may turn from a defeat into a new victory for the programme.

Examples abound. There were many experiments in the eighteenth century which were, as a matter of historico-sociological fact, widely accepted as 'crucial' evidence against Galileo's law of free fall, and Newton's theory of gravitation. In the nineteenth century there were several 'crucial experiments' based on measurements of light velocity which 'disproved' the corpuscular theory and which turned out later to be erroneous in the light of relativity theory. These 'crucial experiments' were later deleted from the justificationist textbooks as manifestations of shameful short-sightedness or even of envy. (Recently they reappeared in some new textbooks, this time to illustrate the inescapable irrationality of scientific fashions.) However, in those cases in which ostensibly 'crucial experiments' were indeed later borne out by the defeat of the programme, historians charged those who resisted them with stupidity, jealousy, or unjustified adulation of the father of the research programme in question. (Fashionable 'sociologists of knowledge' – or 'psychologists of knowledge' – tend to

* From Imre Lakatos, 'Falsification and the Methodology of Scientific Research Programmes', pp. 173–177 in Imre Lakatos and Alan Musgrave (eds) *Criticism and the Growth of Knowledge*, Cambridge University Press, 1970. Reproduced by permission.

explain positions in purely social or psychological terms when, as a matter of fact, they are determined by rationality principles. A typical example is the explanation of Einstein's opposition to Bohr's complementarity principle on the ground that 'in 1926 Einstein was forty-seven years old. Forty-seven may be the prime of life, but not for physicists'.)

In the light of my considerations, the idea of instant rationality can be seen to be utopian. But this utopian idea is a hallmark of most brands of epistemology. Justificationists wanted scientific theories to be proved even before they were published; probabilists hoped a machine could flash up instantly the value (degree of confirmation) of a theory, given the evidence; naive falsificationists hoped that elimination at least was the instant result of the verdict of experiment. I hope I have shown that all these theories of instant rationality – and instant learning – fail. The case studies of this section show that rationality works much slower than most people tend to think, and, even then, fallibly. Minerva's owl flies at dusk. I also hope I have shown that the continuity in science, the tenacity of some theories, the rationality of a certain amount of dogmatism, can only be explained if we construe science as a battleground of research programmes rather than of isolated theories. One can understand very little of the growth of science when our paradigm of a chunk of scientific knowledge is an isolated theory like 'All swans are white', standing aloof, without being embedded in a major research programme. My account implies a new criterion of demarcation between 'mature science', consisting of research programmes, and 'immature science' consisting of a mere patched up pattern of trial and error. For instance, we may have a conjecture, have it refuted and then rescued by an auxiliary hypothesis which is not ad hoc in the senses which we had earlier discussed. It may predict novel facts some of which may even be corroborated. Yet one may achieve such 'progress' with a patched up, arbitrary series of disconnected theories. Good scientists will not find such makeshift progress satisfactory; they may even reject it as not genuinely scientific. They will call such auxiliary hypotheses merely 'formal', 'arbitrary', 'empirical', 'semi-empirical', or even 'ad hoc'.

Mature science consists of research programmes in which not only novel facts but, in an important sense, also novel auxiliary theories, are anticipated; mature science – unlike pedestrian trial-and-error – has 'heuristic power'. Let us remember that in the positive heuristic of a powerful programme there is, right at the start, a general outline of how to build the protective belts: this heuristic power generates the autonomy of theoretical science.

This requirement of continuous growth is my rational reconstruction of the widely acknowledged requirement of 'unity' or 'beauty' of science. It highlights the weakness of two – apparently very different – types of theorizing. First, it shows up the weakness of programmes which, like Marxism or Freudism, are, no doubt, 'unified', which give a major sketch of the sort of auxiliary theories they are going to use in absorbing anomalies, but which unfailingly devise their actual auxiliary theories in the wake of facts without, at the same time, anticipating others. (What novel fact has Marxism predicted since, say, 1917?) Secondly, it hits patched-up, unimaginative series of pedestrian 'empirical' adjustments which are so frequent, for instance, in modern social psychology. Such adjustments may, with the help of so-called 'statistical techniques', make some 'novel' predictions and may even conjure up some irrelevant grains of truth in them. But this theorizing has no unifying idea, no heuristic power, no continuity. They do not add up to a genuine research programme and are, on the whole, worthless.

My account of scientific rationality, although based on Popper's, leads away from some of his general ideas. I endorse to some extent both Le Roy's conventionalism with regard to theories and Popper's conventionalism with regard to basic propositions. In this view scientists (and as I have shown, mathematicians too) are not irrational when they tend to ignore counterexamples or as they prefer to call them, 'recalcitrant' or 'residual' instances, and follow the sequence of problems as prescribed by the positive heuristic of their programme, and elaborate – and apply – their theories regardless. Contrary to Popper's falsificationist morality, scientists frequently and rationally claim 'that the experimental results are not reliable, or that the discrepancies which are asserted to exist between the experimental results and the theory are only apparent and that they will disappear with the advance of our understanding'. When doing so, they may not be 'adopting the very reverse of that critical attitude which . . . is the proper one for the scientist'. Indeed, Popper is right in stressing that 'the dogmatic attitude of sticking to a theory as long as possible is of considerable significance. Without it we could never find out what is in a theory – we should give the theory up before we had a real opportunity of finding out its strength; and in consequence no theory would ever be able to play its role of bringing order into the world, of preparing us for future events, of drawing our attention to events we should otherwise never observe'. Thus the 'dogmatism' of 'normal science' does not prevent growth as long as we combine it with the Popperian recognition that there is good, progressive normal science and that there is bad, degenerating normal science, and as long as we retain the determination to eliminate, under certain objectively defined conditions, some research programmes.

The dogmatic attitude in science – which would explain its stable periods – was described by Kuhn as a prime feature of 'normal science'. But Kuhn's conceptual framework for dealing with continuity in science is socio-psychological: mine is normative. I look at continuity in science through 'Popperian spectacles'. Where Kuhn sees 'paradigms', I also see rational 'research programmes'.

14

PAUL FEYERABEND
Against method* (1975)

The idea of a method that contains firm, unchanging, and absolutely binding principles for conducting the business of science meets considerable difficulty when confronted with the results of historical research. We find then, that there is not a single
rule, however plausible, and however firmly grounded in epistemology, that is not
violated at some time or other. It becomes evident that such violations are not accidental events, they are not results of insufficient knowledge or of inattention which
might have been avoided. On the contrary, we see that they are necessary for progress.
Indeed, one of the most striking features of recent discussions in the history and
philosophy of science is the realization that events and developments, such as the
invention of atomism in antiquity, the Copernican Revolution, the rise of modern
atomism (kinetic theory; dispersion theory; stereochemistry; quantum theory), the
gradual emergence of the wave theory of light, occurred only because some thinkers
either decided not to be bound by certain 'obvious' methodological rules, or because
they unwittingly broke them.

This liberal practice, I repeat, is not just a fact of the history of science. It is both
reasonable and absolutely necessary for the growth of knowledge. More specifically,
one can show the following: given any rule, however 'fundamental' or 'necessary' for
science, there are always circumstances when it is advisable not only to ignore the rule,
but to adopt its opposite. For example, there are circumstances when it is advisable to
introduce, elaborate, and defend ad hoc hypotheses, or hypotheses which contradict
well-established and generally accepted experimental results, or hypotheses whose
content is smaller than the content of the existing and empirically adequate alternative,
or self-inconsistent hypotheses, and so on.

There are even circumstances – and they occur rather frequently – when argument loses its forward-looking aspect and becomes a hindrance to progress. Nobody
would claim that the teaching of small children is exclusively a matter of argument
(though argument may enter into it, and should enter into it to a larger extent than is

* From *Against Method: Outline of an Anarchist Theory of Knowledge*, New Left Books, London, 1975,
pp. 23–28. Reproduced with permission by Verso.

customary), and almost everyone now agrees that what looks like a result of reason – the mastery of a language, the existence of a richly articulated perceptual world, logical ability – is due partly to indoctrination and partly to a process of growth that proceeds with the force of natural law. And where arguments do seem to have an effect, this is more often due to their physical repetition than to their semantic content.

Having admitted this much, we must also concede the possibility of non-argumentative growth in the adult as well as in (the theoretical parts of) institutions such as science, religion, prostitution, and so on. We certainly cannot take it for granted that what is possible for a small child – to acquire new modes of behaviour on the slightest provocation, to slide into them without any noticeable effort – is beyond the reach of his elders. One should rather expect that catastrophic changes in the physical environment, wars, the breakdown of encompassing systems of morality, political revolutions, will transform adult reaction patterns as well, including import-ant patterns of argumentation. Such a transformation may again be an entirely natural process and the only function of a rational argument may lie in the fact that it increases the mental tension that precedes and causes the behavioural outburst.

Now, if there are events, not necessarily arguments which cause us to adopt new standards, including new and more complex forms of argumentation, is it then not up to the defenders of the status quo to provide, not just counter-arguments, but also contrary causes? ('Virtue without terror is ineffective', says Robespierre.) And if the old forms of argumentation turn out to be too weak a cause, must not these defenders either give up or resort to stronger and more 'irrational' means? (It is very difficult, and perhaps entirely impossible, to combat the effects of brainwashing by argument.) Even the most puritanical rationalist will then be forced to stop reasoning and to use propaganda and coercion, not because some of his reasons have ceased to be valid, but because the psychological conditions which make them effective, and capable of influencing others, have disappeared. And what is the use of an argument that leaves people unmoved?

Of course, the problem never arises quite in this form. The teaching of standards and their defence never consists merely in putting them before the mind of the stu-dent and making them as clear as possible. The standards are supposed to have maximal causal efficacy as well. This makes it very difficult indeed to distinguish between the logical force and the material effect of an argument. Just as a well-trained pet will obey his master no matter how great the confusion in which he finds himself, and no matter how urgent the need to adopt new patterns of behaviour, so in the very same way a well-trained rationalist will obey the mental image of his master, he will conform to the standards of argumentation he has learned, he will adhere to these standards no matter how great the confusion in which he finds himself, and he will be quite incapable of realizing that what he regards as the 'voice of reason' is but a causal after-effect of the training he has received. He will be quite unable to discover that the appeal to reason to which he succumbs so readily is nothing but a political manoeuvre.

That interests, forces, propaganda and brainwashing techniques play a much greater role than is commonly believed in the growth of our knowledge and in the growth of science, can also be seen from an analysis of the relation between idea and action. It is often taken for granted that a clear and distinct understanding of new ideas precedes, and should precede, their formulation and their institutional expression. (An investigation starts with a problem, says Popper.) First, we have an idea, or a problem, then we act, i.e. either speak, or build, or destroy. Yet this is certainly not the way in which small children develop. They use words, they combine them, they play with them, until they grasp a meaning that has so far been beyond their reach. And the initial playful activity is an essential prerequisite of the final act of understanding. There is no reason why this mechanism should cease to function in the adult. We must expect, for example, that the idea of liberty could be made clear only by means of the very same actions, which were supposed to create liberty. Creation of a thing, and creation plus full understanding of a correct idea of the thing, are very often parts of one and the same indivisible process and cannot be separated without bringing the process to a stop. The process itself is not guided by a well-defined programme, and cannot be guided by such a programme, for it contains the conditions for the realization of all possible programmes. It is guided rather by a vague urge, by a 'passion' (Kierkegaard). The passion gives rise to specific behaviour which in turn creates the circumstances and the ideas necessary for analysing and explaining the process, for making it 'rational'.

The development of the Copernican point of view from Galileo to the twentieth century is a perfect example of the situation I want to describe. We start with a strong belief that runs counter to contemporary reason and contemporary experience. The belief spreads and finds support in other beliefs which are equally unreasonable, if not more so (law of inertia; the telescope). Research now gets deflected in new directions, new kinds of instruments are built, 'evidence' is related to theories in new ways until there arises an ideology that is rich enough to provide independent arguments for any particular part of it and mobile enough to find such arguments whenever they seem to be required. We can say today that Galileo was on the right track, for his persistent pursuit of what once seemed to be a silly cosmology has by now created the material needed to defend it against all those who will accept a view only if it is told in a certain way and who will trust it only if it contains certain magical phrases, called 'observational reports'. And this is not an exception – it is the normal case: theories become clear and 'reasonable' only after incoherent parts of them have been used for a long time. Such unreasonable, nonsensical, unmethodical foreplay thus turns out to be an unavoidable precondition of clarity and of empirical success.

Now, when we attempt to describe and to understand developments of this kind in a general way, we are, of course, obliged to appeal to the existing forms of speech which do not take them into account and which must be distorted, misused, beaten into new patterns in order to fit unforeseen situations (without a constant misuse of language there can not be any discovery, any progress). 'Moreover, since the traditional categories are the gospel of everyday thinking (including ordinary scientific thinking) and of everyday practice, [such an attempt at understanding] in effect presents rules and forms of false thinking and action – false, that is, from the standpoint of (scientific) common sense.' This is how dialectical thinking arises as a form of thought that 'dissolves into nothing the detailed determinations of the understanding', formal logic included.

(Incidentally, it should be pointed out that my frequent use of such words as 'progress', 'advance', 'improvement', etc., does not mean that I claim to possess special knowledge about what is good and what is bad in the sciences and that I want to impose this knowledge upon my readers. Everyone can read the terms in his own way and in accordance with the tradition to which he belongs. Thus for an empiricist, 'progress' will mean transition to a theory that provides direct empirical tests for most of its basic assumptions. Some people believe the quantum theory to be a theory of this kind. For others, 'progress' may mean unification and harmony, perhaps even at the expense of empirical adequacy. This is how Einstein viewed the general theory of relativity. And my thesis is that anarchism helps to achieve progress in any one of the senses one cares to choose. Even a law-and-order science will succeed only if anarchistic moves are occasionally allowed to take place.)

It is clear, then, that the idea of a fixed method, or of a fixed theory of rationality, rests on too naive a view of man and his social surroundings. To those who look at the rich material provided by history, and who are not intent on impoverishing it in order to please their lower instincts, their craving for intellectual security in the form of clarity, precision, 'objectivity', 'truth', it will become clear that there is only one principle that can be defended under all circumstances and in all stages of human development. It is the principle: anything goes.

This abstract principle must now be examined and explained in concrete detail.

PART 2

The interpretative tradition

Introduction: a general outline

The focus in this part is on the interpretative tradition, yet the narrative line according to which the readings are presented derives in large part from the trajectory of the periodically renewed epistemological-methodological controversy in which interpretation or 'understanding' figured strongly in opposition to 'explanation'. To avoid the impression that understanding is simply a reaction against explanation, however, it is necessary to recall immediately that the interpretative tradition has a long history preceding the outbreak of the controversy for the first time in the late nineteenth century. Considering that the controversy passed through four clearly distinguishable phases in the course of the twentieth century, the selected texts are divided into a corresponding number of broad groups. Readings 15 to 18 offer a glimpse into the interpretative tradition in the context of the first phase of the so-called 'explanation-understanding controversy' which was started by Wilhelm Dilthey in 1883 and still determined discussions in the early twentieth century. The second set of selections, readings 19 to 22, document contributions beyond the first phase, including ones articulating issues central to the second phase of the controversy, particularly that of Alfred Schutz. The third set, readings 23 to 29, covers the interpretative tradition in the context of the revival of the explanation-understanding controversy in the late twentieth century in close connection with the Anglo-American 'interpretative turn' due to the dissolution of positivism and the emergence of post-empiricism, and its intertwinement with and reinforcement by a new spurt of development in the Continental interpretative or hermeneutic tradition since the publication of Hans-Georg Gadamer's *Truth and Method* in 1960. The fourth set, readings 30 to 32, covers the emergence of a distinctive cognitive and reflexive approach in social science that developed in the wake of the earlier phenomenological and hermeneutic philosophies. In the readings this is represented by Aaron Cicourel, Harold Garfinkel and Erving Goffman, who all advocated in different ways the need for social science to address common-sense forms of knowledge.

By elaborating, against the background of a long-standing concern with interpretation and hermeneutics on the European Continent, on the distinction between explanation and understanding first made by Johann Gustav Droysen some 35 years earlier, Wilhelm Dilthey in 1883 gave rise to a wide-ranging and historically significant epistemological-methodological debate in which those representing the understanding or interpretative historical, human, cultural and social sciences clashed with their positivist and scientistic counterparts over questions of the philosophy of science. As against the explanatory methodology of the natural sciences, Dilthey, in what he believed to be an answer to John Stuart Mill's exposition of 'the logic of the moral sciences', posed understanding as being characteristic of the so-called '*Geisteswissenschaften*'. Whereas Dilthey in his earlier work grasped the philosophical foundations of these human sciences in terms of psychological understanding, his later work gives evidence of a change towards an emphasis on the interpretation and understanding of objectivations of the human mind or spirit such as the frameworks or structures of meaning of human expressions and cultural products. The neo-Kantians, particularly Wilhelm Windelband and Heinrich Rickert, but also Georg Simmel and later Max Weber, took up in modified form Dilthey's arguments regarding the epistemological and methodological independence of the *Geisteswissenschaften*. Attempting to correct Dilthey's psychologism and the relativism and historicism of his objectivism, Windelband and Rickert focused understanding in the cultural sciences, by contrast with psychological and physical explanation in the nomological sciences, on the irreal yet valid meaning of individual human cultural achievements. Weber took this a step further. Regarding the social sciences as interpretative cultural sciences with a generalizing thrust, he tried to clarify the interrelation or combination of understanding and explanation within these sciences rather than continuing to insist on the difference between the two epistemological-methodological orientations as such. In this manner, he arrived at his proposal of a '*verstehende Soziologie*', an understanding or interpretative sociology. This was accompanied, however, by a denial of the need for any further philosophical clarification of the foundations of the social sciences in favour of decisionism instead.

While these attempts to establish the historical, human, cultural and social sciences independently of the natural sciences were targeted by positivists as a matter of meaningless metaphysics or even of ideological obfuscation and obscurantism inspired partly by reactionary clerical and partly by German, romantic, anti-Western motives, from the 1920s the epistemological-methodological theme of understanding or interpretation was carried forward with renewed motivation, energy and instruments. Both new intellectual departures and sociopolitical developments on the Continent, especially in Germany, after the First World War played a significant role here. Karl Mannheim, for instance, animated by the emergence of Bolshevism and National Socialism as well as the ideological conflicts of the Weimar Republic, developed an understanding or interpretative sociology of cultural documents and products of all sorts which nevertheless sought to give a neutral explanation of their intrinsic thought or knowledge content by linking them to extrinsic structural patterns of social life and social processes. He was opposed by members of the Frankfurt School such as Max Horkheimer and Theodor Adorno (to be reviewed in Part 3), who incorporated an interpretative approach in a critical one from a more committed left-wing position. Alfred Schutz, in turn, set about to clarify systematically the philosophical foundations of interpretative sociology by underpinning and correcting

Weber's proposal by means of a theory of the constitution and interpretation of meaning deriving from Edmund Husserl's phenomenology. Being central to the second phase of the explanation-understanding controversy, Schutz took on and entered into exchanges with his neo-positivist critics, such as for instance Hempel and Nagel (see Part 1), who argued from a unified science perspective that understanding or interpretation is at best a pre-scientific psychological and heuristic device serving deductive-nomological explanation or, at least, the systematization of scientific knowledge, and therefore could not fulfil the demands of an epistemological-methodological foundation for the social sciences.

The next context in which the interpretative tradition came to the fore is the revival of the explanation-understanding controversy in the late twentieth century. This development was related to the so-called 'interpretative turn' which came about due to the analogical renewal in the Anglo-American world, stimulated by the dissolution of positivism and the emergence of post-empiricism, of arguments and positions characteristic of the Continental interpretative tradition. Of central significance here were Quine's holism, Morris' pragmatics and especially Wittgenstein's language game analysis (see Part 1). Peter Winch's post-Wittgensteinian recuperation of 'interpretative' or 'understanding' sociology is paradigmatic of this new departure. Remarkably, this new departure became intimately intertwined with, and was reinforced by, the controversy between Hans-Georg Gadamer representing philosophical hermeneutics and Jürgen Habermas representing critical theory, which contributed to a marked development in the interpretative tradition. The links between otherwise quite disparate authors such as for instance Winch, Gadamer, Habermas, Paul Ricoeur and Charles Taylor offer a glimpse of this rather complex confluence and intertwinement of the Anglo-American interpretative turn and the Continental interpretative or hermeneutic tradition.

Finally, a fourth development can be identified with the rise of ethnomethodology and a sociology of knowledge inspired by phenomenology and hermeneutics. In this, largely American tradition, knowledge is seen as having a basis in everyday life to the point that it is knowledge as sense-making that offers the basic structures of social integration. This approach, which emerged in opposition to both positivism and Parsons' structural functionalism, can broadly be summed up as entailing a cognitive turn that led to a more reflexive conception of knowledge and a knowing subject. It is particularly represented by the work of Aaron Cicourel, Harold Garfinkel and Erving Goffman who in their different ways were all centrally interested in cognitive processes and structures operative in everyday life. Their work illustrates the rejection of methodological individualism and collectivism in favour of a methodological situationalism. In this respect, the methodological individualism that underlay Weber's interpretative approach was abandoned and the Schutzean phenomenological approach was also radicalized. The cognitive turn amounted to a rejection of the centrality of explanation as the primary purpose of social science. The legacy of this radicalized hermeneutics was that the meaning of a social fact must be seen in terms of the cognitive processes, definitions, tacit forms of understanding, and practical reasonings that are constitutive of it.

The selected texts

Let us now, against the background of this narrative framework of the interpretative tradition, briefly consider each of the selected texts.

Understanding and positivism

Wilhelm Dilthey (1833–1911), a leading German philosopher of his time, made the concern with the philosophical foundations of what he called the *Geisteswissenschaften*, or the human sciences, the central prong of his work and, indeed, in this area offered his most original and certainly very influential contribution. In the selected text, he attempts to show that the endeavour of interpreters and scholars in many different fields to work the everyday phenomenon of the understanding of others up into a more formal set of rules in the form of the 'art of interpretation' or 'hermeneutics' has as long and respectable a tradition as the natural sciences. Rather than only a historical account, however, he asserts a sharp methodological difference between the understanding or interpretative human sciences and the experimenting natural sciences, and then advances his characteristic claim that 'hermeneutics' in the sense of 'the methodology of the interpretation of [the] written records . . . of human existence' provides 'a solution to the whole general problem' of the philosophical foundations of the human sciences.

Georg Simmel (1858–1918), one of the most creative and influential late nineteenth- and early twentieth-century philosophical diagnosticians of the times, gave much attention to the problem of the philosophical foundations of the social sciences. The two selected texts both bear out this interest of his. In the first on historical understanding, he argues that there is a continuity between everyday understanding and historical understanding or between 'praxis' and 'history as a science', and on that basis proposes the development of 'understanding' as 'the methodology of the historical sciences'. The second text is devoted to providing a philosophical foundation for sociology, what he calls a clarification of 'sociological apriorities' or 'the epistemology of sociology', which can be regarded as the exact opposite of Durkheim's presented in Part 1. On the basis of a fundamental difference between nature and society and, hence, between 'things' or 'objects' and the 'psychological processes [and] processes of interaction' constituting 'sociation', he argues that sociology requires 'a methodology which is wholly different' from that of the natural sciences. Since sociation is 'grounded in understanding' involving people who 'are themselves conscious and synthesizing units', a natural scientific type of observational methodology aiming at a 'theoretical picture' is unsuited to the study of society. The only appropriate methodology is one that allows us to grasp 'the inner significance of sociation itself', including 'the categories and the cognitive requirements of the subjective psyche' and the participants' 'knowing' or 'cognizing' of their 'being sociated'.

Max Weber (1864–1920), the classical German sociologist, was less interested in the epistemological problems exercising Dilthey and the neo-Kantians than in clarifying the methodological foundations of his own practice of science. In the selected text, nevertheless, he not only clearly exhibits his neo-Kantian orientation but also draws a sharp distinction between the natural and the social sciences in terms of their divergent cognitive interests. His basic orientation is apparent from his central interest in 'social science [as] an empirical science of concrete reality (*Wirklichkeitswissenschaft*)', while he insists that 'the decisive feature of the methodology of the cultural sciences' is their concern with the 'cultural significance' of the phenomena of life they study which can neither be derived from nor rendered intelligible by 'a system of analytical laws' (*Gesetzesbegriffen*), as in the case of the natural sciences. Such cultural significance derives from the fact that the object of the social sciences is constituted, on the basis of a 'value-orientation', as something meaningful rather than lawful in accordance with the 'historically variable' 'cultural problems' and corresponding 'evaluative ideas' (*Wertideen*) accepted in a particular epoch. In Weber's view, this unique focus on significance or meaningfulness does not preclude the use of explanation, whether by 'imputation' or even by 'subsumption [under] causal laws', in the social sciences. Yet such explanatory methodology is at best only a 'heuristic means' that sub-serves the 'rendering intelligible' or understanding of the significant phenomena in question. In the earlier part of the selected reading, Weber puts forward his well-known argument in favour of a sharp distinction between 'empirical science' and 'value-judgments'. Various critics have raised the question, however, whether his postulate of value-freedom does not stand in a relation of tension to his principle of value-orientation mentioned earlier. Without admitting ideologies, delusions and wishful thinking to science, there are those who are convinced that the strict formulation of value-freedom in the social sciences has its roots in Weber's unjustifiable desire to preserve an area of unarguable choice in which decisionism holds sway. In the text, he indeed insists that 'the validity of values' is 'a matter of faith' and repeatedly submits that the application of scientific knowledge in 'the making of a decision' requires an 'acting, willing person [who] weighs and chooses from among the values involved according to his own conscience and his personal view of the world'. Weber's decisionism is abundantly clear from his suggestion that the employment of scientific knowledge in the organization of modern society is not a matter of deliberation but rather the prerogative of the leader. The essay should be read in the light of being published when the editorship of the *Archiv für Sozialwissenschaft* was transferred to Max Weber, Edgar Jaffé and Werner Sombart. In it Weber attempts to set out the policy of the new editorship.

Sigmund Freud (1856–1939), the founder of psychoanalysis, initially developed his new departure in the context of the influence of the interpretative tradition, hermeneutics in particular, in the German-speaking world in the late nineteenth century. The first selection, from his *The Interpretation of Dreams*, published in 1900, gives evidence of the hermeneutic nature of dream analysis. As against the positivist tendency to fix on the immediately given content, he proposes to consider dreams as complexes of meaningful symbols calling for interpretation. The psychoanalyst interpretatively translates unconscious motives functioning as causes into intelligible motives, which, once understood by the patient, changes the latter's behaviour. In the second selection, dating from 1932, Freud adopts a defensive position which contrasts sharply with this notion of the hermeneutic interpretation of dreams. In response to numerous criticisms directed against him during the heyday of neo-positivism for entertaining an unscientific '*Weltanschauung*' in the sense of an all-embracing, unverifiable or irrefutable philosophy of life, he here seeks to present psychoanalysis as a legitimate 'branch of science'. Not only does he invoke the neo-positivist unified science ideal, 'the unified nature of the explanation of the universe', but he also portrays psycho-analysis as making 'the spirit and mind . . . the subject of scientific investigation in exactly the same way as any non-human entities'. This places us squarely in the second context within which the interpretative tradition asserted itself.

Understanding and neo-positivism

Ernst Cassirer (1874–1945), a German neo-Kantian philosopher who emigrated to the USA in 1941, initially focused on the natural sciences but later developed a philosophy of symbolic forms and also put forward a philosophy of the cultural sciences. The selected text, however, was taken from his important early book *Substance and Function* since Cassirer here advances arguments about scientific concept formation that can be regarded as perhaps the first coherent presentation of a relational approach which runs counter to positivism. His shift of emphasis from substance, whether objects, things or individual actors, to the relations between them instead proved extremely influential, not only in the case of sociologists such as Karl Mannheim (see the next reading) and Norbert Elias in the 1920s and 1930s, but also much later in the case of Pierre Bourdieu (see Parts 5 and 6). Starting with a critique of theories of abstraction which move from 'the particular to the universal' and thus pass over the quality of the individual elements in order to focus on 'the uniformity of the given', Cassirer instead emphasizes 'the relations established between the indi-vidual elements', their 'connection by implication', 'the form of connection', the 'uni-versal *rule* for the connection of the particulars' and hence the 'concrete universality', 'concrete totality' with its own 'generating principle' or 'systematic whole which takes up into itself the peculiarities of all the species and develops them according to a rule'. Cassirer's relationalism provided the basis for Kurt Lewin's field theory and even seems to have anticipated Wittgenstein's notion of language games (see Reading 10).

Karl Mannheim (1887–1947) was a Hungarian Jew who studied in Germany in a neo-Kantian and phenomenological context and as professor of sociology in Frank-furt, who transformed Marx's theory of ideology into the sociology of knowledge and was forced into exile in England in 1933 after his dismissal by the Nazis. In the selected text, Mannheim assumes the earlier established difference between the cultural-social sciences and the exact natural sciences but presents it as a distinction between abstract, decontextualized, functional thought, operating without consider-ations of the ends it serves, and embodied, embedded, context-bound thought con-cerned with consciousness as formed by particular historical circumstances, including consideration of ends. Rather than merely asserting this methodological contrast and insisting on the interpretation and understanding of the qualitative or meaningful nature of the sociocultural world, however, he analyses the latter to show that qualita-tive and meaningful phenomena are generated by social relations and processes, including 'competition' and 'conflict'. His focus is specifically on the process of competition in which social agents struggle over a common stake, what he (with Heidegger) calls 'the public interpretation of reality'. The main thrust of his argument is that not only ordinary everyday understandings, historical interpretations and political views gain ascendancy and become established in society in this manner, but also interpretations in the cultural and social sciences. A decade or so later, Mannheim was convinced that knowledge in the natural sciences achieved dominance in precisely the same way. Although not directly drawing on Mannheim, both Kuhn and Lakatos (see Part 1) would later display a similar understanding of competition in the context of the natural sciences.

Alfred Schutz (1899–1959), an Austrian banking legal counsel and sociologist who emigrated to the USA in the 1930s when Hitler rose to power, was single-mindedly concerned with bringing Husserl's phenomenological perspective to bear on the philosophy of the social sciences. Initially, this took the form of bringing together phenomenology and Weberian interpretative sociology, but once in the USA he also took account of relevant American developments, including not only pragmatism and symbolic interactionism but also neo-positivism. This made him a central contributor to the second phase of the explanation-understanding controversy. Schutz opens the selected text with a brief review and critical evaluation of the first phase of the controversy, but then enters the second phase by targeting logical positivism – more particularly, singling out Nagel's (see Part 1) criticism of the Weberian view of the social sciences as seeking to understand social phenomena in terms of meaningful categories of human experience. He objects not only to the 'monopolistic imperialism' of logical positivism, which entailed both a 'disregard' for the social sciences and an indiscriminate extension of the 'logic of the natural sciences' to the social sciences, but also to the complete misunderstanding and misrepresentation of understanding as irredeemably subjective and uncontrollable 'introspection' concerned with 'psychic states' and the 'imputation of emotions, attitudes and purposes' to actors. The core of his criticism, however, is that logical positivism, in so far as it admits only overtly observable behaviour and thus identifies experience with sensory observation, operates with the rather narrow 'model' of 'situations in which the acting individual is given to the observer in what is commonly called a face-to-face relationship'. This means that logical positivism excludes social scientific study yet in respect of science as a social enterprise nevertheless takes for granted the larger part of social reality which is precisely the object of study of the social sciences. Whereas logical positivism focuses on sensorily observable overt behaviour, social reality or the lifeworld (*Lebenswelt*) is an intersubjective world of meaning which is carried in interaction or intercommunication and understood from the inside by the participants, including the social scientist. Rather than sensory experience mediated through observation, therefore, the social sciences proceed on the basis of communicative experience mediated by understanding. For Schutz, this implies that 'understanding or *Verstehen*' refers to more than merely the interpretative methodology of the social sciences. In the first instance, it is the largely taken for granted 'experiential form in which common-sense thinking takes cognizance of the socio-cultural world', the specific meaning and relevance structure of the lifeworld, which provides the basic level of first degree constructs upon which the 'constructs of the second degree' of the social sciences are built through the mediation of communicative experience – Giddens' later so-called 'double hermeneutic' relation. Like Weber (see above), Schutz takes pains to acknowledge the relative right of the observation of regularities, explanation and prediction in the social sciences, but this does not prevent him from reasserting a fundamental methodological divide based on 'an essential difference in the structure of the thought objects or mental constructs' of the social and natural sciences respectively: 'The world of nature, as explored by the natural scientist, does not "mean" anything to the molecules, atoms, and electrons therein. The observational field of the social scientist, however, namely social reality, has a specific meaning and relevance structure for the human beings living, acting, and thinking therein'.

Maurice Merleau-Ponty (1908–61), the leading French philosopher of his time who exhibited an intense interest in the social sciences, sociology in particular, in the selected text presents a phenomenological position which is comparable to Schutz, in various respects. Central here is his emphasis on what he calls 'the experience . . . of intersubjectivity' against the background of criticisms of positivism and neo-positivism under such titles as 'the mere recording of facts', 'empiricism', 'objectivism' and 'scientism'. But this text was selected in particular because Merleau-Ponty here attacks the '*cordon sanitaire*' constituting the 'segregated system' or apartheid of sociology and philosophy which was maintained by neo-positivism – and, we may add, is still today advocated by others (e.g. the Elias school). According to him, philosophy is necessary to sociology. Philosophy as the 'consciousness of intersubjectivity' comes into play 'every time [the sociologist] is required not only to record but comprehend the facts', and is 'a constant reminder of [sociology's] tasks', being 'the vigilance which does not let us forget the source of all knowledge'.

The interpretative or hermeneutic turn

Martin Heidegger (1889–1976), the major German philosopher of the first half of the twentieth century, made a signal contribution with his book *Being and Time* (1927) which would eventually alter the Continental hermeneutic or interpretative tradition fundamentally. In the key Section 31 on 'understanding' (*Verstehen*), where he spells out the concept of 'being-able-to-be-in-the-world' (*In-der-Welt-sein*), he prepared the ground for pulling the rug from under traditional epistemological and methodological theories by emphasizing the priority of possibility over actuality. But it is in such later writings as the essay 'The age of the world picture' (1938), an excerpt of which is presented below, that he drew the radical conclusion from his earlier work. In this text, he exposes western metaphysics, which had started with Plato's emphasis on *eidos*, meaning 'aspect' or 'view', as having culminated in 'the modern age', where the world has become something that can be represented or pictured, objectified, mastered, manipulated and exploited by the moderns from their peculiar subjective point of view purely for their own humanistic purposes. It is this unitary technical character of modernity that accounts for the fact that 'science as research' is at the heart of the modern project of 'calculating, planning, and molding of all things' – not merely the natural sciences but also the human sciences, indeed, all the sciences in so far as they 'picture' and 'set up' the world and thus make it amenable to 'planning and calculating and adjusting and making secure'. Towards the end of the essay, under the title of the 'shadow of the modern world' or the 'incalculable', Heidegger invokes the unthought of process which makes possible and opens up the space of modernity where alone – by contrast with science – the truth is to be found. In one way or another, this dimension would later provide a starting point for both Gadamer (in the reading below) in Germany and Derrida (see Part 5) in France.

Peter Winch (1926–97), an English philosopher who drew out the implications of Wittgenstein's philosophy of language games for the social sciences, in a surprising and controversial move not only brought the analytic philosophy of ordinary language into contact with the Continental hermeneutic tradition but, in so doing, also provided a new language-philosophical justification for understanding or interpretative sociology. In the selection, from *The Idea of a Social Science and its Relation to Philosophy* (1958), Winch rejects Wittgenstein and his followers' separation of philosophy and science in favour of connecting or even identifying philosophy and science with one another. Instead of their 'underlabourer conception' according to which philosophy is a 'purely negative' activity of 'clearing up linguistic confusions' bedeviling 'positive . . . empirical science', he proposes to transform philosophy into the science of language games or a priori forms of understanding of reality which, as he makes clear later in the book, is equivalent to understanding or interpretative sociology. The new relation he establishes between philosophy and science entails, therefore, the identification of understanding or interpretative sociology and epistemology: sociology as the science of language games or forms of life is not 'empirical research' or a generalizing social science, but rather philosophy in the sense of the epistemological analysis of forms of understanding or 'a priori conceptual analysis'. In the selected text, accordingly, Winch attacks not only Wittgenstein and his followers, but also positivists and logical empiricists or logical positivists who focus on 'the properties of objects, their causes and effects' and 'statements about reality' while losing sight of what is thus presupposed, namely 'the continuing truth of most of our generalizations' or a priori forms of understanding – emphasized also by phenomenologists such as Schutz and Merleau-Ponty. Later in the book, Winch criticizes the line of positivist social science from Mill to Durkheim and Pareto, and through a critical appropriation of Dilthey and Weber seeks to recuperate understanding social science, with understanding being reconceptualized in terms of Wittgenstein's notion of following a rule (see Part 1).

Hans-Georg Gadamer (1900–2002), building on Heidegger's existential ontology and his later concern with language, made an unparalleled contribution to the rejuvenation and reorientation of the Continental hermeneutic tradition with his main work *Truth and Method* (1960) and thus established himself as the leading hermeneutic philosopher of the late twentieth century. Pursuing Heidegger's work to its logical conclusion, he undertook to render the epistemological-methodological distinction between explanation and understanding obsolete by shifting to the more fundamental level of historically shaped, linguistically structured understanding. This strategy is readily apparent both from the title of his main work and from the excerpt presented here. 'Philosophical hermeneutics', as he calls his approach, avoids the attempt to devise an alternative methodology to the absolutized methodology of the natural sciences, as did for instance Dilthey, but rather opposes the modern absolutization of 'scientific method' as such in the form of positivism or objectivism, irrespective of whether in the case of the natural sciences or of the human sciences. Rather than being attained by 'method', the hermeneutical problem of understanding concerns 'truth' which is contained in 'our own historicity' – i.e. in the fact that we are historical beings who are shaped by history and whose self-knowledge is never complete – asserting itself in the 'presuppositions . . . that govern [the] understanding' of tradition, history, texts, strange phenomena or alterity'. Once the problem is grasped at this deeper level, according to Gadamer, it should be clear that understanding consists neither in 'the empathy of one individual for another', as Dilthey tended to think, nor in 'subordinating another person to our own standards', as positivists or behaviourists (see Part 1) hold. Rather, understanding is a constantly continuing 'process' in the form of an 'encounter [involving] the experience of tension between the text and the present' in which 'a real fusing of horizons' occurs in such a way that a 'higher universality that overcomes our own particularity but also that of the other', 'something of living value' for the future, ensues. For Gadamer, 'historically effective consciousness', which makes such a fusion of horizons and hence the disclosure of truth possible, is 'the central problem of hermeneutics'. It is on the basis of the fundamental nature and pervasiveness of the process of understanding defended in the selected text that he later submitted that hermeneutics enjoys incontrovertible universal significance.

Jürgen Habermas (1929–), the leading second generation representative of the Frankfurt tradition of critical theory (see Part 3), together with Karl-Otto Apel, was responsible through a penetrating analysis of Gadamer's work for bringing hermeneutics into late twentieth-century discussions of the epistemology and methodology of the social sciences. In fact, the so-called 'Habermas-Gadamer debate' proved to be one of the most important methodological debates of the time in the social sciences. In the selected text, an excerpt from one of the key texts of the debate, he focuses his criticism directly on Gadamer's claim that hermeneutic understanding is universal and, in the process, effects a radical twist in the hermeneutical tradition by introducing a new form of 'depth-hermeneutical interpretation' useful to the 'critique of ideologies' – what he also refers to as 'hermeneutical understanding that has been extended into critique' or simply a 'critically enlightened hermeneutic'. Habermas takes exception to Gadamer's claim that all understanding of meaning is context-dependent in the sense that we are and remain inescapably and irredeemably caught up in the authority and dogmatic recognition of tradition. His principal criticism is directed against Gadamer's 'ontologization of language' in the sense of making it into an all-pervasive and all-enveloping reality and his 'hypostatization of the context of tradition' in the sense of reifying it into an all-dominant superior knowledge and dogmatic authority. Habermas does not necessarily disagree with the hermeneutic claim to universality, for he accepts that 'everyday language remains the last meta-language' or the final language in which we could resolve problems of understanding. But he submits that such a universal claim can be maintained only if it is simultaneously acknowledged that language is the medium of both understanding and systematically distorted communication, and that it is possible to break through the context of tradition by reflectively and critically exposing its authority as at times dogmatically disguising domination and force. It is on the basis of such 'meta-hermeneutic experience . . . of distorted communication' and 'critique as a penetrating form of understanding which does not rebound off delusions' or 'explanatory understanding' (which he admits should not themselves be overstated or overextended into a 'false claim to universality'), that Habermas insists, as against Gadamer, on the emancipatory potential of a critically enlightened hermeneutic.

Paul Ricoeur (1913–), one of the leading philosophers of post-war France whose work is characterized by playing a mediating role between different schools of thought, in the selected reading evaluates the Habermas-Gadamer debate with a view to clarifying the relations between hermeneutics and critique. Ricoeur's principal concern is to dissolve 'false antinomies' between the 'hermeneutics of tradition' or past-oriented 'ontology of prior understanding', on the one hand, and the 'critique of ideology' or a future-oriented 'eschatology of freedom' on the other hand, which threaten to dominate the debate between Gadamer and Habermas. This he does by highlighting the 'common ground' shared by the two approaches in a 'philosophical anthropology' which accounts for human beings' care about both understanding and critique. Despite this common ground, however, Ricoeur insists that hermeneutics and critique each speak from 'a different place', the former from 'attention to cultural heritages' and the latter from 'where labour, power and language are intertwined', and hence that they should not be conflated. It is this grasp of the relative right of each that allows him then to reject 'the ruinous dichotomy, inherited from Dilthey, between "explanation" and "understanding" ' and to assert a 'dialectic' between hermeneutics and ideology critique – a relation of mediation envisaged earlier by Habermas and Apel. For many, these conclusions pointed in the direction of a critical hermeneutics.

Charles Taylor (1931–) is a Canadian political philosopher who exhibits strong leanings toward Continental developments and does not shrink from a sharp criticism of the Anglo-American philosophy of social science. Calling upon Dilthey, Gadamer, Ricoeur and Habermas, he makes a strong case in the selected text for the necessity of hermeneutical human or social sciences – 'hermeneutical sciences of man' in his old-fashioned language – against the background of the inadequacy of 'the orthodox view' inspired by the natural sciences. In both traditional positivism and logical positivism, according to him, a 'level of certainty' had been demanded – in the former case through the 'empiricist' emphasis on the securing of 'brute data' by 'induction' and in the latter through the addition of the 'rationalist' requirement of deductive or 'logical and mathematical inference' – which is not only inappropriate in the human or social sciences but has actually led to 'sterile' results. Taking on board the 'uncertainty [forming] an ineradicable part of our epistemological predicament', he clarifies the three basic conditions of human or social sciences which proceed by way of interpretation: first, they deal with an object that is meaningful, whether in a coherent or incoherent form; second, they regard meaning as being generated by expression and being embodied in and carried by signifiers; and, finally, they assume that there is a subject, however problematic it might be to identify it, who is responsible for the expression and hence whose meaning it is, as well as an audience to whom the expression is addressed and for whom it makes sense.

Clifford Geertz (1926–), an American anthropologist who has made an influential contribution to the interpretation of culture with his methodological concept of 'thick description', opens the selected text by contrasting his conception of 'interpretative . . . social science' with 'experimental science'. Yet his real adversary is not the natural sciences, but the scientistic theory of mind and knowledge, referred to also by Taylor in his essay (see above), which emerged in the Anglo-American world in the context of the post-empiricist situation following upon the dissolution of positivism. According to this 'cognitive' approach, culture consists of mental phenomena which call for analysis by a formal methodology on the model of mathematics and logic. The focus is thus on 'psychological structures', on the one hand, and on 'systematic rules, an ethnographic algorithm', on the other. By contrast, Geertz is convinced that meaning is something 'public' rather than private, and accordingly proposes a 'semiotic' or 'symbolic' concept of culture embracing 'socially established structures of meaning in terms of which people do . . . things'. In the classic essay from which the reading is selected, Geertz argues that the interpretation of culture must be a 'thick interpretation'. The term, borrowed from the philosopher Gilbert Ryle, refers to the way in which meaning is understood by reference to the wider cultural context. In this respect a 'thick interpretation' is a contrast to a 'thin interpretation', which is decontextualized. Ethnographic description, he argues, is also a form of 'thick interpretation', albeit of a second or third order. 'Analysis', Geertz argues, 'is sorting out the structures of signification' (or the 'cultural codes') in which 'social discourse' is inscribed. 'Description', if it is sensitive to all the forms of meaning and is 'microscopic' in its attention to detail, is for Geertz necessarily interpretation.

Hermeneutics and reflexivity

Aaron Cicourel was Professor of Sociology at Cornell University and later at the University of California, San Diego. His major works are *Method and Measurement in Sociology* (1964), from which the present reading is taken, and *Cognitive Sociology* (1973). This reading can be taken as an early example of an explicit reflexive approach in sociology. Cicourel's argument is that method in social science cannot be reduced to being the measurement and observation of data but must be capable of taking account of the commmon-sense knowledge of the social actor where knowledge assumptions are made but in 'implicit' and 'unstated' cognitive forms. The book attempts, as he wrote in the Preface, 'to specify the problems that sociology must address if researchers are to achieve a more basic level of interaction between theory, method, structure and meaning; between the perceived object, the meaning attached to it, the acts whereby object constancy is achieved, and the physical description of the object; between the rules of the game and "rules" of everyday life; and finally, between the social scene, as perceived and interpreted by its members at some point in time as a world taken for granted and known in an unquestioned way, and the world which can become problematic in the course of interaction because of potential and actual contingencies'. In this respect Cicourel is following in the footsteps of Alfred Schutz, who also advocated the interaction of two levels of knowledge: first-order common-sense and second-order social scientific – what Giddens later called 'double hermeneutic' (see Reading 53). Cicourel argues that much of positivistic social science fails to appreciate that its measurement systems are based on the very indeterminate first-order level of knowledge and are thus a good deal more unreliable than is often assumed. The implication is that social science must be more reflexive in its approach. This text can also be seen as pointing to a cognitive conception of knowledge, i.e. something that is socially constructed on two levels, the everyday and the scientific, and is cognitively organized or structured.

Harold Garfinkel (1917–) is the founder of ethnomethodology and was a very prominent sociologist in the 1960s when he taught at the University of California, Los Angeles. He was a student of Talcott Parsons at Harvard but became influenced by the phenomenology of Alfred Schutz. His most well-known book is *Studies in Ethnomethodology* (1967), a work that led to an emphasis in social research on language and the micro-dimension, and away from the macro-dimensions of large-scale structures and the historical process of modernity that characterized Parsons' structural functionalism as well as Marxism. He and his followers focused on ethnomethods in order to study the forms of knowledge, interpretative structures and cognitive rules in everyday life. Central to his approach was the idea of 'the reflexivity of accounts' by which he meant that people in everyday life make sense of the world and their situation in it. Scientific knowledge must be capable of eliciting such forms of reflexivity. In the classic article chosen, Garfinkel explores the double level of rationality, showing that in everyday life forms of rationality are present which, while being different from scientific forms of rationality, are nonetheless to be seen as rationalities. He begins by listing 14 aspects of rationality, arguing that the last four are strictly speaking scientific rationalities and generally absent from everyday life. In this way, he opposes the conventional assumption of equating rationality exclusively with science. The implication of this is that, for Garfinkel, the social scientist must take into account the situational context of the social actor who is a rational and self-interpreting agency. Nevertheless, he held to a conception of scientific knowledge that ultimately transcended the tacit and practical forms of knowledge in everyday life.

Erving Goffman (1922–82) was born and educated in Canada and later taught at the University of California and the University of Pennsylvania. His most well-known book is *The Presentation of Self in Everyday Life* (1956), but by the 1990s it was clear that his most systematic work, *Frame Analysis: An Essay on the Organization of Experience* (1974), had begun to have a growing impact. His work was characterized by a strong emphasis on social interaction and, like Garfinkel, the situation-boundness of practical knowledge. Unlike the latter, however, he did not adhere to a strict separation of scientific rationality and everyday rationality. Like Cicourel, Goffman was also concerned with the cognitive organization of communicative experience, but unlike Cicourel he elaborated this in much more detail by means of his concept of 'frame'. The reading selected here is an excerpt from a chapter, 'Primary Frameworks', in his book *Frame Analysis*. In it Goffman identifies what he calls 'primary frameworks' as the basic cognitive structures of culture. Such cognitive frameworks organize our experience and thus shape our everyday understanding in providing structures to locate, perceive, identify, describe and interpret the world, including nature, society and ourselves. They are cultural rules systems which give form to the world for people in everyday life. Goffmann distinguishes between social and natural primary frameworks and suggests that in contemporary American society there may be an incomplete sharing of social frameworks. The significance of his approach to knowledge has recently been recognized with the revival of the sociology of knowledge and the idea of reflexivity as well as the emergence of a cognitive epistemology (see Part 6).

15

WILHELM DILTHEY
The development of hermeneutics* (1900)

In a previous work I have considered how to describe the process by which individual works of art, in particular of poetry, are produced. Now we must ask if it is possible to study individual human beings and particular forms of human existence scientifically and how this can be done.

This is a question of the greatest significance, for our actions always presuppose the understanding of other people and a great deal of human happiness springs from empathy with the mental life of others. Indeed, philology and history rest on the assumption that the understanding of the unique can be made objective. The historical sense based on this assumption enables man to recapture the whole of his past; he can look across all the barriers of his own age at past cultures and increase his happiness by drawing strength from them and enjoying their charm. While the systematic human studies derive general laws and comprehensive patterns from the objective apprehension of the unique they still rest on understanding and interpretation. These disciplines, therefore, like history, depend for their certainty on the possibility of giving general validity to the understanding of the unique. So, from the beginning, we are facing a problem which distinguishes the human studies from the physical sciences.

No doubt the human studies have the advantage over the physical sciences because their subject is not merely an appearance given to the senses, a mere reflection in the mind of some outer reality, but inner reality directly experienced in all its complexity. Here we are not considering what difficulties, arising from the way in which this reality is experienced, obstruct objective apprehension but a further problem that inner experience of my own states can never, by itself, make me aware of my own individuality. Only by comparing myself to others and becoming conscious of how I differ from them can I experience my own individuality. However Goethe is, unfortunately, right when he notes how difficult it is to gain this most important of our experiences, and how imperfect our insight into the extent, nature and limit of our

* From Wilhelm Dilthey, 'The Rise of Hermeneutics' in *Wilhelm Dilthey: Selected Writings*, edited, translated and introduced by H.P. Rickman, Cambridge University Press, 1976, pp. 247–249. Reprinted with permission of the translator and publisher.

powers always remains. We are mainly aware of the inner life of others only through the impact of their gestures, sounds and acts on our senses. We have to reconstruct the inner source of the signs which strike our senses. Everything: material, structure, even the most individual features of this reconstruction, have to be supplied by transferring them from our own lives. How, then, can an individually structured consciousness reconstruct – and thereby know objectively – the distinct individuality of another? What kind of process is this which steps so strangely into the midst of the other cognitive processes?

We call the process by which we recognize some inner content from signs received by the senses understanding. This is how the word is used and a much-needed, fixed psychological terminology can only be established when every firmly coined, clearly and usefully circumscribed expression is used by writers consistently. Understanding of nature – *interpretatio naturae* – is a figurative expression. Even awareness of our own state of mind cannot properly be called understanding. It is true I may say: I can't understand how I could do that; I don't understand myself any longer. But then I mean that an expression of my nature which has been externalized confronts me as something alien that I cannot interpret, or else that I have got into a state at which I gaze astonished as if it were foreign to me. Understanding is the process of recognizing a mental state from a sense-given sign by which it is expressed.

Understanding ranges from the apprehension of childish patter to understanding *Hamlet* or the *Critique of Pure Reason*. The same human spirit speaks to us from stone, marble, musical compositions, gestures, words and writings, from actions, economic arrangements and constitutions, and has to be interpreted. This process of understanding must always have common characteristics because it is determined by common conditions and means of its own, and remains the same in its basic features. If, for example, I want to understand Leonardo I must interpret actions, pictures and writings in one homogeneous process.

Understanding shows different degrees which are, to start with, determined by interest. If the interest is limited so is the understanding. We listen impatiently to some explanations if all we want to know about is one point of practical importance and are not interested in the inner life of the speaker. In other cases we strain to get inside a speaker through every facial expression or word. But even the most strenuous attention can only give rise to a systematic process with a controllable degree of objectivity if the expression has been given permanent form so that we can repeatedly return to it. Such systematic understanding of recorded expressions we call exegesis or interpretation. In this sense there is also an art of interpreting sculptures or pictures. F.A. Wolf called for a hermeneutic and critique in archaeology. Welcker advocated it and Preller tried to develop it. But Preller emphasized that such interpretations of non-verbal works depended on explanations from literature.

Because it is in language alone human inwardness finds its complete, exhaustive and objectively comprehensible expression that literature is immeasurably significant for our understanding of intellectual life and history. The art of understanding therefore centres on the interpretation of written records of human existence.

Therefore, the exegesis – and the critical treatment inseparably linked with it – of these records formed the starting-point of philology. This is essentially a personal skill and virtuosity in the treatment of written records; any interpretation of monuments or

historically transmitted actions can only flourish in relation to this skill and its products. We can make mistakes about the motives of historical agents, indeed these agents
may themselves mislead us about their motives; but the work of a great poet or
explorer, of a religious genius or genuine philosopher can only be the true expression
of his mental life; in human society, full of lies, such work is always true and can
therefore – in contrast to other permanent expressions – be interpreted with complete
objectivity. Indeed it throws light on the other artistic records of an age and on the
historical actions of contemporaries.

This art of interpretation has developed just as slowly, gradually and in as orderly
a way as, for example, the questioning of nature by experiment. It originated and
survives in the personal, inspired virtuosity of philologists. Naturally it is mainly
transmitted through personal contact with the great masters of interpretation or their
work. But every skill also proceeds according to rules which teach us to overcome
difficulties and embody what can be transmitted of a personal skill. So the art of
interpretation gives rise to the formulation of rules. The conflict between such rules
and the struggle between different schools about the interpretation of vital works
produces a need to justify the rules and this gives rise to hermeneutics, which is the
methodology of the interpretation of written records.

Because it determines the possibility of valid interpretation by means of an analysis of understanding, it penetrates to the solution of the whole general problem with
which this exposition started. Understanding takes its place beside the analysis of
inner experience and both together demonstrate the possibility and limits of general
knowledge in the human studies in so far as it is determined by the way in which we
are originally presented with mental facts.

I shall document this orderly progress from the history of hermeneutics, by showing how philological virtuosity arose from the need for deep and valid understanding.
This gave rise to rules which were purposefully organized and systematized according
to the state of scholarship in a given period, and finally an assured starting-point for
making these rules was found in the analysis of understanding.

16

GEORG SIMMEL
On the nature of historical understanding* (1918)

The relationship between one mind and another that we call understanding is a fundamental process of human life. The manner in which this process fuses the receptivity and the characteristic and spontaneous activity of human life can only be experienced. It is not susceptible to further analysis. The kind of understanding which is peculiar to history is embedded in our view of understanding in general. In the forms and procedures which the mind develops in order to satisfy the practical demands and further the purposes of life, there are fragmentary, prototypical traces of our intellectual, purely mental activities. For this same reason, prototypical forms of history as a science are significantly prefigured in the structures and methods with which praxis pieces together the images of the past. These images of the past are conditions for the continuation of life itself. Every step of our lives rests upon consciousness of the past. Without some measure of this awareness, life would be utterly inconceivable. But this is not a consciousness of the past as the vast, formless of the totality of the material of life that is contained in memory or tradition. On the contrary, the practical purposes served by the consciousness of the past depend upon an analysis and synthesis of the material of life, its classification under concepts and into sequences, the emphasis and de-emphasis, interpretation and supplementation of this material. In this case, many different theoretical categories serve a nontheoretical interest. These theoretical categories are as continuously integrated into the purposive structures of life as any coordinations of movements, drives, or reflexes.

Consider the categories which form the raw material of life into an intellectually perspicuous, logically meaningful – and, therefore, above all, practically useful – system. Suppose that these categories are detached from this utilitarian function and acquire an intrinsic and autonomous theoretical interest in which the images of the past are structured with a new completeness and with reference to their own definitive values. This is the source of history as a science. There is a sense in which each of us is always his own autobiographer in embryo. Seen from the inverse perspective, this is

* From Georg Simmel 'On the Nature of Historical Understanding' in *Essays on Interpretation in Social Science*, Totowa, New Jersey: Rowman and Littlefield, 1980, pp. 97–98. Translated and edited by Guy Oakes. Reproduced by permission of Guy Oakes.

why, as scientific historians, we systematize and complete the attitudes and forms of prescientific life. On the basis of this completely general reciprocal relationship, insight into historical understanding is dependent upon insight into this other kind of understanding: how it happens that one man understands another. Although the premises and the methods, the interest and the subject matter may be very different, ultimately our understanding of the Apostle Paul and Louis XIV is essentially the same as our understanding of a personal acquaintance.

All understanding has the structure of an integral synthesis of two elements. Prior to the synthesis, these elements are discrete or independent. There is a given empirical phenomenon which, as such, has not yet been understood. The person for whom this phenomenon is a datum supplies the second element. This is the interpretive conception. This interpretive conception may be his own idea, or he may take it from some other source and assimilate it. The interpretive conception – as we might put it – penetrates the given phenomenon and constitutes it as an element that is understood. In some cases, this second mental element – the interpretive idea – is an autonomous object of consciousness. In other cases, it is perceptible only by reference to its results: the interpretation of the given phenomenon. There are three typical forms of the fundamental relationship between these two elements. All three forms are translated from their more or less extensive prescientific employment into the methodology of the historical sciences.

How is society possible?* (1908)

Kant asked and answered the fundamental question of his philosophy, 'How is nature possible?' He could do so only because nature for him was nothing but the representation of nature. It was so not merely in the sense that 'the world is my representation' and that we can therefore speak of nature too as only a content of consciousness, but also in the sense that what we call nature is the special way in which the mind assembles, orders, and shapes sense perceptions. These given perceptions of color, taste, tone, temperature, resistance, and smell pass through our consciousness in the accidental sequence of our subjective experience. In themselves, they are not yet nature. They rather become nature, and they do so through the activity of the mind which combines them into objects and series of objects, into substances and attributes, and into causal connections. In their immediate givenness, Kant held, the elements of the world do not have the interdependence which alone makes them intelligible as the unity of nature's laws. It is this interdependence which transforms the world fragments – in themselves incoherent and unstructured – into nature.

The Kantian image of the world grows from a most peculiar play of contrasts. On the one hand, sense impressions are purely subjective: they depend upon a physicopsychical organization (which may differ from individual to individual) and upon

* From 'How is Society Possible?', translated by Kurt Wolff, in *Georg Simmel, 1885–1918, A Collection of Essays and a Bibliography*, edited by Kurt Wolff. Ohio State University Press, 1959. Reprinted with permission of Kurt Wolff. Pp. 337–42.

the contingency of their provocations. They become objects as they are absorbed by the forms of our intellects and are transformed thereby into fixed regularities and into a consistent picture of 'nature.' On the other hand, these perceptions are what is really 'given,' the content of the world which we must simply accept, and the guarantee of an existence that is independent of us. Thus it is precisely the fact that our intellect forms perceptions into objects, systems, and uniformities which strikes us as subjective, that is, as something which we add to the given, as intellectual functions which, though unchangeable themselves, would have constructed a nature with a different content had they had different sense materials to work upon. For Kant, nature is a particular way of cognizing, a picture growing through and in our cognitive categories. Therefore, the question, 'How is nature possible?' – that is, 'What conditions are necessary for nature to be?' – is resolved by means of an inquiry into the forms which constitute the essence of our intellect. It is they which call forth nature itself.

It is very suggestive to treat as an analogous matter the question of the aprioristic conditions under which society is possible. Here, also, we find individual elements. In a certain sense, they too, like sense perceptions, stay forever isolated from one another. They, likewise, are synthesized into the unity of society only by means of a conscious process which correlates the individual existence of the single element with that of the other, and which does so in certain forms and according to certain rules. However, there is a decisive difference between the unity of a society and the unity of nature. It is this: In the Kantian view (which we follow here), the unity of nature emerges in the observing subject exclusively; it is produced exclusively by him in the sense materials, and on the basis of sense materials, which are in themselves heterogeneous. By contrast, the unity of society needs no observer. It is directly realized by its own elements because these elements are themselves conscious and synthesizing units. Kant's axiom that connection, since it is the exclusive product of the subject, cannot inhere in things themselves, does not apply here. For societal connection immediately occurs in the 'things,' that is, the individuals. As a synthesis, it too, of course, remains something purely psychological. It has no parallels with spatial things and their interaction. Societal unification needs no factors outside its own component elements, the individuals. Each of them exercises the function which the psychic energy of the observer exercises in regard to external nature: the consciousness of constituting with the others a unity is actually all there is to this unity. This does not mean, of course, that each member of a society is conscious of such an abstract notion of unity. It means that he is absorbed in innumerable, specific relations and in the feeling and the knowledge of determining others and of being determined by them. On the other hand, it should be noted that it is quite possible for an observing outsider to perform an additional synthesis of the persons making up the society. This synthesis would proceed as if these persons were spatial elements, but it is based only upon the observer himself. The determination of which aspect of the externally observable is to be comprehended as a unity depends not only on the immediate and strictly objective content of the observable but also upon the categories and the cognitive requirements of the subjective psyche. Again, however, society, by contrast, is the objective unit which needs no outside observer.

Things in nature are further apart than individuals are. In the spatial world, each element occupies a place it cannot share with any other. Here, there is nothing analogous to human unity, which is grounded in understanding, love, or common work. On the other hand, spatial elements fuse in the observer's consciousness into a unity that is not attained by the assemblage of individuals. For here, the objects of the synthesis are independent beings, psychic centers, personal units. They therefore resist the absolute fusion (in an observer's mind) to which, by contrast, the 'self-lessness' of inanimate things must yield. Thus, a number of people is a unit to a much greater extent, really, but to a much lesser extent, ideally, than are the units 'décor,' which is formed by table, chairs, couch, carpet, and mirror, or 'landscape' (or its 'picture' in a painting), which is made up of river, meadow, trees, and house.

Society is 'my representation' – something dependent upon the activity of con-sciousness – in quite a different sense from that in which the external world is. For the other individual has for me the same reality which I have myself, and this reality is very different from that of a material thing. Kant insists that I am precisely as certain of the existence of spatial objects as I am of my own existence. But by 'my own existence' he can understand only the particular contents of my subjective life. For its basis, the very basis of representation, the feeling of the existing ego, is unconditional and unshakable to a degree not attained by any representation of a material object. This very certainty, however, whether we can account for it or not, also extends to the you. And as the cause or as the effect of this certainty, we feel the you as something independent of our representation of it, as something that exists with exactly the same autonomy as does our own existence. And yet, this selfness of the other does not preclude his being made our representation. In other words, something which can by no means be resolved into our representation, nevertheless becomes its content, and thus its product.

This phenomenon is the fundamental psychologico-epistemological paradigm and problem of sociation. Within our own consciousness we very clearly distinguish between two things. One is the basic character of the ego, the precondition of all representing, which does not have the problematic nature of its contents, a nature which can never be completely eliminated; and the other is these contents themselves. In their coming and going, in their doubtfulness and corrigibility, all of these contents always present themselves as the mere products of the former, products of that abso-lute and ultimate force and existence which is our psychic being. And although we also think the other mind, we must nevertheless ascribe to it the very conditions, or rather freedom from conditions, of our own ego. We think that the other mind has the same maximum degree of reality, as distinguished from its mere contents, which our own self possesses, as distinguished from its contents.

Owing to these circumstances, the question of how society is possible implies a methodology which is wholly different from that for the question of how nature is possible. The latter question is answered by the forms of cognition, through which the subject synthesizes the given elements into nature. By contrast, the former is answered by the conditions which reside a priori in the elements themselves, through which they combine, in reality, into the synthesis, society. In a certain sense, the entire content of this book [*Soziologie*], as it is developed on the basis of the principle enunciated, is the beginning of the answer to this question. For it inquires into the processes – those which, ultimately, take place in the individuals themselves – that condition the exist-ence of the individuals as society. It investigates these processes, not as antecedent causes of this result, but as part of the synthesis to which we give the inclusive name of 'society.'

But the question of how society is possible must be understood in a still more fundamental sense. I said that, in the case of nature, the achieving of the synthetic unity is a function of the observing mind, whereas, in the case of society, that function is an aspect of society itself. To be sure, consciousness of the abstract principle that he is forming society is not present in the individual. Nevertheless, every individual knows that the other is tied to him – however much this knowledge of the other as fellow sociate, this grasp of the whole complex as society, is usually realized only on the basis of particular, concrete contents. Perhaps, however, this is not different from the 'unity of cognition.' As far as our conscious processes are concerned, we proceed by arranging one concrete content alongside another, and we are distinctly conscious of the unity itself only in rare and later abstractions. The questions, then, are these: What, quite generally and a priori, is the basis or presupposition which lies behind the fact that particular, concrete processes in the individual consciousness are actually processes of sociation? Which elements in them account for the fact that (to put it abstractly) their achievement is the production of a societal unit out of individuals?

The sociological apriorities envisaged are likely to have the same twofold significance as those which make nature possible. On the one hand, they more or less completely determine the actual processes of sociation as functions or energies of psychological processes. On the other hand, they are the ideational, logical presuppositions for the perfect society (which is perhaps never realized in this perfection, however). We find a parallel in the law of causation. On the one hand, it inheres and is effective in the actual processes of cognition. On the other hand, it constitutes truth as the ideal system of perfect cognition. And it does so irrespective of whether or not this truth obtains in the temporal and relatively accidental psychological dynamics in which causation actually operates – irrespective, that is, of the greater or lesser degree to which the actual, consciously held truth approximates the ideally valid truth.

To ask whether such an inquiry into the conditions of the process of sociation should or should not be called an epistemological inquiry is merely a question of terminology. The phenomenon which arises from these conditions and which receives its norms from their forms does not consist of cognitions but of concrete processes and actual situations. Nevertheless, what I have in mind here and what (as the general idea of sociation) must be examined in regard to its conditions is something cognitive, namely, the consciousness of sociating or of being sociated. This consciousness is perhaps better called a 'knowing' than a 'cognizing.' For here, the subject is not confronting an object of which he will gradually gain a theoretical picture. The consciousness of sociation is, rather, the immediate agent, the inner significance, of sociation itself. It is the processes of interaction which signify the fact of being sociated to the individual – not the abstract fact, to be sure, but a fact capable of abstract expression. What forms must be at the basis of this fact? What specific categories are there that man must bring along, so to speak, so that this consciousness may arise? And what, therefore, are the forms which come to the fore in the consciousness once this consciousness has arisen (namely, society as a fact of knowledge)? The discussion of these questions may well be called the epistemology of society.

17

MAX WEBER
"Objectivity" in social science* (1904)

We all know that our science, as is the case with every science treating the institutions and events of human culture, (with the possible exception of political history) first arose in connection with *practical* considerations. Its most immediate and often sole purpose was the attainment of value-judgments concerning measures of State economic policy. It was a "technique" in the same sense as, for instance, the clinical disciplines in the medical sciences are. It has now become known how this situation was gradually modified. This modification was not, however, accompanied by a formulation of the logical (*prinzipielle*) distinction between "existential knowledge," i.e., knowledge of what "is," and "normative knowledge," i.e., knowledge of what "should be." The formulation of this distinction was hampered, first, by the view that immutably invariant natural laws – later, by the view that an unambiguous evolutionary principle – governed economic life and that accordingly, *what was normatively right* was identical – in the former case with the immutably *existent* and in the latter with the inevitably *emergent*. With the awakening of the historical sense, a combination of ethical evolutionism and historical relativism became the predominant attitude in our science. This attitude sought to deprive ethical norms of their formal character and through the incorporation of the totality of cultural values into the "ethical" (*Sittlichen*) sphere tried to give a *substantive content* to ethical norms. It was hoped thereby to raise economics to the status of an "ethical science" with empirical foundations. To the extent that an "ethical" label was given to all possible cultural ideals, the particular autonomy of the ethical imperative was obliterated, without however increasing the "objective" validity of those ideals. Nonetheless we can and must forego a discussion of the principles at issue. We merely point out that even today the confused opinion that economics does and should derive value-judgments from a specifically "economic point of view" has not disappeared but is especially current, quite understandably, among men of practical affairs.

* Reprinted with the permission of The Free Press, a Division of Simon & Schuster, Inc., from *The Methodology of the Social Sciences* by Max Weber, translated and edited by Edward A. Shils and Henry A. Finch. Copyright © 1949 by The Free Press. Copyright © renewed 1977 by Edward Shils. Pp. 51–58, 72–85.

Our journal as the representative of an empirical specialized discipline must, as we wish to show shortly, reject this view in principle. It must do so because, in our opinion, it can never be the task of an empirical science to provide binding norms and ideals from which directives for immediate practical activity can be derived.

What is the implication of this proposition? It is certainly not that value-judgments are to be withdrawn from scientific discussion in general simply because in the last analysis they rest on certain ideals and are therefore "subjective" in origin. Practical action and the aims of our journal would always reject such a proposition. Criticism is not to be suspended in the presence of value-judgments. The problem is rather: what is the meaning and purpose of the scientific criticism of ideals and value-judgments? This requires a somewhat more detailed analysis.

All serious reflection about the ultimate elements of meaningful human conduct is oriented primarily in terms of the categories "end" and "means." We desire something concretely either "for its own sake" or as a means of achieving something else which is more highly desired. The question of the appropriateness of the means for achieving a given end is undoubtedly accessible to scientific analysis. Inasmuch as we are able to determine (within the present limits of our knowledge) which means for the achievement of a proposed end are appropriate or inappropriate, we can in this way estimate the chances of attaining a certain end by certain available means. In this way we can indirectly criticize the setting of the end itself as practically meaningful (on the basis of the existing historical situation) or as meaningless with reference to existing conditions. Furthermore, when the possibility of attaining a proposed end appears to exist, we can determine (naturally within the limits of our existing knowledge) the consequences which the application of the means to be used will produce in addition to the eventual attainment of the proposed end, as a result of the interdependence of all events. We can then provide the acting person with the ability to weigh and compare the undesirable as over against the desirable consequences of his action. Thus, we can answer the question: what will the attainment of a desired end "cost" in terms of the predictable loss of other values? Since, in the vast majority of cases, every goal that is striven for does "cost" or can "cost" something in this sense, the weighing of the goal in terms of the incidental consequences of the action which realizes it cannot be omitted from the deliberation of persons who act with a sense of responsibility. One of the most important functions of the *technical criticism* which we have been discussing thus far is to make this sort of analysis possible. To apply the results of this analysis in the making of a decision, however, is not a task which science can undertake; it is rather the task of the acting, willing person: he weighs and chooses from among the values involved according to his own conscience and his personal view of the world. Science can make him realize that all action and naturally, according to the circumstances, inaction imply in their consequences the espousal of certain values – and herewith what is today so willingly overlooked – the rejection of certain others. The act of choice itself is his own responsibility.

We can also offer the person, who makes a choice, insight into the significance of the desired object. We can teach him to think in terms of the context and the meaning of the ends he desires, and among which he chooses. We do this through making explicit and developing in a logically consistent manner the "ideas" which actually do or which can underlie the concrete end. It is self-evident that one of the most important tasks of every science of cultural life is to arrive at a rational understanding of these "ideas" for which men either really or allegedly struggle. This does not overstep the boundaries of a science which strives for an "analytical ordering of empirical reality," although the methods which are used in this interpretation of cultural (*geistiger*) values are not "inductions" in the usual sense. At any rate, this task falls at least partly beyond the limits of economics as defined according to the conventional division of labor. It belongs among the tasks of social philosophy. However, the historical influence of ideas in the development of social life has been and still is so great that our journal cannot renounce this task. It shall rather regard the investigation of this phenomenon as one of its most important obligations.

But the scientific treatment of value-judgments may not only understand and empathically analyze (*nacherleben*) the desired ends and the ideals which underlie them; it can also "judge" them critically. This criticism can of course have only a dialectical character, i.e., it can be no more than a formal logical judgment of historically given value-judgments and ideas, a testing of the ideals according to the postulate of the internal consistency of the desired end. It can, insofar is it sets itself this goal, aid the acting willing person in attaining self-clarification concerning the final axioms from which his desired ends are derived. It can assist him in becoming aware of the ultimate standards of value which he does not make explicit to himself or, which he must presuppose in order to be logical. The elevation of these ultimate standards, which are manifested in concrete value-judgments, to the level of explicitness is the utmost that the scientific treatment of value-judgments can do without entering into the realm of speculation. As to whether the person expressing these value-judgments should adhere to these ultimate standards is his personal affair; it involves will and conscience, not empirical knowledge.

An empirical science cannot tell anyone what he *should* do – but rather what he can do – and under certain circumstances what he wishes to do. It is true that in our sciences, personal value-judgments have tended to influence scientific arguments without being explicitly admitted. They have brought about continual confusion and have caused various interpretations to be placed on scientific arguments even in the sphere of the determination of simple casual interconnections among facts according to whether the results increased or decreased the chances of realizing one's personal ideals, i.e., the possibility of desiring a certain thing. Even the editors and the collaborators of our journal will regard "nothing human as alien" to them in this respect. But it is a long way from this acknowledgement of human frailty to the belief in an "ethical" science of economics, which would derive ideals from its subject matter and produce concrete norms by applying general ethical imperatives. It is true that we regard as *objectively* valuable those innermost elements of the "personality," those highest and most ultimate value-judgments which determine our conduct and give meaning and significance to our life. We can indeed espouse these values only when they appear to us as valid, as derived from our highest values and when they are developed in the struggle against the difficulties which life presents. Certainly, the dignity of the "personality" lies in the fact that for it there exist values about which it organizes its life; even if these values are in certain cases concentrated exclusively within the sphere of the person's "individuality," then "self-realization" in *those* interests for which it claims *validity* as *values*, is the idea with respect to which its whole existence is oriented. Only on the assumption of belief in the validity of values is the attempt to espouse value-judgments meaningful. However, to *judge* the *validity* of such values is a matter of faith. It may perhaps be a task for the speculative interpretation of life and the universe in quest of their meaning. But it certainly does not fall within the province of an empirical science in the sense in which it is to be practised here. The empirically demonstrable fact that these ultimate ends undergo historical changes and are debatable does not affect this distinction between empirical science and value-judgments, contrary to what is often thought. For even the knowledge of the most certain proposition of our theoretical sciences – e.g., the exact natural sciences or mathematics – is, like the cultivation and refinement of the conscience, a product of culture. However, when we call to mind the practical problems of economic and social policy (in the usual sense), we see that there are many, indeed countless, practical questions in the discussion of which there seems to be general agreement about the self-evident character of certain goals. Among these we may mention emergency credit, the concrete problems of social hygiene, poor relief, factory inspection, industrial courts, employment exchanges, large sections of protective labor legislation – in short, all those issues in which, at least in appearance, only the means for the attainment of the goal are at issue. But even if we were to mistake the illusion of self-evidence for truth – which science can never do without damaging itself – and wished to view the conflicts immediately arising from attempts at practical realization as purely technical questions of expediency – which would very often be incorrect – even in this case we would have to recognize that this illusion of the self-evidence of normative standards of value is dissipated as soon as we pass from the concrete problems of philanthropic and protective social and economic services to problems of economic and social policy. The distinctive characteristic of a problem of social *policy* is indeed the fact that it cannot be resolved merely on the basis of purely technical considerations which assume already settled ends. Normative standards of value can and must be the objects of *dispute* in a discussion of a problem of social policy because the problem lies in the domain of general cultural values. And the conflict occurs not merely, as we are too easily inclined to believe today, between "class interest" but between general views on life and the universe as well. This latter point, however, does not lessen the truth that the particular ultimate value-judgment which the individual espouses is decided among other factors and certainly to a quite significant degree by the degree of affinity between it and his class interests – accepting for the time being this only superficially unambiguous term. One thing is certain under all circumstances, namely, the more "general" the problem involved, i.e., in this case, the broader its cultural *significance*, the less subject it is to a single unambiguous answer on the basis of the data of empirical sciences and the greater the role played by value-ideas (*Wertideen*) and the ultimate and highest personal axioms of belief. It is simply naive to believe, although there are many specialists who even now occasionally do, that it is possible to establish and to demonstrate as scientifically valid "a principle" for practical social science from which the norms for the solution of practical problems can be unambiguously derived. However much the social sciences need the discussion of practical problems in terms of fundamental principles, i.e., the reduction of unreflective value-judgments to the premises from which they are logically derived and however much our journal intends to devote itself specially to them –

certainly the creation of a lowest common denominator for our problems in the form of generally valid ultimate value-judgments cannot be its task or in general the task of any empirical science. Such a thing would not only be impracticable; it would be entirely meaningless as well. Whatever the interpretation of the basis and the nature of the validity of the ethical imperatives, it is certain that from them, as from the norms for the concretely conditioned conduct of the *individual, cultural values* cannot be unambiguously derived as being normatively desirable; it can do so the less, the more inclusive are the values concerned. Only positive religions – or more precisely expressed: dogmatically bound *sects* – are able to confer on the content of *cultural values* the status of unconditionally valid *ethical* imperatives. Outside these sects, cultural ideals which the individual wishes to realize and ethical obligations which he *should* fulfil do not, in principle, share the same status. The fate of an epoch which has eaten of the tree of knowledge is that it must know that we cannot learn the *meaning* of the world from the results of its analysis, be it ever so perfect; it must rather be in a position to create this meaning itself. It must recognize that general views of life and the universe can never be the products of increasing empirical knowledge, and that the highest ideals, which move us most forcefully, are always formed only in the struggle with other ideals which are just as sacred to others as ours are to us.

Only an optimistic syncretism, such as is, at times, the product of evolutionary-historical relativism, can theoretically delude itself about the profound seriousness of this situation or practically shirk its consequences. It can, to be sure, be just as obligatory subjectively for the practical politician, in the individual case, to mediate between antagonistic points of view as to take sides with one of them. But this has nothing whatsoever to do with scientific "objectivity.' *Scientifically the "middle course" is not truer even by a hair's breadth*, than the most extreme party ideals of the right or left. Nowhere are the interests of science more poorly served in the long run than in those situations where one refuses to see uncomfortable facts and the realities of life in all their starkness. The *Archiv* will struggle relentlessly against the severe self-deception which asserts that through the synthesis of several party points of view, or by following a line between them, practical norms of scientific validity can be arrived at. It is necessary to do this because, since this piece of self-deception tries to mask its standards of value in relativisitic terms, it is more dangerous to the freedom of speech than the former naive faith of parties in the scientific "demonstrability" of their dogmas. The capacity to distinguish between empirical knowledge and value-judgements, and the fulfillment of the scientific duty to see the factual truth as well as the practical duty to stand up for your own ideals constitute the program to which we wish to adhere with ever increasing firmness . . .

. . . There is no absolutely "objective" scientific analysis of culture – or put perhaps more narrowly but certainly not essentially differently for our purposes – of "social phenomena" independent of special and "one-sided" viewpoints according to which – expressly or tacitly, consciously or unconsciously – they are selected, analyzed and organized for expository purposes. The reasons for this lie in the character of the cognitive goal of all research in social science which seeks to transcend the purely formal treatment of the legal or conventional norms regulating social life.

The type of social science in which we are interested is an empirical science of concrete reality (*Wirklichkeitswissenschaft*). Our aim is the understanding of the characteristic uniqueness of the reality in which we move. We wish to understand on the one hand the relationships and the cultural significance of individual events in their contemporary manifestations and on the other the causes of their being historically so and not otherwise. Now, as soon as we attempt to reflect about the way in which life confronts us in immediate concrete situations, it presents an infinite multiplicity of successively and coexistently emerging and disappearing events, both "within" and "outside" ourselves. The absolute infinitude of this multiplicity is seen to remain undiminished even when our attention is focused on a single "object," for instance, a concrete act of exchange, as soon as we seriously attempt an exhaustive description of all the individual components of this "individual phenomena," to say nothing of explaining it casually. All the analysis of infinite reality which the finite human mind can conduct rests on the tacit assumption that only a finite portion of this reality constitutes the object of scientific investigation, and that only it is "important" in the sense of being "worthy of being known." But what are the criteria by which this segment is selected? It has often been thought that the decisive criterion in the cultural sciences, too, was in the last analysis, the "regular" recurrence of certain casual relationships. The "laws" which we are able to perceive in the infinitely manifold stream of events must – according to this conception – contain the scientifically "essential" aspect of reality. As soon as we have shown some causal relationship to be a "law," i.e., if we have shown it to be universally valid by means of comprehensive historical induction or have made it immediately and tangibly plausible according to our subjective experience, a great number of similar cases order themselves under the formula thus attained. Those elements in each individual event which are left unaccounted for by the selection of their elements subsumable under the "law" are considered as scientifically unintegrated residues which will be taken care of in the further perfection of the system of "laws." Alternatively they will be viewed as "accidental" and therefore scientifically unimportant because they do not fit into the structure of the "law;" in other words, they are not typical of the event and hence can only be the objects of "idle curiosity."

Accordingly, even among the followers of the Historical School we continually find the attitude which declares that the ideal which all the sciences, including the cultural sciences, serve and towards which they should strive even in the remote future is a system of propositions from which reality can be "deduced." As is well known, a leading natural scientist believed that he could designate the (factually unattainable) ideal goal of such a treatment of cultural reality as a sort of "astronomical" knowledge.

Let us not, for our part, spare ourselves the trouble of examining these matters more closely – however often they have already been discussed. The first thing that impresses one is that the "astronomical'" knowledge which was referred to is not a system of laws at all. On the contrary, the laws which it presupposes have been taken from other disciplines like mechanics. But it too concerns itself with the question of the individual consequence which the working of these laws in an unique configuration produces, since it is these individual configurations which are significant for us. Every individual constellation which it "explains" or predicts is causally explicable only as the consequence of another equally individual constellation which has preceded it. As far back as we may go into the grey mist of the far-off past, the reality to which the laws apply always remains equally individual, equally undeducible from laws. A cosmic "primeval state" which had no individual character or less individual character than the cosmic reality of the present would naturally be a meaningless notion. But is there not some trace of similar ideas in our field in those propositions sometimes derived from natural law and sometimes verified by the observation of "primitives," concerning an economic-social "primeval state" free from historical "accidents," and characterized by phenomena such as "primitive agrarian communism," sexual "promiscuity," etc., from which individual historical development emerges by a sort of fall from grace into concreteness?

The social-scientific interest has its point of departure, of course, in the real, i.e., concrete, individually-structured configuration of our cultural life in its universal relationships which are themselves no less individually structured, and in its development out of other social cultural conditions, which themselves are obviously likewise individually structured. It is clear here that the situation which we illustrated by reference to astronomy as a limiting case (which is regularly drawn on by logicians for the same purpose) appears in a more accentuated form. Whereas in astronomy, the heavenly bodies are of interest to us only in their quantitative and exact aspects, the qualitative aspect of phenomena concerns us in the social sciences. To this should be added that in the social sciences we are concerned with psychological and intellectual (*geistig*) phenomena the empathic understanding of which is naturally a problem of a specifically different type from those which the schemes of the exact natural sciences in general can or seek to solve. Despite that, this distinction in itself is not a distinction in principle, as it seems at first glance. Aside from pure mechanics, even the exact natural sciences do not proceed without qualitative categories. Furthermore, in our own field we encounter the idea (which is obviously distorted) that at least the phenomena characteristic of a money-economy – which are basic to our culture – are quantifiable and on that account subject to formulation as "laws." Finally it depends on the breadth or narowness of one's definition of "law" as to whether one will also include regularities which because they are not quantifiable are not subject to numerical analysis. Especially insofar as the influence of psychological and intellectual (*geistige*) factors is concerned, it does not in any case exclude the establishment of rules governing rational conduct. Above all, the point of view still persists which claims that the task of psychology is to play a role comparable to mathematics for the *Geisteswissenschaften* [the human sciences] in the sense that it analyzes the complicated phenomena of social life into their psychic conditions and effects, reduces them to their most elementary possible psychic factors and then analyzes their functional interdependences. Thereby, a sort of "Chemistry" if not "mechanics" of the psychic foundations of social life would be created. Whether such investigations can produce valuable and – what is something else – useful results for the cultural sciences, we cannot decide here. But this would be irrelevant to the question as to whether the aim of social-economic knowledge in our sense, i.e., knowledge of reality with respect to its cultural significance and its casual relationships, can be attained through the quest for recurrent sequences. Let us assume that we have succeeded by means of psychology or otherwise in analyzing all the observed and imaginable relationships of social phenomena into some ultimate elementary "factors," that we have made an exhaustive analysis and classification of them and then formulated rigorously exact laws covering their behavior. What would be the significance of these results for our knowledge of the historically given culture or any individual phase thereof, such as capitalism, in its development and cultural significance? As an analytical tool, it would be as useful as a textbook of organic chemical combinations would be for our knowledge of the biogenetic aspect of the animal and plant world. In each case, certainly an important and useful preliminary step would have been taken. In neither case can concrete reality be deduced from "laws" and "factors." This is not because some higher mysterious powers reside in living phenomena (such as "dominants," "entelechies," or whatever they might be called). This, however, is a problem in its own right. The real reason is that the analysis of reality is concerned with the configuration into which those (hypothetical!) "factors" are arranged to form a cultural phenomenon which is historically significant to us. Furthermore, if we wish to "explain" this individual configuration "causally" we must invoke other equally individual configurations on the basis of which we will explain it with the aid of those (hypothetical!) "laws."

The determination of those (hypothetical) "laws" and "factors" would in any case only be the first of the many operations which would lead us to the desired type of knowledge. The analysis of the historically given individual configuration of those "factors" and their significant concrete interaction, conditioned by their historical context and especially the rendering intelligible of the basis and type of this significance would be the next task to be achieved. This task must be achieved, it is true, by the utilization of the preliminary analysis but it is nonetheless an entirely new and distinct task. The tracing as far into the past as possible of the individual features of these historically evolved configurations which are contemporaneously significant, and their historical explanation by antecedent and equally individual configurations would be the third task. Finally the prediction of possible future constellations would be a conceivable fourth task.

For all these purposes, clear concepts and the knowledge of those (hypothetical) "laws" are obviously of great value as heuristic means – but only as such. Indeed they are quite indispensable for this purpose. But even in this function their limitations become evident at a decisive point. In stating this, we arrive at the decisive feature of the method of the cultural sciences. We have designated as "cultural sciences" those disciplines which analyze the phenomena of life in terms of their cultural significance. The significance of a configuration of cultural phenomena and the basis of this significance cannot however be derived and rendered intelligible by a system of analytical laws (*Gesetzesbegriffen*), however perfect it may be, since the significance of cultural events presupposes a value-orientation towards these events. The concept of culture is a value-concept. Empirical reality becomes "culture" to us because and insofar as we relate it to value ideas. It includes those segments and only those segments of reality which have become significant to us because of this value-relevance. Only a small portion of existing concrete reality is colored by our value-conditioned interest and it alone is significant to us. It is significant because it reveals relationships which are important to us due to their connection with our values. Only because and to the extent that this is the case is it worthwhile for us to know it in its individual features. We cannot discover, however, what is meaningful to us by means of a "presuppositionless!" investigation of empirical data. Rather perception of its meaningfulness to us is the presupposition of its becoming an object of investigation.

Meaningfulness naturally does not coincide with laws as such, and the more general the law the less the coincidence. For the specific meaning which a phenomenon has for us is naturally not to be found in those relationships which it shares with many other phenomena.

The focus of attention on reality under the guidance of values which lend it significance and the selection and ordering of the phenomena which are thus affected in the light of their cultural significance is entirely different from the analysis of reality in terms of laws and general concepts. Neither of these two types of the analysis of reality has any necessary logical relationship with the other. They can coincide in individual instances but it would be most disastrous if their occasional coincidence caused us to think that they were not distinct in principle. The cultural significance of a phenomenon, e.g., the significance of exchange in a money economy, can be the fact that it exists on a mass scale as a fundamental component of modern culture. But the historical fact that it plays this role must be causally explained in order to render its cultural significance understandable. The analysis of the general aspects of exchange and the technique of the market is a – highly important and indispensable – preliminary task. For not only does this type of analysis leave unanswered the question as to how exchange historically acquired its fundamental significance in the modern world; but above all else, the fact with which we are primarily concerned, namely, the cultural significance of the money economy, for the sake of which we are interested in the description of exchange technique and for the sake of which alone a science exists which deals with that technique – is not derivable from any "law." The generic features of exchange, purchase, etc., interest the jurist – but we are concerned with the analysis of the cultural significance of the concrete historical fact that today exchange exists on a mass scale. When we require an explanation, when we wish to understand what distinguishes the social-economic aspects of our culture for instance from that of antiquity in which exchange showed precisely the same generic traits as it does today and when we raise the question as to where the significance of "money economy" lies, logical principles of quite heterogeneous derivation enter into the investigation. We will apply those concepts with which we are provided by the investigation of the general features of economic mass phenomena – indeed, insofar as they are relevant to the meaningful aspects of our culture, we shall use them as means of exposition. The goal of our investigation is not reached through the exposition of those laws and concepts, precise as it may be. The question as to what should be the object of universal conceptualization cannot be decided "presuppositionlessly" but only with reference to the significance which certain segments of that infinite multiplicity which we call "commerce" have for culture. We seek knowledge of an historical phenomenon, meaning by historical: significant in its individuality (*Eigenart*). And the decisive element in this is that only through the presupposition that a finite part alone of the infinite variety of phenomena is significant, does the knowledge of an individual phenomenon become logically meaningful. Even with the widest imaginable knowledge of "laws," we are helpless in the face of the question: how is the causal explanation of an individual fact possible – since a description of even the smallest slice of reality can never be exhaustive? The number and type of causes which have influenced any given event are always infinite and there is nothing in the things themselves to set some of them apart as alone meriting attention. A chaos of "existential judgments" about countless individual events would be the only result of a serious attempt to analyse reality "without presuppositions." And even this result is only seemingly possible, since every single perception discloses on closer examination an infinite number of constituent perceptions which can never be exhaustively expressed in a judgment. Order is brought into this chaos only on the condition that in every case only a part of concrete reality is interesting and significant to us, because only it is related to the cultural values with which we approach reality. Only certain sides of the infinitely complex concrete phenomenon, namely those to which we attribute a general cultural significance, are therefore worthwhile knowing. They alone are objects of causal explanation. And even this causal explanation evinces the same character; an exhaustive causal investigation of any concrete phenomena in its full reality is not only practically impossible – it is simply nonsense. We select only those causes to which are to be imputed in the individual case, the "essential" feature of an event.

Where the individuality of a phenomenon is concerned, the question of causality is not a question of laws but of concrete causal relationships; it is not a question of the subsumption of the event under some general rubric as a representative case but of its imputation as a consequence of some constellation. It is in brief a question of imputation. Wherever the causal explanation of a "cultural phenomenon" – an "historical individual" is under consideration, the knowledge of causal laws is not the end of the investigation but only a means. It facilitates and renders possible the causal imputation to their concrete causes of those components of a phenomenon the individuality of which is culturally significant. So far and only so far as it achieves this, is it valuable for our knowledge of concrete relationships. And the more "general," i.e., the more abstract the laws, the less they can contribute to the causal imputation of individual phenomena and, more indirectly, to the understanding of the significance of cultural events.

What is the consequence of all this?

Naturally, it does not imply that the knowledge of universal propositions, the construction of abstract concepts, the knowledge of regularities and the attempt to formulate "laws" have no scientific justification in the cultural sciences. Quite the contrary, if the causal knowledge of the historians consists of the imputation of concrete effects to concrete causes, a valid imputation of any individual effect without the application of "nomological" knowledge – i.e., the knowedge of recurrent causal sequences – would in general be impossible. Whether a single individual component of a relationship is, in a concrete case, to be assigned causal responsibility for an effect, the causal explanation of which is at issue, can in doubtful cases be determined only by estimating the effects which we generally expect from it and from the other components of the same complex which are relevant to the explanation. In other words, the "adequate" effects of the causal elements involved must be considered in arriving at any such conclusion. The extent to which the historian (in the widest sense of the word) can perform this imputation in a reasonably certain manner with his imagination sharpened by personal experience and trained in analytic methods and the extent to which he must have recourse to the aid of special disciplines which make it possible, varies with the individual case. Everywhere, however, and hence also in the sphere of complicated economic processes, the more certain and the more comprehensive our general knowledge the greater is the certainty of imputation. This proposition is not in the least affected by the fact that even in the case of all so-called "economic laws" without exception, we are concerned here not with "laws" in the narrower exact natural science sense, but with adequate causal relationships expressed in rules and with the application of the category of "objective possibility." The establishment of such regularities is not the end but rather the means of knowledge. It is entirely a question of expediency, to be settled separately for each individual case, whether a regularly recurrent causal relationship of everyday experience should be formulated into a "law." Laws are important and valuable in the exact natural sciences, in the measure that those sciences are universally valid. For the knowledge of historical phenomena in their concreteness, the most general laws, because they are most devoid of content are also the least valuable. The more comprehensive the validity, or scope, of a term, the more it leads us away from the richness of reality since in order to include the common elements of the largest possible number of phenomena, it must necessarily be as abstract as possible and hence devoid of content. In the cultural sciences, the knowledge of the universal or general is never valuable in itself.

The conclusion which follows from the above is that an "objective" analysis of cultural events, which proceeds according to the thesis that the ideal of science is the reduction of empirical reality of "laws," is meaningless. It is not meaningless, as is often maintained, because cultural or psychic events for instance are "objectively" less governed by laws. It is meaningless for a number of other reasons. Firstly, because the knowledge of social laws is not knowledge of social reality but is rather one of the various aids used by our minds for attaining this end; secondly, because knowledge of cultural events is inconceivable except on a basis of the significance which the concrete constellations of reality have for us in certain individual concrete situations. In which sense and in which situations this is the case is not revealed to us by any law; it is decided according to the value-ideas in the light of which we view "culture" in each individual case. "Culture" is a finite segment of the meaningless infinity of the world process, a segment on which human beings confer meaning and significance. This is true even for the human being who views a particular culture as a mortal enemy and who seeks to "return to nature." He can attain this point of view only after viewing the culture in which he lives from the standpoint of his values, and finding it "too soft." This is the purely logical-formal fact which is involved when we speak of the logically necessary rootedness of all historical entities (*historische Individuen*) in "evaluative ideas." The transcendental presupposition of every cultural science lies not in our finding a certain culture or any "culture" in general to be valuable but rather in the fact that we are cultural beings, endowed with the capacity and the will to take a deliberate attitude towards the world and to lend it significance. Whatever this significance may be, it will lead us to judge certain phenomena of human existence in its light and to respond to them as being (positively or negatively) meaningful. Whatever may be the content of this attitude these phenomena have cultural significance for us and on this significance alone rests its scientific interest. Thus when we speak here of the conditioning of cultural knowledge through evaluative ideas (*Wertideen*) (following the terminology of modern logic), it is done in the hope that we will not be subject to crude misunderstandings such as the opinion that cultural significance should be attributed only to valuable phenomena. Prostitution is a cultural phenomenon just as much as religion or money. All three are cultural phenomena only because and only insofar as their existence and the form which they historically assume touch directly or indirectly on our cultural interests and arouse our striving for knowledge concerning problems brought into focus by the evaluative ideas which give significance to the fragment of reality analyzed by those concepts.

All knowledge of cultural reality, as may be seen, is always knowledge from particular points of view. When we require from the historian and social research worker as an elementary presupposition that they distinguish the important from the trivial and that they should have the necessary "point of view" for this distinction, we mean that they must understand how to relate the events of the real world consciously or unconsciously to universal "cultural values" and to select out those relationships which are significant for us. If the notion that those standpoints can be derived from the "facts themselves" continually recurs, it is due to the naive self-deception of the specialist who is unaware that it is due to the evaluative ideas with which he unconsciously approaches his subject matter, that he has selected from an absolute infinity a tiny portion with the study of which he concerns himself. In connection with this selection of individual special "aspects" of the event which always and everywhere occurs, consciously or unconsciously, there also occurs that element of cultural-scientific work which is referred to by the often-heard assertion that the "personal" element of a scientific work is what is really valuable in it, and that personality must be expressed in every work if its existence is to be justified. To be sure, without the investigator's evaluative ideas, there would be no principle of selection of subject-matter and no meaningful knowledge of the concrete reality. Just as without the investigator's conviction regarding the significance of particular cultural facts, every attempt to analyze concrete reality is absolutely meaningless, so the direction of his personal belief, the refraction of values in the prism of his mind, gives direction to his work. And the values to which the scientific genius relates the object of his inquiry may determine, i.e., decide, the "conception" of a whole epoch, not only concerning what is regarded as "valuable" but also concerning what is significant or insignificant, "important" or "unimportant" in the phenomena.

Accordingly, cultural science in our sense involves "subjective," presuppositions insofar as it concerns itself only with those components of reality which have some relationship, however indirect, to events to which we attach cultural significance. Nonetheless, it is entirely causal knowledge exactly in the same sense as the knowledge of significant concrete (*individueller*) natural events which have a qualitative character. Among the many confusions which the over-reaching tendency of a formal-juristic outlook has brought about in the cultural sciences, there has recently appeared the attempt to "refute" the "materialistic conception of history" by a series of clever but fallacious arguments which state that since all economic life must take place in legally or conventionally regulated forms, all economic "development" must take the form of striving for the creation of new legal forms. Hence, it is said to be intelligible only through ethical maxims and is on this account essentially different from every type of "natural" development. Accordingly the knowledge of economic development is said to be "teleological" in character. Without wishing to discuss the meaning of the ambiguous term "development," or the logically no less ambiguous term "teleology" in the social sciences, it should be stated that such knowledge need not be "teleological" in the sense assumed by this point of view. The cultural signifi- cance of normatively regulated legal relations and even norms themselves can undergo fundamental revolutionary changes even under conditions of the formal identity of the prevailing legal norms. Indeed, if one wishes to lose one's self for a moment in phantasies about the future, one might theoretically imagine, let us say, the "socialization of the means of production" unaccompanied by any conscious "striv- ing" towards this result, and without even the disappearance or addition of a single paragraph of our legal code; the statistical frequency of certain legally regulated rela- tionships might be changed fundamentally, and in many cases, even disappear entirely; a great number of legal norms might become practically meaningless and their whole cultural significance changed beyond identification. *De lege ferenda* discus- sions may be justifiably disregarded by the "materialistic conception of history" since its central proposition is the indeed inevitable change in the significance of legal institutions. Those who view the painstaking labor of causally understanding histor- ical reality as of secondary importance can disregard it, but it is impossible to supplant it by any type of "teleology." From our viewpoint, "purpose" is the conception of an effect which becomes a cause of an action. Since we take into account every cause which produces or can produce a significant effect, we also consider this one. Its specific significance consists only in the fact that we not only observe human conduct but can and desire to understand it.

Undoubtedly, all evaluative ideas are "subjective." Between the "historical" interest in a family chronicle and that in the development of the greatest conceivable cultural phenomena which were and are common to a nation or to mankind over long epochs, there exists an infinite gradation of "significance" arranged into an order which differs for each of us. And they are, naturally, historically variable in accord- ance with the character of the culture and the ideas which rule men's minds. But it obviously does not follow from this that research in the cultural sciences can only have results which are "subjective" in the sense that they are valid for one person and not for others. Only the degree to which they interest different persons varies. In other words, the choice of the object of investigation and the extent or depth to which this investigation attempts to penetrate into the infinite causal web, are determined by the evaluative ideas which dominate the investigator and his age. In the method of investi- gation, the guiding "point of view" is of great importance for the construction of the conceptual scheme which will be used in the investigation. In the mode of their use, however, the investigator is obviously bound by the norms of our thought just as much here as elsewhere. For scientific truth is precisely what is valid for all who seek the truth.

However, there emerges from this the meaninglessness of the idea which prevails occasionally even among historians, namely, that the goal of the cultural sciences, however far it may be from realization, is to construct a closed system of concepts, in which reality is synthesized in some sort of permanently and universally valid classifi- cation and from which it can again be deduced. The stream of immeasurable events flows unendingly towards eternity. The cultural problems which move men form themselves ever anew and in different colors, and the boundaries of that area in the infinite stream of concrete events which acquires meaning and significance for us, i.e., which becomes an "historical individual," are constantly subject to change. The intellectual contexts from which it is viewed and scientifically analyzed shift. The points of departure of the cultural sciences remain changeable throughout the limitless future as long as a Chinese ossification of intellectual life does not render mankind incapable of setting new questions to the eternally inexhaustible flow of life. A systematic science of culture, even only in the sense of a definitive, objectively valid, systematic fixation of the problems which it should treat, would be senseless in itself. Such an attempt could only produce a collection of numerous, specifically particularized, heterogeneous and disparate viewpoints in the light of which reality becomes "culture" through being significant in its unique character.

18

SIGMUND FREUD

The dream-work* (1900)

Every attempt that has hitherto been made to solve the problem of dreams has dealt directly with their *manifest* content as it is presented in our memory. All such attempts have endeavoured to arrive at an interpretation of dreams from their manifest content or (if no interpretation was attempted) to form a judgement as to their nature on the basis of that same manifest content. We are alone in taking something else into account. We have introduced a new class of psychical material between the manifest content of dreams and the conclusions of our enquiry: namely, their *latent* content, or (as we say) the 'dream-thoughts', arrived at by means of our procedure. It is from these dream-thoughts and not from a dream's manifest content that we disentangle its meaning. We are thus presented with a new task which had no previous existence: the task, that is, of investigating the relations between the manifest content of dreams and the latent dream-thoughts, and of tracing out the processes by which the latter have been changed into the former.

The dream-thoughts and the dream-content are presented to us like two versions of the same subject-matter in two different languages. Or, more properly, the dream-content seems like a transcript of the dream-thoughts into another mode of expression, whose characters and syntactic laws it is our business to discover by comparing the original and the translation. The dream-thoughts are immediately comprehensible, as soon as we have learnt them. The dream-content, on the other hand, is expressed as it were in a pictographic script, the characters of which have to be transposed individually into the language of the dream-thoughts. If we attempted to read these characters according to their pictorial value instead of according to their symbolic relation, we should clearly be led into error. Suppose I have a picture-puzzle, a rebus, in front of me. It depicts a house with a boat on its roof, a single letter of the

* From *The Interpretation of Dreams*, pp. 277–278, by Sigmund Freud. Sigmund Freud © Copyrights, The Institute of Psychoanalysis and the Hogarth Press for permission to quote from *The Standard Edition of the Complete Psychological Works of Sigmund Freud*, translated and edited by James Stratchey. Reprinted by permission of The Random House Group. Published in the United States by Basic Books, Inc., 1965 by arrangement with George Allen & Unwin, Ltd and the Hogarth Press, Ltd. Reprinted by permission of Basic Books, a member of Perseus Books, L.L.C.

alphabet, the figure of a running man whose head has been conjured away, and so on. Now I might be misled into raising objections and declaring that the picture as a whole and its corriporient parts are nonsensical. A boat has no business to be on the roof of a house, and a headless man cannot run. Moreover, the man is bigger than the house; and if the whole picture is intended to represent a landscape, letters of the alphabet are out of place in it since such objects do not occur in nature. But obviously we can only form a proper judgement of the rebus if we put aside criticisms such as these of the whole composition and its parts and if, instead, we try to replace each separate element by a syllable or word that can be represented by that element in some way or other. The words which are put together in this way are no longer nonsensical but may form a poetical phrase of the greatest beauty and significance. A dream is a picture-puzzle of the greatest beauty and significance. A dream is a picture-puzzle of this sort and our predecessors in the field of dream interpretation have made the mistake of treating the rebus as a pictorial composition: and as such it has seemed to them nonsensical and worthless.

A philosophy of life* (1932)

. . . In the last lecture we were occupied with trivial everyday affairs, with putting, as it were, our modest house in order. We will now take a bold step, and risk an answer to a question which has repeatedly been raised in non-analytic quarters, namely, the question whether psycho-analysis leads to any particular *Weltanschauung*, and if so, to what.

'*Weltanschauung*' is, I am afraid, a specifically German notion, which it would be difficult to translate into a foreign language. If I attempt to give you a definition of the word, it can hardly fail to strike you as inept. By *Weltanschauung*, then, I mean an intellectual construction which gives a unified solution of all the problems of our existence in virtue of a comprehensive hypothesis, a construction, therefore, in which no question is left open and in which everything in which we are interested finds a place. It is easy to see that the possession of such a *Weltanschauung* is one of the ideal wishes of mankind. When one believes in such a thing, one feels secure in life, one knows what one ought to strive after, and how one ought to organize one's emotions and interests to the best purpose.

If that is what is meant by a *Weltanschauung*, then the question is an easy one for psycho-analysis to answer. As a specialized science, a branch of psychology – 'depth-psychology' or psychology of the unconscious – it is quite unsuited to form a *Weltanschauung* of its own; it must accept that of science in general. The scientific

* From *New Introductory Lectures on Psychoanalysis*, pp. 202–205, 232–233, by Sigmund Freud, translated by James Stratchey. Copyright © 1965, 1964 by James Stratchey. Used by permission of W.W. Norton & Company, Inc for US rights. Sigmund Freud © Copyrights, The Institute of Psychoanalysis and the Hogarth Press for permission to quote from *The Standard Edition of the Complete Psychological Works of Sigmund Freud*, translated and edited by James Stratchey. Reprinted by permission of The Random House Group.

Weltanschauung is, however, markedly at variance with our definition. The unified nature of the explanation of the universe is, it is true, accepted by science, but only as a programme whose fulfilment is postponed to the future. Otherwise it is distinguished by negative characteristics, by a limitation to what is, at any given time, knowable, and a categorical rejection of certain elements which are alien to it. It asserts that there is no other source of knowledge of the universe but the intellectual manipulation of carefully verified observations, in fact, what is called research, and that no knowledge can be obtained from revelation, intuition or inspiration. It appears that this way of looking at things came very near to receiving general acceptance during the last century or two. It has been reserved for the present century to raise the objection that such a *Weltanschauung* is both empty and unsatisfying, that it overlooks all the spiritual demands of man, and all the needs of the human mind.

This objection cannot be too strongly repudiated. It cannot be supported for a moment, for the spirit and the mind are the subject of scientific investigation in exactly the same way as any non-human entities. Psycho-analysis has a peculiar right to speak on behalf of the scientific *Weltanschauung* in this connection, because it cannot be accused of neglecting the part occupied by the mind in the universe. The contribution of psycho-analysis to science consists precisely in having extended research to the region of the mind. Certainly without such a psychology science would be very incomplete. But if we add to science the investigation of the intellectual and emotional functions of men (and animals), we find that nothing has been altered as regards the general position of science, that there are no new sources of knowledge or methods of research. Intuition and inspiration would be such, if they existed; but they can safely be counted as illusions, as fulfilments of wishes. It is easy to see, moreover, that the qualities which, as we have shown, are expected of a *Weltanschauung* have a purely emotional basis. Science takes account of the fact that the mind of man creates such demands and is ready to trace their source, but it has not the slightest ground for thinking them justified. On the contrary, it does well to distinguish carefully between illusion (the results of emotional demands of that kind) and knowledge.

This does not at all imply that we need push these wishes contemptuously aside, or under-estimate their value in the lives of human beings. We are prepared to take notice of the fulfilments they have achieved for themselves in the creations of art and in the systems of religion and philosophy; but we cannot overlook the fact that it would be wrong and highly inexpedient to allow such things to be carried over into the domain of knowledge. For in that way one would open the door which gives access to the region of the psychoses, whether individual or group psychoses, and one would drain off from these tendencies valuable energy which is directed towards reality and which seeks by means of reality to satisfy wishes and needs as far as this is possible.

From the point of view of science we must necessarily make use of our critical powers in this direction, and not be afraid to reject and deny. It is inadmissible to declare that science is one field of human intellectual activity, and that religion and philosophy are others, at least as valuable, and that science has no business to interfere with the other two, that they all have an equal claim to truth, and that everyone is free to choose whence he shall draw his convictions and in what he shall place his belief. Such an attitude is considered particularly respectable, tolerant, broad-minded and free from narrow prejudices. Unfortunately it is not tenable; it shares all the pernicious qualities of an entirely unscientific *Weltanschauung* and in practice comes to much the same thing. The bare fact is that truth cannot be tolerant and cannot admit compromise or limitations, that scientific research looks on the whole field of human activity as its own, and must adopt an uncompromisingly critical attitude towards any other power that seeks to usurp any part of its province . . .

Let me in conclusion sum up what I had to say about the relation of psychoanalysis to the question of a *Weltanschauung*. Psycho-analysis is not, in my opinion, in a position to create a *Weltanschauung* of its own. It has no need to do so, for it is a branch of science, and can subscribe to the scientific *Weltanschauung*. The latter, however, hardly merits such a high-sounding name, for it does not take everything into its scope, it is incomplete and it makes no claim to being comprehensive or to constituting a system. Scientific thought is still in its infancy; there are very many of the great problems with which it has as yet been unable to cope. A *Weltanschauung* based upon science has, apart from the emphasis it lays upon the real world, essentially negative characteristics, such as that it limits itself to truth and rejects illusions. Those of our fellow-men who are dissatisfied with this state of things and who desire something more for their momentary peace of mind may look for it where they can find it. We shall not blame them for doing so; but we cannot help them and cannot change our own way of thinking on their account.

19

ERNST CASSIRER
From a critique of abstraction to relationalism* (1910)

If we merely follow the traditional rule for passing from the particular to the universal, we reach the paradoxical result that thought, in so far as it mounts from lower to higher and more inclusive concepts, moves in mere negations. The essential act here presupposed is that we drop certain determinations, which we had hitherto held; that we abstract from them and exclude them from consideration as irrelevant. What enables the mind to form concepts is just its fortunate gift of forgetfulness, its inability to grasp the individual differences everywhere present in the particular cases. If all the memory images, which remained with us from previous experiences, were fully determinate, if they recalled the vanished content of consciousness in its full, concrete and living nature, they would never be taken as completely similar to the new impression and would thus not blend into a unity with the latter. Only the inexactness of reproduction, which never retains the whole of the earlier impression but merely its hazy outline, renders possible this unification of elements that are in themselves dissimilar. Thus all formation of concepts begins with the substitution of a generalized image for the individual sensuous intuition, and in place of the actual perception the substitution of its imperfect and faded remainder. If we adhere strictly to this conception, we reach the strange result that all the logical labor which we apply to a given sensuous intuition serves only to separate us more and more from it. Instead of reaching a deeper comprehension of its import and structure, we reach only a superficial schema from which all peculiar traits of the particular case have vanished . . . The genuine concept does not disregard the peculiarities and particularities which it holds under it, but seeks to show the necessity of the occurrence and connection of just these particularities. What it gives is a universal *rule* for the connection of the particulars themselves . . . The individual case is not excluded from consideration, but is fixed and retained as a perfectly determinate step in a general process of change. It is evident anew that the characteristic feature of the concept is not the 'universality' of a presentation, but the universal validity of a principle of serial order. We do not

* From Ernst Cassirer, *Substance and Function & Einstein's Theory of Relativity.* The Open Court Publishing Company, Chicago, 1923, pp. 18–26. Reproduced with permission.

isolate any abstract part whatever from the manifold before us, but we create for its members a definite relation by thinking of them as bound together by an inclusive law. And the further we proceed in this and the more firmly this connection according to laws is established, so much the clearer does the unambiguous determination of the particular stand forth . . . Modern expositions of logic have attempted to take account of this circumstance by opposing – in accordance with a well-known distinction of Hegel's – abstract universality to concrete universality . . . Abstract universality belongs to the genus in so far as, considered in and for itself, it neglects all specific differences; concrete universality, on the contrary, belongs to the systematic whole (*Gesamtbegriff*) which takes up into itself the peculiarities of all the species and develops them according to a rule . . .

. . . If we carry through the above rule to the end, it obliges us to retain, in place of the particular 'marks' which are neglected in the formation of the concept, the systematic totality (*Inbegriff*) to which those marks belong as special determinations. We can abstract from the particular color only if we retain the total series of colors in general as a fundamental schema, with respect to which we consider the concept determined, which we are forming. We represent this systematic totality (*Inbegriff*) when we substitute for the constant particular 'marks', variable terms, such as stand for the total group of possible values which the different 'marks' can assume. Thus it becomes evident that the falling aside of the particular determinations is only in appearance a purely negative process. In truth, what seems to be cancelled in this way is maintained in another form and under a different logical category. As long as we believe that all determinateness consists in constant 'marks' in things and their attributes, every process of logical generalization must indeed appear an impoverishment of the conceptual content. But precisely to the extent that the concept is freed of all thing-like being, its peculiar functional character is revealed. Fixed properties are replaced by universal rules that permit us to survey a total series of possible determinations at a single glance. This transformation, this change into a new form of logical being, constitutes the real positive achievement of abstraction. We do not proceed from a series $\alpha\alpha_1\beta_1$, $\alpha\alpha_2\beta_2$, $\alpha\alpha_3\beta_3$ . . . directly to their common constitutive α, but replace the totality of individual members α by a variable expression κ, the totality of individual members β by a variable expression γ. In this way we unify the whole system in the expression $\alpha \kappa \gamma$ . . . which can be changed into the concrete totality (*Allheit*) of the members of the series by a continuous transformation, and which therefore perfectly represents the structure and logical divisions of the concept.

. . . The first phase of every construction of concepts . . . does indeed involve the separating out of a certain universal on the basis of the uniformity with which its content recurs amid varying particulars; but this uniformity of the given, though perhaps the original, is not the sole condition which enables us to mark off the objects of our presentations. In the progress of thought, the consciousness of uniformity is rather supplemented by the consciousness of necessary connection; and this supplementation goes so far that ultimately we are not dependent upon a number of repetitions to establish a concept . . . In contrast to objects of sense-perception, which we can designate as 'objects of the first order', there now appear 'objects of the second order', whose logical character is determined solely by the form of connection from which they proceed. In general, wherever we unify the objects of our thought into a single object, we create a new 'object of the second order', whose total content is expressed in the relations established between the individual elements by the act of unification. This type of thought . . . breaks through the old schema of the formation of concepts; for instead of the community of 'marks', the unification of elements in a concept is decided by their 'connection by implication'. And this criterion . . . proves on closer analysis to be the real logical prius; for we have already seen that 'abstraction' remains aimless and unmeaning if it does not consider the elements from which it takes the concept to be from the first arranged and connected by a certain relation.

. . . By the side of what the content is in its material, sensuous structure, there appears what it means in the system of knowledge; and thus, its meaning develops out of the various logical 'acts' which can be attached to the content. These 'acts', which differentiate the sensuously unitary content by imprinting upon it different objectively directed 'intentions', are . . . peculiar forms of consciousness, such as cannot be reduced to the consciousness of sensation or perception. If we are still to speak of abstraction as that to which the concept owes its being, nevertheless its meaning is now totally different from that of the customary sensationalistic doctrine; for abstraction is no longer a uniform and undifferentiated attention to a given content, but the intelligent accomplishment of the most diversified and mutually independent acts of thought, each of which involves a particular sort of meaning of the content, a special direction of objective reference . . . This identity of reference . . . under which the comparison takes place, is, however, something distinctive and new as regards the compared contents themselves. The difference between these contents, on the one hand, and the conceptual 'species', on the other, by which we unify them, is an irreducible fact; it is categorical and belongs to the 'form of consciousness'. In fact, it is a new expression of the characteristic contrast between the *member of the series* and the *form of the series*. The content of the concept cannot be dissolved into the elements of its extension, because the two do not lie on the same plane but belong in principle to different dimensions. The meaning of the law that connects the individual members is not to be exhausted by the enumeration of any number of instances of the law; for such enumeration lacks the *generating principle* that enables us to connect the individual members into a functional whole. If I know the relation according to which $a\ b\ c$ . . . are ordered, I can deduce them by reflection and isolate them as objects of thought; it is impossible, on the other hand, to discover the special character of the connecting relation from the mere juxtaposition of a, b, c in presentation. In this conception there is no danger of hypostasizing the pure concept, of giving it an independent reality along with the particular things. The serial form $F(a, b, c\ \ldots)$. which connects the members of a manifold obviously cannot be thought after the fashion of an individual a or b or c, without thereby losing its peculiar character. Its 'being' consists exclusively in the logical determination by which it is clearly differentiated from other possible serial forms ϕ, ψ, . . .; and this determination can only be expressed by a synthetic act of definition, and not by a simple sensuous intuition. . . .

20

KARL MANNHEIM
Competition as a cultural phenomenon* (1929)

There are two extreme points of view regarding the role of competition in intellectual life. There are those who refuse to ascribe more than a peripheral role to it, over against those who see in cultural creations nothing but a by-product of the social process of competition. My own position is somewhere in the middle between these two extremes. To give a more exact idea of my position with regard to these extreme views: while the first school of thought considers the role of competition in intellectual life as peripheral, and the second as determinant, in my own view, it is co-determinant.

I do not propose, however, to pursue this train of thought any farther, although the epistemological problems just alluded to are certainly germane to my subject. For reasons of economy and to keep the discussion at a factual level, I would suggest disregarding all questions of epistemological validity for the time being. I shall make a few remarks about these things at the end of my talk, but I would ask you to pay attention in the first place to what I have to say about the purely sociological aspects of my subject.

My assertion that the form which competition among intellectually creative subjects assumes at a given time is a co-determinant of the visible cultural pattern is closely connected with a more sweeping conviction many of you share, namely, that not only competition, but also all other social relations and processes comprising the prevailing pattern of social life are determinants of the mental life corresponding to that particular social structure. To use a somewhat bold shorthand formula: we recognize here the problem of sociology of the mind, as one capable of unambiguous formulation and of detailed empirical examination.

Whereas the generation which lived through the French Revolution and went through the corresponding process of reflection had as its task the development of a 'phenomenology of the spirit' and of a philosophy of history showing, for the first time, the dynamics and the morphology of the mind and the role of the historical

* From Karl Mannheim, 'Competition as a Cultural Phenomenon' in *Essays on the Sociology of Knowledge*, edited by Paul Kecskemeti, London, Routledge & Kegan Paul, 1952, pp. 192–198. Reproduced with permission.

moment as a co-determinant of the content of intellectual products, it seems to me to be at least one of the primary tasks devolving upon our generation, owing to the historical circumstances of our time, to promote understanding for the role of the life of the social body as a determinant of mental phenomena.

Certain problems of hoary antiquity assume a surprising meaning if seen in this new context. Thus problems such as those which Wegelin had already pondered – what intellectual currents really are, what factors determine their inner rhythm – for the first time become to a large degree amenable to a solution if viewed from this angle.

I think a consistent application of the method of sociological analysis to mental life will show that many phenomena originally diagnosed as manifestations of imma-nent laws of the mind may be explained in terms of the prevailing structural pattern of determination within society. It seems to me, then, that I am not following a false trail if I assume that the so-called 'dialectical' (as distinct from the unilinear, continuous) form of evolution and change in mental life can be largely traced back to two very simple structural determinants of social character: to the existence of generations, and to the existence of the phenomenon of competition with which it is our task to deal here.

So much for introduction, as a preliminary survey of the subject. After this more general discussion, however, I hope you will bear with me if I go on to examine only a rather narrowly circumscribed segment of the field to which my subject belongs. In the interests of concreteness, I shall now formulate my problem in more specialized terms. First I shall make a few preparatory remarks.

To begin with, I should like to delimit, examine, and describe, somewhat in the manner of a physician, the area of demonstration, the field in which competition is to be shown to operate.

I do not propose to determine the role competition plays in mental life as a whole, but only in the realm of thought, and even here, I shall not be concerned with all thought, but only with a special kind of thought – not that of the exact natural sci-ences, but only a particular kind of thought which I would like to call existentially-determined. Within this concept of existentially-determined thought are included historical thought (the way in which man interprets history, and the way in which he presents it to others), political thought, thought in the cultural and social sciences, and also ordinary everyday thought.

The simplest way to describe this type of thought is to contrast it with thought as it appears in the exact natural sciences. There are the following differences;

(a) in the case of existentially-determined thought, the results of the thought process are partly determined by the nature of the thinking subject;

(b) in the natural sciences, thinking is carried on, in idea at least, by an abstract 'consciousness as such' in us, whereas in existentially-determined thought, it is – to use Dilthey's phrase – 'the whole man' who is thinking.

What does this mean more exactly? The difference can be shown very clearly with a simple example. In the thought '2 + 2 = 4' there is no indication as to who did the thinking, and where. On the other hand, it is possible to tell in the case of existentially-determined thought, not only from its content, but also from its logical form and the categoreal apparatus involved, whether the thinker has approached historical and social reality from the point of view of the 'historical school', of 'Western positivism', or of Marxism.

Here arises an important point. We shall see in this a defect of existentially-determined thinking only if we adopt a methodology based upon the exact natural sciences as a model. I would urge, as against this, that each type of thinking should be understood in terms of its own innermost nature. That certain items of knowledge are incapable of an absolute interpretation and formulation does not mean that they are abitrary and subjective, but only that they are a function of a particular viewpoint or perspective; that is to say, that certain qualitative features of an object encountered in the living process of history are accessible only to minds of a certain structure. There are certain qualitatively distinguished features of historically existing objects that are open to perception only by a consciousness as formed and devised by particular historical circumstances. This idea of the 'existential relativity' of certain items of knowledge – which the phenomenological school, along with a few others, is now developing with increasing clarity – is far from implying a relativism under which everybody and nobody is right; what it implies is rather a relationism which says that certain (qualitative) truths cannot even be grasped, or formulated, except in the framework of an existential correlation between subject and object. This means, in our context, that certain insights concerning some qualitative aspect of the living process of history are available to consciousness only as formed by certain historical and social circumstances, so that the historico-social formation of the thinking and knowing subject assumes epistemological importance.

So much for existentially-determined thought: our area of demonstration at present. Now for the problem: what are we maintaining as our thesis? Firstly, that in thought (from now on, this term always means existentially-determined thought) competition can be shown to operate; and, secondly, that it can be shown to be a co-determinant in the process of its formation. The first question which confronts us as we try to develop these theses is the following: does the process of thinking, of struggling for truth, involve at all a competition?

We can be certain that our formulation of the problem will expose us to the criticism that we are projecting specifically economic categories into the mental sphere, and our first task must be to meet this criticism. This reproach, however plausible it may seem at first sight, and happily as it meets the view of those who like to see in the kingdom of the mind the unchallenged domain of absolute unconditional creation, must be rejected as beside the point. Actually, it seems to me that the reverse is the case. Nothing is being generalized from the economic sphere: on the contrary, when the Physiocrats and Adam Smith demonstrated the important role of competition in economic life, they were in fact only discovering a general social relationship in the particular context of the economic system. The 'general social' – meaning the interplay of vital forces between the individuals of a group – became visible at first in the economic sphere, and if we deliberately adopt the course of employing economic categories in the formulation of social interrelationships in the mental sphere, this is because until now the existence of the social was most easily discerned in its economic manifestations. The ultimate aim, however, must be to strip our categorial apparatus of anything specifically economic in order to grasp the social fact *sui generis*.

To accept the proposition that the phenomenon of competition is also to be found in the mental sphere, does not imply that theoretical conflict is nothing but the reflection of current social competition, but simply that theoretical conflict also is a manifestation of the 'general social'.

Phenomenologically speaking, theoretical conflict is a self-contained sphere, as is also social conflict in the more general sense. It is not enough, however, always to keep things apart and to keep watch over the jurisdictions of the various spheres. We must explore the interpenetration, the togetherness of these 'planes of experience', the separation of which is merely a matter of phenomenality and often does not go beyond the immediate datum. Once this is seen, the question becomes: how is theoretical conflict related to social conflict?

The correctness of our thesis that competition does operate in mental life – that is, in existentially-determined thinking – can perhaps be shown in the easiest way by demonstrating some of the generally typical features of competition as such in intellectual life.

In the first place, it is clear that in the case of historical thought, as in that of all existentially-determined thought, we are faced with rivalry between different parties seeking an identical goal, and also with what von Wiese has called 'a discrepancy of the lowest degree'. Other general characteristics of competition can also be shown to be present in existentially-determined thinking, the tendency either to degenerate into conflict, to turn into fight, or to change into a relationship of association. It would not be difficult to demonstrate in existentially-determined thought also the two types of competition defined by Oppenheimer – hostile contest and peaceful rivalry. Finally, as regards the social agents of competition, individuals, groups, and abstract collectives can all take over this function, and it could be shown how far thought, and the principle of competition operative within it, assume different forms according to whether the competing parties are groups or individuals. The American writer Ross has put forward some very useful observations on this point, in particular as to competition between institutions.

It is thus clear that the characteristics of the general sociological phenomenon of competition are also to be met within existentially-determined thought. There is only one difficulty – how can we show that, in existentially-determined thinking, the various parties seek identical goals? What is the appropriate formulation of competition in the sphere of thought? How can we define existentially-determined thought in such a way that the sociological factor of competition comes to the fore? Further, what can we take to be the identical goal sought by competitors in the sphere of existentially-determined thought?

It appears that the different parties are all competing for the possession of the correct social diagnosis (*Sicht*), or at least for the prestige which goes with the possession of this correct diagnosis. Or, to use a more pregnant term to characterize this identical goal: the competing parties are always struggling to influence what the phenomenologist Heidegger calls the 'public interpretation of reality'. I do not suggest, of course, that Heidegger, as a philosopher, would agree with the sociological theory I am propounding.

Philosophy, ladies and gentlemen, may look at this matter differently; but from the point of view of the social sciences, every historical, ideological, sociological piece of knowledge (even should it prove to be Absolute Truth itself), is clearly rooted in and carried by the desire for power and recognition of particular social groups who want to make their interpretation of the world the universal one.

To this, sociology and the cultural sciences make no exception; for in them we see only the old battle for universal acceptance of a particular interpretation of reality, carried on with modern scientific weapons. One may accept or reject the thesis that all pre-sociological interpretations of reality were based on gratuitous belief or superstition, and that our concept of reality is the only scientific and correct one. But even those who accept this thesis unconditionally must admit that the process in the course of which scientific interpretations gain ascendancy in a society has the same structure as the process in the course of which pre-scientific modes of interpretation had achieved dominance; that is to say, even the 'correct', 'scientific', interpretation did not arise out of a pure, contemplative desire for knowledge, but fulfilled the age-old function of helping some group find its way about in the surrounding world. It emerged and exists in exactly the same way as the pre-scientific modes of orientation – that is, as a function of the interplay of vital forces.

The nature of the generally accepted interpretation of the world at any given time is of decisive importance in determining the particular nature of the stage of historical evolution reached at that time. This is not merely a matter of the so-called 'public opinion' which is commonly recognized as a superficial phenomenon of collective psychology, but of the inventory of our set of fundamental meanings in terms of which we experience the outside world as well as our own inner responses.

Man, when he lives in the world rather than in complete aloofness – and we will not discuss here whether any such complete aloofness, involving complete indifference toward the prevailing interpretation of reality, is at all conceivable – does not exist in a world in general, but in a world of meanings, interpreted in a particular way.

The philosopher Heidegger calls this collective subject who supplies us with the prevailing public interpretation of reality *'das Man'* – the 'They'. This is the 'They' that is meant in the French expressions – such as *Que dit-on*, or *Que dira-t-on*-but it is not merely the collective subject responsible for gossip and tittle-tattle, but also that profounder Something which always interprets the world somehow, whether in its superficiality or its depths, and which causes us always to meet the world in a preconceived form. We step at birth into a ready-interpreted world, a world which has already been made understandable, every part of which has been given meaning, so that no gaps are left. What Life means, what Birth and Death mean, and what one's attitude toward certain feelings and thoughts should be – all that is already more or less definitely laid down for us: something – this 'They' – has gone before us, apparently determined that nothing should be left for us to do in this respect.

The philosopher looks at this 'They', this secretive Something, but he is not interested to find out how it arose; and it is just at this point, where the philosopher stops, that the work of the sociologist beings.

Sociological analysis shows that this public interepretation of reality is not simply 'there'; nor, on the other hand, is it the result of a 'systematic thinking out'; it is the stake for which men fight. And the struggle is not guided by motives of pure contemplative thirst for knowledge. Different interpretations of the world for the most part correspond to the particular positions the various groups occupy in their struggle for power. In answering the question how this 'They', this publicly prevailing interpretation of reality actually comes into being, I would mention four kinds:

(1) on the basis of a consensus of opinion, of spontaneous co-operation between individuals and groups;

(2) on the basis of the monoply-position of one particular group;

(3) on the basis of competition between many groups, each determined to impose on others their particular interpretation of the world. (We shall call this case 'atomistic competition', although we must add that a point is never reached where atomization is complete, so that individuals compete with individuals, and completely independent thinking groups with others equally isolated);

(4) on the basis of a concentration round one point view of a number of formerly atomistic competing groups, as a result of which competition as a whole is gradually concentrated around a few poles which become more and more dominant.

As you see, public interpreations of reality, just like any other objective cultural product, come into being through the intermediary of social relationships and processes.

21

ALFRED SCHUTZ
Concept and theory formation in the social sciences* (1954)

The title of my paper refers intentionally to that of a Symposium held in December, 1952, at the annual meeting of the American Philosophical Association. Ernest Nagel and Carl G. Hempel contributed highly stimulating comments on the problem involved, formulated in the careful and lucid way so characteristic of these scholars. Their topic is a controversy which for more than half a century has split not only logicians and methodologists but also social scientists into two schools of thought. One of these holds that the methods of the natural sciences which have brought about such magnificent results are the only scientific ones and that they alone, therefore, have to be applied in their entirety to the study of human affairs. Failure to do so, it has been maintained, prevented the social sciences from developing systems of explanatory theory comparable in precision to those offered by the natural sciences and makes debatable the empirical work of theories developed in restricted domains such as economics.

The other school of thought feels that there is a basic difference in the structure of the social world and the world of nature. This feeling led to the other extreme, namely the conclusion that the methods of the social sciences are *toto coelo* different from those of the natural sciences. In order to support this position a variety of arguments was proffered. It has been maintained that the social sciences are idiographic, characterized by individualizing conceptualization and seeking singular assertory propositions, whereas the natural sciences are nomothetic, characterized by generalizing conceptualization and seeking general apodictic propositions. The latter have to deal with constant relations of magnitude which can be measured and can perform experiments, whereas neither measurement nor experiment is practicable in the social sciences. In general, it is held that the natural sciences have to deal with material objects and processes, the social sciences, however, with psychological and intellectual ones and that, therefore, the method of the former consists in explaining, that of the latter in understanding.

* From 'Concept and Theory Formation in the Social Sciences', by Alfred Schutz, *The Journal of Philosophy*, Vol. LI, no. 9, 1954, pp. 257–267. Reproduced by permission of the publisher.

Admittedly, most of these highly generalized statements are untenable under closer examination, and this for several reasons. Some proponents of the characterized arguments had a rather erroneous concept of the methods of the natural sciences. Others were inclined to identify the methodological situation in one particular social science with the method of the social sciences in general. Because history has to deal with unique and non-recurrent events, it was contended that all social sciences are restricted to singular assertory proposition. Because experiments are hardly possible in cultural anthropology, the fact was ignored that social psychologists can successfully use laboratory experiments at least to a certain extent. Finally, and this is the most important point, these arguments disregard the fact that a set of rules for scientific procedure is equally valid for all empirical sciences whether they deal with objects of nature or with human affairs. Here and there, the principles of controlled inference and verification by fellow-scientists and the theoretical ideals of unity, simplicity, universality, and precision prevail.

This unsatisfactory state of affairs results chiefly from the fact that the development of the modern social sciences occurred during a period in which the science of logic was mostly concerned with the logic of the natural sciences. In a kind of monopolistic imperialism the methods of the latter were frequently declared to be the only scientific ones and the particular problems which social scientists encountered in their work were disregarded. Left without help and guidance in their revolt against this dogmatism, the students of human affairs had to develop their own conceptions of what they believed to be the methodology of the social sciences. They did it without sufficient philosophical knowledge and stopped their effort when they reached a level of generalization which seemed to justify their deeply felt conviction that the goal of their inquiry could not be reached by adopting the methods of the natural sciences without modification or implementation. No wonder that their arguments are frequently ill-founded, their formulations insufficient, and that many misunderstandings obfuscate the controversy. Not what social scientists said but what they meant is therefore our main concern in the following.

The writings of the late Felix Kaufmann and the more recent contributions by Nagel and Hempel have criticized many fallacies in the arguments proposed by social scientists and prepared the ground for another approach to the problem. I shall here concentrate on Professor Nagel's criticism of the claim made by Max Weber and his school that the social sciences seek to 'understand' social phenomena in terms of 'meaningful' categories of human experience and that, therefore, the 'causal functional' approach of the natural sciences is not applicable in social inquiry. This school, as Dr. Nagel sees it, maintains that all socially significant human behavior is an expression of motivated psychic states, that in consequence the social scientist cannot be satisfied with viewing social processes simply as concatenations of 'externally related' events, and that the establishment of correlations or even of universal relations of concomitance cannot be his ultimate goal. On the contrary, he must construct 'ideal types' or 'models of motivations' in terms of which he seeks to 'understand' overt social behavior by imputing springs of action to the actors involved in it. If I understand Professor Nagel's criticism correctly, he maintains:

1.   That these springs of action are not accessible to sensory observation. It follows

and has frequently been stated that the social scientist must imaginatively identify himself with the participants and view the situation which they face as the actors themselves view it. Surely, however, we need not undergo other men's psychic experiences in order to know that they have them or in order to predict their overt behavior.

2. That the imputation of emotions, attitudes, and purposes as an explanation of overt behaviour is a twofold hypothesis: it assumes that the agents participating in some social phenomenon are in certain psychological states; and it assumes also definite relations of concomitance between such states, and between such states and overt behavior. Yet none of the psychological states which we imagine the subjects of our study to possess may in reality be theirs, and even if our imputations should be correct none of the overt actions which allegedly issue from those states may appear to us understandable or reasonable.

3. That we do not 'understand' the nature and operations of human motives and their issuance in overt behavior more adequately than the 'external' causal relations. If if by meaningful explanation we assert merely than a particular action is an instance of a pattern of behavior which human beings exhibit under a variety of circumstances and that, since some of the relevant circumstances are realized in the given situation, a person can be expected to manifest a certain form of that pattern, then there is no sharp gulf separating such explanations from those involving merely 'external' knowledge of causal connections. It is possible to gain knowledge of the actions of men on the evidence supplied by their overt behavior just as it is possible to discover and know the atomic constitution of water on the evidence supplied by the physical and chemical behavior of that substance. Hence the rejection of a purely 'objective' or 'behavioristic' social science by the proponents of 'meaningful connections' as the goal of social sciences is unwarranted.

Since I shall have to disagree with Nagel's and Hempel's findings in several questions of a fundamental nature, I might be permitted to start with a brief summary of the no less important points in which I find myself happily in full agreement with them. I agree with Professor Nagel that all empirical knowledge involves discovery through processes of controlled inference, and that it must be statable in propositional form and capable of being verified by anyone who is prepared to make the effort to do so through observation – although I do not believe, as Professor Nagel does, that this observation has to be sensory in the precise meaning of this term. Moreover, I agree with him that 'theory' means in all empirical sciences the explicit formulation of determinate relations between a set of variables in terms of which a fairly extensive class of empirically ascertainable regularities can be explained. Furthermore, I agree wholeheartedly with his statement that neither the fact that these regularities have in the social sciences a rather narrowly restricted universality, nor the fact that they permit prediction only to a rather limited extent, constitutes a basic difference between the social and the natural sciences, since many branches of the latter show the same features. As I shall try to show later on, it seems to me that Professor Nagel misunderstands Max Weber's postulate of subjective interpretation. Nevertheless, he is right in stating that a method which would require that the individual scientific observer identify himself with the social agent observed in order to understand the motives of the latter, or a method which would refer the selection of the facts observed and their interpretation to the private value system of the particular observer, would merely lead to an uncontrollable private and subjective image in the mind of this particular student of human affairs, but never to a scientific theory. I merely submit that I do not know of any social scientist of stature who ever advocated such a concept of subjectivity as that criticized by Professor Nagel. Most certainly this was not the position of Max Weber.

Yet I submit also that our authors are prevented from grasping the point of vital concern to social scientists by their basic philosophy of sensationalistic empiricism or logical positivism, which identifies experience with sensory observation and which assumes that the only alternative to controllable and, therefore, objective sensory observation is that of subjective and, therefore, uncontrollable and unverifiable introspection. This is certainly not the place to renew the age-old controversy relating to the hidden presuppositions and implied metaphysical assumptions of this basic philosophy. On the other hand, in order to account for my own position, I should have to treat at length certain principles of phenomenology. Instead of doing so, I propose to defend a few rather simple propositions.

1. The primary goal of the social sciences is to obtain organized knowledge of social reality. By the term 'social reality' I wish to be understood the sum total of objects and occurrences within the social cultural world as experienced by the common-sense thinking of men living their daily lives among their fellow-men, connected with them in manifold relations of interaction. It is the world of cultural objects and social institutions into which we all are born, within which we have to find our bearings, and with which we have to come to terms. From the outset, we, the actors on the social scene, experience the world we live in as a world both of nature and of culture, not as a private but as an intersubjective one, that is, as a world common to all of us, either actually given or potentially accessible to everyone; and this involves intercommunication and language.

2. All forms of naturalism and logical empiricism simply take for granted this social reality which is the proper object of the social sciences. Intersubjectivity, interaction, intercommunication, and language are simply presupposed as the unclarified foundations of these theories. They assume, as it were, that the social scientist has already solved his fundamental problem, before scientific inquiry starts. To be sure, Dewey emphasized, with a clarity worthy of this eminent philosopher, that all inquiry starts and ends within the social cultural matrix; to be sure, Professor Nagel is fully aware of the fact that science and its self-correcting process is a social enterprise. But the postulate to describe and explain human behavior in terms of controllable sensory observation stops short before the description and explanation of the process by which scientist B controls and verifies the observational findings of scientist A and the conclusions drawn by him. In order to do so, B has to know what A has observed, what the goal of his inquiry is, why he thought the observed fact worthy of being observed, i.e., relevant to the scientific problem at hand, etc. This knowledge is commonly called understanding. The explanation of how such a mutual understanding of

human beings might occur is apparently left to the social scientist. But whatever his explanation might be, one thing is sure, namely, that such an intersubjective understanding between scientist B and scientist A occurs neither by scientist B's observations of scientist A's overt behavior, nor by introspection performed by B, nor by identification of B with A. To translate this argument into the language dear to logical positivism, this means, as Felix Kaufmann has shown, that so-called protocol propositions about the psycho-physical world.

3. The identification of experiences with sensory observations in general and of the experiences of overt action in particular (and this is what Nagel proposes) excludes several dimensions of social reality from all possible inquiry.

(a) Even an ideally refined behaviorism can, as has been pointed out for instance by George H. Mead, merely explain the behavior of the observed, not of the observing behaviorist.

(b) The same overt behavior (say a tribal pagent as it can be captured by the movie-camera) may have an entirely different meaning to the performers. What interests the social scientist is merely whether it is a way dance, a barter trade, the reception of a friendly ambassador, or something else of this sort.

(c) Moreover, the concept of human action in terms of common-sense thinking and of the social sciences includes what may be called 'negative actions' i.e., intentional refraining from acting, which of course, escapes sensory observation. Not to sell certain merchandise at a given price is doubtless as economic an action as to sell it.

(d) Furthermore, as W.I. Thomas has shown, social reality contains elements of beliefs and convictions which are real because so defined by the participants and which escape sensory observation. To the inhabitants of Salem in the seventeenth century, witchcraft was not a delusion but an element of their social reality and is as such open to investigation by the social scientist.

(e) Finally, and this is the most important point, the postulate of sensory observation of overt human behaviour takes as a model a particular and relatively small sector of the social world, namely, situations in which the acting individual is given to the observer in what is commonly called a face-to-face relationship. But there are many other dimensions of the social world in which situations of this kind do not prevail. If we put a letter in the mailbox we assume that anonymous fellow-men, called postmen, will perform a series of manipulations, unknown and unobservable to us, with the effect that the addressee, possibly also unknown to us, will receive the message and react in a way which also escapes our sensory observation; and the result of all this is that we receive the book we have ordered. Or if I read an editorial stating that France fears the re-armament of Germany, I know perfectly well what this statement means without knowing the editorialist and even without knowing a Frenchman or a German, let alone without observing their overt behavior.

In terms of common-sense thinking in everyday life men have knowledge of these various dimensions of the social world in which they live. To be sure, this knowledge is not only fragmentary since it is restricted principally to certain sectors of this world, it is also frequently inconsistent in itself and shows all degrees of clarity and distinctness from full insight or 'knowledge-about,' as James called it, through 'knowledge of acquaintance' or mere familiarity, to blind belief in things just taken for granted. In this respect there are considerable differences from individual to individual and from social group to social group. Yet, in spite of all these inadequacies, common-sense knowledge of everyday life is sufficient for coming to terms with fellow-men, cultural objects, social institutions – in brief, with social reality. This is so, because the world (the natural and the social one) is from the outset an intersubjective world and because, as shall be pointed out later on, our knowledge of it is in various ways socialized. Moreover, the social world is experienced from the outset as a meaningful one. The other's body is not experienced as an organism but as a fellow-man, its overt behavior not as an occurrence in the space-time of the outer world, but as our fellow-man's action. We normally 'know' what the other does, wherefore he does it, why he does it at this particular time and in these particular circumstances. That means that we experience our fellow-man's action in terms of his motives and goals. And in the same way we experience cultural objects in terms of the human action of which they are the result. A tool, for example, is not experienced as a thing in the outer world (which of course it is also) but in terms of the purpose for which it was designed by more or less anonymous fellow-men and its possible use by others.

The fact that in common-sense thinking we take for granted our actual or potential knowledge of the meaning of human actions and their products, is, so I submit, precisely what social scientists want to express if they speak of understanding or *Verstehen* as a technique of dealing with human affairs. *Verstehen* is, thus, primarily not a method used by the social scientist, but the particular experiential form in which common-sense thinking takes cognizance of the social cultural world. It has nothing to do with introspection, it is a result of processes of learning or acculturation in the same way as the common-sense experience of the so-called natural world. *Verstehen* is, moreover, by no means a private affair of the observer which cannot be controlled by the experiences of other observers. It is controllable at least to the same extent to which the private sensory perceptions of an individual are controllable by any other individual under certain conditions. You have just to think of the discussion by a trial-jury whether the defendant has shown 'pre-meditated malice' or 'intent' in killing a person, whether he was capable of knowing the consequences of his deed, etc. Here we even have certain 'rules of procedure' furnished by the 'rules of evidence' in the juridical sense and a kind of verification of the findings resulting from processes of *Verstehen* by the Appellate Court, etc. Moreover, predictions based on *Verstehen* are continuously and with high success made in common-sense thinking. There is more than a fair chance that a duly stamped and addressed letter put in a New York mailbox will reach the addressee in Chicago.

Nevertheless, both defenders and critics of the process of *Verstehen* maintain, and with good reason, that *Verstehen* is 'subjective'. Unfortunately, however, this term is used by each party in a different sense. The critics of *Verstehen* call it subjective, because they hold that understanding the motives of another person's action depends upon the private, uncontrollable, and unverifiable intuition of the observer or refers to their private value system. The social scientists, such as Max Weber, however, call *Verstehen* subjective because its goal is to find out what the actor 'means' in his action, in contrast to the meaning which this action has for the actor's partner or a neutral observer. This is the origin of Max Weber's famous postulate of subjective interpretation, of which more will have to be said in what follows. The whole discussion suffers from the failure to distinguish clearly between *Verstehen* (1) as the experiential form of common-sense knowledge of human affairs, (2) as an epistemological problem, and (3) as a method peculiar to the social sciences.

So far we have concentrated on *Verstehen* as the way in which common-sense thinking finds its bearing within the social world and comes to terms with it. As to the epistemological question: 'How is such understanding or *Verstehen* possible?' I have to answer, alluding to a statement Kant made in another context, that it is a 'scandal of philosophy' that so far the problem of our knowledge of other minds and, in connection therewith, of the intersubjectivity of our experience of the natural as well as the socio-cultural world, has not found a satisfactory solution and that, until rather recent times, this problem has even escaped the attention of philosophers. But the solution of this most difficult problem of philosophical interpretation is one of the first things taken for granted in our common-sense thinking and practically solved without any difficulty in each of our everyday actions. And since human beings are born of mothers and not concocted in retorts, the experience of the existence of other human beings and of the meaning of their actions is certainly the first and most original empirical observation man makes.

On the other hand, philosophers as different as James, Bergson, Dewey, Husserl, and Whitehead agree that the common-sense knowledge of everyday life is the unquestioned but always questionable background within which inquiry starts and within which alone it can be carried out. It is this *Lebenswelt* [Lifeworld], as Husserl calls it, within which, according to him, all scientific and even logical concepts originate; it is the social matrix within which, according to Dewey, unclarified situations emerge, which have to be transformed by the process of inquiry into warranted assertibility; and Whitehead has pointed out that it is the aim of science to produce a theory which agrees with experience by explaining the thought-objects constructed by common sense through the mental constructs or thought objects of science. For all these thinkers agree that any knowledge of the world, in common-sense thinking as well as in science, involves mental constructs, syntheses, generalizations, formalizations, idealizations specific to the respective level of thought organization. The concept of Nature, for instance, with which the natural sciences have to deal is, as Husserl has shown, an idealizing abstraction from the *Lebenswelt*, an abstraction which, on principle and of course legitimately, excludes persons with their personal life and all objects of culture which originate as such in practical human activity. Exactly this layer of the *Lebenswelt*, however, from which the natural sciences have to abstract, is the social reality which the social sciences have to investigate.

This insight sheds a light on certain methodological problems peculiar to the social sciences. To begin with, it appears that the assumption that the strict adoption of the principles of concept and theory formation prevailing in the natural sciences will lead to reliable knowledge of the social reality, is inconsistent in itself. If a theory can be developed on such principles, say in the form of an ideally refined behaviorism

– and it is certainly possible to imagine this – then it will not tell us anything about social reality as experienced by men in everyday life. As Professor Nagel himself admits, it will be highly abstract, and its concepts will apparently be remote from the obvious and familiar traits found in any society. On the other hand, a theory which aims at explaining social reality has to develop particular devices foreign to the natural sciences in order to agree with the common-sense experience of the social world. This is indeed what all theoretical sciences of human affairs – economics, sociology, the sciences of law, linguistics, cultural anthropology, etc. – have done.

This state of affairs is founded on the fact that there is an essential difference in the structure of the thought objects or mental constructs formed by the social sciences and those formed by the natural sciences. It is up to the natural scientist and to him alone to define, in accordance with the procedural rules of his science, his observational field, and to determine the facts, data, and events within it which are relevant for his problem or scientific purpose at hand. Neither are those facts and events pre-selected, nor is the observational field pre-interpreted. The world of nature, as explored by the natural scientist, does not 'mean' anything to the molecules, atoms, and electrons therein. The observational field of the social scientist, however, namely the social reality, has a specific meaning and relevance structure for the human beings living, acting, and thinking therein. By a series of common-sense constructs they have pre-selected and pre-interpreted this world which they experience as the reality of their daily lives. It is these thought objects of theirs which determine their behavior by motivating it. The thought objects constructed by the social scientist, in order to grasp this social reality, have to be founded upon the thought objects constructed by the common-sense thinking of men, living their daily life within their social world. Thus, the constructs of the social sciences are, so to speak, constructs of the second degree, namely constructs of the constructs made by the actors on the social scene, whose behavior the social scientist has to observe and to explain in accordance with the procedural rules of his science.

22

MAURICE MERLEAU-PONTY
The philosopher and sociology* (1960)

Philosophy and sociology have long lived under a segregated system which has succeeded in concealing their rivalry only by refusing them any meeting-ground, impeding their growth, making them incomprehensible to one another, and thus placing culture in a situation of permanent crisis. As always, the spirit of inquiry has gotten around these interdicts; and it seems to us that both philosophy and sociology have now progressed far enough to warrant a re-examination of their relationships.

We would also like to call attention to the thought Husserl gave to these problems. Husserl seems to us to be exemplary in that he may have realized better than anyone else that all forms of thought are in a certain sense interdependent. We need neither tear down the behavioral sciences to lay the foundations of philosophy, nor tear down philosophy to lay the foundations of the behavioral sciences. Every science secretes an ontology; every ontology anticipates a body of knowledge. It is up to us to come to terms with this situation and see to it that both philosophy and science are possible.

The segregation of philosophy and sociology has perhaps nowhere been described in the terms in which we are going to state it. Fortunately, the practices of philosophers and sociologists are often less exclusive than their principles. Yet this segregation nevertheless constitutes a part of a certain common sense of philosophers and sociologists which, by reducing philosophy and the behavioral sciences to what it believes is their ideal type, ultimately endangers scientific knowledge just as much as philosophical reflection.

Even though all the great philosophies are recognizable by their attempt to think about the mind *and its dependency* – ideas and their movement, understanding and sensibility – there is a myth about philosophy which presents it as an authoritarian affirmation of the mind's absolute autonomy. Philosophy so conceived is no longer an inquiry. It is a certain body of doctrines, made to assure an absolutely *unfettered* spirit in full possession of itself and its ideas. In another connection, there is a myth about scientific knowledge which expects to attain from the mere recording of facts not only

* From 'The Philosopher and Sociology' by Maurice Merleau-Ponty, *Signs*. Northwestern University Press, 1964, pp. 98–101, 111–113. Translated by Richard C. McCleary. Reprinted with permission.

the science of the things of the world but also the science of that science – a sociology of knowledge (conceived in an empiricist fashion) which should make the universe of facts self-contained by including even the ideas we invent to interpret the facts, and thus rids us, so to speak, of ourselves. These two myths contain one another in their very antagonism. For even though the philosopher and the sociologist are opposed to one another, they at least agree upon a delimitation of boundaries which assures them of never meeting. But if the *cordon sanitaire* were removed, philosophy and sociology would destroy one another. Even now, they battle for our minds. Segregation is cold war.

In this atmosphere, any investigation which seeks to take both ideas and facts into account is immediately bifurcated. Facts, instead of being taken as the spur and warrant for a constructive effort to reach their inner dynamics, are worshipped as a sort of peremptory grace which reveals all truth. And ideas are exempted as a matter of principle from all confrontation with our experience of the world, others, and ourselves. The movement back and forth from facts to ideas and from ideas to facts is discredited as a bastard process – neither science nor philosophy – which denies scientists the final interpretation of the very facts that they have taken the pains to assemble, and which compromises philosophy with the always provisional results of scientific research.

We must be fully aware of the *obscurantist* consequences of this rigid segregation. If 'mixed' investigations really have the inconveniences we have just mentioned, then we shall have to admit that a simultaneously philosophical and scientific view of experience is impossible, and that philosophy and sociology can attain certain knowledge only if they ignore one another. We shall have to hide from the scientist that 'idealization' of brute fact which is nevertheless the essence of his work. He will have to ignore the deciphering of meanings which is his reason for being, the construction of intellectual models of reality without which there would no more be any sociology today than there would formerly have been Galilean physics. We shall have to put the blinders of Baconian or 'Millian' induction back on the scientist, even though his own investigations obviously do not follow these canonical recipes. Consequently, he will pretend to approach social fact as if it were alien to him, as if his study owed nothing to the experience which, as social subject, he has of intersubjectivity.

Under the pretext that as a matter of fact sociology is not yet constructed with this lived experience but is instead an analysis, an explicit formulation and objectification of it which reverses our initial consciousness of social relationships (and ultimately shows that these experienced social relationships are very special variants of a dynamics we are originally unaware of and can learn about only in contact with other cultural formations), objectivism forgets another evident fact. We can expand our experience of social relationships and get a proper view of them only by analogy or contrast with those we have lived. We can do so, in short only by subjecting the social relationships we have experienced to an *imaginary variation*. These lived relationships will no doubt take on a new meaning in comparison with this imaginary variation (as the fall of a body on an inclined plane is put in a new light by the ideal concept of free fall), but they will provide it with all the sociological meaning it can have.

Anthropology teaches us that in such and such cultures children treat certain cousins as their 'kin,' and facts of this sort allow us ultimately to draw up a diagram of the kinship structure in the civilization under consideration. But the correlations thus noted give only the silhouette or contour of kinship structures in that civilization, a cross-section of behavior patterns which are nominally defined as those of 'kinship' at certain significant but still anonymous points X. . . ., Y. . . ., Z. . . . In short, these correlations do not yet have a sociological meaning. As long as we have not succeeded in installing ourselves in the institution which they delimit, in understanding the style of kinship which all these facts allude to and *the sense in which* certain subjects in that culture perceive other subjects of their generation as their 'kin,' and finally, in grasping the basic personal and interpersonal structure and the institutional relationships with nature and others which make the established correlations possible, the formulas which sum up these correlations could just as well represent a given physical or chemical process of the same form. Let us make it perfectly clear that the underlying dynamics of the social whole is certainly not *given* with our narrow experience of living among others, yet it is only by throwing this experience in and out of focus that we succeed in representing it to ourselves, just as the generalized number remains number for us only through the link which binds it to the whole number of elementary arithmetic . . .

It is essential never to cut sociological inquiry off from our experience of social subjects (which of course includes not only what we have experienced ourselves but also the behavior we perceive through the gestures, tales, or writings of our fellow men). For the sociologist's equations begin to represent something social only at the moment when the correlations they express are connected to one another and enveloped in a certain unique *view* of the social and of nature which is characteristic of the society under consideration and has come to be institutionalized in it as the hidden principle of all its overt functioning – even though this view may be rather different than the official conceptions which are current in that society. If objectivism or scientism were ever to succeed in depriving sociology of all recourse to significations, it would save it from 'philosophy' only by shutting it off from knowledge of its object. Then we might do mathematics in the social, but we would not have the mathematics *of* the society being considered. The sociologist philosophizes every time he is required to not only record but comprehend the facts. At the moment of interpretation, he is himself already a philosopher. This means that the professional philosopher is not disqualified to reinterpret facts he has not observed himself, if these facts say something more and different than what the scientist has seen in them. As Husserl says, eidetic analysis of the physical thing did not begin with phenomenology but with Galileo. And reciprocally, the philosopher has the right to read and interpret Galileo . . .

Ultimately our situation is what links us to the whole of human experience, no less than what separates us from it. 'Science' and 'sociology' will designate the efforts to construct ideal variables which objectify and schematize the functioning of this effective communication. We shall call 'philosophy'' the consciousness we must maintain – as our consciousness of the ultimate reality whose funtioning our theoretical constructions retrace but could not possibly replace – of the open and successive community of *alter egos* living, speaking, and thinking in one another's presence and in relation to nature as we sense its presence behind, around, and before us at the limits of our historical field.

Thus philosophy is not defined by a peculiar domain of its own. Like sociology, it only speaks about the world, men, and mind. It is distinguished by a certain *mode* of consciousness we have of others, of nature, or of ourselves. It is nature and man in the present, not 'flattened out' (Hegel) in a derivative objectivity but such as they are presented in our present cognitive and active commerce with them. Philosophy is nature in us, the others in us, and we in them. Accordingly, we must not simply say that philosophy is compatible with sociology, but that it is necessary to it as a constant reminder of its tasks; and that each time the sociologist returns to the living sources of his knowledge, to what operates within him as a means of understanding the forms of culture most remote from him, he practices philosophy spontaneously. Philosophy is not a particular body of knowledge; it is the vigilance which does not let us forget the source of all knowledge . . .

Philosophy's role as consciousness of rationality in contingency is no insignificant residue. In the last analysis, only the philosophical consciousness of intersubjectivity enables us to understand scientific knowledge. Without this philosophical conscious- ness, scientific knowledge remains indefinitely in suspense, always deferred until the termination of discussions of causality which, having to do with man, are by their nature interminable. We wonder for example whether social relationships are (as psychoanalytic sociology would have it) only the amplification and generalization of the sexual-aggressive drama, or whether on the contrary this drama itself (in the form described by psychoanalysis) is only a particular case of the institutional relationships of Western societies. These discussions have the value of inducing the sociologists to make observations, of revealing facts, and of giving rise to analyses and insights. But they admit of no conclusion as long as we remain on the level of causal and 'objective' thought, since we can neither reduce one of the causal chains to nothing nor think of them together as causal chains. We can hold that both these views are true (as they are) only on the condition that we move to an a-causal mode of thought, which is philosophy. For there are two truths which must be grasped simultaneously. The individual drama takes place among roles which are already inscribed in the total institutional structure, so that from the beginning of his life the child proceeds – simply by perceiving the attentions paid to him and the utensils surrounding him – to a deciphering of meanings which from the outset generalizes his own drama into a drama of his culture. And yet it is the whole symbolic consciousness which in the last analysis elaborates what the child lives or does not live, suffers or does not suffer, feels or does not feel. Consequently, there is not a single detail of his most individual history which does not contribute something to that personal significance he will manifest when (having first thought and lived as he thought best, and perceived according to his culture's imagery) he finally comes to the point of reversing the relationship and slipping into the meanings of his speech and his behavior, converting even the most secret aspects of his experience into culture. From the causal point of view it is unthinkable that this centripetal movement and this centrifugal movement are compossible. These reversals, these 'meta morphoses,' this proximity and distance of the past and present (of the archaic and the 'modern'), this way that cultural time and space roll up on themselves, and this perpetual overdetermination of human events which makes the social fact (no matter how singular the local, or temporal conditions) always appear to us as a variant of a single life that ours is also part of, and makes every *other person another ourself* for us – all these things become conceivable or even visible to the philosophical attitude alone.

Philosophy is indeed, and always, a break with objectivism and a return from *constructa* to lived experience, from the world to ourselves. It is just that this indispensable and characteristic step no longer transports it into the rarified atmosphere of introspection or into a realm numerically distinct from that of science. It no longer makes philosophy the rival of scientific knowledge, now that we have recognized that the 'interior' it brings us back to is not a 'private life' but an intersubjectivity that gradually connects us ever closer to the whole of history. When I discover that the social is not simply an object but to begin with my situation, and when I awaken within myself the consciousness of this social-which-is- mine, then my whole synchrony becomes present to me, through that synchrony I become capable of really thinking about the whole past as the synchrony it has been in its time, and all the convergent and discordant action of the historical community is effectively given to me in my living present. Giving up systematic philosophy as an explanatory device does not reduce philosophy to the rank of an auxiliary or a propagandist in the service of objective knowledge; for philosophy has a dimension of its own, the dimension of coexistence – not as a *fait accompli* and an object of contemplation, but as the milieu and perpetual event of the universal *praxis*. Philosophy is irreplaceable because it reveals to us both the movement by which lives become truths, and the circularity of that singular being who in a certain sense already *is* everything he *happens to think*.

23

MARTIN HEIDEGGER
The age of the world picture* (1938)

When we reflect on the modern age, we are questioning concerning the modern world picture (*Weltbild*). We characterize the latter by throwing it into relief over against the medieval and the ancient world pictures. But why do we ask concerning a world picture in our interpreting of a historical age? Does every period of history have its world picture, and indeed in such a way as to concern itself from time to time about that world picture? Or is this, after all, only a modern kind of representing, this asking concerning a world picture?

What is a world picture? Obviously a picture of the world. But what does 'world' mean here? What does 'picture' mean? 'World' serves here as a name for what is, in its entirety. The name is not limited to the cosmos, to nature. History also belongs to the world. Yet even nature and history, and both interpenetrating in their underlying and transcending of one another, do not exhaust the world. In this designation the ground of the world is meant also, no matter how its relation to the world is thought.

With the word 'picture' we think first of all of a copy of something. Accordingly, the world picture would be a painting, so to speak, of what is as a whole. But 'world picture' means more than this. We mean by it the world itself, the world as such, what is, in its entirety, just as it is normative and binding for us. 'Picture' here does not mean some imitation, but rather what sounds forth in the colloquial expression, 'We get the picture' (literally, we are in the picture) concerning something. This means the matter stands before us exactly as it stands with it for us. 'To get into the picture' (literally, to put oneself into the picture) with respect to something means to set whatever is, itself, in place before oneself just in the way that it stands with it, and to have it fixedly before oneself as set up in this way. But a decisive determinant in the essence of the picture is still missing. 'We get the picture' concerning something does not mean only that what is, is set before us, is represented to us, in general, but that what is stands before us – in all that belongs to it and all that stands together in it – as a system. 'To get the picture' throbs with being acquainted with something, with being

* From 'The Age of the World Picture', in *The Question Concerning Technology and Other Essays* by Martin Heidegger. English language copyright © 1977 by Harper & Row, Publishers, Inc. Reprinted by permission of HarperCollins Publishers Inc. Pp. 128–136.

equipped and prepared for it. Where the world becomes picture, what is, in its entirety, is juxtaposed as that for which man is prepared and which, correspondingly, he therefore intends to bring before himself and have before himself, and consequently intends in a decisive sense to set in place before himself. Hence world picture, when understood essentially, does not mean a picture of the world but the world conceived and grasped as picture. What is, in its entirety, is now taken in such a way that it first is in being and only is in being to the extent that it is set up by man, who represents and sets forth. Wherever we have the world picture, an essential decision takes place regarding what is, in its entirety. The Being of whatever is, is sought and found in the representedness of the latter.

However, everywhere that whatever is, is not interpreted in this way, the world also cannot enter into a picture; there can be no world picture. The fact that whatever is comes into being in and through representedness transforms the age in which this occurs into a new age in contrast with the preceding one. The expressions 'world picture of the modern age' and 'modern world picture' both mean the same thing and both assume something that never could have been before, namely, a medieval and an ancient world picture. The world picture does not change from an earlier medieval one into a modern one, but rather the fact that the world becomes picture at all is what distinguishes the essence of the modern age (*der Neuzeit*). For the Middle Ages, in contrast, that which is, is the *ens creatum*, that which is created by the personal Creator-God as the highest cause. Here, to be in being means to belong within a specific rank of the order of what has been created – a rank appointed from the beginning – and as thus caused, to correspond to the cause of creation (*analogia entis*). But never does the Being of that which is consist here in the fact that it is brought before man as the objective, in the fact that it is placed in the realm of man's knowing and of his having disposal, and that it is in being only in this way.

The modern interpretation of that which is, is even further from the interpretation characteristic of the Greeks. One of the oldest pronouncements of Greek thinking regarding the Being of that which is runs: *To gar auto noein estin te kai einai*. This sentence of Parmenides means: The apprehending of whatever is belongs to Being because it is demanded and determined by Being. That which is, is that which arises and opens itself, which, as what presences, comes upon man as the one who presences, i.e., comes upon the one who himself opens himself to what presences in that he apprehends it. That which is does not come into being at all through the fact that man first looks upon it, in the sense of a representing that has the character of subjective perception. Rather, man is the one who is looked upon by that which is; he is the one who is – in company with itself – gathered toward presencing, by that which opens itself. To be beheld by what is, to be included and maintained within its openness and in that way to be borne along by it, to be driven about by its oppositions and marked by its discord – that is the essence of man in the great age of the Greeks. Therefore, in order to fulfill his essence, Greek man must gather (*legein*) and save (*sozein*), catch up and preserve, what opens itself in its openness, and he must remain exposed (*aletheuein*) to all its sundering confusions. Greek man is as the one who apprehends (*der Vernehmer*) that which is, and this is why in the age of the Greeks the world cannot become picture. Yet, on the other hand, that the beingness of whatever is, is defined for Plato as *eidos* (aspect, view) is the presupposition, destined far in advance and long ruling indirectly in concealment, for the world's having to become picture.

In distinction from Greek apprehending, modern representing, whose meaning the word *repraesentatio* first brings to its earliest expression, intends something quite different. Here to represent (*vor-stellen*) means to bring what is present at hand (*das Vorhandene*) before oneself as something standing over against, to relate it to oneself, to the one representing it, and to force it back into this relationship to oneself as the normative realm. Wherever this happens, man 'gets into the picture' in precedence over whatever is. But in that man puts himself into the picture in this way, he puts himself into the scene, i.e., into the open sphere of that which is generally and publicly represented. Therewith man sets himself up as the setting in which whatever is must henceforth set itself forth, must present itself (*sich . . . präsentieren*), i.e., be picture. Man becomes the representative (*der Repräsentant*) of that which is, in the sense of that which has the character of object.

But the newness in this event by no means consists in the fact that now the position of man in the midst of what is, is an entirely different one in contrast to that of medieval and ancient man. What is decisive is that man himself expressly takes up this position as one constituted by himself, that he intentionally maintains it as that taken up by himself, and that he makes it secure as the solid footing for a possible development of humanity. Now for the first time is there any such thing as a 'position' of man. Man depends upon himself the way in which he must take his stand in relation to whatever is as the objective. There begins that way of being human which mans the realm of human capability as a domain given over to measuring and executing, for the purpose of gaining mastery over that which is as a whole. The age that is determined from out of this event is, when viewed in retrospect, not only a new one in contrast with the one that is past, but it settles itself firmly in place expressly as the new. To be new is peculiar to the world that has become picture.

When, accordingly, the picture character of the world is made clear as the representedness of that which is, then in order fully to grasp the modern essence of representedness we must track out and expose the original naming power of the worn-out word and concept 'to represent' (*vorstellen*): to set out before oneself and to set forth in relation to oneself. Through this, whatever is comes to a stand as object and in that way alone receives the seal of Being. That the world becomes picture is one and the same event with the event of man's becoming *subiectum* in the midst of that which is.

Only because and insofar as man actually and essentially has become subject is it necessary for him, as a consequence, to confront the explicit question: Is it as an 'I' confined to its own preferences and freed into its own arbitrary choosing or as the 'we' of society; is it as an individual or as a community; is it as a personality within the community or as a mere group member in the corporate body; is it as a state and nation and as a people or as the common humanity of modern man, that man will and ought to be the subject that in his modern essence he already is? Only where man is essentially already subject does there exist the possibility of his slipping into the aberration of subjectivism in the sense of individualism. But also, only where man remains subject does the positive struggle against individualism and for the community as the sphere of those goals that govern all achievement and usefulness have any meaning.

The interweaving of these two events, which for the modern age is decisive – that the world is transformed into picture and man into *subiectum* – throws light at the same time on the grounding event of modern history, an event that at first glance seems almost absurd. Namely, the more extensively and the more effectually the world stands at man's disposal as conquered, and the more objectively the object appears, all the more subjectively, i.e., the more importunately, does the *subiectum* rise up, and all the more impetuously, too, do observation of and teaching about the world change into a doctrine of man, into anthropology. It is no wonder that humanism first arises where the world becomes picture. It would have been just as impossible for a humanism to have gained currency in the great age of the Greeks as it would have been impossible to have had anything like a world picture in that age. Humanism, therefore, in the more strict historiographical sense, is nothing but a moral-aesthetic anthropology. The name 'anthropology' as used here does not mean just some investigation of man by a natural science. Nor does it mean the doctrine established within Christian theology of man created, fallen, and redeemed. It designates that philosophical interpretation of man which explains and evaluates whatever is, in its entirety, from the standpoint of man and in relation to man.

The increasingly exclusive rooting of the interpretation of the world in anthropology, which has set in since the end of the eighteenth century, finds its expression in the fact that the fundamental stance of man in relation to what is, in its entirety, is defined as a world view (*Weltanschauung*). Since that time this word has been admitted into common usage. As soon as the world becomes picture, the position of man is conceived as a world view. To be sure, the phrase 'world view' is open to misunderstanding, as though it were merely a matter here of a passive contemplation of the world. For this reason, already in the nineteenth century it was emphasized with justification that 'world view' also meant and even meant primarily 'view of life.' The fact that, despite this, the phrase 'world view' asserts itself as the name for the position of man in the midst of all that is, is proof of how decisively the world became picture as soon as man brought his life as *subiectum* into precedence over other centers of relationship. This means: whatever is, is considered to be in being only to the degree and to the extent that it is taken into and referred back to this life, i.e., is lived out, and becomes life-experience. Just as unsuited to the Greek spirit as every humanism had to be, just so impossible was a medieval world view, and just as absurd is a Catholic world view. Just as necessarily and legitimately as everything must change into life-experience for modern man the more unlimitedly he takes charge of the shaping of his essence, just so certainly could the Greeks at the Olympian festivals never have had life-experiences.

The fundamental event of the modern age is the conquest of the world as picture. The word 'picture' (*Bild*) now means the structured image (*Gebild*) that is the creature of man's producing which represents and sets before. In such producing man contends for the position in which he can be that particular being who gives the measure and draws up the guidelines for everything that is. Because this position secures, organizes, and articulates itself as a world view, the modern relationship to that which is, is one that becomes, in its decisive unfolding, a confrontation of world views; and indeed not of random world views, but only of those that have already taken up the fundamental position of man that is most extreme, and have done so with the utmost resoluteness. For the sake of this struggle of world views and in keeping with its meaning, man brings into play his unlimited power for the calculating, planning, and molding of all things. Science as research is an absolutely necessary form of this establishing of self in the world; it is one of the pathways upon which the modern age rages toward fulfillment of its essence, with a velocity unknown to the participants. With this struggle of world views the modern age first enters into the part of its history that is the most decisive and probably the most capable of enduring.

A sign of this event is that everywhere and in the most varied forms and disguises the gigantic is making its appearance. In so doing, it evidences itself simultaneously in the tendency toward the increasingly small. We have only to think of numbers in atomic physics. The gigantic presses forward in a form that actually seems to make it disappear – in the annihilation of great distances by the airplane, in the setting before us of foreign and remote worlds in their everydayness, which is produced at random through radio by a flick of the hand. Yet we think too superficially if we suppose that the gigantic is only the endlessly extended emptiness of the purely quantitative. We think too little if we find that the gigantic, in the form of continual not-ever-having-been-here-yet, originates only in a blind mania for exaggerating and excelling. We do not think at all if we believe we have explained this phenomenon of the gigantic with the catchword 'Americanism'.

The gigantic is rather that through which the quantitative becomes a special quality and thus a remarkable kind of greatness. Each historical age is not only great in a distinctive way in contrast to others; it also has, in each instance, its own concept of greatness. But as soon as the gigantic in planning and calculating and adjusting and making secure shifts over out of the quantitative and becomes a special quality, then what is gigantic, and what can seemingly always be calculated completely, becomes, precisely through this, incalculable. This becoming incalculable remains the invisible shadow that is cast around all things everywhere when man has been transformed into *subiectum* and the world into picture.

By means of this shadow the modern world extends itself out into a space withdrawn from representation, and so lends to the incalculable the determinateness peculiar to it, as well as a historical uniqueness. This shadow, however, points to something else, which it is denied to us of today to know. But man will never be able to experience and ponder this that is denied so long as he dawdles about in the mere negating of the age. The flight into tradition, out of a combination of humility and presumption, can bring about nothing in itself other than self-deception and blindness in relation to the historical moment.

Man will know, i.e., carefully safeguard into its truth, that which is incalculable, only in creative questioning and shaping out of the power of genuine reflection. Reflection transports the man of the future into that 'between' in which he belongs to Being and yet remains a stranger amid that which is . . .

24

PETER WINCH
Philosophy and science* (1958)

I want to argue . . . that the philosophies of science, art, politics etc. – subjects which I will call the 'peripheral' philosophical disciplines – lose their philosophical character if unrelated to epistemology and metaphysics. But before I can show this in detail, I must first attempt to examine the philosophical foundations of the underlabourer conception of philosophy.

That conception is in large part a reaction against the 'master-scientist' view of the philosopher, according to which philosophy is in direct competition with science and aims at constructing or refuting scientific theories by purely a priori reasoning. This is an idea which is justly ridiculed; the absurdities to which it may lead are amply illustrated in Hegel's amateur pseudo-scientific speculations. Its philosophical refutation was provided by Hume:

> If we would satisfy ourselves . . . concerning the nature of that evidence, which assures us of matters of fact, we must enquire how we arrive at the knowledge of cause and effect. I shall venture to affirm, as a general proposition, which admits of no exception, that the knowledge of this relation is not, in any instance, attained by reasonings a priori; but arises entirely from experience, when we find that any particular objects are constantly conjoined with each other. Let an object be presented to a man of never so strong natural reason and abilities; if that object be entirely new to him, he will not be able, by the most accurate examination of its sensible qualities, to discover any of its causes or effects.
>
> (*Enquiry into Human Nature*, Section IV, Part I.)

Now this is admirable as a critique of a priori pseudoscience. But the argument has also frequently been misapplied in order to attack a priori philosophizing of a sort which is quite legitimate. The argument runs as follows: new discoveries about real matters of fact can only be established by experimental methods; no purely a priori

* From *The Idea of a Social Science and its Relation to Philosophy* by Peter Winch, Routledge & Kegan Paul, 1958, pp. 7–18. Reprinted with permission.

process of thinking is sufficient for this. But since it is science which uses experimental methods, while philosophy is purely a priori, it follows that the investigation of reality must be left to science. On the other hand, philosophy has traditionally claimed, at least in large part, to consist in the investigation of the nature of reality; either, therefore, traditional philosophy was attempting to do something which its methods of investigation could never possibly achieve, and must be abandoned; or else it was mistaken about its own nature, and the purport of its investigations must be drastically reinterpreted.

Now the argument on which this dilemma is based is fallacious: it contains an undistributed middle term. The phrase 'the investigation of the nature of reality' is ambiguous, and whereas Hume's argument applies perfectly well to what that phrase conveys when applied to scientific investigation, it is a mere *ignoratio elenchi* as applied to philosophy. The difference between the respective aims of the scientist and the philosopher might be expressed as follows. Whereas the scientist investigates the nature, causes and effects of particular real things and processes, the philosopher is concerned with the nature of reality as such and in general. Burnet puts the point very well in his book on *Greek Philosophy* when he points out . . . that the sense in which the philosopher asks 'What is real?' involves the problem of man's relation to reality, which takes us beyond pure science. 'We have to ask whether the mind of man can have any contact with reality at all, and, if it can, what difference this will make to his life'. Now to think that this question of Burnet's could be settled by experimental methods involves just as serious a mistake as to think that philosophy, with its a priori methods of reasoning, could possibly compete with experimental science on its own ground. For it is not an empirical question at all, but a conceptual one. It has to do with the force of the concept of reality. An appeal to the results of an experiment would necessarily beg the important question, since the philosopher would be bound to ask by what token those results themselves are accepted as 'reality'. Of course, this simply exasperates the experimental scientist – rightly so, from the point of view of his own aims and interests. But the force of the philosophical question cannot be grasped in terms of the preconceptions of experimental science. It cannot be answered by generalizing from particular instances since a particular answer to the philosophical question is already implied in the acceptance of those instances as 'real'.

The whole issue was symbolically dramatized on a celebrated occasion in 1939 when Professor G. E. Moore gave a lecture to the British Academy entitled 'Proof of an External World'. Moore's 'proof' ran roughly as follows. He held up each of his hands in succession, saying 'Here is one hand and here is another; therefore at least two external objects exist; therefore an external world exists'. In arguing thus Moore seemed to be treating the question 'Does an external world exist?' as similar in form to the question 'Do animals with a single horn growing out of their snout exist?' This of course would be conclusively settled by the production of two rhinoceri. But the bearing of Moore's argument on the philosophical question of the existence of an external world is not as simple as the bearing of the production of two rhinoceri on the other question. For, of course, philosophical doubt about the existence of an external world covers the two hands which Moore produced in the same way as it covers everything else. The whole question is: Do objects like Moore's two hands qualify as inhabitants of an external world? This is not to say that Moore's argument is completely beside the point; what is wrong is to regard it as an experimental 'proof', for it is not like anything one finds in an experimental discipline. Moore was not making an experiment; he was reminding his audience of something, reminding them of the way in which the expression 'external object' is in fact used. And his reminder indicated that the issue in philosophy is not to prove or disprove the existence of a world of external objects but rather to elucidate the concept of externality. That there is a connection between this issue and the central philosophical problem about the general nature of reality is, I think, obvious.

The philosopher's concern with language

So much, at present, for the relation between philosophy and science. But I have yet to show why the rejection of the master-scientist conception of the philosopher need not, and should not, lead to the underlabourer conception. I have spoken of Moore reminding us how certain expressions are in fact used; and I have emphasized how important in philosophy is the notion of elucidating a concept. These are ways of speaking which prima facie fit the underlabourer conception very well. And in fact what is wrong with that conception in general is to be looked for not so much in any downright false doctrine as in a systematically mistaken emphasis.

Philosophical issues do, to a large extent, turn on the correct use of certain linguistic expressions; the elucidation of a concept is, to a large extent, the clearing up of linguistic confusions. Nevertheless, the philosopher's concern is not with correct usage as such and not all linguistic confusions are equally relevant to philosophy. They are relevant only in so far as the discussion of them is designed to throw light on the question how far reality is intelligible and what difference would the fact that he could have a grasp of reality make to the life of man. So we have to ask how questions of language, and what kinds of question about language, are likely to bear upon these issues.

To ask whether reality is intelligible is to ask about the relation between thought and reality. In considering the nature of thought one is led also to consider the nature of language. Inseparably bound up with the question whether reality is intelligible, therefore, is the question of how language is connected with reality, of what it is to say something. In fact the philosopher's interest in language lies not so much in the solution of particular linguistic confusions for their own sakes, as in the solution of confusions about the nature of language in general.

I will elaborate this point polemically, referring to T. D. Weldon's *Vocabulary of Politics*. I choose this book because in it Weldon uses his interpretation of the concern which philosophy has with language to support a conception of the relations between philosophy and the study of society, which is fundamentally at variance with the conception to be commended in this monograph. Weldon's view is based on an interpretation of recent developments in philosophy in this country. What has occurred, he says, is that 'philosophers have become extremely self-conscious about language. They have come to realise that many of the problems which their predecessors have found insuperable arose not from anything mysterious or inexplicable in the world but from the eccentricities of the language in which we try to describe the world' (85: Chapter I). The problems of social and political philosophy, therefore, arise from the eccentricities of the language in which we try to describe social and political institutions, rather than from anything mysterious in those institutions themselves. In accordance with the underlabourer conception of philosophy, which Weldon is here faithfully following, he regards philosophy as having a purely negative role to play in advancing our understanding of social life. Any positive advances in this understanding must be contributed by the methods of empirical science rather than by those of philosophy. There is no hint that discussion of the central questions of metaphysics and epistemology themselves may (as I shall later argue) have light to throw on the nature of human societies.

In fact those questions are cavalierly brushed aside in the very statement of Weldon's position. To assume at the outset that one can make a sharp distinction between 'the world' and 'the language in which we try to describe the world', to the extent of saying that the problems of philosophy do not arise at all out of the former but only out of the latter, is to beg the whole question of philosophy.

Weldon would no doubt reply that this question has already been settled in a sense favourable to his position by those philosophers who contributed to the developments of which he is speaking. But even if we overlook the important fact that philosophical issues can never be settled in that way, that the results of other men's philosophizing cannot be assumed in one's own philosophical work as can scientific theories established by other men/ – even, I say, if we overlook this, the work of Wittgenstein, the most outstanding contributor to the philosophical development in question, is just misinterpreted if it is taken to support Weldon's way of speaking. This is obvious enough in relation to Wittgenstein's *Tractatus Logico-Philosophicus*, as can be seen from two representative quotations. 'To give the essence of proposition means to give the essence of all description, therefore the essence of the world' (86: 5.4711). 'That the world is my world shows itself in the fact that the limits of my language (of the only language I can understand) mean the limits of my world' (Ibid.: 5.62).

It is true that these ideas in the *Tractatus* are connected with a theory of language which Wittgenstein afterwards rejected and which Weldon would also reject. But Wittgenstein's methods of argument in the later *Philosophical Investigations* are equally incompatible with any easy distinction between the world and language. This comes out clearly in his treatment of the concept of seeing an object as something: for example, seeing the picture of an arrow as in flight. The following passage is characteristic of Wittgenstein's whole approach:

> In the triangle I can see now this as apex, that as base – now this as apex, that as base. Clearly the words 'Now I am seeing this as the apex' cannot so far mean anything to a learner who has only just met the concepts of apex, base, and so on. But I do not mean this as an empirical proposition.
>
> 'Now he's seeing it like this', 'now like that' would only be said of someone capable of making certain applications of the figure quite freely.
>
> The substratum of this experience is the mastery of a technique.
>
> But how queer for this to be the logical condition of someone's having such and such an experience! After all, you don't say that one only 'has toothache' if one is capable of doing such-and-such. From this it follows that we cannot be

dealing with the same concept of experience here. It is a different though related concept.

It is only if someone can do, has learnt, is master of, such-and-such, that it makes sense to say he has had this experience.

And if this sounds crazy, you need to reflect that the concept of seeing is modified here. (A similar consideration is often necessary to get rid of a feeling of dizziness in mathematics.) We talk, we utter words, and only later get a picture of their life.

(Philosophical Investigations: II, xi.)

We cannot say then, with Weldon, that the problems of philosophy arise out of language rather than out of the world, because in discussing language philosophically we are in fact discussing what counts as belonging to the world. Our idea of what belongs to the realm of reality is given for us in the language that we use. The concepts we have settle for us the form of the experience we have of the world. It may be worth reminding ourselves of the truism that when we speak of the world we are speaking of what we in fact mean by the expression 'the world': there is no way of getting outside the concepts in terms of which we think of the world, which is what Weldon is trying to do in his statements about the nature of philosophical problems. The world is for us what is presented through those concepts. That is not to say that our concepts may not change; but when they do, that means that our concept of the world has changed too.

Conceptual and empirical enquiries

This misunderstanding of the way in which philosophical treatments of linguistic confusions are also elucidations of the nature of reality leads to inadequacies in the actual methods used for treating such questions. Empiricists like Weldon systematically underemphasize the extent of what may be said a priori: for them all statements about reality must be empirical or they are unfounded, and a priori statements are 'about linguistic usage' as opposed to being 'about reality'. But if the integrity of science is endangered by the over-estimation of the a priori, against which Hume legitimately fought, it is no less true that philosophy is crippled by its underestimation: by mistaking conceptual enquiries into what it makes sense to say for empirical enquiries which must wait upon experience for their solution.

The misunderstanding is well illustrated in the following passage from Hume himself. He is discussing the extent and nature of our knowledge of what will happen in the future and arguing that nothing in the future can be logically guaranteed for us by our knowledge of what has been observed to happen in the past.

In vain do you pretend to have learned the nature of bodies from past experience. Their secret nature, and consequently all their effects and influence may change, without any change in their sensible qualities. This happens sometimes, and with regard to some objects: Why may it not happen always and with regard to all objects? What logic, what process of argument secures you against this supposition?

(Philosophical Investigations: Section IV, Part II.)

Hume assumes here that since a statement about the uniform behaviour of some objects is a straightforward empirical matter which may at any time be upset by future experience, the same must be true of a statement about the uniform behaviour of all objects. This assumption is very compelling. Its compellingness derives from a healthy unwillingness to admit that anyone can legislate a priori concerning the course of future experience on the basis of purely logical considerations. And of course we cannot thus legislate against a breakdown in the regular order of nature, such as would make scientific work impossible and destroy speech, thought, and even life. But we can and must legislate a priori against the possibility of describing such a situation in the terms which Hume attempts to use: in terms, that is, of the properties of objects, their causes and effects. For were the order of nature to break down in that way these terms would be no longer applicable. Because there may be minor, or even major, variations within such an order without our whole conceptual apparatus being upset, it does not follow that we can use our existing apparatus (and what other are we to use?) to describe a breakdown in the order of nature as a whole. This is not merely verbal quibbling. For the whole philosophical purport of enquiries like Hume's is to clarify those concepts which are fundamental to our conception of reality, like object, property of an object, cause and effect. To point out that the use of such notions necessarily presupposes the continuing truth of most of our generalizations about the behaviour of the world we live in is of central importance to such an undertaking.

The importance of this issue for the philosophy of the social sciences will become more apparent later on. I shall argue, for instance, that many of the more important theoretical issues which have been raised in those studies belong to philosophy rather than to science and are, therefore, to be settled by a priori conceptual analysis rather than by empirical research. For example, the question of what constitutes social behaviour is a demand for an elucidation of the concept of social behaviour. In dealing with questions of this sort there should be no question of 'waiting to see' what empirical research will show us; it is a matter of tracing the implications of the concepts we use.

25

HANS-GEORG GADAMER
Hermeneutical understanding* (1960)

Historical interest is directed not only toward the historical phenomenon and the traditionary work but also, secondarily, toward their effect in history (which also includes the history of research); the history of effect is generally regarded as a mere supplement to historical inquiry, from Hermann Grimm's *Raffael* to Gundolf and beyond – though it has occasioned many valuable insights. To this extent, history of effect is not new. But to require an inquiry into history of effect every time a work of art or an aspect of the tradition is led out of the twilight region between tradition and history so that it can be seen clearly and openly in terms of its own meaning – this is a new demand (addressed not to research, but to its methodological consciousness) that proceeds inevitably from thinking historical consciousness through.

It is not, of course, a hermeneutical requirement in the sense of the traditional conception of hermeneutics. I am not saying that historical inquiry should develop inquiry into the history of effect as a kind of inquiry separate from understanding the work itself. The requirement is of a more theoretical kind. Historical consciousness must become conscious that in the apparent immediacy with which it approaches a work of art or a traditionary text, there is also another kind of inquiry in play, albeit unrecognized and unregulated. If we are trying to understand a historical phenomenon from the historical distance that is characteristic of our hermeneutical situation, we are always already affected by history. It determines in advance both what seems to us worth inquiring about and what will appear as an object of investigation, and we more or less forget half of what is really there – in fact, we miss the whole truth of the phenomenon – when we take its immediate appearance as the whole truth.

In our understanding, which we imagine is so innocent because its results seem so self-evident, the other presents itself so much in terms of our own selves that there is no longer a question of self and other. In relying on its critical method, historical objectivism conceals the fact that historical consciousness is itself situated in the web of historical effects. By means of methodical critique it does away with the

* From *Truth and Method* by Hans-Georg Gadamer, The Crossroad Publishing Corporation, New York, 1989, Second, Revised Edition, pp. 300–307. Reprinted by permission of Sheed and Ward.

arbitrariness of 'relevant' appropriations of the past, but it preserves its good conscience by failing to recognize the presuppositions – certainly not arbitrary, but still fundamental – that govern its own understanding, and hence falls short of reaching that truth which, despite the finite nature of our understanding, could be reached. In this respect, historical objectivism resembles statistics, which are such excellent means of propaganda because they let the 'facts' speak and hence simulate an objectivity that in reality depends on the legitimacy of the questions asked.

We are not saying, then, that history of effect must be developed as a new independent discipline ancillary to the human sciences, but that we should learn to understand ourselves better and recognize that in all understanding, whether we are expressly aware of it or not, the efficacy of history is at work. When a naive faith in scientific method denies the existence of effective history, there can be an actual deformation of knowledge. We are familiar with this from the history of science, where it appears as the irrefutable proof of something that is obviously false. But on the whole the power of effective history does not depend on its being recognized. This, precisely, is the power of history over finite human consciousness, namely that it prevails even where faith in method leads one to deny one's own historicity. Our need to become conscious of effective history is urgent because it is necessary for scientific consciousness. But this does not mean it can ever be absolutely fulfilled. That we should become completely aware of effective history is just as hybrid a statement as when Hegel speaks of absolute knowledge, in which history would become completely transparent to itself and hence be raised to the level of a concept. Rather, historically effected consciousness (*wirkungsgeschichtliches Bewußtsein*) is an element in the act of understanding itself and, as we shall see, is already effectual in finding the right questions to ask.

Consciousness of being affected by history (*wirkungsgeschichtliches Bewußtsein*) is primarily consciousness of the hermeneutical situation. To acquire an awareness of a situation is, however, always a task of peculiar difficulty. The very idea of a situation means that we are not standing outside it and hence are unable to have any objective knowledge of it. We always find ourselves within a situation, and throwing light on it is a task that is never entirely finished. This is also true of the hermeneutic situation – i.e., the situation in which we find ourselves with regard to the tradition that we are trying to understand. The illumination of this situation – reflection on effective history – can never be completely achieved; yet the fact that it cannot be completed is due not to a deficiency in reflection but to the essence of the historical being that we are. To be historically means that knowledge of oneself can never be complete. All self-knowledge arises from what is historically pregiven, what with Hegel we call 'substance,' because it underlies all subjective intentions and actions, and hence both prescribes and limits every possibility for understanding any tradition whatsoever in its historical alterity. This almost defines the aim of philosophical hermeneutics: its task is to retrace the path of Hegel's phenomenology of mind until we discover in all that is subjective the substantiality that determines it.

Every finite present has its limitations. We define the concept of 'situation' by saying that it represents a standpoint that limits the possibility of vision. Hence essential to the concept of situation is the concept of 'horizon.' The horizon is the range of vision that includes everything that can be seen from a particular vantage point.

Applying this to the thinking mind, we speak of narrowness of horizon, of the possible expansion of horizon, of the opening up of new horizons, and so forth. Since Nietzsche and Husserl, the word has been used in philosophy to characterize the way in which thought is tied to its finite determinacy, and the way one's range of vision is gradually expanded. A person who has no horizon does not see far enough and hence overvalues what is nearest to him. On the other hand, 'to have a horizon' means not being limited to what is nearby but being able to see beyond it. A person who has a horizon knows the relative significance of everything within this horizon, whether it is near or far, great or small. Similarly, working out the hermeneutical situation means acquiring the right horizon of inquiry for the questions evoked by the encounter with tradition.

In the sphere of historical understanding, too, we speak of horizons, especially when referring to the claim of historical consciousness to see the past in its own terms, not in terms of our contemporary criteria and prejudices but within its own historical horizon. The task of historical understanding also involves acquiring an appropriate historical horizon, so that what we are trying to understand can be seen in its true dimensions. If we fail to transpose ourselves into the historical horizon from which the traditionary text speaks, we will misunderstand the significance of what it has to say to us. To that extent this seems a legitimate hermeneutical requirement: we must place ourselves in the other situation in order to understand it. We may wonder, however, whether this phrase is adequate to describe the understanding that is required of us. The same is true of a conversation that we have with someone simply in order to get to know him – i.e., to discover where he is coming from and his horizon. This is not a true conversation – that is, we are not seeking agreement on some subject – because the specific contents of the conversation are only a means to get to know the horizon of the other person. Examples are oral examinations and certain kinds of conversation between doctor and patient. Historical consciousness is clearly doing something similar when it transposes itself into the situation of the past and thereby claims to have acquired the right historical horizon. In a conversation, when we have discovered the other person's standpoint and horizon, his ideas become intelligible without our necessarily having to agree with him; so also when someone thinks historically, he comes to understand the meaning of what has been handed down without necessarily agreeing with it or seeing himself in it.

In both cases, the person understanding has, as it were, stopped trying to reach an agreement. He himself cannot be reached. By factoring the other person's standpoint into what he is claiming to say, we are making our own standpoint safely unattainable. In considering the origin of historical thinking, we have seen that in fact it makes this ambiguous transition from means to ends – i.e., it makes an end of what is only a means. The text that is understood historically is forced to abandon its claim to be saying something true. We think we understand when we see the past from a historical standpoint – i.e., transpose ourselves into the historical situation and try to reconstruct the historical horizon. In fact, however, we have given up the claim to find in the past any truth that is valid and intelligible for ourselves. Acknowledging the otherness of the other in this way, making him the object of objective knowledge, involves the fundamental suspension of his claim to truth. However, the question is whether this description really fits the hermeneutical phenomenon. Are there really two different horizons here – the horizon in which the person seeking to understand lives and the historical horizon within which he places himself? Is it a correct description of the art of historical understanding to say that we learn to transpose ourselves into alien horizons? Are there such things as closed horizons, in this sense? We recall Nietzsche's complaint against historicism that it destroyed the horizon bounded by myth in which alone a culture is able to live. Is the horizon of one's own present time ever closed in this way, and can a historical situation be imagined that has this kind of closed horizon?

Or is this a romantic refraction, a kind of Robinson Crusoe dream of historical enlightenment, the fiction of an unattainable island, as artificial as Crusoe himself – i.e., as the alleged primacy of the solus ipse? Just as the individual is never simply an individual because he is always in understanding with others, so too the closed horizon that is supposed to enclose a culture is an abstraction. The historical movement of human life consists in the fact that it is never absolutely bound to any one standpoint, and hence can never have a truly closed horizon. The horizon is, rather, something into which we move and that moves with us. Horizons change for a person who is moving. Thus the horizon of the past, out of which all human life lives and which exists in the form of tradition, is always in motion. The surrounding horizon is not set in motion by historical consciousness. But in it this motion becomes aware of itself.

When our historical consciousness transposes itself into historical horizons, this does not entail passing into alien worlds unconnected in any way with our own; instead, they together constitute the one great horizon that moves from within and that, beyond the frontiers of the present, embraces the historical depths of our self-consciousness. Everything contained in historical consciousness is in fact embraced by a single historical horizon. Our own past and that other past toward which our historical consciousness is directed help to shape this moving horizon out of which human life always lives and which determines it as heritage and tradition.

Understanding tradition undoubtedly requires a historical horizon, then. But it is not the case that we acquire this horizon by transposing ourselves into a historical situation. Rather, we must always already have a horizon in order to be able to transpose ourselves into a situation. For what do we mean by 'transposing ourselves'? Certainly not just disregarding ourselves. This is necessary, of course, insofar as we must imagine the other situation. But into this other situation we must bring, precisely, ourselves. Only this is the full meaning of 'transposing ourselves.' If we put ourselves in someone else's shoes, for example, then we will understand him – i.e., become aware of the otherness, the indissoluble individuality of the other person – by putting ourselves in his position.

Transposing ourselves consists neither in the empathy of one individual for another nor in subordinating another person to our own standards; rather, it always involves rising to a higher universality that overcomes not only our own particularity but also that of the other. The concept of 'horizon' suggests itself because it expresses the superior breadth of vision that the person who is trying to understand must have. To acquire a horizon means that one learns to look beyond what is close at hand – not in order to look away from it but to see it better, within a larger whole and in truer proportion. To speak, with Nietzsche, of the many changing horizons into which historical consciousness teaches us to place ourselves is not a correct description. If we disregard ourselves in this way, we have no historical horizon. Nietzsche's view that historical study is deleterious to life is not, in fact, directed against historical consciousness as such, but against the self-alienation it undergoes when it regards the method of modern historical science as its own true nature. We have already pointed out that a truly historical consciousness always sees its own present in such a way that it sees itself, as well as the historically other, within the right relationships. It requires a special effort to acquire a historical horizon. We are always affected, in hope and fear, by what is nearest to us, and hence we approach the testimony of the past under its influence. Thus it is constantly necessary to guard against overhastily assimilating the past to our own expectations of meaning. Only then can we listen to tradition in a way that permits it to make its own meaning heard.

We have shown above that this is a process of foregrounding (*abheben*). Let us consider what this idea of foregrounding involves. It is always reciprocal. Whatever is being foregrounded must be foregrounded from something else, which, in turn, must be foregrounded from it. Thus all foregrounding also makes visible that from which something is foregrounded. We have described this above as the way prejudices are brought into play. We started by saying that a hermeneutical situation is determined by the prejudices that we bring with us. They constitute, then, the horizon of a particular present, for they represent that beyond which it is impossible to see. But now it is important to avoid the error of thinking that the horizon of the present consists of a fixed set of opinions and valuations, and that the otherness of the past can be foregrounded from it as from a fixed ground.

In fact the horizon of the present is continually in the process of being formed because we are continually having to test all our prejudices. An important part of this testing occurs in encountering the past and in understanding the tradition from which we come. Hence the horizon of the present cannot be formed without the past. There is no more an isolated horizon of the present in itself than there are historical horizons which have to be acquired. Rather, understanding is always the fusion of these horizons supposedly existing by themselves. We are familiar with the power of this kind of fusion chiefly from earlier times and their naivete about themselves and their heritage. In a tradition this process of fusion is continually going on, for there old and new are always combining into something of living value, without either being explicitly foregrounded from the other.

If, however, there is no such thing as these distinct horizons, why do we speak of the fusion of horizons and not simply of the formation of the one horizon, whose bounds are set in the depths of tradition? To ask the question means that we are recognizing that understanding becomes a scholarly task only under special circumstances and that it is necessary to work out these circumstances as a hermeneutical situation. Every encounter with tradition that takes place within historical consciousness involves the experience of a tension between the text and the present. The hermeneutic task consists in not covering up this tension by attempting a naive assimilation of the two but in consciously bringing it out. This is why it is part of the hermeneutic approach to project a historical horizon that is different from the horizon of the present. Historical consciousness is aware of its own otherness and hence foregrounds the horizon of the past from its own. On the other hand, it is itself, as we are trying to show, only something superimposed upon continuing tradition, and hence it immediately recombines with what it has foregrounded itself from in order to become one with itself again in the unity of the historical horizon that it thus acquires.

Projecting a historical horizon, then, is only one phase in the process of understanding; it does not become solidified into the self-alienation of a past consciousness, but is overtaken by our own present horizon of understanding. In the process of understanding, a real fusing of horizons occurs – which means that as the historical horizon is projected, it is simultaneously superseded. To bring about this fusion in a regulated way is the task of what we called historically effected consciousness. Although this task was obscured by aesthetic-historical positivism following on the heels of romantic hermeneutics, it is, in fact, the central problem of hermeneutics. It is the problem of application, which is to be found in all understanding.

26

JÜRGEN HABERMAS
The hermeneutic claim to universality* (1973)

Hermeneutics refers to an 'ability' we acquire to the extent to which we learn to 'master' a natural language: the art of understanding linguistically communicable meaning and to render it comprehensible in cases of distorted communication. The understanding of meaning is directed at the semantic content of speech as well as the meaning-content of written forms or even of non-linguistic symbolic systems, in so far as their meaning-content can, in principle, be expressed in words. It is no accident that we speak of the art of understanding and of making-oneself-understood, since the ability to interpret meaning, which every language-user possesses, can be stylized and developed into an artistic skill. This art is symmetric with the art of convincing and persuading in situations where decisions have to be reached on practical questions. Rhetoric, too, is based on an ability which is part of the communicative competence of every language user and which can be stylized into a special skill. Rhetoric and hermeneutics have both emerged as teachable arts which methodically discipline and cultivate a natural ability.

This is not so in the case of a philosophical hermeneutic: it is not a practical skill guided by rules but a critique, for its reflexive engagement brings to consciousness experiences of our language which we gain in the course of exercising our communicative competence, that is, by moving within language. It is because rhetoric and hermeneutics serve the instruction and disciplined development of communicative competence that hermeneutic reflection can draw on this sphere of experience. But the reflection upon skilled understanding and making-oneself-understood on the one hand (1), and upon convincing and persuading on the other (2), does not serve the establishing of a teachable art, but the philosophical consideration of the structure of everyday communication.

(1) The art of understanding and making-oneself-understood provides a philosophical hermeneutic with its characteristic insight that the means of natural language are, in principle, sufficient for elucidating the sense of any symbolic complex, however

* From 'The Hermeneutic Claim to Universality' by Jürgen Habermas, in Josef Bleicher, *Hermeneutics, as Method, Philosophy and Critique*, Routledge & Kegan Paul, 1980, translated by Josef Bleicher. Reproduced with permission of the publisher. Pp. 181–182, 190–192, 202–211.

unfamiliar and inaccessible it may initially appear. We are able to translate from any language into any language. We are able to make sense of objectivations of the most remote epoch and the most distant civilization by relating them to the familiar, i.e. pre-understood, context of our own world. At the same time, the actual distance to other traditions is part of the horizon of every natural language. In addition, the already understood context of one's own world can at any time be exposed as being questionable; it is, potentially, incomprehensible. Hermeneutic experience is circumscribed by the conjunction of these two moments: the intersubjectivity of everyday communication is principally as unlimited as it is restricted; it is unlimited because it can be extended *ad libitum*; it is restricted because it can never be completely achieved. This applies to contemporary communication both within a socioculturally homogeneous language community and across the distance between different classes, civilizations and epochs.

Hermeneutic experience brings to consciousness the position of a speaking subject *vis-à-vis* his language. He can draw upon the self-referentiality of natural languages for paraphrasing any changes metacommunicatively . . .

Hermeneutic consciousness remains incomplete as long as it does not include a reflection upon the limits of hermeneutic understanding. The experience of a hermeneutical limitation refers to specifically incomprehensible expressions. This specific incomprehensibility cannot be overcome by the exercise, however skilful, of one's naturally acquired communicative competence; its stubbornness can be regarded as an indication that it cannot be explained by sole reference to the structure of everyday communication that hermeneutic philosophy has brought to light.

In this case it is not the objectivity of linguistic tradition, the finite horizon of a linguistically articulated understanding of life, the potential incomprehensibility of what is implicitly regarded as self-evident, that stands in the way of the interpretative effort.

In cases where understanding proves difficult owing to great cultural, temporal or social distance it is still possible for us to state in principle what additional information we require in order to fully understand: we know that we have to decipher an alphabet, get to know a vocabulary or rules of application which are specific to their context. Within the limits of tolerance of normal everyday communication it is possible for us to determine what we do not-yet-know when we try to make sense of an incomprehensible complex of meaning. This hermeneutic consciousness proves inadequate in the case of systematically distorted communication: incomprehensibility is here the result of a defective organization of speech itself. Openly pathological speech defects which are apparent, for example, among psychotics, can be disregarded by hermeneutics without impairment of its self-conception. The area of applicability of hermeneutics is congruent with the limits of normal everyday speech, as long as pathological cases are excluded. The self-conception of hermeneutics can only be shaken when it appears that patterns of systematically distorted communication are also in evidence in 'normal', let us call it pathologically unobtrusive, speech. This is the case in the pseudo-communication in which the participants cannot recognize a breakdown in their communication; only an external observer notices that they misunderstand one another. Pseudo-communication generates a system of misunderstandings that cannot be recognized as such under the appearance of a false consensus.

Hermeneutics has taught us that we are always a participant as long as we move within the natural language and that we cannot step outside the role of a reflective partner. There is, therefore, no general criterion available to us which would allow us to determine when we are subject to the false consciousness of a pseudo-normal understanding and consider something as a difficulty that can be resolved by hermeneutical means when, in fact, it requires systematic explanation. The experience of the limit of hermeneutics consists of the recognition of systematically generated misunderstanding as such – without, at first, being able to 'grasp' it.

Freud has drawn on this experience of systematically distorted communication in order to demarcate a sphere of specifically incomprehensible expressions. He always regarded dreams as the 'standard model' for those phenomena which themselves extend innocuous pseudo-communication and parapraxes in everyday life to the pathological manifestations of neuroses, mental illness and psychosomatic complaints. In his writings on the theory of civilization Freud extended the sphere of systematically distorted communication and he used the insights gained in dealing with clinical phenomena as a key for pseudonormality, i.e. the hidden pathology of societal systems. We shall first of all focus on the sphere of neurotic manifestations that has received the fullest explanation.

There are available three criteria for demarcating neurotically distorted, which here means specifically incomprehensible, forms of expression. On the level of linguistic symbols, distorted communication is apparent in the application of rules which deviate from the publicly accepted rule-system. It is possible for an isolated semantic content or complete fields of meaning, in extreme cases even the syntax, to be affected. Freud examined the content of dreams mainly in relation to condensation, displacement, a-grammaticality and the role of contraries. On the level of the behaviour, a deformed language game is noticeable because of its rigidity and compulsion to repeat. Stereotyped patterns of behaviour recur in situations with the same stimuli which give rise to affective impulses. This inflexibility is an indication that the semantic content of a symbol has lost its specifically linguistic situational independence. When we consider the system of distorted communication as a whole it becomes apparent that there exists a characteristic discrepancy between the levels of communication: the usual congruence between linguistic symbols, actions and accompanying expressions has disintegrated. Neurotic symptoms are merely the most stubborn and manifest evidence of this dissonance. No matter on what level of communication these symptoms appear – in linguistic expression, body-language or compulsive behaviour – it is always the case that a content, which has been excommunicated from its public usage, assumes independence. This content expresses an intention which remains incomprehensible according to the rules of public communication, and is, in this sense, privatized; but it also remains inaccessible to its author. There exists within the self a barrier to communication between the 'I' who is linguistically competent and who participates in intersubjectively established language-games, and that 'inner exile' (Freud) that is represented by the symbolic system of a private or protogenal language . . .

It is now possible to answer our original question: explanatory understanding, in the sense of the depth-hermeneutical decoding of specifically inadequate expressions, does not only necessitate the skilled application of naturally acquired communicative competence, as it is the case with elementary hermeneutical understanding, but also presupposes a theory of communicative competence. The latter covers the forms of the intersubjectivity of language and causes of its deformation. I cannot say that a theory of communicative competence has up until now been attempted in a satisfactory way, never mind been explicitly developed. Freud's metapsychology would have to be freed of its scientistic self-miscomprehension before it could be utilized as a part of a meta-hermeneutic. I would say, however, that each depth-hermeneutical interpretation of systematically distorted communication, irrespective of whether it appears in an analytic encounter or informally, implicitly relies on those demanding theoretical assumptions which can only be developed and justified within the framework of a theory of communicative competence . . .

What follows from this hermeneutic claim to universality? Is it not the case that the theoretical language of a meta-hermeneutic is subject to the same reservation as all other theories: that a given non-reconstructed everyday language remains the last metalanguage? And would not the application of general interpretations, which are deducible from such theories, to material given in everyday language still require basic hermeneutical understanding which is not replaceable by any generalized measuring procedure? Neither of these questions would any longer have to be answered in accordance with the hermeneutic claim to universality if the knowing subject, who necessarily has to draw on his previously acquired linguistic competence, could assure himself explicitly of this competence in the course of a theoretical reconstruction. We have so far bracketed this problem of a general theory of natural language. But we can already refer to this competence, which the analyst (and the critic of ideologies) has to employ factually in the disclosure of specifically incomprehensible expressions, in advance of all theory construction. Already the implicit knowledge of the conditions of systematically distorted communication, which is presupposed in an actual form in the depth-hermeneutical use of communicative competence, is sufficient for the questioning of the ontological self-understanding of the philosophical hermeneutic which Gadamer propounds by following Heidegger.

Gadamer turns the context-dependency of the understanding of meaning, which hermeneutic philosophy has brought to consciousness and which requires us always to proceed from a pre-understanding that is supported by tradition as well as to continuously form a new pre-understanding in the course of being corrected, to the ontologically inevitable primacy of linguistic tradition. Gadamer poses the question: 'Is the phenomenon of understanding adequately defined when I state that to understand is to avoid misunderstanding? Is it not, rather, the case that something like a 'supporting consensus' precedes all misunderstanding? We can agree on the answer, which is to be given in the affirmative, but not on how to define this preceding consensus. If I understand correctly, then Gadamer is of the opinion that the hermeneutical clarification of incomprehensible or misunderstood expressions always has to lead back to a consensus that has already been reliably established through converging tradition. This tradition is objective in relation to us in the sense that we cannot confront it with a principled claim to truth. The pre-judgmental structure of understanding not only prohibits us from questioning that factually established consensus which underlies our misunderstanding and incomprehension, but makes such an undertaking appear senseless. It is a hermeneutical requirement that we refer to a concrete pre-understanding which itself, in the last analysis, goes back to the process of socialization, i.e. the introduction into a shared tradition. None of them is, in principle, beyond criticism; but neither can they be questioned abstractly. This would only be possible if we could examine a consensus that has been achieved through mutual understanding by, as it were, looking into it from the side and subjecting it, behind the backs of the participants, to renewed demands for legitimation. But we can only make demands of this kind in the face of the participants by entering into a dialogue with them. In this case we submit, yet again, to the hermeneutic demand to accept, for the time being, the clarifying consensus which the resumed dialogue might arrive at, as a supporting agreement. It would be senseless to abstractly suspect this agreement, which, admittedly, is contingent of being false consciousness since we cannot transcend the dialogue which we are. This leads Gadamer to conclude to the ontological priority of linguistic tradition over all possible critique; we can consequently criticize specific traditions only on the basis that we are part of the comprehensive context of the tradition of a language.

On first sight, these considerations seem plausible. They can, however, be shaken by the depth-hermeneutical insight that a consensus achieved by seemingly 'reasonable' means may well be the result of pseudo-communication. Albrecht Wellmer has pointed out that the Enlightenment tradition generalized this insight which is hostile to tradition. However much the Enlightenment was interested in communication, it still demanded that Reason be recognized as the principle of communication, free from force in the face of the real experience of communication distorted by force: 'The Enlightenment knew what a philosophical hermeneutic forgets – that the "dialogue" which we, according to Gadamer, "are", is also a context of domination and as such precisely no dialogue . . . The universal claim of the hermeneutic approach [can only] be maintained if it is realized at the outset that the context of tradition as a locus of possible truth and factual agreement is, at the same time, the locus of factual untruth and continued force.'

It would only be legitimate for us to equate the supporting consensus which, according to Gadamer, always precedes any failure at mutual understanding with a given factual agreement, if we could be certain that each consensus arrived at in the medium of linguistic tradition has been achieved without compulsion and distortion. But we learn from depth-hermeneutic experience that the dogmatism of the context of tradition is subject not only to the objectivity of language in general but also to the repressivity of forces which deform the intersubjectivity of agreement as such and which systematically distort everyday communication. It is for this reason that every consensus, as the outcome of an understanding of meaning, is, in principle, suspect of having been enforced through pseudo-communication: in earlier days, people talked about delusion when misunderstanding and self-misunderstanding continued unaffected under the appearance of factual agreement. Insight into the prejudgmental structure of the understanding of meaning does not cover the identification of actually achieved consensus with a true one. It, rather, leads to the ontologization of language and to the hypostatization of the context of tradition. A critically enlightened hermeneutic that differentiates between insight and delusion incorporates the meta-hermeneutic awareness of the conditions for the possibility of systematically distorted communication. It connects the process of understanding to the principle of rational discourse, according to which truth would only be guaranteed by that kind of consensus which was achieved under the idealized conditions of unlimited communication free from domination and could be maintained over time.

K.-O. Apel rightly emphasized that hermeneutical understanding can, at the same time, lead to the critical ascertainment of truth only to the extent to which it follows the regulative principle: to try to establish universal agreement within the framework of an unlimited community of interpreters. Only this principle can make sure that the hermeneutic effort does not cease until we are aware of deceptions within a forcible consensus and of the systematic distortion behind seemingly accidental misunderstanding. If the understanding of meaning is not to remain *a fortiori* indifferent towards the idea of truth then we have to anticipate, together with the concept of a kind of truth which measures itself on an idealized consensus achieved in unlimited communication free from domination, also the structures of solidary co-existence in communication free from force. Truth is that characteristic compulsion towards unforced universal recognition; the latter is itself tied to an ideal speech situation, i.e. a form of life, which makes possible unforced universal agreement. The critical understanding of meaning thus has to take upon itself the formal anticipation of a true life. This has already been expressed by G. H. Mead:

> Universal discourse is the formal ideal of communication. If communication can be carried through and made perfect, then there would exist the kind of democracy . . . in which each individual would carry just the response in himself that he knows he calls out in the community. That is what makes communication in the significant sense the organising process in the community.

The idea of truth, which measures itself on a true consensus, implies the idea of the true life. We could also say: it includes the idea of being-of-age (*Mündigkeit*). It is only the formal anticipation of an idealized dialogue, as the form of life to be realized in the future, which guarantees the ultimate supporting and contra-factual agreement that already unites us; in relation to it we can criticize every factual agreement, should it be a false one, as false consciousness. It is, however, only when we can show that the anticipation of possible truth and a true life is constitutive for every linguistic communication which is not monological that we are in a position not merely to demand but to justify that regulative principle of understanding. Basic meta-hermeneutic experience makes us aware of the fact that critique, as a penetrating form of understanding which does not rebound off delusions, orients itself on the concept of ideal consensus and thereby follows the regulative principle of rational discourse. But to justify the view that we not only do, but indeed have to, engage in that formal anticipation in the course of every penetrating understanding, it is not enough to merely refer to experience alone. To attempt a systematic justification we have to develop the implicit knowledge, that always and already guides the depth-hermeneutical analysis of language, into a theory which would enable us to deduce the principle of rational discourse from the logic of everyday language and regard it as the necessary regulative for any actual discourse, however distorted it may be.

Even without anticipating a general theory of natural language, the above considerations would suffice to criticize two conceptions which follow not so much from hermeneutics itself but from what seems to me to be a false ontological self-understanding of it.

(1) Gadamer deduced the rehabilitation of prejudice from his hermeneutic insight into the pre-judgmental structure of understanding. He does not see any opposition between authority and reason. The authority of tradition does not assert itself blindly but only through its reflective recognition by those who, while being part of tradition themselves, understand and develop it through application. In response to my criticism, Gadamer clarifies his position once again: 'I grant that authority exercises force in an infinite number of forms of domination . . . But this view of obedience to authority cannot tell us why these forms all represent ordered states of affairs and not the disorder of the brachial use of force. It seems to me to follow necessarily when I consider recognition as being determined in actual situations of authority . . . One only needs to study such events as the loss or decay of authority . . . to see what authority is and what sustains it; it is not dogmatic force but dogmatic recognition. But what is dogmatic recognition, however, if it is not that one concedes to authority a superiority of knowledge.'

The dogmatic recognition of tradition, and this means the acceptance of the truth-claims of this tradition, can be equated with knowledge itself only when freedom from force and unrestricted agreement about tradition have already been secured within this tradition. Gadamer's argument presupposes that legitimizing recognition and the consensus on which authority is founded can arise and develop free from force. The experience of distorted communication contradicts this presupposition. Force can, in any case, acquire permanence only through the objective semblance of an unforced pseudo-communicative agreement. Force that is legitimated in such a way we call, with Max Weber, authority. It is for this reason that there has to be that principle proviso of a universal agreement free from domination in order to make the fundamental distinction between dogmatic recognition and true consensus. Reason, in the sense of the principle of rational discourse, represents the rock which factual authorities have so far been more likely to crash against than build upon.

(2) If, then, such opposition between authority and reason does in fact exist, as the Enlightenment has always claimed, and if it cannot be superseded by hermeneutic means, it follows that the attempt to impose fundamental restrictions upon the inter-prepter's commitment to enlightenment becomes problematic, too. Gadamer has, in addition, derived the re-absorption of the moment of enlightenment into the horizon of currently existing convictions, from his insight into the pre-judgmental structure of understanding. The interpreter's ability to understand the author better than he had understood himself is limited by the accepted and traditionally established certitudes of the socio-cultural life-world of which he is part:

How does the psychoanalyst's knowledge relate to his position within the social reality to which he belongs? The emancipatory reflection which he initiates in his patients necessitates that he inquires into the more conscious surface interpret-ations, breaks through masked self-understanding, sees through the repressive function of social taboos. But when he conducts this reflection in situations which are outside the legitimate sphere of an analyst and where he is himself a partner in social interaction, then he is acting out of part. Anyone who sees through his social partners to something hidden to them, i.e. who does not take their role-acting seriously, is a 'spoilsport' who will be avoided. The emancipatory potential of reflection which the psychoanalyst draws on therefore has to find its limit in the social consciousness within which both the analyst and his patient are in agreement with everyone else. As hermeneutic reflection has shown us, social communality, despite existing tensions and defects, always refers us back to a consensus on the basis of which it exists.

There is, however, reason to assume that the background consensus of estab-lished traditions and of language-games may be a forced consensus which resulted from pseudo-communication; this may be so not only in the individual, pathological case of disturbed family systems, but also in societal systems. The range of a hermen-eutical understanding that has been extended into critique must, consequently, not be tied to the radius of convictions existing within a tradition. A depth-hermeneutic which adheres to the regulative principle of rational discourse has to seek out remain-ing natural-historical traces of distorted communication which are still contained even within fundamental agreements and recognized legitimations; and since it can find them there, too, it follows that any privatization of its commitment to enlightenment, and the restriction of the critique of ideology to the role of a treatment as it is insti-tutionalized in the analyst-patient relationship, would be incompatible with its methodic point of departure. The enlightenment, which results from radical under-standing, is always political. It is, of course, true that criticism is always tied to the context of tradition which it reflects. Gadamer's hermeneutic reservations are justified against monological self-certainty which merely arrogates to itself the title of critique. There is no validation of depth-hermeneutical interpretation outside of the self-reflection of all participants that is successfully achieved in a dialogue. The hypo-thetical status of general interpretations leads, indeed, to a priori limitations in the selection of ways in which the given immanent commitment of critical understanding to enlightenment can at any time be realized.

In present conditions it may be more urgent to indicate the limits of the false claim to universality made by criticism rather than that of the hermeneutic claim to universality. Where the dispute about the grounds for justification is concerned, however, it is necessary to critically examine the latter claim, too.

27

PAUL RICOEUR
Towards a critical hermeneutic: hermeneutics and the critique of ideology* (1973)

... The principal protagonists in the debate are, on the side of hermeneutics, Hans-Georg Gadamer; and on the side of critique, Jürgen Habermas. The dossier of their polemic is now public, partially reproduced in the little volume entitled *Hermeneutik und Ideologiekritik*. It is from this dossier that I shall extract the lines of force which characterise the conflict between hermeneutics and the critical theory of ideology. I shall take the assessment of tradition by each of these philosophies as the touchstone of the debate. In contrast to the positive assessment by hermeneutics, the theory of ideology adopts a suspicious approach, seeing tradition as merely the systematically distorted expression of communication under unacknowledged conditions of violence. The choice of this touchstone has the advantage of bringing to the fore a confrontation which bears upon the 'claim to universality' of hermeneutics. For the critique of ideology is of interest insofar as it is a non-hermeneutical discipline, situated outside the sphere of competence of a science or philosophy of interpretation, and marking the fundamental limit of the latter.

In the first part of this essay, I shall restrict myself to presenting the contents of the dossier. I shall do so in terms of a simple alternative: either hermeneutics or the critique of ideology. I shall reserve for the second part a more personal reflection, centred on the following two questions: (1) Can hermeneutic philosophy account for the legitimate demand of the critique of ideology, and if so at what price? Must it sacrifice its claim to universality and undertake a profound reformulation of its programme and its project? (2) On what condition is the critique of ideology possible? Can it, in the last analysis, be detached from hermeneutic presuppositions?

I hasten to say that no plan of annexation, no syncretism, will preside over this debate. I readily admit, along with Gadamer, that each of the two theories speaks from a different place; but I hope to show that each can recognise the other's claim to universality in a way which marks the place of one in the structure of the other ...

* From Paul Ricoeur 'Hermeneutics and the Critique of Ideology', pp. 63–64 and 90–100, edited and translated by John Brookshire Thompson, in *Paul Ricoeur: Hermeneutics and the Human Sciences*, Cambridge: Cambridge University Press, 1981. Reproduced by permission of John Thompson and the publisher.

1. Critical reflection on hermeneutics

. . . I shall note to begin with that the recognition of a critical instance is a vague desire constantly reiterated, but constantly aborted, within hermeneutics. From Heidegger onwards, hermeneutics is wholly engaged in going back to the foundations, a movement which leads from the epistemological question concerning the conditions of possibility of the human sciences to the ontological structure of understanding. It may be asked, however, whether the return route from ontology to epistemology is possible. For it is only along this route that one could confirm the assertion that questions of exegetico-historical critique are 'derivative', and that the hermeneutical circle, in the sense of the exegetes, is 'founded' on the fundamental anticipatory structure of understanding . . .

It seems to me that Gadamer's hermeneutics is prevented from embarking upon this route, not simply because, as with Heidegger, all effort of thought is invested in the radicalisation of the problem of foundation, but because the hermeneutical experience itself discourages the recognition of any critical instance.

The primary experience of this hermeneutics, determining the very place from which it raises its claim to universality, involves the refutation of the 'alienating distanciation' – *Verfremdung* – which commands the objectifying attitude of the human sciences. Henceforth the entire work assumes a dichotomous character which is indicated even in the title, *Truth and Method*, wherein the disjunction overrides the conjunction. It is this initial dichotomous situation which, it seems to me, prevents Gadamer from really recognising the critical instance and hence rendering justice to the critique of ideology, which is the modern post-Marxist expression of the critical instance. My own interrogation proceeds from this observation. Would it not be appropriate to shift the initial locus of the hermeneutical question, to reformulate the question in such a way that a certain dialectic between the experience of belonging and alienating distanciation becomes the mainspring, the key to the inner life, of hermeneutics?

The idea of such a shift in the initial locus of the hermeneutical question is suggested by the history of hermeneutics itself. Throughout this history, the emphasis has always come back to exegesis or philology, that is, to the sort of relation with tradition which is based on the mediation of texts, or documents and monuments which have a status comparable to texts. Schleiermacher was exegete of the New Testament and translator of Plato. Dilthey located the specificity of interpretation (*Auslegung*), as contrasted with the direct understanding of the other (*Verstehen*), in the phenomenon of fixation by writing and, more generally, of inscription.

In thus reverting to the problematic of the text, to exegesis and philology, we appear at first sight to restrict the aim and the scope of hermeneutics. However, since any claim to universality is raised from somewhere, we may expect that the restoration of the link between hermeneutics and exegesis will reveal its own universal features which, without really contradicting Gadamer's hermeneutics, will rectify it in a manner decisive for the debate with the critique of ideology.

I should like to sketch four themes which constitute a sort of critical supplementation to the hermeneutics of tradition.

(a) The distanciation in which this hermeneutics tends to see a sort of ontological fall from grace appears as a positive component of being for the text; it characteristically belongs to interpretation, not as its contrary but as its condition. The moment of distanciation is implied by fixation in writing and by all comparable phenomena in the sphere of the transmission of discourse. Writing is not simply a matter of the material fixation of discourse; for fixation is the condition of a much more fundamental phenomenon, that of the autonomy of the text. A threefold autonomy: with respect to the intention of the author; with respect to the cultural situation and all the sociological conditions of the production of the text; and finally, with respect to the original addressee. What the text signifies no longer coincides with what the author meant; verbal meaning and mental meaning have different destinies. This first form of autonomy already implies the possibility that the 'matter of the text' may escape from the author's restricted intentional horizon, and that the world of the text may explode the world of its author. What is true of psychological conditions is also true of sociological conditions, even though he who is prepared to liquidate the author is less prepared to perform the same operation in the sociological sphere. The peculiarity of the literary work, and indeed of the work as such, is nevertheless to transcend its own psycho-sociological conditions of production and thereby to open itself to an unlimited series of readings, themselves situated in socio-cultural contexts which are always different. In short, the work decontextualises itself, from the sociological as well as the psychological point of view, and is able to recontextualise itself differently in the act of reading. It follows that the mediation of the text cannot be treated as an extension of the dialogical situation. For in dialogue, the *vis-à-vis* of discourse is given in advance by the setting itself; with writing, the original addressee is transcended. The work itself creates an audience, which potentially includes anyone who can read.

The emancipation of the text constitutes the most fundamental condition for the recognition of a critical instance at the heart of interpretation; for distanciation now belongs to the mediation itself.

In a sense, these remarks only extend what Gadamer himself says, on the one hand, about 'temporal distance' which, as we have seen above, is one aspect of 'consciousness exposed to the efficacy of history'; and on the other hand, about *Schriftlichkeit* which, according to Gadamer himself, adds new features to *Sprachlichkeit*. But at the same time as this analysis extends Gadamer's, it shifts the emphasis somewhat. For the distanciation revealed by writing is already present in discourse itself, which contains the seeds of the distanciation of the said from the saying, to follow Hegel's famous analysis at the beginning of *The Phenomenology of Mind*: the saying vanishes, but the said persists. In this respect, writing does not represent a radical revolution in the constitution of discourse, but only accomplishes the latter's profoundest aim.

(b) If hermeneutics is to account for a critical instance in terms of its own premises, then it must satisfy a second condition: it must overcome the ruinous dichotomy, inherited from Dilthey, between 'explanation' and 'understanding'. As is well known, this dichotomy arises from the conviction that any explanatory attitude is borrowed from the methodology of the natural sciences and illegitimately extended to the human sciences. However, the appearance of semiological models in the field of the text convinces us that all explanation is not naturalistic or causal. The semiological models, applied in particular to the theory of the narrative, are borrowed from the domain of language itself, by extension from units smaller than the sentence to units larger than the sentence (poems, narratives, etc.). Here discourse must be placed under the category, no longer of writing but rather of the work, that is, under a category which pertains to praxis, to labour. Discourse is characterised by the fact that it can be produced as a work displaying structure and form. Even more than writing, the production of discourse as a work involves an objectification that enables it to be read in existential conditions which are always new. But in contrast to the simple discourse of conversation, which enters into the spontaneous movement of question and answer, discourse as a work 'takes hold' in structures calling for a description and an explanation that mediate 'understanding'. We are here in a situation similar to that described by Habermas: reconstruction is the path of understanding. However, this situation is not peculiar to psychoanalysis and to all that Habermas designates by the term 'depth hermeneutics'; it is the condition of the work in general. So if there is a hermeneutics – and here I oppose those forms of structuralism which would remain at the explanatory level – it must be constituted across the mediation rather than against the current of structural explanation. For it is the task of understanding to bring to discourse what is initially given as structure. It is necessary to have gone as far as possible along the route of objectification, to the point where structural analysis discloses the depth semantics of a text, before one can claim to 'understand' the text in terms of the 'matter' which speaks therefrom. The matter of the text is not what a naive reading of the text reveals, but what the formal arrangement of the text mediates. If that is so, then truth and method do not constitute a disjunction but rather a dialectical process.

(c) The hermeneutics of texts turns towards the critique of ideology in a third way. It seems to me that the properly hermeneutical moment arises when the interrogation, transgressing the closure of the text, is carried towards what Gadamer himself called 'the matter of the text', namely the sort of world opened up by it. This can be called the referential moment, in allusion to the Fregean distinction between sense and reference. The sense of the work is its internal organisation, whereas the reference is the mode of being unfolded in front of the text.

It may be noted in passing that the most decisive break with Romantic hermeneutics is here; what is sought is no longer an intention hidden behind the text, but a world unfolded in front of it. The power of the text to open a dimension of reality implies in principle a recourse against any given reality and thereby the possibility of a critique of the real. It is in poetic discourse that this subversive power is most alive. The strategy of this discourse involves holding two moments in equilibrium: suspending the reference of ordinary language and releasing a second order reference, which is another name for what we have designated above as the world opened up by the work. In the case of poetry, fiction is the path of redescription; or to speak as Aristotle does in the *Poetics*, the creation of a mythos, of a 'fable', is the path of mimesis, of creative imitation.

Here again we are developing a theme sketched by Gadamer himself, particularly in his magnificent pages on play. But in pressing to the end this meditation on the relation between fiction and redescription, we introduce a critical theme which the hermeneutics of tradition tends to cast beyond its frontiers. The critical theme was nevertheless present in the Heideggerian analysis of understanding. Recall how Heidegger conjoins understanding to the notion of 'the projection of my ownmost possibilities'; this signifies that the mode of being of the world opened up by the text is the mode of the possible, or better of the power-to-be: therein resides the subversive force of the imaginary. The paradox of poetic reference consists precisely in the fact that reality is redescribed only insofar as discourse is raised to fiction.

A hermeneutics of the power-to-be thus turns itself towards a critique of ideology, of which it constitutes the most fundamental possibility. Distanciation, at the same time, emerges at the heart of reference: poetic discourse distances itself from everyday reality, aiming towards being as power-to-be.

(d) In a final way, the hermeneutics of texts indicates the place for a critique of ideology. This final point pertains to the status of subjectivity in interpretation. For if the primary concern of hermeneutics is not to discover an intention hidden behind the text but to unfold a world in front of it, then authentic self-understanding is something which, as Heidegger and Gadamer wish to say, can be instructed by the 'matter of the text'. The relation to the world of the text takes the place of the relation to the subjectivity of the author, and at the same time the problem of the subjectivity of the reader is displaced. To understand is not to project oneself into the text but to expose oneself to it; it is to receive a self enlarged by the appropriation of the proposed worlds which interpretation unfolds. In sum, it is the matter of the text which gives the reader his dimension of subjectivity; understanding is thus no longer a constitution of which the subject possesses the key. Pressing this suggestion to the end, we must say that the subjectivity of the reader is no less held in suspense, no less potentialised, than the very world which the text unfolds. In other words, if fiction is a fundamental dimension of the reference of the text, it is equally a fundamental dimension of the subjectivity of the reader: in reading, I 'unrealise myself'. Reading introduces me to imaginative variations of the ego. The metamorphosis of the world in play is also the playful metamorphosis of the ego.

In the idea of the 'imaginative variation of the ego', I see the most fundamental possibility for a critique of the illusions of the subject. This link could remain hidden or undeveloped in a hermeneutics of tradition which introduced prematurely a concept of appropriation (*Aneignung*) directed against alienating distanciation. However, if distanciation from oneself is not a fault to be combated, but rather the condition of possibility of understanding oneself in front of the text, then appropriation is the dialectical counterpart of distanciation. Thus the critique of ideology can be assumed by a concept of self-understanding which organically implies a critique of the illusions of the subject. Distanciation from oneself demands that the appropriation of the proposed worlds offered by the text passes through the disappropriation of the self. The critique of false consciousness can thus become an integral part of hermeneutics, conferring upon the critique of ideology that meta-hermeneutical dimension which Habermas assigns to it.

2. Hermeneutical reflection on critique

I should like now to offer a similar reflection on the critique of ideology, with the aim of assessing the latter's claim to universality. I do not expect this reflection to return the critique of ideology to the fold of hermeneutics, but rather to confirm Gadamer's view that the two 'universalities', that of hermeneutics and that of the critique of ideology, are interpenetrating. The question could also be presented in Habermas's terms: on what conditions can critique be formulated as meta-hermeneutics? I propose to follow the order of the theses in terms of which I sketched Habermas's thought.

(1) I shall begin with the theory of interests which underlies the critique of the ideologies of transcendental phenomenology and positivism. It may be asked what authorises the following theses: that all *Forschung* is governed by an interest which establishes a prejudicial frame of reference for its field of meaning; that there are three such interests (and not one or two or four): namely, the technical interest, the practical interest and the interest in emancipation; that these interests are anchored in the natural history of the human species, but that they mark the emergence of man out of nature, taking form in the spheres of labour, power and language; that in self-reflection, knowledge and interest are one; that the unity of knowledge and interest is attested to in a dialectic which discerns the historical traces of the repression of dialogue and which reconstructs what has been suppressed.

Are these 'theses' empirically justifiable? No, for then they would fall under the yoke of the empirical-analytic sciences which pertain to one interest, the technical interest. Are these theses a 'theory', in the sense given to this word by psychoanalysis for example, that is, in the sense of a network of explanatory hypotheses permitting the reconstruction of a primitive scene? No, for then they would become regional theses as in any theory and would again be justified by one interest, the interest in emancipation perhaps; and the justification would become circular.

Is it not necessary to recognise henceforth that the disclosure of interests at the roots of knowledge, the hierarchical ordering of interests and their connection to the trilogy of labour-power-language, are dependent upon a philosophical anthropology similar to Heidegger's *Analytic of Dasein*, and more particularly to his hermeneutics of 'care'? If that is so, then these interests are neither observables, nor theoretical entities like the ego, the super-ego and the id in Freud's work, but rather 'existentiales'. Their analysis depends upon hermeneutics, insofar as they are at once 'the closest' and 'the most concealed', so that they must be disclosed in order to be recognised.

The analysis of interests could be called 'meta-hermeneutical', if it is supposed that hermeneutics is primarily a hermeneutics of discourse, indeed an idealism of lingual life. But we have seen that it has nothing to do with this, that the hermeneutics of pre-understanding is fundamentally a hermeneutics of finitude. Hence I am quite willing to say that the critique of ideology raises its claim from a different place than hermeneutics, namely from the place where labour, power and language are inter-twined. But the two claims cross on a common ground: the hermeneutics of finitude, which secures a priori the correlation between the concept of prejudice and that of ideology.

(2) I should like now to consider afresh the pact which Habermas establishes between critical social science and the interest in emancipation. We have sharply contrasted the positions of the critical social and the historical-hermeneutic sciences, the latter inclining towards recognition of the authority of traditions rather than towards revolutionary action against oppression.

Here the question which hermeneutics addresses to the critique of ideology is this: can you assign the interest in emancipation a status as distinct as you suppose with respect to the interest which animates the historical-hermeneutic sciences? The distinction is asserted so dogmatically that it seems to create a gulf between the interest in emancipation and the ethical interest. But the concrete analyses of Habermas himself belie this dogmatic aim. It is striking that the distortions which psychoanalysis describes and explains are interpreted, at the meta-hermeneutical level where Habermas places them, as distortions of communicative competence. Everything suggests that the distortions relevant to the critique of ideology also operate at this level. Recall how Habermas reinterprets Marxism on the basis of a dialectic between instrumental and communicative action. It is at the heart of communicative action that the institutionalisation of human relations undergoes the reification which renders it unrecognisable to the participants of communication. It follows that all distortions, those which psychoanalysis discovers as well as those which the critique of ideology denounces, are distortions of the communicative capacity of men.

So can the interest in emancipation be treated as a distinct interest? It seems not, especially if one considers that taken positively as a proper motif and no longer negatively in terms of the reifications which it combats, this interest has no other content than the ideal of unrestricted and unconstrained communication. The interest in emancipation would be quite empty and abstract if it were not situated on the same plane as the historical-hermeneutic sciences, that is, on the plane of communicative action. But if that is so, can a critique of distortions be separated from the communicative experience itself, from the place where it begins, where it is real and where it is exemplary? The task of the hermeneutics of tradition is to remind the critique of ideology that man can project his emancipation and anticipate an unlimited and unconstrained communication only on the basis of the creative reinterpretation of cultural heritage. If we had no experience of communication, however restricted and mutilated it was, how could we wish it to prevail for all men and at all institutional levels of the social nexus? It seems to me that critique can be neither the first instance nor the last. Distortions can be criticised only in the name of a consensus which we cannot anticipate merely emptily, in the manner of a regulative idea, unless that idea is exemplified; and one of the very places of exemplification of the ideal of communication is precisely our capacity to overcome cultural distance in the interpretation of works received from the past. He who is unable to reinterpret his past may also be incapable of projecting concretely his interest in emancipation.

(3) I arrive at the third point of disagreement between the hermeneutics of tradition and the critique of ideology. It concerns the abyss which seems to separate simple misunderstanding from pathological or ideological distortion. I shall not reconsider the arguments, already mentioned above, which tend to attenuate the difference between misunderstanding and distortion; a depth-hermeneutics is still a

hermeneutics, even if it is called meta-hermeneutical. I should like instead to emphasise an aspect of the theory of ideology which owes nothing to the parallel with psychoanalysis. A large part of Habermas's work is addressed, not to the theory of ideology taken abstractly, but to contemporary ideologies. Now when the theory of ideology is thus developed concretely in terms of a critique of the present, it reveals aspects which call for a concrete – and not simply a theoretical – rapprochement between the interest in emancipation and the interest in communication.

For what is, according to Habermas, the dominant ideology of the present day? His answer is close to that of Herbert Marcuse and Jacques Ellul: it is the ideology of science and technology. Here I shall not discuss Habermas's interpretation of advanced capitalism and of developed industrial societies; I shall go straight to the principal characteristic which, in my view, imperiously returns the theory of ideology to the hermeneutical field. In modern industrial society, according to Habermas, the traditional legitimations and basic beliefs once used for the justification of power have been replaced by an ideology of science and technology. The modern state is a state dedicated no longer to representing the interests of an oppressing class, but rather to eliminating the dysfunctions of the industrial system. To justify surplus-value by concealing its mechanism is thus no longer the primary legitimating function of ideology, as it was in the epoch of liberal capitalism described by Marx, quite simply because surplus-value is no longer the principal source of productivity and its appropriation the dominant feature of the system. The dominant feature of the system is the productivity of rationality itself, incorporated into self-regulating systems; what is to be legitimated, therefore, is the maintenance and growth of the system itself. It is precisely for this purpose that the scientific-technological apparatus has become an ideology, that is, a legitimation of the relations of domination and inequality which are necessary for the functioning of the industrial system, but which are concealed beneath all sorts of gratifications provided by the system. The modern ideology thus differs appreciably from that described by Marx, which prevailed only during the short period of liberal capitalism and possessed no universality in time. Nothing now remains of pre-bourgeois ideology, and bourgeois ideology was expressly linked to the camouflaging of domination in the legal institution of the free labour contract.

Granted this description of the modern ideology, what does it signify in terms of interest? It signifies that the sub-system of instrumental action has ceased to be a sub-system, and that its categories have overrun the sphere of communicative action. Therein consists the famous 'rationalisation' of which Max Weber spoke: not only does rationality conquer new domains of instrumental action, but it subjugates the domain of communicative action. Max Weber described this phenomenon in terms of 'disenchantment' and 'secularisation'; Habermas describes it as the obliteration of the difference between the plane of instrumental action, which is also that of labour, and the plane of communicative action, which is also that of agreed norms, symbolic exchanges, personality structures and rational decision-making procedures. In the modern capitalist system, which here seems identical with the industrial system as such, the ancient Greek question of the 'good life' is abolished in favour of the functioning of a manipulated system. The problems of praxis linked to communication – in particular the desire to submit important political questions to public discussion and democratic decision – have not disappeared; they persist, but in a repressed form.

Precisely because their elimination is not automatic and the need for legitimation remains unfulfilled, there is still the need for an ideology to legitimate the authority that secures the functioning of the system; science and technology today assume this ideological role.

But the question which hermeneutics then addresses to the critique of contemporary ideology is this: granted that ideology today consists in disguising the difference between the normative order of communicative action and bureaucratic conditioning, hence in dissolving the sphere of interaction mediated by language into the structures of instrumental action, how can the interest in emancipation remain anything other than a pious vow, save by embodying it in the reawakening of communicative action itself? And upon what will you concretely support the reawakening of communicative action, if not upon the creative renewal of cultural heritage?

(4) The inelectable link between the reawakening of political responsibility and reanimation of traditional sources of communicative action leads me to say a few words, in conclusion, about what appeared to be the most formidable difference between the hermeneutical consciousness and the critical consciousness. The first, we said, is turned towards a consensus which precedes us and, in this sense, which exists; the second anticipates a future freedom in the form of a regulative idea which is not a reality but an ideal, the ideal of unrestricted and unconstrained communication. With this apparent antithesis, we reach the liveliest but perhaps the most futile point in the debate. For in the end, hermeneutics will say, from where do you speak when you appeal to *Selbstreflexion*, if it is not from the place that you yourself have denounced as a non-place, the non-place of the transcendental subject? It is indeed from the basis of a tradition that you speak. This tradition is not perhaps the same as Gadamer's; it is perhaps that of the *Aufklärung*, whereas Gadamer's would be Romanticism. But it is a tradition nonetheless, the tradition of emancipation rather than that of recollection. Critique is also a tradition. I would even say that it plunges into the most impressive tradition, that of liberating acts, of the Exodus and the Resurrection. Perhaps there would be no more interest in emancipation, no more anticipation of freedom, if the Exodus and the Resurrection were effaced from the memory of mankind . . .

If that is so, then nothing is more deceptive than the alleged antinomy between an ontology of prior understanding and an eschatology of freedom. We have encountered these false antinomies elsewhere: as if it were necessary to choose between reminiscence and hope! In theological terms, eschatology is nothing without the recitation of acts of deliverance from the past.

In sketching this dialectic of the recollection of tradition and the anticipation of freedom, I do not want in any way to abolish the difference between hermeneutics and the critique of ideology. Each has a privileged place and, if I may say so, different regional preferences: on the one hand, an attention to cultural heritages, focused most decidedly perhaps on the theory of the text; on the other hand, a theory of institutions and of phenomena of domination, focused on the analysis of reifications and alienations. Insofar as each must always be regionalised in order to endow their claims to universality with a concrete character, their differences must be preserved against any conflationist tendency. But it is the task of philosophical reflection to eliminate deceptive antinomies which would oppose the interest in the reinterpretation of cultural heritages received from the past and the interest in the futuristic projections of a liberated humanity.

The moment these two interests become radically separate, then hermeneutics and critique will themselves be no more than . . . ideologies!

28

CHARLES TAYLOR
Interpretation and the sciences of man* (1971)

Is there a sense in which interpretation is essential to explanation in the sciences of man? The view that it is, that there is an unavoidably 'hermeneutical' component in the sciences of man, goes back to Dilthey. But recently the question has come again to the fore, for instance, in the work of Gadamer, in Ricœur's interpretation of Freud, and in the writings of Habermas.

Interpretation, in the sense relevant to hermeneutics, is an attempt to make clear, to make sense of an object of study. This object must, therefore, be a text, or a text-analogue, which in some way is confused, incomplete, cloudy, seemingly contradictory – in one way or another, unclear. The interpretation aims to bring to light an underlying coherence or sense.

This means that any science which can be called 'hermeneutical,' even in an extended sense, must be dealing with one or another of the confusing interrelated forms of meaning. Let us try to see a little more clearly what this involves.

1) We need, first, an object or field of objects, about which we can speak in terms of coherence or its absence, of making sense or nonsense.

2) Second, we need to be able to make a distinction, even if only a relative one, between the sense or coherence made, and its embodiment in a particular field of carriers or signifiers. For otherwise, the task of making clear what is fragmentary or confused would be radically impossible. No sense could be given to this idea. We have to be able to make for our interpretations claims of the order: the meaning confusedly present in this text or text-analogue is clearly expressed here. The meaning, in other words, is one which admits of more than one expression, and, in this sense, a distinction must be possible between meaning and expression.

The point of the above qualification, that this distinction may be only relative, is that there are cases where no clear, unambiguous, nonarbitrary line can be drawn between what is said and its expression. It can be plausibly argued (I think convincingly although there isn't space to go into it here) that this is the normal and

* From Charles Taylor, 'Interpretation and the Sciences of Man', in *Review of Metaphysics*, Vol. 25, No. 1, 1971, pp. 3–10. Reproduced with permission.

fundamental condition of meaningful expression, that exact synonymy, or equivalence of meaning, is a rare and localized achievement of specialized languages or uses of civilization. But this, if true (and I think it is), doesn't do away with the distinction between meaning and expression. Even if there is an important sense in which a meaning re-expressed in a new medium cannot be declared identical, this by no means entails that we can give no sense to the project of expressing a meaning in a new way. It does of course raise an interesting and difficult question about what can be meant by expressing it in a clearer way: what is the 'it' which is clarified if equivalence is denied? I hope to return to this in examining interpretation in the sciences of man.

Hence the object of a science of interpretation must be describable in terms of sense and nonsense, coherence and its absence; and must admit of a distinction between meaning and its expression.

3) There is also a third condition it must meet. We can speak of sense or coherence, and of their different embodiments, in connection with such phenomena as gestalts, or patterns in rock formations, or snow crystals, where the notion of expression has no real warrant. What is lacking here is the notion of a subject for whom these meanings are. Without such a subject, the choice of criteria of sameness and difference, the choice among the different forms of coherence which can be identified in a given pattern, among the different conceptual fields in which it can be seen, is arbitrary.

In a text or text-analogue, on the other hand, we are trying to make explicit the meaning expressed, and this means expressed by or for a subject or subjects. The notion of expression refers us to that of a subject. The identification of the subject is by no means necessarily unproblematical, as we shall see further on; it may be one of the most difficult problems, an area in which prevailing epistemological prejudice may blind us to the nature of our object of study. I think this has been the case, as I will show below. And moreover, the identification of a subject does not assure us of a clear and absolute distinction between meaning and expression as we saw above. But any such distinction, even a relative one, is without any anchor at all, is totally arbitrary, without appeal to a subject.

The object of a science of interpretation must thus have: sense, distinguishable from its expression, which is for or by a subject.

Before going on to see in what way, if any, these conditions are realized in the sciences of man, I think it would be useful to set out more clearly what rides on this question, why it matters whether or not we think of the sciences of man as hermeneutical, what the issue is at stake here.

The issue here is at root an epistemological one. But it is inextricable from an ontological one, and, hence, cannot but be relevant to our notions of science and of the proper conduct of inquiry. We might say that it is an ontological issue which has been argued ever since the seventeenth century in terms of epistemological considerations which have appeared to some to be unanswerable.

The case could be put in these terms: what are the criteria of judgment in a hermeneutical science? A successful interpretation is one which makes clear the meaning originally present in a confused, fragmentary, cloudy form. But how does one know that this interpretation is correct? Presumably because it makes sense of the original text: what is strange, mystifying, puzzling, contradictory is no longer so, is accounted for. The interpretation appeals throughout to our understanding of the 'language' of expression, which understanding allows us to see that this expression is puzzling, that it is in contradiction to that other, etc., and that these difficulties are cleared up when the meaning is expressed in a new way.

But this appeal to our understanding seems to be crucially inadequate. What if someone does not 'see' the adequacy of our interpretation, does not accept our reading? We try to show him how it makes sense of the original non- or partial sense. But for him to follow us he must read the original language as we do, he must recognize these expressions as puzzling in a certain way, and hence be looking for a solution to our problem. If he does not, what can we do? The answer, it would seem, can only be more of the same. We have to show him through the reading of other expressions why this expression must be read in the way we propose. But success here requires that he follow us in these other readings, and so on, it would seem, potentially forever. We cannot escape an ultimate appeal to a common understanding of the expressions, of the 'language' involved. This is one way of trying to express what has been called the 'hermeneutical circle.' What we are trying to establish is a certain reading of text or expressions, and what we appeal to as our grounds for this reading can only be other readings. The circle can also be put in terms of part-whole relations: we are trying to establish a reading for the whole text, and for this we appeal to readings of its partial expressions; and yet because we are dealing with meaning, with making sense, where expressions only make sense or not in relation to others, the readings of partial expressions depend on those of others, and ultimately of the whole.

Put in forensic terms, as we started to do above, we can only convince an interlocutor if at some point he shares our understanding of the language concerned. If he does not, there is no further step to take in rational argument; we can try to awaken these intuitions in him, or we can simply give up; argument will advance us no further. But of course the forensic predicament can be transferred into my own judging: if I am this ill-equipped to convince a stubborn interlocutor, how can I convince myself? how can I be sure? Maybe my intuitions are wrong or distorted, maybe I am locked into a circle of illusion.

Now one, and perhaps the only sane response to this would be to say that such uncertainty is an ineradicable part of our epistemological predicament. That even to characterize it as 'uncertainty' is to adopt an absurdly severe criterion of 'certainty,' which deprives the concept of any sensible use. But this has not been the only or even the main response of our philosophical tradition. And it is another response which has had an important and far-reaching effect on the sciences of man. The demand has been for a level of certainty which can only be attained by breaking beyond the circle. There are two ways in which this break-out has been envisaged. The first might be called the 'rationalist' one and could be thought to reach a culmination in Hegel. It does not involve a negation of intuition, or of our understanding of meaning, but rather aspires to attainment of an understanding of such clarity that it would carry with it the certainty of the undeniable. In Hegel's case, for instance, our full understanding of the whole in 'thought' carries with it a grasp of its inner necessity, such that we see how it could not be otherwise. No higher grade of certainty is conceivable.

For this aspiration the word 'break-out' is badly chosen; the aim is rather to bring understanding to an inner clarity which is absolute.

The other way, which we can call 'empiricist,' is a genuine attempt to go beyond the circle of our own interpretations, to get beyond subjectivity. The attempt is to reconstruct knowledge in such a way that there is no need to make final appeal to readings or judgments which cannot be checked further. That is why the basic building block of knowledge on this view is the impression, or sense-datum, a unit of information which is not the deliverance of a judgment, which has by definition no element in it of reading or interpretation, which is a brute datum. The highest ambition would be to build our knowledge from such building blocks by judgments which could be anchored in a certainty beyond subjective intuition. This is what underlies the attraction of the notion of the association of ideas, or if the same procedure is viewed as a method, induction. If the original acquisition of the units of information is not the fruit of judgment or interpretation, then the constatation that two such elements occur together need not either be the fruit of interpretation, of a reading or intuition which cannot be checked. For if the occurrence of a single element is a brute datum, then so is the co-occurrence of two such elements. The path to true knowledge would then repose crucially on the correct recording of such co-occurrences.

This is what lies behind an ideal of verification which is central to an important tradition in the philosophy of science, whose main contemporary protagonists are the logical empiricists. Verification must be grounded ultimately in the acquisition of brute data. By 'brute data,' I mean here and throughout data whose validity cannot be questioned by offering another interpretation or reading, data whose credibility cannot be founded or undermined by further reasoning. If such a difference of interpretation can arise over given data, then it must be possible to structure the argument so as to distinguish the basic, brute data from the inferences made on the basis of them.

The inferences themselves, of course, to be valid must similarly be beyond the challenge of a rival interpretation. Here the logical empiricists added to the armory of traditional empiricism which set great store by the method of induction, the whole domain of logical and mathematical inference which had been central to the rationalist position (with Leibniz at least, although not with Hegel), and which offered another brand of unquestionable certainty.

Of course, mathematical inference and empirical verification were combined in such a way that two theories or more could be verified of the same domain of facts. But this was a consequence to which logical empiricism was willing to accommodate itself. As for the surplus meaning in a theory which could not be rigorously co-ordinated with brute data, it was considered to be quite outside the logic of verification.

As a theory of perception, this epistemology gave rise to all sorts of problems, not least of which was the perpetual threat of skepticism and solipsism inseparable from a conception of the basic data of knowledge as brute data, beyond investigation. As a theory of perception, however, it seems largely a thing of the past, in spite of a surprising recrudescence in the Anglo-Saxon world in the thirties and forties. But there is no doubt that it goes marching on, among other places, as a theory of how the human mind and human knowledge actually function.

In a sense, the contemporary period has seen a better, more rigorous statement of what this epistemology is about in the form of computer-influenced theories of intelligence. These try to model intelligence as consisting of operations on machine-recognizable input which could themselves be matched by programs which could be run on machines. The machine criterion provides us with our assurance against an appeal to intuition or interpretations which cannot be understood by fully explicit procedures operating on brute data – the input.

The progress of natural science has lent great credibility to this epistemology, since it can be plausibly reconstructed on this model, as for instance has been done by the logical empiricists. And, of course, the temptation has been overwhelming to reconstruct the sciences of man on the same model; or rather to launch them in lines of inquiry that fit this paradigm, since they are constantly said to be in their 'infancy.' Psychology, where an earlier vogue of behaviorism is being replaced by a boom of computer-based models, is far from the only case.

The form this epistemological bias – one might say obsession – takes is different for different sciences. Later I would like to look at a particular case, the study of politics, where the issue can be followed out. But in general, the empiricist orientation must be hostile to a conduct of inquiry which is based on interpretation, and which encounters the hermeneutical circle as this was characterized above. This cannot meet the requirements of intersubjective, non-arbitrary verification which it considers essential to science. And along with the epistemological stance goes the ontological belief that reality must be susceptible to understanding and explanation by science so understood. From this follows a certain set of notions of what the sciences of man must be.

On the other hand, many, including myself, would like to argue that these notions about the sciences of man are sterile, that we cannot come to understand important dimensions of human life within the bounds set by this epistemological orientation. This dispute is of course familiar to all in at least some of its ramifications. What I want to claim is that the issue can be fruitfully posed in terms of the notion of interpretation as I began to outline it above.

I think this way of putting the question is useful because it allows us at once to bring to the surface the powerful epistemological beliefs which underlie the orthodox view of the sciences of man in our academy, and to make explicit the notion of our epistemological predicament implicit in the opposing thesis. This is in fact rather more way-out and shocking to the tradition of scientific thought than is often admitted or realized by the opponents of narrow scientism. It may not strengthen the case of the opposition to bring out fully what is involved in a hermeneutical science as far as convincing waverers is concerned, but a gain in clarity is surely worth a thinning of the ranks – at least in philosophy.

29

CLIFFORD GEERTZ
The thick description of culture* (1973)

The concept of culture I espouse, and whose utility the essays below attempt to demonstrate, is essentially a semiotic one. Believing, with Max Weber, that man is an animal suspended in webs of significance he himself has spun, I take culture to be those webs, and the analysis of it to be therefore not an experimental science in search of law but an interpretive one in search of meaning. It is explication I am after, construing social expressions on their surface enigmatical. But this pronouncement, a doctrine in a clause, demands itself some explication.

Operationalism as a methodological dogma never made much sense so far as the social sciences are concerned, and except for a few rather too well-swept corners – Skinnerian behaviorism, intelligence testing, and so on – it is largely dead now. But it had, for all that, an important point to make, which, however we may feel about trying to define charisma or alienation in terms of operations, retains a certain force: if you want to understand what a science is, you should look in the first instance not at its theories or its findings, and certainly not at what its apologists say about it; you should look at what the practitioners of it do . . .

. . . ethnography is thick description. What the ethnographer is in fact faced with – except when (as, of course, he must do) he is pursuing the more automatized routines of data collection – is a multiplicity of complex conceptual structures, many of them superimposed upon or knotted into one another, which are at once strange, irregular, and inexplicit, and which he must contrive somehow first to grasp and then to render. And this is true at the most down-to-earth, jungle field work levels of his activity: interviewing informants, observing rituals, eliciting kin terms, tracing property lines, censusing households . . . writing his journal. Doing ethnography is like trying to read (in the sense of 'construct a reading of') a manuscript – foreign, faded, full of ellipses, incoherencies, suspicious emendations, and tendentious commentaries, but written not in conventionalized graphs of sound but in transient examples of shaped behavior . . .

* From 'Thick Description: Toward an Interpretative Theory of Culture' by Clifford Geertz in *The Interpretation of Cultures: Selected Essays*, Basic Books, 1973. Printed with permission by HarperCollins Publishers, 1973, pp. 5, 10–13.

Culture, this acted document, thus is public, like a burlesqued wink or a mock sheep raid. Though ideational, it does not exist in someone's head; though unphysical, it is not an occult entity. The interminable, because unterminable, debate within anthropology as to whether culture is 'subjective' or 'objective,' together with the mutual exchange of intellectual insults ('idealist!' – 'materialist!'; 'mentalist!' – 'behaviorist!'; 'impressionist!' – 'positivist!') which accompanies it, is wholly misconceived. Once human behavior is seen as (most of the time; there are true twitches) symbolic action – action which, like phonation in speech, pigment in painting, line in writing, or sonance in music, signifies – the question as to whether culture is patterned conduct or a frame of mind, or even the two somehow mixed together, loses sense. The thing to ask about a burlesqued wink or a mock sheep raid is not what their ontological status is. It is the same as that of rocks on the one hand and dreams on the other – they are things of this world. The thing to ask is what their import is: what it is, ridicule or challenge, irony or anger, snobbery or pride, that, in their occurrence and through their agency, is getting said.

This may seem like an obvious truth, but there are a number of ways to obscure it. One is to imagine that culture is a self-contained 'superorganic' reality with forces and purposes of its own; that is, to reify it. Another is to claim that it consists in the brute pattern of behavioral events we observe in fact to occur in some identifiable community or other; that is, to reduce it. But though both these confusions still exist, and doubtless will be always with us, the main source of theoretical muddlement in contemporary anthropology is a view which developed in reaction to them and is right now very widely held – namely, that, to quote Ward Goodenough, perhaps its leading proponent, 'culture [is located] in the minds and hearts of men.'

Variously called ethnoscience, componential analysis, or cognitive anthropology (a terminological wavering which reflects a deeper uncertainty), this school of thought holds that culture is composed of psychological structures by means of which individuals or groups of individuals guide their behavior. 'A society's culture,' to quote Goodenough again, this time in a passage which has become the *locus classicus* of the whole movement, 'consists of whatever it is one has to know or believe in order to operate in a manner acceptable to its members.' And from this view of what culture is follows a view, equally assured, of what describing it is – the writing out of systematic rules, an ethnographic algorithm, which, if followed, would make it possible so to operate, to pass (physical appearance aside) for a native. In such a way, extreme subjectivism is married to extreme formalism, with the expected result: an explosion of debate as to whether particular analyses (which come in the form of taxonomies, paradigms, tables, trees, and other ingenuities) reflect what the natives 'really' think or are merely clever simulations, logically equivalent but substantively different, of what they think.

As, on first glance, this approach may look close enough to the one being developed here to be mistaken for it, it is useful to be explicit as to what divides them. If, leaving our winks and sheep behind for the moment, we take, say, a Beethoven quartet as an, admittedly rather special but, for these purposes, nicely illustrative, sample of culture, no one would, I think, identify it with its score, with the skills and knowledge needed to play it, with the understanding of it possessed by its performers or auditors, nor, to take care, *en passant*, of the reductionists and reifiers, with a particular performance of it or with some mysterious entity transcending material existence. The 'no one' is perhaps too strong here, for there are always incorrigibles. But that a Beethoven quartet is a temporally developed tonal structure, a coherent sequence of modeled sound – in a word, music – and not anybody's knowledge of or belief about anything, including how to play it, is a proposition to which most people are, upon reflection, likely to assent.

To play the violin it is necessary to possess certain habits, skills, knowledge, and talents, to be in the mood to play, and (as the old joke goes) to have a violin. But violin playing is neither the habits, skills, knowledge, and so on, nor the mood, nor (the notion believers in 'material culture' apparently embrace) the violin. To make a trade pact in Morocco, you have to do certain things in certain ways (among others, cut, while chanting Quranic Arabic, the throat of a lamb before the assembled, undeformed, adult male members of your tribe) and to be possessed of certain psychological characteristics (among others, a desire for distant things). But a trade pact is neither the throat cutting nor the desire, though it is real enough, as seven kinsmen of our Marmusha sheikh discovered when, on an earlier occasion, they were executed by him following the theft of one mangy, essentially valueless sheepskin from Cohen.

Culture is public because meaning is. You can't wink (or burlesque one) without knowing what counts as winking or how, physically, to contract your eyelids, and you can't conduct a sheep raid (or mimic one) without knowing what it is to steal a sheep and how practically to go about it. But to draw from such truths the conclusion that knowing how to wink is winking and knowing how to steal a sheep is sheep raiding is to betray as deep a confusion as, taking thin descriptions for thick, to identify winking with eyelid contractions or sheep raiding with chasing woolly animals out of pastures. The cognitivist fallacy – that culture consists (to quote another spokesman for the movement, Stephen Tyler) of 'mental phenomena which can [he means "should"] be analyzed by formal methods similar to those of mathematics and logic' – is as destructive of an effective use of the concept as are the behaviorist and idealist fallacies to which it is a misdrawn correction. Perhaps, as its errors are more sophisticated and its distortions subtler, it is even more so.

The generalized attack on privacy theories of meaning is, since early Husserl and late Wittgenstein, so much a part of modern thought that it need not be developed once more here. What is necessary is to see to it that the news of it reaches anthropology; and in particular that it is made clear that to say that culture consists of socially established structures of meaning in terms of which people do such things as signal conspiracies and join them or perceive insults and answer them, is no more to say that it is a psychological phenomenon, a characteristic of someone's mind, personality, cognitive structure, or whatever, than to say that Tantrism, genetics, the progressive form of the verb, the classification of wines, the Common Law, or the notion of 'a conditional curse' . . . is. What, in a place like Morocco, most prevents those of us who grew up winking other winks or attending other sheep from grasping what people are up to is not ignorance as to how cognition works (though, especially as, one assumes, it works the same among them as it does among us, it would greatly help to have less of that too) as a lack of familiarity with the imaginative universe within which their acts are signs. As Wittgenstein has been invoked, he may as well be quoted:

'We . . . say of some people that they are transparent to us. It is, however, important as regards this observation that one human being can be a complete enigma to another. We learn this when we come into a strange country with entirely strange traditions; and, what is more, even given a mastery of the country's language. We do not understand the people. (And not because of not knowing what they are saying to themselves.) We cannot find our feet with them.'

30

AARON CICOUREL
Method and measurement* (1964)

I have assumed throughout the book that the nature of collective life – its social institutions such as kinship and bureaucratic organization, its ecological arrangements, both the areal distribution of living conditions (residence and work) and the physical distance which in part determines the formation of primary or secondary relations, and general norms and values which are explicit – is then the distinct subject matter of sociology and it provides us with a set of boundary conditions which we assume determines or sets limits upon social conduct and life in general. But a large part of collective life is also problematic to define because of its essentially oral tradition and because even its formally stated written tradition is subject to the differential perception and interpretation of actors variously distributed in the social structures. Thus, what is written about policy, ideology, values, norms, and even scientific knowledge about natural events and objects does not describe what determines the actor's conduct because of problematic features in the social action scene. The oral tradition which characterizes institutional norms and values and ideologies can be viewed as policy statements that are sometimes perceived as explicit, but they are frequently implicit and unstated although conversation or concrete action may make them explicit. Thus, the very questionaire items posed about implicit values, norms, and ideologies may crystallize some of their relatively amorphous properties. I have focused on the unstated, including both stable and problematic, features of social action because they are the most difficult to measure by means of methodological devices available to the sociologist. I have argued that because of their dependence for stability on the actor's perception and interpretation of them, the measurement of the stated and formal features of everyday life (even after assuming that social institutions and ecological arrangements delimit the forms of collective life) and, especially, the unstated conditions of everyday life are sufficiently indeterminate to raise serious questions about the measurement systems now in use. I have also implied that some

* Reprinted with the permission of The Free Press, a Division of Simon & Schuster, Inc., from *Method and Measurement in Sociology* by Aaron V. Cicourel. Copyright © 1964 by The Free Press. Pp. 221–224.

forms of everyday life may never be measured very precisely because of the innovative elements in social action.

Our actor is a constructed type in the sense used by Max Weber. We are in the business of constructing an actor and subtypes which we imagine to be gifted with consciousness. But this consciousness is restricted precisely to those theoretical features which hopefully are relevant to operational procedures and empirical confirmation by observation. To this fictitious consciousness the observer assigns typical cultural motives for achieving future action and typical cultural motives imputed to others for understanding their action. In addition we construct what Schutz calls 'course-of-action types' (i.e., typical patterns of behavior) which we impute to anonymous others we do not know. These course-of-action types include invariant motives which presumably govern the others' actions. Schutz continues:

> Yet these models of actors are not human beings living within their biographical situation in the social world of everyday life. Strictly speaking, they do not have any biography or any history, and the situation into which they are placed is not a situation defined by them but defined by their creator, the social scientist. He has created these puppets or homunculi to manipulate them for his purpose. A merely specious consciousness is imputed to them by the scientist which is constructed in such a way that its presupposed stock of knowledge at hand (including the ascribed set of invariant motives) would make actions originating therefrom subjectively understandable, provided that these actions were performed by real actors within the social world. But the puppet and his artificial consciousness is not subjected to the ontological conditions of human beings. The homunculus was not born, he does not grow up, and he will not die. He has no hopes and no fears; he does not know anxiety as the chief motive of all his deeds. He is not free in the sense that his acting could transgress the limits his creator, the social scientist, has predetermined. He cannot, therefore, have other conflicts of interests and motives than those the social scientist has imputed to him. He cannot err, if to err is not his typical destiny. He cannot choose, except among the alternatives the social scientist has put before him as standing to his choice.
>
> (Alfred Schutz, 'Common-Sense and Scientific Interpretation of Human Action', *Philosophy and Phenomenological Research*, 14, 1953, p. 32)

The model of the actor outlined by Schutz enables the social scientist to make explicit the inner horizon of ('subjective') social action as defined by Weber. The construction of typical motives, roles, cues, constancies, unstated meanings, and so forth permits their possible manipulation under experimental or quasi-experimental conditions.

The sociological observer, therefore, who fails to conceptualize the elements of common-sense acts in everyday life, is using an implicit model of the actor which is confounded by the fact that his observations and inferences interact, in unknown ways, with his own biographical situation within the social world. The very conditions of obtaining data require that he make use of typical motives, cues, roles, etc., and the typical meanings he imputes to them, yet the structures of these common-sense courses of action are notions which the sociological observer takes for granted, treats as self-evident. But they are just the notions which the sociologist must analyze and study empirically if he desires rigorous measurement. The distributions he now constructs relegate such notions to a taken-for-granted status or to some latent continuum. Therefore, the observations which go to make up a distribution of, say, types of cities, responses to questionnaire items, or occupational prestige categories are only half of the picture. The distribution merely represents the 'outer' horizon for which operational procedures have been devised. Yet the 'meaning' of the distribution relies upon common-sense knowledge which includes the observer's typification of the world as it is founded in his own biographical situation, and his formalization of the actor's typification which is inextricably woven into his response. Both sets of typifications must be objects of sociological inquiry.

The inner horizon of idiomatic expressions, course-of-action motives, institutional and innovational language, and the like remain unclarified in the sociologist's distributions. The observations which are coded into dichotomies, fourfold tables, ordinal scales, zero-order correlations, and distributions in general reveal only half of the story; the 'bottom half' has been taken for granted, relegated to a 'latent continuum,' yet informs the observer's description and inferences about the 'top half' represented by 'rigorous' measurement devices. It is the lack of explicit conceptualization and observation on the 'bottom half' which makes measurement in sociology metaphorical and not literal. The difficulty is to be found in the lack of adequate conceptualization and the use of measurement axioms which do not correspond to the structure of social action.

Conventional measurement systems may have a moderate correspondence with the institutional features of everyday life.

31

HAROLD GARFINKEL
Rational properties of scientific and common-sense activities* (1960)

The program of his discipline requires that the sociologist scientifically describe a world that includes as problematical phenomena not only the other person's actions, but the other person's knowledge of the world. As a result, the sociologist cannot avoid some working decision with respect to the various phenomena intended by the term 'rationality.'

Commonly, sociological researchers decide on a definition of rationality by selecting one or more features from among the properties of scientific activity as it is ideally described and understood. The definition is then used methodologically to aid the researcher in deciding the realistic, pathological, prejudiced, delusional, mythical, magical, ritual, and similar features of everyday conduct, thinking and beliefs.

But because sociologists find with such overwhelming frequency that effective, persistent, and stable actions and social structures occur despite obvious discrepancies between the lay person's and the ideal scientist's knowledge and procedures, they have found that the rational properties which their definitions discriminated are empirically uninteresting. They have preferred instead to study the features and conditions of non-rationality in human conduct. The result is that in most of the available theories of social action and social structure rational actions are assigned residual status.

With the hope of correcting a trend, it is the purpose of this paper to remedy this residual status by re-introducing as a problem for empirical inquiry (a) the various rational properties of conduct, as well as (b) the conditions of a social system under which various rational behaviors occur.

* From Harold Garfinkel 'Rational Properties of Scientific and Common-sense Activities', *Behavioural Science*, 5(1) 1960, pp. 72–76, 79, 82. Produced with permission.

Rational behaviours

'Rationality' has been used to designate many different ways of behavior. A list of such behaviors can be made without treating any one as definitive of the term 'rationality.' Alfred Schutz' classical paper on the problem of rationality ('The Problem of Rationality in the Social World', *Economica*, 10, 130–149, 1943) inventories these meanings and is our point of departure.

When the various meanings of the term which Schutz inventoried are phrased as descriptions of conduct, the following list of behaviors results. In the remainder of the paper, these behaviours will be referred to as 'the rationalities.'

1. Categorizing and comparing. It is commonplace for a person to search his experience for a situation with which to compare the one he addresses. Sometimes rationality refers to the fact that he searches the two situations with regard to their comparability, and sometimes to his concern for making matters comparable. To say that a person addresses the tasks of comparison is equivalent to saying that he treats a situation or a person or a problem as an instance of a type. Thereby the notion of a 'degree of rationality' is encountered. The extensiveness of a person's concern with classification, the frequency of this activity, the success with which he engages in it are frequently the behaviors meant by saying that one person's activities are more rational than another's.

2. Tolerable error. It is possible for a person to 'require' varying degrees of 'goodness of fit' between an observation and a theory in terms of which he names, measures, describes, or otherwise intends the sense of his observation as a datum. He may pay a little or a lot of attention to the degree of fit. On one occasion he will allow a literary allusion to describe what has occurred. On another occasion and for the same occurrences he may search the mathematical journals for a model to order them. It is sometimes said, then, that one person is rational while another is not or is less so, when that person pays closer attention than does his neighbor to the degree of fit between what he has observed and what he intends as his finding.

3. Search for 'means.' Rationality is sometimes used to mean that a person reviews rules of procedures which in the past yielded the practical effects now desired. Sometimes it is the fact that a person seeks to transfer rules of practice which had a payoff in situations of like character; sometimes it is the frequency of this effort; at other times the rational character of his actions refers to the person's ability or inclination to employ in a present situation techniques that worked in other situations.

4. Analysis of alternatives and consequences. Frequently the term rationality is used to call attention to the fact that a person, in assessing a situation, anticipates the alterations which his actions will produce. Not only the fact that he 'rehearses in imagination' the various courses of action which will have occurred; but the care, attention, time, and elaborateness of analysis paid to alternative courses of action are frequent references. With respect to the activity of 'rehearsing in imagination' the competing lines of actions-that-will-have-been-completed, the clarity, extent of

detail, the number of alternatives, the vividness and the amount of information which fills out each of the schemata of competing lines of action are often the intended features in calling a person's actions 'rational.'

5. Strategy. Prior to the actual occasion of choice a person may assign to a set of alternative courses of action the conditions under which any one of them is to be followed. Von Neuman and Morgenstern (*Theory of Games and Economic Behaviour,* Princeton, 1947) have called the set of such decisions a player's strategy. The set of such decisions can be called the strategy character of the actor's anticipations. A person whose anticipations are handled with the belief that his circumstances tomorrow will be like those he has known in the past is sometimes said to be acting with less rationality than the one who addresses alternatively possible future states of his present situation by the use of a manual of 'what-to-do-in-case-ofs.'

6. Concern for timing. When we say that a person intends through his behaviors to realize a future state of affairs, we frequently mean that the person entertains an expectations of the scheduling of events. The concern for timing involves the extent to which he takes a position with regard to the possible ways in which events can occur temporally. A definite and restricted frame of scheduled possibilities is compared with a 'lesser rationality' that consists of the person orienting the future fall of events under the aspect of 'anything can happen.'

7. Predictability. Highly specific expectations of time scheduling can be accompanied by a concern with the predicatible character of a situation. A person may seek preliminary information about the situation in order to establish some empirical constants, or he may attempt to make the situation predictable by examining the logical properties of the constructs he uses in 'defining' it or by reviewing the rules that govern the use of his constructs. Accordingly, making the situation predictable means taking whatever measures are possible to reduce 'surprise.' Both the desire for 'surprise in small amounts' and the use of whatever measures yield it are frequently the behaviors intended by the term rationality.

8. Rules of procedure. Sometimes rationality refers to rules of procedure and inference in terms of which a person decides the correctness of his judgements, inferences, perceptions and characterizations. Such rules define the distinct ways in which a thing may be known – distinctions, for example, between fact, supposition, evidence, illustration, and conjecture. For our purposes two important classes of such rules of correct decisions may be distinguished: 'Cartesian' rules and 'tribal' rules. Cartesian rules propose that a decision is correct because the person followed the rules without respect for persons, i.e., that the decision was made without regard for social affiliation. By contrast, 'tribal' rules provide that a decision is or is not correct according to whether certain interpersonal solidarities are respected as conditions of the decision. The person counts his decision right or wrong in accordance with whom it is referentially important that he be in agreement.

The term rationality is frequently used to refer to the application of Cartesian rules of decision. Because conventions may impose constraints on such decision making, the extent to which the constraints are suppressed, controlled, or rendered ineffective or irrelevant is another frequent meaning of rationality.

9. Choice. Sometimes the fact that a person is aware of the actual possibility of exercising a choice and sometimes the fact that he chooses, are popular meanings of rationality.

10. Grounds of choice. The grounds upon which a person exercises a choice among alternatives as well as the grounds he uses to legitimize a choice are frequently pointed out as rational features of an action. Several different behavioral meanings of the term 'grounds' need to be discriminated.

(a) Rational grounds sometimes refer exclusively to the scientific corpus of information as an inventory of propositions which is treated by the person as correct grounds of further inference and action.

(b) Rational grounds sometimes refer to such properties of a person's knowledge as the 'fine' or 'gross' structure of the characterizations he uses, or whether the 'inventory' consists of a set of stories as compared with universal empirical laws, or the extent to which the materials are codified, or whether the corpus in use accords with the corpus of scientific propositions.

(c) Grounds of a person's choice may be those which he quite literally finds through retrospectively interpreting a present outcome. For example, in the effort to determine what was 'really' decided at a prior time, a person may realize such grounds in the course of historicizing an outcome. Thus, if a present datum is treated as an-answer-to-some-question, the datum may motivate the original question. Selecting, arranging, and unifying the historical context of an action after its occurrence so as to present a publicly acceptable or coherent account of it is a familiar meaning of 'rationalization.'

11. Compatibility of ends-means relationships with principles of formal logic. A person may treat a contemplated course of action as an arrangement of steps in the solution of a problem. He may arrange these steps as a set of 'means-ends' relationships but count the problem solved only if these relationships are accomplished without violating the ideal of full compatibility with the principles of formal scientific logic and the rules of scientific procedure. The fact that he may do so, the frequency with which he does so, his persistence in treating problems in this way, or the success that he enjoys in following such procedures, are alternative ways of specifying the rationality of his actions.

12. Semantic clarity and distinctness. Reference is often made to a person's attempt to treat the semantic clarity of a construction as a variable with a maximum value which must be approximated as a required step in solving the problem of constructing a credible definition of a situation. A person who withholds credence until the condition of approximate maximum value has been met is frequently said to be more rational than another who will lend credence to a mystery. A person may assign a high

priority to the tasks of clarifying the constructs which make up a definition of a situation and of deciding the compatibility of such constructs with meanings intended in terminologies employed by others. On the other hand, a person may pay little attention to such tasks. The former action is sometimes said to be more rational than the latter.

13. Clarity and distinctness 'for its own sake.' Schutz points out that a concern for distinctness that is adequate for person's purposes. Different possible relationships, ideal or actual, between (a) a concern for clarity and (b) the purposes which the clarity of the construct serves reveal additional behavioral meanings of rationality. Two variables are involved: (1) how highly one esteems clarification for its own sake, and (2) the value assigned by the person to the accomplishment of a project. One relationship between these variables makes the task of clarification itself the project to be accomplished. This is the meaning of 'clarification for its own sake.' But the relationship between the two variables may be treated by a person as consisting in some degree of independent variability. Such a relationship would be meant when treating as an ideal 'clarification that is sufficient for present purposes.' Rationality frequently means a high degree of dependence of one upon the other. Such a dependence when treated as a rule of investigative or interpretive conduct is sometimes meant in the distinction between 'pure' and 'applied' research and theory.

14. Compatibility of the definition of a situation with scientific knowledge. A person can allow what he treats as 'matters of fact' to be criticized in terms of their compatibility with the body of scientific findings. The 'allowed legitimacy of such criticism' means that in the case of a demonstrated discrepancy between what the person treats as correct grounds of inference (the meaning of 'fact') and what has been demonstrated as correct, the former will be changed to accommodate to the latter. Thus a person's actions are said to be rational to the extent that he accommodates or is prepared to accommodate to what is scientifically the case.

Frequently rationality refers to the person's feelings that accompany his conduct, e.g. 'affective neutrality,' 'unemotional,' 'detached,' 'disinterested,' and 'impersonal.' For the theoretical tasks of this paper, however, the fact that a person has such feelings is uninteresting. It is of interest, however, that a person uses his feelings about his environment to recommend the sensible character of the thing he is talking about or the warrant of a finding. There is nothing that prohibits a scientific investigator from being passionately hopeful that his hypothesis will be confirmed. He is prohibited, however, from using his passionate hope or his detachment of feeling to recommend the sense or warrant of a proposition. A person who treats his feelings about a matter as irrelevant to its sense or warrant is sometimes said to be acting rationally, while a person who recommends sense and warrant by invoking his feelings is said to act with less rationality. This holds, however, only for ideally described scientific activities.

Scientific rationalities

The foregoing rationalities may be used to construct an image of a person as a type of behavior. A person can be conceived who may search a present situation for its points of comparability to situations that he knew in the past and may search his past experience for formulas that have yielded the practical effects he now seeks to bring about. In this task he may pay close attention to these points of comparability. He may anticipate the consequences of his acting according to the formulas that recommend themselves to him. He may 'rehearse in imagination' various competing lines of action. He may assign to each alternative, by a decision made prior to the actual occasion of choice, the conditions under which any one of the alternatives is to be followed. Along with such structurings of experience as these, the person may intend through his behaviors to realize a projected outcome. This may involve his paying specific attention to the predictable characteristics of the situation that he seeks to manipulate. His actions may involve the exercise of choice between two or more means for the same ends or of a choice between ends. He may decide the correctness of his choice by invoking empirical laws. And so on.

In extending the features of this behavioral type to incorporate all of the preceding rationalities, a distinction arises between the interests of everyday life and the interests of scientific theorizing. Where a person's actions are governed by the 'attitude of daily life,' all of the rationalities can occur with four important exceptions. Phrased as ideal maxims of conduct, these excepted rationalities state that the projected steps in the solution of a problem or the accomplishment of a task, i.e., the 'means-ends relationships,' be constructed in such a way (1) that they remain in full compatibility with the rules that define scientifically correct decisions of grammar and procedure; (2) that all the elements be conceived in full clearness and distinctness; (3) that the clarification of both the body of knowledge as well as the rules of investigative and interpretive procedure be treated as a first priority project; and (4) that the projected steps contain only scientifically verifiable assumptions that have to be in full compatibility with the whole of scientific knowledge. The behavioral correlates of these maxims were described before as rationalities 11 through 14. For ease of reference I shall refer to these four as 'the scientific rationalities.'

It is the crux of this paper and of a research program that would follow if its arguments are correct, that the scientific rationalities, in fact, occur as stable properties of actions and as sanctionable ideals only in the case of actions governed by the attitude of scientific theorizing. By contrast, actions governed by the attitude of daily life are marked by the specific absence of these rationalities either as stable properties or as sanctionable ideals. Where actions and social structures governed by the presuppositions of everyday life are concerned, attempts to stabilize these features or to compel adherence through socially systematic administration of rewards and punishments are the operations required to multiply the anomic features of interaction. All of the other rationalities, 1 through 10, however, can occur in actions governed by either attitude, both as stable properties and sanctionable ideals.

The preceding assertions are meant as empirical matters not as doctrinal ones. The reconstruction of the 'problem of rationality' proposed by this paper depends upon the warranted character of these assertions. Their test depends upon a viable distinction between the 'attitude of daily life' and the 'attitude of scientific theorizing.' . . .

Methodology

It is the scientific rationalities which writers on social organization and decision making commonly refer to as features of 'rational choice.' It is proposed here, however, that the scientific rationalities are neither properties of nor sanctionable ideals of choices exercised within the affairs governed by the presuppositions of everyday life. If the scientific rationalities are neither stable properties nor sanctionable ideals of everyday life, then the troubles encountered by researchers and theorists with respect to the concepts of organizational purposes, the role of knowledge and ignorance in interaction, the difficulties in handling meaningful messages in mathematical theories of communication, the anomalies found in studies of betting behavior, the difficulties in rationalizing the concept of abnormality in light of cross-cultural materials may be troubles of their own devising. The troubles would be due not to the complexities of the subject matter, but to the insistence on conceiving actions in accordance with scientific conceits instead of looking to the actual rationalities that persons' behaviors, in fact, exhibit in the course of managing their practical affairs . . .

It has been the purpose of this paper to recommend the hypothesis that the scientific rationalities can be employed only as ineffective ideals in the actions governed by the presuppositions of everyday life. The scientific rationalities are neither stable features nor sanctionable ideals of daily routines, and any attempt to stabilize these properties or to enforce conformity to them in the conduct of everyday affairs will magnify the senseless character of a person's behavioral environment and multiply the anomic features of the system of interaction.

Bold as the statement may be, it does no violence whatever; and, in fact, it is entirely compatible with current sociological discourse and current sociological theories and findings. Sociologists have long been concerned with the task of describing the conditions of organized social life under which the phenomena of rationality in conduct occur. One of these conditions is continually documented in sociological writings: routine as a necessary condition of rational action. Max Weber, in his neglected distinction between substantive rationality and formal rationality, and almost alone among sociological theorists, used the distinction between the two sets of rationalities throughout his work, although he proposed the distinction on the basis of a keen methodological intuition rather than on empirical grounds.

The relationships between routine and rationality are incongruous ones if they are viewed either according to everyday common sense or according to most philosophical teachings. But sociological inquiry accepts almost as a truism that the ability of a person to act 'rationally' – that is, the ability of a person in conducting his everyday affairs to calculate, to project alternative plans of action, to select before the actual fall of events the conditions under which he will follow one plan or another, to give priority in a selection of means to their technical efficacy and the rest – depends upon the fact that the person must be able literally to take for granted, to take under trust, a vast array of features of the social order. In order to treat rationally the 1/10th of his situation that, like an iceberg, appears above the water, he must be able to treat the 9/10ths that lies below as an unquestioned and, even more interestingly, as an unquestionable background of matters that are demonstrably relevant to his calculation, but which appear without being noticed. In his famous discussion of the normative backgrounds of activity, Emile Durkheim made much of the point that the validity and understandability of the stated terms of a contract depended upon the unstated terms that the contracting parties took for granted as binding upon their action.

The sociologist refers to these trusted, taken for granted, background features of the person's situation, that is, the routine aspects of the situation that permit 'rational action,' as mores and folkways. Among sociologists the mores depict the ways in which routine is a condition for the appearance of rational action or, in psychiatric terms, for the operativeness of the 'reality principle.' The mores have been used, thereby, to show how the stability of social routine is a condition which enables persons in the course of their everyday affairs to recognize each other's actions, beliefs, aspirations, feelings, and the like as reasonable, normal, legitimate, understandable, and realistic.

32

ERVING GOFFMAN
Primary frameworks* (1974)

When the individual in our Western society recognizes a particular event, he tends, whatever else he does, to imply in this response (and in effect employ) one or more frameworks or schemata of interpretation of a kind that can be called primary. I say primary because application of such a framework or perspective is seen by those who apply it as not depending on or harking back to some prior or 'original' interpretation; indeed a primary framework is one that is seen as rendering what would otherwise be a meaningless aspect of the scene into something that is meaningful.

Primary frameworks vary in degree of organization. Some are neatly presentable as a system of entities, postulates, and rules; others – indeed, most others – appear to have no apparent articulated shape, providing only a lore of understanding, an approach, a perspective. Whatever the degree of organization, however, each primary framework allows its user to locate, perceive, identify, and label a seemingly infinite number of concrete occurrences defined in its terms. He is likely to be unaware of such organized features as the framework has and unable to describe the framework with any completeness if asked, yet these handicaps are no bar to his easily and fully applying it.

In daily life in our society a tolerably clear distinction is sensed, if not made, between two broad classes of primary frameworks: natural and social. Natural frameworks identify occurrences seen as undirected, unoriented, unanimated, unguided, 'purely physical.' Such unguided events are ones understood to be due totally, from start to finish, to 'natural' determinants. It is seen that no willful agency causally and intentionally interferes, that no actor continuously guides the outcome. Success or failure in regard to these events is not imaginable; no negative or positive sanctions are involved. Full determinism and determinateness prevail. There is some understanding that events perceived in one such schema can be reductively translated into ones perceived in a more 'fundamental' framework and that some premises, such as the notion of the conservation of energy or that of a single, irreversible time, will be shared

* From 'Primary Frameworks' in *Frame Analysis: An Essay in the Organization of Experience* by Erving Goffman, New York: Harper & Row. Copyright © 1974 by Erving Goffman. Pp. 21–28.

by all. Elegant versions of these natural frameworks are found, of course, in the physical and biological sciences. An ordinary example would be the state of the weather as given in a report.

Social frameworks, on the other hand, provide background understanding for events that incorporate the will, aim, and controlling effort of an intelligence, a live agency, the chief one being the human being. Such an agency is anything but implacable; it can be coaxed, flattered, affronted, and threatened. What it does can be described as 'guided doings.' These doings subject the doer to 'standards,' to social appraisal of his action based on its honesty, efficiency, economy, safety, elegance, tactfulness, good taste, and so forth. A serial management of consequentiality is sustained, that is, continuous corrective control, becoming most apparent when action is unexpectedly blocked or deflected and special compensatory effort is required. Motive and intent are involved, and their imputation helps select which of the various social frameworks of understanding is to be applied. An example of a guided doing would be the newscast reporting of the weather. So one deals here with deeds, not mere events. (We support some perceivedly basic distinctions within the social sphere, such as that between human and animal purposiveness, but more of this later.) We use the same term, 'causality,' to refer to the blind effect of nature and the intended effect of man, the first seen as an infinitely extended chain of caused and causing effects and the second something that somehow begins with a mental decision.

In our society we feel that intelligent agents have the capacity to gear into the ongoing natural world and exploit its determinacy, providing only that natural design is respected. Moreover, it is felt that, with the possible exception of pure fantasy or thought, whatever an agent seeks to do will be continuously conditioned by natural constraints, and that effective doing will require the exploitation, not the neglect, of this condition. Even when two persons play checkers by keeping the board in their heads, they will still have to convey information concerning moves, this exchange requiring physically competent, willful use of the voice in speech or the hand in writing. The assumption is, then, that although natural events occur without intelligent intervention, intelligent doings cannot be accomplished effectively without entrance into the natural order. Thus any segment of a socially guided doing can be partly analyzed within a natural schema.

Guided doings appear, then, to allow for two kinds of understanding. One, more or less common to all doings, pertains to the patent manipulation of the natural world in accordance with the special constraints that natural occurrings impose; the other understanding pertains to the special worlds in which the actor can become involved, which, of course, vary considerably. Thus each play in checkers involves two radically different bases for guidance: one pertains to quite physical matters – to the physical management of the vehicle, not the sign; the other pertains to the very social world of opposing positions that the play has generated, wherein a move can equally well be made by voice, gesture, or the mails, or by physically shifting a checker by the fist, any combination of fingers, or the right elbow. Behavior at the board can easily be separated into making moves and shifting checkers. And an easy distinction can be drawn between a clumsy move, one that ill considers the strategic positions of the two players, and a move made clumsily, one that has been badly executed according to local social standards for accomplishing physical acts. Observe that although an adult with a newly acquired prosthetic device might play checkers fully mindful of the physical task involved, ordinary players do not. Decisions as to which move to make are problematic and significant; pushing the checker once the decision is made is neither. On the other hand, there are guided doings such as fixing a sink or clearing a sidewalk in which sustained, conscious effort is given to manipulating the physical world, the doing itself taking on the identity of an 'instrumental procedure,' a task, a 'purely utilitarian' activity – a doing the purpose of which cannot be easily separated from the physical means employed to accomplish it.

All social frameworks involve rules, but differently. For example, a checker move is informed by rules of the game, most of which will be applied in any one complete playing through of the game; the physical manipulation of a checker, on the other hand, involves a framework informing small bodily movements, and this framework, if indeed it is possible to speak in terms of a or one framework, might well be manifest only partially during the playing of a game. So, too, although the rules for checkers and the rules of vehicular traffic can be (and are) well enough explicated within the confines of a small booklet, there is a difference: the game of checkers incorporates an understanding of the governing purpose of the participants, whereas the traffic code does not establish where we are to travel or why we should want to, but merely the restraints we are to observe in getting there.

In sum, then, we tend to perceive events in terms of primary frameworks, and the type of framework we employ provides a way of describing the event to which it is applied. When the sun comes up, a natural event; when the blind is pulled down in order to avoid what has come up, a guided doing. When a coroner asks the cause of death, he wants an answer phrased in the natural schema of physiology; when he asks the manner of death, he wants a dramatically social answer, one that describes what is quite possibly part of an intent.

The idea of a primary framework is, then, the first concept that is needed: I wish it were more satisfactory. For example, there is the embarrassing fact that during any one moment of activity, an individual is likely to apply several frameworks. ('We waited till the rain stopped and then started the game again.') Of course, sometimes a particular framework is chiefly relevant and provides a first answer to the question 'What is it that's going on here?' The answer: an event or deed described within some primary framework. Then one can begin to worry about the microanalytic issues of what is meant by 'we,' 'it,' and 'here' and how the implied consensus is accomplished.

Now a further consideration is necessary. When an x and y axis can be located as the framework within which to identify a given point, or a checkerboard is brought to mind as a matrix within which to locate a move, the notion of a primary framework is clear enough, although even here there is the issue of the dependency of a particular framework upon our understanding of frameworks of that type. When one looks at some ordinary happening in daily life, say, a passing greeting or a customer's request for the price of an article, an identification of the primary framework is, as already suggested, very considerably more problematic. Here indeed is where the writers in the tradition I am employing have quietly fallen down. To speak here of 'everyday life' or, as Schutz does, of the 'world of wide-awake practical realities' is merely to take a shot in the dark. As suggested, a multitude of frameworks may be involved or none at all. To proceed, however, an operating fiction might be accepted, at least temporarily, namely, that acts of daily living are understandable because of some primary framework (or frameworks) that informs them and that getting at this schema will not be a trivial task or, hopefully, an impossible one.

In describing primary frameworks so far I have limited attention to those that are assumed (explicitly or in effect) by the individual in deciding what it is that is going on, given, of course, his particular interests. The individual, it is true, can be 'wrong' in his interpretations, that is, misguided, out of touch, inappropriate, and so forth. 'Wrong' interpretations will be considered throughout. Here I want only to mention the belief that in many cases the individual in our society is effective in his use of particular frameworks. The elements and processes he assumes in his reading of the activity often are ones that the activity itself manifests – and why not, since social life itself is often organized as something that individuals will be able to understand and deal with. A correspondence or isomorphism is thus claimed between perception and the organization of what is perceived, in spite of the fact that there are likely to be many valid principles of organization that could but don't inform perception. And just as others in our society find this an effective claim, so do I . . .

Taken all together, the primary frameworks of a particular social group constitute a central element of its culture, especially insofar as understandings emerge concerning principal classes of schemata, the relations of these classes to one another, and the sum total of forces and agents that these interpretive designs acknowledge to be loose in the world. One must try to form an image of a group's framework of frameworks – its belief system, its 'cosmology' – even though this is a domain that close students of contemporary social life have usually been happy to give over to others. And note that across a territory like the United States there is an incomplete sharing of these cognitive resources. Persons otherwise quite similar in their beliefs may yet differ in regard to a few assumptions, such as the existence of second sight, divine intervention, and the like. (Belief in God and in the sacredness of His local representatives seems to constitute currently one of the largest bases of dissensus in our society concerning ultimate forces. Tact ordinarily prevents social scientists from discussing the matter.)

PART 3
The critical tradition

Introduction: a general outline

The presentation of the selected readings in this part follows the development of critical theory which, for present purposes, can be divided into three phases. Correspondingly, the readings can be regarded as falling into three distinct groups. Readings 33 (Horkheimer) and 34 (Marcuse), stemming from the second decade after its founding in the early 1920s, represent critical theory in the pre-Second World War context which was characterized by the emergence of Fascism and the ossification of Marxism, on the one hand, and the ascendancy of the neo-positivist philosophy of science, on the other. While the critical theorists had already been engaged in treating positivism as an object of critique, at this stage they did not yet move the debate explicitly to the level of the philosophy of social science. Their epistemological and methodological concerns were nevertheless plain to see. It is only in the 1960s, in the context of the so-called 'Positivist Dispute' and its aftermath signalling the second phase of critical theory, that such a shift would be made quite deliberately and consciously. This is documented by readings 35 to 38. As the leading critical theorists, Jürgen Habermas in particular, came to prominence through the Positivist Dispute, which coincided with the dissolution of positivism, the emergence of post-empiricism, the student movement, and the increasing acknowledgement of different theoretical and methodological approaches in the social sciences, so critical theory also gained international recognition. On this basis, critical theory entered its third phase of development which was characterized by its international reception, as is represented by readings 39 (Roberto Mangabeira Unger) and 40 (Alvin Gouldner).

Critical theory, institutionally embodied in the Institute for Social Research founded originally in 1923 in Frankfurt but forced to go into exile in Geneva and New York and re-established in Frankfurt after the Second World War, was brought to maturity only after Max Horkheimer (1895–1973) had taken over its directorship in 1930 and Herbert Marcuse (1898–1979) had become a member in 1932. Upon the formal accession to his new post, Horkheimer outlined the framework of an interdisciplinary, critical social scientific programme, what he called 'interdisciplinary materialism' which was at once rooted in European philosophy (particularly Kant,

Hegel and Marx), receptive to contemporary research techniques, and focused on current social questions and issues. While an active inner circle around Horkheimer was responsible for the Institute's core achievement, including Pollock, Fromm, Lowenthal and Adorno, who became a member only in 1938, Marcuse proved in the 1930s to be one of critical theory's principal architects. From 1930, Horkheimer published a series of articles, most of them in the Institute's journal *Zeitschrift für Sozialforschung*, in which he set out the principles of the Frankfurt School, complemented by pieces written by other members of the Institute, including Marcuse. In these publications, we witness a battle being fought simultaneously on two different fronts with a view to establishing critical theory as a credible, new, interdisciplinary social scientific departure.

On the one hand, Horkheimer and Marcuse critically renewed their own Hegelian-Marxist tradition which had assumed a dogmatic orthodox form, and on the other they moved in against the conventional conception of social science of the time represented by neo-Kantianism, phenomenology, the sociology of knowledge and above all neo-positivism. Whereas the social scientific weakness of Marxism needed to be overcome, the narrow scientistic rationality of the established scientific enterprise had to be corrected and broadened. The most characteristic achievement of this period was undoubtedly Horkheimer's tradition-founding formulation of critical theory against the background of this relentless exposure of the epistemological, methodological and practical limits of the dominant positions of the time. The critical theorists were also very interested in integrating Freud's social psychology into a more rigorous theory of society.

As exiles due to Fascism, the first generation of critical theorists could hardly have been more acutely aware of the dangers lurking in metaphysical and ideological modes of thinking. Yet in the 1930s, they were actively engaged in criticisms of the determined neo-positivist attempt to cleanse science definitively of metaphysics, including all forms of philosophy. At times, whole articles would be devoted to this task, as in the case of Horkheimer, Marcuse and Adorno, but more often the critical theorists interspersed their writings with efforts to salvage philosophy in so far as it plays a role in the interdisciplinary interrelation of the social sciences, as a placeholder of social scientific problems, or as a repository of normative visions and imaginative vanishing points. Besides its approach to the problem of demarcation, however, positivism itself – both the older form of positivism and in particular the dominant logical positivism or logical empiricism of the time – was an object of direct criticism at the epistemological and methodological as well as the ideological level. For instance, positivism's fixation on the given, its emphasis on sensory-instrumental experience alone, the principles of induction, deduction and verification, its claim to objectivity, neutrality and value-freedom – all were targeted by the critical theorists from a variety of angles. This did not prevent them, however, from incorporating the most advanced techniques into their research, such as for instance on workers and employees, authority and the family, and so forth. On the contrary, they expressly sought to overcome the dissociation of theoretical construction and empirical research. Indeed, at a time when a sharp and disturbing decline of social scientific research occurred in the Weimar Republic, the Frankfurt School stood out as the only exception to the rule. The commitment to bring together theory with both quantitative and qualitative research, which they would maintain for some 30 years, was honoured during their exile in the USA, as many instances of collaboration with American social scientists as well as the mammoth study of the 1950s, *The Authoritarian Personality*, demonstrate.

Upon his return to Germany after the Second World War, Horkheimer resolved to teach German students the most advanced social scientific research methods and techniques within the framework of what he called 'critical research', and in this he was joined by Adorno who produced a series of articles on social research during the first half of the 1950s. A diverse range of research projects using innovative methods was undertaken in the newly established Institute for Social Research, but for various reasons a sharp decline set in around the mid-1950s which led to the unfortunate displacement of the idea of critical research by culture criticism. Against the background of a lack of research collaborators of quality, the paradoxical German phenomenon of the simultaneous reactionary opposition to new techniques and the ascendancy of American-style empirical research, Horkheimer and Adorno effectively withdrew from research, with disastrous consequences. The Positivist Dispute was the watershed.

On the one hand, the lapse of critical theory into cultural criticism without social scientific qualities during the early part of the controversy between 1957 and the early 1960s culminated in the stark opposition of theory to research or the critical focus on society as a whole to all empirical work. The mistaken and misleading alternatives of theoretical and empirical sociology were encouraged by both Karl Popper and Hans Albert, the opponents of the critical theorists in the controversy, but Adorno also reinforced it, while even Habermas' arguments were not free from the contrast. On the other hand, however, this ironic self-obstruction of the dispute made possible a renewed transcendence of the divide, first in critical theory itself, thus marking the second phase in its development, but to a certain extent also more broadly. Whereas empirical research devoid of any theory and pure theory in the form of a conceptual classificatory system had for long tended to operate side by side in the social sciences without taking any interest in one another, the Positivist Dispute had the effect of pointing up the possibility of overcoming this debilitating coexistence. Besides suggestions in his much noted interventions in the controversy, Habermas' writings of the latter half of the 1960s – including *On the Logic of the Social Sciences* (originally 1967) and *Knowledge and Human Interests* (originally 1968) – proved to be decisive, but Karl-Otto Apel also made a significant and extensive contribution, including *Analytic Philosophy of Language and the 'Geisteswissenschaften'* (originally 1965), 'Scientistics, Hermeneutics, Ideology-Critique: Outline of a Philosophy of Science from the Viewpoint of the Anthropology of Knowledge' (1968) and the later 'Types of Social Science in the Light of Cognitive Interests' (1977), partially reproduced below.

From these works it became apparent that the Positivist Dispute had not been about the opposition of theoretical sociology represented by the critical theorists and empirical sociology represented by the positivists, but rather about two divergent forms of the production of social scientific knowledge, each with its own concepts of theory and the empirical dimension and its own combination of the two. Beyond this, moreover, Habermas and Apel separated the different strands still intertwined in a confusing way in the arguments put forward during the Positivist Dispute to show that, rather than two, there are actually three distinct forms of social scientific knowledge production. The first is empirical-analytical social science which constitutes and deals with social reality as an objective-instrumental reality by means of explanation; the second is hermeneutic or understanding social science which approaches social reality as a symbolic-interpretative reality and proceeds by means of interpretation; and finally there is critical social science for which social reality is a normative yet ideologically deformed reality which calls for critique consisting of the mediation and advancement of understanding through a moment of explanation. Basic to this threefold methodological distinction was the concept of cognitive interests. Apel showed that Habermas at times identified too closely with social interests. Be that as it may, Habermas and Apel thus not merely questioned and relativized the notions of empirical sciences and hermeneutical sciences both philosophically and methodologically, but proposed a comprehensive philosophy of the social sciences with a typologically differentiated methodology at its core which Apel has over the years developed most extensively and consistently.

Horkheimer's essays of the 1930s anticipated the basic arguments that were later employed in criticism of positivism and the interpretative tradition. Yet it is in the drastically changed significance acquired in the Positivist Dispute that these arguments in the late 1960s and 1970s entered the widening international debate about the philosophy of the social sciences. Albrecht Wellmer, who was active also within critical theory in the development of the arguments, played an important role in advancing the reception of Habermas' work in particular and critical theory more generally. His book, *Critical Theory of Society* (1969), from which the reading below was selected, was central here, but it had been developed against the background of a penetrating critical analysis of Popper's theory of science published two years earlier. Marcuse's popularity as spokesman of the student movement in the USA and as representative of critical theory's emancipatory concept of science provided favourable conditions for this international reception. On the one hand, critical theory's threefold typologically differentiated methodology proved to be of central significance, as is borne out by the fact that it had become the standard framework for the presentation of the methodology of the social sciences by the 1990s. On the other hand, this was possible only once critical theory's philosophy of the social sciences had been confronted and corrected by exchanges with new post-empiricist (see Part 1), post-Heideggerian hermeneutic (see Part 2) and other later developments. These corrections involved a mitigation of the mistaken opposition of the empirical and the symbolic, a better grasp of nature as self-organizing, a more constructivist approach to nature and more broadly reality, and the mitigation of the sharp division between science and everyday knowledge.

The selected texts

Max Horkheimer (1895–1973), the most important figure in the history of the Frankfurt Institute for Social Research, was a founding member of this institution and as successor of Carl Grünberg became its third director in 1930, officially installed in 1931. In his opening address, 'The Current Condition of Social Philosophy and the Task of an Institute of Social Research', he sketched an interdisciplinary research programme with synthetic goals oriented towards a positive change of society that would be focused by historical-political experience of the age, guided by a materialist theory of society and filled out by substantive empirical work. But since he was convinced that it was necessary for a theory of society to avoid the sheer accumulation of merely empirical material, as was typical of the American social sciences, empirical research was always treated as a means and never as a goal in itself. Horkheimer's inaugural address marked the beginning of a series of some eight articles spelling out the principles of critical theory and distinguishing it epistemologically, methodologic-ally and politically from its liberal, conservative and even socialist competitors – i.e. from positivism, interpretativism and orthodox Marxism respectively. The famous essay 'Traditional and Critical Theory' of 1937, from which the reading below was selected, represents the highpoint of this endeavour by Horkheimer to establish the common epistemological-methodological framework of the critical social science of the Frankfurt School. In the selected excerpt, he criticizes the established social scien-tific practice of his day, whether positivism more generally or the sociology of know-ledge more particularly, as well as its supporting philosophy inspired by the natural sciences, and opposes his own philosophy of critical social science to it. In his view, the conventional position involves a traditional Cartesian approach, typically embodied in a special science (e.g. sociology) within the fragmented division of scientific labour, which assumes a sharp divide between the subject of knowledge as an individual and the object of knowledge as an extrinsic reality consisting of pure factuality governed by logical necessity. Particularly problematic, from his viewpoint, is the series of polarities or dualisms this entails, including subject-object, fact-value and knowledge-action. In its study of social reality, it proceeds, completely unaware of the larger set of relations of which it forms a part, by relating theory in the sense of abstract universal concepts to reality by means of hypotheses deduced from the theory with a view to making a classificatory judgements about which factual relations are likely to occur. Critical social science, by contrast, is a self-aware and reflective practice which, shun-ning all polarities and dualisms, acknowledges that it forms an inherent part of the development of society and hence that the object of study is affected by the social scientist's theory which helps to shape it into a meaningful human necessity. Hork-heimer admits that it is conceivable that it could on occasion make use of the hypothetico-deductive approach, yet at best it would remain but a subordinate aspect of the critical social scientific endeavour to arrive at historically sensitive existential rather than abstract classificatory judgements about society as a process in which the individual's purposefulness, spontaneity, rationality and constructive activity find their rightful place.

Herbert Marcuse (1898–1979), who had studied with Husserl and Heidegger in Freiburg but upon the break with the latter left for Frankfurt, with the help of Husserl joined the Institute for Social Research in 1932, representing with Horkheimer phil-osophy as one of the four core disciplines of the Institute's 'interdisciplinary material-ism'. In 1934 he fled to the USA where he stayed until his death, associating with the Institute in exile during the 1930s, perhaps the most fruitful decade in the history of this institution, and well into the 1940s. It is as one of the Institute's major theoreti-cians, now under Horkheimer's rather than Heidegger's influence, that he published the essay 'Philosophy and Critical Theory' in 1937 from which the excerpt below was selected. In the essay, as the title suggests, he seeks to distinguish critical theory from philosophy in such a way that critical theory nevertheless retains a philosophical core. Simultaneously, he also tries to distinguish critical theory from science as understood by both the philosophy of science and scientistic Marxism, without rejecting critical theory as critical social science. As against philosophy which in its various guises 'leaves everything in the external world as it was', exchanges the 'progressive element of philosophy' for a 'whimsy and uninhibited opportunism' or turns away from contemporary society to 'orient itself toward another realm that does not conflict with the material world', Marcuse links critical theory to the 'practical aim' of the 'creation of a rational society', salvages the lost philosophical emphasis on human potentialities such as 'freedom, happiness and rights', and stresses critical theory's 'constructive character' in so far as it is a factor in the human endeavour of bringing into being a better society. It is specifically against the foil of the constructive character of critical theory that he launches an attack against positivism's predilection for 'making reality into a criterion' and thus to 'simply register and systematize facts'. Critical theory rather retains, in the form of 'constructive concepts', the 'imagination' or 'phantasy' as the core of philosophy which enables us to envision realizable potentialities or possibilities and thus to avoid getting bogged down in the present. The incorporation of this faculty does not imply, however, that critical theory surrenders its scientific character. Critical social science indeed resists the negative implications of science in at least three respects: being reduced to just a 'methodology', being crippled by the 'fateful fetishism of science' deriving from science's entanglement in and perpetuation of 'relations of domination', and finally being colonized by vulgar 'scientific' Marxism. By contrast, critical social science engages in a 'constant critique of scientific aims and methods' and, instead of taking science 'a priori as a conceptual model' for itself and for society, seeks to shape science into something that serves a 'human form' of society.

Theodor W. Adorno (1903–1969), although eight years his junior, had a close relation to Horkheimer since the 1920s, but it is only after he joined up with the Institute in exile in New York in 1938 upon the completion of his studies in Oxford that he became the influential figure in the Frankfurt School with whom we are familiar today. In the lecture on the relation of philosophy and science which he delivered upon entering an academic career at the University of Frankfurt in 1931 a few months after Horkheimer's inaugural address, Adorno gave an intimation of his later well-known 'negative dialectics' and against that background sketched some of his own epistemological and methodological ideas. Circumstances had changed to such an extent, according to him, that it was no longer possible to study the social process in a systematic manner. Presenting itself in fragments and trails, the analysis of society could proceed only by means of tracking or ascertaining traces which methodologically in turn called for a monographic approach focusing through immanent analysis on the study of exemplary cases in order to discover the general in the particular. Adorno always maintained this predilection of his, also after his return from exile. This is apparent not only from the important series of some ten articles on the social sciences, sociology and empirical research dating from the first years after his return to Frankfurt and published in the 1950s, but also from the remainder of his work up to his death in 1969. The selected reading is an excerpt from one of the ten articles mentioned above, 'Sociology and Empirical Research' dating from 1957 which marks the beginning of the controversy which would come to a head in 1961 and become known as the Positivist Dispute. Starting from different practices in sociology, Adorno in the text sharply distinguishes the 'critical theory of society' from the positivist 'empirical social science' in its different varieties, all of which are based on the social scientifically inappropriate 'natural scientific model'. While he criticizes empirical social science severely and at length, he simultaneously also offers a critique of ' "interpretative" sociology' or sociology as a 'cultural science'. The basic problem with these different directions is that, unlike critical social science, they neglect to start from and always return to the 'societal conditions' of investigated social phenomena which can be accessed through the historically specific 'living experience' of society and account both for the 'genesis of the existing forms' and for the 'tendency which reaches beyond them'. Interpretative sociology, on the one hand, uncritically takes the substratum of understanding as unified and meaningful and thus overlooks the fact that it has already been deformed by the 'obduracy of society' which 'continually reduces human beings to objects and transforms their condition into 'second nature'. Empirical social science, on the other hand, approaches social reality as a harmonious object consisting of generally classifiable, atomistic, brute facts which it unreflectively and blindly seeks to reproduce and mirror and through hypotheses attempts to forecast in their regularly expected consequences. In Adorno's view, this implies that it operates with an undialectical 'hypostatized method' which merely duplicates a reified and distorted reality and thus at best serves administrative purposes and at worst takes the form of an ideology which helps to perpetuate unchanged the existing state of affairs. Critical social science, by contrast, is a reflective approach which constructs its object, the 'societal totality', from 'living experience', the historical development of societal relationships and conditions within the horizon of the future, and hence the 'tension of the possible and the real'. Rather than the scientistic 'dichotomy of induction and deduction', therefore, Adorno insists that it proceeds dialectically, combining these moments in such a way that critical social science is willing to employ both 'quantitative and qualitative' methods and techniques to further its own philosophically inspired and theoretically guided 'immanent analysis'.

Jürgen Habermas (1929–), perhaps the single most influential philosopher and sociologist of the second half of the twentieth century, inherited the mantle of the Frankfurt School from Horkheimer, Adorno and Marcuse and thus became the leading second generation critical theorist. Since their student days, he has been fundamentally influenced by his friend, colleague and collaborator Apel, who is seven years his senior. Due to his readiness to engage in debates and his generally brilliant contributions, Habermas has had a wide-ranging impact, besides philosophy and theology, on virtually all humanities and social science disciplines – particularly their epistemological and methodological self-understanding. His incisive contributions to the Positivist Dispute of the early 1960s first brought him to prominence, but it is through his subsequent related writings, such as *On the Logic of the Social Sciences* (1967, translation 1988), the inaugural address 'Knowledge and Human Interests' (1965, translation 1972) and the book *Knowledge and Human Interests* (1968, translation

1972) spelling out his theory of cognitive interests, that he was able to shape the philosophy of the social sciences. This was reinforced by his leading role in a series of debates, including the so-called Habermas-Gadamer debate and Habermas-Luhmann debate. However, due to difficulties in his attempt to formulate epistemology directly in the form of social theory – i.e. identifying cognitive interests too directly with social interests and conceiving of critical social science too immediately as emancipatory – he felt compelled in the early 1970s to modify his position by placing the social sciences on a linguistic or more broadly a communicative and discourse theoretical footing. It is only very recently, more precisely in 1999 (see Part 6), that he has sought to clarify philosophically what this implies. These reflections benefited from Habermas' practice of social scientific research. Between 1971 and 1981, he was director of the Max Planck Institute in Starnberg, near Munich, where a large number of research projects were conducted within an institution organized in a particular manner. What we learn from all this regarding the practical implications of his philosophy of the social sciences is that Habermas remained committed to the practice of social scientific research along the lines of the early Frankfurt School's 'interdisciplinary materialism' and that it involved both quantitative and qualitative analysis within a broad critical thrust. In the first of the two selected texts, an extract from his inaugural lecture, Habermas introduces his theory of the three 'technical', 'practical' and 'emancipatory' cognitive or 'knowledge-constitutive interests' which are rooted in 'work', 'language' and 'power' or mastery (*Herrschaft*) and guide research in the 'empirical-analytical', the 'historical-hermeneutical' and the social sciences, particularly 'critical social science'. This he does against the background of a broad attack on the 'illusion of objectivism' or 'positivistic self-understanding of the sciences' – i.e. naturalistic instrumentalism in empirical-analytic science and historicism in the historical-hermeneutic sciences – by showing that it not only overlooks the cognitive interest which makes each of the different categories of science transcendentally possible, but also abandons the 'dimension in which acting subjects could arrive rationally at agreement about goals and purposes'. According to Habermas, it would be possible to outgrow the resulting world of arbitrariness and instrumentalism in which we live today and to move in the direction of an 'emancipated society' only if critical social science is allowed its full sway and we come to recognize that the sciences, far from just being a matter of gaining technical control over objectified processes and of keeping particular traditions alive, are a crucial factor in actually realizing a society in which the members are free, autonomous and responsible and organize their world through 'non-authoritarian and universally practiced dialogue'. In the second text, Habermas links up directly with Horkheimer's 'interdisciplinary materialism' and in the process also reframes Marcuse's statement of the relation between philosophy and critical theory. Starting from the theory of communicative action, critical social science no longer depends for its normative reference point on the ideology critique of modern culture, but enters into a cooperative relation with philosophy. Critical social science takes the form of a 'reconstructive science' in which 'the operations of empirical science and of philosophical conceptual analysis intermesh'. He draws reconstructions of 'pre-theoretical knowledge' about, for instance, structural change or development from philosophy and builds it into 'empirical theories', thus rendering them 'fallibilistic', and seeks to establish a 'coherence' between the philosophical and scientific components which would allow it to engage in a 'critique of deformations' in the realization of available potentialities for the organization of society. That Habermas does not operate with the conventional understanding of 'empirical science' is indicated by the fact that he understands the empirical in the broad sense of including not only objective material but also symbolic material and hidden forces in need of being ferreted out; and he insists that the experience which guides critical social science is not simply sensory and instrumental or even communicative experience but rather the living experience of society as a totality. We gain this experience through the emergence of an 'objective challenge', a 'provocative threat' or 'problem situations' which problematize our 'background knowledge' and compel us to transform it into 'explicit knowledge'. Critical social science is 'conscious of the self-referentiality of its calling' and accordingly proceeds 'reflectively' only to the extent that it is alive to this fundamental kind of experience which Horkheimer already took to be characteristic of critical theory.

In the second reading, which is from the conclusion to his later and important two volume *Theory of Communicative Action* (1981), Habermas argues, in response to the new social movements of the period, that a critical theory of society must be grounded less on cognitive interests than on communicative processes in society more generally. In this respect he moves more decisively beyond the old critical theory and its assumptions about modernity.

Karl-Otto Apel (1922–), Professor of Philosophy at the University of Frankfurt from the early 1970s to his retirement in 1990 and one of Germany's internationally best-known philosophers of social science, since the Positivist Dispute played a leading role together with Habermas in the defence and development of critical theory, and over many years exhibited a particular interest in the philosophy of the social sciences. Indeed, he is the critical theorist who has contributed by far the most to the philosophy of science, particularly critical social science. On the one hand, he embedded this philosophy of science in an 'anthropology of knowledge' which was in turn incorporated in a broad 'transcendental pragmatic' philosophical framework (see Part 4). On the other, he acted as an internal critic of the Frankfurt tradition of critical theory in general and of Habermas in particular, and in the process provided many of the leading ideas for the creative continuation of critical theory. In the reading, an excerpt from a long essay on different types of social science, we witness these different sides of Apel's contribution. Starting from the centrality of 'leading interests of knowledge' and proceeding to a philosophy of science offering an alternative to the positivism of logical empiricism and Popper (see Part 1) but also to an advanced hermeneutic position such as Ricoeur's (see Part 2), he elaborates the concept in a highly differentiated way well beyond Habermas' earlier account. This involves emphasizing the element of the constitution of the object of study or constructivism more strongly and conceiving of reality, including nature, in a more differentiated way. On this basis, he is able to make a distinction not only between natural and social science; but also among four different types of social science: 'quasi-nomological behavioural science', focusing on 'regularities' and hence the 'explanation and prediction' of behaviour, and 'quasi-biologistic functionalist systems theory', focusing on society as part of a self-organizing nature, which stand in a relationship of 'complementarity' to 'hermeneutical science of communicative understanding', and finally the 'critical-reconstructive social sciences', focusing on the explicative inter-pretation of ambiguous symbols or the critique of ideology, social institutions or technocracy with a view to re-establishing communicative understanding, which are characterized by a 'dialectical mediation' of understanding through explanation.

Albrecht Wellmer (1933–), former Professor of Philosophy at the University of Konstanz, who initially studied mathematics and physics and subsequently phil-osophy and sociology, was closely associated with Adorno and Habermas at the time of the Positivist Dispute and its aftermath in the late 1960s. It is in this context that he produced both his critical analysis of Popper's contribution to the philosophy of science in *Methodologie als Erkenntnistheorie* (1967) and his presentation of develop-ments in critical theory from the early Frankfurt to the later Frankfurt School via the Positivist Dispute in *Critical Theory of Society* (1969), from which the selected text was taken. In the 1960s, as well as later, Wellmer played the role of the meticulous and penetrating internal critic who sought to strengthen the central ideas of critical theory as much as possible. In the extract he does just this by clarifying the relation between science and critique against background of Horkheimer and Adorno's seminal *Dia-lectic of Enlightenment* (originally 1944, translation 1972) and the controversy about the philosophy of social science in the Positivist Dispute. Arguing with Adorno that both society and sociology have a 'dual nature', he reinforces Horkheimer's distinc-tion between traditional and critical theory and provides backing from Habermas and Apel's emphasis of an emancipatory or 'liberating interest in cognition' in the case of critical social science by showing that the controversy about the philosophy of social science has an extra-scientific or 'practical core' of which positivism in particular and the sociological tradition from Comte to Parsons in general remain oblivious. It is encapsulated in the question, considering 'social experience', whether sociology should 'accept society in the particular form in which it functions' or whether it should instead 'strive for the transformation of its fundamental structures'.

Roberto Mangabeira Unger (1947–) was born in Rio de Janeiro and has been long active in Brazilian politics. He is Professor in the Harvard Law School and a promin-ent social and political theorist who took up the critical theory perspective in the process of its international diffusion in the wake of the Positivist Dispute. Applying this perspective in his book *Knowledge and Politics* (1975), he showed that the positiv-ist assumption of a value-free social science is deceptively misleading. Positivism itself, including the idea of a value-free social science, is the product of a certain sociohistorical climate. In the excerpt, which was selected from the book mentioned above, Unger argues, while operating against the background of the characteristic insight of the critical theorists into the central significance of the historical-political or living experience of society as a whole, that liberalism is the climate in question. Given the 'tyranny' which liberalism as a 'metaphysical conception of the mind and society' exercises over our minds, he suggests that it is impossible to come to terms with the various positions in and controversies about the philosophy of social science unless one adopts a self-conscious critical orientation toward liberalism – our sociohistorical climate.

Alvin Gouldner (1920–1980) was born in New York and was Professor of Sociology at Columbia University and later Max Weber Research Professor of Social Theory at Washington University, St Louis. He was founding editor of the journal *Theory and Society* and author several influential books, such *The Dialectic of Ideology and Technology* (1976) and *The Future of Intellectuals and the Rise of the New Class* (1979) but it was the book from which the extract has been selected, *The Coming Crisis of Western Sociology* (1970), that established his fame for a new generation of 'radical' sociologists who sought an alternative to the rigid conformism of postitivistic social science with its assumption of 'methodological dualism', the separation of theory and practice and the reduction of knowledge to information. In the selected text, Gouldner advocates a reflexive sociology conceived of as a recovery of the political nature of social science. The book as a whole – which expressed a combination of Marxist and Weberian approaches – was a significant development in the formation of a radical sociology beyond the narrow confines of Marxism. One of its major messages was that the personal is political and that radical knowledge is necessarily reflexive. Reflexivity is part of the transformative project of radical politics. Gouldner argues that it has as its aim the transformation of the sociologist's self-awareness in bringing the self into the domain of science. Sociologists, he argues, must acquire the habit of viewing their own beliefs in the same way as they view those held by others. The reflexive thesis is of broader significance for social science beyond sociology in that Gouldner argues that a reflexive social science is not defined by its subject matter but by the relation it establishes between the researcher as a self or person and as a scientist.

33

MAX HORKHEIMER
Traditional and critical theory* (1937)

In traditional theoretical thinking, the genesis of particular objective facts, the practical application of the conceptual systems by which it grasps the facts, and the role of such systems in action, are all taken to be external to the theoretical thinking itself. This alienation, which finds expression in philosophical terminology as the separation of value and research, knowledge and action, and other polarities, protects the savant from the tensions we have indicated and provides an assured framework for his activity. Yet a kind of thinking which does not accept this framework seems to have the ground taken out from under it. If a theoretical procedure does not take the form of determining objective facts with the help of the simplest and most differentiated conceptual systems available, what can it be but an aimless intellectual game, half conceptual poetry, half impotent expression of states of mind? The investigation into the social conditioning of facts and theories may indeed be a research problem, perhaps even a whole field for theoretical work, but how can such studies be radically different from other specialized efforts? Research into ideologies, or sociology of knowledge, which has been taken over from the critical theory of society and established as a special discipline, is not opposed either in its aim or in its other ambitions to the usual activities that go on within classificatory science.

In this reaction to critical theory, the self-awareness of thought as such is reduced to the discovery of the relationship that exists between intellectual positions and their social location. Yet the structure of the critical attitude, inasmuch as its intentions go beyond prevailing social ways of acting, is no more closely related to social disciplines thus conceived than it is to natural science. Its opposition to the traditional concept of theory springs in general from a difference not so much of objects as of subjects. For men of the critical mind, the facts, as they emerge from the work of society, are not extrinsic in the same degree as they are for the savant or for members of other professions who all think like little savants. The latter look towards a new kind of organization of work. But in so far as the objective realities given in perception are

* From 'Traditional and Critical Theory' by Max Horkheimer in *Critical Theory: Selected Essays*, The Seabury Press, New York, 1972, pp. 208–211, 224–229. Reprinted with permission by The Continuum Publishing Group.

conceived as products which in principle should be under human control and, in the future at least, will in fact come under it, these realities lose the character of pure factuality.

The scholarly specialist 'as' scientist regards social reality and its products as extrinsic to him, and 'as' citizen exercises his interest in them through political articles, membership in political parties or social service organizations, and participation in elections. But he does not unify these two activities, and his other activities as well, except, at best, by psychological interpretation. Critical thinking, on the contrary, is motivated today by the effort really to transcend the tension and to abolish the opposition between the individual's purposefulness, spontaneity, and rationality, and those work-process relationships on which society is built. Critical thought has a concept of man as in conflict with himself until this opposition is removed. If activity governed by reason is proper to man, then existent social practice, which forms the individual's life down to its least details, is inhuman, and this inhumanity affects everything that goes on in the society. There will always be something that is extrinsic to man's intellectual and material activity, namely nature as the totality of as yet unmastered elements with which society must deal. But when situations which really depend on man alone, the relationships of men in their work, and the course of man's own history are also accounted part of 'nature,' the resultant extrinsicality is not only not a suprahistorical eternal category (even pure nature in the sense described is not that), but it is a sign of contemptible weakness. To surrender to such weakness is nonhuman and irrational.

Bourgeois thought is so constituted that in reflection on the subject which exercises such thought a logical necessity forces it to recognize an ego which imagines itself to be autonomous. Bourgeois thought is essentially abstract, and its principle is an individuality which inflatedly believes itself to be the ground of the world or even to be the world without qualification, an individuality separated off from events. The direct contrary of such an outlook is the attitude which holds the individual to be the unproblematic expression of an already constituted society; an example would be a nationalist ideology. Here the rhetorical 'we' is taken seriously; speech is accepted as the organ of the community. In the internally rent society of our day, such thinking, except in social questions, sees nonexistent unanimities and is illusory.

Critical thought and its theory are opposed to both the types of thinking just described. Critical thinking is the function neither of the isolated individual nor of a sum-total of individuals. Its subject is rather a definite individual in his real relation to other individuals and groups, in his conflict with a particular class, and, finally, in the resultant web of relationships with the social totality and with nature. The subject is no mathematical point like the ego of bourgeois philosophy; his activity is the construction of the social present. Furthermore, the thinking subject is not the place where knowledge and object coincide, nor consequently the starting-point for attaining absolute knowledge. Such an illusion about the thinking subject, under which idealism has lived since Descartes, is ideology in the strict sense, for in it the limited freedom of the bourgeois individual puts on the illusory form of perfect freedom and autonomy. As a matter of fact, however, in a society which is untransparent and without self-awareness the ego, whether active simply as thinker or active in other ways as well, is unsure of itself too. In reflection on man, subject and object are sundered; their identity lies in the future, not in the present. The method leading to such an identification may be called explanation in Cartesian language, but in genuinely critical thought explanation signifies not only a logical process but a concrete historical one as well. In the course of it both the social structure as a whole and the relation of the theoretician to society are altered, that is both the subject and the role of thought are changed. The acceptance of an essential unchangeableness between subject, theory, and object thus distinguishes the Cartesian conception from every kind of dialectical logic . . .

Our consideration of the various functions of traditional and critical theory brings to light the difference in their logical structure. The primary propositions of traditional theory define universal concepts under which all facts in the field in question are to be subsumed; for example, the concept of a physical process in physics or an organic process in biology. In between primary propositions and facts there is the hierarchy of genera and species with their relations of subordination. Facts are individual cases, examples, or embodiments of classes. There are no differences due to time between the unities in the system. Electricity does not exist prior to an electrical field, nor a field prior to electricity, any more than wolf as such exists before or after particular wolves. As far as an individual knower is concerned there may be one or other temporal sequence among such relationships, but no such sequence exists in the objects themselves.

Furthermore, physics has also ceased to regard more general characteristics as causes or forces hidden in the concrete facts and to hypostatize these logical relationships; it is only sociology that is still unclear on this point. If new classes are added to the system or other changes are introduced, this is not usually regarded as proof that the determinations made earlier are necessarily too rigid and must turn out to be inadequate, for the relationship to the object or even the object itself may change without losing its identity. Changes are taken rather as an indication that our earlier knowledge was deficient or as a substitution of some aspects of an object for others, as a map, for example, may become dated because forests have been cut down, new cities built, or different borders drawn. In discursive logic, or logic of the understanding, the evolution of living beings is conceived in the same way. This person is now a child, then an adult; for such logic this can only mean that there is an abiding stable nucleus, 'this person,' who successively possesses the attributes of being a child and an adult. For positivism, of course, there is simply no identity: first there is a child, later there is an adult, and the two are simply distinct complexes of facts. But this view cannot come to grips with the fact that a person changes and yet is identical with himself.

The critical theory of society also begins with abstract determinations; in dealing with the present era it begins with the characterization of an economy based on exchange. The concepts Marx uses, such as commodity, value, and money, can function as genera when, for example, concrete social relations are judged to be relations of exchange and when there is question of the commodity character of goods. But the theory is not satisfied to relate concepts of reality by way of hypotheses. The theory begins with an outline of the mechanism by which bourgeois society, after dismantling feudal regulations, the guild system, and vassalage, did not immediately fall apart under the pressure of its own anarchic principle but managed to survive. The regulatory effects of exchange are brought out on which bourgeois economy is founded.

The conception of the interaction of society and nature, which is already exercising its influence here, as well as the idea of a unified period of society, of its self-preservation, and so on, spring from a radical analysis, guided by concern for the future, of the historical process. The relation of the primary conceptual interconnections to the world of facts is not essentially a relation of classes to instances. It is because of its inner dynamism that the exchange relationship, which the theory outlines, dominates social reality, as, for example, the assimilation of food largely dominates the organic life of plant and brute beast.

In critical theory, as in traditional theory, more specific elements must be introduced in order to move from fundamental structure to concrete reality. But such an intercalation of more detailed factors – for example the existence of large money reserves, the diffusion of these in sectors of society that are still precapitalist, foreign trade – is not accomplished by simple deduction as in theory that has been simplified for specialized use. Instead, every step rests on knowledge of man and nature which is stored up in the sciences and in historical experience. This is obvious, of course, for the theory of industrial technology. But in other areas too a detailed knowledge of how men react is applied throughout the doctrinal developments to which we have been referring. For example, the statement that under certain conditions the lowest strata of society have the most children plays an important role in explaining how the bourgeois society built on exchange necessarily leads to capitalism with its army of industrial reserves and its crises. To give the psychological reasons behind the observed fact about the lower classes is left to traditional science.

Thus the critical theory of society begins with the idea of the simple exchange of commodities and defines the idea with the help of relatively universal concepts. It then moves further, using all knowledge available and taking suitable material from the research of others as well as from specialized research. Without denying its own principles as established by the special discipline of political economy, the theory shows how an exchange economy, given the condition of men (which, of course, changes under the very influence of such an economy), must necessarily lead to a heightening of those social tensions which in the present historical era lead in turn to wars and revolutions.

The necessity just mentioned, as well as the abstractness of the concepts, are both like and unlike the same phenomena in traditional theory. In both types of theory there is a strict deduction if the claim of validity for general definitions is shown to include a claim that certain factual relations will occur. For example, if you are dealing with electricity, such and such an event must occur because such and such characteristics belong to the very concept of electricity. To the extent that the critical theory of society deduces present conditions from the concept of simple exchange, it includes this kind of necessity, although it is relatively unimportant that the hypothetical form of statement be used. That is, the stress is not on the idea that wherever a society based on simple exchange prevails, capitalism must develop-although this is true. The stress is rather on the fact that the existent capitalist society, which has spread all over the world from Europe and for which the theory is declared valid, derives from the basic relation of exchange. Even the classificatory judgments of specialized science have a fundamentally hypothetical character, and existential judgments are allowed, if at all, only in certain areas, namely the descriptive and practical parts of the discipline. But the critical theory of society is, in its totality, the unfolding of a single existential judgment. To put it in broad terms, the theory says that the basic form of the historically given commodity economy on which modern history rests contains in itself the internal and external tensions of the modern era; it generates these tensions over and over again in an increasingly heightened form; and after a period of progress, development of human powers, and emancipation for the individual, after an enormous extension of human control over nature, it finally hinders further development and drives humanity into a new barbarism.

The individual steps within the theory are, at least in intention, as rigorous as the deductions in a specialized scientific theory; each is an element in the building up of that comprehensive existential judgment. Particular parts of the theory can be changed into general or specific hypothetical judgments and applied after the fashion of traditional theory; for example, the idea that increasing productivity usually devalues capital. In many areas of the theory there thus arise propositions the relation of which to reality is difficult to determine. From the fact that the representation of a unified object is true as a whole, it is possible to conclude only under special conditions the extent to which isolated parts of the representation can validly be applied, in their isolation, to isolated parts of the object. The problem that arises as soon as particular propositions of the critical theory are applied to unique or recurring events in contemporary society has to do not with the truth of the theory but with how suitable the theory is for traditional kinds of intellectual operation with progressively extended goals. The special sciences, and especially contemporary political economics, are unable to derive practical profit from the fragmentary questions they discuss. But this incapacity is due neither to these sciences nor to critical theory alone, but to their specific role in relation to reality.

Even the critical theory, which stands in opposition to other theories, derives its statements about real relationships from basic universal concepts, as we have indicated, and therefore presents the relationships as necessary. Thus both kinds of theoretical structure are alike when it comes to logical necessity. But there is a difference as soon as we turn from logical to real necessity, the necessity involved in factual sequences. The biologist's statement that internal processes cause a plant to wither or that certain processes in the human organism lead to its destruction leaves untouched the question whether any influences can alter the character of these processes or change them totally. Even when an illness is said to be curable, the fact that the necessary curative measures are actually taken is regarded as purely extrinsic to the curability, a matter of technology and therefore nonessential as far as the theory as such is concerned. The necessity which rules society can be regarded as biological in the sense described, and the unique character of critical theory can therefore be called in question on the grounds that in biology as in other natural sciences particular sequences of events can be theoretically constructed just as they are in the critical theory of society. The development of society, in this view, would simply be a particular series of events, for the presentation of which conclusions from various other areas of research are used, just as a doctor in the course of an illness or a geologist dealing with the earth's prehistory has to apply various other disciplines. Society here would be the individual reality which is evaluated on the basis of theories in the special sciences.

However many valid analogies there may be between these different intellectual endeavors, there is nonetheless a decisive difference when it comes to the relation of subject and object and therefore to the necessity of the event being judged. The object with which the scientific specialist deals is not affected at all by his own theory. Subject and object are kept strictly apart. Even if it turns out that at a later point in time the objective event is influenced by human intervention, to science this is just another fact. The objective occurrence is independent of the theory, and this independence is part of its necessity: the observer as such can effect no change in the object. A consciously critical attitude, however, is part of the development of society: the construing of the course of history as the necessary product of an economic mechanism simultaneously contains both a protest against this order of things, a protest generated by the order itself, and the idea of self-determination for the human race, that is the idea of a state of affairs in which man's actions no longer flow from a mechanism but from his own decision. The judgment passed on the necessity inherent in the previous course of events implies here a struggle to change it from a blind to a meaningful necessity. If we think of the object of the theory in separation from the theory, we falsify it and fall into quietism or conformism. Every part of the theory presupposes the critique of the existing order and the struggle against it along lines determined by the theory itself.

34

HERBERT MARCUSE
Philosophy and critical theory* (1937)

. . . The interest of philosophy, concern with man, had found its new form in the interest of critical social theory. There is no philosophy alongside and outside this theory. For the philosophical construction of reason is replaced by the creation of a rational society. The philosophical ideals of a better world and of true Being are incorporated into the practical aim of struggling mankind, where they take on a human form.

What, however, if the development outlined by the theory does not occur? What if the forces that were to bring about the transformation are suppressed and appear to be defeated? Little as the theory's truth is thereby contradicted, it nevertheless appears then in a new light which illuminates new aspects and elements of its object. The new situation gives a new import to many demands and indices of the theory, whose changed function accords it in a more intensive sense the character of 'critical theory.' Its critique is also directed at the avoidance of its full economic and political demands by many who invoke it. This situation compels theory anew to a sharper emphasis on its concern with the potentialities of man and with the individual's freedom, happiness, and rights contained in all of its analyses. For the theory, these are exclusively potentialities of the concrete social situation. They become relevant only as economic and political questions and as such bear on human relations in the productive process, the distribution of the product of social labor, and men's active participation in the economic and political administration of the whole. The more elements of the theory become reality – not only as the old order's evolution confirms the theory's predictions, but as the transition to the new order begins – the more urgent becomes the question of what the theory intended as its goal. For here, unlike in philosophical systems, human freedom is no phantom or arbitrary inwardness that leaves everything in the external world as it was. Rather, freedom here means a real potentiality, a social relationship on whose realization human destiny depends. At the given stage of development, the constructive character of critical theory emerges

* From 'Philosophy and Critical Theory' in *Negations: Essays in Critical Theory* by Herbert Marcuse. Copyright © 1968 by Herbert Marcuse. Translations from German copyright © 1968 by Beacon Press. Reprinted by permission of Beacon Press, Boston. Pp. 142–143, 153–156.

anew. From the beginning it did more than simply register and systematize facts. Its impulse came from the force with which it spoke against the facts and confronted bad facticity with its better potentialities. Like philosophy, it opposes making reality into a criterion in the manner of complacent positivism. But unlike philosophy, it always derives its goals only from present tendencies of the social process. Therefore it has no fear of the utopia that the new order is denounced as being. When truth cannot be realized within the established social order, it always appears to the latter as mere utopia. This transcendence speaks not against, but for, its truth. The utopian element was long the only progressive element in philosophy, as in the constructions of the best state and the highest pleasure, of perfect happiness and perpetual peace. The obstinacy that comes from adhering to truth against all appearances has given way in contemporary philosophy to whimsy and uninhibited opportunism. Critical theory preserves obstinacy as a genuine quality of philosophical thought . . .

Critical theory's interest in the liberation of mankind binds it to certain ancient truths. It is at one with philosophy in maintaining that man can be more than a manipulable subject in the production process of class society. To the extent that philosophy has nevertheless made its peace with man's determination by economic conditions, it has allied itself with repression. That is the bad materialism that under-lies the edifice of idealism: the consolation that in the material world everything is in order as it is. (Even when it has not been the personal conviction of the philosopher, this consolation has arisen almost automatically as part of the mode of thought of bourgeois idealism and constitutes its ultimate affinity with its time.) The other prem-ise of this materialism is that the mind is not to make its demands in this world, but is to orient itself toward another realm that does not conflict with the material world. The materialism of bourgeois practice can quite easily come to terms with this atti-tude. The bad materialism of philosophy is overcome in the materialist theory of society. The latter opposes not only the production relations that gave rise to bad materialism, but every form of production that dominates man instead of being dom-inated by him: this idealism underlies its materialism. Its constructive concepts, too, have a residue of abstractness as long as the reality toward which they are directed is not yet given. Here, however, abstractness results not from avoiding the status quo, but from orientation toward the future status of man. It cannot be supplanted by another, correct theory of the established order (as idealist abstractness was replaced by the critique of political economy). It cannot be succeeded by a new theory, but only by rational reality itself. The abyss between rational and present reality cannot be bridged by conceptual thought. In order to retain what is not yet present as a goal in the present, phantasy is required. The essential connection of phantasy with phil-osophy is evident from the function attributed to it by philosophers, especially Aristotle and Kant, under the title of 'imagination.' Owing to its unique capacity to 'intuit' an object though the latter be not present and to create something new out of given material of cognition, imagination denotes a considerable degree of independ-ence from the given, of freedom amid a world of unfreedom. In surpassing what is present, it can anticipate the future. It is true that when Kant characterizes this 'fundamental faculty of the human soul' as the a priori basis of all knowledge, this restriction to the a priori diverts once again from the future to what is always past. Imagination succumbs to the general degradation of phantasy. To free it for the construction of a more beautiful and happier world remains the prerogative of children and fools. True, in phantasy one can imagine anything. But critical theory does not envision an endless horizon of possibilities.

The freedom of imagination disappears to the extent that real freedom becomes a real possibility. The limits of phantasy are thus no longer universal laws of essence (as the last bourgeois theory of knowledge that took seriously the meaning of phantasy so defined them), but technical limits in the strictest sense. They are prescribed by the level of technological development. What critical theory is engaged in is not the depiction of a future world, although the response of phantasy to such a challenge would not perhaps be quite as absurd as we are led to believe. If phantasy were set free to answer, with precise reference to already existing technical material, the fundamental philosophical questions asked by Kant, all of sociology would be terrified at the utopian character of its answers. And yet the answers that phantasy could provide would be very close to the truth, certainly closer than those yielded by the rigorous conceptual analyses of philosophical anthropology. For it would determine what man is on the basis of what he really can be tomorrow. In replying to the question, 'What may I hope?', it would point less to eternal bliss and inner freedom than to the already possible unfolding and fulfillment of needs and wants. In a situation where such a future is a real possibility, phantasy is an important instrument in the task of continually holding the goal up to view. Phantasy does not relate to the other cognitive faculties as illusion to truth (which in fact, when it plumes itself on being the only truth, can perceive the truth of the future only as illusion). Without phantasy, all philosophical knowledge remains in the grip of the present or the past and severed from the future, which is the only link between philosophy and the real history of mankind.

Strong emphasis on the role of phantasy seems to contradict the rigorously scientific character that critical theory has always made a criterion of its concepts. This demand for scientific objectivity has brought materialist theory into unusual accord with idealist rationalism. While the latter could pursue its concern with man only in abstraction from given facts, it attempted to undo this abstractness by associating itself with science. Science never seriously called use-value into question. In their anxiety about scientific objectivity, the Neo-Kantians are at one with Kant, as is Husserl with Descartes. How science was applied, whether its utility and productivity guaranteed its higher truth or were instead signs of general inhumanity – philosophy did not ask itself these questions. It was chiefly interested in the methodology of the sciences. The critical theory of society maintained primarily that the only task left for philosophy was elaborating the most general results of the sciences. It, too, took as its basis the viewpoint that science had sufficiently demonstrated its ability to serve the development of the productive forces and to open up new potentialities of a richer existence. But while the alliance between idealist philosophy and science was burdened from the beginning with sins engendered by the dependence of the sciences on established relations of domination, the critical theory of society presupposes the disengagement of science from this order. Thus the fateful fetishism of science is avoided here in principle. But this does not dispense the theory from a constant critique of scientific aims and methods which takes into account every new social situation. Scientific objectivity as such is never a sufficient guarantee of truth, especially in a situation where the truth speaks as strongly against the facts and is as well hidden behind them as today. Scientific predictability does not coincide with the futuristic mode in which the truth exists. Even the development of the productive forces and the evolution of technology know no uninterrupted progression from the old to the new society. For here, too, man himself is to determine progress: not 'socialist' man, whose spiritual and moral regeneration is supposed to constitute the basis for planning the planners (a view that overlooks that 'socialist' planning presupposes the disappearance of the abstract separation both of the subject from his activity and of the subject as universal from each individual subject), but the association of those men who bring about the transformation. Since what is to become of science and technology depends on them, science and technology cannot serve a priori as a conceptual model for critical theory.

Critical theory is, last but not least, critical of itself and of the social forces that make up its own basis. The philosophical element in the theory is a form of protest against the new 'Economism,' which would isolate the economic struggle and separate the economic from the political sphere. At an early stage, this view was countered with the criticism that the determining factors are the given situation of the entire society, the interrelationships of the various social strata, and relations of political power. The transformation of the economic structure must so reshape the organization of the entire society that, with the abolition of economic antagonisms between groups and individuals, the political sphere becomes to a great extent independent and determines the development of society. With the disappearance of the state, political relations would then become, in a hitherto unknown sense, general human relations: the organization of the administration of social wealth in the interest of liberated mankind.

35

THEODOR W. ADORNO
Sociology and empirical research* (1969)

The modes of procedure assembled under the name of sociology as an academic discipline are united in an extremely abstract sense, namely, in that all of them in some way deal with society. But neither their object nor their method is uniform. Some apply to societal totality and its laws of movement, others, in pointed opposition, apply to individual social phenomena which one relates to a concept of society at the cost of ostracization for being speculative. Accordingly, the methods vary. In the former case, insight into the societal context is supposed to follow from structural basic conditions, such as the exchange relationship. In the latter, such an endeavour, even though it may in no way desire to justify the factual from the standpoint of an autocratic mind, is dismissed as philosophical residue in the development of science, and is to give way to the mere establishment of what is the case. Historically divergent models underlie both conceptions. The theory of society originated in philosophy whilst, at the same time, it attempts to reformulate the questions posed by the latter by defining society as the substratum which traditional philosophy called eternal essences or spirit. Just as philosophy mistrusted the deceit of appearances and sought after interpretation, so the more smoothly the façade of society presents itself, the more profoundly does theory mistrust it. Theory seeks to give a name to what secretly holds the machinery together. The ardent desire for thought, to which the senseless-ness of what merely exists was once unbearable, has become secularized in the desire for disenchantment. It seeks to raise the stone under which the monster lies brooding. In such knowledge alone meaning has been preserved for us. Sociological research into facts opposes such a desire. Disenchantment of the kind that Max Weber accepted, is merely a special case of sorcery for such research, and reflection upon that which governs secretly and would have to be changed, is viewed as a mere waste of time on the way towards the alteration of the manifest. This is especially the case since what nowadays generally bears the name empirical social science has taken, more or less avowedly since Comte's positivism, the natural sciences as its model. The

* From Theodor W. Adorno, 'Sociology and Empirical Research', in Theodor W. Adorno et al., *The Positivist Dispute in German Sociology*, Heinemann, 1976, pp. 68–70, 73–77, 84–86.

two tendencies refuse to be reduced to a common denominator. Theoretical reflections upon society as a whole cannot be completely realized by empirical findings; they seek to evade the latter just as spirits evade para-psychological experimental arrangements. Each particular view of society as a whole necessarily transcends its scattered facts. The first condition for construction of the totality is a concept of the object (*Sache*), around which the disparate data are organized. From the living experience, and not from one already established according to the societally installed control mechanisms, from the memory of what has been conceived in the past, from the unswerving consequence of one's own reflection, this construction must always bring the concept to bear on the material and reshape it in contact with the latter. But if theory is not to fall prey to the dogmatism over whose discovery scepticism – now elevated to a prohibition on thought – is always ready to rejoice, then theory may not rest here. It must transform the concepts which it brings, as it were, from outside into those which the object has of itself, into what the object, left to itself, seeks to be, and confront it with what it is. It must dissolve the rigidity of the temporally and spatially fixed object into a field of tension of the possible and the real: each one, in order to exist, is dependent upon the other. In other words, theory is indisputably critical. But, for this reason, hypotheses derived from it – forecasts of what can be regularly expected – are not completely sufficient for it. What can merely be expected is itself a piece of societal activity, and is incommensurable with the goal of criticism. The cheap satisfaction that things actually come about in the manner which the theory of society had suspected, ought not to delude the theory, that, as soon as it appears as a hypothesis, it alters its inner composition. The isolated observation through which it is verified belongs, in turn, to the context of delusion which it desires to penetrate. The concretization and certainty gained must be paid for with a loss in penetrating force; as fas as the principle is concerned it will be reduced to the phenomenon against which it is tested. But if, conversely, one wishes to proceed in accordance with general scientific custom from individual investigations to the totality of society then one gains, at best, classificatory higher concepts, but not those which express the life of society itself. The category 'a society based on the division of labour in general' is higher and more general than 'capitalistic society' – but it is not more substantial. Rather, it is less substantial and tells us less about the life of the people and what threatens them. This does not mean, however, that a logically lower category such as 'urbanism' would say more. Neither upwards nor downwards do sociological levels of abstraction correspond simply to the societal knowledge value. For this reason, one can expect so little from their systematic standardization by means of a model such as Parsons' 'functional' model. But still less can be expected from the promises repeatedly made, and postponed since sociological prehistory, of a synthesis of the theoretical and the empirical, which falsely equate theory with formal unity and refuse to admit that a theory of society, purged of the substantive contents, displaces all its emphases. It should be remembered how indifferent recourse to the 'group' is as opposed to recourse to industrial society. Societal theory formation, based on the model of classificatory systems, substitutes the thinnest conceptual residue for what gives society its law. The empirical and the theoretical cannot be registered on a continuum. Compared with the presumption of insight into the essence of modern society, empirical contributions are like drops in the ocean. But according to the empirical rules of the game, empirical proofs for central structural laws remain, in any case, contestable. It is not a matter of smoothing out such divergences and harmonizing them. Only a harmonistic view of society could induce one to such an attempt. Instead, the tensions must be brought to a head in a fruitful manner. . . .

It is in the nature of society itself that the natural scientific model cannot be happily and unreservedly transferred to it. But although the ideology suggests otherwise, and this is rationalized by the reactionary opposition to new techniques in Germany, this is not because the dignity of man, for the gradual abolition of which mankind is avidly working, would be excluded from methods which regard him as a part of nature. Instead, it is more true to say that mankind commits a flagrant sin in so far as man's claim to domination represses the remembrance of his natural being and thus perpetuates blind natural spontaneity (*Naturwüchsigkeit*) than when human beings are reminded of their natural instincts (*Naturhaftigkeit*). 'Sociology is not a cultural science (*Geisteswissenschaft*).' In so far as the obduracy of society continually reduces human beings to objects and transforms their condition into 'second nature', methods which find it guilty of doing just this are not sacrilegious. The lack of freedom in the methods serves freedom by attesting wordlessly to the predominant lack of freedom. The enraged, indignant protests and the subtler defensive gestures provoked by Kinsey's investigations are the most powerful argument for Kinsey. Wherever human beings are, in fact, reduced under the pressure of conditions to the 'amphibious' mode of reaction, as they are in their capacity as compulsive consumers of the mass media and other regimented joys, opinion research, which infuriates lixiviated humanism, is better suited to them than, for instance, an 'interpretative' sociology. For, the substratum of understanding, namely human behavior, which is in itself unified and meaningful, has already been replaced in the human subjects themselves by mere reaction. A social science which is both atomistic, and ascends through classification from the atoms to generalities, is the Medusan mirror to a society which is both atomized and organized according to abstract classificatory concepts, namely those of administration. But in order to become true, this *adaequatio rei atque cogitationis* requires self-reflection. Its legitimation is solely critical. In that moment in which one hypostatizes that state which research methods both grasp and express as the immanent reason of science, instead of making it the object of one's thought, one contributes intentionally or otherwise to its perpetuation. Then, empirical social research wrongly takes the epiphenomenon – what the world has made of us – for the object itself. In its application, there exists a presupposition which should not be deduced from the demands of the method but rather the state of society, that is, historically. The hypostatized method postulates the reified consciousness of the people tested. If a questionnaire inquires into musical taste and, in so doing, offers a choice between the categories 'classical' and 'popular', then it rightly believes that it has ascertained that the audience in question listens in accordance with these categories. Similarly, one automatically recognizes, without reflection, when one turns on the radio, whether one has found a popular music programme, or what is considered serious music, or the background music to a religious act. But as long as the societal conditions for such forms of reaction are not met, the correct finding is also misleading. It suggests that the division of musical experience into 'classical' and 'popular' is final and even natural. But the societally relevant question only arises with this division, with its perpetuation as something self-evident, and necessarily implies the question whether the perception of music under the a priori sectors most acutely affects the spontaneous experience of the perceived. Only the insight into the genesis of the existing forms of reaction and their relationship to the meaning of that experienced would permit one to decipher the phenomenon registered. The predominant empiricist habit, however, would reject any discussion of the objective meaning of the particular work of art, and would discuss such meaning as a mere subjective projection by the listeners and relegate the structure to the mere 'stimulus' of a psychological experimental arrangement. In this manner, it would, from the outset, exclude the possibility of discussing the relationship between the masses and the products forced upon them by the culture industry. Ultimately, the products themselves would be defined through the reactions of the masses whose relation to the products was under discussion. But it is all the more urgent today to proceed beyond the isolated study since, with the hold of the media on the population growing stronger, the preformation of their consciousness also increases so that there is scarcely a gap left which might permit an awareness of this very pre-formation. Even such a positivistic sociologist as Durkheim, who in his rejection of *Verstehen* was in agreement with social research, had good reason for associating the statistical laws, to which he also adhered, with the 'contrainte sociale' and even for recognizing in the latter the criterion of society's general law-like nature. Contemporary social research denies this connection and thereby also sacrifices the connection between its generalizations and concrete, societal determinations of structure. But if such perspectives are pushed aside and considered to be the task of special investigations which must be carried out at some point, then scientific mirroring indeed remains a mere duplication, the reified apperception of the hypostatized, thereby distorting the object through duplication itself. It enchants that which is mediated into something immediate. As a corrective, it is not then sufficient simply to distinguish descriptively between the 'collective realm' and the 'individual realm', as Durkheim intended, but rather the relationship between the two realms must be mediated and must itself be grounded theoretically. The opposition between quantitative and qualitative analysis is not absolute. It is not the last word in the matter. It is well known that whoever quantifies must always first abstract from qualitative differences in the elements, and everything that is societally individual contains the general determinations for which the quantitative generalizations are valid. The proper categories of the latter are always qualitative. A method which does not do justice to this fact and rejects qualitative analysis as incompatible with the essence of the collective realm distorts what it should investigate. Society is one. Even where the major societal forces have not yet made their influence felt, the 'undeveloped' spheres are functionally inter-related with those spheres which have advanced towards rationality and uniform socialization (*Vergesellschaftung*). Sociology, which disregards this and remains content with such weak and inadequate concepts as induction and deduction, supports what exists in the over-zealous attempt to say what exists. Such sociology becomes ideology in the strict sense – a necessary illusion. It is illusion since the diversity of methods does not encompass the unity of the object and conceals it behind so-called factors into which the object is broken up for the sake of convenience; it is necessary since the object, society, fears nothing more than to be called by name, and therefore it automatically encourages and tolerates only such knowledge of itself that slides off its back without any impact. The conceptual dichotomy of induction and deduction is the scientistic substitute for dialectics. But just as a binding theory of society must have fully immersed itself in its material, so the fact to be processed must itself throw light on the societal totality by virtue of the process which apprehends it. If, however, the method has already rendered it a *factum brutum*, then no light can subsequently penetrate it. In the rigid opposition and complementation of formal sociology and the blind establishment of facts, the relationship between the general and the particular disappears. But society draws its life from this relationship, which therefore provides sociology with its only humanly worthy object. If one subsequently adds together what has been separated, then the material relationship is stood upon its head by the gradation of the method. The eagerness to quantify immediately even the qualitative findings is not fortuitous. Science wishes to rid the world of the tension between the general and the particular by means of its consistent system, but the world gains its unity from inconsistency . . .

Empirical social research cannot evade the fact that all the given factors investigated, the subjective no less than the objective relations, are mediated through society. The given, the facts which, in accordance with its methods, it encounters as something final, are not themselves final but rather are conditioned. Consequently, empirical social research cannot confuse the roots of its knowledge – the givenness of facts which is the concern of its method – with the real basis, a being in-itself of facts, their immediacy as such, their fundamental character. It can protect itself against such a confusion in that it is able to dissolve the immediacy of the data through refinement of the method. This accounts for the significance of motivational analyses although they remain under the spell of subjective reaction. They can indeed seldom rest upon direct questions; and correlations indicate functional connections but do not elucidate causal dependencies. Consequently, the development of indirect methods is, in principle, the opportunity for empirical social research to reach beyond the mere observation and preparation of superficial facts. The cognitive problem of its self-critical development remains, namely that the facts ascertained do not faithfully reflect the underlying societal conditions but rather they simultaneously constitute the veil by means of which these conditions, of necessity, disguise themselves. For the findings of what is called – not without good reason – 'opinion research' Hegel's formulation in his *Philosophy of Right* concerning public opinion is generally valid: it deserves to be respected and despised in equal measure. It must be respected since even ideologies, necessary false consciousness, are a part of social reality with which anyone who wishes to recognize the latter must be acquainted. But it must be despised since its claim to truth must be criticized. Empirical social research itself becomes ideology as soon as it posits public opinion as being absolute. This is the fault of an unreflectedly nominalistic concept of truth which wrongly equates the '*volonté de tous*' with truth in general, since a different truth cannot be ascertained. This tendency is particularly marked in American empirical social research. But it should not be dogmatically confronted with the mere assertion of a '*volonté générale*' as a truth in-itself, for instance in the form of postulated 'values.' Such a procedure would be loaded with the same arbitrariness as the installation of popular opinion as objectively valid. Historically, since Robespierre, the establishment of the '*volonté générale*' by decree has possibly caused even more harm than the concept-free assumption of a '*volonté de tous.*' The only way out of the fateful alternative was provided by immanent analysis; the analysis of the consistency or inconsistency of opinion in itself and of its relationship to reality (*Sache*), not however the abstract antithesis of the objectively valid and of opinion. Opinion should not be rejected with Platonic arrogance, but rather its untruth is to be derived from the truth: from the supporting societal relationship and ultimately from the latter's own untruth. On the other hand, however, average opinion does not represent an approximate value of truth, but instead the socially average illusion. In the latter, there participate what unreflective social research imagines to be its *ens realissimum*: those questioned, the human subjects. Their own nature, their being as subjects, depends upon the objectivity, upon the mechanisms which they obey, and which constitute their concept. This can only be determined, however, if one perceives in the facts themselves the tendency which reaches out beyond them. That is the function of philosophy in empirical social research. If it is not realized or suppressed, if merely the facts are reproduced then such a reproduction is at the same time a corruption of facts into ideology.

36

JÜRGEN HABERMAS
Knowledge and human interests* (1965)

In the empirical-analytic sciences the frame of reference that prejudges the meaning of possible statements establishes rules both for the construction of theories and for their critical testing. Theories comprise hypothetico-deductive connections of propositions, which permit the deduction of lawlike hypotheses with empirical content. The latter can be interpreted as statements about the covariance of observable events; given a set of initial conditions, they make predictions possible. Empirical-analytic knowledge is thus possible predictive knowledge. However, the meaning of such predictions, that is their technical exploitability, is established only by the rules according to which we apply theories to reality.

In controlled observation, which often takes the form of an experiment, we generate initial conditions and measure the results of operations carried out under these conditions. Empiricism attempts to ground the objectivist illusion in observations expressed in basic statements. These observations are supposed to be reliable in providing immediate evidence without the admixture of subjectivity. In reality basic statements are not simple representations of facts in themselves, but express the success or failure of our operations. We can say that facts and the relations between them are apprehended descriptively. But this way of talking must not conceal that as such the facts relevant to the empirical sciences are first constituted through an a priori organization of our experience in the behavioral system of instrumental action.

Taken together, these two factors, that is the logical structure of admissible systems of propositions and the type of conditions for corroboration, suggest that theories of the empirical sciences disclose reality subject to the constitutive interest in the possible securing and expansion, through information, of feedback-monitored action. This is the cognitive interest in technical control over objectified processes.

The historical-hermeneutic sciences gain knowledge in a different methodological framework. Here the meaning of the validity of propositions is not constituted in the frame of reference of technical control. The levels of formalized language and

* From 'Knowledge and Human Interests: A General Perspective', Appendix to *Knowledge and Human Interests* by Jürgen Habermas, 2nd edition, Heinemann, 1972, pp. 308–317.

Not from evidence

objectified experience have not yet been divorced. For theories are not constructed deductively and experience is not organized with regard to the success of operations. Access to the facts is provided by the understanding of meaning, not observation. The verification of lawlike hypotheses in the empirical-analytic sciences has its counterpart here in the interpretation of texts. Thus the rules of hermeneutics determine the possible meaning of the validity of statements of the cultural sciences.

Historicism has taken the understanding of meaning, in which mental facts are supposed to be given in direct evidence, and grafted onto it the objectivist illusion of pure theory. It appears as though the interpreter transposes himself into the horizon of the world or language from which a text derives its meaning. But here, too, the facts are first constituted in relation to the standards that establish them. Just as positivist self-understanding does not take into account explicitly the connection between measurement operations and feedback control, so it eliminates from consideration the interpreter's pre-understanding. Hermeneutic knowledge is always mediated through this pre-understanding, which is derived from the interpreter's initial situation. The world of traditional meaning discloses itself to the interpreter only to the extent that his own world becomes clarified at the same time. The subject of understanding establishes communication between both worlds. He comprehends the substantive content of tradition by applying tradition to himself and his situation.

If, however, methodological rules unite interpretation and application in this way, then this suggests that hermeneutic inquiry discloses reality subject to a constitutive interest in the preservation and expansion of the intersubjectivity of possible action-orienting mutual understanding. The understanding of meaning is directed in its very structure toward the attainment of possible consensus among actors in the framework of a self-understanding derived from tradition. This we shall call the practical cognitive interest, in contrast to the technical.

The systematic sciences of social action, that is economics, sociology, and political science, have the goal, as do the empirical-analytic sciences, of producing nomological knowledge. A critical social science, however, will not remain satisfied with this. It is concerned with going beyond this goal to determine when theoretical statements grasp invariant regularities of social action as such and when they express ideologically frozen relations of dependence that can in principle be transformed. To the extent that this is the case, the critique of ideology, as well, moreover, as psychoanalysis, take into account that information about lawlike connections sets off a process of reflection in the consciousness of those whom the laws are about. Thus the level of unreflected consciousness, which is one of the initial conditions of such laws, can be transformed. Of course, to this end a critically mediated knowledge of laws cannot through reflection alone render a law itself inoperative, but it can render it inapplicable.

The methodological framework that determines the meaning of the validity of critical propositions of this category is established by the concept of self-reflection. The latter releases the subject from dependence on hypostatized powers. Self-reflection is determined by an emancipatory cognitive interest. Critically oriented sciences share this interest with philosophy. However, as long as philosophy remains caught in ontology, it is itself subject to an objectivism that disguises the connection of its knowledge with the human interest in autonomy and responsibility (*Mündigkeit*).

There is only one way in which it can acquire the power that it vainly claims for itself in virtue of its seeming freedom from presuppositions: by acknowledging its dependence on this interest and turning against its own illusion of pure theory the critique it directs at the objectivism of the sciences.

The concept of knowledge-constitutive human interests already conjoins the two elements whose relation still has to be explained: knowledge and interest. From everyday experience we know that ideas serve often enough to furnish our actions with justifying motives in place of the real ones. What is called rationalization at this level is called ideology at the level of collective action. In both cases the manifest content of statements is falsified by consciousness' unreflected tie to interests, despite its illusion of autonomy. The discipline of trained thought thus correctly aims at excluding such interests. In all the sciences routines have been developed that guard against the subjectivity of opinion, and a new discipline, the sociology of knowledge, has emerged to counter the uncontrolled influence of interests on a deeper level, which derive less from the individual than from the objective situation of social groups. But this accounts for only one side of the problem. Because science must secure the objectivity of its statements against the pressure and seduction of particular interests, it deludes itself about the fundamental interests to which it owes not only its impetus but the conditions of possible objectivity themselves.

Orientation toward technical control, toward mutual understanding in the conduct of life, and toward emancipation from seemingly 'natural' constraint establish the specific viewpoints from which we can apprehend reality as such in any way whatsoever. By becoming aware of the impossibility of getting beyond these transcendental limits, a part of nature acquires, through us, autonomy in nature. If knowledge could ever outwit its innate human interest, it would be by comprehending that the mediation of subject and object that philosophical consciousness attributes exclusively to its own synthesis is produced originally by interests. The mind can become aware of this natural basis reflexively. Nevertheless, its power extends into the very logic of inquiry. Representations and descriptions are never independent of standards. And the choice of these standards is based on attitudes that require critical consideration by means of arguments, because they cannot be either logically deduced or empirically demonstrated. Fundamental methodological decisions, for example such basic distinctions as those between categorial and noncategorial being, between analytic and synthetic statements, or between descriptive and emotive meaning, have the singular character of being neither arbitrary nor compelling. They prove appropriate or inappropriate. For their criterion is the metalogical necessity of interests that we can neither prescribe nor represent, but with which we must instead come to terms. Therefore my first thesis is this: The achievements of the transcendental subject have their basis in the natural history of the human species.

Taken by itself this thesis could lead to the misunderstanding that reason is an organ of adaptation for men just as claws and teeth are for animals. True, it does serve this function. But the human interests that have emerged in man's natural history, to which we have traced back the three knowledge-constitutive interests, derive both from nature and from the cultural break with nature. Along with the tendency to realize natural drives they have incorporated the tendency toward release from the constraint of nature. Even the interest in self-preservation, natural as it seems, is represented by a social system that compensates for the lacks in man's organic equipment and secures his historical existence against the force of nature threatening from without. But society is not only a system of self-preservation. An enticing natural force, present in the individual as libido, has detached itself from the behavioral system of self-preservation and urges toward utopian fulfillment. These individual demands, which do not initially accord with the requirement of collective self-preservation, are also absorbed by the social system. That is why the cognitive processes to which social life is indissolubly linked function not only as means to the reproduction of life; for in equal measure they themselves determine the definitions of this life. What may appear as naked survival is always in its roots a historical phenomenon. For it is subject to the criterion of what a society intends for itself as the good life. My second thesis is thus that knowledge equally serves as an instrument and transcends mere self-preservation.

The specific viewpoints from which, with transcendental necessity, we apprehend reality ground three categories of possible knowledge: information that expands our power of technical control; interpretations that make possible the orientation of action within common traditions; and analyses that free consciousness from its dependence on hypostatized powers. These viewpoints originate in the interest structure of a species that is linked in its roots to definite means of social organization: work, language, and power. The human species secures its existence in systems of social labor and self-assertion through violence, through tradition-bound social life in ordinary-language communication, and with the aid of ego identities that at every level of individuation reconsolidate the consciousness of the individual in relation to the norms of the group. Accordingly the interests constitutive of knowledge are linked to the functions of an ego that adapts itself to its external conditions through learning processes, is initiated into the communication system of a social life-world by means of self-formative processes, and constructs an identity in the conflict between instinctual aims and social constraints. In turn these achievements become part of the productive forces accumulated by a society, the cultural tradition through which a society interprets itself, and the legitimations that a society accepts or criticizes. My third thesis is thus that knowledge-constitutive interests take form in the medium of work, language, and power.

However, the configuration of knowledge and interest is not the same in all categories. It is true that at this level it is always illusory to suppose an autonomy, free of presuppositions, in which knowing first grasps reality theoretically, only to be taken subsequently into the service of interests alien to it. But the mind can always reflect back upon the interest structure that joins subject and object a priori: this is reserved to self-reflection. If the latter cannot cancel out interest, it can to a certain extent make up for it.

It is no accident that the standards of self-reflection are exempted from the singular state of suspension in which those of all other cognitive processes require critical evaluation. They possess theoretical certainty. The human interest in autonomy and responsibility is not mere fancy, for it can be apprehended a priori. What raises us out of nature is the only thing whose nature we can know: language. Through its structure, autonomy and responsibility are posited for us. Our first sentence expresses unequivocally the intention of universal and unconstrained consensus. Taken together, autonomy and responsibility constitute the only Idea the we possess a priori in the sense of the philosophical tradition. Perhaps that is why the language of German Idealism, according to which 'reason' contains both will and consciousness as its elements, is not quite obsolete. Reason also means the will to reason. In self-reflection knowledge for the sake of knowledge attains congruence with the interest in autonomy and responsibility. The emancipatory cognitive interest aims at the pursuit of reflection as such. My fourth thesis is thus that in the power of self-reflection, knowledge and interest are one.

However, only in an emancipated society, whose members' autonomy and responsibility had been realized, would communication have developed into the non-authoritarian and universally practiced dialogue from which both our model of reciprocally constituted ego identity and our idea of true consensus are always implicitly derived. To this extent the truth of statements is based on anticipating the realization of the good life. The ontological illusion of pure theory behind which knowledge-constitutive interests become invisible promotes the fiction that Socratic dialogue is possible everywhere and at any time. From the beginning philosophy has presumed that the autonomy and responsibility posited with the structure of language are not only anticipated but real. It is pure theory, wanting to derive everything from itself, that succumbs to unacknowledged external conditions and becomes ideological. Only when philosophy discovers in the dialectical course of history the traces of violence that deform repeated attempts at dialogue and recurrently close off the path to unconstrained communication does it further the process whose suspension it otherwise legitimates: mankind's evolution toward autonomy and responsibility. My fifth thesis is thus that the unity of knowledge and interest proves itself in a dialectic that takes the historical traces of suppressed dialogue and reconstructs what has been suppressed.

The sciences have retained one characteristic of philosophy: the illusion of pure theory. This illusion does not determine the practice of scientific research but only its self-understanding. And to the extent that this self-understanding reacts back upon scientific practice, it even has its point.

The glory of the sciences is their unswerving application of their methods without reflecting on knowledge-constitutive interests. From knowing not what they do methodologically, they are that much surer of their discipline, that is of methodical progress within an unproblematic framework. False consciousness has a protective function. For the sciences lack the means of dealing with the risks that appear once the connection of knowledge and human interest has been comprehended on the level of self-reflection. It was possible for fascism to give birth to the freak of a national physics and Stalinism to that of a Soviet Marxist genetics (which deserves to be taken more seriously than the former) only because the illusion of objectivism was lacking. It would have been able to provide immunity against the more dangerous bewitchments of misguided reflection.

But the praise of objectivism has its limits. Husserl's critique was right to attack it, if not with the right means. As soon as the objectivist illusion is turned into an affirmative *Weltanschauung*, methodologically unconscious necessity is perverted to the dubious virtue of a scientific profession of faith. Objectivism in no way prevents the sciences from intervening in the conduct of life, as Husserl thought it did. They are integrated into it in any case. But they do not of themselves develop their practical efficacy in the direction of a growing rationality of action.

Instead, the positivist self-understanding of the nomological sciences lends countenance to the substitution of technology for enlightened action. It directs the utilization of scientific information from an illusory viewpoint, namely that the practical mastery of history can be reduced to technical control of objectified processes. The objectivist self-understanding of the hermeneutic sciences is of no lesser consequence. It defends sterilized knowledge against the reflected appropriation of active traditions and locks up history in a museum. Guided by the objectivist attitude of theory as the image of facts, the nomological and hermeneutical sciences reinforce each other with regard to their practical consequences. The latter displace our connection with tradition into the realm of the arbitrary, while the former, on the levelled-off basis of the repression of history, squeeze the conduct of life into the behavioral system of instrumental action. The dimension in which acting subjects could arrive rationally at agreement about goals and purposes is surrendered to the obscure area of mere decision among reified value systems and irrational beliefs. When this dimension, abandoned by all men of good will, is subjected to reflection that relates to history objectivistically, as did the philosophical tradition, then positivism triumphs at the highest level of thought, as with Comte. This happens when critique uncritically abdicates its own connection with the emancipatory knowledge-constitutive interest in favor of pure theory. This sort of high-flown critique projects the undecided process of the evolution of the human species onto the level of a philosophy of history that dogmatically issues instructions for action. A delusive philosophy of history, however, is only the obverse of deluded decisionism. Bureaucratically prescribed partisanship goes only too well with contemplatively misunderstood value freedom.

These practical consequences of a restricted, scientistic consciousness of the sciences can be countered by a critique that destroys the illusion of objectivism. Contrary to Husserl's expectations, objectivism is eliminated not through the power of renewed theoria but through demonstrating what it conceals: the connection of knowledge and interest. Philosophy remains true to its classic tradition by renouncing it. The insight that the truth of statements is linked in the last analysis to the intention of the good and true life can be preserved today only on the ruins of ontology. However even this philosophy remains a specialty alongside of the sciences and outside public consciousness as long as the heritage that it has critically abandoned lives on in the positivistic self-understanding of the sciences.

The tasks of a critical theory* (1981)

In this work I have tried to introduce a theory of communicative action that clarifies the normative foundations of a critical theory of society. The theory of communicative action is meant to provide an alternative to the philosophy of history on which earlier critical theory still relied, but which is no longer tenable. It is intended as a framework within which interdisciplinary research on the selective pattern of capitalist modernization can be taken up once again. The illustrative observations (a) through (d) were meant to make this claim plausible. The two additional themes (e) and (f) are a reminder that the investigation of what Marx called 'real abstraction' has to do with the social-scientific tasks of a theory of modernity, not the philosophical. Social theory need no longer ascertain the normative contents of bourgeois culture, of art and of philosophical thought, in an indirect way, that is, by way of a critique of ideology. With the concept of a communicative reason ingrained in the use of language oriented to reaching understanding, it again expects from philosophy that it take on systematic tasks. The social sciences can enter into a cooperative relation with a philosophy that has taken up the task of working on a theory of rationality.

It is no different with modern culture as a whole than it was with the physics of Newton and his heirs: modern culture is as little in need of a philosophical grounding as science. As we have seen, in the modern period culture gave rise of itself to those structures of rationality that Weber then discovered and described as value spheres. With modern science, with positive law and principled secular ethics, with autonomous art and institutionalized art criticism, three moments of reason crystallized without help from philosophy. Even without the guidance of the critiques of pure and practical reason, the sons and daughters of modernity learned how to divide up and develop further the cultural tradition under these different aspects of rationality – as questions of truth, justice, or taste. More and more the sciences dropped the elements of worldviews and do without an interpretation of nature and history as a whole. Cognitive ethics separates off problems of the good life and concentrates on strictly deontological, universalizable aspects, so that what remains from the Good is only the Just. And an art that has become autonomous pushes toward an ever purer expression of the basic aesthetic experiences of a subjectivity that is decentered and removed from the spatiotemporal structures of everyday life. Subjectivity frees itself here from the conventions of daily perception and of purposive activity, from the imperatives of work and of what is merely useful.

These magnificent 'one-sidednesses,' which are the signature of modernity, need no foundation and no justification in the sense of a transcendental grounding, but they do call for a self-understanding regarding the character of this knowledge. Two questions must be answered: (i) whether a reason that has objectively split up into its

* From *The Theory of Communicative Action*, Volume 2 by Jürgen Habermas. Translator's preface and translation Copyright © 1987 by Beacon Press. Originally published as *Theorie des kommunikativen Handelns*, Band 2: *Zur Kritik der funktionalistischen Vernuft*, Copyright © 1981 by Suhrkamp Verlag, Franfurt am Main. Reprinted by permission of Beacon Press, Boston and by permission of Blackwell Publishers, Oxford. Pp. 396–403.

moments can still preserve its unity, and (ii) how expert cultures can be mediated with everyday practice. The reflections offered in the first and third chapters [of Volume 1 of *The Theory of Communicative Action*] are intended as a provisional account of how formal pragmatics can deal with these questions. With that as a basis, the theory of science, the theory of law and morality, and aesthetics, in cooperation with the corresponding historical disciplines, can then reconstruct both the emergence and the internal history of those modern complexes of knowledge that have been differentiated out, each under a different single aspect of validity – truth, normative rightness, or authenticity.

The mediation of the moments of reason is no less a problem than the separation of the aspects of rationality under which questions of truth, justice, and taste were differentiated from one another. The only protection against an empiricist abridgement of the rationality problematic is a steadfast pursuit of the tortuous routes along which science, morality, and art communicate with one another. In each of these spheres, differentiation processes are accompanied by countermovements that, under the primacy of one dominant aspect of validity, bring back in again the two aspects that were at first excluded. Thus nonobjectivist approaches to research within the human sciences bring viewpoints of moral and aesthetic critique to bear – without threatening the primacy of questions of truth; only in this way is critical social theory made possible. Within universalistic ethics the discussion of the ethics of responsibility and the stronger consideration given to hedonistic motives bring the calculation of consequences and the interpretation of needs into play – and they lie in the domains of the cognitive and the expressive; in this way materialist ideas can come in without threatening the autonomy of the moral. Finally, post-avant-garde art is characterized by the coexistence of tendencies toward realism and engagement with those authentic continuations of classical modern art that distilled out the independent logic of the aesthetic; in realist art and *l'art engagé*, moments of the cognitive and of the moral-practical come into play again in art itself, and at the level of the wealth of forms that the avant-garde set free. It seems as if the radically differentiated moments of reason want in such countermovements to point toward a unity – not a unity that could be had at the level of worldviews, but one that might be established this side of expert cultures, in a nonreified communicative everyday practice.

How does this sort of affirmative role for philosophy square with the reserve that critical theory always maintained in regard to both the established scientific enterprise and the systematic pretensions of philosophy? Is not such a theory of rationality open to the same objections that pragmatism and hermeneutics have brought against every kind of foundationalism? Do not investigations that employ the concept of communicative reason without blushing bespeak universalistic justificatory claims that will have to fall to those – only too well grounded – metaphilosophical doubts about theories of absolute origins and ultimate grounds? Have not both the historicist enlightenment and materialism forced philosophy into a self-modesty for which the tasks of a theory of rationality must already appear extravagant? The theory of communicative action aims at the moment of unconditionality that, with criticizable validity claims, is built into the conditions of processes of consensus formation. As claims they transcend all limitations of space and time, all the provincial limitations of the given context. Rather than answer these questions here with arguments already set out in the introductory chapter [to Volume 1], I shall close by adding two methodological arguments that speak against the suspicion that the theory of communicative action is guilty of foundationalist claims.

First we must see how philosophy changes its role when it enters into cooperation with the sciences. As the 'feeder' (*Zubringer*) for a theory of rationality, it finds itself in a division of labor with reconstructive sciences; these sciences take up the pretheoretical knowledge of competently judging, acting, and speaking subjects, as well as the collective knowledge of traditions, in order to get at the most general features of the rationality of experience and judgment, action and mutual understanding in language. In this context, reconstructions undertaken with philosophical means also retain a hypothetical character; precisely because of their strong universalistic claims, they are open to further, indirect testing. This can take place in such a way that the reconstructions of universal and necessary presuppositions of communicative action, of argumentative speech, of experience and of objectivating thought, of moral judgments and of aesthetic critique, enter into empirical theories that are supposed to explain other phenomena – for example, the ontogenesis of language and of communicative abilities, of moral judgment and social competence; the structural transformation of religious-metaphysical worldviews; the development of legal systems or of forms of social integration generally.

From the perspective of the history of theory, I have taken up the work of Mead, Weber, and Durkheim and tried to show how in their approaches, which are simultaneously empirical and reconstructive, the operations of empirical science and of philosophical conceptual analysis intermesh. The best example of this cooperative division of labor is Piaget's genetic theory of knowledge.

A philosophy that opens its results to indirect testing in this way is guided by the fallibilistic consciousness that the theory of rationality it once wanted to develop on its own can now be sought only in the felicitous coherence of different theoretical fragments. Coherence is the sole criterion of considered choice at the level on which mutually fitting theories stand to one another in relations of supplementing and reciprocally presupposing, for it is only the individual propositions derivable from theories that are true or false. Once we have dropped foundationalist claims, we can no longer expect a hierarchy of sciences; theories – whether social-scientific or philosophical in origin – have to fit with one another, unless one puts the other in a problematic light and we have to see whether it suffices to revise the one or the other.

The test case for a theory of rationality with which the modern understanding of the world is to ascertain its own universality would certainly include throwing light on the opaque figures of mythical thought, clarifying the bizarre expressions of alien cultures, and indeed in such a way that we not only comprehend the learning processes that separate 'us' from 'them,' but also become aware of what we have unlearned in the course of this learning. A theory of society that does not close itself off a priori to this possibility of unlearning has to be critical also in relation to the preunderstanding that accrues to it from its own social setting, that is, it has to be open to self-criticism. Processes of unlearning can be gotten at through a critique of deformations that are rooted in the selective exploitation of a potential for rationality and mutual understanding that was once available but is now buried over.

There is also another reason why the theory of society based on the theory of communicative action cannot stray into foundationalist byways. Insofar as it refers to structures of the lifeworld, it has to explicate a background knowledge over which no one can dispose at will. The lifeworld is at first 'given' to the theoretician (as it is to the layperson) as his or her own, and in a paradoxical manner. The mode of preunderstanding or of intuitive knowledge of the lifeworld from within which we live together, act and speak with one another, stands in peculiar contrast, as we have seen, to the explicit knowledge of something. The horizontal knowledge that communicative everyday practice tacitly carries with it is paradigmatic for the certainty with which the lifeworld background is present; yet it does not satisfy the criterion of knowledge that stands in internal relation to validity claims and can therefore be criticized. That which stands beyond all doubt seems as if it could never become problematic; as what is simply unproblematic, a lifeworld can at most fall apart. It is only under the pressure of approaching problems that relevant components of such background knowledge are torn out of their unquestioned familiarity and brought to consciousness as something in need of being ascertained. It takes an earthquake to make us aware that we had regarded the ground on which we stand everyday as unshakable. Even in situations of this sort, only a small segment of our background knowledge becomes uncertain and is set loose after having been enclosed in complex traditions, in solidaric relations, in competences. If the objective occasion arises for us to arrive at some understanding about a situation that has become problematic, background knowledge is transformed into explicit knowledge only in a piecemeal manner.

This has an important methodological implication for sciences that have to do with cultural tradition, social integration, and the socialization of individuals – an implication that became clear to pragmatism and to hermeneutic philosophy, each in its own way, as they came to doubt the possibility of Cartesian doubt. Alfred Schutz, who so convincingly depicted the lifeworld's mode of unquestioned familiarity, nevertheless missed just this problem: whether a lifeworld, in its opaque take-for-grantedness, eludes the phenomenologist's inquiring gaze or is opened up to it does not depend on just *choosing* to adopt a theoretical attitude. The totality of the background knowledge constitutive for the construction of the lifeworld is no more at his disposition than at that of any social scientist – unless an objective challenge arises, in the face of which the lifeworld as a whole becomes problematic. Thus a theory that wants to ascertain the general structures of the lifeworld cannot adopt a transcendental approach; it can only hope to be equal to the *ratio essendi* of its object when there are grounds for assuming that the objective context of life in which the theoretician finds himself is opening up to him its ratio *cognoscendi*.

This implication accords with the point behind Horkheimer's critique of science in his programmatic essay 'Traditional and Critical Theory': 'The traditional idea of theory is abstracted from scientific activity as it is carried on within the division of labor at a particular stage in the latter's development. It corresponds to the activity of the scholar which takes place alongside all the other activities of a society, but in no immediately clear connection with them. In this view of theory, therefore, the real social function of science is not made manifest; it conveys not what theory means in human life, but only what it means in the isolated sphere in which, for historical reasons, it comes into existence.' As opposed to this, critical social theory is to become conscious of the self-referentiality of its calling; it knows that in and through the very act of knowing it belongs to the objective context of life that it strives to grasp. The context of its emergence does not remain external to the theory; rather, the theory takes this reflectively up into itself: 'In this intellectual activity the needs and goals, the experiences and skills, the customs and tendencies of the contemporary form of human existence have all played their part.' The same holds true for the context of application: 'As the influence of the subject matter on the theory, so also the application of the theory to the subject matter is not only an intrascientific process but a social one as well.'

In his famous methodological introduction to his critique of political economy of 1857, Marx applied the type of reflection called for by Horkheimer to one of his central concepts. He explained there why the basic assumptions of political economy rest on a seemingly simple abstraction, which is in fact quite difficult:

> It was an immense step forward for Adam Smith to throw out every limiting specification of wealth-creating activity – not only manufacturing, or commercial, or agricultural labor, but one as well as the others, labor in general. With the abstract universality of wealthcreating activity we now have the universality of the object defined as wealth, the product as such or again labor as such, but labor as past objectified labor. How difficult and great this transition was may be seen from how Adam Smith himself from time to time still falls back into the Physiocratic system. Now it might seem that all that had been achieved thereby was to discover the abstract expression for the simplest and most ancient relation in which human beings – in whatever form of society – play the role of producers. This is correct in one respect. Not in another . . . Indifference toward specific labors corresponds to a form of society in which individuals can with ease transfer from one labor to another, and where the specific kind is a matter of chance for them, hence of indifference. Not only the category 'labor,' but labor in reality has here become the means of creating wealth in general, and has ceased to be organically linked with particular individuals in any specific form. Such a state of affairs is at its most developed in the modern form of existence of bourgeois society – in the United States. Here, then, for the first time, the point of departure of modern economics, namely the abstraction of the category 'labor,' 'labor as such,' labor pure and simple, becomes true in practice.

Smith was able to lay the foundations of modern economics only after a mode of production arose that, like the capitalist mode with its differentiation of an economic system steered via exchange value, forced a transformation of concrete activities into abstract performances, intruded into the world of work with this real abstraction, and thereby created a problem for the workers themselves: 'Thus the simplest abstraction which modern economics places at the head of its discussions and which expresses an immeasurably ancient relation valid in all forms of society, nevertheless achieves practical truth as an abstraction only as a category of the most modern society.'

A theory of society that claims universality for its basic concepts, without being allowed simply to bring them to bear upon their object in a conventional manner, remains caught up in the self-referentiality that Marx demonstrated in connection with the concept of abstract labor. As I have argued above, when labor is rendered abstract and indifferent, we have a special case of the transference of communicatively structured domains of action over to media-steered interaction. This interpretation decodes the deformations of the lifeworld with the help of another category, namely, 'communicative action.' What Marx showed to be the case in regard to the category of labor holds true for this as well: 'how even the most abstract categories, despite their validity – precisely because of their abstractness – for all epochs, are nevertheless, in the specific character of this abstraction, themselves likewise a product of historical relations, and possess their full validity only for and within these relations.' The theory of communicative action can explain why this is so: the development of society must itself give rise to the problem situations that objectively afford contemporaries a privileged access to the general structures of the lifeworld.

The theory of modernity that I have here sketched in broad strokes permits us to recognize the following: In modern societies there is such an expansion of the scope of contingency for interaction loosed from normative contexts that the inner logic of communicative action 'becomes practically true' in the deinstitutionalized forms of intercourse of the familial private sphere as well as in a public sphere stamped by the mass media. At the same time, the systemic imperatives of autonomous subsystems penetrate into the lifeworld and, through monetarization and bureaucratization, force an assimilation of communicative action to formally organized domains of action – even in areas where the action-coordinating mechanism of reaching understanding is functionally necessary. It may be that this provocative threat, this challenge that places the symbolic structures of the lifeworld as a whole in question, can account for why they have become accessible to us.

37

KARL-OTTO APEL
Types of social science in light of human cognitive interests* (1977)

... The idea of leading interests of knowledge, in my opinion, makes up the characteristic core of a philosophy of science that understands itself as an alternative to the so-called modern theory of science, that is, to the neopositivistic conception of a logic of unified science. Tracing back the different questions and methods of science to different leading interests of knowledge means indeed denying the claim to a unification of scientific methodology by logical reductionism. But this does not imply the disavowal of any kind of unity of science. At this point the first misunderstanding has to be dissolved. And this may be done, I think, by a distinction between the problematics of a differentiated constitution of the meaning of possible objects of experience on the one hand and the problematics of a discursive reflection upon the validity claims of all results of scientific inquiry on the other hand. Although the latter question cannot be settled without carefully taking into regard the different meanings of validity claims, it nevertheless shows the ultimate unity of all sciences as lying in their universal truth claims to be reconfirmed by a universal intersubjective consensus to be reached by discursive arguments ...

After this first preliminary remark, it becomes possible to cope with a second misunderstanding: If the leading interests of knowledge are to be considered as conditions of the possibility for the meaning-constitution of possible objects of experience, then they may obviously not be simply equated with external motivations which may promote or even corrupt scientific enterprises. Whereas the latter interests are to be considered only as causes with regard to the possibility of scientific knowledge (although they might be reasons of action for individual scientists), the leading interests of knowledge are not only and not primarily to be considered as causes of the factual performance of science but rather as reasons or normative conditions of the possibility of the methical meanings of typically differentiated scientific questions (although it must and may easily be admitted that, in the long run, they fulfill also a causal or energetic function in the evolution of human knowledge, being the force

* From 'Types of Social Science in the Light of Human Interests of Knowledge' by Karl-Otto Apel, originally published in *Social Research*, 44 (3), 1977, pp. 425–444, 460–470. Reprinted by permission of the author and publisher.

behind at least part of the external motivations of scientific enterprises). Therefore the leading interests of knowledge, in contradistinction to merely external motiv- ations, are not (primarily) a topic for 'science of science,' which as an empiric social science has to explore the external steerings of science by its environments, but it is rather a topic of a transcendental reflection upon those conditions of the possibility of human knowledge that were not taken into account by Kant's transcendental ideal- ism, which in a sense presupposes that a pure mind or consciousness could constitute such a thing as a world of significant meanings for us. Indeed, I take the problematics of leading interests of knowledge as a topic of a transcendental pragmatics of language which comprises an anthropology of knowledge.

The preceding two remarks imply that the conception of leading interests of knowledge cannot be defended within the frame of a pure 'logic of science,' as it was often equated with modern theory of science in the last decades. Modern 'logic of science' – as it was primarily developed under the paradigm of 'logical empiricism' but also along the lines of a Popperian unified methodology – presupposes that all questions concerning the constitution of knowledge may be treated as questions con- cerning the empirical genesis of knowledge and hence, being questions of the empiric- pragmatic context of discovery, may be separated from the genuine questions of a logic of science concerning the context of justification of knowledge. As against this already classical dichotomy we must insist on the thesis that the conception of leading interests of knowing belongs to the extended context of the Kantian and Husserlian question as to the transcendental conditions of the possibility of a constitution of meaningful objects of experience. This question, concretized as it is by the conception of knowledge-interests as normative conditions of the possibility of meaning- constitution, may not be answered within the empiric-pragmatic 'context of dis- covery' but rather in the context of a transcendental-pragmatic reflection upon the internal connections between possible experiences, possible ways of practical world- commitments, and possible contexts of language games. In other words, the concep- tion of knowledge-interests is a topic of a transcendental-pragmatic supplementation or integration of the current 'logic of science,' being at the same time a transformation of the traditional transcendental theory of knowledge or epistemology. As such it no longer takes the theoretical subject-object relation for granted but calls it into ques- tion as a relation that has to be mediated by practical commitment in order to be a primordial sphere of typically different constitutions of meaningful objects of experience.

Hence, from the present point of view, the fashionable talk about the theory- impregnatedness of all experiential data does not suffice to overcome the naiveté of logical empiricism. For, instead of taking theories for granted, it is first necessary to ask about the conditions of the possibility of the constitution of theories as possible systematizations of synthetic achievements of cognition. And this might be done under the heuristic assumption that the different synthetic achievements of the differ- ent sciences – for example, causal explanation, functionalistic explanation, under- standing of good reasons (sometimes called teleological or rational explanation) – are not intelligible as synthetic achievements of cognition, if they are to be reduced to a unitary logical model of, say, deductive or inductive nomological explanation. For the synthetic achievements of cognition may be dependent on the different categories of posing questions which again may be considered as expressing different leading interests of knowledge.

Now, after these general and abstract remarks concerning the meaning and function of the conception of leading interests of knowledge, it might be time to introduce those three fundamental interests of knowledge that, according to Habermas's and my opinion, must be presupposed in a systematic account of the conditions of the possibility of the constitution of meaningful objects of human experience:

1. The interest in controlling an objectified environmental world;

2. The interest in communicative understanding;

3. The interest in critically emancipatory self-reflection.

The first knowledge-interest may be called practical in the sense of being related to technical praxis in a wide sense . . . The interest in controlling an objectified environmental world may however be sublimed, and as such it goes far beyond its manipulative paradigm, comprising, for example, all theoretical objectifying of world pictures and being even presupposed in our present attempt of a philosophical disposing of leading interests of knowledge in a very abstract model of their structure. In German this wide range of a controlling knowledge may be expressed by the term *Verfügungswissen.*

The second knowledge-interest may be called practical in the Aristotelian sense of the word 'praxis' because in its origin it is not restricted to meaning-understanding and interpretation in the abstractive sense of, say, modern philology, but comprises the interest of coming to agreement with other people in human interaction . . . The German word *Verständigung* encompasses both the understanding of meaning and the coming to agreement, and by this ambiguity it is capable of expressing the whole concern of the second knowledge-interest by the term *Verständigungs-Interesse.*

The third leading interest of knowledge may be called practical in the sense of being related to an evolutionary or revolutionary praxis of changing the human quasi-nature, be it that of individuals or that of society, as a consequence of a process of enlightenment, that is, of overcoming inner constraints of compulsions by critical self-reflection . . .

Concerning these three fundamental interests of knowledge I would claim that they can be systematically grounded as normative conditions of the possibility of meaningful experience within the frame of a transcendental pragmatics of language games. And this implies the further claim that all conceivable internal, meaning-constitutive interests of knowledge may be derived, in a sense, from the three fundamental knowledge-interests or from possible typical combinations or dialectical mediations of them. In this context it might be heuristically supposed that, on the one hand and in one sense, all three leading internal interests are presupposed in all methodological forms or types of scientific inquiries but that, on the other hand and in another sense, certain types of science (in their constitutive questions and methodical devices) are paradigmatically determined by just one of the three fundamental interests. And, moreover, it might be supposed that there are typical figures of thought constituting methodological devices that might be derived from different types of combinations or dialectical mediations of the three fundamental interests of know-ledge. Now, this is what I want to show in this paper with respect to the social sciences, this term being understood in a very broad sense such that quasi-physicalistic 'behavioral sciences' and quasi-biological 'system-theories' might be subsumed under that label as well as, for instance, historic-hermeneutical *Geisteswissenschaften* and historic-critical social sciences, in the sense of, say, sociological critique of institutions and of ideology and in the sense of psychoanalysis. Being thematized in this wide range, the social sciences provide a particularly favorable field of demonstration for the conception of leading interests of knowledge; for the fact that the same human society may become an object of knowledge according to very different method-ological perspectives in my opinion supports the thesis that neither a pure logic of science nor an ontology of the essential regions of possible objects of knowledge in the pre-Kantian sense (e.g., in the sense of Thomism or of Hartmann or of orthodox dialectical materialism) is able to do justice to the interrelationship between the struc-ture of being and the normative conditions of possible constitution of meaningful objects of human experience and hence of methodical questions of the sciences in the broadest sense of this word . . .

From these considerations we may derive the following thesis: Understanding and explanation, so it turns out now, are complementary forms of knowledge corresponding to complementary leading interests of knowledge. That is to say,

1. They supplement each other within the whole household of human know-ledge, so to speak. At the same time,

2. They exclude each other as different interests or intentions of asking questions. And,

3. For both reasons, they cannot be reduced to each other. By this comple-mentarity thesis we have fixed a first ideal-typical constellation of possible methods of knowledge according to a corresponding constellation of leading interests of knowledge. And this fundamental polarized constellation might serve us as a first orientation for a further ideal-typical differentiation of possible methods of human knowledge.

Focusing now on the social sciences in a broad sense, we may apply the point of view of the complementarity thesis in a two-fold way. First, we may, in the light of that thesis, look for criteria for distinguishing between common presuppositions of all social sciences, on the one hand, and natural sciences, especially physics, on the other hand. Second, we may try, in the light of the same thesis, to find criteria of a methodological differentiation within the social sciences themselves, say between those that spring from a quasi-physicalistic interest of nomological explanation of objectified social processes and those that methodically incorporate and elaborate on the hermeneutical interest in improving or reestablishing communicative understanding between differ-ent contemporary language-games and sociocultural forms of life or between those of the present and those of the past.

The first way of looking at things may show that the ontological difference be-tween the entities made into the object of science – for example, between human beings capable of intentional actions and communication with the scientists and mute physical things – still are to be considered as a reason for methodological differentiation of knowledge, that is, they are to be considered as a factor that cannot be eliminated by the knowledge-interests on the side of the scientists but, on the contrary, already on the level of the object-constitution favors certain corresponding knowledge-interests and resists or even definitely limits the realization of certain other knowledge-interests.

The second way of looking at things, on the other hand, may show that the leading interests of knowledge are indeed normative conditions of the possibility of object-constitution and thus far are reasons of a methodological differentiation of knowledge not only in conformity with certain correspondences between kinds of interests and kinds of ontological entities but also, to a certain extent, in spite of them – for example, insofar as the same human beings or the same activities of the human society may become the object or topic of very different types of methodological approaches corresponding to different leading interests of knowledge.

Now, as I said, both these considerations of the relationship between the nature of being and the object-constitution according to leading interests of knowledge shall be applications of the complementarity thesis. That is to say, they are merely concerned with the two complementary knowledge-interests in controlling objectified processes, on the one hand, and in communicative understanding, on the other hand. In order to show the function of the third leading interest of knowledge – namely, that of critical-emancipatory self-reflection – we shall have to supplement the complementarity thesis itself by that of a dialectical mediation between communicative understanding and a quasi-naturalistic explanation. And this methodological figure of thought may be shown, I think, to correspond to an intrinsic constitution of human nature as well as to an ethical demand concerning an interest of man in himself, that is, of critical-emancipatory self-knowledge. It may be considered as the characteristic methodological device of the critical-reconstructive social sciences, including sociological critique of ideology and institutional self-alienations of man as well as psychoanalysis.

Methodological differences between natural science and social science

Regarding the differences between natural science and social science in general that are constituted both by the nature of being and by the complementarity of knowledge-interests corresponding to the nature of being, the following critiera might be discussed in a short overview:

1. A fundamental precondition of the constitution of nature as an object of experimental explanatory physics in the moden sense is, I think, defined by the possibility of a complete objectification of nature with regard to the presupposed epistemological subject-object relation, whereas all social sciences, even those that provide the basis for social technology, are only allowed to perform certain secondary methodological objectifications but may not totally objectify their human subject-objects, so to speak, in order to prevent losing them as intentional objects of knowledge . . . The reason why not even quasi-physicalistic empirical social sciences are allowed to totally objectify

human behavior in the sense of a complete renunciation of understanding is exposed by a further criterion for a necessary distinction between the methodology of all social sciences and that of natural science.

2. Natural science as explanatory science must renounce all kinds of communicative and teleological understanding because it must suppose that the regularities of nature are not rules (or even norms) which may be followed or not, or followed in a false way, by nature as a subject of teleological action, but that they are laws determining the behavior of natural objects in the sense of causal or statistical necessity.

In contradistinction to this situation, the social sciences are, in principle, to be considered as sciences confronted with a 'subject-object,' so to speak. That is to say, they must, at least in a first approach, suppose that there are regularities, constitutive for the specific character of their objects, that must be considered as rules or norms followed more or less intentionally (although not necessarily in a conscious way) by human subjects of actions; and that means that they might also be not followed or incorrectly followed in exceptional cases.

Methodological consequences of this necessary presupposition concerning the object-constitution may be formulated in the following theses:

(1) The social sciences cannot restrict themselves to imposing hypothetical regularities from outside their objects and to testing these hypotheses by communication-free observation. For they cannot, on principle, infer from an observed correspondence between a regularity imposed from outside and observed behavior that the regularity is a rule followed by the objects as subjects of actions, for the imposed regularity can always, on principle, be made so complicated that it must fit to the observed behavior (not to speak of the heuristical impossibility of discovering rules of social behavior, say, e.g., of so-called 'institutional facts,' just by observation in the light of nomological theories, i.e., without presupposing communicative understanding).

(2) Little as the social sciences may infer the existence of rules from observed correspondences of imposed regularities and observed behaviour, they may as little infer from observed deviations of human behaviour from supposed regularities that these regularities do not express a valid rule, usually followed, or even a norm that is valid although it is not often followed.

(3) Hence, it follows that the social sciences must insist on the presupposition that their hypotheses concerning rules of behavior must rest on an understanding that, on principle, could be proved valid by a participation of the scientist in that rule game (language-game in the wide sense of Wittgenstein) which he must suppose as context of the hypothetical rules.

(4) This involves among other things that all knowledge of social science, in contradistinction to knowledge of natural science, is in a twofold way mediated by language, or even in a twofold way mediated by theories; once by the language-game and the theory of scientists and, besides that, by the language-game, and sometimes even by the theory, in the light of which the human

subject-objects understand their own rule-following behavior. Hence the decisive achievement of cognition must in this case consist in the methodical bridging between the two language-games, or even theories, by communicative understanding to be tested, in principle, by communicative participation in supposed language-games.

As illustrations of the criteria of a fundamental difference between natural science and social science presented thus far, we may mention the following examples which refer to those cases of explanatory social sciences that may be considered as methodological limit cases in the sense of quasi-natural science but nonetheless must fulfill the methodological limit cases for all social sciences:

(1) Mathematical linguistics in the sense of Chomsky's generative-transformational grammar may claim to provide a nomological-explanatory theory for human language-universals and linguistic competence by deriving the restrictions of possible grammars to be generated by man from a biological law of human nature; nevertheless, as a social science, whose experiential data are delivered by human speech-acts and texts, generative linguistics has also to understand and to reconstruct in a normatively correct way those rules of grammatical sentences that competent native speakers may be able to reconfirm as rules on the basis of their intuition (notwithstanding the difficulties caused by possible misunderstandings between the linguists and the native speakers). Chomsky even presupposes explicitly that the linguist must reconstruct precisely that grammar which previously has been unconsciously constructed by the competent speaker himself. This would mean that even explanatory linguistics as limit case of social science proves the methodological thesis that all knowledge of social science must in a twofold way be mediated by language, or even by theory. What I have said thus far about Chomsky's linguistic theory seems to hold good also for other proposed explanatory theories of human competences, say of logic-mathematical, cognitive, communicative and role-taking competences of man. Nomological explanations, if they should be possible at all on the basis of supposed biological programings, must in all these cases at least be combined with normative reconstructions which have to be proved correct by communicative understanding between the social scientist and his 'subject-object' (which sometimes may be the scientist himself).

(2) Another limit case of social science that nevertheless illustrates the criteria presented thus far is represented by those behavioral sciences that owe the laws and antecedent conditions of their quasi-nomological explanations to logical transformations of maxims, aims, and beliefs into a so-called volitional-cognitive causal complex, by which the behavior seems to be determined. Also in this case it is required, on principle, that the correctness of having understood the presupposed maxims, aims, and beliefs can be tested by communication – for example, by questions, interviews, etc. And this hermeneutical presupposition cannot be considered along with Hempel

as only a matter of psychological-heuristic relevance – that is, as being dispensable, on principle. For the contrary is shown by every case where the hermeneutical presupposition of understanding people's mentality cannot be taken as a matter of course – for example, in the case of economic projects in developing countries.

Nevertheless, the results of quasi-nomological behavioral sciences – for example, explanations and predictions of consumers' behavior under certain situational conditions – look like results of natural science and may indeed be considered as a limit case of social science. The reason for this fact becomes intelligible in light of a further general criterion of difference between social science and natural science.

(3) Pure natural science – that is, physics – need not deal with the world as history in a proper sense. By this I do not mean that there is no dimension of irreversibility, and hence of a history of nature to be dealt with by physics. It is true, I think, that physics has to deal with irreversibility of nature in the sense of the second principle of thermodynamics – that is, in the sense of the increase of entropy. But in this very sense of irreversibility physics may suppose nature's being definitely determined concerning its future and thus having no history in a sense that would resist nomological objectification.

Contrary to this, social science, insofar as it is concerned, on principle, with the history of human society, must presuppose history in a structural sense that resists nomological objectification. For it must not only suppose irreversibility in the sense of a statistically determined process but irreversibility in the sense of man's progress of knowledge influencing the process of history in an irreversible manner . . .

Types of social science and the critical-emancipatory interest of knowledge

At this point, however, where we are looking for a compensation of social-technological power of manipulation by another type of social sciences, we must reflect upon the fact that the complementarity thesis rests on an idealization which is necessary, but not sufficient, in order to understand the whole scope of possible leading interests of knowledge underlying different types of social science. The idealization involved in the complementarity thesis has its paradigm in the esoteric community of scientific investigators and, moreover, in the esoteric community of argumentative discourse, where the communication partners must consider each other as pure subjects of thought and speech and hence as limit instances of the objectifiable world, so to speak. They are thereby anticipating an ideal situation where only two complementary leading interests of knowledge would be justified – namely, the interest in controlling (by explanation and prediction) an objectified environmental world and the interest in communicative understanding between the cosubjects of argumentative discourse. Now, this idealization disregards or embezzles, so to speak, the fact that human beings interacting in social relations are in no case those pure co-subjects of understanding as it is presupposed in the esoteric situation of argumentative discourse.

What I have in mind now is not simply the fact that the human subjects of thought and speech can be made the objects of quasi-nomological behavioral science, as we have already noticed. This fact by no means contradicts the ideal complementarity situation, since in any case of an objectification of human behavior there has to be presupposed a community of cosubjects of science that corresponds to the anticipated ideal of a pure communication community. This very anticipation, however, is at the same time a necessary presupposition of arguing and a counterfactual presupposition that contradicts at least the present state of human self-understanding and hence of communicative competence. For even as subjects of knowledge and as co-subjects of communicative understanding we are not (or not yet) transparent to ourselves, and our speech is not the pure expression of our intentions by public symbols as intersubjective vehicles of unambiguous meanings. Rather, we are as subjects of understanding more or less alienated to ourselves and to our self-understanding, and our speech is ambiguous insofar as it always expresses both connotations that cannot be unambiguously expressed by individual speakers, because their self-understanding in terms of public language underlies idiosyncratic restrictions and connotations that cannot be expressed by public language at all.

Now, by these two dimensions of speech ambiguity due to speech restriction I tried to intimate two dimensions of human self-alienation by splitting off of unconscious motivations and hence of ex-communicated meanings, so to speak: one concerning the individual person and his or her communicative competence, and one concerning the society as a communication community that functions as the subject of the public conventions of language-games and hence of a public world and self-understanding of men. And, although these two dimensions of self-alienation are to be considered as interconnected, their overtly pathological aspects have first been noted separately in two quite different and initially rather antagonistic new disciplines of human science, Freudian psychoanalysis on the one hand and Marxian critique of ideology on the other hand. In the present context I want to suggest that these two disciplines should be understood under the common label of critical-reconstructive social science and that their methodological approach may be explicated by tracing it down to a common leading interest of knowledge – that is, to the interest in critical-emancipatory self-reflection. And I want to show that, corresponding to this peculiar leading interest of knowledge, there is a peculiar methodological figure of thought underlying both psychoanalysis and critique of ideology as it is part of a critical sociohistorical reconstruction of the state of society.

Now, in the context of our present approach it is no matter of course that a peculiar knowledge interest and methodological figure of thought has to be postulated to account for so-called critical-reconstructive social sciences. Rather the necessity of this postulate has to be shown by confronting the approach of critical-reconstructive social science to that of quasi-physicalistic behavioral science and to hermeneutical science of communicative understanding . . . I can be rather brief, I think, in defending the thesis that critical-reconstructive social science cannot be reduced to quasi-physicalistic behavioral science, or speaking more loosely, and generally, to so-called empiric-analytic social science in the sense of the unified logic or methodology of science. For the propagators and absolutizers of that type of social science have often shrewdly remarked that neither psychoanalysis nor critique in the sense of Marx fits the methodological standards of an experimental, nomological-explanatory science, as for example to the postulate of yielding consequences in form of conditional predictions to be tested by repeatable experiments based on observations by exchangeable observers, etc. Thus, for example, Karl Popper at the beginning of his career in Vienna came to distinguish Marxism and Freudian psychoanalysis as pseudoscience from Einsteinian physics as a paradigm of science underlying possible falsifications by yielding risky testable consequences. Very similar criticism was directed against Marxism and psychoanalysis along the lines of a Carnap-Hempel-Nagel logic of unified science. Now, it almost goes without saying that I cannot see much sense in defending both types of critical-reconstructive social sciences against reproaches that rest on a systematic disregard of the rise of the leading questions of different sciences from different leading interests of knowledge. The usual issue of the scientistic defenses of Marxism and psychoanalysis at best represents a bad approximation to the prestige-paradigm of (quasi-natural) science at the cost of the characteristic features of a critical-reconstructive project of inquiry, springing from an interest in emancipatory self-reflection.

Thus it seems intelligible from what we have said about the impossibility, in principle, of nomological explanation to be tested by repeatable experiments with respect to history (i.e., history of the human species and life-history of single persons) that neither the Marxian conception of historical necessity nor the Freudian quasi-causal explanations of neurotic symptoms within the context of a life-history may be conceived of as applications of universal laws and special marginal conditions to explaining and predicting certain classes of observable phenomena to be tested by exchangeable observers in repeatable experiments. The crucial significance of explicative interpreting ambiguous symbols in psychoanalysis as well as in critique of ideology (from the critique of religious myths to that of the myths of everyday life in late capitalism and state socialism) may suggest from the outset that critical-reconstructive social science is rather concerned with improving or reestablishing communicative understanding than with nomological explanation; and it is clear, even from a Carnapian point of view, that all kinds of explication of the meaning of symbols are different, on principle, from explanation according to laws, since an unambiguous system of symbols is already presupposed for nomological explanation.

Now, at this point, it seems as if the critical-reconstructive social sciences were to be understood along with the hermeneutic sciences, and that is to say from the point of view of the leading interest in communicative understanding being complementary to the interest in explanatory and predictive control of objectified processes. This point of view has indeed inspired some important philosophical reinterpretations of Freudian psychoanalysis, especially within the frame of hermeneutic phenomenology; and also humanistic reconstructions of Marxism or neo-Marxism in western Europe were more or less influenced by hermeneutic points of view. Regarding psycho-analysis, it is, in fact, hard to contest that hermeneutic procedures, similar to text interpretation, play a crucial role in its context; or speaking more precisely: since psychoanalysts try not only to interpret the ambiguous meanings of everyday language and of religious and poetical texts but, moreover, so-called dream texts and even neurotic symptoms as a paralanguage of bodily expressions, it may seem that they differ from normal hermeneuticians (interpreters) only by going beyond the realm of traditional text interpretation, widening, so to speak, the program of hermeneutics into that of a 'depth hermeneutics' (*Tiefenhermeneutik*).

It might seem plausible, at this stage of our consideration, to redefine the whole business of hermeneutics by supposing that not just communicative understanding of symbols but interpreting of ambiguous symbols is the task of hermeneutics, whereas unambiguous symbols of artificial formalized languages of logics and mathematics and even symbols of everyday language, rendered unambiguous by the pragmatical context of understanding, do not pose problems for hermeneutics. The latter distinction was indeed introduced by Dilthey, who emphasized that methodical-hermeneutic understanding can constitute itself only where the meanings of delivered texts, works, or institutions have become unintelligible; and the redefinition of hermeneutics in terms of interpretation of ambiguous symbols was proposed by Ricoeur. Hence it seems plausible that psychoanalysis might be considered as the very paradigm of hermeneutics.

However, for reasons still to be explicated, I cannot follow this suggestion, which would involve a merely bipolarized or complementaristic architectonics of epistemology. I don't wish to renounce the distinction made by Dilthey between purely logical and pragmatical understanding, on the one side, and methodical-hermeneutic understanding on the other side, but I do not think that the ambiguity of symbols as it is presupposed in psychoanalysis should be considered as the paradigm for hermeneutics in general. The reason for questioning this latter suggestion is provided, I think, by the fact that the ambiguity of symbols in psychoanalysis (say the ambiguity of the symbols in dreams, not to speak of psychosomatic symptoms) is not only a topic of hermeneutic interpretation but at the same time also the object of quasi-causal and quasi-functional explanation in terms of quasi-nomological theory of energetic processes that are as such precluded from hermeneutic understanding by the reification, so to speak, of split-off motives into compulsory behavior.

Here also a methodological analogy between psychoanalysis and neo-Marxist critical reconstruction of social history seems to become apparent, insofar as the latter must presuppose causally determined reified processes of a human pseudonature in order to supplement historical hermeneutics and to mediate, so to speak, a deeper understanding of human history, and of the ideological self-understandings of history, through a quasi-naturalistic explanation of the causally determined reified processes. In both cases the critical analyst must go behind the whole sphere of communicative understanding; that is to say, he must not only try to render dark and ambiguous texts intelligible by meaning-interpolations of a philological kind; but he must rather change his attitude to the human utterances insofar as he interpolates meanings that are not supposed to be accessible to the (intentional self-understanding of the) subjects of the interpreted utterances. In doing so, the analyst at least partially suspends the relation of communicative understanding between himself and his subject-object and replaces it by the subject-object relation of quasi-naturalistic explanation.

Now, this attitude, which is characteristic and indispensable for the critical-reconstructive social sciences, is excluded, it seems to me, by the idea of pure hermeneutics and is even abhorred by the typical hermeneuticians for good reasons. For hermeneuticians must stick to the idea that human utterances and texts, works of art, religion, philosophy, and science, are sources of a possible disclosure of valid truth and hence subjects of learning to the interpreter. The systematic tension between this attitude and that of the critical social sciences becomes immediately clear if one reflects on the fact that psychoanalysts and critics of ideology must presuppose a communicative understanding among themselves, and in this context an interpretation of texts – say, for example, of their own critical tradition of Freud and Marx – which is different, in principle, from that understanding of ambiguous symbols that is mediated by a quasi-naturalistic phase of causal explanation, and nevertheless may be mediated and improved by hermeneutic methods in the usual sense. By this reflection the methodological point of the complementarity thesis is reestablished, so to speak, in the back of critical social science.

At this point of our consideration, one could think that the methodical structure of the critical social sciences must, after all, be very similar to that of the quasi-nomological behavioral sciences, in view of the fact that in both cases the relation of communicative interaction and understanding is partially suspended in favor of a quasi-naturalistic objectification and explanation. However, within the frame of my approach, this conjecture of analogy proves to be precipitous and superficial; for it does not take into regard the very different constellations of the leading interests of knowledge and methodological figures of thought in both cases.

In the case of quasi-nomological behavioral science, the leading interest is directed to control over objectified and predictable processes as the final result of the whole procedure of inquiry, and, corresponding to this interest, the proper aim of knowledge is quasi-nomological explanation as a basis for social technology, whereas communicative understanding of reasons of human actions is only a heuristic means, although an indispensable one, in order to frame explanatory hypotheses. Thus the methodological figure of thought is characterized by a dialectical mediation of explanatory knowledge through communicative understanding.

The contrary is true in the case of the critical-reconstructive social sciences – for example, in psychoanalysis and critique of ideology. In this case the leading interest of knowledge is not directed to control of objectified processes but to deepening of self-understanding by critical-emancipatory self-reflection, and hence the proper aim of the methodical procedure is not to win quasi-nomological knowledge of human behavior; but quasi-causal explanation is on its part only a heuristic means of deepening human self-understanding. Hence the methodological figure of thought corresponding to the leading knowledge-interest of critical social science is characterized by a dialectical mediation of human self-understanding, and thus also of communicative understanding, through quasi-naturalistic causal explanation.

In order to show that this issue of my analysis is not only a lofty play of construction but actually opens an epistemological and methodological dimension that is inaccessible, in principle, to a pure logic of science, one should reflect upon the different role played by self-reflection of the human subject-objects of science in both cases: In the case of quasi-nomological behavioral science relevant self-reflection of the subject-objects in the sense of self-application of conditioned predictions can only disturb, in the sense of Merton's paradox, the subject-object relation presupposed by controllable experiments, and therefore it has to be eliminated as far as possible for methodological reasons, as I have pointed out already. On the contrary, in the case of critical social science, particularly in the paradigmatical case of psychoanalysis, self-reflection on the side of the human subject-objects of knowledge is intentionally provoked for methodological reasons, because it is the very vehicle of the dialectical mediation of deepening self-understanding through quasi-causal explanation of split-off reified compulsory processes. (In this case reflective self-application of the explanatory theory to the effect of changing the behavior of the human subject-objects of inquiry is not only no obstacle but, on the contrary, is intended as the very therapeutic aim of the analysis which is at the same time a test of the truth claim of the analysis. For, in case of a full success of the emancipatory self-reflection, the very causes of compulsory behavior that were supposed by quasi-causal explanation are eliminated by the reflective self-application of that explanation by its subject-object. And this effect is not considered as self-destroying prophecy of a conditional prediction but rather as a self-applicative verification of the truth-claim of the analysis.)

Facing this remarkable inversion of the methodological device of behavioral science by psychoanalysis, and imagining that this methodological figure of thought might, on principle, also hold good in the case of a possible sociological critique of ideology connected with a critique of social institutions, one might come to the conclusion that critical social science is the very counterpart of quasi-nomological behavioral science – a counterpart that might also fulfill the compensatory function with respect to the danger of a technocracy based on conditioning manipulation of behavior.

38

ALBRECHT WELLMER
Critical theory of society* (1969)

I have attempted, in conjunction with the previous criticism of Marx, to indicate once more the historical background against which Western European intellectuals have tried since the twenties to bring an 'unmodified' Marx into currency again, in contrast to ossified official Party discussion. Since then, 'critical Marxism' has become a privileged possession of radical intellectuals, at first in the capitalist countries and, since the end of World War II, to an increasing extent in the socialist countries too. The isolation of this critical Marxism from political praxis has begun to give way only in the last few years. One characteristic seems to be common despite all fundamental differences, from Korsch, the philosophers of the Frankfurt School, Sartre and Marcuse, to the theoreticians of the Marxism of Warsaw, Prague and Zagreb: that, as the expression of oppositionist tendencies, it is required implicitly or explicitly to oppose the objectivistic trends of Marx's philosophy of history; that it espouses the claims of individuals to autonomy and happiness as against the historically effective tendencies to the totalization of technical and bureaucratic rationality; that (here quite un-Marxist) it espouses 'morality' as against the 'course of the world.' This post-revolutionary critical Marxism has as yet led to no theory that (in regard to historical concretion and empirical contents) can be put side by side with that of Marx. Nevertheless, taken as a whole, it is yet another confirmation of the need for an ideology-critical examination of Marx's theory itself, which (with the acumen of the conservative) Hans Freyer expressed forty years ago. In Marx's intensification of 'Hegel's ethics as naturalism,' and in his turning of the ' "necessity of the cause," that is, the necessity of reason, into the causal mechanism of social movement' Freyer hears the call-sign of an age which 'applied all forms of thought, particularly those inherited from German idealism (having wrested them into a naturalistic shape), to all areas of reality, even to social facts and the forms of thought proper to the physical sciences.' However overstated this criticism may be, the 'possibility of establishing a just society' is in fact a prejudgement that puts Marxist theory (to a greater extent

* From *Critical Theory of Society* by Albrecht Wellmer. Continuum, New York, 1971, pp. 127–135. Reprinted with permission.

than its creators would have wished) in line with the other great sociological 'draft theories' of the nineteenth century – but now in a negative sense: 'As every social reality is, so it thinks.'

I shall now return to the Frankfurt School's critique of positivism and make use of these last insights. At the beginning of this essay, I presented the early Horkheimer's theory, corresponding to the contemporary self-conception of Marxist intellectuals, from the viewpoint of a return to the 'authentic,' 'dialectical' Marx. It is now evident that this return was already a wholly critical one. Horkheimer's criticism of capitalist society is already fundamentally a 'critique of instrumental reason'; the instrumentalization of reason, which Horkheimer observed in bourgeois science, is perceived to be the interdiction of reason in view of the increasingly universal growth of conditions of domination, and the exchange principle of bourgeois society is interpreted as the fullest expression of this instrumentalized reason. Already implicit here is a criticism of the objectivistic tendencies of Marx's conception of revolution; it appears in the distinction between different forms of revolutionary struggle, in the criticism of the bureaucratic rigidity of the socialist movement, in the demand for the union of spontaneity and discipline and for the anticipation of future solidarity in the organization of the revolutionary struggle, and, finally, in the criticism of the objectivistic 'misunderstanding' of Marx's theory itself. What Horkheimer still represents here as a genuine interpretation of Marx, has already been conditioned by the insight that the revolution has to break through a closed world of technical rationality and reified relations, and therefore that it does not only have to carry out the laws of such a world by means of a mere shifting of the centers of power. Even in the early Horkheimer, the link is broken that in Marx joined the critique of political economy to the theory of revolution. However, this is already a first step towards what proved so characteristic of the later Frankfurt School – the displacement of the critique of political economy by which the main component of a revolutionary theory becomes the instrument of an ideology criticism suspicious of political practice.

In *The Dialectics of Enlightenment*, which Horkheimer and Adorno completed in 1944, while in exile, its authors established the consequences of their critical interpretation of Marx and of recent historical experiences. *The Dialectics of Enlightenment* is a fascinating attempt to produce a profound historico-philosophical critique of capitalist society – so profound that it grapples both with the liberal capitalism criticized by Marx and with its state-capitalist and state-interventionist heirs, and incorporates them in a proficient conceptual framework. Marx saw the cause of the reification of all social relations in the unleasing of the exchange rationality in bourgeois society. Inasmuch as he associated this rationality with a specific form of ownership, he saw the abrogation of this form of property as productive of a consequent removal of reification; therefore, Horkheimer and Adorno detach the criticism of exchange rationality from its fundamental exposition in terms of labor value in the criticism of political economy, and translate it into a criticism of instrumental reason: the criticism of instrumental reason replaces the criticism of political economy in terms of trends, and the criticism of political economy becomes a criticism of technical civilization.

The theoretical significance of this process is immense. The dialectics of alienation and emancipation that Marx identified is now revealed in all its implications, in such a way that the theoretical resolution of this dialectics is shown to be obstructed by a theory of revolution on the Marxian pattern. According to Marx, the social systems produced by men must turn into an external authority over the reified sub- jects, in order to permit development of the material resources which will ultimately allow men to make their own history with the will and consciousness of freely social- ized individuals. However, since for Marx the dialectical union of social existence and consciousness ultimately became a unilateral determining relationship, he could describe the history of self-sacrifice and emancipation only in accordance with that external destiny which men were themselves preparing by building a class society; by the same logic of self-preservation that brought men to involve themselves in this external destiny, they must also eventually liberate themselves from it. Horkheimer faced Marx with the other side of the picture. The external fate in which men have had to involve themselves for the sake of emancipation from their natural corruption, is at the same time their inner destiny; a destiny which reason sustains through its own efforts. Ultimately, the subjects for whose sake the subjection, reification and demy- thization of nature were begun, are themselves so repressed, reified and disenchanted in self-regard, that even their emancipatory efforts become the contrary: the confirm- ation of the context of delusion in which they are imprisoned. The cancellation of an animistic image of the world already saw the foundation of the dialectics of enlightenment which, in capitalist industrial society, is taken to the point where 'man is anthropomorphized for man.' 'The ratio which supplants mimesis is not simply its opposite. It is itself mimesis: mimesis unto death. The subjective spirit which cancels the animation of nature, exerts power over a despiritualized nature only by imitating its rigidity, and despiritualizing itself in turn.'

Horkheimer and Adorno (who know their Freud) emphasize that 'the power of control over non-human nature and over other men' was repeatedly paid for by the 'denial of nature in man.' 'This very denial, the nucleus of all civilizing rationality, is the cancer-cell of a proliferating mythic irrationality; with the denial of nature in man, not only the goal of the external conquest of nature, but the goal of man's own individual life is distorted and rendered unintelligible. As soon as man discards his awareness that he himself is nature, all the aims for which he goes on living – social progress, the enhancement of all material and spiritual powers, even consciousness itself – are as nothing, and the enthroning of the means as an end (which in late capitalism develops to a degree tantamount to open insanity) is already perceptible even in the prehistory of subjectivity. Man's mastery over himself, which is the basis of his self, is almost without exception the destruction of the individual as subject, thus negating the very purpose of that mastery.' Admittedly, just as the productive forces arising under the enslaving pressures of a class society are the condition for social wealth and hence the pre-condition of a state of life without domination, so the subjection of nature in man is the pre-condition of personal autonomy: it is part of the mechanism of formation of an ego-consciousness. But the consequence of the world- historical identity of both processes has been that the reification of individuals has advanced to the same extent as the objectification of external nature; in the end, the individual subjects are no longer there who alone would be able to 'appropriate to themselves' the promised social wealth.

Therefore, for Horkheimer and Adorno, 'Enlightenment' becomes a world-historical project of the human species, in which the species simultaneous creates itself and threatens its own destruction; its ultimate aim is social freedom, happiness and the independence of the individual, but its secret logic aims at the extinction of the self-liberating subjects and the self-elevation of social bondage and constraint. From this viewpoint, the various metamorphoses of capitalist society that with Marx's approach were equally incomprehensible, can now be shown to be in fact accomplishments of the law of movement of this capitalist society – the ways in which the law of increasing objectification is fulfilled. Odysseus and the Marquis de Sade's Juliette become key figures in a process of enlightenment at the self-destructive end of which enlightenment degenerates into mass deception.

Critical theory therefore establishes, in contradistinction to Marx, that the fateful process of 'rationalization' of all processes of social life does not find its preordained end in an emancipated society, but – in accordance with its inward logic – is compelled instead to end in the opposite of emancipation: in the subjection of men, too, to the domination over nature that they themselves have achieved. But then 'revolution' is no longer conceivable as the conscious and collective fulfillment of an objectifiable historical necessity. 'Revolution' in the sense of a liberation from the natural history of man is far more something which results from an enlightenment of enlightened reason about its own nature – and that something is the breakingthrough of the dialectics of enlightenment of which revolutions to date were mere blind agents.

This radicalization of Marx's philosophy of history, by means of which (a long way from Marx's 'technical humanism' [cf. Klages]) the unleashing of technical rationality is perceived to be the most decisive of all forms of domination of men by men, anticipates some of the basic ideas of Marcuse. It reveals somber prospects for reified men. For their integration into the universal context of delusion is so inclusive that even the most serious efforts of liberation run the danger of confirming and stabilizing the existing power structure. The possibility of a 'praxis that will bring about a revolutionary transformation' therefore depends on the self-abandonment of the enlightenment in its 'positivistic aspect' being comprehended appropriately, and on thought reaching enlightenment about itself when it addresses itself to the domination in itself that is at the same time 'nature unreconciled.' Only this kind of self-conscious thought, which was from the start the only form in which enlightenment was opposed to domination, Horkheimer and Adorno believe has the power to break through that 'necessity' which socialism prematurely glorified as the 'guarantor of freedom to come.' Critical theory therefore remains the pioneer and conscience of a revolutionary, transforming praxis. But the future subjects of that praxis are no longer to be discerned so simply; the possibility of their existing is dependent solely on the 'intransigence of theory in regard to the lack of consciousness which allows society to adopt an inflexible pattern of thought.' With a resignation born of the experience of insanity systematized, the authors of The Dialectics of Enlightenment come finally to the question of the very possibility of enlightenment: 'If it is possible today to speak to anyone [in this regard], then we pass on the responsibility not to the so-called masses, and not to the individual (who is powerless) but to an imaginary witness – lest it disappear with us entirely.'

The Dialectics of Enlightenment has a key position in regard to the later development of the critical theory of the Frankfurt School. Attention to the basic ideas of these 'philosophical fragments' (the sub-title of the book) should help in further elucidation of the problem upon which my meta-theoretical discussion up to now has centered: the question of the mutual relationship of 'science' and 'criticism.' Adorno and Horkheimer take seriously the claim of Marx's theory to the status of ideology criticism; as against Marx's scientistic self-misconception they rely on his declared intention to reveal behind the mere 'apparent forms' of capitalist commodity-society its 'essential nature' – which means too, its 'unnatural essence.' This insistence on the distinction between essence and appearance is equally an insistence on the 'dual nature' of society and sociology, which positivism denies. Adorno remarked on this again in one of his last essays: 'Sociology enjoys a dual nature: in it the subject of all knowledge, society, [. . .] is simultaneously the object. Society is subjective because it refers back to the men who form it, and also because it refers its principles of organization back to subjective consciousness. [. . .] It is objective, because by reason of its supporting structure its own subjectivity remains unintelligible to it, because it has no total subject and through its organization prevents one from being established. However, a dual nature of this kind modifies the attitude of socio-scientific knowledge to its object – a fact that positivism does not acknowledge. It treats society, potentially the self-determining subject, unceremoniously as if it were an object to be determined from without.' In this way, the practical core of the theory of science controversy between 'traditional' and 'critical' theory, to which the early Horkheimer had already referred, is revealed anew: Critical social theory lives by the anticipation of a 'total social subject'; only on the basis of this anticipation is it able to conceive the apparent forms of a social disorder or 'unnatural essence' of society; the validity of its findings is bound up with the efficacy of a liberating interest in cognition – in knowing. Whether sociology 'as science is to accept society in the particular form in which it functions in any given case, as it has been traditionally represented as doing from Comte to Talcott Parsons, or whether – from the basis of social experience – it strives for the transformation of its fundamental structures, determines scientific theory in all categories and is therefore scarcely to be decided in terms of scientific theory.'

39

ROBERTO MANGABEIRA UNGER
The critical argument* (1975)

The hypothesis from which the discussion starts is that the present state of our psychological and political ideas is similar in one fundamental respect to the situation of European social thought in the mid-seventeenth century. Then as now, partial critiques of a still dominant tradition could not be taken further without being changed into a total critique of that tradition

Many movements, from the nominalism of Ockham to the political doctrines of Machiavelli and the epistemology of Descartes, had worked to subvert the foundations of classical metaphysics in its scholastic form. But it was in the work of Thomas Hobbes, of his contemporaries, and of his successors that the ancient political and psychological theories of the schools were first criticized as a whole. Only then did it become fully clear that theorists had not yet freed themselves from the medieval Aristotle; that the framework of thought within which they worked suffered from defects and carried consequences of which they were not previously aware; that the ideas about mind and about society which defined this kind of thought formed a single system; and that this body of doctrines turned on certain metaphysical principles. The attempt to come to terms with the implications of these insights produced a new system of ideas, the liberal doctrine, which rivaled and even surpassed in coherence and generality the tradition it displaced. The novel theory, at first the possession of a tiny band of thinkers, increasingly became the common property of broader social groups and the basis of the modern social sciences.

Now as then, a unified set of ideas has been refined and rejected piecemeal. Our approaches to social study are nothing but partial assaults on a mode of thought they have neither repudiated nor understood in its entirety. Again, however, a study of the main difficulties faced by these traditions shows the unbroken tyranny that the classical theory, in this case the liberal doctrine, exercises over the minds of those who believe they have extricated themselves from its clutches.

If this view of our predicament is correct, our initial efforts should be devoted to

* Reprinted with the permission of The Free Press, a Division of Simon & Schuster, Inc., from *Knowledge and Politics* by Roberto Mangabeira Unger. Copyright © 1975 by Roberto Mangabeira Unger. Pp. 5–7.

defining with as much precision as possible the ideas that determine and limit the possibilities of our thinking. Liberalism must be seen all of a piece, not just as a set of doctrines about the disposition of power and wealth, but as a metaphysical conception of the mind and society. Only then can its true nature be understood, and its secret empire overthrown.

The very first step is to reconstruct the design of the whole doctrine, and to understand the relationship of its different parts. Until we draw the map of the system, we shall misunderstand our own ideas by failing to apprehend their premises and implications. Moreover, we shall be condemned to accept incoherent views of whose incoherence we are unaware or to acquiesce in paradoxes we suppose inescapable when they are just the consequences of postulates on which we need not rely. Lastly, one who regards as disparate principles what are in fact different aspects of a single doctrine will be deluded into imagining it possible to dispose of one without rejecting all the others, or to accept one without conforming to the rest.

The claims of the critique may be summarized in the following eleven propositions. First, a large number of the views about knowledge, epistemology, human nature (psychology in the strict sense), and morals (ethics) that we share in our everyday experience and use in our social studies can be accounted for by a much smaller number of principles, premises, or postulates than are commonly thought necessary. I shall deal with these assumptions under the name of liberal psychology. Second, these principles of psychology (or of the theory of knowledge) depend upon one another. If any one of them is false, the others cannot be true, and the truth of any one implies the truth of the others. The sense of the interdependence is analogized to a relation of logical entailment. But the inadequacies of the analogy will be pointed out, as will the requirements of the effort to move beyond it. Third, these principles of psychology lead to an antinomy in our conception of the relation between reason and desire in the moral life, an antinomy that subverts the idea of personality with which moral beings cannot dispense. Liberal psychology justifies two kinds of conceptions of the self and of morals that are inconsistent with one another; cannot be reconciled on the basis of the premises from which they are derived; and are equally untenable. Fourth, the elucidation of our moral beliefs, of many of our political ideas, and especially of those most basic to the liberal doctrine can be reduced to a small number of postulates. Fifth, these postulates require each other in the same sense that the principles of psychology do. Sixth, liberal political theory, as the system of these principles, generates an antinomy in the conception of the relation between public rules and private ends. This antinomy in the liberal doctrine is fatal to its hope of solving the problems of freedom and public order as those problems are defined by the doctrine itself, and it leads to conflicting, irreconcilable, and equally unsatisfactory theories of society. Seventh, the principles of the psychology and of the political doctrine presuppose one another. Properly understood, they constitute a single body of thought. Eighth, this system of ideas is inadequate. It results in basic and insoluble paradoxes; its principles, considered in their interrelationships, are unsound as accounts of experience and as moral standards. Ninth, one can begin to imagine the rudiments of a better alternative to the liberal doctrine, but this alternative should not be mistaken for the liberal view set upside down. Tenth, a particular conception of the relationship between parts and wholes in knowledge and in society plays a central role in liberal thought, and must be revised in any superior theory of mind and politics. Eleventh, to solve the antinomies of liberal thought, replace its view of parts and wholes, and work toward a different system of psychological and political ideas, we must abandon the manner in which our modern schools conceive the relationship of universals to particulars.

40

ALVIN GOULDNER
Towards a reflexive sociology* (1970)

Sociologists are no more ready than other men to cast a cold eye on their own doings. No more than others are they ready, willing, or able to tell us what they are really doing and to distinguish this firmly from what they should be doing. Professional courtesy stifles intellectual curiosity; guild interests frown upon the washing of dirty linen in public; the teeth of piety bite the tongue of truth. Yet, first and foremost, a Reflexive Sociology is concerned with what sociologists want to do and with what, in fact, they actually do in the world

The intellectual development of sociology during the last two decades or so, especially the growth of the sociologies of occupations and of science, is, when fused with the larger perspectives of the older sociology of knowledge, one promising basis for the development of a Reflexive Sociology. We have already seen some of the first stirrings of a Reflexive Sociology, in one form or another. Indeed, I believe we have already also seen the emergence of defensive reactions that, in effect, seek to contain the impact of a Reflexive Sociology by defining it as just one other technical specialty within sociology.

What sociologists now most require from a Reflexive Sociology, however, is not just one more specialization, not just another topic for panel meetings at professional conventions, and not just another burbling little stream of technical reports about the sociological profession's origins, educational characteristics, patterns of productivity, political preferences, communication networks, nor even about its fads, foibles, and phonies. For there are ways and ways of conducting and reporting such studies. There are ways that do not touch and quicken us but may, instead, deaden us to the disorders we bear; by allowing us to talk about them with a ventriloquist's voice, they only create an illusion of self-confrontation that serves to disguise a new form of self-celebration. The historical mission of a Reflexive Sociology as I conceive it, however, would be to transform the sociologist, to penetrate deeply into his daily life and work, enriching them with new sensitivities, and to raise the sociologist's self-awareness to a new historical level.

* From *The Coming Crisis of Western Sociology* by Alvin W. Gouldner. Copyright © 1970 by Alvin W. Gouldner. Reprinted by permission of Basic Books, a member of Perseus Books, L.L.C, pp. 488–500.

To the extent that it succeeds in this, and in order to succeed in it, a Reflexive Sociology is and would need to be a radical sociology. Radical, because it would recognize that knowledge of the world cannot be advanced apart from the sociologist's knowledge of himself and his position in the social world, or apart from his efforts to change these. Radical, because it seeks to transform as well as to know the alien world outside the sociologist as well the alien world inside of him. Radical, because it would accept the fact that the roots of sociology pass through the sociologist as a total man, and that the question he must confront, therefore, is not merely how to work but how to live.

The historical mission of a Reflexive Sociology is to transcend sociology as it now exists. In deepening our understanding of our own sociological selves and of our position in the world, we can, I believe, simultaneously help to produce a new breed of sociologists who can also better understand other men and their social worlds. A Reflexive Sociology means that we sociologists must – at the very least – acquire the ingrained habit of viewing our own beliefs as we now view those held by others.

It will be difficult for many sociologists to accept that we presently know little or nothing about ourselves or other sociologists or, in point of fact, that we know little about how one piece of social research, or one sociologist, comes to be esteemed while another is disparaged or ignored. The temptation is great to conceal our ignorance of this process behind a glib affirmation of the proprieties and to pretend that there is no one here but us scientists. In other words, one of the basic reasons we deceive ourselves and lie to others is because we are moral men. Sociologists, like other men, confuse the moral answer with the empirical and, indeed, often prefer it to the empirical. Much of our noble talk about the importance of 'truth for its own sake' is often a tacit way of saying that we want the truth about others, at whatever cost it may be to them. A Reflexive Sociology, however, implies that sociologists must surrender the assumption, as wrongheaded as it is human, that others believe out of need while we believe – only or primarily – because of the dictates of logic and evidence.

A systematic and dogged insistence upon seeing ourselves as we see others would, I have suggested, transform not only our view of ourselves but also our view of others. We would increasingly recognize the depth of our kinship with those whom we study. They would no longer be viewable as alien others or as mere objects for our superior technique and insight; they could, instead, be seen as brother sociologists, each attempting with his varying degree of skill, energy, and talent to understand social reality. In this respect, all men are basically akin to those whom we usually acknowledge as professional 'colleagues,' who are no less diversified in their talents and competence. With the development of a Reflexive Sociology that avoids becoming molded into just another technical specialty, such rigor as sociology attains may be blended with a touch of mercy, and such skills as sociologists possess may come to yield not only information but perhaps even a modest measure of wisdom.

The development of a Reflexive Sociology, in sum, requires that sociologists cease acting as if they thought of subjects and objects, sociologists who study and 'laymen' who are studied, as two distinct breeds of men. There is only one breed of man. But so long as we are without a Reflexive Sociology, we will act upon the tacit dualistic premise that there are two, regardless of how monistic our professions of methodological faith.

I conceive of Reflexive Sociology as requiring an empirical dimension which might foster a large variety of researches about sociology and sociologists, their occupational roles, their career 'hangups,' their establishments, power systems, sub-cultures, and their place in the larger social world. Indeed, my emphasis on the empir-ical character of a Reflexive Sociology and my insistence that the methodological morality of social science not be confused with the description of its social system and cultures, may seem to express a Positivistic bias. Yet while I believe that a Reflexive Sociology must have an empirical dimension, I do not conceive of this as providing a factual basis that determines the character of its guiding theory. Which is to say that I do not conceive of the theory of a Reflexive Sociology merely as an induction from researches or from 'facts.' And more important, I do not conceive of these researches or their factual output as being 'value-free,' for I would hope that their originating motives and terminating consequences would embody and advance certain specific values. A Reflexive Sociology would be a moral sociology.

Perhaps this can be adumbrated by clarifying my conception of the ultimate objective or goal of a Reflexive Sociology, in regard to both its theory and its researches. The nominal objective of any scientific enterprise is to extend knowledge of some part of the world. The difficulty with this conception, however, resides in the ambiguity of its core notion, namely, 'knowledge.' This ambiguity is of long standing, especially in the social sciences, where it has been particularly acute. Although expressible in different ways, this ambiguity will be formulated here as meaning that knowledge may be, and has been, conceived of as either 'information' or 'awareness.'

Since the nineteenth century, when a distinction was formulated between the natural sciences, on the one hand, and the cultural or human sciences, on the other, this implicit ambiguity in the meaning of 'knowledge' was imported into the social sciences and has remained at the core of certain of its fundamental controversies. Those believing that the social sciences were a 'natural' science, like physics or biol-ogy, took an essentially Positivistic view, holding that they should be pursued with the same methods and objectives as the physical sciences. They largely conceived of knowledge as 'information,' as empirically confirmed assertions about 'reality,' whose scientific value derived from their implications for rational theory and whose larger social value derived from technologies based upon them. In short, science thus con-strued aimed at producing information, either for its own sake or to enhance power over the surrounding world: to know in order to control.

So long as this was a conception of the physical (as distinct from the social) sciences, it was an ideology (1) behind which all 'humanity' might unite in a common effort to subdue a 'nature' that was implicitly regarded as external to man, and (2) with which to promote technologies that could transform the universe into the usable resource of mankind as a whole. Such a conception of science was based upon an assumption of the essential unity and the common interests of mankind as a species. It was also a tacitly parochial conception of the relationship of the human species to others; it postulated humanity's lordship over the rest of the universe and its right to use the entire universe for its own benefit, a right tempered only by the species' expedient concern for its own long-range welfare. If such a view of science was an expression of the unthinking ethnocentrism of an expanding animal species, it was also an historical summit of this species' idealism; limitations were ignored in the flush of an optimistic sense that the newly realized universalism of science constituted an advance over narrower and more ancient parochialisms – and so it was.

The humanistic parochialism of science, with its premised unity of mankind, created problems, however, when the effort was made to apply science to the study of mankind itself. It did so partly because national or class differences then became acutely visible, but also, and perhaps more important, because men now expected to use social science to 'control' men themselves, as they were already using physical science to control 'nature.' Such a view of social science premised that a man might be known, used, and controlled like any other thing: it 'thingafied' man. The use of the physical sciences as a model fostered just such a conception of the social sciences, all the more so as they were developing in the context of an increasingly utilitarian culture.

This view of the social sciences was fostered by French Positivism. In opposition to it, largely under German auspices and the Romantic Movement with its full-scale critique of utilitarian culture, there emerged a different conception of social science. This required a different method, for example, *verstehen*, clinical intuition, or historical empathy – an inward closeness to the object studied rather than an antiseptic distance from it, an inward communion with it rather than an external manipulation of it. This conception of social science held that its ultimate goal was not neutral 'information' about social reality, but rather such knowledge as was relevant to men's own changing interests, hopes, and values and as would enhance men's awareness of their place in the social world rather than simply facilitating their control over it.

In this conception of social science both the inquiring subject and the studied object are seen not only as mutually interrelated but also as mutually constituted. The entire world of social objects is seen as constituted by men, by the shared meanings bestowed and confirmed by men themselves, rather than as substances eternally fixed and existent apart from them. The social world, therefore, is to be known not simply by 'discovery' of some external fact, not only by looking outward, but also by opening oneself inward. Awareness of the self is seen as an indispensable avenue to awareness of the social world. For there is no knowledge of the world that is not a knowledge of our own experience with it and our relation to it.

In a knowing conceived as awareness, the concern is not with 'discovering' the truth about a social world regarded as external to the knower, but with seeing truth as growing out of the knower's encounter with the world and his effort to order his experience with it. The knower's knowing of himself – of who, what, and where he is – on the one hand, and of others and their social worlds, on the other, are two sides of a single process.

Insofar as social reality is seen as contingent in part on the effort, the character, and the position of the knower, the search for knowledge about social worlds is also contingent upon the knower's self-awareness. To know others he cannot simply study them, but must also listen to and confront himself. Knowing as awareness involves not a simple impersonal effort of segmented 'role players,' but a personalized effort by whole, embodied men. The character and quality of such knowing is molded not only by a man's technical skills or even by his intelligence alone, but also by all that he is and wants, by his courage no less than his talent, by his passion no less than his objectivity. It depends on all that a man does and lives. In the last analysis, if a man wants to change what he knows he must change how he lives; he must change his praxis in the world.

Knowing as the pursuit of information, however, conceives of the resultant knowledge as depersonalized; as a product that can be found in a card file, a book, a library, a colleague, or some other 'storage bank.' Such knowledge does not have to be recallable by a specific knower and, indeed, does not have to be in the mind of any person; all that need be known about it is its 'location.' Knowledge as information, then, is the attribute of a culture rather than of a person; its meaning, pursuit, and consequence are all depersonalized. Knowledge as awareness, however, is quite another matter, for it has no existence apart from the persons that pursue and express it. Awareness is an attribute of persons, even though it is influenced by the location of these persons in specific cultures or in parts of a social structure. A culture may assist or hinder in attaining awareness, but a culture as such cannot be aware.

Awareness entails a relationship between persons and information; yet information, while necessary to, is not sufficient for awareness. Awareness turns on the attitude of persons toward information and is related to their ability to hold onto and to use information. The crux of the matter is that information is rarely neutral in its implication for men's purposes, hopes, or values. Information, therefore, tends to be experienced – even if not expressly defined – as either 'friendly' or 'hostile,' as consonant or dissonant with a man's purposes. It is the relation of information to a man's purposes, not what it is 'in itself,' that makes information hostile or friendly. News of the stability of a government is hostile information to a revolutionary but friendly to a conservative. An openness to and a capacity to use hostile information is awareness. Awareness is an openness to bad news, and is born of a capacity to overcome resistance to its acceptance or use. This is inevitably linked, at some vital point, with an ability to know and to control the self in the face of threat. The pursuit of awareness, then, even in the world of modern technology, remains rooted in the most ancient of virtues. The quality of a social scientist's work remains dependent upon the quality of his manhood.

Whether 'hostile information' refers directly to some state of the larger world itself, or, rather, to the deficiencies of an established, perhaps technical, system of information about the world, an openness to it always requires a measure of self-knowledge and courage. The self of a scholar may be as deeply and personally invested in his work on information systems as is a revolutionary's on a political system. Both have conceptions of their work that may, at some point, be maintained only through the blunting of their awareness. A politician's capacity to accept and use hostile information about his own political efforts and situation is often referred to as his 'realism.' A scholar's ability to accept and use hostile information about his own view of social reality, and his efforts to know it, is part of what is usually called his 'objectivity.'

As a program for a Reflexive Sociology, then, this implies that: (1) The conduct of researches is only a necessary but not a sufficient condition for the maturation of the sociological enterprise. What is needed is a new praxis that transforms the person of the sociologist. (2) The ultimate goal of a Reflexive Sociology is the deepening of the sociologist's own awareness, of who and what he is, in a specific society at any given time, and of how both his social role and his personal praxis affect his work as a sociologist. (3) Its work seeks to deepen the sociologist's self-awareness as well as his ability to produce valid-reliable bits of information about the social world of others. (4) Therefore, a Reflexive Sociology requires not only valid-reliable bits of information about the world of sociology, and not only a methodology or a set of technical skills for procuring this. It also requires a persistent commitment to the value of that awareness which expresses itself through all stages of work, as well as auxiliary skills or arrangements that will enable the sociologist's self to be open to hostile information.

Conventional Positivism premises that the self is treacherous and that, so long as it remains in contact with the information system, its primary effect is to bias or distort it. It is assumed, therefore, that the way to defend the information system is to insulate it from the scholar's self by generating distance and by stressing impersonal detachment from the objects studied. From the standpoint of a Reflexive Sociology, however, the assumption that the self can be sealed off from information systems is mythological. The assumption that the self affects the information system solely in a distorting manner is one-sided: it fails to see that the self may also be a source both of valid insight that enriches study and of motivation that energizes it. A Reflexive Sociology looks, therefore, to the deepening of the self's capacity to recognize that it views certain information as hostile, to recognize the various dodges that it uses to deny, ignore, or camouflage information that is hostile to it, and to the strengthening of its capacity to accept and to use hostile information. In short, what Reflexive Sociology seeks is not an insulation but a transformation of the sociologist's self, and hence of his praxis in the world.

A Reflexive Sociology, then, is not characterized by what it studies. It is distinguished neither by the persons and the problems studied nor even by the techniques and instruments used in studying them. It is characterized, rather, by the relationship it establishes between being a sociologist and being a person, between the role and the man performing it. A Reflexive Sociology embodies a critique of the conventional conception of segregated scholarly roles and has a vision of an alternative. It aims at transforming the sociologist's relation to his work.

Since the 1920s when American sociology began to be institutionalized within universities, it has held firmly to one operating methodological assumption, despite the other changes it has undergone. This assumption can be called 'Methodological Dualism.' Methodological Dualism focuses on the differences between the social scientist and those whom he observes; it tends to ignore their similarities by taking them as given or by confining them to the sociologist's subsidiary attention. Methodological Dualism calls for the separation of subject and object, and it views their mutual contact with concern and fear. It enjoins the sociologist to be detached from the world he studies. It warns him of the dangers of 'over rapport.' It sees his involvement with his 'subjects' primarily from the standpoint of its contaminating effect upon the information system.

Methodological Dualism is based upon a fear; but this is a fear not so much of those being studied as of the sociologist's own self. Methodological Dualism is, at bottom, concerned to constitute a strategy for coping with the feared vulnerability of the scholar's self. It strives to free him from disgust, pity, anger, from egoism or moral outrage, from his passions and his interests, on the supposition that it is a bloodless and disembodied mind that works best. It also seeks to insulate the scholar from the values and interests of his other roles and commitments, on the dubious assumption that these can never be anything but blinders. It assumes that feeling is the blood enemy of intelligence, and that there can be an unfeeling, unsentimental knower. Methodological Dualism is, in fine, based on the tacit assumption that the goal of sociology is knowledge conceived as information. Correspondingly, it serves as a powerful inhibitor of the sociologist's awareness, for it paradoxically presupposes that the sociologist may rightfully be changed as a person by everything except the very intellectual work which is at the center of his existence. In effect, Methodological Dualism prohibits the sociologist from changing in response to the social worlds that he studies and knows best; it requires him to finish his research with the same self, the same biases and commitments, as those with which he began it.

Methodological Dualism is based on the myth that social worlds are merely 'mirrored' in the sociologist's work, rather than seeing them as conceptually constituted by the sociologist's cognitive commitments and all his other interests. The Methodological Dualist commonly conceives his goal to be the study of social worlds in their 'natural' or uncontaminated state. In effect, he says, like the photographer, 'Don't mind me; just be natural, carry on as if I were not here.' What this ignores, however, is that the reaction of the group under study to the sociologist is just as real and revealing of its 'true' character as its reaction to any other stimulus, and, furthermore, that the sociologist's own reaction to the group is a form of behavior as relevant and significant for social science as is anyone else's. There is not as great a difference between the sociologist and those he studies as the sociologist seems to think, even with respect to an intellectual interest in knowing social worlds. Those being studied are also avid students of human relations; they too have their social theories and conduct their investigations.

Believing that he should not influence or change the group he studies – except in those limited ways that he plans during experimentation – the sociologist would also like to believe that he does not. He prefers to believe that he is what he should be, according to his methodological morality. He thus commonly fails to attend to the ramifying range of influences that he actually exerts upon social worlds and, to that extent, he obscures what, in point of fact, he does and is. The notion that research can be 'contaminated' premises that there is research that is not contaminated. From the standpoint of a Reflexive Sociology, however, all research is 'contaminated,' for all are conducted from the standpoint of limited perspectives and all entail relationships that may influence both parties to it.

Methodological Dualism entails a fantasy of the sociologist's Godlike invisibility and of his Olympian power to influence – or not influence – those around him, as he pleases. In contrast, the Methodological Monism of a Reflexive Sociology believes that sociologists are really only mortal; that they inevitably change others and are changed by them, in planned and unanticipated ways, during their efforts to know them; and that knowing and changing are distinguishable but not separable processes. The aim of the Reflexive Sociologist, then, is not to remove his influence on others but to know it, which requires that he must become aware of himself as both knower and as agent of change. He cannot know others unless he also knows his intentions toward and his effects upon them; he cannot know others without knowing himself, his place in the world, and the forces – in society and in himself – to which he is subjected.

Methodological Dualism stresses the 'contamination' possible in the research process itself; it sees the main danger to 'objectivity' in the interaction between those studying and those studied. In effect, this is the narrow perspective of an interpersonal social psychology that ignores the biasing effects of the larger society and the powerful influences it exerts upon the sociologist's work through the intervening mechanism of his career and other interests. What Methodological Dualism ignores is that the sociologist does not only enter into consequential relations with those whom he studies, but that these relations themselves operate within the orbit of the relations that the sociologist has with those who, directly or indirectly, finance his researches and control his occupational life and the establishments within which he works. In ignoring these larger influences, Methodological Dualism in effect boggles at a gnat but swallows a camel. Its claim to 'objectivity' is, in effect, commonly made in such a way as to give least offense to those who most subvert it.

A Reflexive Sociology, for its part, recognizes that there is an inevitable tendency for any social system to curtail the sociologist's autonomy in at least two ways: to transform him either into an ideologue of the status quo and an apologist for its policies, or into a technician acting instrumentally on behalf of its interests. A Reflexive Sociology recognizes that the status quo often exerts such influences by the differential rewards – essentially, research funding, academic prestige, and income-earning opportunities – that it selectively provides for scholarly activities acceptable and useful to it. The most fundamental control device of any stable social system is not its use of crude force, or even of other, nonviolent forms of punishment, but its continuing distribution of mundane rewards. It is not simply power that an hegemonic elite seeks and uses, but an authority that is rooted in the readiness of others to credit its good intentions, to cease contention when it has rendered its decision, to accept its conception of social reality, and to reject alternatives at variance with the status quo.

The most effective strategy possessed by any stable social system and its hegemonic elites to induce such conformity is to make it worthwhile. What elites prefer is not craven expedience, but pious opportunism. Conformity with the basic principle of establishment politics – that is, accepting the image of social reality held by the hegemonic elite or at least one compatible with it – is, however, nothing less than a betrayal of the most fundamental objectives of any sociology. The price paid is the dulling of the sociologist's awareness; it is a surrender in the struggle to know those social worlds that are and those that might be.

Reflexive Sociology, then, rests upon an awareness of a fundamental paradox: namely, that those who supply the greatest resources for the institutional development of sociology are precisely those who most distort its quest for knowledge. And a Reflexive Sociology is aware that this is not the peculiarity of any one type of established social system, but is common to them all. While a Reflexive Sociology assumes that any sociology develops only under certain social conditions which it is deeply committed to know, it also recognizes that elites and institutions seek something in return for the support they provide sociology. It recognizes that the development of sociology depends on a societal support that permits growth in certain directions but simultaneously limits it in other ways and thus warps its character. In short, every social system is bent upon crippling the very sociology to which it gives birth. A claim to 'objectivity' made by a sociology that does not acknowledge this contradiction, and which lacks a concrete understanding of the manner in which its own hegemonic institutions and elites are a fundamental danger to it, is a tacit testimonial to the successful hegemony of that system over that sociology. It evidences a failure to achieve that very objectivity to which it so proudly pledges allegiance.

A Reflexive Sociology can grasp this hostile information: all the powers-that-be are inimical to the highest ideals of sociology. At the same time, it further recognizes that most often these are not external dangers, for they produce their most powerful effect when allied with the dispositions and career interests internal to sociologists themselves. A Reflexive Sociology is fully aware that sociology is most deeply distorted because and when the sociologist himself is a willing party to this. A Reflexive Sociology therefore prefers the seeming naivete of 'soul-searching' to the genuine vulgarity of 'soul-selling.'.

Insofar as a Reflexive Sociology focuses on the problem of dealing with hostile information, it confronts the problem of a 'value-free' sociology from two directions. On the one hand, it denies the possibility and, indeed, questions the worth of a value-free sociology. On the other hand, it also sees the dangers, no less than the gains, of a value-committed sociology; for men may and do reject information discrepant with the things they value. It recognizes that men's highest values, no less than their basest impulses, may make liars of them. Nonetheless, a Reflexive Sociology accepts the dangers of a value commitment, for it prefers the risk of ending in distortion to beginning in it, as does a dogmatic and arid value-free sociology.

Again, insofar as a Reflexive Sociology centers on the problem of hostile information, it has a distinctive awareness of the ideological implications and political resonance of sociological work. It recognizes that under different conditions an ideology may have different effects upon awareness; it may be liberating or repressive, may increase or inhibit awareness. Moreover, the specific problems or aspects of the social world that an ideology can make us aware of also change over time. A Reflexive Sociology must, therefore, have an historical sensitivity that alerts it to the possibility that yesterday's ideologies may no longer enlighten but may now blind us. For since hostile information entails a relation between an information system and the purposes of men, what is hostile will change with the changing purposes that men pursue and with the changing problems that their pursuit encounters under new conditions. What was formerly hostile information may cease to be so; and what was hitherto friendly may become hostile. Thus, for a part of the middle class – the new 'swinging' middle class – as the 'sexual revolution' has progressed, Freudianism has ceased to be the liberating force it once was. Furthermore, insofar as Freudianism becomes part of a larger movement that interprets social and political dissent as symptomatic of mental illness, it increasingly becomes an instrument of social control and begins to play a sociologically repressive role.

Similarly, the 'good news' and the liberating effects of the scientific revolution may now also need to be seen as an historically limited liberation. What is now required is to confront that hostile information which suggests that the scientific revolution has, under present social conditions, opened the prospect of global self-destruction and, more generally, that science has become an instrument through which almost all contemporary industrial social systems maintain themselves. What made Nazi Germany blind was, among other things, its irrational racial ideology; but what made it uniquely dangerous and destructive was its effective mobilization of modern science and technology on behalf of this. This was an extreme case; but it is far from the only instance in which modern societies use science as an instrument of domination, in much the same way that rulers of the 'ancient regimes' of the eighteenth and nineteenth centuries once used institutional religion. Despite this, however, the conventional Western view of science is still largely that of the Enlightenment, seeing it as a source of cultural liberation and human welfare that is marred only occasionally, marginally, accidentally.

PART 4
Pragmatism, semiotics and transcendental pragmatics

Introduction: a general outline

The readings presented in this part have been selected with the aim of offering the reader a sense of pragmatism, from its formulation in the early twentieth century on the basis of Peirce's work during the second half of the nineteenth century, to its acquisition of increasing significance for the philosophy of the social sciences in the late twentieth century. The first text marks the origin of pragmatism or 'pragmaticism', as Peirce called it to distinguish his own version from the one put forward by James and others. The second and third texts cover the extension of pragmatism to the social sciences accomplished by such authors as Mead, Dewey and Mills during the second and third decades of the twentieth century, here represented by the latter two. The third records the rehabilitation of 'semiotic' or the pragmatist theory of signs by Morris in the late 1930s and 1940s. Finally, the incorporation of pragmatism into a broad and enhanced philosophical framework for the social sciences is presented, here as put forward by Apel but also represented by Habermas as well as Bernstein (both taken up again in Part 6), which played a significant role in establishing relations among different philosophies of the social sciences in the late twentieth century.

Pragmatism is sometimes regarded as a philosophical movement closely related or allied to positivism, but often it is even treated as being merely a variant of positivism. This is due to a number of different factors. They include the significant impact of pragmatism on logical empiricism, as can be seen in the contributions of for example Popper, Morris and Quine (see Part 1), and the widespread acceptance in pragmatism of apparently the same principle of empiricism as is ascribed to by positivists and neo-positivists – i.e. the principle according to which experience forms the basis of all knowledge. Rather than the similarities, however, it is the differences separating pragmatism from positivism which stand out. Some authors therefore insist that we should not allow the taken-for-granted view of the scientific method to lead us into misunderstanding pragmatism. Indeed, many a reputable commentator had been misled in this way by scientism, including Horkheimer and even Adorno (see Part 3).

What principally characterizes pragmatism, as is suggested by the Greek word πραγμα (*pragma*) meaning action, is its emphasis on human beings as agents and their practical relations to the world. According to this view, science is produced by inquirers who are understood as agents maintaining a use orientation, creative beings employing language and using knowledge to open up possibilities, some of which could be realized. This contrasts sharply with the positivist view of the scientist as spectator with a reference orientation, a contemplative being observing externally given objects and seeking to obtain eternal knowledge about them. At a deeper level, the difference between pragmatism and positivism resides in pragmatism's origin in Peirce's critique of Descartes and the overcoming of precisely those Cartesian dualisms which are presupposed by modern western philosophy, including positivism – dualisms such as subject and object, body and mind, perception and conceptualization, theory and fact, fact and value, deduction and induction, reality and copy, nature and culture, individual and society, sign and signified, and so forth. The overcoming of these dualisms means that pragmatism entails the rejection of some of the basic guiding ideas which inform not only the positivist philosophy of science but also the interpretative (see Part 3) and the structuralist (see Part 5) traditions. Among them are ideas such as the subject of knowledge as an individual, observation as presuppositionless activity, truth as a picture or representation corresponding with reality, knowledge as being built up of observation and logical inference, social science as being exclusively concerned with culture and hence the interpretation and understanding of symbolic meaning, knowledge as involving an arbitrary or conventional twofold sign relation, and so on. Pragmatism, by contrast, takes a very different position. It stresses the anchorage of knowledge in real collective problems, and knowledge as being dependent on the mediation of signs, which means that it regards knowledge as being social by nature. Accordingly, it focuses on the development of knowledge which it sees as taking place in different ways and in a variety of contexts. Knowledge develops not only through the individual scientist's creative (neither induction nor deduction but) 'abduction' or drawing of synthetic conclusions, but also and in particular through the cooperative search for truth in the scientific community by means of processes of interpretation and discussion or argumentation, and more broadly through the creative collective overcoming of action problems. That this does not merely involve the accumulation of scientific knowledge is apparent from the fact that pragmatism is above all concerned with the way in which the overcoming of collective problems and the concurrent development of knowledge simultaneously realize and enhance democracy.

Pragmatism was founded by the outstanding nineteenth- and early twentieth-century American philosopher Charles Sanders Peirce, who had put forward his basic pragmatist ideas in a series of essays published already as early as 1868 but developed them in their classical form in the period between 1871 and 1884. His follower William James, who in the late nineteenth century proclaimed Pierce as the founder of this philosophical movement, was responsible for popularizing this new departure and in the process generating quite a wide-ranging response in Europe.

However, being satisfied neither with James's nominalistic and subjectivistic emphasis, nor with the largely misguided resonance created by the popularized version, Peirce preferred the title 'pragmaticism' – 'which is ugly enough to be safe from kidnappers' – rather than 'pragmatism'. During the first part of the twentieth century, pragmatism was pursued and elaborated by Josiah Royce, John Dewey, George Herbert Mead, C.I. Lewis, Charles Morris and others. Although Morris brought pragmatism to bear on logical empiricism and central elements were also appropriated by authors such as Popper, Quine, Toulmin and Kuhn (See Part 1), and although Dewey and Mead brought it into the philosophy of the social sciences, with an author like C. Wright Mills drawing still more specific conclusions in respect of sociology – despite all this, pragmatism had for decades been pushed to the background in American universities. At best, pragmatism enjoyed only a partial transposition into the philosophy of the social sciences, being largely implicitly operative in the Chicago School or later languishing in an undifferentiated and fragmentary form in symbolic interactionism. Since the 1970s, however, it has undergone a renaissance in American philosophy and indeed more broadly, by no means without consequences for the philosophy of the social sciences.

An American philosopher who since the early 1970s consistently made a contribution to the revitalization of pragmatism is Richard Bernstein, author of *Praxis and Action* (1971) and later *The Restructuring of Social and Political Theory* (1976), *Beyond Objectivism and Relativism* (1983) and *The New Constellation* (1991). The most decisive impetus toward the renewed development of pragmatism, however, came from Richard Rorty when in the late 1970s he elevated Dewey to the level of one of the three most significant philosophers of the century – the others being Wittgenstein and Heidegger. This intervention gave rise to the so-called 'neo-pragmatist' movement, associated with the name of Rorty, which represents a certain Heideggerianization and thus to some extent a hermeneutic dissipation of pragmatism which dovetails with the postmodernist perspective. Due to the radical reduction of boundaries between disciplines and genres, for instance between science and literature, there is little or no room for a philosophy of social science as such within this framework. To be fair, Rorty does differ from Heidegger and the French representatives of postmodernism in so far as he holds to a version of Peirce's pragmatic maxim: 'We know there must be a better way to do things than this; let us look for it together' – the collective first person pronoun implying 'the desire to extend the forum to "us" as far as we can'. Besides Bernstein and Rorty, two closely associated German authors, with whom Bernstein has some relation, historically played a decisive role in the renaissance of pragmatism: Karl-Otto Apel and Jürgen Habermas, the leading second generation critical theorists presented in Part 3. Apel was responsible for introducing Peirce and making him known in Germany through two volumes of the American philosopher's writings issued in 1967 and 1970, accompanied by an influential introduction which was also published as a separate book, in English entitled, *Charles S. Peirce: From Pragmatism to Pragmaticism* (German 1975, English 1981) – what Bernstein regards as not only 'one of the most thoughtful, sophisticated, and illuminating studies of Peirce', but also as 'one of the best introductions to Peirce in any language'. On the basis of the pioneering work of Peirce, Apel then developed the very important approach he calls 'transcendental pragmatics', which embraces the social sciences and at the same time connects them to public practical discourse and thus democracy. Habermas' appropriation of Peirce is reflected in *Knowledge and Human Interests* in his investigation of Peirce's anti-positivistic logic of science as well as in other writings in which he, with reference to Apel, identifies with Peirce's pragmatic-semiotic transformation of epistemology. From the point of view of the philosophy of the social sciences, Apel's contribution to the revitalization of pragmatism is all the more important since he also brings to the fore, by going back to Peirce, Royce and very critically to Morris, the pragmatist theory of signs, or semiotics, which opens a perspective on knowledge and the social world and provides a framework for the social sciences which is appreciably different from the structuralist theory of signs (see Part 5) and makes a link with public communication and discourse. In a series of works from the late 1970s, the 1980s and the early 1990s, Bernstein sought from the American side to mobilize these Continental contributions for the revitalization of what he calls the 'pragmatic legacy' (see Part 6) in a way that is relevant to the further development of the philosophy of social science.

The selected texts

Charles S. Peirce (1839–1914), who was professionally a practicing scientist, is considered by many to be America's most original and greatest philosopher and is even called 'the Kant of America'. He developed the philosophical programme of pragmatism between his late twenties and mid-forties, when he virtually disappeared from the scene in the wake of his publicly unexplained dismissal from Johns Hopkins University, living for some 15 years in almost total isolation in Milford, Pennsylvania, only to be brought into the spotlight in his sixties after having been proclaimed as the founder of pragmatism. Although some of his classical essays had been known at the time, and although James and Dewey had made reference to him in their writings, the names of the latter two classical representatives became associated with pragmatism instead. Even his coming to prominence in the first part of the twentieth century had not been sufficient to make a big difference in this underestimation of his original contribution. While authors like Popper, Morris, Quine, Sellars and Putnam acknowledged aspects of his work, it is only since the 1970s that a more comprehensive appreciation of Peirce has begun to evolve. The selected text represents the fourth and last stage in Peirce's development, dating from the early twentieth century. It is an excerpt from a dictionary article in which Peirce was required to give a definition of pragmatism, but at the same time he also uses the opportunity to distinguish his thinking from that of James. The centrepiece of Peirce's clarification of pragmatism is the pragmatic 'maxim' according to which one can grasp the meaning of a concept by engaging in a 'practical consideration', – i.e. by taking account of the 'upshot' or 'effects' of the concept or the 'practical consequences' that might conceivably result from it. Instead of vague ontological speculations, therefore, he suggests that from a pragmatic perspective the meaning of a concept should be regarded in connection with possible practically relevant situations and thus with reference to possible action. For the sake of clarity, Peirce contrasts this position of his with James'. In terms of his psychological or existential interpretation of pragmatism as assuming that 'the end of man is action', James emphasizes the immediate translation of concepts into action. But Peirce objects that it is less a matter of immediate action than the ends of action that call for consideration. The same objection would apply also to Dewey's tendency towards instrumentalism. Rather than a psychological or instrumental matter, therefore, pragmatism concerns the fact 'that action wants an end, and that that end must be something of a general description', which implies that the pragmatic maxim 'would direct us towards something different from practical facts, namely, to general ideas, as the interpreters of our thought' and the guides of our actions. In order to distinguish his position still further, Peirce places the pragmatic maxim in a broad philosophical or 'metaphysical' system or 'architectonic' to which the 'evolutionary process' of the 'growth' or the 'development of concrete reasonableness' is central. While the aged Peirce's sweeping speculative assumption of the complete priority of natural evolution contained in the notion of concrete reasonableness is unquestionably unwarranted, his abiding related idea of the indefinite community of investigators and deliberate agents serving as the ultimate general idea giving direction to and guiding our thoughts and actions is of the utmost importance. Through 'reasoning' involving 'feeling' ('firstness' or spontaneity), 'experience' ('secondness' or actuality) and the interpretation and 'communication' of meaning ('thirdness' or possibility), humans are not only able to grasp the possible practical consequences of their ideas and actions, but they are also in a propitious position to fit their ideas and actions into a larger pattern contributing to a more appropriate and reasonable organization of their world.

John Dewey (1859–1952), one of the leading American philosophers of his time, in fact studied at Johns Hopkins University while Peirce was lecturing there, yet it took some years before he exchanged his initial Hegelian idealism for pragmatism, in the process becoming deeply indebted to Peirce. Like his slightly younger contemporary, George Herbert Mead, Dewey extended pragmatism to the social and political field, but unlike Mead he wrote explicitly and at some length about the philosophy of the social sciences. Although he gave serious attention to such topics as education, art and religion, he is by comparison with Peirce regarded as having been the representative of a more instrumentalist version of pragmatism. It is in this vein that pragmatism conjures up an association with the name of Dewey in the American mind, whereas in Europe Peirce comes to mind first. In the selected reading, Dewey in keeping with the pragmatist abhorrence of Cartesian dualism writes on social inquiry with a view to overcoming the customary 'separation of practice and theory'. His central claim, therefore, is that the 'connection of social inquiry . . . with practice is intrinsic, not external'. Throughout the piece there are indications that he structures his argument according to Peirce's pragmatic maxim (see Peirce above). He regards social inquiry, accordingly, as starting from problems which emerge from real social situations of conflict and confusion, the meaning of which can be understood only with reference to the alternative possible ends of resolving such conflict and confusion and hence the projected consequences of the activities necessary to achieve this. This means that social inquiry always proceeds in accordance with an 'indispensable . . . end-in-view' which makes possible the discrimination of the relevant object, shapes the hypothesis or plan and policy for dealing with the problem, directs what one should look for, guides observation, dictates what counts as facts, and determines what values would come into play in the resolution of the problem. On the basis of this pragmatist philosophy of social science, he criticizes two dominant modes of procedure which are largely responsible for reproducing the gap between theory and practice. On the one hand, Dewey shows that social scientists are not just prevented from transforming problematic social situations into 'definitely formulated problems' suited to social inquiry by practical or political pressures which treat problem situations as though they are already well understood and determined, but they even accept and themselves perpetuate such an unscientific way of defining problems. At the same time, the kind of moralistic prejudgment involved in such unscientific problem definitions, often cloaked by a claim to value-freedom, is inimical to the kind of evaluation which necessarily plays a role in the social scientific selection and determination of problems with reference to some end-in-view. On the other hand, he criticizes social scientists for their ready and widespread adoption of the misguided empiricist or positivist view of social scientific methodology as proceeding from the assumption: 'The facts are out there and only need to be observed, assembled and arranged to give rise to suitable and grounded generalizations'. In Dewey's view, social scientists generally speaking do not find facts ready-made but need to constitute them within the context of a problematic social situation with reference to an end-in-view. But he insists further, quite contrary to, for example, Durkheim (see Part 1), that a 'social fact' forms part of social reality as a 'process' or 'sequential course of changes', which means that it is something 'inherently historical', 'temporal' and thus 'changing anyhow in some direction'. The social scientist must be able not only to stay focused on such a moving target, but also to 'indicate the intervening activities which will give the movement (and hence its consequences) a different direction' – i.e. towards the 'existential resolution of the conflicting social situation'. While Dewey admits that social scientists can learn from the way in which natural scientists undertake scientific inquiry, he is critical of a slavish adoption of the natural science model, particularly a superficially and anachronistically interpreted model. He regards both natural and social sciences to be guided by an end-in-view, but insists on a basic difference between them. Unlike 'physical inquiry' which proceeds relatively isolated from social factors, the pursuit of the ends of social inquiry includes as part of itself the whole set of implicated social relations, from the social scientist who conducts the inquiry, through the social subjects serving as the object of inquiry, to those who are involved in the resolution of the problem, including the public.

Charles Morris (1901–79), who drew heavily on Peirce's pragmatic theory of signs, can be regarded as the twentieth-century founder of the research programme on 'semiotic' or the general theory of signs. Initially, however, he did not become known for his 'semiotic' but rather for his subsidiary proposal to synthesize the logical empiricism diffused in America by the *émigrés* of the Vienna Circle and pragmatism as represented by Mead and Dewey in Chicago. As noted in Part 1, this had had the effect of broadening logical empiricism, which at the time was confined to a dyadic semantic approach, by the incorporation of pragmatics. Neo-positivism never fully overcame its inability to grasp the triadic nature of pragmatics or the sign function, however, and even Morris advocated a behaviouristic approach to semiotic which tended to reduce triadic sign relations to dyadic ones. This is the case not only in his early semiotic manifesto, *Foundations of the Theory of Signs* (1938), but also – and as the title suggests, especially – in his main work, *Signs, Language, and Behaviour* (1946). The reading consists of two texts, the first selected from the early semiotic manifesto, which outlines the idea of 'semiotic', and the second from his main work, offering a more precise restatement of 'pragmatics', 'semantics' and 'syntactics' as marking the 'scope and subdivisions of semiotic'. In the first selection, proceeding from the assumption that human beings are 'sign-using animals', Morris puts forward a 'theory of signs', what he calls 'semiotic', which on the one hand could itself be pursued scientifically and on the other could serve as an 'organon' or basic unifying viewpoint in the philosophy of science. The latter point, however, he interprets narrowly in accordance with neo-positivism as raising the possibility of 'the unification of science', which is further reinforced by the fact that this piece had been published originally in the neo-positivistic *International Encyclopedia of Unified Science*. More important is his analysis of semiotic in terms of 'semiosis', or the process in which something functions as a sign for somebody, and more specifically the threefold sign function taking place within the process. Semiosis is a process of signification and interpretation in which a range of 'relational properties' – for instance, sign vehicle, signified object, whether 'designatum' or 'denotatum', signifying effect, sign-interpreting agent – are mediated through signs in such a way that an interpreter is referred to something and is able to interpret it from a relevant point of view which makes sense to others. In the development of the theory of signs, Morris explicitly adopts 'the standpoint of behavioristics' according to which the agent or interpreter and the interpretation community to which he or she belongs are underplayed in favour of the disinterested observation of external behaviour. This in fact entails a reduction of a three-dimensional, pragmatically integrated semiotic to a two-dimensional behaviouristic semiotic, with the result that he in effect moves away from Pierce's pragmatic semiotic and closer to the quite different structuralist theory of signs or 'semiology' stemming from the work of Saussure (see Part 5). In the second selection, Morris clarifies semiotic by elaborating on the subdivision of the semiotic field into the three basic areas of 'pragmatics', 'semantics' and 'syntactics' first introduced in his earlier work. It is this threefold distinction that allowed Morris in the 1930s to offer pragmatics as an essential extension of the early Wittgenstein's concern with logical form (syntactics) and Tarski and Carnap's logical-semantic frameworks (semantics) (see Part 1). Important to note is that Morris later insists that all modes of signification are of semiotic interest, not only language, least of all the language of science, as in neo-positivism. It is symptomatic of his behaviouristic approach, however, that he, despite stressing the need to 'keep in mind the field of semiotic as a whole', continues to be misled by a narrow interpretation of syntactics, semantics and pragmatics which does not accord with what Apel calls Morris' intended 'pragmatically integrated semiotic'. Typically, the syntactic, semantic and pragmatic dimensions of semiosis are presented as equivalent dyadic relations – syntactics concerning the relation between signs, semantics the relation between sign and object referred to, and pragmatics the relation between signs and their users. As Peirce's (see above) and later Apel's (see below) writings suggest, by contrast, syntactics is one-dimensional (Peirces' 'Firstness'), semantics two-dimensional (Peirce's 'Secondness') and pragmatics three-dimensional in that it is concerned with the concrete process of semiosis in which all these different aspects are related and interwoven (Peirce's 'Thirdness').

C. Wright Mills (1916–62), professor of sociology at Columbia University from 1945 until his early death, was from the start under the influence of his pragmatist mentors and entered an academic career on the basis of a dissertation submitted at the University of Wisconsin which was posthumously published under the title of

Sociology and Pragmatism (1964). Under the impact of Peirce's pragmatic maxim, and Dewey's *Logic: The Theory of Inquiry* (1938) and *Freedom and Culture* (1939), Mills here offers a sociological account of the institutionalization of pragmatism as shaped by Peirce, James and particularly Dewey. It is on the basis of Dewey's conception of language and vocabulary as sets of collective action, which Mills combined with insights drawn from Mannheim (see Part 2 above), Morris (see above) and later also Adorno and Horkheimer (see Part 3), that he was able to translate pragmatism into a philosophically informed sociological approach. The selected reading is one from a series of early essays in which Mills puts forward his sociologized pragmatism. While the theme of situated actions and vocabularies of motive is obviously strongly influenced by Dewey, Mills attacks what he calls Dewey's 'nakedly utilitarian schema', which lacks an understanding of the 'intrinsically social character' of motives, and proposes to correct it by making it more relevant to sociology or, more generally, the social sciences. The essay takes the form of an outline, based on the pragmatist philosophy and a sociological theory of language, of a metatheoretical 'model' for the analysis and 'explanation of social actions' and their 'coordination' in 'social situations'. While Mills is convinced that this pragmatic sociological approach can be applied in different historical epochs and societal structures, he is in particular concerned with delimited problematic or crisis situations, what he calls 'question situations'. In such situations those involved are no longer able to 'live in immediate acts of experience' since they have been compelled through frustration to become reflexive, acquiring 'awareness of self and of motive', and consequently to 'interrupt acts or programs' by raising questions. From such situations emerges a process in which the participants 'vocalize and impute motives to themselves and to others' and thus bring into play 'lingual mechanisms' whereby actions can be specified, integrated and controlled. According to Mills' model, social scientific investigation involves a number of steps. It has to delimit the relevant situation with reference to the 'assent and dissent phase of the conversation' or 'discourse', and within this context it then has to identify the participating actors – for instance, labour leaders, businessmen, radicals and college professors – as well as the different 'motives', 'reasons' or 'justifications' which each of them verbalizes. Once this preliminary step has been taken, the social scientist engages in the construction of typical vocabularies of motive which allows him or her to identify the 'normative . . . frame' of each actor and to analyse the 'varying and competing vocabularies' in the situation and how they are used as 'strategies of action' by those who proffer them. The first social phenomenon which requires explanation here is the strategically and competitively driven process of the 'imputation and avowal of motives' by the different actors in terms of their 'typical vocabularies'. But of even greater importance is the explanation of the social consequences of each of the alternative normatively framed clusters of action and motive as well as the process of competition and conflict between them as a whole. In this respect, the social scientific task is to account for the sense in which such consequences entail, for instance, the exercise of influence over actions, the control of actions, the coordination of actions, the integration of actors, the resolution of conflict and so forth.

Karl-Otto Apel (1922–) was introduced in Part 3 in the context of the critical tradition as the critical theorist who has contributed most to the philosophy of the social sciences. In the reading selected here, he gives a basic outline of his 'transcendental pragmatics' and puts forward the core argument that this new departure represents an 'expansion of the epistemological foundations of the theory [or philosophy] of science'. Transcendental pragmatics is a broad philosophical framework which embraces also an 'anthropology of knowledge' specifying knowledge as something obtainable only by humans as embodied and communicating beings who maintain practical relations and engage with their world. As Apel makes clear, transcendental pragmatics entails a transformation of Kant's philosophy which was still marred by a residue of Cartesian dualism, while he in turn finds inspiration for this transformation in Peirce. Apel retains Kant's transcendental perspective, which counters the positivistic and behaviouristic view that the objects of knowledge are given or positively available by insisting that they are rather constituted by the subject of knowledge and, thus, that this constitutive dimension should be included in the philosophy of science. At the same time, however, he criticizes Kant for conceiving of the subject of knowledge on the one hand exclusively as 'consciousness' to the exclusion of 'practical, bodily . . . world engagement', and on the other exclusively as 'subjective' or individual rather than as 'intersubjective' or being borne by the indefinite communication community. Learning from Peirce's threefold pragmatist theory of signs or semiotic which Morris rehabilitated, Apel also goes beyond Kant and the traditional philosophy of science by conceiving of knowledge as mediated by signs or communication – i.e. knowledge depends on (i) signs which (ii) refer to something in the world and (iii) give something to understand to a community of interpreters. By adopting the title 'transcendental pragmatics' rather than simply 'pragmatism' (or 'pragmaticism'), as does Peirce, or 'pragmatics', as does Morris, however, he sets himself off against both these authors. In his introduction to the German edition of Morris' main work, *Signs, Language, and Behavior* (1946, German edition 1981), Apel criticizes the latter for his behaviouristic reduction of semiotics and his related adoption of value-free scientism. Peirce comes in for a parallel criticism. In his many writings – for example *Towards a Transformation of Philosophy* (1980) – on Peirce's development of Kant, Apel argues that Peirce's concept of community remained too tied to the scientific community to really grasp the necessary and unavoidable notion of an ideal, indefinite or unlimited community of communication and interpretation. While the pragmatists Josiah Royce and George Herbert Mead in one way or another both acknowledged this latter notion, its consistent elaboration is an achievement forming part of Apel's transcendental pragmatics. It is the incorporation of this inescapable transcendental presupposition of all knowledge into the philosophy of the social sciences that enables Apel to avoid the scientistic, instrumentalist and behaviouristic trap into which many pragmatists so readily fall. By starting from practical, bodily engagement with the world, on the one hand, transcendental pragmatics identifies basic ways in which human beings constitute meaning and categorically pose questions, and thus it allows us to distinguish between different kinds of knowledge and, by extension, different sciences and forms of inquiry. By incorporating the vanishing point of an unrealized communication community, on the other hand, transcendental pragmatics compels us never to forget that all cognitive processes and the acquisition and use of knowledge, over and above being communicatively mediated, form part of an ongoing and incomplete process in which all human beings are potentially implicated.

41

CHARLES S. PEIRCE
A definition of pragmatic and pragmatism* (1902)

1. Pragmatic anthropology, according to Kant, is practical ethics. Pragmatic horizon is the adaptation of our general knowledge to influencing our morals.

2. The opinion that metaphysics is to be largely cleared up by the application of the following maxim for attaining clearness of apprehension: 'Consider what effects, that might conceivably have practical bearings, we conceive the object of our conception to have. Then, our conception of these effects is the whole of our conception of the object.' [The doctrine that the whole 'meaning' of a conception expresses itself in practical consequences, consequences either in the shape of conduct to be recommended, or in that of experiences to be expected, if the conception be true; which consequences would be different if it were untrue, and must be different from the consequences by which the meaning of other conceptions is in turn expressed. If a second conception should not appear to have other consequences, then it must really be only the first conception under a different name. In methodology it is certain that to trace and compare their respective consequences is an admirable way of establishing the differing meanings of different conceptions.]

3. This maxim was first proposed by C. S. Peirce in the *Popular Science Monthly* for January, 1878 (xii. 287); and he explained how it was to be applied to the doctrine of reality. The writer was led to the maxim by the reflection upon Kant's *Critique of Pure Reason*. Substantially the same way of dealing with ontology seems to have been practised by the Stoics. The writer subsequently saw that the principle might easily be misapplied, so as to sweep away the whole doctrine of incommensurables, and, in fact, the whole Weierstrassian way of regarding the calculus. In 1896 William James

* Reprinted by permission of the publisher from *Collected Papers of Charles Sanders Peirce, Vol. 5, Pragmatism and Pragmaticism*, edited by Charles Hartshore and Paul Weiss, pp. 1–6, Cambridge, Mass: The Belknap Press of Harvard University Press, Copyright © 1934, 1935 by the President and Fellows of Harward College. This was originally an entry written by C.S. Peirce in a *Dictionary of Philosophy and Psychology*, edited by J.M. Baldwin, New York, Macmillan, 1902. This explains why he used the third person in referring to himself.

published his *Will to Believe*, and later his *Philosophical Conceptions* and *Practical Results*, which pushed this method to such extremes as must tend to give us pause. The doctrine appears to assume that the end of man is action – a stoical axiom which, to the present writer at the age of sixty, does not recommend itself so forcibly as it did at thirty. If it be admitted, on the contrary, that action wants an end, and that that end must be something of a general description, then the spirit of the maxim itself, which is that we must look to the upshot of our concepts in order rightly to apprehend them, would direct us towards something different from practical facts, namely, to general ideas, as the true interpreters of our thought. Nevertheless, the maxim has approved itself to the writer, after many years of trial, as of great utility in leading to a relatively high grade of clearness of thought. He would venture to suggest that it should always be put into practice with conscientious thoroughness, but that, when that has been done, and not before, a still higher grade of clearness of thought can be attained by remembering that the only ultimate good which the practical facts to which it directs attention can subserve is to further the development of concrete reasonableness; so that the meaning of the concept does not lie in any individual reactions at all, but in the manner in which those reactions contribute to that development. Indeed, in the article of 1878, above referred to, the writer practised better than he preached; for he applied the stoical maxim most unstoically, in such a sense as to insist upon the reality of the objects of general ideas in their generality.

4. A widely current opinion during the last quarter of a century has been that reasonableness is not a good thing in itself, but only for the sake of something else. Whether it be so or not seems to be a synthetical question, not to be settled by an appeal to the principle of contradiction – as if a reason for reasonableness were absurd. Almost everybody will now agree that the ultimate good lies in the evolutionary process in some way. If so, it is not in individual reactions in their segregation, but in something general or continuous. Synechism is founded on the notion that the coalescence, the becoming continuous, the becoming governed by laws, the becoming instinct with general ideas, are but phases of one and the same process of the growth of reasonableness. This is first shown to be true with mathematical exactitude in the field of logic, and is thence inferred to hold good metaphysically. It is not opposed to pragmatism in the manner in which C.S. Peirce applied it, but includes that procedure as a step.

The architectonic construction of pragmatism

5. . . . Pragmatism was not a theory which special circumstances has led its authors to entertain. It has been designed and constructed, to use the expression of Kant, architectonically. Just as a civil engineer, before erecting a bridge, a ship, or a house, will think of the different properties of all materials, and will use no iron, stone, or cement, that has not been subjected to tests; and will put them together in ways minutely considered, so, in constructing the doctrine of pragmatism the properties of all indecomposable concepts were examined and the ways in which they could be compounded. Then the purpose of the proposed doctrine having been analyzed, it was constructed out of the appropriate concepts so as to fulfill that purpose. In this way,

the truth of it was proved. There are subsidiary confirmations of its truth; but it is believed that there is no other independent way of strictly proving it . . .

6. But first, what is its purpose? What is it expected to accomplish? It is expected to bring to an end those prolonged disputes of philosophers which no observations of facts could settle, and yet in which each side claims to prove that the other side is in the wrong. Pragmatism maintains that in those cases the disputants must be at cross-purposes. They either attach different meanings to words, or else one side or the other (or both) uses a word without any definite meaning. What is wanted, therefore, is a method for ascertaining the real meaning of any concept, doctrine, proposition, word, or other sign. The object of a sign is one thing; its meaning is another. Its object is the thing or occasion, however indefinite, to which it is to be applied. Its meaning is the idea which it attaches to that object, whether by way of mere supposition, or as a command, or as an assertion.

7. Now every simple idea is composed of one of three classes; and a compound idea is in most cases predominantly of one of those classes. Namely, it may, in the first place, be a quality of feeling, which is positively such as it is, and is indescribable; which attaches to one object regardless of every other; and which is *sui generis* and incapable, in its own being, of comparison with any other feeling, because in comparisons it is representations of feelings and not the very feelings themselves that are compared. Or, in the second place, the idea may be that of a single happening or fact, which is attached at once to two objects, as an experience, for example, is attached to the experiencer and to the object experienced. Or, in the third place, it is the idea of a sign or communication conveyed by one person to another (or to himself at a later time) in regard to a certain object well known to both . . . Now the bottom meaning of a sign cannot be the idea of a sign, since that latter sign must itself have a meaning which would thereby become the meaning of the original sign. We may therefore conclude that the ultimate meaning of any sign consists either in an idea predominantly of feeling or in one predominantly of acting and being acted on. For there ought to be no hesitation in assenting to the view that all those ideas which attach essentially to two objects take their rise from the experience of volition and from the experience of the perception of phenomena which resist direct efforts of the will to annul or modify them.

8. But pragmatism does not undertake to say in what the meanings of all signs consist, but merely to lay down a method of determining the meanings of intellectual concepts, that is, of those upon which reasonings may turn. Now all reasoning that is not utterly vague, all that ought to figure in a philosophical discussion involves, and turns upon, precise necessary reasoning. Such reasoning is included in the sphere of mathematics, as modern mathematicians conceive their science. 'Mathematics,' said Benjamin Peirce, as early as 1870, 'is the science which draws necessary conclusions'; and subsequent writers have substantially accepted this definition, limiting it, perhaps, to precise conclusions. The reasoning of mathematics is now well understood. It consists in forming an image of the conditions of the problem, associated with which are certain general permissions to modify the image, as well as certain general

assumptions that certain things are impossible. Under the permissions, certain experiments are performed upon the image, and the assumed impossibilities involve their always resulting in the same general way. The superior certainty of the mathematician's results, as compared, for example, with those of the chemist, are due to two circumstances. First, the mathematician's experiments being conducted in the imagination upon objects of his own creation, cost next to nothing; while those of the chemist cost dear. Secondly, the assurance of the mathematician is due to his reasoning only concerning hypothetical conditions, so that his results have the generality of his conditions; while the chemist's experiments relating to what will happen as a matter of fact are always open to the doubt whether unknown conditions may not alter. Thus, the mathematician knows that a column of figures will add up the same, whether it be set down in black ink or in red; because he goes on the assumption that the sum of any two numbers of which one is M and the other one more than N will be one more than the sum of M and N; and this assumption says nothing about the color of the ink. The chemist assumes that when he mixes two liquids in a test-tube, there will or will not be a precipitate whether the Dowager Empress of China happens to sneeze at the time, because his experience has always been that laboratory experiments are not affected by such distant conditions. Still, the solar system is moving through space at a great rate, and there is a bare possibility that it may just then have entered a region in which sneezing has very surprising force.

9. Such reasonings and all reasonings turn upon the idea that if one exerts certain kinds of volition, one will undergo in return certain compulsory perceptions. Now this sort of consideration, namely, that certain lines of conduct will entail certain kinds of inevitable experiences is what is called a 'practical consideration.' Hence is justified the maxim, belief in which constitutes pragmatism; namely,

In order to ascertain the meaning of an intellectual conception one should consider what practical consequences might conceivably result by necessity from the truth of that conception; and the sum of these consequences will constitute the entire meaning of the conception.

42

JOHN DEWEY
Social inquiry* (1938)

1. Most current social inquiry is marked, as analytic examination will disclose, by the dominance of one or the other of two modes of procedure, which, in their contrast with one another, illustrate the separation of practice and theory. On the practical side, or among persons directly occupied with management of practical affairs, it is commonly assumed that the problems which exist are already definite in their main features. When this assumption is made, it follows that the business of inquiry is but to ascertain the best method of solving them. The consequence of this assumption is that the work of analytic discrimination, which is necessary to convert a problematic situation into a set of conditions forming a definite problem, is largely foregone. The inevitable result is that methods for resolving problematic situations are proposed without any clear conception of the material in which projects and plans are to be applied and to take effect. The further result is that often difficulties are intensified. For additional obstructions to intelligent action are created; or else, in alleviating some symptoms, new troubles are generated. Survey of political problems and the methods by which they are dealt with, in both domestic and international fields, will disclose any number of pertinent illustrations.

The contrast at this point with methods in physical inquiry is striking. For, in the latter, a large part of the techniques employed have to do with determination of the nature of the problem by means of methods that procure a wide range of data, that determine their pertinency as evidential, that ensure their accuracy by devices of measurement, and that arrange them in the order which past inquiry has shown to be most likely to indicate appropriate modes of procedure. Controlled analytic observation, involving systematic comparison-contrast, is accordingly a matter of course in the subjects that have achieved scientific status. The futility of attempting to solve a problem whose conditions have not been determined is taken for granted.

The analogy between social practice and medical practice as it was conducted before the rise of techniques of clinical observation and record, is close enough to be instructive. In both, there is the assumption that gross observation suffices to

* From John Dewey, *Logic, the Theory of Inquiry*, Henry Holt, 1938, pp. 493–499.

ascertain the nature of the trouble. Except in unusually obscure cases, symptoms sufficiently large and coarse to be readily observable sufficed in medical practice to supply the data that were used as means of diagnosis. It is now recognized that choice of remedial measures looking to restoration of health is haphazard until the conditions which constitute the trouble or disease have been determined as completely and accurately as possible. The primary problem is, then, to institute the techniques of observation and record that provide the data taken to be evidential and testing. The lesson, as far as method of social inquiry is concerned, is the prime necessity for development of techniques of analytic observation and comparison, so that problematic social situations may be resolved into definitely formulated problems.

One of the many obstructions in the way of satisfying the logical conditions of scientific method should receive special notice. Serious social troubles tend to be interpreted in moral terms. That the situations themselves are profoundly moral in their causes and consequences, in the genuine sense of moral, need not be denied. But conversion of the situations investigated into definite problems, that can be intelligently dealt with, demands objective intellectual formulation of conditions; and such a formulation demands in turn complete abstraction from the qualities of sin and righteousness, of vicious and virtuous motives, that are so readily attributed to individuals, groups, classes, nations. There was a time when desirable and obnoxious physical phenomena were attributed to the benevolence and malevolence of overruling powers. There was a time when diseases were attributed to the machinations of personal enemies. Spinoza's contention that the occurrence of moral evils should be treated upon the same basis and plane as the occurrence of thunderstorms is justifiable on the ground of the requirements of scientific method, independently of its context in his own philosophic system. For such procedure is the only way in which they can be formulated objectively or in terms of selected and ordered conditions. And such formulation is the sole mode of approach through which plans of remedial procedure can be projected in objective terms. Approach to human problems in terms of moral blame and moral approbation, of wickedness or righteousness, is probably the greatest single obstacle now existing to development of competent methods in the field of social subject-matter.

2. When we turn from consideration of the methods of inquiry currently employed in political and many administrative matters, to the methods that are adopted in the professed name of social science, we find quite an opposite state of affairs. We come upon an assumption which if it were made explicitly formulated would take some such shape as 'The facts are out there and only need to be observed, assembled and arranged to give rise to suitable and grounded generalizations.' Investigators of physical phenomena often speak and write in similar fashion. But analysis of what they do as distinct from what they say yields a very different result. Before, however, considering this point I shall discuss a closely connected assumption, namely the assumption that in order to base conclusions upon the facts and only the facts, all evaluative procedures must be strictly ruled out.

This assumption on the part of those engaged, in the name of science, in social investigation derives in the minds of those who entertain it from a sound principle. It springs, at least in large measure, from realization of the harm that has been wrought by forming social judgments on the ground of moral preconceptions, conceptions of what is right and wrong, vicious and virtuous. As has just been stated, this procedure inevitably prejudices the institution of relevant significant data, the statement of the problems that are to be solved, and the methods by which they may be solved. The soundness of the principle that moral condemnation and approbation should be excluded from the operations of obtaining and weighing material data and from the operations by which conceptions for dealing with the data are instituted, is, however, often converted into the notion that all evaluations should be excluded. This conversion is, however, effected only through the intermediary of a thoroughly fallacious notion; the notion, namely, that the moral blames and approvals in question are evaluative and that they exhaust the field of evaluation. For they are not evaluative in any logical sense of evaluation. They are not even judgments in the logical sense of judgment. For they rest upon some preconception of ends that should or ought to be attained. This preconception excludes ends (consequences) from the field of inquiry and reduces inquiry at its very best to the truncated and distorted business of finding out means for realizing objectives already settled upon. Judgment which is actually judgment (that satisfies the logical conditions of judgment) institutes means-consequences (ends) in strict conjugate relation to each other. Ends have to be adjudged (evaluated) on the basis of the available means by which they can be attained just as much as existential materials have to be adjudged (evaluated) with respect to their function as material means of effecting a resolved situation. For an end-in-view is itself a means, namely, a procedural means.

The idea that 'the end justifies the means' is in as bad repute in moral theory as its adoption is a commonplace of political practice. The doctrine may be given a strictly logical formulation, and when so formulated its inherent defect becomes evident. From the logical standpoint, it rests upon the postulate that some end is already so fixedly given that it is outside the scope of inquiry, so that the only problem for inquiry is to ascertain and manipulate the materials by which the end may be attained. The hypothetical and directive function of ends-in-view as procedural means is thus ignored and a fundamental logical condition of inquiry is violated. Only an end-in-view that is treated as a hypothesis (by which discrimination and ordering of existential material is operatively effected) can by any logical possibility determine the existential materials that are means. In all fields but the social, the notion that the correct solution is already given and that it only remains to find the facts that prove it is so thoroughly discredited that those who act upon it are regarded as pretenders, or as cranks who are trying to impose some pet notion upon facts. But in social matters, those who claim that they are in possession of the one sure solution of social problems often set themselves up as being peculiarly scientific while others are floundering around in an 'empirical' morass. Only recognition in both theory and practice that ends to be attained (ends-in-view) are of the nature of hypotheses and that hypotheses have to be formed and tested in strict correlativity with existential conditions as means, can alter current habits of dealing with social issues.

What has been said indicates the valid meaning of evaluation in inquiry in general and also shows the necessity of evaluative judgments in social inquiry. The need for selective discrimination of certain existential or factual material to be data proves that an evaluative estimate is operating. The notion that evaluation is concerned only with ends and that, with the ruling out of moral ends, evaluative judgments are ruled out rests, then, upon a profound misconception of the nature of the logical conditions and constituents of all scientific inquiry. All competent and authentic inquiry demands that out of the complex welter of existential and potentially observable and recordable material, certain material be selected and weighed as data or the 'facts of the case.' This process is one of adjudgment, of appraisal or evaluation. On the other end, there is, as has been just stated, no evaluation when ends are taken to be already given. An idea of an end to be reached, an end-in-view, is logically indispensable in discrimination of existential material as the evidential and testing facts of the case. Without it, there is no guide for observation; without it, one can have no conception of what one should look for or even is looking for. One 'fact' would be just as good as another – that is, good for nothing in control of inquiry and formation and in settlement of a problem.

3. What has been said has direct bearing upon another assumption which underlies a considerable part of allegedly scientific social inquiry; the idea, namely, that facts are just there and need only to be observed accurately and be assembled in sufficient number to warrant generalizations. A generalization in the form of a hypothesis is a prerequisite condition of selection and ordering of material as facts. A generalization is quite as much an antecedent of observation and assemblage of facts as it is a consequence of observing and assembling them. Or, more correctly stated, no generalization can emerge as a warranted conclusion unless a generalization in the form of a hypothesis has previously exercised control of the operations of discriminative selection and (synthetic) ordering of material to form the facts of and for a problem. To return to the point suggested earlier: What scientific inquirers do, as distinct from what they say, is to execute certain operations of experimentation – which are operations of doing and making – that modify antecedently given existential conditions so that the results of the transformation are facts which are relevant and weighty in solution of a given problem. Operations of experimentation are cases of blind trial and error which at best only succeed in suggesting a hypothesis to be later tried except as they are themselves directed by a hypothesis about a solution.

The assumption that social inquiry is scientific if proper techniques of observation and record (preferably statistical) are employed (the standard of propriety being set by borrowing from techniques used in physical science), thus fails to observe the logical conditions which in physical science give the techniques of observing and measuring their standing and force. This point will be developed by considering the idea, which is current, that social inquiry is scientific only when complete renunciation of any reference to practical affairs is made its precondition. Discussion of this fallacy (fallacious from the strictly logical point of view) will start from a consideration of the nature of the problems of social inquiry.

Institution of problems

A genuine problem is one set by existential problematic situations. In social inquiry, genuine problems are set only by actual social situations which are themselves conflicting and confused. Social conflicts and confusions exist in fact before problems for inquiry exist. The latter are intellectualizations in inquiry of these 'practical' troubles and difficulties. The intellectual determinations can be tested and warranted only by doing something about the problematic existential situations out of which they arise, so as to transform it in the direction of an ordered situation. The connection of social inquiry, as to social data and as to conceptual generalizations, with practice is intrinsic not external. Any problem of scientific inquiry that does not grow out of actual (or 'practical') social conditions is factitious; it is arbitrarily set by the inquirer instead of being objectively produced and controlled. All the techniques of observation employed in the advanced sciences may be conformed to, including the use of the best statistical methods to calculate probable errors, etc., and yet the material ascertained be scientifically 'dead,' i.e., irrelevant to a genuine issue, so that concern with it is hardly more than a form of intellectual busy work. That which is observed, no matter how carefully and no matter how accurate the record, is capable of being understood only in terms of projected consequences of activities. In fine, problems with which inquiry into social subject-matter is concerned must, if they satisfy the conditions of scientific method, (1) grow out of actual social tensions, needs, 'troubles'; (2) have their subject-matter determined by the conditions that are material means of bringing about a unified situation, and (3) be related to some hypothesis, which is a plan and policy for existential resolution of the conflicting social situation.

Determination of facts in social science

This topic has, of necessity, been anticipated in the foregoing discussion which has shown that facts are such in a logical sense only as they serve to delimit a problem in a way that affords indication and test of proposed solutions. Two involved considerations will, however, be explicitly dealt with.

1. Since transformation of a problematic situation (a confused situation whose constituents conflict with one another) is effected by interaction of specially discriminated existential conditions, facts have to be determined in their dual function as obstacles and as resources; that is, with reference to operations of negation (elimination) and affirmation, the latter being determination of materials as positively agreeing with or reinforcing one another. No existing situation can be modified without counteracting obstructive and deflecting forces that render a given situation confused and conflicting. Operations of elimination are indispensable. Nor can an objectively unified situation be instituted except as the positive factors of existing conditions are released and ordered so as to move the direction of the objective consequence desired. Otherwise, ends-in-view are utopian and 'idealistic,' in the sentimental sense of the latter word. Realistic social thinking is precisely the mode of observation which discriminates adverse and favorable conditions in an existing situation, 'adverse' and 'favorable' being understood in connection with the end proposed. 'Realism' does not mean apprehension of the existing situation *in toto*, but selective discrimination of conditions as obstructive and as resources; i.e., as negative and positive. When it is said 'We must take conditions as they are' the statement is either a logical truism or a fallacy which then operates as an excuse for inaction. It is a truism if it is understood

to mean that existing conditions are the material, and the only material, of analytic observation. But if it is taken to mean that 'conditions as they are' are final for judgment as to what can or should be done, there results complete abnegation of intelligent direction of both observation and action. For conditions in any doubtful and undesirable situation are never all of a piece – otherwise there would be no conflict or confusion involved – and, moreover, they are never so fixed that no change in them can be effected. In actual fact, they are themselves changing anyhow in some direction, so that the problem is to institute modes of interaction among them which will produce changes in the direction that leads to the proposed objective consequence.

2. That conditions are never completely fixed means that they are in process – that, in any case, they are moving toward the production of a state of affairs which is going to be different in some respect. The purpose of the operations of observation which differentiate conditions into obstructive factors and positive resources is precisely to indicate the intervening activities which will give the movement (and hence its consequences) a different form from what it would take if it were left to itself; that is, movement toward a proposed unified existential situation.

The result of taking facts as finished and over with is more serious in inquiry into social phenomena than it is with respect to physical objects. For the former phenomena are inherently historical. But in physics, although universal conceptions are defined and kinds are described in reference to some final existential application, they are free from the necessity of any immediate application. Every social phenomenon, however, is itself a sequential course of changes, and hence a fact isolated from the history of which it is a moving constituent loses the qualities that make it distinctively social. Generic propositions are indispensable in order to determine the unique sequence of events, but as far as the latter is interpreted wholly in terms of general and universal propositions, it loses that unique individuality in virtue of which it is a historic and social fact. A physical fact may be treated as a 'case.' Any account of, say, the assassination of Julius Caesar assuredly involves the generic conceptions of assassination, conspiracy, political ambition, human beings, of which it is an exemplifying case and it cannot be reported and accounted for without the use of such general conceptions. But treatment of it as just and merely a case eliminates its qualities that make it a social fact. The conceptions are indispensable but they are indispensable as means for determining a non-recurring temporal sequence. Even in physics 'laws' are in their logical import ultimately means of selecting and linking together events which form an individual temporal sequence.

It was just affirmed that social phenomena are historical, or of the nature of individual temporal sequences. Argument in support of this assumption is superfluous if 'history' is understood to include the present. No one would dream of questioning that the social phenomena which constitute the rise of the papacy, the industrial revolution, the rise of cultural and political nationalism, are historical. It cannot be denied that what is now going on in the countries of the world, in their domestic institutions and foreign relations, will be the material of history in the future. It is absurd to suppose that history includes events that happened up to yesterday but does not take in those occurring today. As there are no temporal gaps in a historically determined sequence, so there are none in social phenomena that are determined by inquiry for the latter constitute a developing course of events. Hence, although observation and assemblage of materials in isolation from their movement into an eventual consequence may yield 'facts' of some sort, the latter will not be facts in any social sense of that word, since they will be non-historical.

This consideration reinforces the conclusion already drawn: Inquiry into social phenomena involves judgments of evaluation, for they can be understood only in terms of eventuations to which they are capable of moving. Hence, there are as many possible interpretations in the abstract as there are possible kinds of consequences. This statement does not entail carrying over into social phenomena a teleology that has been outmoded in the case of physical phenomena. It does not imply that there is some purpose ruling social events or that they are moving to a predetermined goal. The meaning is that any problematic situation, when it is analyzed, presents, in connection with the idea of operations to be performed, alternative possible ends in the sense of terminating consequences. Even in physical inquiry, what the inquirer observes and the conceptions he entertains are controlled by an objective purpose – that of attaining a resolved situation. The difference between physical and social inquiry does not reside in the presence or absence of an end-in-view, formulated in terms of possible consequences. It consists in the respective subject-matters of the purposes. This difference makes a great practical difference in the conduct of inquiry: a difference in the kind of operations to be performed in instituting the subject-matters that in their interactions will resolve a situation. In the case of social inquiry, associated activities are directly involved in the operations to be performed; these associated activities enter into the idea of any proposed solution. The practical difficulties in the way of securing the agreements in actual association that are necessary for the required activity are great. In physical matters, the inquirer may reach the outcome in his laboratory or observatory. Utilization of the conclusions of others is indispensable, and others must be able to attain similar conclusions by use of materials and methods similar to those employed by the individual investigator. His activity is socially conditioned in its beginning and close. But in physical inquiry the conditioning social factors are relatively indirect, while in solution of social problems they are directly involved. Any hypothesis as to a social end must include as part of itself the idea of organized association among those who are to execute the operations it formulates and directs.

Evaluative judgments, judgments of better and worse about the means to be employed, material and procedural, are required. The evils in current social judgments of ends and policies arise, as has been said, from importations of judgments of value from outside of inquiry. The evils spring from the fact that the values employed are not determined in and by the process of inquiry: for it is assumed that certain ends have an inherent value so unquestionable that they regulate and validate the means employed, instead of ends being determined on the basis of existing conditions as obstacles-resources. Social inquiry, in order to satisfy the conditions of scientific method, must judge certain objective consequences to be the end which is worth attaining under the given conditions. But, to repeat, this statement does not mean what it is often said to mean: Namely, that ends and values can be assumed outside of scientific inquiry so that the latter is then confined to determination of the means best calculated to arrive at the realization of such values. On the contrary, it means that ends in their capacity of values can be validly determined only on the basis of the tensions, obstructions and positive potentialities that are found, by controlled observation, to exist in the actual situation.

43

CHARLES MORRIS
Foundations of the theory of signs* (1938)

Men are the dominant sign-using animals. Animals other than man do, of course, respond to certain things as signs of something else, but such signs do not attain the complexity and elaboration which is found in human speech, writing, art, testing devices, medical diagnosis, and signaling instruments. Science and signs are insepar-ably interconnected, since science both presents men with more reliable signs and embodies its results in systems of signs. Human civilization is dependent upon signs and systems of signs, and the human mind is inseparable from the functioning of signs – if indeed mentality is not to be identified with such functioning.

It is doubtful if signs have ever before been so vigorously studied by so many persons and from so many points of view. The army of investigators includes lin-guists, logicians, philosophers, psychologists, biologists, anthropologists, psycho-pathologists, aestheticians, and sociologists. There is lacking, however, a theoretical structure simple in outline and yet comprehensive enough to embrace the results obtained from different points of view and to unite them into a unified and consistent whole. It is the purpose of the present study to suggest this unifying point of view and to sketch the contours of the science of signs. This can be done only in a fragmentary fashion, partly because of the limitations of space, partly because of the undeveloped state of the science itself, but mainly because of the purpose which such a study aims to serve by its inclusion in this Encyclopedia.

Semiotic has a double relation to the sciences: it is both a science among the sciences and an instrument of the sciences. The significance of semiotic as a science lies in the fact that it is a step in the unification of science, since it supplies the foundations for any special science of signs, such as linguistics, logic, mathematics, rhetoric, and (to some extent at least) aesthetics. The concept of sign may prove to be of importance in the unification of the social, psychological, and humanistic sciences in so far as these are distinguished from the physical and biological sciences. And since it will be shown that signs are simply the objects studied by the biological and

* From 'Foundations of the Theory of Signs', *International Encylopedia of Unified Science*, vol. 1, no. 2, pp. 79–84. Reproduced by permission of University of Chicago Press.

physical sciences related in certain complex functional processes, any such unification of the formal sciences on the one hand, and the social, psychological, and humanistic sciences on the other, would provide relevant material for the unification of these two sets of sciences with the physical and biological sciences. Semiotic may thus be of importance in a program for the unification of science, though the exact nature and extent of this importance is yet to be determined.

But if semiotic is a science co-ordinate with the other sciences, studying things or the properties of things in their function of serving as signs, it is also the instrument of all sciences, since every science makes use of and expresses its results in terms of signs. Hence metascience (the science of science) must use semiotic as an organon. It was noticed in the essay 'Scientific Empiricism' (Vol. I, No. 1) that it is possible to include without remainder the study of science under the study of the language of science, since the study of that language involves not merely the study of its formal structure but its relation to objects designated and to the persons who use it. From this point of view the entire Encyclopedia, as a scientific study of science, is a study of the language of science. But since nothing can be studied without signs denoting the objects in the field to be studied, a study of the language of science must make use of signs referring to signs – and semiotic must supply the relevant signs and principles for carrying on this study. Semiotic supplies a general language applicable to any special language or sign, and so applicable to the language of science and specific signs which are used in science.

The interest in presenting semiotic as a science and as part of the unification of science must here be restricted by the practical motive of carrying the analysis only so far and in such directions as to supply a tool for the work of the Encyclopedia, i.e., to supply a language in which to talk about, and in so doing to improve, the language of science. Other studies would be necessary to show concretely the results of sign analysis applied to special sciences and the general significance for the unification of science of this type of analysis. But even without detailed documentation it has become clear to many persons today that man – including scientific man – must free himself from the web of words which he has spun and that language – including scientific language – is greatly in need of purification, simplification, and systematization. The theory of signs is a useful instrument for such debabelization.

The process in which something functions as a sign may be called semiosis. This process, in a tradition which goes back to the Greeks, has commonly been regarded as involving three (or four) factors: that which acts as a sign, that which the sign refers to, and that effect on some interpreter in virtue of which the thing in question is a sign to that interpreter. These three components in semiosis may be called, respectively, the sign vehicle, the designatum, and the interpretant; the interpreter may be included as a fourth factor. These terms make explicit the factors left undesignated in the common statement that a sign refers to something for someone.

A dog responds by the type of behavior (I) involved in the hunting of chipmunks (D) to a certain sound (S); a traveler prepares himself to deal appropriately (I) with the geographical region (D) in virtue of the letter (S) received from a friend. In such cases S is the sign vehicle (and a sign in virtue of its functioning), D the designatum, and I the interpretant of the interpreter. The most effective characterization of a sign is the following: S is a sign of D for I to the degree that I takes account of D in virtue of the presence of S. Thus in semiosis something takes account of something else mediately, i.e., by means of a third something. Semiosis is accordingly a mediated-taking-account-of. The mediators are sign vehicles; the takings-account-of are interpretants; the agents of the process are interpreters; what is taken account of are designata. There are several comments to be made about this formulation.

It should be clear that the terms 'sign,' 'designatum,' 'interpretant,' and 'interpreter' involve one another, since they are simply ways of referring to aspects of the process of semiosis. Objects need not be referred to by signs, but there are no designata unless there is such reference; something is a sign only because it is interpreted as a sign of something by some interpreter; a taking-account-of-something is an interpretant only in so far as it is evoked by something functioning as a sign; an object is an interpreter only as it mediately takes account of something. The properties of being a sign, a designatum, an interpreter, or an interpretant are relational properties which things take on by participating in the functional process of semiosis. Semiotic, then, is not concerned with the study of a particular kind of object, but with ordinary objects in so far (and only in so far) as they participate in semiosis. The importance of this point will become progressively clearer.

Signs which refer to the same object need not have the same designata, since that which is taken account of in the object may differ for various interpreters. A sign of an object may, at one theoretical extreme, simply turn the interpreter of the sign upon the object, while at the other extreme it would allow the interpreter to take account of all the characteristics of the object in question in the absence of the object itself. There is thus a potential sign continuum in which with respect to every object or situation all degrees of semiosis may be expressed, and the question as to what the designatum of a sign is in any given situation is the question of what characteristics of the object or situation are actually taken account of in virtue of the presence of the sign vehicle alone.

A sign must have a designatum; yet obviously every sign does not, in fact, refer to an actual existent object. The difficulties which these statements may occasion are only apparent difficulties and need no introduction of a metaphysical realm of 'subsistence' for their solution. Since 'designatum' is a semiotical term, there cannot be designata without semiosis – but there can be objects without there being semiosis. The designatum of a sign is the kind of object which the sign applies to, i.e., the objects with the properties which the interpreter takes account of through the presence of the sign vehicle. And the taking-account-of may occur without there actually being objects or situations with the characteristics taken account of. This is true even in the case of pointing: one can for certain purposes point without pointing to anything. No contradiction arises in saying that every sign has a designatum but not every sign refers to an actual existent. Where what is referred to actually exists as referred to the object of reference is a denotatum. It thus becomes clear that, while every sign has a designatum, not every sign has a denotatum. A designatum is not a thing, but a kind of object or class of objects – and a class may have many members, or one member, or no members. The denotata are the members of the class. This distinction makes explicable the fact that one may reach in the icebox for an apple that is not there and make preparations for living on an island that may never have existed or has long since disappeared beneath the sea.

As a last comment on the definition of sign, it should be noted that the general theory of signs need not commit itself to any specific theory of what is involved in taking account of something through the use of a sign. Indeed, it may be possible to take 'mediated-taking-account-of' as the single primitive term for the axiomatic development of semiotic. Nevertheless, the account which has been given lends itself to treatment from the point of view of behavioristics, and this point of view will be adopted in what follows. This interpretation of the definition of sign is not, however, necessary. It is adopted here because such a point of view has in some form or other (though not in the form of Watsonian behaviorism) become widespread among psychologists, and because many of the difficulties which the history of semiotic reveals seem to be due to the fact that through most of its history semiotic linked itself with the faculty and introspective psychologies. From the point of view of behavioristics, to take account of D by the presence of S involves responding to D in virtue of a response to S. As will be made clear later, it is not necessary to deny 'private experiences' of the process of semiosis or of other processes, but it is necessary from the standpoint of behavioristics to deny that such experiences are of central importance or that the fact of their existence makes the objective study of semiosis (and hence of sign, designatum, and interpretant) impossible or even incomplete.

Pragmatics and semantics* (1946)

We have now surveyed the range of material with which a science of signs must deal. There remains only the task of bringing to a sharper focus the scope of this science and of indicating its theoretical and practical importance.

Those readers who are familiar with the literature of semiotic may have been surprised that the terms 'pragmatics', 'semantics', and 'syntactics' – so widely current in this literature – have not figured in our account. Their absence up to this point has, however, been deliberate. These terms have already taken on an ambiguity which threatens to cloud rather than illumine the problems of this field, being used by some writers to designate subdivisions of semiotic itself and by others to designate kinds of signs in the object languages with which semiotic deals. Otto Neurath warned years ago that these terms would engender pseudo-problems and distract attention from genuine problems; the course of events has proved in part the legitimacy of his fears. Yet these terms, if carefully introduced, serve to mark the scope and subdivisions of semiotic, and may now be added to our terminology.

In *Foundations of the Theory of Signs* (p. 6), the three terms in question were defined as follows: pragmatics as the study of 'the relation of signs to interpreters', semantics as the study of 'the relations of signs to the objects to which the signs are applicable', syntactics as the study of 'the formal relations of signs to one another'. Later analysis has shown that these definitions need refinement. Even as they stand,

* From Charles Morris, 'Signs, Language, and Behaviour' in Charles Morris *Writings on the General Theory of Signs*, Mouton, The Hague, 1971, pp. 301–311.

however, they give no warrant for their utilization as a classification of kinds of signs ('pragmatical signs', 'semantical signs', 'syntactical signs'); such extension of their signification is questionable, since it may blur the distinction between signs in various modes of signifying and the signs which make up pragmatics, semantics, and syntactics conceived as the three divisions of semiotic. Hence we shall not employ such an expression as 'syntactical sign', since doubt can then arise whether it designates a kind of sign (say, formators) or a sign within the part of semiotic distinguished as syntactics. The terms 'pragmatics', 'semantics', and 'syntactics' need clarification, however, even when restricted to differentiations of the field of semiotic.

Carnap formulates these distinctions in the following way:

> If we are analyzing a language, then we are concerned, of course, with expressions. But we need not necessarily also deal with speakers and designata. Although these factors are present whenever language is used, we may abstract from one or both of them in what we intend to say about the language in question. Accordingly, we distinguish three fields of investigation of languages. If in an investigation explicit reference is made to the speaker, or, to put it in more general terms, to the user of a language, then we assign it to the field of pragmatics. (Whether in this case reference to designata is made or not makes no difference for this classification.) If we abstract from the user of the language and analyze only the expressions and their designata, we are in the field of semantics. And if, finally, we abstract from the designata also and analyze only the relations between the expressions, we are in (logical) syntax. The whole science of language, consisting of the three parts mentioned, is called semiotic.
>
> (*Introduction to Semantics*, p. 9.)

In terms of the approach of the present study, the indicated division of the fields of semiotic needs certain further alterations: the restriction of semiotic to a study of language must be removed, the study of the structure of languages other than the scientific must be made possible, other modes of signification than the designative must be dealt with in semantics, and this in turn requires some modification of the formulation of pragmatics.

The following definitions retain the essential features of the prevailing classification, while freeing it from certain restrictions and ambiguities: pragmatics is that portion of semiotic which deals with the origin, uses, and effects of signs within the behaviour in which they occur; semantics deals with the signification of signs in all modes of signifying; syntactics deals with combinations of signs without regard for their specific significations or their relation to the behaviour in which they occur.

When so conceived, pragmatics, semantics, and syntactics are all interpretable within a behaviourally oriented semiotic, syntactics studying the ways in which signs are combined, semantics studying the signification of signs, and so the interpretant behaviour without which there is no signification, pragmatics studying the origin, uses, and effects of signs within the total behaviour of the interpreters of signs. The difference lies not in the presence or absence of behaviour but in the sector of behaviour under consideration. The full account of signs will involve all three considerations. It is legitimate and often convenient to speak of a particular semiotical investigation as falling within pragmatics, semantics, or syntactics. Nevertheless, in general it is more important to keep in mind the field of semiotic as a whole, and to bring to bear upon specific problems all that is relevant to their solution. The present study has deliberately preferred to emphasize the unity of semiotic rather than break each problem into its pragmatical, semantical, and syntactical components.

There is another current distinction which offers no difficulty in terms of this analysis: the distinction between pure and descriptive semiotic.

This distinction simply marks the difference between the formative discourse of semiotic and its designative discourse, that is, the difference between semiotic as logic and semiotic as scientific discourse. Semiotic, as a language to talk scientifically about signs, will have its own formative ascriptors (such as 'Every sign has an interpretant') and such ascriptors belong to logic; it will also consist of designative ascriptors (such as statements as to what signs signify to certain persons, how signs are combined in a specific language, the origin, uses, and effects of specific signs), and such ascriptors constitute semiotic as a natural science. This distinction applies to each of the subdivisions of semiotic: hence we can distinguish pure and descriptive pragmatics, pure and descriptive semantics, pure and descriptive syntactics. The application of semiotic as an instrument may be called applied semiotic.

Does semiotic signify itself? An affirmative answer can be given to this question, without contradictions arising, provided we recognize that no sign denotes its own signification. This assertion, itself part of logic, is an analytic formative ascriptor: since the signification of a sign gives the conditions of denotation for a sign, the signification of a sign is not itself a denotatum of the sign. So while no statement denotes all significations, there is no signification about which a statement cannot be made. In this way a statement can be made within semiotic about any sign, including the signs of this book, though no body of statements about signs is the totality of statements which can be made about signs.

A programme for linguistics

Our discussion of signs, even of language signs, has another noticeable peculiarity: it has not been couched in the terminology current in linguistics. 'Subject', 'object', 'predicate', 'noun', 'verb', 'word', 'sentence', 'modification', 'voice', 'phonology', 'morphology': such terms have been deliberately avoided. This has not been done to disparage the work of the professional linguist – for certainly he of all persons has carried farthest the scientific study of language – but in order to raise in an explicit form the relation of linguistics to semiotic, and to suggest a programme by which the terminology of the linguist can be grounded on the basic terms of semiotic. Only the linguist himself can carry out this programme.

The justification for this programme lies in the present state of linguistics itself. For decades linguists have expressed dissatisfaction with the traditional terminology in which they have talked about the spoken and written languages with which they have been concerned. And many proposals have been made for rebuilding this terminology on new foundations. The issue concerns the nature of the metalanguage in which the linguist is to talk about languages. The problem has arisen largely as the result of the study of languages other than those for which the traditional terminology was designed. This terminology appeared in Western linguistic science through attention to such languages as Greek and Latin within the Indo-European family of languages, and has been influenced at many points by the work of philosophers and logicians who themselves lived within this linguistic tradition. As attention widened to include languages in Asia, Africa, and America of widely diverse families, the parochial and limited character of the traditional linguistic metalanguage became obvious. The linguist found himself somewhat in the situation of early students of comparative religion who tried to describe the religions of the world in terms of one particular religious tradition. If one attempts to avoid this difficulty of talking about all languages in terms of one set of languages, or in terms of one philosophical or logical point of view, the problem then becomes acute: on what foundation is linguistics to erect its own metalanguage? This problem cannot be evaded by merely describing various languages, because a description of any language must be made in some terms or other. And any attempt to solve the problem means a reconstruction of linguistics at its foundations.

The suggestion here made is that semiotic provides the metalanguage for linguistics, and that the terminology of linguistics is to be defined by linguists on the basis of the terms of semiotic. In this way one could describe all languages of the world in a uniform terminology which would make possible a scientific comparative linguistics. A number of linguists have moved steadily in this direction, as mention of the names of Edward Sapir, Alan Gardiner, Leonard Bloomfield and Manuel J. Andrade indicates. And from the side of a general theory of signs, such philosophers, logicians and psychologists as Peirce, Cassirer, Reichenbach, Carnap and Bühler have been increasingly attentive to the material furnished by linguists. The carrying out of this programme consistently and in detail would mean the emergence of a semiotically grounded science of linguistics. Since this work requires the expert training of the linguist, it does not fall within the province of this study; it is for this reason that we have not employed the current terminology of linguistics nor attempted to define this terminology in our terms nor proposed a new terminology. We must be content to indicate a programme the carrying out of which will require the co-operation of the general semiotician and the specialized linguist.

A language is completely described in terms of the signification of its simple and compound signs, the restrictions which are imposed on sign combinations, and the way the language operates in the behaviour of its interpreters. These distinctions are those of semantics, syntactics, and pragmatics; hence these studies, when limited to languages, would constitute the three main divisions of linguistic science. They should in the interest of clarity replace the prevailing classifications, such as the frequent classification of linguistics into phonology and semantics, semantics being divided into grammar and lexicon, and grammar into syntax and morphology. The term 'grammar' is as we have seen especially ambiguous, covering for most linguists both syntactical and semantical considerations (usually the signification of formators but not that of lexicators).

The linguist interested in a semiotical foundation of linguistics would then employ the terms of semantics, pragmatics and syntactics in describing and comparing languages, and where these terms are insufficient, introduce the terms he needs upon the basis of the terms of semiotic. Thus the term 'phoneme' seems to designate in a spoken language any sound which is a non-significant component of signs and yet which is influential in signification; 'i' and 'a' are two phonemes in a language if and only if there are two signs in the language which differ only in these respects and yet have different significations (as 'bit' and 'bat' in English). The term 'sentence' seems to coincide with 'dominant ascriptor', the kinds of sentences corresponding to the kinds of ascriptors. The term 'word' on the other hand corresponds to no single semiotical term; so if it is to be retained it would have to be defined, presumably syntactically in terms of the degree of freedom which certain sign combinations have within ascriptors. Similarly for 'parts of speech', a notion which seems to be con-nected with the limitation upon the mode of signifying open to certain signs in sign combinations; in a language where there are no such constant limitations on signs there would be no 'parts of speech', though a given sign might signify in one ascriptor 'adjectivally', in another 'nominally', and so forth. In such ways linguistics would build up its terminology on a semiotical basis. What terms it will need and how they will be defined is a matter which must be left to linguists themselves. But if linguistics pro-ceeds in this manner it will gain a metalanguage adequate to talk about all languages and not biased toward only one set of languages. Linguistics will also secure the advantages of a behavioural foundation freeing it from the mentalistic categories which have hindered and even now hinder its scientific advance.

My own confidence in the feasibility of this programme is due to years of fruitful discussion with the linguist and anthropologist, Manuel J. Andrade. Andrade's early death prevented him from writing the book on the science of language which he had set himself as his life work. But he had himself gone a long way toward developing a semiotically grounded linguistics, much farther than any studies yet made in this field. He distinguished a number of 'linguistic offices' which signs fulfilled – referential offices (under which he distinguished onomastic, deictic, and declarative), pragmatic offices, and formal offices. In terms of these offices – which are akin to the distinction of the modes of signifying – and the limitations imposed on signs in sign combin-ations, he defined various classes of signs (linguistical, functional, semantical, and grammatical) and distinguished parts of speech as grammatical classes involving functional differences (that is, in our terms combinatory differences plus differences in mode of signifying). In a similar spirit he attempted to deal with all the phenomena which the linguist studies. I mention his terms, without attempting to elucidate them here, merely to show that his programme involved the building of the whole of lin-guistics upon semiotical foundations; he believed that in this way linguistics would obtain a metalanguage appropriate to the description and comparison of all lan-guages. It is to be hoped that some of his students will attempt to reconstruct his views and to carry further the project whose completion was prevented by his sudden death.

Semiotic as unification of science

The scope of semiotic has now been sufficiently explicated: semiotic is the science of signs, whether animal or human, language or non-language, true or false, adequate or inadequate, healthy or pathic. There remains for consideration the question of the theoretical and practical importance of this discipline. Its theoretical import will be discussed in relation to the question as to the role of semiotic in the unification of knowledge, and in particular in its bearing upon the treatment of psychology, human-istic studies and philosophy in such unification; its practical import will be discussed in relation to the problems of the orientation of the individual, social organization, and education.

As a science, semiotic shares whatever importance a science has. As it develops it will furnish increasingly reliable knowledge about sign-processes. Men have sought this knowledge in various ways in many cultures over many centuries; a scientific approach to this field but continues in this domain the development which is charac-teristic of every science – astronomy, chemistry, medicine, sociology, psychology and all the rest. A scientific semiotic is at the minimum simply one more extension of scientific techniques to fields of human interest. It needs no special justification to those who have the scientific enterprise at heart.

But beyond this, semiotic has a special importance in any programme for the unification (systematization) of scientific knowledge. The tendency toward the unifi-cation of science is inherent in scientific activity, since science is not content with a mere collection of statements known to be true, but aims at an organization of its knowledge. This unification occurs at two levels: on the one hand scientists seek knowledge concerning a subject matter which for various historical reasons has been broken up into separate fields studied by separate groups of investigators. Historically, for instance, the process of cell division has been studied by biologists and the process of surface tensions by physicists; today the biophysicist seeks comprehensive laws of surface tension which will apply to cell division. The other level of the unification of science is distinctively semiotical: it takes the existing language of science and seeks whatever relations can be found between the terms of the special sciences and between the laws of these sciences; this activity is essentially the descriptive semiotic of the language of science, though it may issue in suggestions for the improvement of this language. Semiotic serves in the unification of science at both levels: it provides a comprehensive language for talking about a field of phenomena (sign phenomena) which has been looked at piecemeal by various special disciplines; it provides an instrument for analysis of the relations between all special scientific languages. It is both a phase in the unification of science and an instrument for describing and furthering the unification of science.

The sense in which semiotic is itself a phase of the unification of knowledge should be evident from all that precedes, and needs no elaboration. For our discussions have brought together material which has been approached in isolation by philosophers, logicians, linguists, estheticians, sociologists, anthropologists, psychol-ogists and psychiatrists, and they show, at least in principle, how this material may be organized under a common terminology within a general theory of behaviour.

The role which such a science performs in the study of the relations between all other sciences needs, however, to be considered in some detail. In the unity of science movement, as represented by the *International Encyclopedia of Unified Science*, there are four major points at which difficulties and doubts have arisen: the relation of the 'formal sciences' to the 'natural sciences', the relation of psychology to the biological and physical sciences, the relation of humanistic studies to science, and the relation of philosophy to systematized knowledge. Semiotic throws considerable light on all these problems and facilitates a thoroughgoing unification of scientific knowledge. The first of the problems – the relation of the 'formal sciences' to the 'natural sciences' – has already been discussed tangentially, and needs only to be restated in terms of the present context. The question is whether a unification of science can in principle eventuate in one system of terms and laws or whether an encyclopedia of unified science would stand on the shelf in two volumes, one a unification of logic and mathematics on the pattern of Russell and Whitehead's *Principia Mathematica*, the other a unification of the sciences of nature on the pattern of Newton's *Philosophiae Naturalis Principia Mathematica*.

The difficulty in a straightforward answer to this question comes in part from the ambiguity in the terms 'unification' and 'science'. The work of Russell and Whitehead shows that it is possible to bring into one system of postulates and theorems many systems of formative ascriptors which have had an independent origin and development; it does not show that all systems of mathematics are part of a single system which includes, say, Euclidean and non-Euclidean geometries. In the same way the work of Newton showed that statements about the motion of astronomical bodies and statements about the motions of bodies on the earth were instances of general laws of motion; it did not show that there were no mutually exclusive languages possible for physics. The unification of science then does not mean that there are no alternative languages, but that it is possible to some extent at present, and to an unknown extent in the future, to construct a single language applicable to various subject matters and allowing the formulation of general laws holding for these subject matters. Unified science is systematized science; it does not exclude the possibility of alternative systematizations.

Now in this sense of unification it seems possible to unify (systematize) mathematics and natural science, and semiotic is itself the evidence of this possibility. For semiotic provides a set of terms applicable to all signs and hence to the signs of both mathematics and natural science. This does not mean that the signs of these two domains are the same kind of signs; the distinction between formative ascriptors and designative ascriptors protects us from this error. Nor does it mean that mathematics is a natural science; mathematical discourse is distinguished in our account from scientific discourse, just as, say, poetic discourse is distinguished from scientific discourse. But it does mean that insofar as we have knowledge about mathematics this knowledge is essentially of the same kind as all scientific knowledge, resting in this case on evidence drawn from the signification of signs; hence this knowledge is in principle incorporable within a system of unified science. If we do not confuse the existence of various types of discourse with knowledge, the recognition that mathematics is not physics or poetry, and that a Euclidean geometry is not a non-Euclidean geometry, is no obstacle to the unification of knowledge. How far this unification can in fact be carried out remains an open question; semiotic, even its present stage, should give some assurance of the feasibility of the programme.

So with regard to our first problem we conclude that the confusing distinction between the 'formal sciences' and the 'natural sciences' should be couched rather in terms of the legitimate distinction between mathematical discourse and scientific discourse, and that when this is done no obstacle is presented by this difference for the unification of scientific knowledge. Language has its mathematical portion and its scientific portion; the nature of each and their relations can be scientifically studied within semiotic, itself a language with a mathematical subdivision (logic or pure semiotic) and a scientific subdivision (descriptive semiotic). The fact that mathematics is used by a scientist and yet is itself not knowledge of the subject matter which the scientist studies raises no more of a problem than the fact that the microscope used by a scientist is not itself a scientific statement or a part of his scientific knowledge. And since semiotic is itself a science, its nature and its relations to other sciences can in turn be studied scientifically. Semiotic then is not only a science incorporable within unified science, but is able both to show the distinctive character of mathematics and the possibility of a single unified science which includes knowledge of mathematics along with knowledge of other subject matters.

44

C. WRIGHT MILLS
Situated actions and vocabularies of motive* (1940)

The major reorientation of recent theory and observation in sociology of language emerged with the overthrow of the Wundtian notion that language has as its function the 'expression' of prior elements within the individual. The postulate underlying modern study of language is the simple one that we must approach linguistic behavior, not by referring it to private states in individuals, but by observing its social function of coordinating diverse actions. Rather than expressing something which is prior and in the person, language is taken by other persons as an indicator of future actions.

Within this perspective there are suggestions concerning problems of motivation. It is the purpose of this paper to outline an analytic model for the explanation of motives which is based on a sociological theory of language and a sociological psychology.

As over against the inferential conception of motives as subjective 'springs' of action, motives may be considered as typical vocabularies having ascertainable functions in delimited societal situations. Human actors do vocalize and impute motives to themselves and to others. To explain behavior by referring it to an inferred and abstract 'motive' is one thing. To analyze the observable lingual mechanisms of motive imputation and avowal as they function in conduct is quite another. Rather than fixed elements 'in' an individual, motives are the terms with which interpretation of conduct by social actors proceeds. This imputation and avowal of motives by actors are social phenomena to be explained. The differing reasons men give for their actions are not themselves without reasons.

First, we must demarcate the general conditions under which such motive imputation and avowal seem to occur. Next, we must give a characterization of motive in denotable terms and an explanatory paradigm of why certain motives are verbalized rather than others. Then, we must indicate mechanisms of the linkage of vocabularies of motive to systems of action. What we want is an analysis of the integrating, controlling, and specifying function a certain type of speech fulfils in socially situated actions.

* Originally published in the *American Sociological Review*, 5, 1940, pp. 904–913.

The generic situation in which imputation and avowal of motives arise, involves, first, the social conduct or the (stated) programs of languaged creatures, i.e., programs and actions oriented with reference to the actions and talk of others; second, the avowal and imputation of motives is concomitant with the speech form known as the 'question.' Situations back of questions typically involve alternative or unexpected programs or actions which phases analytically denote 'crises.' The question is distinguished in that it usually elicits another verbal action, not a motor response. The question is an element in conversation. Conversation may be concerned with the factual features of a situation as they are seen or believed to be or it may seek to integrate and promote a set of diverse social actions with reference to the situation and its normative pattern of expectations. It is in this latter assent and dissent phase of conversation that persuasive and dissuasive speech and vocabulary arise. For men live in immediate acts of experience and their attentions are directed outside themselves until acts are in some way frustrated. It is then that awareness of self and of motive occur. The 'question' is a lingual index of such conditions. The avowal and imputation of motives are features of such conversations as arise in 'question' situations.

Motives are imputed or avowed as answers to questions interrupting acts or programs. Motives are words. Generically, to what do they refer? They do not denote any elements 'in' individuals. They stand for anticipated situational consequences of questioned conduct. Intention or purpose (stated as a 'program') is awareness of anticipated consequence; motives are names for consequential situations, and surrogates for actions leading to them. Behind questions are possible alternative actions with their terminal consequences. 'Our introspective words for motives are rough, shorthand descriptions for certain typical patterns of discrepant and conflicting stimuli.'

The model of purposive conduct associated with Dewey's name may briefly be stated. Individuals confronted with 'alternative acts' perform one or the other of them on the basis of the differential consequences which they anticipate. This nakedly utilitarian schema is inadequate because: (a) the 'alternative acts' of social conduct 'appear' most often in lingual form, as a question, stated by one's self or by another; (b) it is more adequate to say that individuals act in terms of anticipation of named consequences.

Among such names and in some technologically oriented lines of action there may appear such terms as 'useful,' 'practical,' 'serviceable,' etc., terms so 'ultimate' to the pragmatists, and also to certain sectors of the American population in these delimited situations. However, there are other areas of population with different vocabularies of motives. The choice of lines of action is accompanied by representations, and selection among them, of their situational termini. Men discern situations with particular vocabularies, and it is in terms of some delimited vocabulary that they anticipate consequences of conduct. Stable vocabularies of motives link anticipated consequences and specific actions. There is no need to invoke 'psychological' terms like 'desire' or 'wish' as explanatory, since they themselves must be explained socially. Anticipation is a subvocal or overt naming of terminal phases and/or social consequences of conduct. When an individual names consequences, he elicits the behaviors for which the name is a re-integrative cue. In a societal situation, implicit in the names for consequences is the social dimension of motives. Through such vocabularies, types of societal controls operate. Also, the terms in which the question is asked often will contain both alternatives: 'Love or Duty?', 'Business or Pleasure?' Institutionally different situations have different vocabularies of motive appropriate to their respective behaviors.

This sociological conception of motives as relatively stable lingual phases of delimited situations is quite consistent with Mead's program to approach conduct socially and from the outside. It keeps clearly in mind that 'both motives and actions very often originate not from within but from the situation in which individuals find themselves . . .' It translates the question of 'why' into a 'how' that is answerable in terms of a situation and its typal vocabulary of motives, i.e., those which conventionally accompany that type situation and function as cues and justifications for normative actions in it.

It has been indicated that the question is usually an index to the avowal and imputation of motives. Max Weber defines motive as a complex of meaning, which appears to the actor himself or to the observer to be an adequate ground for his conduct. The aspect of motive which this conception grasps is its intrinsically social character. A satisfactory or adequate motive is one that satisfies the questioners of an act or program, whether it be the other's or the actor's. As a word, a motive tends to be one which is to the actor and to the other members of a situation an unquestioned answer to questions concerning social and lingual conduct. A stable motive is an ultimate in justificatory conversation. The words which in a type situation will fulfil this function are circumscribed by the vocabulary of motives acceptable for such situations. Motives are accepted justifications for present, future, or past programs or acts.

To term them justification is not to deny their efficacy. Often anticipations of acceptable justifications will control conduct. ('If I did this, what could I say? What would they say?') Decisions may be, wholly or in part, delimited by answers to such queries.

A man may begin an act for one motive. In the course of it, he may adopt an ancillary motive. This does not mean that the second apologetic motive is inefficacious. The vocalized expectation of an act, its 'reason,' is not only a mediating condition of the act but it is a proximate and controlling condition for which the term 'cause' is not inappropriate. It may strengthen the act of the actor. It may win new allies for his act.

When they appeal to others involved in one's act, motives are strategies of action. In many social actions, others must agree, tacitly or explicitly. Thus, acts often will be abandoned if no reason can be found that others will accept. Diplomacy in choice of motive often controls the diplomat. Diplomatic choice of motive is part of the attempt to motivate acts for other members in a situation. Such pronounced motives undo snarls and integrate social actions. Such diplomacy does not necessarily imply intentional lies. It merely indicates that an appropriate vocabulary of motives will be utilized – that they are conditions for certain lines of conduct.

When an agent vocalizes or imputes motives, he is not trying to describe his experienced social action. He is not merely stating 'reasons.' He is influencing others – and himself. Often he is finding new 'reasons' which will mediate action. Thus, we need not treat an action as discrepant from 'its' verbalization, for in many cases, the verbalization is a new act. In such cases, there is not a discrepancy between an act and 'its' verbalization, but a difference between two disparate actions, motor-social and verbal. This additional (or 'ex *post facto*') lingualization may involve appeal to a vocabulary of motives associated with a norm with which both members of the situation are in agreement. As such, it is an integrative factor in future phases of the original social action or in other acts. By resolving conflicts, motives are efficacious. Often, if 'reasons' were not given, an act would not occur, nor would diverse actions be integrated. Motives are common grounds for mediated behaviors . . .

The motives actually used in justifying or criticizing an act definitely link it to situations, integrate one man's action with another's, and line up conduct with norms. The societally sustained motive-surrogates of situations are both constraints and inducements. It is a hypothesis worthy and capable of test that typal vocabularies of motives for different situations are significant determinants of conduct. As lingual segments of social action, motives orient actions by enabling discrimination between their objects. Adjectives such as 'good,' 'pleasant,' and 'bad' promote action or deter it. When they constitute components of a vocabulary of motives, i.e., are typical and relatively unquestioned accompaniments of typal situations, such words often function as directives and incentives by virtue of their being the judgments of others as anticipated by the actor. In this sense motives are 'social instruments, i.e., data by modifying which the agent will be able to influence [himself or others].' The 'control' of others is not usually direct but rather through manipulation of a field of objects. We influence a man by naming his acts or imputing motives to them – or to 'him.' The motives accompanying institutions of war, e.g., are not 'the causes' of war, but they do promote continued integrated participation, and they vary from one war to the next. Working vocabularies of motive have careers that are woven through changing institutional fabrics . . .

Within the perspective under consideration, the verbalized motive is not used as an index of something in the individual but as a basis of inference for a typal vocabulary of motives of a situated action. When we ask for the 'real attitude' rather than the 'opinion,' for the 'real motive' rather than the 'rationalization,' all we can meaningfully be asking for is the controlling speech form which was incipiently or overtly presented in the performed act or series of acts. There is no way to plumb behind verbalization into an individual and directly check our motive-mongering, but there is an empirical way in which we can guide and limit, in given historical situations, investigations of motives. That is by the construction of typal vocabularies of motives that are extant in types of situations and actions. Imputation of motives may be controlled by reference to the typical constellation of motives which are observed to be societally linked with classes of situated actions. Some of the 'real' motives that have been imputed to actors were not even known to them. As I see it, motives are circumscribed by the vocabulary of the actor. The only source for a terminology of motives is the vocabularies of motives actually and usually verbalized by actors in specific situations . . .

A labor leader says he performs a certain act because he wants to get higher standards of living for the workers. A business man says that this is rationalization, or a lie; that it is really because he wants more money for himself from the workers. A radical says a college professor will not engage in radical movements because he is afraid for his job, and besides, is a 'reactionary.' The college professor says it is because he just likes to find out how things work. What is reason for one man is rationalization for another. The variable is the accepted vocabulary of motives, the ultimates of discourse, of each man's dominant group about whose opinion he cares. Determination of such groups, their location and character, would enable delimitation and methodological control of assignment of motives for specific acts.

Stress on this idea will lead us to investigations of the compartmentalization of operative motives in personalities according to situation and the general types and conditions of vocabularies of motives in various types of societies. The motivational structures of individuals and the patterns of their purposes are relative to societal frames. We might, e.g., study motives along stratified or occupational lines. Max Weber has observed: '. . . that in a free society the motives which induce people to work vary with . . . different social classes . . . There is normally a graduated scale of motives by which men from different social classes are driven to work. When a man changes ranks, he switches from one set of motives to another.'

The lingual ties which hold them together react on persons to constitute frameworks of disposition and motive. Recently, Talcott Parsons has indicated, by reference to differences in actions in the professions and in business, that one cannot leap from 'economic analysis to ultimate motivations; the institutional patterns always constitute one crucial element of the problem.' It is my suggestion that we may analyze, index, and guage this element by focusing upon those specific verbal appendages of variant institutionalized actions which have been referred to as vocabularies of motive.

In folk societies, the constellations of motives connected with various sectors of behavior would tend to be typically stable and remain associated only with their sector. In typically primary, sacred, and rural societies, the motives of persons would be regularly compartmentalized. Vocabularies of motives ordered to different situations stabilize and guide behavior and expectation of the reactions of others. In their appropriate situations, verbalized motives are not typically questioned. In secondary, secular, and urban structures, varying and competing vocabularies of motives operate coterminously and the situations to which they are appropriate are not clearly demarcated. Motives once unquestioned for defined situations are now questioned. Various motives can release similar acts in a given situation. Hence, variously situated persons are confused and guess which motive 'activated' the person. Such questioning has resulted intellectually in such movements as psychoanalysis with its dogma of rationalization and its systematic motive-mongering. Such intellectual phenomena are underlaid by split and conflicting sections of an individuated society which is characterized by the existence of competing vocabularies of motive. Intricate constellations of motives, for example, are components of business enterprise in America. Such patterns have encroached on the old style vocabulary of the virtuous relation of men and women: duty, love, kindness. Among certain classes, the romantic, virtuous, and pecuniary motives are confused. The asking of the question: 'Marriage for love or money?' is significant, for the pecuniary is now a constant and almost ubiquitous motive, a common denominator of many others.

Back of 'mixed motives' and 'motivational conflicts' are competing or discrepant situational patterns and their respective vocabularies of motive. With shifting and interstitial situations, each of several alternatives may belong to disparate systems of action which have differing vocabularies of motives appropriate to them. Such conflicts manifest vocabulary patterns that have overlapped in a marginal individual and are not easily compartmentalized in clear-cut situations.

Besides giving promise of explaining an area of lingual and societal fact, a further advantage of this view of motives is that with it we should be able to give sociological accounts of other theories (terminologies) of motivation. This is a task for sociology of knowledge. Here I can refer only to a few theories. I have already referred to the Freudian terminology of motives. It is apparent that these motives are those of an upper bourgeois patriarchal group with strong sexual and individualistic orientation. When introspecting on the couches of Freud, patients used the only vocabulary of motives they knew; Freud got his hunch and guided further talk. Mittenzwey has dealt with similar points at length. Widely diffused in a postwar epoch, psychoanalysis was never popular in France where control of sexual behavior is not puritanical. To converted individuals who have become accustomed to the psychoanalytic terminology of motives, all others seem self-deceptive.

In like manner, to many believers in Marxism's terminology of power, struggle, and economic motives, all others, including Freud's, are due to hypocrisy or ignorance. An individual who has assimilated thoroughly only business congeries of motives will attempt to apply these motives to all situations, home and wife included. It should be noted that the business terminology of motives has its intellectual articulation, even as psychoanalysis and Marxism have.

It is significant that since the Socratic period many 'theories of motivation' have been linked with ethical and religious terminologies. Motive is that in man which leads him to do good or evil. Under the aegis of religious institutions, men use vocabularies of moral motives: they call acts and programs 'good' and 'bad,' and impute these qualities to the soul. Such lingual behavior is part of the process of social control. Institutional practices and their vocabularies of motive exercise control over delimited ranges of possible situations. One could make a typal catalog of religious motives from widely read religious texts, and test its explanatory power in various denominations and sects.

In many situations of contemporary America, conduct is controlled and integrated by hedonistic language. For large population sectors in certain situations, pleasure and pain are now unquestioned motives. For given periods and societies, these situations should be empirically determined. Pleasure and pain should not be reified and imputed to human nature as underlying principles of all action. Note that hedonism as a psychological and an ethical doctrine gained impetus in the modern world at about the time when older moral-religious motives were being debunked and simply discarded by 'middle class' thinkers. Back of the hedonistic terminology lay an emergent social pattern and a new vocabulary of motives. The shift of unchallenged motives which gripped the communities of Europe was climaxed when, in reconciliation, the older religious and the hedonistic terminologies were identified: the 'good' is the 'pleasant.' The conditioning situation was similar in the Hellenistic world with the hedonism of the Cyrenaics and Epicureans.

What is needed is to take all these terminologies of motive and locate them as vocabularies of motive in historic epochs and specified situations. Motives are of no value apart from the delimited societal situations for which they are the appropriate vocabularies. They must be situated. At best, socially unlocated terminologies of motives represent unfinished attempts to block out social areas of motive imputation and avowal. Motives vary in content and character with historical epochs and societal structures.

Rather than interpreting actions and language as external manifestations of subjective and deeper lying elements in individuals, the research task is the locating of particular types of action within typal frames of normative actions and socially situated clusters of motive. There is no explanatory value in subsuming various vocabularies of motives under some terminology or list. Such procedure merely confuses the task of explaining specific cases. The languages of situations as given must be considered a valuable portion of the data to be interpreted and related to their conditions. To simplify these vocabularies of motive into a socially abstracted terminology is to destroy the legitimate use of motive in the explanation of social actions.

45

KARL-OTTO APEL
Transcendental pragmatics* (1979)

We can now reconstrue the critical point of transcendental reflection on the subjective conditions of the possibility of an objectively valid knowledge of nature: We must abandon the aspiration of knowing 'things-in-themselves,' that is, knowing things that, in principle, cannot be the objects of possible experience. We must abandon the attempt to lift ourselves in cognition to a position outside the world from which its structure can be grasped in purely theoretical, ontological terms, that is, apart from practical, bodily (*leibhaft*) engagement in the sense of categorial lines of questioning. Overcoming the precritical attitude of theoretic or dogmatic ontology, however, does not imply renouncing the knowledge of things as they are in themselves in favor of the knowledge of mere appearances. Rather, it means that one ceases to orient the meaning of knowledge toward a paradigm of knowledge that is not possible for us. In transcendental-pragmatic reflection, one attains a radically new conception of possible knowledge and of the real, possible objects of knowledge. Instead of 'things-in-themselves' conceived without reflection on the subjective conditions of their possibility, but nonetheless considered objects of knowledge, we have the concept of natural things as objects of possible experience occurring, in principle, under the conditions of subjective experience and knowable in themselves. Instead of an ontological knowledge *sub specie aeternitatis*, which is conceived independently of engagement (*theoria*, in Aristotle's sense), we have a theoretical knowledge of nature which, as experience, is fundamentally connected to meaning-constitutive bodily and practical engagement (although it remains open to hermeneutic and transcendental reflection). This is nature as the existence of things insofar as they are objects of why-questions understood in causal analytic terms.

These results have the following implications for causal explanation and the subjective conditions of its possibility: In the first place, one must abandon the precritical attitude that Hume still retains, according to which something like causal necessity could be conceived under ontological-theoretical premises and hence established as

* From *Understanding and Explanation: A Transcendental-Pragmatic Perspective* by Karl-Otto Apel, MIT Press, 1984, pp. 64–67, 190–191. Reprinted by permission.

the possible object of passive observation. As Hume and the neo-Humeans or neo-positivists have shown, under such premises the categorial concept of causal necessity and causal law presupposed in natural scientific experiment can be neither philosophically confirmed nor explicated. The transcendental-pragmatic significance of this insight becomes clear only when it is generalized to all categorial constitutions of objects and relations: under the assumption of a purely passive or observational distance to the world – that is, apart from the standpoints that arise from a practical engagement in it (standpoints underlying the inquiry into and understanding of something as something in relation to) – we can acquire no preconception as to knowledge of an a priori necessary structure of the world of experience.

In light of the world engagement presupposed here as the necessary condition of the constitution of meaning, the Kantian position of transcendental idealism must be seen as a residue of theoretical ontology. More precisely, it has to be understood as an ontological-metaphysical residue of Cartesian dualism and be transcendentally-pragmatically superseded. The philosopher wishing to comprehend the possibility of causal necessity cannot raise himself above the real world in his interpretive acts and interrogative viewpoints in such a way that he is forced to conceive of the subjective conditions of a possible experience of nature, not as acts of experimental interference but as the objectifiability of nature and its openness to explanation through causal laws. In so doing, he delivers up the real world, including the 'phenomenal' aspects of human action within the real world, to causal nomological determinism, so that the freedom of morally responsible action must be derived from a cause outside or behind the world – that is, from an intelligible will of which it has to be presupposed: (1) that it can begin a series of successive things or states, and (2) that it can alter nothing in the world of appearance, for such a capacity would confuse and disconnect everything, thus making impossible nature as the object of causal explanation.

The philosopher who wishes to grasp the possibility of causal necessity must assume the standpoint of transcendental-pragmatic reflection. That is, the philosopher must recognize that the subjective conditions of action are not components of the objectifiable world (which can be observed and explained in theoretical, causal-analytic terms) but still belong to the comprehensible real world. In this way he will achieve the position Kant describes in analyzing the thesis of freedom in the antinomy of freedom and causal determinism: 'to admit within the course of the world different series as capable in their causality of beginning of themselves,' that is, 'attribute to their substances a power of acting from freedom.' Under this premise, as the subjective condition of experimental action, causal necessity can be postulated as the relation between successive phenomena or states within closed systems of which one can, in principle, suppose they could be set in motion by experimenters through manipulatively producing their initial conditions. Again, in the sense of the thesis of freedom in Kant's antinomy, one can claim of such systems that their initiation 'does not form part of the succession of purely natural effects' as 'the mere continuation of them.' Rather, 'in regard of its happening, natural causes exercise over it no determining influence whatsoever.' In experiment we must, in fact, assume that without our active interference no already existent state of nature changes into the initial state of the system we set in motion.

Determinism thus proves to reflect an illegitimate totalization of the structure of an objectifiable fragment of the world of experience, an extrapolation that presupposes the freedom of action in experiment. This means, however, that determinism, as a metaphysical absolutization of causal necessity, is a 'pretranscendental-pragmatic' product of metaphysical theory – whether in the sense of a pre-Kantian ontology that does not reflect on the subjective conditions of the possibility of experimental experience, as in the case of Laplace, or in that of Kant's transcendental idealism, which, in a quasi-Cartesian manner, divides the conditions within consciousness of the categories and their graphic schematization from the corresponding conditions of bodily action.

If transcendental-pragmatic reflection thus overcomes the premise of an ontological metaphysics that intends to explain the world theoretically, entirely in terms of a position outside it, then the prospect emerges of simplifying Kant's architectonic with regard to problems of transcendental philosophy. In distinguishing between (1) the merely phenomenal domain of knowable natural processes, (2) the transcendental domain of acts of understanding that can only be formally reflected upon, the acts of the 'I' in the sense of transcendental apperception, and (3) the unknowable but intelligible domain of free actions which are also the theme of ethics, Kant's complicated architectonic is scarcely compatible with his own critical intentions. In place of this architectonic, the position of transcendental pragmatics emphasizes the fundamental difference between that which can be explained and that which can be understood. It thereby opens the possibility of establishing a relation between knowledge of the world governed by natural laws and the different knowledge of the world of practical reason and morality . . .

In what follows I shall recall an insight to which I have already referred. I shall attempt to show the validity of a transcendental-pragmatic expansion of the epistemological foundations of the theory of science as a way to resolve the problems we have discussed.

We begin with the perspective of the logico-semantic method of explicating explanation as 'scientific systematizations.' In terms of semiotics and the logic of relations, one can characterize the approach of transcendental pragmatics as one that expands the two-place expression of a relation, 'x explains y' into the three-place expression 'x explains y for the subject of knowledge z.' This expansion, however, is not to be understood as an empirical pragmatics of the subjective context of cognitive achievements, so that, for example, one would have to discriminate between the different everyday explanations for schoolchildren, members of different professions, and social groups or cultures. Rather, the expansion is based, in principle, on the three-place character of the sign relation (Peirce), and thus on linguistically mediated acts of knowledge. Thus we go back to the subjective context in which explanations and other acts of knowledge are interpreted only insofar as they contain the subjective-intersubjective conditions of the possibility of constituting both the meaning of forms of human inquiry and, therefore, the possible meaning of cognitive achievements in general, as answers to forms of inquiry. In the present context it is important to note among meaning-constitutive conditions especially the 'knowledge-constitutive interests' that can be presumed to be interwoven with language games and forms of ongoing practice in ideal-typical ways. My argument is that these ideal-typical connections between cognitive interests, language games, and forms of ongoing practice can be considered the transcendental-pragmatic conditions of the constitution of the world of experience, and that they go beyond the forms or functions of the pure contemplation and pure understanding presupposed by Kant's transcendental idealism. This argument must be valid if the constitution of anything like 'meaning' or of the categorial viewpoints for possible inquiries is to be made intelligible to human beings; a pure consciousness can win no meaning from the world. Nevertheless, although this consideration of the anthropologically contingent factors within the transcendental function goes beyond Kant's 'transcendental psychology,' it is not concerned with the causes that advance or impede cognitive enterprises; those are, rather, the subject of research for an external, empirical psychology or sociology of science. Instead, it is concerned with the internal reasons or grounds of the possibility of substantive and significant knowledge.

PART 5

The structuralist controversy: language, discourse and practice

Introduction: a general outline

This section concerns one of the major traditions in French social thought in the second half of the twentieth century. It represents a striking contrast to the American pragmatic tradition discussed in Part 4, for in place of the latter's concern with social action and language as a creative expression of human agency, the linguistic turn in French thought tended to reduce language to structure. The communicative component of action that was central to the approach of Peirce through Dewey and Morris to Apel hardly figured in the work of some of the leading French philosophers since the 1950s whose concern was a recovery of structure, the preoccupation with which was one of the central and defining tenets of French social science since Emile Durkheim. But the new structuralism was one that went far beyond Durkheim's.

Durkheim, it will be recalled, favoured an approach that strongly stressed the objectivity and determining power of structures, those coercive 'social facts' that constitute what he called the reality of the social, the basic feature of which was, under the conditions of modernity, differentiation. While Durkheim had no conception of the linguistic nature of society, this was introduced by the French-speaking Swiss linguist, Ferdinand de Saussure (1857–1913), whose *Course in General Linguistics* (based on lectures given in Geneva between 1906 and 1911) greatly influenced subsequent thinking in the French-speaking world, leading to what in effect was a continuation of the Durkheimean structuralist approach. According to Saussure – in whose work there was also the distinct presence of Marx's materialism – all of reality is essentially mediated by language, which accordingly is a social entity. However, in what was to be the new science of structural linguistics a conception of language developed that, while emphasizing the material nature of language, had no place for agency because speakers draw from pre-existing linguistic codes. In this view, the human actor is merely the voice through which language speaks. What changes is not the codes themselves, but the combinations of them. The structuralist linguists did not emphasize the threefold nature of the sign as did Peirce and Morris (see Part 4), but its twofold composition as a relation between signifiers and in which the signified becomes another signifer. What was eliminated from the sign was an interpreting subject.

The true significance of Saussure became apparent in the work of the French anthropologist, Claude Lévi-Strauss who laid the foundations of a new thinking in France that renounced human subjectivity. Of course, Lévi-Strauss did not need Saussaure to develop a structuralist approach, as this was one of the major traditions in anthropology, especially associated with Radcliff-Brown's structural anthropology. The impact of Saussaure, who Lévi-Strauss encountered through the work of the Russian linguist Jakobson, lay in conceiving of language as a system of structures which perform social functions based on relations of exchange. Indeed, Lévi-Strauss saw social relations as shaped by relations of exchange, not unlike the basic structures of language. What in effect he announced the end of was an approach centred on meaning and agency, but also one that stressed the centrality of functions – structural anthropology since the linguistic turn was not functional structuralism, which in the form of Parsonian sociological theory was the orthodoxy in the USA. For Lévi-Strauss what was crucial was systems of classification rather than functionalism. Moving beyond the prevailing concern with functionalism, he opened a scenario of the radical indeterminacy of all systems of classification and, crucially, the suggestion that the modern western forms of classification are nothing but variations of some basic codes out of which all of civilization is constructed. With this went a critique of evolution, the idea of progress and the triumph of the human will. It also represented the end of the Durkheimean legacy, since what structural anthropology was proclaiming was the essential unity of the social world and the unity of the primitive and modern minds.

For all these reasons, his work, while being initially within anthropology, brought about a revolution in modern thought. His ideas were taken up by many thinkers in France, especially in philosophy and in the theory of the human and social sciences, who wanted an exit from the dominant traditions in post Second World War French thought, namely Marxism, existentialism and phenomenology. Structural anthropology offered the prospect, especially to the social sciences, of escaping from the humanist assumptions of the older approaches, such as the view that history has a meaning, that history is the narrative of a subject and that the sciences of man can reveal the truth of the historical meaning contained in the unfolding of this narrative. Lévi-Strauss' structuralism demolished these myths of modernist thought and his ideas were taken up by a wide range of philosophers, ranging from the structuralist Marxist, Louis Althusser, to Michel Foucault, the nascent historian of the human sciences, and the philosopher Jacques Derrida to the literary theorist Roland Barthes and the psychoanalyst Jacques Lacan.

But the new movement in fact turned in upon itself and became known not as 'structuralism' but as 'poststructuralism'. The French structuralist tradition from Emile Durkheim and Ferdinand de Saussure to Claude Lévi-Strauss incited a reaction that led to the most influential movement in the social thought of the late twentieth century, namely poststructuralism as represented in the mature thought of Michel Foucault and, increasingly, in the work of Jacques Derrida. Many of these thinkers abandoned the structuralism of Lévi-Strauss, for whom there could be no reality other than that shaped by the relatively rigid and universal principles of exchange. They also rejected his belief in the universality of human nature. The new generation of post-Lévi-Straussean thinkers were more 'deconstructive' than structuralist. Many of them were explicitly Marxist (Louis Althusser, Roland Barthes) and others such as Foucault and Derrida saw the poststructuralist movement as the continuation of the Marxist 'permanent revolution' in the domain of language, thought and culture.

Poststructuralism is best seen as a method of deconstruction, the aim of which is to break up the established structures of thought – discourses, especially those of the sciences – that sustain power relations. The Anglo-American term 'poststructuralism' in any case was the term that was used to describe the new philosophy, which while having its origins in the structuralist tradition was in fact much broader, for in addition to wedding the linguistic tradition of Saussure to Durkheimean structuralism, the poststructuralists also brought in the crucial dimension of Freud and Nietzsche, figures who replaced the older canonical figures of Hegel and Marx, and later Heidegger. Freud suggested an approach that would stress the subterranean forces in the psyche and the need for a depth hermeneutics, albeit it one that would shed the illusion of the emancipation of the subject from power. Nietzsche – who was read increasingly in a neo-Heideggerian direction – suggested a more far-reaching critique of European modernity than was contained in the Marxist critique of political economy. Together Freud and Nietzsche would bring poststructuralism in the direction of a radical critique of western thought and institutions which would culminate in the postmodern movement. Although often conflated, postmodernism had a later beginning (in the 1980s), but one that was initiated by the poststructuralist movement. At this point the poststructuralist movement dissipated and a new beginning was made, as is clearly evidenced by a reorientation in Foucault's thinking and a different range of thinkers taking the lead, namely Jean Baudrillard and Jean-Francois Lyotard.

Deconstruction as method has been closely associated with the work of Jacques Derrida. His major works, *Of Grammatology* and *Writing and Difference*, based on essays written between 1959 and 1967, advocated more strongly than Foucault a deconstructive approach to language that had huge implications for the social sciences. Although initially an approach designed for literary theory and philosophy, Derrida's deconstructivism had a wider relevance for the social sciences in that it hastened the cultural turn, central to which was the recognition of the role of language in social relations. Derrida's approach aimed to reveal the multiple levels of meaning contained within language, which is never neutral but pervaded by relations of power. Unlike Foucault, Derrida was primarily concerned with liberating texts, and thus readings, from the power of speech, for he saw speech as restraining the creative power of discourse. In this respect, his method was designed only to reveal a multiplicity of readings, whereas Foucault's aim was much broader and ultimately more far-reaching.

It would be a mistake to see French social thought as entirely dominated by the poststructuralist appropriation of structuralism. In the characterization of the debate on method in France in the final decades of the twentieth century in this section the story is one of a threefold reaction to Lévi-Strauss's structuralism and the structuralism of the entire Durkheimean heritage. The first reaction to be discussed is that of genetic structuralism, which is represented in psychology by Jean Piaget (1896–1980) and in the social and human sciences by Lucien Goldmann (1913–1970). Genetic structuralism in general sought to preserve a link between agency and structure. Piaget wrote about the processes by which human intelligence is acquired, proposing a transformative conception of structure based on concepts of self-regulation. Goldmann rejected the anti-humanism of the prevailing structuralist movement and tried to retain a connection with praxis, the human dimension of agency in the shaping of structures. Like Piaget, he was primarily concerned to explain how change occurs and especially how forms of consciousness – intellectual movements, for instance – relate to material forms of life, such as class.

However, there is no denying the more powerful impact of Michel Foucault and that of the other major French thinker of his generation, Pierre Bourdieu, who together constitute the most consequential French thinkers since Durkheim, both offering different solutions to the problems posed by structuralism. Although differing greatly from the poststructuralist philosophers, Bourdieu, who denied he was a philosopher, was heavily influenced by Lévi-Strauss and operated within a structuralist framework until well into the 1960s, breaking with it only gradually, and, some would say, never entirely. While Foucault's impact in the human and social sciences has been wider than Bourdieu's, the latter has undoubtedly represented the Durkheim tradition within sociology and offers a distinctive approach that more successfully avoids the pitfalls that plagued the Foucauldian method in its various moments, from the early structuralist approach, which Foucault called 'archaeological', to the later 'genealogical' and more explicitly deconstructive approach. In the reading below, Bourdieu's repudiation of Lévi-Strauss is evident in his preference for an approach that is more concerned with practices than with discourses. In this respect, Bourdieu – who will be returned to in Part 6 under the general heading of reflexivity – offered a different and more decisive route out of structuralism than Foucault's, whose concern with discourse as a configuration of power relations never fully broke from the structuralist distrust of agency. Yet, within Foucault's work always lay the suggestion that the discursive constitution of society, of subjectivity and of the power of knowledge itself was relational and constituted out of practices that could in principle render the functioning of discourse disruptive for the maintenance of order and thus that every system of power contained within it particular forms of resistance. But Foucault never fully took up this question of resistance beyond the recognition that power entails resistance. Nor did he consider the possibility of scientific knowledge leading to truth, with the result that the deconstructive method ultimately plunged the social and human sciences into a long-term crisis.

In this respect, Bourdieu's legacy complements the absence of agency in Foucault and brings to completion the historical and cultural turn in modern French thought initiated by Foucault. The basic idea underlying Bourdieu's approach is a view of social life as one constantly pervaded by struggles over social recognition which arise in response to the basic social reality of inequality. In these struggles, individuals and groups are striving to augment their power which derives from the various forms of capital – economic, social and cultural – they possess. Rejecting the primacy of structure and of discourse, he sees all of social life as mediated by practices. In *The Logic of Practice* (1980) Bourdieu, while continuing the French tradition of seeing structures as systems of classification, avoided the dualism of agency and structure by moving primacy to 'practices'. Practices mediate between objective structures and the intentional activity of action and are grounded in the 'habitus': 'The theory of practice as practice insists, contrary to positivist materialism, that the objects of knowledge are constructed, not passively recorded, and contrary to intellectualist idealism, that the principle of this construction is the system of structured, structuring dispositions, the *habitus*, which is constituted in practice and is always oriented towards practical functions'. For Bourdieu, structuralism is no better than positivism, but the solution is not a retreat into subjectivism:

> It is possible to step down from the sovereign viewpoint from which objectivist idealism orders the world, as Marx demands in the *Theses on Feuerbach*, but without having to abandon it to the 'active aspect' of apprehension of the world by reducing knowledge to a mere recording. To do this, one has to situate oneself *within* 'real activity as such', that is, in the practical relation to the world, the preoccupied, active presence in the world through which the world imposes its presence, with its urgencies, its things to be done and said, things made to be said, which directly govern words and deeds without ever unfolding as a spectacle. One has to escape from realism of the structure, to which objectivism, a necessary stage in breaking with primary experience and constructing the objective relationships, necessarily leads when it hypostatizes these relations by treating them as realities already constituted outside of the history of the group – without falling back into subjectivism, which is quite incapable of giving an account of the necessity of the social world.
>
> (*The Logic of Practice*, 1980/1990: 52)

The term that might best characterize Bourdieu's approach is constructivist-structuralism, especially in so far as he sought to link rules to a conception of practice. However, in the view of many of his critics, Bourdieu never fully reconciled the tension between the structuralist and constructivist dimensions in his thinking.

In the readings selected in this section, the structuralist approach is presented as best represented by the structuralist anthropologist Claude Lévi-Strauss and the threefold reaction to it, first by Lucien Goldmann and his version of what has been known as genetic structuralism, second by the major initiators of the poststructuralist movement, Foucault and Derrida, and third by Pierre Bourdieu's theory of the logic of practice.

The selected texts

Claude Lévi-Strauss (1908–) was born in Belgium but grew up and was educated in France before spending many years in Brazil, as Professor of Anthropology at the University of Sao Paulo. By the time of his appointment to the prestigious Chair of Social Anthropology, Collège de France in 1959 he had written several influential works in anthropology, including *Structural Anthropology* (1958) and *The Elementary Structures of Kinship* (1959). Between then and his entry to the French Academy in 1973 Lévi-Strauss shaped the movement that was to be known as poststructuralism, which defined itself in terms of a critical appropriation of his writings. The two selected extracts are from *Structural Anthropology* (respectively Chapters 2 and 3) and derive from essays published earlier. In these readings we have clear evidence of his preoccupation with structure as mediated by language. In the first extract he shows that structural linguistics, as advocated by Saussure and Jakobson, can offer anthropology a 'rigorous method'. He believes more progress has been made in linguistics than in the social sciences and that the social sciences should learn from linguistics, which is revolutionizing all the social sciences, not just anthropology. He goes so far as to proclaim: 'Structural linguistics will certainly play the same renovating role with respect to the social sciences that nuclear physics, for example, has played for the physical sciences'. The reading argues that collaboration between social science and linguistics is no longer loose but essential. In this text and in the following one Lévi-Strauss establishes the critical contribution of structural linguistics, namely the relational rather than the functional significance of social roles. Thus structures are essential relations of 'elements of meaning', rather like 'phonemes', those basic units of meaning in linguistic theory. In the second extract, he begins by reiterating the contribution of structural linguistics to a rigorous scientific method that does not require hermeneutic interpretation, since what is being studied is not subjectively or intersubjectively created meaning but structures of meaning which can be uncovered with almost mathematical precision. He goes on to apply this structuralist method to the study of kinship systems and marriage rules in different civilizations, showing the different systems of combination that result from some very basic rules.

Lucien Goldmann (1913–1979) was born in Romania and was a student of Georg Lukács before moving to Paris where he spent most of his professional career, in which he became one of the important western Marxists working in the area of cultural theory. His major work is *The Hidden God* (1979), a study of the seventeenth-century Jansenist movement and its leading figures, Racine and Pascal. As noted above, his genetic structuralism marked him off from both the scientific structuralism of orthodox Marxism and from the linguistic structuralism adocated by Lévi-Strauss and his followers as well as the structural Marxism of Louis Althusser. In the short selected extract from the Preface to the new edition of the *The Human Sciences and Philosophy* (1969) Goldmann distances himself from the overly formalistic approach of Lévi-Strauss and bemoans the dominance of the structuralist movement in French social science in the 1960s because it led to an 'ahumanistic, ahistorical and aphilosophical attitude' which was stifling 'a truly critical social sociology'. Rather than dismiss the concepts of structure and function, he seeks to link structure and function in a more dynamic way in order to explain the historical nature of the social.

Michel Foucault (1926–1984) began his career as a psychiatrist but soon turned against the medical profession in early works such as *Madness and Civilization* (1961) and the *Birth of the Clinic* (1963). He was influenced by such post-war French thinkers as Dumézil, Cavailles, Canguilhem and Bachelard and was also inspired by Nietzsche, Bataille and Freud. By the time he became Professor of the 'History of Systems of Thought' at the Collège de France in 1969, he had already become one of France's best known intellectuals, although it was in the USA from the early 1980s that his thought had it greatest impact, providing the intellectual foundations for the postmodernist movement in the social sciences and philosophy. His major books were *The Order of Things: An Archaeology of the Human Sciences* (1966), *Discipline and Punish* (1975) and *The History of Sexuality* (3 vols) (1976, 1984 and 1984). The first extract is from the Preface to *The Order of Things*. It is a striking example of his earlier work, illustrating his self-styled 'archaeological' method, the aim of which was to reveal the structures of power constituting the fixed and secure 'orders' of 'classification' of western thought and institutions. It can be contrasted with Lévi-Strauss' text in seeking to show less the 'grid' of rigid relations between codes and more the hidden space of language that deviates from the fixed order of dominant cultural codes and uncovers western culture's major ruptures and 'discontinuities'. Foucault identifies as his aim the uncovering of the structures of the epistemological field of science, its *episteme*, after the method of 'archaeology', to demonstrate that the birth of modern thought – following the collapse of the 'Classical Age's' (generally the Renaissance) notion of representation – was accompanied by a new entity which was constituted by science: namely 'man', or subjectivity and with it a new historicity. The Preface concludes with the often-cited passage in which Foucault announces the inevitable disappearance of that subjectivity brought into being by modernity. This more explicit attack on subjectivity is more apparent in the second extract, which dates from a lecture given in 1976 at the Collège de France. In this reading we see how Foucault defines his position, as distinct from Marxist critique, as one concerned with a 'non-economic analysis of power'. His approach is based on the 'local character of criticism' which aims at the 'insurrection of subjugated knowledges' which have been buried by structuralist approaches. The text is particularly significant in that it introduces into the domain of knowledge what positivism and structuralism excludes, namely struggles, conflicts, naïve and popular knowledges, all that is 'marginal' and hidden. With this, Foucault announces his new approach, which he calls, after Nietszche, 'genealogy', which is designed less to uncover structures of power than a 'historical knowledge of struggles'. In this respect, he abandons the last vestiges of structuralism that may have been contained in his initial archaeological approach for an 'anti-science' which would write the history of medicine from the perspective of the patient rather than the doctor and all the privileged systems of truth that modern science has established. However, it is to be noted that he retains archaeology as a method which is rather to be supplemented with the normative-critical politics of genealogy. The reading concludes with some discussion of power, which was to be his main concern in the following years when he applied more fully the theory of the discursive formation of modern subjectivity in systems of knowledge.

Jacques Derrida (1930–) was born in Algeria and studied and taught in Paris and the USA. His numerous books have been very influential in disciplines in philosophy and literary criticism and have had a considerable impact on postmodern social science. Derrida's work – which is deeply influenced by Nietzsche, Heidegger, Freud and Bataille – has been the principal inspiration of deconstruction, which can be compared to Foucault's genealogical method in its concern to question the received wisdom of the dominant frameworks of thought. Like Foucault, he has been a pivotal figure in reorienting interpretative approaches beyond hermeneutics, which has traditionally been overladen with assumptions of truth and subjectivity. The method of deconstruction aims to show the multiple and indeterminate levels of meaning in a text, the reading of which can never be complete since the text is never reducible to a founding subjectivity, an origin, an author or a sovereign legislator and can never be closed by the reader. In essence, it is an approach that sees texts – all works of writing – as relatively free-floating and productive of meaning, which cannot be related to intentionality. It is a view of the method of interpretation that departs radically from all traditional approaches. In the selected text, written in characteristic Derridean elliptical style, but lacking the obscurity of his later writing, we find one of the most famous examples of the deconstructive method. The essay, 'Structure, Sign and Play in the Discourses of the Human Sciences' was originally a lecture given at Johns Hopkins University in 1966 and became a classic statement of poststructuralism because in it Derrida was perceived as distancing his thinking from Lévi-Strauss' belief in the redeeming power of science to explain the world by a rigorous method. It was in any case a very influential essay, effectively introducing poststructuralist thought into the Anglo-American academic world as an alternative to neo-positivism, Parsonian structural functionalism and the New Criticism. The text commences by introducing the idea of 'play' as something inherent in all structures, which Derrida recasts as 'discourse'. The coherence and stability of structure consists of a dominant centre being established. However, the centre is an illusion and is constantly being displaced by other centres in a process of 'dislocation', 'transformations' and 'decentring'. Derrida introduced his famous notion of 'decentring', which defines the method of deconstruction, to find alternative experiences and ways of thinking to the dominant ones from western metaphysics to structuralism. However, and it is one of the chief aims of the essay to spell this out, there is no privileged point outside the discourse, which can be decentred only from a point within it. In this he dismisses Lévi-Strauss' belief in science as capable of transcending culture.

Pierre Bourdieu (1930–2002) had, by the time of his death in 2002, become the most important French sociologist since Durkheim, and with Foucault, a figure of enormous importance in the reorientation of the social sciences in the last three decades of the twentieth century. He was born in the south-east of France and was trained as an anthropologist. He increasingly turned to sociology, publishing such classic works as *Distinction: A Social Critique of the Judgement of Taste* (1979) and *Homo Academicus* (1984), and although he was very hostile to philosophers, in particular the poststructuralist generation, his writings took on a pronounced philosophical nature, as was apparent in his last major work, *Pascalian Meditations* (1997). One of his later works, *The Political Ontology of Martin Heidegger* (1989), demolished the reputation of one of the key philosophical figures behind what was an increasingly neo-Heideggerian current in postmodernism, now chiefly represented by Jacques Derrida and increasingly by Richard Rorty. The selected text from his methodological work, *The Logic of Practice* (1980), presents Bourdieu's position against Lévi-Strauss' structuralism. In it Bourdieu argues for a less rigid conception of structure to allow for the constructive activity of agency (which he calls practice) and a corresponding reflexivity on the part of the social scientist who cannot claim to occupy an external position. While Lévi-Strauss believed the structures of myth, kinship etc. always solved logical problems, Bourdieu is of the view that there is always a certain 'indeterminacy' in structure and in the relation of science to social structures. The significance of the reading is that he marks the point at which subjectivity re-enters the domain of science whose method must become reflexive. The full consequences of this turn to the subject under the conditions of reflexivity will be looked at in Part 6.

46

CLAUDE LÉVI-STRAUSS

Structural analysis in linguistics and in anthropology* (1958)

Linguistics occupies a special place among the social sciences, to whose ranks it unquestionably belongs. It is not merely a social science like the others, but, rather, the one in which by far the greatest progress has been made. It is probably the only one which can truly claim to be a science and which has achieved both the formulation of an empirical method and an understanding of the nature of the data submitted to its analysis. This privileged position carries with it several obligations. The linguist will often find scientists from related but different disciplines drawing inspiration from his example and trying to follow his lead. *Noblesse oblige.* A linguistic journal like *Word* cannot confine itself to the illustration of strictly linguistic theories and points of view. It must also welcome psychologists, sociologists, and anthropologists eager to learn from modern linguistics the road which leads to the empirical knowledge of social phenomena. As Marcel Mauss wrote already forty years ago: 'Sociology would certainly have progressed much further if it had everywhere followed the lead of the linguists . . .' The close methodological analogy which exists between the two disciplines imposes a special obligation of collaboration upon them.

Ever since the work of Schrader it has been unnecessary to demonstrate the assistance which linguistics can render to the anthropologist in the study of kinship. It was a linguist and a philologist (Schrader and Rose) who showed the improbability of the hypothesis of matrilineal survivals in the family in antiquity, to which so many anthropologists still clung at that time. The linguist provides the anthropologist with etymologies which permit him to establish between certain kinship terms relationships that were not immediately apparent. The anthropologist, on the other hand, can bring to the attention of the linguist customs, prescriptions, and prohibitions that help him to understand the persistence of certain features of language or the instability of terms or groups of terms. At a meeting of the Linguistic Circle of New York, Julien Bonfante once illustrated this point of view by reviewing the etymology of the word for uncle in several Romance languages. The Greek οειος corresponds in Italian,

* From Claude Lévi-Strauss, 'Structural Analysis in Linguistics and in Anthropology', *Structural Anthropology.* New York: Basic Books, 1963, pp. 31–34. Reprinted with the permission of Claude Lévi-Strauss.

Spanish and Portuguese to *zio* and *tio*; and he added that in certain regions of Italy the uncle is called *barba*. The 'beard', the 'divine' uncle – what a wealth of suggestions for the anthropologist! The investigations of the late A.M. Hocart into the religious character of the avuncular relationship and the 'theft of the sacrifice' by the maternal kinsmen immediately come to mind. Whatever interpretation is given to the data collected by Hocart (and his own interpretation is not entirely satisfactory), there is no doubt that the linguist contributes to the solution of the problem by revealing the tenacious survival in contemporary vocabulary of relationships which have long since disappeared. At the same time, the anthropologist explains to the linguist the bases of etymology and confirms its validity. Paul K. Benedict, in examining, as a linguist, the kinship systems of Southeast Asia, was able to make an important contribution to the anthropology of the family in that area.

But linguists and anthropologists follow their own paths independently. They halt, no doubt, from time to time to communicate to one another certain of their findings; these findings, however, derive from different operations, and no effort is made to enable one group to benefit from the technical and methodological advances of the other. This attitude might have been justified in the era when linguistic research leaned most heavily on historical analysis. In relation to the anthropological research conducted during the same period, the difference was one of degree rather than of kind. The linguists employed a more rigorous method, and their findings were established on more solid grounds; the sociologists could follow their example in 'renouncing consideration of the spatial distribution of contemporary types as a basis for their classifications.' But, after all, anthropology and sociology were looking to linguistics only for insights; nothing foretold a revelation.

The advent of structural linguistics completely changed this situation. Not only did it renew linguistic perspectives; a transformation of this magnitude is not limited to a single discipline. Structural linguistics will certainly play the same renovating role with respect to the social sciences that nuclear physics, for example, has played for the physical sciences. In what does this revolution consist, as we try to assess its broadest implications? N. Troubetzkoy, the illustrious founder of structural linguistics, himself furnished the answer to this question. In one programmatic statement, he reduced the structural method to four basic operations. First, structural linguistics shifts from the study of conscious linguistic phenomena to study of their unconscious infrastructure; second, it does not treat terms as independent entities, taking instead as its basis of analysis the relations between terms; third, it introduces the concept of system – 'Modern phonemics does not merely proclaim that phonemes are always part of a system; it shows concrete phonemic systems and elucidates their structure' – ; finally, structural linguistics aims at discovering general laws, either by induction 'or ... by logical deduction, which would give them an absolute character.'

Thus, for the first time, a social science is able to formulate necessary relationships. This is the meaning of Troubetzkoy's last point, while the preceding rules show how linguistics must proceed in order to attain this end. It is not for us to show that Troubetzkoy's claims are justified. The vast majority of modern linguists seem sufficiently agreed on this point. But when an event of this importance takes place in one of the sciences of man, it is not only permissible for, but required of, representatives of related disciplines immediately to examine its consequences and its possible application to phenomena of another order.

New perspectives then open up. We are no longer dealing with an occasional collaboration where the linguist and the anthropologist, each working by himself, occasionally communicate those findings which each thinks may interest the other. In the study of kinship problems (and, no doubt, the study of other problems as well), the anthropologist finds himself in a situation which formally resembles that of the structural linguist. Like phonemes, kinship terms are elements of meaning; like phonemes, they acquire meaning only if they are integrated into systems. 'Kinship systems,' like 'phonemic systems,' are built by the mind on the level of unconscious thought. Finally, the recurrence of kinship patterns, marriage rules, similar prescribed attitudes between certain types of relatives, and so forth, in scattered regions of the globe and in fundamentally different societies, leads us to believe that, in the case of kinship as well as linguistics, the observable phenomena result from the action of laws which are general but implicit. The problem can therefore be formulated as follows: Although they belong to another order of reality, kinship phenomena are of the same type as linguistic phenomena. Can the anthropologist, using a method analogous in form (if not in content) to the method used in structural linguistics, achieve the same kind of progress in his own science as that which has taken place in linguistics?

We shall be even more strongly inclined to follow this path after an additional observation has been made. The study of kinship problems is today broached in the same terms and seems to be in the throes of the same difficulties as was linguistics on the eve of the structuralist revolution. There is a striking analogy between certain attempts by Rivers and the old linguistics, which sought its explanatory principles first of all in history. In both cases, it is solely (or almost solely) diachronic analysis which must account for synchronic phenomena. Troubetzkoy, comparing structural linguistics and the old linguistics, defines structural linguistics as a 'systematic structuralism and universalism,' which he contrasts with the individualism and 'atomism' of former schools. And when he considers diachronic analysis, his perspective is a profoundly modified one: 'The evolution of a phonemic system at any given moment is directed by the tendency toward a goal . . .'

Language and the analysis of social laws* (1951)

In a recent work, whose importance from the point of view of the future of the social sciences can hardly be overestimated, Wiener poses, and resolves in the negative, the question of a possible extension to the social sciences of the mathematical methods of prediction which have made possible the construction of the great modern electronic machines. He justifies his position by two arguments.

---

* From Claude Lévi-Strauss, 'Language and the Analysis of Social Laws', *Structural Anthropology*. New York: Basic Books, 1963, pp. 55–56. Reprinted with the permission of Claude Lévi-Strauss.

In the first place, he maintains that the nature of the social sciences is such that it is inevitable that their very development have repercussions on the object of their investigation. The coupling of the observer with the observed phenomenon is well known to contemporary scientific thought, and, in a sense, it illustrates a universal situation. But it is negligible in fields which are ripe for the most advanced mathematical investigation; as, for example, in astrophysics, where the object has such vast dimensions that the influence of the observer need not be taken into account, or in atomic physics, where the object is so small that we are interested only in average mass effects in which the effect of bias on the part of the observer plays no role. In the field of the social sciences, on the contrary, the object of study is necessarily affected by the intervention of the observer, and the resulting modifications are on the same scale as the phenomena that are studied.

In the second place, Wiener observes that the phenomena subjected to sociological or anthropological inquiry are defined within our own sphere of interests; they concern questions of the life, education, career, and death of individuals. Therefore the statistical runs available for the study of a given phenomenon are always far too short to lay the foundation of a valid induction. Mathematical analysis in the field of social science, he concludes, can bring results which should be of as little interest to the social scientist as those of the statistical study of a gas would be to an individual about the size of a molecule.

These objections seem difficult to refute when they are examined in terms of the investigations toward which their author has directed them, the data of research monographs and of applied anthropology. In such cases, we are dealing with a study of individual behavior, directed by an observer who is himself an individual; or with a study of a culture, a national character, or a pattern, by an observer who cannot dissociate himself completely from his culture, or from the culture out of which his working hypotheses and his methods of observation, which are themselves cultural patterns, are derived.

There is, however, at least one area of the social sciences where Wiener's objections do not seem to be applicable, where the conditions which he sets as a requirement for a valid mathematical study seem to be rigorously met. This is the field of language, when studied in the light of structural linguistics, with particular reference to phonemics.

Language is a social phenomenon; and, of all social phenomena, it is the one which manifests to the greatest degree two fundamental characteristics which make it susceptible of scientific study. In the first place, much of linguistic behavior lies on the level of unconscious thought. When we speak, we are not conscious of the syntactic and morphological laws of our language. Moreover, we are not ordinarily conscious of the phonemes that we employ to convey different meanings; and we are rarely, if ever, conscious of the phonological oppositions which reduce each phoneme to a bundle of distinctive features. This absence of consciousness, moreover, still holds when we do become aware of the grammar or the phonemics of our language. For, while this awareness is the privilege of the scholar, language, as a matter of fact, lives and develops only as a collective construct; and even the scholar's linguistic knowledge always remains dissociated from his experience as a speaking agent, for his mode of speech is not affected by his ability to interpret his language on a higher level. We may say, then, that insofar as language is concerned we need not fear the influence of the observer on the observed phenomenon, because the observer cannot modify the phenomenon merely by becoming conscious of it.

Furthermore, as regards Wiener's second point, we know that language appeared very early in human history. Therefore, even if we can study it scientifically only when written documents are available, writing itself goes back a considerable distance and furnishes long enough runs to make language a valid subject for mathematical analysis. For example, the series we have at our disposal in studying Indo-European, Semitic, or Sino-Tibetan languages is about four or five thousand years old. And, where a comparable temporal dimension is lacking, the multiplicity of coexistent forms furnishes, for several other linguistic families, a spatial dimension that is no less valuable.

We thus find in language a social phenomenon that manifests both independence of the observer and long statistical runs, which would seem to indicate that language is a phenomenon fully qualified to satisfy the demands of mathematicians for the type of analysis Wiener suggests.

It is, in fact, difficult to see why certain linguistic problems could not be solved by modern calculating machines. With knowledge of the phonological structure of a language and the laws which govern the groupings of consonants and vowels, a student could easily use a machine to compute all the combinations of phonemes constituting the words of n syllables existing in the vocabulary, or even the number of combinations compatible with the structure of the language under consideration, such as previously defined. With a machine into which would be 'fed' the equations regulating the types of structures with which phonemics usually deals, the repertory of sound which human speech organs can emit, and the minimal differential values, determined by psycho-physiological methods, which distinguish between the phonemes closest to one another, one would doubtless be able to obtain a computation of the totality of phonological structures for n oppositions (n being as high as one wished). One could thus construct a sort of periodic table of linguistic structures that would be comparable to the table of elements which Mendeleieff introduced into modern chemistry. It would then remain for us only to check the place of known languages in this table, to identify the positions and the relationships of the languages whose first-hand study is still too imperfect to give us a proper theoretical knowledge of them, and to discover the place of languages that have disappeared or are unknown, yet to come, or simply possible.

To add a last example: Jakobson has suggested that a language may possess several coexisting phonological structures, each of which may intervene in a different kind of grammatical operation. Since there must obviously be a relationship between the different structural modalities of the same language, we arrive at the concept of a 'metastructure' which would be something like the law of the group (*loi du groupe*) consisting of its modal structures. If all of these modalities could be analyzed by our machine, established mathematical methods would permit it to construct the 'metastructure' of the language, which would in certain complex cases be so intricate as to make it difficult, if not impossible, to achieve on the basis of purely empirical investigation.

The problem under discussion here can, then, be defined as follows. Among all social phenomena, language alone has thus far been studied in a manner which permits it to serve as the object of truly scientific analysis, allowing us to understand its formative process and to predict its mode of change. This results from modern researches into the problems of phonemics, which have reached beyond the superficial conscious and historical expression of linguistic phenomena to attain fundamental and objective realities consisting of systems of relations which are the products of unconscious thought processes. The question which now arises is this: Is it possible to effect a similar reduction in the analysis of other forms of social phenomena? If so, would this analysis lead to the same result? And if the answer to this last question is in the affirmative, can we conclude that all forms of social life are substantially of the same nature – that is, do they consist of systems of behavior that represent the projection, on the level of conscious and socialized thought, of universal laws which regulate the unconscious activities of the mind? Obviously, no attempt can be made here to do more than to sketch this problem by indicating certain points of reference and projecting the principal lines along which its orientation might be effective.

Some of the researches of Kroeber appear to be of the greatest importance in suggesting approaches to our problem, particularly his work on changes in the styles of women's dress. Fashion actually is, in the highest degree, a phenomenon that depends on the unconscious activity of the mind. We rarely take note of why a particular style pleases us or falls into disuse. Kroeber has demonstrated that this seemingly arbitrary evolution follows definite laws. These laws cannot be reached by purely empirical observation, or by intuitive consideration of phenomena, but result from measuring some basic relationships between the various elements of costume. The relationship thus obtained can be expressed in terms of mathematical functions, whose values, calculated at a given moment, make prediction possible.

Kroeber has thus shown how even such a highly arbitrary aspect of social behavior is susceptible of scientific study. His method may be usefully compared not only with that of structural linguistics, but also with that of the natural sciences. There is a remarkable analogy between these researches and those of a contemporary biologist, G. Teissier, on the growth of the organs of certain crustaceans. Teissier has shown that, in order to formulate the laws of this growth, it is necessary to consider the relative dimensions of the component parts of the claws, and not the exterior forms of those organs. Here, relationships allow us to derive constants – termed parameters – from which it is possible to derive the laws which govern the development of these organisms. The object of a scientific zoology, in these terms, is thus not ultimately concerned with the forms of animals and their organs as they are usually perceived, but with the establishment of certain abstract and measurable relationships, which constitute the basic nature of the phenomena under study.

An analogous method has been followed in studying certain features of social organization, particularly marriage rules and kinship systems. It has been shown that the complete set of marriage regulations operating in human societies, and usually classified under different headings, such as incest prohibitions, preferential forms of marriage, and the like, can be interpreted as being so many different ways of insuring the circulation of women within the social group or of substituting the mechanism of a sociologically determined affinity for that of a biologically determined consanguinity. Proceeding from this hypothesis, it would only be necessary to make a mathematical study of every possible type of exchange between *n* partners to enable one almost automatically to arrive at every type of marriage rule actually operating in living societies and, eventually, to discover other rules that are merely possible; one would also understand their function and the relationship between each type and the others.

This approach was fully validated by the demonstration, reached by pure deduction, that the mechanisms of reciprocity known to classical anthropology – namely, those based on dual organization and exchange-marriage between two partners or partners whose number is a multiple of two – are but a special instance of a wider kind of reciprocity between any number of partners. This fact has tended to remain unnoticed, because the partners in those matings, instead of giving and receiving from each other, do not give to those from whom they receive and do not receive from those to whom they give. They give to and receive from different partners to whom they are bound by a relationship that operates only in one direction.

This type of organization, no less important than the moiety system, has thus far been observed and described only imperfectly and incidentally. Starting with the results of mathematical study, data had to be compiled; thus, the real extension of the system was shown and its first theoretical analysis offered. At the same time, it became possible to explain the more general features of marriage rules such as preferential marriage between bilateral cross-cousins or with only one kind of cross-cousin, on the father's side (patrilateral), or on that of the mother (matrilateral). Thus, for example, though such customs had been unintelligible to anthropologists, they were perfectly clear when regarded as illustrating different modalities of the laws of exchange. In turn, these were reduced to a still more basic relationship between the rules of residence and the rules of descent. Now, these results can be achieved only by treating marriage regulations and kinship systems as a kind of language, a set of processes permitting the establishment, between individuals and groups, of a certain type of communication. That the mediating factor, in this case, should be the women of the group, who are circulated between clans, lineages, or families, in place of the words of the group, which are circulated between individuals, does not at all change the fact that the essential aspect of the phenomenon is identical in both cases.

We may now ask whether, in extending the concept of communication so as to make it include exogamy and the rules flowing from the prohibition of incest, we may not, reciprocally, achieve insight into a problem that is still very obscure, that of the origin of language. For marriage regulations, in relation to language, represent a much more crude and archaic complex. It is generally recognized that words are signs; but poets are practically the only ones who know that words were also once values. As against this, women are held by the social group to be values of the most essential kind, though we have difficulty in understanding how these values become integrated in systems endowed with a significant function. This ambiguity is clearly manifested in the reactions of persons who, on the basis of the analysis of social structures referred to, have laid against it the charge of 'anti-feminism,' because women are referred to as objects. Of course, it may be disturbing to some to have women conceived as mere parts of a meaningful system. However, one should keep in mind that the processes by which phonemes and words have lost – even though in an illusory manner – their character of value, to become reduced to pure signs, will never lead to the same results in matters concerning women. For words do not speak, while women do; as producers of signs, women can never be reduced to the status of symbols or tokens. But it is for this very reason that the position of women, as actually found in this system of communication between men that is made up of marriage regulations and kinship nomenclature, may afford us a workable image of the type of relationships that could have existed at a very early period in the development of language, between human beings and their words. As in the case of women, the original impulse which compelled men to exchange words must be sought for in that split representation that pertains to the symbolic function. For, since certain terms are simultaneously perceived as having a value both for the speaker and the listener, the only way to resolve this contradiction is in the exchange of complementary values, to which all social existence is reduced.

These speculations may be judged utopian. Yet, if one considers that the assumptions made here are legitimate, a very important consequence follows, one that is susceptible of immediate verification. That is, the question may be raised whether the different aspects of social life (including even art and religion) cannot only be studied by the methods of, and with the help of concepts similar to those employed in linguistics, but also whether they do not constitute phenomena whose inmost nature is the same as that of language. That is, in the words of Voegelin, we may ask whether there are not only 'operational' but also 'substantial comparabilities' between language and culture.

How can this hypothesis be verified? It will be necessary to develop the analysis of the different features of social life, either for a given society or for a complex of societies, so that a deep enough level can be reached to make it possible to cross from one to the other; or to express the specific structure of each in terms of a sort of general language, valid for each system separately and for all of them taken together. It would thus be possible to ascertain if one had reached their inner nature and to determine if this pertained to the same kind of reality. In order to develop this point, an experiment can be attempted. It will consist, on the part of the anthropologist, in translating the basic features of the kinship systems from different parts of the world into terms general enough to be meaningful to the linguist, and thus be equally applicable by the linguist to the description of languages from the same regions. Both could thus ascertain whether or not different types of communication systems in the same societies – that is, kinship and language – are or are not caused by identical unconscious structures. Should this be the case, we could be assured of having reached a truly fundamental formulation.

If then, a substantial identity were assumed to exist between language structure and kinship systems, one should find, in the following regions of the world, languages whose structures would be of a type comparable to kinship systems in the following terms:

(1) Indo-European: As concerns the kinship systems, we find that the marriage regulations of our contemporary civilization are entirely based on the principle that, a few negative prescriptions being granted, the density and fluidity of the population will achieve by itself the same results which other societies have sought in more complicated sets of rules; i.e., social cohesion obtained by marriage in degrees far removed or even impossible to trace. This statistical solution has its origin in a typical

feature of most ancient Indo-European systems. These belong, in the author's terminology, to a simple formula of generalized reciprocity (*formule simple de l'échange généralisé*). However, instead of prevailing between lineages, this formula operates between more complex units of the bratsvo type, which actually are clusters of lineages, each of which enjoys a certain freedom within the rigid framework of general reciprocity effective at the cluster level. Therefore, it can be said that a characteristic feature of Indo-European kinship structure lies in the fact that a problem set in simple terms always admits of many solutions.

Should the linguistic structure be homologous with the kinship structure it would thus be possible to express the basic feature of Indo-European languages as follows: The languages have simple structures, utilizing numerous elements. The opposition between the simplicity of the structure and the multiplicity of elements is expressed in the fact that several elements compete to occupy the same positions in the structure.

(2) Sino-Tibetan kinship systems exhibit quite a different type of complexity. They belong to or derive directly from the simplest form of general reciprocity, namely, mother's brother's daughter marriage, so that, as has been shown, while this type of marriage insures social cohesion in the simplest way, at the same time it permits this to be indefinitely extended so as to include any number of participants.

Translated into more general terms applicable to language that would correspond to the following linguistic pattern, we may say that the structure is complex, while the elements are few, a feature that may be related to the tonal structure of these languages.

(3) The typical feature of African kinship systems is the extension of the bridewealth system, coupled with a rather frequent prohibition on marriage with the wife's brother's wife. The joint result is a system of general recriprocity more complex than the mother's brother's daughter system, while the types of unions resulting from the circulation of the marriage-price approaches, to some extent, the statistical mechanism operating in our own society.

Therefore one could say that African languages have several modalities corresponding in general to a position intermediate between (1) and (2).

(4) The widely recognized features of the Oceanic kinship systems seem to lead to the following formulation of the basic characteristics of the linguistic pattern: simple structure and few elements.

(5) The originality of American Indian kinship systems lies in the so-called Crow-Omaha type, which should be carefully distinguished from other types showing the same disregard for generation levels. The important point with the Crow-Omaha type is not that two kinds of cross-cousins are classified in different generation levels, but rather that they are classified with consanguineous kin instead of with affinal kin (as is the case, for instance, in the Miwok system). But systems of the Miwok type belong equally to the Old and the New World; while the differential systems just referred to as Crow-Omaha are, apart from a few exceptions, typical only for the New World. It can be shown that this quite exceptional feature of the Crow-Omaha system resulted from

the simultaneous application of the two simple formulas of reciprocity, both special and general (*échange restreint* and *échange généralisé*), which elsewhere in the world were generally considered to be incompatible. It thus became possible to achieve marriage within remote degrees by using simultaneously two simple formulas, each of which independently applied could have led only to different kinds of cross-cousin marriages.

The linguistic pattern corresponding to this situation is that certain of the American Indian languages offer a relatively high number of elements which succeed in becoming organized into relatively simple structures by the structures' assuming asymmetrical forms.

It should be kept in mind that in the above highly tentative experiment the anthropologist proceeds from what is known to him to what is unknown: namely, from kinship structures to linguistic structures. Whether or not the differential characteristics thus outlined have a meaning insofar as the respective languages are concerned remains for the linguist to decide. The author, being a social anthropologist and not a linguist, can only try to explain briefly to which specific features of kinship systems he is referring in this attempt toward a generalized formulation. Since the general lines of his interpretation have been fully developed elsewhere, short sketches were deemed sufficient for the purpose of this paper.

If the general characteristics of the kinship systems of given geographical areas, which we have tried to bring into juxtaposition with equally general characteristics of the linguistic structures of those areas, are recognized by linguists as an approach to equivalences of their own observations, then it will be apparent, in terms of our preceding discussion, that we are much closer to understanding the fundamental characteristics of social life than we have been accustomed to think.

The road will then be open for a comparative structural analysis of customs, institutions, and accepted patterns of behavior. We shall be in a position to understand basic similarities between forms of social life, such as language, art, law, and religion, that on the surface seem to differ greatly. At the same time, we shall have the hope of overcoming the opposition between the collective nature of culture and its manifestations in the individual, since the so-called 'collective consciousness' would, in the final analysis, be no more than the expression, on the level of individual thought and behavior, of certain time and space modalities of the universal laws which make up the unconscious activity of the mind.

47

LUCIEN GOLDMANN
The human sciences and philosophy* (1966)

. . . By contrast, Lévi-Strauss, an exceptionally sophisticated theorist whose links with contemporary society are certainly unconscious and involuntary and are mediatized in complex ways, represents current tendencies in thought in a different manner: he is the exponent of a formalistic system that tends to eliminate in a radical way all interest in history and the problem of meaning . . .

For the moment, however, we must remain content with a mere mention of the most important of the intellectual and methodological principles which seem to us to confirm the ahistorical nature of the greater part of current sociological reflection: the disjunction of the ideas of structure and function. If structures in fact characterize the reactions of men to different problems which their relations with the surrounding social and natural world raise, these structures always fulfil, in a particular context, a function within a larger social structure. And when the situation changes, they cease to fulfil this function and thus lose their rational character, which leads men to abandon them and to replace them with new and different structures. It is thus that the indissoluble link between structure and function, resulting from the relatively durable nature of functions and the relatively provisional nature of structures, constitutes the motive power of history or, to put it another way, the historical character of human behaviour. Thus, if one separates structure from function, he has already committed himself to the creation of either an ahistorical and formalistic structuralism or a functionalism with the same orientation. The structuralism will be oriented towards the investigation of the most generalized structures of thought, which can be found in all social forms and which are never affected by historical changes, thereby eliminating by its very methodology the historical element from its field of study. The functionalism, which is interested only in the conservative nature of every institution and mode of behaviour within a given society, illuminates it by revealing its 'functional' aspect, but never confronts the problem of change. These are but two sides of one coin. The manner in which the functionalist designates what he calls 'dysfunctions' indicates how these have only a negative character for him; these dysfunctions are related only

* From *The Human Sciences and Philosophy* by Lucien Goldman, Jonathan Cape, London, 1969, pp. 12–15.

to the society under study, without considering whether what is designated as 'dys-
functional' might not perhaps be a new functionality in process of constitution in
relation to a new social order or at least in relation to a new social situation. The very
use of the term 'dysfunction' indicates the limits of this perspective, limits which are
ultimately the same as those of non-genetic structuralism: the methodological denial
of any historical dimension to social facts.

48

MICHEL FOUCAULT
The order of things* (1966)

When we establish a considered classification, when we say that a cat and a dog resemble each other less than two greyhounds do, even if both are tame or embalmed, even if both are frenzied, even if both have just broken the water pitcher, what is the ground on which we are able to establish the validity of this classification with complete certainty? On what 'table', according to what grid of identities, similitudes, analogies, have we become accustomed to sort out so many different and similar things? What is this coherence – which, as is immediately apparent, is neither determined by an a priori and necessary concatenation, nor imposed on us by immediately perceptible contents? For it is not a question of linking consequences, but of grouping and isolating, of analysing, of matching and pigeon-holing concrete contents; there is nothing more tentative, nothing more empirical (superficially, at least) than the process of establishing an order among things; nothing that demands a sharper eye or a surer, better-articulated language; nothing that more insistently requires that one allow oneself to be carried along by the proliferation of qualities and forms. And yet an eye not consciously prepared might well group together certain similar figures and distinguish between others on the basis of such and such a difference: in fact, there is no similitude and no distinction, even for the wholly untrained perception, that is not the result of a precise operation and of the application of a preliminary criterion. A 'system of elements' – a definition of the segments by which the resemblances and differences can be shown, the types of variation by which those segments can be affected, and, lastly, the threshold above which there is a difference and below which there is a similitude – is indispensable for the establishment of even the simplest form of order. Order is, at one and the same time, that which is given in things as their inner law, the hidden network that determines the way they confront one another, and also that which has no existence except in the grid created by a glance, an examination, a language; and it is only in the blank spaces of this grid that order manifests

* From the Preface, *The Order of Things: An Archaeology of the Human Sciences* by Michel Foucault. Copyright © 1965 by Random House, Inc., New York. Originally published in French as *Les mots et les choses*. Copyright © 1966 by editions Gallimard. Reprinted by permission of Georges Borchardt, Inc., for editions Gallimard and by Routledge, London and New York. Pp. xix–xxiv.

itself in depth as though already there, waiting in silence for the moment of its expression.

The fundamental codes of a culture – those governing its language, its schemas of perception, its exchanges, its techniques, its values, the hierarchy of its practices – establish for every man, from the very first, the empirical orders with which he will be dealing and within which he will be at home. At the other extremity of thought, there are the scientific theories or the philosophical interpretations which explain why order exists in general, what universal law it obeys, what principle can account for it, and why this particular order has been established and not some other. But between these two regions, so distant from one another, lies a domain which, even though its role is mainly an intermediary one, is nonetheless fundamental: it is more confused, more obscure, and probably less easy to analyse. It is here that a culture, imperceptibly deviating from the empirical orders prescribed for it by its primary codes, instituting an initial separation from them, causes them to lose their original transparency, relinquishes its immediate and invisible powers, frees itself sufficiently to discover that these orders are perhaps not the only possible ones or the best ones; this culture then finds itself faced with the stark fact that there exists, below the level of its spontaneous orders, things that are in themselves capable of being ordered, that belong to a certain unspoken order; the fact, in short, that order exists. As though emancipating itself to some extent from its linguistic, perceptual, and practical grids, the culture super-imposed on them another kind of grid which neutralized them, which by this super-imposition both revealed and excluded them at the same time, so that the culture, by this very process, came face to face with order in its primary state. It is on the basis of this newly perceived order that the codes of language, perception, and practice are criticized and rendered partially invalid. It is on the basis of this order, taken as a firm foundation, that general theories as to the ordering of things, and the interpretation that such an ordering involves, will be constructed. Thus, between the already 'encoded' eye and reflexive knowledge there is a middle region which liberates order itself: it is here that it appears, according to the culture and the age in question, continuous and graduated or discontinuous and piecemeal, linked to space or consti-tuted anew at each instant by the driving force of time, related to a series of variables or defined by separate systems of coherences, composed of resemblances which are either successive or corresponding, organized around increasing differences, etc. This middle region, then, in so far as it makes manifest the modes of being of order, can be posited as the most fundamental of all: anterior to words, perceptions, and gestures, which are then taken to be more or less exact, more or less happy, expressions of it (which is why this experience of order in its pure primary state always plays a critical role); more solid, more archaic, less dubious, always more 'true' than the theories that attempt to give those expressions explicit form, exhaustive application, or philo-sophical foundation. Thus, in every culture, between the use of what one might call the ordering codes and reflections upon order itself, there is the pure experience of order and of its modes of being.

The present study is an attempt to analyse that experience. I am concerned to show its developments, since the sixteenth century, in the mainstream of a culture such as ours: in what way, as one traces – against the current, as it were – language as it has been spoken, natural creatures as they have been perceived and grouped together, and exchanges as they have been practised; in what way, then, our culture has made manifest the existence of order, and how, to the modalities of that order, the exchanges owed their laws, the living beings their constants, the words their sequence and their representative value; what modalities of order have been recognized, posited, linked with space and time, in order to create the positive basis of knowledge as we find it employed in grammar and philology, in natural history and biology, in the study of wealth and political economy. Quite obviously, such an analysis does not belong to the history of ideas or of science: it is rather an inquiry whose aim is to rediscover on what basis knowledge and theory became possible; within what space of order knowledge was constituted; on the basis of what historical a priori, and in the element of what positivity, ideas could appear, sciences be established, experience be reflected in philosophies, rationalities be formed, only, perhaps, to dissolve and vanish soon afterwards. I am not concerned, therefore, to describe the progress of knowledge towards an objectivity in which today's science can finally be recognized; what I am attempting to bring to light is the epistemological field, the episteme in which knowledge, envisaged apart from all criteria having reference to its rational value or to its objective forms, grounds its positivity and thereby manifests a history which is not that of its growing perfection, but rather that of its conditions of possibility; in this account, what should appear are those configurations within the space of knowledge which have given rise to the diverse forms of empirical science. Such an enterprise is not so much a history, in the traditional meaning of that word, as an 'archaeology'.

Now, this archaeological inquiry has revealed two great discontinuities in the episteme of Western culture: the first inaugurates the Classical age (roughly half-way through the seventeenth century) and the second, at the beginning of the nineteenth century, marks the beginning of the modern age. The order on the basis of which we think today does not have the same mode of being as that of the Classical thinkers. Despite the impression we may have of an almost uninterrupted development of the European ratio from the Renaissance to our own day, despite our possible belief that the classifications of Linnaeus, modified to a greater or lesser degree, can still lay claim to some sort of validity, that Condillac's theory of value can be recognized to some extent in nineteenth-century marginalism, that Keynes was well aware of the affinities between his own analyses and those of Cantillon, that the language of general grammar (as exemplified in the authors of Port-Royal or in Bauzée) is not so very far removed from our own – all this quasi-continuity on the level of ideas and themes is doubtless only a surface appearance; on the archaeological level, we see that the system of positivities was transformed in a wholesale fashion at the end of the eighteenth and beginning of the nineteenth century. Not that reason made any progress: it was simply that the mode of being of things, and of the order that divided them up before presenting them to the understanding, was profoundly altered. If the natural history of Tournefort, Linnaeus, and Buffon can be related to anything at all other than itself, it is not to biology, to Cuvier's comparative anatomy, or to Darwin's theory of evolution, but to Bauzée's general grammar, to the analysis of money and wealth as found in the works of Law, or Véron de Fortbonnais, or Turgot. Perhaps knowledge succeeds in engendering knowledge, ideas in transforming themselves and actively modifying one another (but how? – historians have not yet enlightened us on this point); one thing, in any case, is certain: archaeology, addressing itself to the general space of knowledge, to its configurations, and to the mode of being of the things that appear in it, defines systems of simultaneity, as well as the series of mutations necessary and sufficient to circumscribe the threshold of a new positivity.

In this way, analysis has been able to show the coherence that existed, throughout the Classical age, between the theory of representation and the theories of language, of the natural orders, and of wealth and value. It is this configuration that, from the nineteenth century onward, changes entirely; the theory of representation disappears as the universal foundation of all possible orders; language as the spontaneous tabula, the primary grid of things, as an indispensable link between representation and things, is eclipsed in its turn; a profound historicity penetrates into the heart of things, isolates and defines them in their own coherence, imposes upon them the forms of order implied by the continuity of time; the analysis of exchange and money gives way to the study of production, that of the organism takes precedence over the search for taxonomic characteristics, and, above all, language loses its privileged position and becomes, in its turn, a historical form coherent with the density of its own past. But as things become increasingly reflexive, seeking the principle of their intelligibility only in their own development, and abandoning the space of representation, man enters in his turn, and for the first time, the field of Western knowledge. Strangely enough, man – the study of whom is supposed by the naïve to be the oldest investigation since Socrates – is probably no more than a kind of rift in the order of things, or, in any case, a configuration whose outlines are determined by the new position he has so recently taken up in the field of knowledge. Whence all the chimeras of the new humanisms, all the facile solutions of an 'anthropology' understood as a universal reflection on man, half-empirical, half-philosophical. It is comforting, however, and a source of profound relief to think that man is only a recent invention, a figure not yet two centuries old, a new wrinkle in our knowledge, and that he will disappear again as soon as that knowledge has discovered a new form.

It is evident that the present study is, in a sense, an echo of my undertaking to write a history of madness in the Classical age; it has the same articulations in time, taking the end of the Renaissance as its starting-point, then encountering, at the beginning of the nineteenth century, just as my history of madness did, the threshold of a modernity that we have not yet left behind. But whereas in the history of madness I was investigating the way in which a culture can determine in a massive, general form the difference that limits it, I am concerned here with observing how a culture experiences the propinquity of things, how it establishes the tabula of their relationships and the order by which they must be considered. I am concerned, in short, with a history of resemblance: on what conditions was Classical thought able to reflect relations of similarity or equivalence between things, relations that would provide a foundation and a justification for their words, their classifications, their systems of exchange? What historical a priori provided the starting-point from which it was possible to define the great checkerboard of distinct identities established against the confused, undefined, faceless, and, as it were, indifferent background of differences? The history of madness would be the history of the Other – of that which, for a given culture, is at once interior and foreign, therefore to be excluded (so as to exorcize the interior danger) but by being shut away (in order to reduce its otherness); whereas the history of the order imposed on things would be the history of the Same – of that which, for a given culture, is both dispersed and related, therefore to be distinguished by kinds and to be collected together into identities.

And if one considers that disease is at one and the same time disorder – the existence of a perilous otherness within the human body, at the very heart of life – and a natural phenomenon with its own constants, resemblances, and types, one can see what scope there would be for an archaeology of the medical point of view. From the limit-experience of the Other to the constituent forms of medical knowledge, and from the latter to the order of things and the conceptions of the Same, what is available to archaeological analysis is the whole of Classical knowledge, or rather the threshold that separates us from Classical thought and constitutes our modernity. It was upon this threshold that the strange figure of knowledge called man first appeared and revealed a space proper to the human sciences. In attempting to uncover the deepest strata of Western culture, I am restoring to our silent and apparently immobile soil its rifts, its instability, its flaws; and it is the same ground that is once more stirring under our feet.

Power/knowledge* (1976)

. . . So, the main point to be gleaned from these events of the last fifteen years, their predominant feature, is the *local* character of criticism. That should not, I believe, be taken to mean that its qualities are those of an obtuse, naive or primitive empiricism; nor is it a soggy eclecticism, an opportunism that laps up any and every kind of theoretical approach; nor does it mean a self-imposed ascetism which taken by itself would reduce to the worst kind of theoretical impoverishment. I believe that what this essentially local character of criticism indicates in reality is an autonomous, non-centralised kind of theoretical production, one that is to say whose validity is not dependent on the approval of the established regimes of thought.

It is here that we touch upon another feature of these events that has been manifest for some time now: it seems to me that this local criticism has proceeded by means of what one might term 'a return of knowledge'. What I mean by that phrase is this: it is a fact that we have repeatedly encountered, at least at a superficial level, in the course of most recent times, an entire thematic to the effect that it is not theory but life that matters, not knowledge but reality, not books but money etc.; but it also seems to me that over and above, and arising out of this thematic, there is something else to which we are witness, and which we might describe as an *insurrection of subjugated knowledges*.

By subjugated knowledges I mean two things: on the one hand, I am referring to the historical contents that have been buried and disguised in a functionalist coherence or formal systemisation. Concretely, it is not a semiology of the life of the asylum, it is not even a sociology of delinquency, that has made it possible to produce an

* From *Power/Knowledge: Selected Interviews and Other Writings 1972–1977* by Michel Foucault, edited by Colin Gordon, copyright © 1972, 1975, 1976, 1977 by Michel Foucault. This collection © 1980 by the Harvester Press. Used by permission of Pantheon Books, a division of Random House, Inc. Pp. 81–92.

effective criticism of the asylum and likewise of the prison, but rather the immediate emergence of historical contents. And this is simply because only the historical contents allow us to rediscover the ruptural effects of conflict and struggle that the order imposed by functionalist or systematising thought is designed to mask. Subjugated knowledges are thus those blocs of historical knowledge which were present but disguised within the body of functionalist and systematising theory and which criticism – which obviously draws upon scholarship – has been able to reveal.

On the other hand, I believe that by subjugated knowledges one should understand something else, something which in a sense is altogether different, namely, a whole set of knowledges that have been disqualified as inadequate to their task or insufficiently elaborated: naive knowledges, located low down on the hierarchy, beneath the required level of cognition or scientificity. I also believe that it is through the re-emergence of these low-ranking knowledges, these unqualified, even directly disqualified knowledges (such as that of the psychiatric patient, of the ill person, of the nurse, of the doctor – parallel and marginal as they are to the knowledge of medicine – that of the delinquent etc.), and which involve what I would call a popular knowledge (*le savoir des gens*) though it is far from being a general commonsense knowledge, but is on the contrary a particular, local, regional knowledge, a differential knowledge incapable of unanimity and which owes its force only to the harshness with which it is opposed by everything surrounding it – that it is through the re-appearance of this knowledge, of these local popular knowledges, these disqualified knowledges, that criticism performs its work.

However, there is a strange kind of paradox in the desire to assign to this same category of subjugated knowledges what are on the one hand the products of meticulous, erudite, exact historical knowledge, and on the other hand local and specific knowledges which have no common meaning and which are in some fashion allowed to fall into disuse whenever they are not effectively and explicitly maintained in themselves. Well, it seems to me that our critical discourses of the last fifteen years have in effect discovered their essential force in this association between the buried knowledges of erudition and those disqualified from the hierarchy of knowledges and sciences.

In the two cases – in the case of the erudite as in that of the disqualified knowledges – with what in fact were these buried, subjugated knowledges really concerned? They were concerned with a *historical knowledge of struggles*. In the specialised areas of erudition as in the disqualified popular knowledge there lay the memory of hostile encounters which even up to this day have been confined to the margins of knowledge.

What emerges out of this is something one might call a genealogy, or rather a multiplicity of genealogical researches, a painstaking rediscovery of struggles together with the rude memory of their conflicts. And these genealogies, that are the combined product of an erudite knowledge and a popular knowledge, were not possible and could not even have been attempted except on one condition, namely that the tyranny of globalising discourses with their hierarchy and all their privileges of a theoretical *avant-garde* was eliminated.

Let us give the term *genealogy* to the union of erudite knowledge and local memories which allows us to establish a historical knowledge of struggles and to make use of this knowledge tactically today. This then will be a provisional definition of the genealogies which I have attempted to compile with you over the last few years.

You are well aware that this research activity, which one can thus call genealogical, has nothing at all to do with an opposition between the abstract unity of theory and the concrete multiplicity of facts. It has nothing at all to do with a disqualification of the speculative dimension which opposes to it, in the name of some kind of scientism, the rigour of well established knowledges. It is not therefore via an empiricism that the genealogical project unfolds, nor even via a positivism in the ordinary sense of that term. What it really does is to entertain the claims to attention of local, discontinuous, disqualified, illegitimate knowledges against the claims of a unitary body of theory which would filter, hierarchise and order them in the name of some true knowledge and some arbitrary idea of what constitutes a science and its objects. Genealogies are therefore not positivistic returns to a more careful or exact form of science. They are precisely anti-sciences. Not that they vindicate a lyrical right to ignorance or non-knowledge: it is not that they are concerned to deny knowledge or that they esteem the virtues of direct cognition and base their practice upon an immediate experience that escapes encapsulation in knowledge. It is not that with which we are concerned. We are concerned, rather, with the insurrection of knowledges that are opposed primarily not to the contents, methods or concepts of a science, but to the effects of the central-ising powers which are linked to the institution and functioning of an organised scientific discourse within a society such as ours. Nor does it basically matter all that much that this institutionalisation of scientific discourse is embodied in a university, or, more generally, in an educational apparatus, in a theoretical-commercial institu-tion such as psychoanalysis or within the framework of reference that is provided by a political system such as Marxism; for it is really against the effects of the power of a discourse that is considered to be scientific that the genealogy must wage its struggle.

To be more precise, I would remind you how numerous have been those who for many years now, probably for more than half a century, have questioned whether Marxism was, or was not, a science. One might say that the same issue has been posed, and continues to be posed, in the case of psychoanalysis, or even worse, in that of the semiology of literary texts. But to all these demands of: 'Is it or is it not a science?', the genealogies or the genealogists would reply: 'If you really want to know, the fault lies in your very determination to make a science out of Marxism or psycho-analysis or this or that study'. If we have any objection against Marxism, it lies in the fact that it could effectively be a science. In more detailed terms, I would say that even before we can know the extent to which something such as Marxism or psycho-analysis can be compared to a scientific practice in its everyday functioning, its rules of construction, its working concepts, that even before we can pose the question of a formal and structural analogy between Marxist or psychoanalytic discourse, it is surely necessary to question ourselves about our aspirations to the kind of power that is presumed to accompany such a science. It is surely the following kinds of question that would need to be posed: What types of knowledge do you want to disqualify in the very instant of your demand: 'Is it a science'? Which speaking, discoursing sub-jects – which subjects of experience and knowledge – do you then want to 'diminish' when you say: 'I who conduct this discourse am conducting a scientific discourse, and I am a scientist'? Which theoretical-political *avant garde* do you want to enthrone in order to isolate it from all the discontinuous forms of knowledge that circulate about it? When I see you straining to establish the scientificity of Marxism I do not really think that you are demonstrating once and for all that Marxism has a rational structure and that therefore its propositions are the outcome of verifiable procedures; for me you are doing something altogether different, you are investing Marxist discourses and those who uphold them with the effects of a power which the West since Medieval times has attributed to science and has reserved for those engaged in scientific discourse.

By comparison, then, and in contrast to the various projects which aim to inscribe knowledges in the hierarchical order of power associated with science, a genealogy should be seen as a kind of attempt to emancipate historical knowledges from that subjection, to render them, that is, capable of opposition and of struggle against the coercion of a theoretical, unitary, formal and scientific discourse. It is based on a reactivation of local knowledges – of minor knowledges, as Deleuze might call them – in opposition to the scientific hierarchisation of knowledges and the effects intrinsic to their power: this, then, is the project of these disordered and fragmentary genealogies. If we were to characterise it in two terms, then 'archaeology' would be the appropriate methodology of this analysis of local discursivities, and 'genealogy' would be the tactics whereby, on the basis of the descriptions of these local discursivities, the subjected knowledges which were thus released would be brought into play.

So much can be said by way of establishing the nature of the project as a whole. I would have you consider all these fragments of research, all these discourses, which are simultaneously both superimposed and discontinuous, which I have continued obstinately to pursue for some four or five years now, as elements of these genealogies which have been composed – and by no means by myself alone – in the course of the last fifteen years. At this point, however, a problem arises, and a question: why not continue to pursue a theory which in its discontinuity is so attractive and plausible, albeit so little verifiable? Why not continue to settle upon some aspect of psychiatry or of the theory of sexuality etc.? It is true, one could continue (and in a certain sense I shall try to do so) if it were not for a certain number of changes in the current situation. By this I mean that it could be that in the course of the last five, ten or even fifteen years, things have assumed a different complexion – the contest could be said to present a different physiognomy. Is the relation of forces today still such as to allow these disinterred knowledges some kind of autonomous life? Can they be isolated by these means from every subjugating relationship? What force do they have taken in themselves? And, after all, is it not perhaps the case that these fragments of genealogies are no sooner brought to light, that the particular elements of the knowledge that one seeks to disinter are no sooner accredited and put into circulation, than they run the risk of re-codification, re-colonisation? In fact, those unitary discourses, which first disqualified and then ignored them when they made their appearance, are, it seems, quite ready now to annex them, to take them back within the fold of their own discourse and to invest them with everything this implies in terms of their effects of knowledge and power. And if we want to protect these only lately liberated fragments are we not in danger of ourselves constructing, with our own hands, that unitary discourse to which we are invited, perhaps to lure us into a trap, by those who say to us: 'All this is fine, but where are you heading? What kind of unity are you after?' The temptation, up to a certain point, is to reply: 'Well, we just go on, in a cumulative fashion; after all, the moment at which we risk colonisation has not yet arrived'. One could even attempt to throw out a challenge: 'Just try to colonise us then!' Or one might say, for example, 'Has there been, from the time when anti-psychiatry or the genealogy of psychiatric institutions were launched – and it is now a good fifteen years ago – a single Marxist, or a single psychiatrist, who has gone over the same ground in his own terms and shown that these genealogies that we produced were false, inadequately elaborated, poorly articulated and ill-founded?' In fact, as things stand in reality, these collected fragments of a genealogy remain as they have always been, surrounded by a prudent silence. At most, the only arguments that we have heard against them have been of the kind I believe were voiced by Monsieur Juquin: 'All this is all very well, but Soviet psychiatry nonetheless remains the foremost in the world'. To which I would reply: 'How right you are; Soviet psychiatry is indeed the foremost in the world and it is precisely that which one would hold against it'.

The silence, or rather the prudence, with which the unitary theories avoid the genealogy of knowledges might therefore be a good reason to continue to pursue it. Then at least one could proceed to multiply the genealogical fragments in the form of so many traps, demands, challenges, what you will. But in the long run, it is probably over-optimistic – if we are thinking in terms of a contest that of knowledge against the effects of the power of scientific discourse – to regard the silence of one's adversaries as indicative of a fear we have inspired in them. For perhaps the silence of the enemy – and here at the very least we have a methodological or tactical principle that it is always useful to bear in mind – can also be the index of our failure to produce any such fear at all. At all events, we must proceed just as if we had not alarmed them at all, in which case it will be no part of our concern to provide a solid and homogeneous theoretical terrain for all these dispersed genealogies, nor to descend upon them from on high with some kind of halo of theory that would unite them. Our task, on the contrary, will be to expose and specify the issue at stake in this opposition, this struggle, this insurrection of knowledges against the institutions and against effects of the knowledge and power that invests scientific discourse.

What is at stake in all these genealogies is the nature of this power which has surged into view in all its violence, aggression and absurdity in the course of the last forty years, contemporaneously, that is, with the collapse of Fascism and the decline of Stalinism. What, we must ask, is this power – or rather, since that is to give a formulation to the question that invites the kind of theoretical coronation of the whole which I am so keen to avoid – what are these various contrivances of power, whose operations extend to such differing levels and sectors of society and are possessed of such manifold ramifications? What are their mechanisms, their effects and their rela-tions? The issue here can, I believe, be crystallised essentially in the following ques-tion: is the analysis of power or of powers to be deduced in one way or another from the economy? Let me make this question and my reasons for posing it somewhat clearer. It is not at all my intention to abstract from what are innumerable and enor-mous differences; yet despite, and even because of these differences, I consider there to be a certain point in common between the juridical, and let us call it, liberal, conception of political power (found in the *philosophes* of the eighteenth century) and the Marxist conception, or at any rate a certain conception currently held to be

Marxist. I would call this common point an economism in the theory of power. By that I mean that in the case of the classic, juridical theory, power is taken to be a right, which one is able to possess like a commodity, and which one can in consequence transfer or alienate, either wholly or partially, through a legal act or through some act that establishes a right, such as takes place through cession or contract. Power is that concrete power which every individual holds, and whose partial or total cession enables political power or sovereignty to be established. This theoretical construction is essentially based on the idea that the constitution of political power obeys the model of a legal transaction involving a contractual type of exchange (hence the clear analogy that runs through all these theories between power and commodities, power and wealth). In the other case – I am thinking here of the general Marxist conception of power – one finds none of all that. Nonetheless, there is something else inherent in this latter conception, something which one might term an economic functionality of power. This economic functionality is present to the extent that power is conceived primarily in terms of the role it plays in the maintenance simultaneously of the relations of production and of a class domination which the development and specific forms of the forces of production have rendered possible. On this view, then, the historical *raison d'être* of political power is to be found in the economy. Broadly speaking, in the first case we have a political power whose formal model is discoverable in the process of exchange, the economic circulation of commodities; in the second case, the historical *raison d'être* of political power and the principle of its concrete forms and actual functioning, is located in the economy. Well then, the problem involved in the researches to which I refer can, I believe, be broken down in the following manner: in the first place, is power always in a subordinate position relative to the economy? Is it always in the service of, and ultimately answerable to, the economy? Is its essential end and purpose to serve the economy? Is it destined to realise, consolidate, maintain and reproduce the relations appropriate to the economy and essential to its functioning? In the second place, is power modelled upon the commodity? Is it something that one possesses, acquires, cedes through force or contract, that one alienates or recovers, that circulates, that voids this or that region? Or, on the contrary, do we need to employ varying tools in its analysis – even, that is, when we allow that it effectively remains the case that the relations of power do indeed remain profoundly enmeshed in and with economic relations and participate with them in a common circuit? If that is the case, it is not the models of functional subordination or formal isomorphism that will characterise the interconnection between politics and the economy. Their indissolubility will be of a different order, one that it will be our task to determine.

What means are available to us today if we seek to conduct a non-economic analysis of power? Very few, I believe. We have in the first place the assertion that power is neither given, nor exchanged, nor recovered, but rather exercised, and that it only exists in action. Again, we have at our disposal another assertion to the effect that power is not primarily the maintenance and reproduction of economic relations, but is above all a relation of force. The questions to be posed would then be these: if power is exercised, what sort of exercise does it involve? In what does it consist? What is its mechanism? There is an immediate answer that many contemporary analyses would appear to offer: power is essentially that which represses. Power represses nature, the instincts, a class, individuals. Though one finds this definition of power as repression endlessly repeated in present day discourse, it is not that discourse which invented it – Hegel first spoke of it, then Freud and later Reich. In any case, it has become almost automatic in the parlance of the times to define power as an organ of repression. So should not the analysis of power be first and foremost an analysis of the mechanisms of repression?

Then again, there is a second reply we might make: if power is properly speaking the way in which relations of forces are deployed and given concrete expression, rather than analysing it in terms of cession, contract or alienation, or functionally in terms of its maintenance of the relations of production, should we not analyse it primarily in terms of struggle, conflict and war? One would then confront the original hypothesis, according to which power is essentially repression, with a second hypothesis to the effect that power is war, a war continued by other means. This reversal of Clausewitz's assertion that war is politics continued by other means has a triple significance: in the first place, it implies that the relations of power that function in a society such as ours essentially rest upon a definite relation of forces that is established at a determinate, historically specifiable moment, in war and by war. Furthermore, if it is true that political power puts an end to war, that it installs, or tries to install, the reign of peace in civil society, this by no means implies that it suspends the effects of war or neutralises the disequilibrium revealed in the final battle. The role of political power, on this hypothesis, is perpetually to re-inscribe this relation through a form of unspoken warfare; to re-inscribe it in social institutions, in economic inequalities, in language, in the bodies themselves of each and every one of us.)

So this would be the first meaning to assign to the inversion of Clausewitz's aphorism that war is politics continued by other means. It consists in seeing politics as sanctioning and upholding the disequilibrium of forces that was displayed in war. But there is also something else that the inversion signifies, namely, that none of the political struggles, the conflicts waged over power, with power, for power, the alterations in the relations of forces, the favouring of certain tendencies, the reinforcements etc., etc., that come about within this 'civil peace' – that none of these phenomena in a political system should be interpreted except as the continuation of war. They should, that is to say, be understood as episodes, factions and displacements in that same war. Even when one writes the history of peace and its institutions, it is always the history of this war that one is writing. The third, and final, meaning to be assigned to the inversion of Clausewitz's aphorism, is that the end result can only be the outcome of war, that is, of a contest of strength, to be decided in the last analyses by recourse to arms. The political battle would cease with this final battle. Only a final battle of that kind would put an end, once and for all, to the exercise of power as continual war.

So, no sooner do we attempt to liberate ourselves from economistic analyses of power, than two solid hypotheses offer themselves: the one argues that the mechanisms of power are those of repression. For convenience sake, I shall term this Reich's hypothesis. The other argues that the basis of the relationship of power lies in the hostile engagement of forces. Again for convenience, I shall call this Nietzsche's hypothesis.

These two hypotheses are not irreconcilable; they even seem to be linked in a

fairly convincing manner. After all, repression could be seen as the political consequence of war, somewhat as oppression, in the classic theory of political right, was
seen as the abuse of sovereignty in the juridical order.

One might thus contrast two major systems of approach to the analysis of power:
in the first place, there is the old system as found in the *philosophes* of the eighteenth
century. The conception of power as an original right that is given up in the establishment of sovereignty, and the contract, as matrix of political power, provide its
points of articulation. A power so constituted risks becoming oppression whenever it
over-extends itself, whenever – that is – it goes beyond the terms of the contract. Thus
we have contract-power, with oppression as its limit, or rather as the transgression of
this limit. In contrast, the other system of approach no longer tries to analyse political
power according to the schema of contract-oppression, but in accordance with that of
war-repression, and, at this point, repression no longer occupies the place that
oppression occupies in relation to the contract, that is, it is not abuse, but is, on the
contrary, the mere effect and continuation of a relation of domination. On this view,
repression is none other than the realisation, within the continual warfare of this
pseudo-peace, of a perpetual relationship of force.

Thus we have two schemes for the analysis of power. The contract-oppression
schema, which is the juridical one, and the domination-repression or war-repression
schema for which the pertinent opposition is not between the legitimate and illegitimate, as in the first schema, but between struggle and submission.

It is obvious that all my work in recent years has been couched in the schema of
struggle-repression, and it is this – which I have hitherto been attempting to apply –
which I have now been forced to reconsider, both because it is still insufficiently
elaborated at a whole number of points, and because I believe that these two notions
of repression and war must themselves be considerably modified if not ultimately
abandoned. In any case, I believe that they must be submitted to closer scrutiny.

I have always been especially diffident of this notion of repression: it is precisely
with reference to those genealogies of which I was speaking just now – of the history
of penal right, of psychiatric power, of the control of infantile sexuality etc. – that I
have tried to demonstrate to you the extent to which the mechanisms that were
brought into operation in these power formations were something quite other, or in
any case something much more, than repression. The need to investigate this notion
of repression more thoroughly springs therefore from the impression I have that it is
wholly inadequate to the analysis of the mechanisms and effects of power that it is so
pervasively used to characterise today.

49

JACQUES DERRIDA
Structure, sign and play in the discourses of the human sciences* (1966)

'We need to interpret interpretations more than to interpret things'

(Montaigne)

Perhaps something has occurred in the history of the concept of structure that could be called an 'event,' if this loaded word did not entail a meaning which it is precisely the function of structural – or structuralist – thought to reduce or to suspect. Let us speak of an 'event,' nevertheless, and let us use quotation marks to serve as a precaution. What would this event be then? Its exterior form would be that of a rupture and a redoubling.

It would be easy enough to show that the concept of structure and even the word 'structure' itself are as old as the *episteme* – that is to say, as old as Western science and Western philosophy – and that their roots thrust deep into the soil of ordinary language, into whose deepest recesses the *episteme* plunges in order to gather them up and to make them part of itself in a metaphorical displacement. Nevertheless, up to the event which I wish to mark out and define, structure – or rather the structurality of structure – although it has always been at work, has always been neutralized or reduced, and this by a process of giving it a center or of referring it to a point of presence, a fixed origin. The function of this center was not only to orient, balance, and organize the structure – one cannot in fact conceive of an unorganized structure – but above all to make sure that the organizing principle of the structure would limit what we might call the play of the structure. By orienting and organizing the coherence of the system, the center of a structure permits the play of its elements inside the total form. And even today the notion of a structure lacking any center represents the unthinkable itself.

Nevertheless, the center also closes off the play which it opens up and makes possible. As center, it is the point at which the substitution of contents, elements, or

* From 'Structure, Sign, and Play in the Discourses of the Human Sciences' in *Writing and Difference* by Jacques Derrida, translated by Alan Bass, published by Routledge & Kegan Paul and University of Chicago Press, 1978. Copyright © 1978 by the University of Chicago Press. Reproduced by permission. Pp. 278–282.

terms is no longer possible. At the center, the permutation or the transformation of elements (which may of course be structures enclosed within a structure) is forbidden. At least this permutation has always remained interdicted (and I am using this word deliberately). Thus it has always been thought that the center, which is by definition unique, constituted that very thing within a structure which while governing the structure, escapes structurality. This is why classical thought concerning structure could say that the center is, paradoxically, within the structure and outside it. The center is at the center of the totality, and yet, since the center does not belong to the totality (is not part of the totality), the totality has its center elsewhere. The center is not the center. The concept of centered structure – although it represents coherence itself, the condition of the *episteme* as philosophy or science – is contradictorily coherent. And as always, coherence in contradiction expresses the force of a desire. The concept of centered structure is in fact the concept of a play based on a fundamental ground, a play constituted on the basis of a fundamental immobility and a reassuring certitude, which itself is beyond the reach of play. And on the basis of this certitude anxiety can be mastered, for anxiety is invariably the result of a certain mode of being implicated in the game, of being caught by the game, of being as it were at stake in the game from the outset. And again on the basis of what we call the center (and which, because it can be either inside or outside, can also indifferently be called the origin or end, *arche* or *telos*), repetitions, substitutions, transformations, and permutations are always taken from a history of meaning (*sens*) – that is, in a word, a history – whose origin may always be reawakened or whose end may always be anticipated in the form of presence. This is why one perhaps could say that the movement of any archaeology, like that of any eschatology, is an accomplice of this reduction of the structurality of structure and always attempts to conceive of structure on the basis of a full presence which is beyond play.

If this is so, the entire history of the concept of structure, before the rupture of which we are speaking, must be thought of as a series of substitutions of center for center, as a linked chain of determinations of the center. Successively, and in a regulated fashion, the center receives different forms or names. The history of metaphysics, like the history of the West, is the history of these metaphors and metonymies. Its matrix – if you will pardon me for demonstrating so little and for being so elliptical in order to come more quickly to my principal theme – is the determination of Being as presence in all senses of this word. It could be shown that all the names related to fundamentals, to principles, or to the center have always designated an invariable presence – *eidos, arche, telos, energeia, ousia* (essence, existence, substance, subject) *aletheia*, transcendentality, consciousness, God, man, and so forth.

The event I called a rupture, the disruption I alluded to at the beginning of this paper, presumably would have come about when the structurality of structure had to begin to be thought, that is to say, repeated, and this is why I said that this disruption was repetition in every sense of the word. Henceforth, it became necessary to think both the law which somehow governed the desire for a center in the constitution of structure, and the process of signification which orders the displacements and substitutions for this law of central presence – but a central presence which has never been itself, has always already been exiled from itself into its own substitute. The substitute does not substitute itself for anything which has somehow existed before it.

Henceforth, it was necessary to begin thinking that there was no center, that the center could not be thought in the form of a present-being, that the center had no natural site, that it was not a fixed locus but a function, a sort of nonlocus in which an infinite number of sign-substitutions came into play. This was the moment when language invaded the universal problematic, the moment when, in the absence of a center or origin, everything became discourse – provided we can agree on this word – that is to say, a system in which the central signified, the original or transcendental signified, is never absolutely present outside a system of differences. The absence of the transcendental signified extends the domain and the play of signification infinitely.

Where and how does this decentering, this thinking the structurality of structure, occur? It would be somewhat naïve to refer to an event, a doctrine, or an author in order to designate this occurrence. It is no doubt part of the totality of an era, our own, but still it has always already begun to proclaim itself and begun to work. Nevertheless, if we wished to choose several 'names,' as indications only, and to recall those authors in whose discourse this occurrence has kept most closely to its most radical formulation, we doubtless would have to cite the Nietzschean critique of metaphysics, the critique of the concepts of Being and truth, for which were substituted the concepts of play, interpretation, and sign (sign without present truth); the Freudian critique of self-presence, that is, the critique of consciousness, of the subject, of self-identity and of self-proximity or self-possession; and, more radically, the Heideggerian destruction of metaphysics, of onto-theology, of the determination of Being as presence. But all these destructive discourses and all their analogues are trapped in a kind of circle. This circle is unique. It describes the form of the relation between the history of metaphysics and the destruction of the history of metaphysics. There is no sense in doing without the concepts of metaphysics in order to shake metaphysics. We have no language – no syntax and no lexicon – which is foreign to this history; we can pronounce not a single destructive proposition which has not already had to slip into the form, the logic, and the implicit postulations of precisely what it seeks to contest. To take one example from many: the metaphysics of presence is shaken with the help of the concept of sign. But, as I suggested a moment ago, as soon as one seeks to demonstrate in this way that there is no transcendental or privileged signified and that the domain or play of signification henceforth has no limit, one must reject even the concept and word 'sign' itself – which is precisely what cannot be done. For the signification 'sign' has always been understood and determined, in its meaning, as sign-of, a signifier referring to a signified, a signifier different from its signified. If one erases the radical difference between signifier and signified, it is the word 'signifier' itself which must be abandoned as a metaphysical concept. When Lévi-Strauss says in the preface to *The Raw and the Cooked* that he has 'sought to transcend the opposition between the sensible and the intelligible by operating from the outset at the level of signs,' the necessity, force, and legitimacy of his act cannot make us forget that the concept of the sign cannot in itself surpass this opposition between the sensible and the intelligible. The concept of the sign, in each of its aspects, has been determined by this opposition throughout the totality of its history. It has lived only on this opposition and its system. But we cannot do without the concept of the sign, for we cannot give up this metaphysical complicity without also giving up the critique we are directing against this complicity, or without the risk of erasing difference in the self-identity of a signified reducing its signifier into itself or, amounting to the same thing, simply expelling its signifier outside itself. For there are two heterogenous ways of erasing the difference between the signifier and the signified: one, the classic way, consists in reducing or deriving the signifier, that is to say, ultimately in submitting the sign to thought; the other, the one we are using here against the first one, consists in putting into question the system in which the preceding reduction functioned: first and foremost, the opposition between the sensible and the intelligible. For the paradox is that the metaphysical reduction of the sign needed the opposition it was reducing. The opposition is systematic with the reduction. And what we are saying here about the sign can be extended to all the concepts and all the sentences of metaphysics, in particular to the discourse on 'structure.' But there are several ways of being caught in this circle. They are all more or less naïve, more or less empirical, more or less systematic, more or less close to the formulation – that is, to the formalization – of this circle. It is these differences which explain the multiplicity of destructive discourses and the disagreement between those who elaborate them. Nietzsche, Freud, and Heidegger, for example, worked within the inherited concepts of metaphysics. Since these concepts are not elements or atoms, and since they are taken from a syntax and a system, every particular borrowing brings along with it the whole of metaphysics. This is what allows these destroyers to destroy each other reciprocally – for example, Heidegger regarding Nietzsche, with as much lucidity and rigor as bad faith and misconstruction, as the last metaphysician, the last 'Platonist.' One could do the same for Heidegger himself, for Freud, or for a number of others. And today no exercise is more widespread.

What is the relevance of this formal schema when we turn to what are called the 'human sciences'? One of them perhaps occupies a privileged place – ethnology. In fact one can assume that ethnology could have been born as a science only at the moment when a decentering had come about: at the moment when European culture – and, in consequence, the history of metaphysics and of its concepts – had been dislocated, driven from its locus, and forced to stop considering itself as the culture of reference. This moment is not first and foremost a moment of philosophical or scientific discourse. It is also a moment which is political, economic, technical, and so forth. One can say with total security that there is nothing fortuitous about the fact that the critique of ethnocentrism – the very condition for ethnology – should be systematically and historically contemporaneous with the destruction of the history of metaphysics. Both belong to one and the same era. Now, ethnology – like any science – comes about within the element of discourse. And it is primarily a European science employing traditional concepts, however much it may struggle against them. Consequently, whether he wants to or not – and this does not depend on a decision on his part – the ethnologist accepts into his discourse the premises of ethnocentrism at the very moment when he denounces them. This necessity is irreducible; it is not a historical contingency. We ought to consider all its implications very carefully. But if no one can escape this necessity, and if no one is therefore responsible for giving in to it, however little he may do so, this does not mean that all the ways of giving in to it are of equal pertinence. The quality and fecundity of a discourse are perhaps measured by the critical rigor with which this relation to the history of metaphysics and to inherited concepts is thought. Here it is a question both of a critical relation to the language of the social sciences and a critical responsibility of the discourse itself. It is a question of explicitly and systematically posing the problem of the status of a discourse which borrows from a heritage the resources necessary for the deconstruction of that heritage itself. A problem of economy and strategy.

If we consider, as an example, the texts of Claude Lévi-Strauss, it is not only because of the privilege accorded to ethnology among the social sciences, nor even because the thought of Lévi-Strauss weighs heavily on the contemporary theoretical situation. It is above all because a certain choice has been declared in the work of Lévi-Strauss and because a certain doctrine has been elaborated there, and precisely, in a more or less explicit manner, as concerns both this critique of language and this critical language in the social sciences.

In order to follow this movement in the text of Lévi-Strauss, let us choose as one guiding thread among others the opposition between nature and culture. Despite all its rejuvenations and disguises, this opposition is congenital to philosophy.

50

PIERRE BOURDIEU
The logic of practice* (1980)

Projecting into the perception of the social world the unthought content inherent in his position in that world, that is, the monopoly of 'thought' which he is granted de facto by the social division of labour and which leads him to identify the work of thought with an effort of expression and verbalization in speech or writing – 'thought and expression are constituted simultaneously', said Merleau-Ponty – the 'thinker' betrays his secret conviction that action is fully performed only when it is understood, interpreted, expressed, by identifying the implicit with the unthought and by denying the status of authentic thought to the tacit and practical thought that is inherent in all 'sensible' action. Language spontaneously becomes the accomplice of this hermeneutic philosophy which leads one to conceive action as something to be deciphered, when it leads one to say, for example, that a gesture or ritual act expresses something, rather than saying, quite simply, that it is 'sensible' (*sensé*) or, as in English, that it 'makes' sense. No doubt because they know and recognize no other thought than the thought of the 'thinker', and cannot grant human dignity without granting what seems to be constitutive of that dignity, anthropologists have never known how to rescue the people they were studying from the barbarism of pre-logic except by identifying them with the most prestigious of their colleagues – logicians or philosophers (I am thinking of the famous title, 'The primitive as philosopher'). As Hocart puts it, 'Long ago [man] ceased merely to live and started to think how he lived; he ceased merely to feel life: he conceived it. Out of all the phenomena contributing to life he formed a concept of life, fertility, prosperity, and vitality'. Claude Lévi-Strauss does just the same when he confers on myth the task of resolving logical problems, of expressing, mediating and masking social contradictions – mainly in some earlier analyses, such '*La geste d'Asdiwal*' – or when he makes it one of the sites where, like Reason in history according to Hegel, the universal Mind thinks itself, thereby offering for observation 'the universal laws which govern the unconscious activities of the mind'.

The indeterminacy surrounding the relationship between the observer's

* From Pierre Bourdieu, *The Logic of Practice*, translated by Richard Nice, Copyright 1989, Polity Press, Cambridge, pp. 36–41. Reproduced by permission of Blackwell Publishers and Stanford University Press.

viewpoint and that of the agents is reflected in the indeterminacy of the relationship between the constructs (diagrams or discourses) that the observer produces to account for practices, and these practices themselves. This uncertainty is intensified by the interferences of the native discourse aimed at expressing or regulating practice – customary rules, official theories, sayings, proverbs, etc. – and by the effects of the mode of thought that is expressed in it. Simply by leaving untouched the question of the principle of production of the regularities that he records and giving free rein to the 'mythopoeic' power of language, which, as Wittgenstein pointed out, constantly slips from the substantive to the substance, objectivist discourse tends to constitute the model constructed to account for practices as a power really capable of determining them. Reifying abstractions (in sentences like 'culture determines the age of weaning'), it treats its constructions – 'culture', 'structures', 'social classes' or 'modes of production' – as realities endowed with a social efficacy. Alternatively, giving concepts the power to act in history as the words that designate them act in the sentences of historical narrative, it personifies collectives and makes them subjects responsible for historical actions (in sentences like 'the bourgeoisie thinks that . . .' or 'the working class refuses to accept'). And, when the question cannot be avoided, it preserves appearances by resorting to systematically ambiguous notions, as linguists say of sentences whose representative content varies systematically with the context of use.

Thus the notion of the rule which can refer indifferently to the regularity immanent in practices (a statistical correlation, for example), the model constructed by science to account for it, or the norm consciously posited and respected by the agents, allows a fictitious reconciliation of mutually contradictory theories of action. I am thinking, of course, of Chomsky, who (in different contexts) describes grammatical rules as instruments of description of language; as systems of norms of which speakers have a certain knowledge; and finally as neuro-physiological mechanisms ('A person who knows a language has represented in his brain some very abstract system of underlying structures along with an abstract system of rules that determine, by free iteration, an infinite range of sound-meaning correspondences'). But it is also instructive to re-read a paragraph from the preface to the second edition of *The Elementary Structures of Kinship*, in which one may assume that particular care has been taken with the vocabulary of norms, models or rules, since the passage deals with the distinction between 'preferential systems' and 'prescriptive systems': 'Conversely, a system which *recommends* marriage with the mother's brother's daughter may be called prescriptive even if the *rule* is seldom observed, since it says what *must* be done. The question of how far and in what proportion the members of a given society *respect the norm* is very interesting, but a different question to that of where this society should properly be placed in a typology. It is sufficient to acknowledge the likelihood that *awareness* of the *rule* inflects *choices* ever so little in the *prescribed* directions, and that the percentage of *conventional* marriages is higher than would be the case if marriages were made *at random*, to be able to recognize what might be called a matrilateral *operator* at work in this society and acting as a pilot: certain alliances at least follow the path which it charts out for them, and this suffices to imprint a specific curve in the genealogical space. No doubt there will be not just one curve but a great number of local curves, merely incipient for the most part, however, and forming closed cycles only in rare and exceptional cases. But the *structural* outlines which emerge here and there will be enough for the system to be used in making a *probabilistic version* of more rigid systems, the notion of which is completely *theoretical* and in which marriage would conform rigorously to *any rule the social group pleases to enunciate*'.

The dominant tonality in this passage, as in the whole preface, is that of the norm, whereas *Structural Anthropology* is written in the language of the model or structure; not that such terms are entirely absent here, since the metaphors organizing the central passage ('operator', 'curve' in 'genealogical space', 'structural outlines') imply the logic of the theoretical model and the equivalence (which is both professed and repudiated) of the model and the norm: 'A preferential system is prescriptive when envisaged at the level of the model, a prescriptive system can only be preferential when envisaged at the level of reality'.

But for the reader who remembers the passages in *Structural Anthropology* on the relationship between language and kinship (for example, ' "Kinship systems", like "phonemic systems", are built up by the mind on the level of unconscious thought') and the imperious way in which 'cultural norms' and all the 'rationalizations' or 'secondary arguments' produced by the natives were rejected in favour of the 'unconscious structures', not to mention the texts asserting the universality of the fundamental rule of exogamy, the concessions made here to 'awareness of the rule' and the dissociation from rigid systems 'the notion of which is entirely theoretical', may come as a surprise, as may this further passage from the same preface: 'It is nonetheless true that the empirical reality of so-called prescriptive systems only takes on its full meaning when related to a *theoretical model worked out by the natives themselves* prior to ethnologists'; or again:

'Those who practise them *know full well* that the spirit of such systems cannot be reduced to the tautological proposition that each group obtains its women from "givers" and gives its women to "takers". They are also *aware* that marriage with the matrilateral cross cousin (mother's brother's daughter) provides the simplest illustration of the rule, the form most likely to *guarantee its survival*. On the other hand, marriage with the patrilateral cross cousin (father's sister's daughter) would violate it irrevocably'.

It is tempting to quote in reply a passage in which Wittgenstein effortlessly brings together all the questions evaded by structural anthropology and, no doubt, more generally by all intellectualism, which transfers the objective truth established by science into a practice that by its very essence rules out the theoretical stance which makes it possible to establish that truth: 'What do I call "the rule by which he proceeds"? – The hypothesis that satisfactorily describes his use of words, which we observe; or the rule which he looks up when he uses signs; or the one which he gives us in reply when we ask what his rule is? – But if observation does not enable us to see any clear rule, and the question brings none to light? – For he did indeed give me a definition when I asked him what he understood by "N", but he was prepared to withdraw and alter it. So how am I to determine the rule according to which he is playing? He does not know it himself. – Or, to ask a better question: What meaning is the expression "the rule by which he proceeds" supposed to have left to it here?'.

To slip from *regularity*, i.e. from what recurs with a certain statistically measurable frequency and from the formula which describes it, to a consciously laid down and consciously respected *ruling* (*règlement*), or to unconscious regulating by a mysterious cerebral or social mechanism, are the two commonest ways of sliding from the model of reality to the reality of the model. In the first case, one moves from a rule which, to take up Quine's distinction between *to fit* and *to guide*, fits the observed regularity in a purely descriptive way, to a rule that governs, directs or orients behaviour – which presupposes that it is known and recognized, and can therefore be stated – thereby succumbing to the most elementary form of legalism, that variety of finalism which is perhaps the most widespread of the spontaneous theories of practice and which consists in proceedings as if practices had as their principle conscious obedience to consciously devised and sanctioned rules. As Ziff puts it:

'Consider the difference between saying "The train is *regularly* two minutes late" and "*As a rule*, the train is two minutes late" . . . There is the suggestion in the later case that the train be two minutes late is as it were in accordance with some policy or plan . . . Rules connect with plans or policies in a way that regularities do not . . . To argue that there must be rules in the natural language is like arguing that roads must be red if they correspond to red lines on a map'.

In the second case, one acquires the means of proceeding as if the principle (if not the end) of the action were the theoretical model one has to construct in order to account for it, without however falling into the most flagrant naiveties of legalism, by settling up as the principle of practices or institutions objectively governed by rules unknown to the agents – significations without a signifying intention, finalities without consciously posited ends, which are so many challenges to the old dilemma of mechanism and finalism – an unconscious defined as a mechanical operator of finality. Thus, discussing Durkheim's attempts to 'explain the genesis of symbolic thought', Lévi-Strauss writes:

'Modern sociologists and psychologists resolve such problems by appealing to the unconscious activity of the mind; but when Durkheim was writing, psychology and modern linguistics had not yet reached their main conclusions. This explains why Durkheim foundered in what he regarded as an irreducible antinomy (in itself a considerable progress over late nineteenth-century thought as exemplified by Spencer): the blindness of history and the finalism of consciousness. Between the two there is *of course the unconscious finality of the mind*'.

It is easy to imagine how minds trained to reject the naivety of finalist explanations and the triviality of causal explanations (particularly 'vulgar' when they invoke economic and social factors) could be fascinated by all the mysterious teleological mechanisms, meaningful and apparently willed products without a producer, which structuralism brought into being by sweeping away the social conditions of production, reproduction and use of symbolic objects in the very process in which it revealed immanent logic. And it is also easy to understand the credit given in advance to Lévi-Strauss's attempt to move beyond the antinomy of action consciously oriented towards rational ends and mechanical reaction to determinations by locating finality in mechanism, with the notion of the unconscious, a kind of *Deus ex machina* which is also a God in the machine.

The naturalization of finality implied in forgetting historical action, which leads one to inscribe the ends of history in the mysteries of a Nature, through the notion of the unconscious, no doubt enabled structural anthropology to appear as the most natural of the social sciences and the most scientific of the metaphysics of nature. 'As the mind *is* also *a thing*, the functioning of this thing teaches us something about the nature of things; even pure reflexion is in the last analysis an internalization of the cosmos'.

One sees the oscillation, in the same sentence, between two contradictory explanations of the postulated identity of mind and nature: an essential identity – the mind is a thing – or an identity acquired through learning – the mind is the internalization of the cosmos. The two theses, which are merged with the help of the ambiguity of another formulation, 'an image of the world inscribed in the architecture of the mind', in any case both exclude individual and collective history. Beneath its air of radical materialism, this philosophy of nature is a philosophy of mind which amounts to a form of idealism. Asserting the universality and eternity of the logical categories that govern 'the unconscious activity of the mind', it ignores the dialectic of social structures and structured, structuring dispositions through which schemes of thought are formed and transformed. These schemes – either logical categories, principles of division which, through the principles of the division of labour, correspond to the structure of the social world (and not the natural world), or temporal structures, imperceptibly inculcated by 'the dull pressure of economic relations' as Marx puts it, that is, by the system of economic and symbolic sanctions associated with a particular position in the economic structures – are one of the mediations through which the objective structures ultimately structure all experience, starting with economic experience, without following the paths of either mechanical determination or adequate consciousness.

If the dialectic of objective structures and incorporated structures which operates in every practical action is ignored, then one necessarily falls into the canonical dilemma, endlessly recurring in new forms in the history of social thought, which condemns those who seek to reject subjectivism, like the present-day structuralist readers of Marx, to fall into the fetishism of social laws. To make transcendent entities, which are to practices as essence to existence, out of the constructions that science resorts to in order to give an account of the structure and meaningful products of the accumulation of innumerable historical actions, is to reduce history to a 'process without a subject', simply replacing the 'creative subject' of subjectivism with an automaton driven by the dead laws of a history of nature. This emanatist vision, which makes a structure – Capital or a Mode of production – into an entelechy developing itself in a process of self-realization, reduces historical agents to the role of 'supports' (*Träger*) of the structure and reduces their actions to mere epiphenomenal manifestations of the structure's own power to develop itself and to determine and overdetermine other structures.

PART 6
New directions and challenges

Introduction: a general outline

The readings in Part 5 traced the gradual demise of positivism in France following the reaction of late twentieth-century thinkers to the structuralism of Lévi-Strauss. While the linguistic turn in French epistemology with Lévi-Strauss' structuralist approach continued the basic positivistic conception of science, this was not to endure: virtually the entire debate on method in France since the 1960s – Lucien Goldmann, Michel Foucault and Pierre Bourdieu – abandoned the basic assumptions of structuralism, thus opening language and culture more generally to new interpretations. All these approaches, in different ways, pointed to the demise not just of positivism, but the possibility of a consensus on method in social science. In the more polemical positions, under the general heading of postmodernism and a variety of anti-foundationalist philosophies, there was a rejection of the authority of the scientific method. With Foucault, the line between power and knowledge was a thin one. Although not all of the new approaches went quite so far, there is a general recognition, which is perhaps best illustrated by Bourdieu, that the scientific method in social science can no longer shield itself from its context and, as a result, the demarcation of science from society, the basis of positivism, becomes increasingly difficult. It is precisely this turn to context that characterizes some of the major debates on method in social science today. In this respect, the premises of the older positivist dispute considered in Parts 1, 2 and 3 of this volume have today been superseded by an entirely new set of assumptions. The central challenge might be summed up in the question whether science can survive the anti-foundationalist current and create a new relationship of knowledge to the world.

In this section we present the major strands that have emerged since the 1980s. In this regard we are moving beyond the immediate horizons of the poststructuralist attack and of the terms of the positivist controversy concerning explanation and understanding. Since the 1980s, but with its origins much earlier, we find a growing debate between constructivism and realism as well as a new debate around relativism and universalism that calls into question some of the presuppositions of critique. When viewed in the longer perspective of the demise of positivism surveyed in the earlier sections of this volume, some general trends can be discerned, and these constitute the basic assumptions of the contemporary epistemological and methodological situation of social science. These can be outlined under the following 12 headings:

1   *Knowledge is historically embedded.* By this is simply meant the recognition that scientific knowledge is historically specific. As is best exemplified in the work of Thomas Kuhn and Michel Foucault, different though these thinkers were, scientific knowledge is embedded in 'paradigms' (Kuhn) or 'discourses' (Foucault) that shift accordingly as major epistemic ruptures occur. This ultimately leads to the incommensurability of historical cultures of knowledge, in the more extreme interpretation. Although not all approaches will share this stronger thesis, virtually every epistemological position today will accept the historical nature of social scientific knowledge.

2   *The relativization of truth.* The intrusion of history into science inevitably led to a certain relativization of truth. The truths of science can no longer be seen as timeless, transhistorical and universal but relative to the scientific context and to the historical location of science in human history. This does not necessarily lead to a rejection of universalism, as in the Enlightenment's proclamation of the timeless nature of science, but to a limited universality. In the work of Apel and Habermas, who reject a Platonic 'covering law universalism' in favour of a Kantian-Peircean 'constructive universalism' (Hauke Brunkhorst), universalism is controlled by hermeneutic experience and interpretative agreement, so that it is possible today only as a limited and highly qualified capacity of critique and reflexivity.

3   *The decline of the neutrality of science.* Knowledge, especially in the social and human sciences, is never neutral but has a valuational dimension built into it. While the explanation-understanding controversy from Dilthey to Weber and beyond was fought around the role of values in sciences, with the proponents of understanding seeking to overcome the separation of facts and values, it was only gradually accepted that science is not neutral. Weber was deeply ambivalent on this. Seeking to rescue as much objectivity as possible for science, the implications of his interpretative approach made a valuational perspective unavoidable. This, too, was the inescapable lesson of Freud's psychoanalytical method, despite all its claims to be a medical science. However, it was not until the advent of critical hermeneutics with Ricoeur, Apel and Habermas that the interpretative tradition accepted what had in fact been central to an older tradition – from Hegel through Marx to critical theory – namely a dialectical relation between science and society. In the American pragmatic tradition from Peirce to Dewey, as discussed in Part 4, science was inherently connected with social practice and the needs of a democratic society. It is increasingly recognized, therefore, that public debate has to be allowed to play a much greater role in science today.

4   *The constitutive nature of theory.* Science is not simply a description of reality, but has a constitutive role. This means that rather than simply providing knowledge of an external reality in the form of a mirror image of it, science in the first place constructs that reality. This assumption has been built into modern epistemology

since Kant and was the basis of Weber's conception of the scientific method as one of ideal types of a reality that was in itself unknowable. For Weber, science must first of all epistemologically and theoretically constitute its object, which in social science will always be an interpretation of an essentially meaningful reality. In the interpretative tradition from Weber onwards, and especially with Schutz, the constitutive role of theory became increasingly emphasized. Habermas and Apel encapsulated the same insight in their theory of cognitive interests, while philosophers of science such as Popper, Piaget, Hanson, Toulmin, Kuhn and Feyerabend formulated it in the so-called 'thesis of theory-ladenness'. For instance, Piaget emphasized that observation is always shot through with theory, Kuhn showed that a paradigm determines what counts as relevant and proper evidence, while the need for a prior theorization of the scientific object was the basis of Popper's critique of induction. Thus, whether for Weber, Popper, Kuhn, Habermas or Bourdieu, facts are first of all constituted by an epistemologically structured theoretical framework.

5   *Knowledge is socially contextualized.* The assumption of the historical location of science and the consequent relativization of truth inevitably opened up a view of science as socially contextualized. The turn to context – under the rubric of locationalism, situationalism, contextualism – is one of the main developments in the epistemology of social science in recent decades. The recognition that science is not demarcated from society demolishes one of the central assumptions of positivism. The demarcation of science from society was likewise one of the central tenets of Popper's critical rationalism, which in opposing other aspects of positivism, such as the priority of induction, did not question this asocial nature of science. While the social contextualization of science is more or less a commonly accepted aspect of science today, views differ greatly on where the limits lie and how far contextualization should be taken. In the more extreme claim, as in certain kinds of contructivism, it is held that all of science is constructed by social actors and that there is no difference between science and other forms of knowledge. Feminism, along with a whole range of standpoints from class and race to gender and ecology, has introduced the salience of the 'standpoint' into science, making it impossible for any normative philosophy to claim an unquestioned standpoint. While many of these notions of standpoint in fact seek the status of foundations based on essentialistic conceptions of identity, on the whole standpoint epistemology has reinforced the general direction towards anti-foundational thinking.

6   *Epistemological uncertainty.* It is increasingly recognized in recent epistemologies of social science that knowledge does not rest on a foundation, but rather involves a self-implicative operation. Gone are the old assumptions connected with the idea of founding such as unity, universality and the ultimate certainty of scientific knowledge. Epistemologically, we can no longer avoid circularity and paradox, while knowledge itself is contested and uncertain. The historical, linguistic and cultural, and more broadly the reflexive, turn in the philosophy of the social sciences has introduced an unavoidable degree of epistemological indeterminacy and uncertainty into the core of science. Increasingly contextualized in other

social discourses, scientific knowledge suffers the same fate that has fallen on most, if not all, normative discourses. Knowledge is not only contested, but there is also less and less consensus on what constitutes method. As Richard Bernstein argues in the reading that follows, fallibilism is an irreversible feature of all of scientific knowledge today, and as Jürgen Habermas insists, the experts have been drawn into legitimation controversies in which publicly acceptable reasons prevail rather than authoritative knowledge as such.

7   *The end of physicalism.* The demise of positivism and the general turn to social and historical context has not led to the death of reality, despite the announcements of the more extreme proponents of postmodernism (such as Jean Baudrillard) or extreme constructivists (such as Bruno Latour or Steve Woolgar). What it has led to is the end of physicalism, at least in its assumption of there being a fixed order of reality external to science, and the redefinition of naturalism. Many of the new philosophies have sought a recovery of a non-physicalist kind of realism, as in Quine's attempt to develop a naturalistic position starting from the participant perspective and the subsequent 'naturalization of epistemology', or Bhaskar's concept of a post-empiricist naturalism. Such post-empiricist conceptions of reality hold that there are multiple orders of reality as well as emergent orders. Reality is not any longer something encapsulated in facts or in general laws that can be observed from a neutral standpoint. This is not just an assumption stemming from social science, but is one that also derives from the natural experimental sciences, which are increasingly seeing nature itself no longer as inert matter but rather as an undivided, multidimensional, processual and even active and creative whole. An increasingly influential view, represented for instance by Luhmann, is that all of reality is characterized by self-organization and thus complexity.

8   *Anti-reductionism.* Post-empiricist philosophies of social science are strongly anti-reductionist. They are opposed not only to the positivist programme of unified science proposing to reduce the language of all science to idealized physics, but also to the positivist tendency, inspired by its principle of empiricism, to lead scientific knowledge back either to the immediate experience of phenomenal entities or to perceptual or physical things or events. The anti-reductionist stance against positivism is reflected also in a general distrust of Marxism's claim to offer an alternative to positivism, given its general tendency to explain social phenomena by reference to class power or capitalism. In this sense, anti-reductionism is simply the recognition of the manifold nature of reality or society and the multiplicity of possible interpretations.

9   *Contingency.* This is a consequence of anti-reductionism and the recognition of the relational nature of reality, including social reality and especially science as a human activity. Contingency is a product, on the one hand, of a world in which chance has replaced necessity, impossibility and determinism, and on the other of a reconstituted social world in which science, as just one activity among others, is surrounded by critical discourses which relativize it and bring the public, in an increasingly significant way, into play. Richard Rorty has been a well known representative of a radicalized hermeneutics that extends contingency into all aspects of society to a point that some of the traditional assumptions of science

are no longer tenable. And towards the end of the twentieth century, a new concept of social contingency, so-called 'triple contingency' (Strydom), has emerged
to capture the role of the public in critical discourses. Contingency has reinforced
assumptions of anti-foundationalism, as Bernstein argues in the first reading of
this section – i.e. the impossibility of securing a fixed and reliable foundation for
scientific knowledge. This is strengthened by the fact that science becomes
increasingly embedded in practical discourses which incorporate scientific
knowledge in appropriate social, ethical and practical frameworks.

10 *Anti-essentialism.* The anti-reductionist tenet is closely linked to anti-essentialism:
the view that the social world cannot be reduced to an essence that is fixed
or unchanging. Anti-essentialism commits social science to the view that social
reality is processual, in flux and multi-faceted.

11 *The world as artifact.* An assumption common to many philosophies of social
science today is that the world is an artifact in the sense of something that is the
product of human creativity. Human beings are seen as being able to create the
world, as in Marx's early notion of *homo faber.* This idea is central not only to
contemporary constructivism, but also to much of realism which also tends to see
the world in terms of a naturalized epistemology.

12 *The decline of disciplinarity.* The transformation of the epistemological assumptions of the sciences has led to a crisis in disciplinarity. This has occurred on two
fronts. The natural, human and social sciences can no longer be so sharply separated from each other as in the tradition of the three cultures of science that grew
out of the institutionalization of science. The social and natural sciences, for
instance, share many concerns as a result of the rise of new discourses (environment, the body, risk) that have problematized the ontological distinction between
humans and nature and are demanding that we treat both in their complexity and
interrelations. All scientific knowledge, irrespective of natural, human or social, is
furthermore increasingly required to pass through the public sphere. Second,
the social sciences have become irreversibly more and more inter-disciplinary,
with research being driven more by problems, ethical-political concerns and
policy directed programmes than by disciplinarily specific traditions concerning
subject domains and particular methods of inquiry. Beyond interdisciplinary
relations, however, questions are today emerging about the potential role of such
new trans-disciplines as semiotics, cybernetics and general systems theory and
their relations to one another.

These assumptions could be regarded as symptoms of a crisis of social science
which is undergoing a major epistemological transformation today, or they may
simply be seen as the signs of a transition. It would be premature to say what will
emerge out of the current reorientation of the social sciences and, therefore, it makes
more sense to see these assumptions as representing the legacy of the twentieth
century; they are thus the challenges and potential elements of a twenty-first century
philosophy of social science.

The readings that follow have been selected with a view to illustrating these
assumptions and challenges as they are expressed in some of the emerging directions.

These directions are particularly evident in the following points around which the readings are broadly grouped: reflexivity, standpoint, rational choice, constructivism, cognitivism and realism. It needs to be said that all the above 12 assumptions are not of course present in any one trend and that these dominant trends are in many cases overlapping. If these assumptions have anything in common, however, it is an understanding of social science as a reflexive relation to an increasingly contingent world. But beyond this concern there is little else that is common to most of these quite different approaches and directions. The following points summarize some of these directions with respect to how they articulate the above-mentioned assumptions. It is to be emphasized that these are not schools of thought but general trends in the philosophy of post-empiricist social science.

Reflexivity

In the wake of the Positivist Dispute, the old transcendental philosophical question of the role of the subject of knowledge in knowledge itself has been introduced into the philosophy of social science. Consequently, the idea of a reflexive social science has become increasingly evident in recent times and the term itself has become a widely used concept in a broad range of contexts, with notions of reflexive modernization, reflexive identity, reflexive communication, reflexive production and reflexive learning increasingly in vogue. The term suggests self-implication or the application of something to itself, and thus in social scientific methodology it indicates an epistemological position in which the researcher questions his/her own role in the research process. In a stronger sense it means self-confrontation. In many ways, the growing adoption of reflexivity in social science is a response to, on the one side, the limits of traditional assumptions about critique and, on the other, the need for social science to express an orientation to the world. Reflexivity avoids the illusions of some of the traditional assumptions of critique in the context of multiple standpoints and normative positions. In this sense, reflexivity is a continuation of critique. It is a response to the growing sense that social science is contextualized in a social and historical milieu, but yet the scientific method entails a certain distance from the social world. The world appears in the constructions of science in a different way than it appears in everyday life. Thus, reflexivity, especially so in the work of Pierre Bourdieu, avoids reducing all scientific knowledge to common-sense knowledge; yet, science must reflexively relate to the world from which it can never entirely separate itself. While in Bourdieu reflexivity is a means of preserving the autonomy of science, a radicalized reflexivity has become apparent in feminist standpoint epistemology. The reading by Anthony Giddens can be located somewhere between these two extremes. For Giddens, reflexivity is primarily increasingly a feature of everyday life but also occurs on a different level within social science.

Standpoint

Since Marx, the critical tradition in social science has assumed the existence of a standpoint outside science from which science obtains its normative direction. This has generally been understood as entailing a certain relation of theory to practice.

While the Marxists generally, but to varying degrees within the different schools, saw this as mediated and not direct, a long-standing assumption was that this standpoint was one related to class, which held a priority over others. Georg Lukács formulated this with particular clarity. In recent decades, radical social science has moved beyond an exclusive orientation around class as the normative standpoint. A whole range of new standpoints have emerged, from gender to race, which constitute the most influential standpoint epistemologies or epistemologies of conviction in recent times. Standpoint epistemology highlights the relativity of truth and the view that knowledge is never neutral but reflects the standpoint of the knower. Feminist standpoint epistemology can be seen as a response to earlier kinds of feminism, such as 'feminist empiricism', which in reflecting the concerns of feminism did not question the nature of method and the assumptions of objectivistic knowledge. It is possible to distinguish three broad categories of feminist standpoint epistemology:

1   *Strong standpoint,* which equates method, truth, objectivity and neutrality with masculine objectivity, postulating women's experience as the starting point and the claim that only women can have knowledge of women. Typically this will have to entail the 'strong' thesis that the researched must be included in the research and that all research is emancipatory for women. In the extreme case, it is the thesis that knowledge is available only from a certain experience.

2   *Weak standpoint* differs from the strong or radical position in that it does not dismiss objectivity and is also more hermeneutic and reflexive. The readings selected below by Dorothy Smith and Donna Haraway are clearly representative of this understanding of standpoint. Haraway, for instance, is as critical of subjectivism as she is of objectivism. Weak standpoint epistemology thus seeks to avoid the tendential essentialism in the stronger forms of standpoint.

3   *Postmodern feminism* represents a move beyond the tendency in the other two versions to reduce standpoint to just one position. While many proponents of postmodern feminism reject attempts to ground knowledge in any form of experience, others, most notably proponents of black and lesbian feminism, simply demand the recognition of multiple and overlapping standpoints. In this respect, gender will have to be reconciled with race and even class. This position is illustrated by the extract from Patricia Hill Collins who represents black feminism.

Despite these differences, standpoint epistemology attempts to give voice to those kinds of human experience that have traditionally been excluded from what is often seen as eurocentric and masculine science. In this sense, it can be seen as a radicalization of consciousness-raising positions in science that began with Marx.

Rational choice

Rational choice emerged in the 1960s around a few seminal texts largely in American social science, but has become increasingly more influential in recent years, especially in economics and political science. While in the view of many it had its roots in Max Weber's theory of action, rational choice is based on the assumption that the social actor, whether the individual or a collectivity, seeks to optimize rational gains within the limits of the objective situation in which the actor finds him, her or itself. Unlike realism, rational choice theory is strongly focused on agency, but like realism it claims to be able to offer an explanatory account of social relations. Undoubtedly, it is this explanatory capacity of rational choice that accounts for much of its popularity. The explanatory models in rational choice differ from positivistic ones in that they are regressive, beginning with outcomes at the macro level which are explained by a series of actions that can be traced back to the actions of individuals. The major early statements of rational choice were Mancur Olson's *The Logic of Collective Action* (1965), Peter Blau's *Exchange and Power in Social Life* (1964) and T.C. Schelling's *Strategy of Conflict* (1960). In the 1980s and 1990s, with major contributions by James Coleman and Jon Elster, rational choice theory, now more closely allied to game theory, became influential due to a shift towards non-cooperative situations and situations where the outcome of an action is never entirely determined by the individual who must take into account the actions of others. Rational choice theories have also become more relevant in the context of contingency, since what is central to these approaches is the availability of information relating to the choices of other actors, as in the so-called 'Prisoner's Dilemma'. Rational choice thus offers a method to explain very real situations, while avoiding reductive and positivistic explanations. Rational choice approaches have been criticized for their methodological individualism, although there is no reason in principle for restricting rational choice explanation to the individual. This is evident from the selected text by Jon Elster. Rational choice approaches have been heavily criticized for their non-sociological view of the social actor who is generally seen as making rational and culturally neutral choices in artificial situations. While being oriented towards explanation, in the view of the critics, rational choice theorists over-stress intentionality and attribute rationality where it might in fact be absent.

Constructivism

As already mentioned, constructivism has become an influential position in the new epistemologies of social science and is fully compatible with most conceptions of reflexivity and with some standpoint epistemologies. However, constructivism takes many forms and frequently goes beyond the assumptions of reflexivity to entail the strong thesis that all of science is constructed by social actors and that social science must be viewed as a reality-creating force.

Many of the epistemological assumptions were inherent in twentieth-century post-empiricist social science which held that science constructs its object and therefore that social reality appears in science in a mediated form. This constructivist assumption was implicit, for instance, in Popper's attack on inductive empiricism with his claim that science does not proceed by means of presuppositionless inquiry but constitutes its object with the aid of epistemological frameworks, theories, concepts and methods. Some of the logical positivists regarded their conventionalist understanding of meaning as constructivist. This constructed view of science was also the idea behind the hypothethico-deductive method. Indeed, the word 'constructivism' had its origins in developments in mathematics. However, the label constructivism cannot be fully applied to these epistemological developments since they lacked the reflexive moment that is characteristic of most kinds of contemporary constructivism. In the social science literature, therefore, the names of Vico and Kant as well as Hegel and Marx are mentioned in connection with the origins of constructivism. Logical positivism and critical rationalism on the whole accepted the social world as it existed. In this respect, contemporary constructivism is different. Moreover, constructivists today deny the normative character of construction.

At least three kinds of constructivism can be identified, with the second being the most influential one:

1 *Social constructionism.* One of the older assumptions of post-empiricist epistemology is that knowledge is not confined to the world of science but is also to be found in the everyday world where social actors cognitively construct their world using cognitive structures. In this view, the social world is socially constructed. A famous example of this is the book *The Social Construction of Reality* (1966) by Peter Berger and Thomas Luckmann. But many of these older approaches were ontological in their concern with social reality which they simply assumed as continuously being in a process of creation by human agency. This conception of constructivism as 'constructionism' is represented in a more reflexive form in the readings by Cicourel, Garfinkel and Goffman in Part 2. A more recent and critical assessment of constructionism is represented in the reading by Ian Hacking. In the case of this reading, however, we see the influence of the much stronger social constructivist school.

2 *Social constructivism* (or scientific constructivism). This is the stronger thesis which advances the central claim that science is constructed by social actors. Today this is generally what is meant by constructivism, a term that has become associated with a wide variety of positions. Beginning with the so-called 'Strong Programme' of the Edinburgh School and the now famous book by David Bloor, *Knowledge and Social Imagery* (1979), the idea emerged that science is not merely influenced by social factors, as the older sociology of knowledge and sociology of science described above claimed, but its actual content, as opposed to its external form, may in fact be socially constructed. This 'strong' thesis became the basis of a new sociology of science and a new interdisciplinary sub-field, science and technology studies. Some of its most well-known classical texts are Steve Woolgar and Bruno Latour's *Laboratory Life: The Construction of Scientific Facts* (1979) and Karin Knorr-Cetina's *The Manufacture of Knowledge: An Essay on the Constructivist and Contextual Nature of Science* (1981). In the extreme view, it is the claim that there is no essential difference between nature and society, a thesis associated with Latour in the famous book *We Have Never Been Modern* (1993). The short extract by Knorr-Cetina summarizes some of the main ideas of strong constructivism. All these accounts, however, share a view of constructivism as a creative process in which elements of some sort get put together in a combination such that an emergent reality – whether problems, issues, facts, etc. – results. For this reason, many of its proponents situate themselves within a broader realism, where what is real is precisely the capacity to construct social and natural worlds.

However, where these authors differ from realism (see below) and from the older generation of constructionists is in their more reflexive stance. Different forms of constructivism or constructionism are defined by their particular choice of conceiving of the process, the agents, the elements, and the make-up of the various combinations of elements and hence the emergent constructs. An example of this is Knorr-Cetina's constructivism which focuses on the internal practices of the scientific enterprise in which transactions, competition, conflicts and negotiations between scientists lead to emergent outcomes such as conceptual orders, theories, diagrams, laboratory phenomena, facts and knowledge. A further example is Steve Fuller's idea of 'social epistemology'.

3   *Radical constructivism* refers to a more specific development. The term was introduced in the 1970s by Ernst von Glaserfeld, but the roots of the tradition in fact lie in cybernetics, particularly the work of Heinz von Foerster on self-organizing and self-observing systems, and in developments associated with Jean Piaget's psychology. It is closely related also to the cognitive biology of Humberto Maturana and Francisco Varela. In the 1980s, it emerged as the most important perspective in mathematics education. Within social science, a major example is Niklas Luhmann, who under the influence of cognitive biology and cybernetics focuses on the processes of construction in which a system engages in relation to its environment. This version of constructivism, like much radical constructivism, can also be called cognitivist due to assumptions about the system being structured or organized in such a way that it can operate in a closed fashion as a selective and information processing entity, with these structures themselves being central to the system's autopoiesis in simultaneity with its presupposed environment or world. This kind of constructivism is called 'radical' because it seeks to bring ontological argumentation back to the source of the argument in a self-referential or reflexive way. In the selected readings Luhmann represents this tradition within social science. It should be noted, however, that radical constructivists regard Luhmann's work as idiosyncratic, while he in turn rejects the adjective 'radical' as unnecessary and instead speaks of 'operative constructivism'.

Constructivism inevitably reaches certain limits. Underlying it is a fairly strong notion of how scientific knowledge is shaped not just by social factors but by social interests too. It rests on a strong notion of agency and of the internal structure of science being shaped by external, social factors. Developments generally associated with constructivism, but ultimately pointing beyond it, have emerged in recent times that suggest the need to distinguish different approaches. For instance, actor-network theory as represented by the work of Latour has now departed from many of the earlier constructivist assumptions, and in the selection of readings below Hacking encourages us to leave constructivism behind. However, constructivism meets its strongest opposition in realism (see p. 376).

Cognitivism

The emergence of the cognitive sciences opened the way for the study of cognition and knowledge beyond such disciplines as epistemology and psychology traditionally concerned with these topics. After a period of gestation dating from the 1940s, the 'cognitive revolution' occurred in 1956 on the basis of cybernetics, computer science, psychology, epistemology, neuroscience and linguistics. The subsequent maturation of the cognitive sciences between 1960 and 1985, in which artificial intelligence as well as Noam Chomsky's linguistics played a part, took place around a computational or cognitivist model according to which the mind was assumed to process information through the manipulation of symbols in accordance with rules. These new ideas were also brought to bear on the social sciences – sociology and anthropology in particular – but of importance here was also the so-called 'Berkeley approach', the concurrent critique of the narrow computational or cognitivist view in terms of a linguistic theory forming part of a theory of action. Social scientific developments at the time such as ethnomethodology (see Garfinkel and Cicourel in Part 2) and the sociology of science (see Knorr-Cetina, below) that were shaped by these new ideas, although also drawing on older phenomenological, linguistic and sociology of knowledge traditions, had a significant impact on the philosophy of social science. In the early 1980s, for instance, the question arose whether and to what extent a 'cognitive turn' had occurred in sociology. At this stage, the computer-based cognitivist model of computation became supplemented and even challenged by an alternative model based on the brain, not as a rule-governed central information processing unit, but as a neural network that changes through experience. What is called 'connectionism', entailing questions of networks, their self-organization and production of emergent properties, now tended to take the place of the initial, rather narrow, cognitivist model.

Whereas social scientific disciplines had played only an ancillary role during the second phase in the development of the cognitive sciences, the current phase – regarded by some as a phase of 'identity crisis' which started in the mid-1980s – opened the door quite widely for the social sciences to play an influential role in the interdisciplinary interactions shaping the future of the cognitive sciences. For instance, the impact of the sociological and anthropological understanding of situated and mediated action on cognitive psychology and computer science has been quite remarkable. Simultaneously, however, the cognitive transformation of the social sciences is also intensifying. Two directions, which bring with them tensions in the cognitive understanding of social science, are clearly visible today. These tendencies are directly related to the broadening of the cognitive science computer model since the late 1980s, in the direction first of the brain and second of the environment. On the one extreme, Luhmann's cognitive programme rests squarely on the cognitive neuroscientific and biological emphasis on the brain as an operationally closed and autopoietic unit. And recently Stephen Turner used connectionism, based on the study of physical processes in the brain, to develop a critical appreciation of social science after cognitive science. While Turner adopts a naturalist and individualist approach that stresses reorganizing neural patterns unique to each individual, Luhmann offers a collectivist and functionalist approach that focuses on closed self-referential systems which create and regulate themselves. At the other extreme are those philosophers of social science who is some sense or another recognize that cognitive systems are situated in an environment with which they are in constant mediated interaction. The older contributions of Garfinkel, Cicourel and Goffman (see Part 2) fit this category, while such different authors as Habermas, Giddens and Fuller also belong here. An interesting case in cognitive science is Francisco Varela's 'enactivism' or pragmatic cognitivism that clearly defines the third stage in the development of the cognitive approach, beyond both the initial strict 'cognitivism' and the later 'connectionism' or 'emergentism'.

Realism

In the philosophical literature, there are large differences of opinion about what is at issue in the long-standing problem of realism and in the late twentieth century a number of different debates about realism emerged. In the philosophy of social science, however, the constructivist turn from the late 1970s and 1980s, and with it many of the assumptions that emerged out of post-empiricist social science, provoked a reaction in the form of realism. It is indeed possible to see this constructivist-realist controversy as replacing the older explanation-understanding controversy. In this new debate, constructivism, with its characteristic emphasis on interpretation, takes the place of understanding, while realism reconstitutes explanation in a new key. Underlying both epistemologies is a general recognition of the passing of the illusions of positivism. Realism has been particularly influential in British philosophy of social science, with some important contributions made by Rom Harré, Mary Hesse and Roy Bhaskar, and within social theory (in particular sociology), realism has found different voices in Martin Hollis, William Outhwaite, Ted Benton, Russell Keat, John Urry, Margaret Archer and Andrew Sayer. As the term suggests, realism is based on the assumption that an external reality exists which is independent of human consciousness yet can nevertheless be known. Unlike traditional forms of positivism or inductive modes of social inquiry, realism does not make the naïve assumption that reality is easily observable. It rather regards reality as morphologically unfolding and hence as 'emergent' and layered, with the result that there can be no simple recourse to observable causes, as in the Humean theory of causation where regular occurrences must be explained in terms of cause and effects. Realists draw attention to the different levels of causation that go beyond reductive cause-effect models of explanation, such as the mechanisms by which effects operate, the powers and properties that they produce and the intricate interlinkages between the different levels of structures which all make causation very complex and thus irreducible to single factors. Many of its representatives regard realism as implying a political practice that is critical by nature. In the selected reading, realism is represented by Roy Bhaskar's particular epistemology of critical realism and is also reflected in the excerpt from Randall Collins, where a more compromising position with constructivism is indicated. Essentially, realism is the thesis that social science must concern itself with underlying structures and must not relinquish the goal of explanation as the key characteristic of all of science. While social scientific realists on the whole are opposed to the projectionism of the constructivist tendency to see society as the outcome of agency, it is important not see realism and constructivism – indeed also cognitivism –

as incompatible. It needs to be emphasized that constructivists are not necessarily idealists – they are not saying that reality is imagined or does not exist, but that reality exists in science only in ways defined by science. The kind of realism that constructivists adhere to is one that sees things as real in their consequences but not in their causes. It is in this respect that constructivists and realists disagree. Constructivists are anti-realist about the nature of causes, which they tend to see as defined by the conceptual systems within science and, moreover, they question the assumptions about truth and falsity.

It is possible to detect a movement towards a reconciliation of realism and constructivism in several developments in recent years – for instance, Rom Harré's embracing of constructivism in his attempt to distinguish himself from his rival Bhaskar, or in Habermas' adoption of a pragmatic realism which nevertheless leaves room for constructivism. In the work of Hilary Putnam and Ian Hacking, the line between realism and constructivism is also very thin. The final reading by Habermas provides a good example of the mediation of realism and constructivism. However, it seems as if he is suggesting that it is in the cognitive dimension that a bridge between these two positions is to be found. For Habermas sees the basic cognitive forms through which we are able to engage in constructive activities geared toward the realization of an inclusive, democratically organized social world as emerging in the first instance from natural historical processes in which we maintain pragmatic relations with reality.

The selected texts

Richard J. Bernstein (1932–) is Professor of Philosophy at the New School for Social Research, New York, and the author of several influential books, including *Praxis and Action* (1971), *Beyond Objectivism and Relativism* (1983), *The Restructuring of Social and Political Theory* (1976) and *The New Constellation: The Ethical-Political Horizons of the Modernity/Postmodernity Debate* (1991). It is from the latter work that the present reading is taken. The reading gives a clear account of the idea of 'anti-foundationalism', which Bernstein traces back to the pragmatic philosophy of Peirce which opposed Cartesianism in the sense of a search for rational foundations (see Part 4). He sees anti-foundationalism as compatible with many non-dogmatic tendencies in modern thought and argues that it does not necessarily lead to extreme forms of relativism or scepticism. Anti-foundationalism is compatible with critical thought, plurality and a social understanding of the self.

Pierre Bourdieu (1930–2002), discussed in Part 5, is a major proponent of reflexivity. In the present reading we find a lucid and strongly argued case for reflexivity as a kind of 'radical doubt'. Bourdieu begins by making a distinction between common-sense and social scientific knowledge. But the latter, while being irreducible to the former, is also not entirely separate from it, for science is a product of the social world. The question is how science can be practiced in a way that does not reduce it to its object. It is in essence for Bourdieu a question of how a critical space for intellectual, academic autonomy can be preserved. The text, too, can be read as a constructivist statement: science necessarily entails the construction of the object, which never appears in a pure, empirical form. But for Bourdieu a constructivist approach will involve a reflexive moment in so far as it requires self-questioning. The social scientist must first of all objectify the object of research and then, to avoid the illusion of total objectivity, subject the scientific process to radical doubt. This reflexivity will also entail the incorporation of the standpoint of the social actor. However, it is to be noted that reflexivity in this sense is different from Gouldner's (see Part 3), which in Bourdieu's terms would be levelling scientific knowledge too much to the standpoint of the subject's self-awarness. In the selected text, Bourdieu refers to how social problems get constructed, even 'officialized' as the issues to be researched and discussed in social science. So, for him, social science is context-bound, but through its methods it can maintain a distance from the pre-theoretical world of common-sense and the official discourses of society. In this way, Bourdieu aims to avoid both object-ivism and subjectivism. It is a conception of reflexivity that is strongly tied to a belief in the ability of science to offer explanatory accounts of social realities which ultimately transcend everyday forms of consciousness. The feminist standpoint texts that follow take much further Bourdieu's attempt to mediate the researcher with the object of research, for in Bourdieu this is a weak reflexivity.

Anthony Giddens (1938–) is one of the leading British social theorists. Although not primarily known for philosophy of social science, the selected text, from his major epistemological and methodological work, *The Constitution of Society* (1984), is a statement of his most well known idea, namely that of the 'double hermeneutic'. This means that the reflexivity of science is built upon the reflexivity of everyday life. Giddens adopts a cognitive hermeneutics that sees everyday life as entailing know-ledge, by which he understands forms of social interpretation. Social actors are 'knowledgeable agents', he argues. Social science is a reflexive operation involving interpretations that are built upon everyday interpretations. His main point, which derives from the phenomenological and hermeneutical traditions of Schutz and Garfinkel, is that 'The concepts that sociological observers invent are "second-order" concepts in so far as they presume certain conceptual capabilities on the part of the actors to whose conduct they refer'. The cognitivist assumptions of his approach are evident in the sentence: 'The social scientist is a communicator, intro-ducing frames of meaning associated with certain contexts of social life to those in others'.

Dorothy Smith (1926–) is one of the most well known writers on the question of method in social science from a feminist perspective. Canadian by nationality, she has studied and taught at the University of California, Berkeley, and in universities in Canada. Her main books include *The Conceptual Practices of Power* (1990) and *The Everyday World as Problematic: A Feminist Sociology* (1987), from which the reading in this section has been taken. In this excerpt, Smith argues against any simplistic equa-tion of the standpoint of women with a worldview or an ideological position that universalizes a particular experience. In this respect, her notion of standpoint epis-temology is anti-reductionist and can be characterized as a method designed to articu-late excluded forms of experience within the limits of a reflexively constituted science. This line of reasoning might be located somewhere between Gouldner's and

Bourdieu's notion of reflexivity. The challenge, as she sees it for feminist methodology, is how to make science reflect women's experience. She offers the argument
that one key dimension in this is the recognition of the exclusion of women's experience from the world of science. The starting point thus must be actual experience in
everyday life.

Donna Haraway (1944–) studied at Yale University and currently teaches at the
University of California, Santa Cruz. Her main works are *Primate Visions: Gender,
Race, and Nature in the World of Modern Science* (1989) and *Simians, Cyborgs and
Women* (1991). The selected reading is an excerpt from an article in the journal
Feminist Studies in 1988 which is a classic statement of a sophisticated standpoint
epistemology. As the title indicates, it concerns the notion of 'situated knowledge', by
which Haraway means that knowledge is socially contextualized rather than being
unlocatable. In her view, responsible science must be capable of being called into
account and this is not possible if it is disconnected from any social context. The text
differs from the preceding one by Dorothy Smith in arguing more strongly for a
perspective 'from below' or, as Haraway puts it, the 'standpoint of the subjugated'.
She argues strongly against relativism, which she regards as a false solution to the
problems of universalism or 'totalization'. Thus standpoint epistemology for her is
within the bounds of scientific objectivity. The reading makes the important point
that objectivity here means expressing modes of contestation, deconstruction and
processes of construction, thus locating the text within the broad span of constructivism. The latter part of the text presents the key notion as to the meaning of objectivity,
namely the 'partial perspective' – the rejection of the totalizing and objectivating
attitude that has been characteristic of positivistic science. This, she also argues,
entails the rejection of feminist essentialistic epistemologies or appeals to identity that
simply substitute one totalizing view for another.

Patricia Hill Collins (1948–) is Professor of African-American studies at the University of Cincinnati and author of an influential work, *Black Feminist Thought* (1990).
The selected text is an excerpt from a much cited article published earlier in *Social
Problems* in 1986, the significance of which is the application of social theory and
philosophy of social science to black feminist thought. The article reveals the epistemological significance of the work of black feminist authors in combining the
standpoints of gender and race, and in this respect advances the debate on standpoint
beyond Haraway. The key concept is that of the 'outsider within': Hill Collins argues
that social science can learn from the experience of black women, who in the academic world are in one sense outsiders, but are also inside the community of scholars.
The understanding of standpoint in this article is a reflexive one, but one mediated by
processes of inclusion and exclusion. In the excerpt, the notion of standpoint is situated in the context of cognitive models and the argument made that one neglected
aspect of these is the process by which an outsider becomes an insider – a process that
Hill Collins thinks opens up important epistemological questions concerning the
nature of social scientific knowledge.

Karin Knorr-Cetina (1944–), since the early 1990s Professor of Sociology at the

University of Bielefeld, Germany, is Austrian with a background in cultural anthropology. Through affiliation with American institutions such as the Ford Foundation (1976–7) and the Institute for Advanced Studies in Princeton (1992–3), she came to have a discernible impact on the philosophy of social science. During the early 1980s she published a number of important works, including *The Manufacture of Knowledge* (1981), *Advances in Social Theory and Methodology* (edited with Aaron Cicourel, 1981) and *Science Observed* (edited with Michael Mulkay, 1983), which played an important part in redirecting the older institutionally oriented sociology of science toward the study of science as culture and practice. In these works, she advanced a particular but influential conception of constructivism which she defends in the selected reading on 'strong constructivism'.

Ian Hacking (1936–) was born in Vancouver and studied at the University of British Columbia and Cambridge University, then held positions at many universities in Europe and America. He is University Professor of Philosophy at the University of Toronto and is also Professor of Philosophy and History of Scientific Concepts at the Collège de France in Paris. He has published extensively in logic and the philosophy of science and his many books include *Probability and Inductive Logic* (2001), *Historical Ontology* (2002), *The Emergence of Probability* (1984) and *What Does Language Matter to Philosophy?* (1975). Some of this recent work has involved influential articles on constructivism, many of which have appeared in his *The Social Construction of What?* (1999). The selected essay is a previously unpublished paper and offers a critical analysis of the application of constructivism in social science.

Steve Fuller (1959–), was born in New York, has a background in the history and philosophy of science and taught at both American and British universities before becoming Professor of Sociology at the University of Warwick in the late 1990s. In the late 1980s he contributed to the forging of the identity of science and technology studies (STS) through the development of his 'social epistemology', the title of a journal he founded in 1987. His books include *Social Epistemology* (1988), *Philosophy, Rhetoric, and the End of Knowledge* (1993), *The Governance of Science* (2000) and *Thomas Kuhn: A Philosophical History for Our Times* (2000). His emphasis on social constructivism and the significance of the public sphere for science is apparent from the selected reading: His social epistemology can also be taken to represent a 'weak naturalism', but one that is closer to Dewey's than to either Quine's or Bhaskar's.

Niklas Luhmann (1927–98), Professor of Sociology at the University of Bielefeld from 1968 until his retirement in the early 1990s, was one of late twentieth-century Germany's most prolific and influential sociologists. Since his reformulation in the early 1980s of his systems functionalism in the so-called 'autopoietic' terms of Humberto Maturana and Francisco Varela's cognitive biology, he exhibited an increasing interest in epistemological questions. Among his most important works in this field are such relatively late books as *Erkenntnis als Konstruktion* (1988), *Soziologische Aufklärung 5: Konstruktivistische Perspektiven* (1990) and *Die Wissenschaft der Gesellschaft* (1992). The selected reading is an excerpt from a paper dating from this period in Luhmann's development which he originally delivered in 1988 at a conference in

Bielefeld on the late twentieth-century scientific revolution centred on the concepts of self-organization and complexity and finding expression in the new constructivist approach. In this text, Luhmann introduces a range of new ideas deriving from cybernetics, developmental and linguistic psychology, biology and cognitive science which thus far have been largely neglected in the social sciences. Against the background of a critique of traditional epistemology and the philosophy of social science, Luhmann opens the text with a clarification of the conditions that have led to the strong emergence of constructivism in the late twentieth century. Although he believes that the conditions are now ripe for the first time for constructivism to come into its own, he attacks extant versions of constructivism, such as those focusing on 'conventions' (e.g. Thomas Kuhn) and 'negotiation' (e.g. Knorr-Cetina). Instead, he proposes a cognitivist constructivism that proceeds from systems theoretical distinctions such as 'system/environment' and 'operation/observation' which he regards as having displaced traditional ones such as 'transcendental/empirical', 'subject/object' and 'being/non-being'. From a cognitive constructivist perspective, according to him, a cognitive system is a 'real (empirical – that is, observable) system in a real world', yet it is 'operationally closed' and therefore 'separated from its environment'. The real world to which the system belongs is indeed all the while presupposed, but it is 'only cognitively . . . approachable' and is thus 'constituted over [the system's own] distinctions' from the point of view of whether the results are 're-usable' for system decisions. Constructivism thus involves a 'de-ontologization of reality' in that it avoids dealing with reality in terms of the ontological question of whether it exists or not.

Roy Bhaskar (1944–), a British philosopher with Indian and British parents, has taught at the Universities of Oxford, Edinburgh and Sussex and is at present Research Fellow at the City University, London, and Linacre College, Oxford. A student of the ex-engineer and philosopher of science Rom Harré, he transformed the latter's metaphysically revanchist Aristotelian realism into an original 'transcendental realism' which he has sought to give a 'practically-oriented' thrust by linking it to Marxism. The resulting 'critical realism' has generated a wide-ranging resonance within Britain but also internationally. His books include *A Realist Theory of Science* (1975, 1978), *The Possibility of Naturalism: A Philosophical Critique of the Contemporary Human Sciences* (1979, 1989) and *Philosophy and the Idea of Freedom* (1991), while Margaret Archer, Bhaskar and others recently edited an anthology on *Critical Realism: Essential Readings* (1998). In the selected reading, an extract from *The Possibility of Naturalism*, Bhaskar criticizes positivism and hermeneutics, what he regards as the two major traditions in the philosophy of social science, for being mirror images of each other and thus sharing the same erroneous presuppositions of empiricism and individualism. Instead, he proposes his own 'transcendental realism' which focuses neither on natural events nor on their social scientific counterpart, behaviour or action, but rather on 'structures' conceived in the essentialist terms of revived Aristotlian metaphysics. On the basis of the resulting non-reductionist and non-scientistic or 'non-positivist naturalism', he claims that, while the social sciences differ from the natural sciences in object, in predicates requiring explanation and in procedure or method, there is a unity of science embracing both categories of discipline. That Bhaskar's emphasis is squarely on science and the philosophy of science as such reveals that he leaves little or no room for the network of communicative or discursive relations in which science is increasingly seen to stand, for instance by such authors as Habermas, Bernstein and Fuller, not to mention Rorty.

Jon Elster (1940–) was born in Oslo and is Robert K. Merton Professor of Social Science at Columbia University, New York. He studied at the Universities of Oslo and Paris V and previously taught at the University of Paris VIII, Oslo and Chicago. His publications include *Ulysses and the Sirens* (1979), *Sour Grapes* (1983), *Making Sense of Marx* (1985), *Nuts and Bolts for the Social Sciences* (1989), *The Cement of Society* (1989), *Local Justice* (1992), *Alchemies of the Mind* (1999) and *Ulysses Unbound* (2000). The chosen text offers a good example of rational choice reasoning. By means of four examples Elster demonstrates the radically subjective nature of social action, which he regards as the basis of society. He argues that social action is primarily intentional and rational. This argument claims to offer social science a means of explanatory reasoning which differs from, for example, functional explanation in that it does not explain the action in terms of outcomes but in terms of intentions.

Randall Collins (1941–) studied at Harvard and the University of California and established his reputation in the sociology of conflict, the sociology of knowledge and sociological theory. He is currently at the University of Pennsylvannia. His major publications include *Conflict Sociology* (1975), *The Credential Society* (1979) and *The Sociology of Philosophies* (1998) from which the present reading derives. The reading argues that constructivism and realism, which are often counterposed, are in fact compatible. Collins argues that constructivism is a meaningless idea if it denies objectivity and thus makes the argument that sociological knowledge concerns realities. However, realism is not opposed to constructivism since much of reality is constituted by cultural and cognitive processes.

Jürgen Habermas (1929–) was introduced in Part 2 and 3 as a major force in the development of different directions in the philosophy of social science in the twentieth century. In the selected text, an excerpt from a book published in his seventieth year, *Wahrheit und Rechtfertigung* (1999), Habermas takes up once again a series of epistemological questions which he had left in abeyance after *Knowledge and Human Interests* (1968, translation 1972) when he was convinced that he could displace them by basing the critical theory of society directly on a linguistic foundation. That he now revisits his earlier 'weak naturalism' and 'transcendental-pragmatic cognitive realism', which he left unattended between the early 1970s and the late 1990s, is an admission that the problem of the transcendental conditions of knowledge does not allow itself to be easily shelved. The viewpoint he adopts for these purposes is what he calls 'Kantian pragmatism' within the framework of the twentieth-century 'linguistic-pragmatic turn'. Arguing against the widely adopted forms of both Quinean naturalism and Heideggerian idealism, Habermas defends a 'weak naturalism' instead. The latter proceeds from the assumption that there is a 'continuity between nature and culture', or an 'analogy' between the natural historical processes giving rise to *Homo sapiens* and human sociocultural forms of life. It is interesting that this analogy is a cognitive one in that it assumes 'a "scale" of learning processes at different levels' which are connected to one another through operative cognitive forms. Through the solution of evolutionary problems, natural historical development gives rise to 'naturally formed structures' possessing 'cognitive import' that in turn make it possible for human beings living in sociocultural forms of life to 'make experiences of and statements about . . . the objective world', to learn and develop knowledge of it, and eventually to pursue in a 'constructivist' manner the realization of a 'social world' of 'well-ordered interpersonal relations' and the 'ever-widening inclusion of other claims and persons' which 'cannot become real without the assistance of the morally acting subjects themselves'. The constraints under which this takes place derive, on the one hand, from the objective world which makes itself felt as 'reality' only pragmatically or in so far as we relate to it through action, and, on the other, from the 'contradictions of social opponents whose value-orientations come into conflict' which calls for the 'rationalizing force of a public and inclusive, violence-free and decentring form of argumentation among equals'. What is of particular interest in these late reflections of Habermas is that he here takes a position which seems to bridge the currently much debated divide between realism and constructivism. For he renews his claim of a 'transcendental-pragmatic cognitive realism' that is based on a 'weak naturalism' yet at the same time makes room for a cognitive 'constructivist thrust' of social subjects within their sociocultural lifeworld who deal not only intelligently with a 'risky and disillusioning reality' but also morally with a 'social world . . . which they themselves design . . . as a universe they themselves still have to realize'.

51

RICHARD J. BERNSTEIN
'Anti-foundationalism'* (1991)

With an eye to the present, let me turn to five interrelated substantive themes that enable us to characterize the pragmatic ethos:

(1) "Anti-foundationalism" is not an expression that the pragmatists used. They certainly did not mean what is sometimes meant today when "anti-foundationalism" is polemically used to attack the very idea of philosophy. Yet I do not think there is an important argument in the anti-foundationalist arsenal that was not anticipated (and sometimes stated in a much more trenchant form) in the remarkable series of articles that Peirce published in 1868. Peirce presents a battery of arguments directed against the idea that knowledge rests upon fixed foundations, and that we possess a special faculty of insight or intuition by which we can know these foundations. Peirce was exposing what has come to be called "the metaphysics of presence." Peirce realized that in criticizing foundationalism he was attacking many of the most cherished doctrines and dogmas that constituted modern philosophy. He makes this clear when he contrasts Cartesianism with the scholasticism that it displaced. He begins his article "Some Consequences of Four Incapacities" by declaring:

> Descartes is the father of modern philosophy, and the spirit of Cartesianism – that which principally distinguishes it from the scholasticism which it displaced – may be compendiously stated as follows:

> 1   It teaches that philosophy must begin with universal doubt, whereas scholasticism had never questioned fundamentals.

> 2   It teaches that the ultimate test of certainty is to be found in individual consciousness; whereas scholasticism had rested on the testimony of sages and of the Catholic Church.

> 3   The multiform argumentation of the Middle Ages is replaced by a single thread of inference depending often on inconspicuous premises.

* From Richard J. Bernstein *The New Constellation: The Ethical-Political Horizons of Modernity/Postmodernity*. MIT Press, 1991, pp. 326–330, 336. Reproduced with permission of the publisher.

4   Scholasticism had its mysteries of faith, but undertook to explain all created things. But there are many facts which Cartesianism not only does not explain but renders absolutely inexplicable, unless to say 'God makes them so' is regarded as an explanation.

In some, or all these respects, most modern philosophers have been, in effect, Cartesians. Now without wishing to return to scholasticism, it seems to me that modern science and modern logic require us to stand upon a very different platform from this.

Peirce realized that his critique of Cartesianism, his elaboration of a different platform that is required by modern science and logic, required a rethinking of every major philosophic problem. For in one fell swoop he sought to demolish the idea that there are or can be any absolute beginnings or endings in philosophy. He sought to exorcize what Dewey later called "the quest for certainty" and the "spectator theory of knowledge." He called into question the privileged status of subjectivity and consciousness that had dominated so much of modern philosophy. He elaborated a theory of signs where interpretants are always and necessarily open to further interpretation, determination, and critical correction.

We find variations on these themes in all the pragmatic thinkers. We can see how subsequent philosophers have continued to refine the anti-foundational arguments adumbrated by Peirce. They are developed further in Quine's own distinctive version of pragmatism and in Wilfrid Sellars' work when he criticizes "the myth of the given" and declares that "empirical knowledge, like its sophisticated extension science, is rational, not because it has a foundation, but because it is a self-correcting enterprise which can put any claim in jeopardy, though not all at once."

(2)   But if we abandon foundationalism and the craving for absolutes, then what is the alternative? There are many who have thought that to give up foundationalism can lead only to some version of skepticism or relativism. But this was not the response of Peirce and the pragmatists. Their alternative to foundationalism was to elaborate a thoroughgoing fallibilism where we realize that although we must begin any inquiry with prejudgments and can never call everything into question at once, nevertheless there is no belief or thesis – no matter how fundamental – that is not open to further interpretation and criticism. Peirce advocated that we displace the "foundation" metaphor with the metaphor of a "cable." In philosophy, as in the sciences, we ought to "trust rather to the multitude and variety of its arguments than to the conclusiveness of any one. Its reasoning should not form a chain which is no stronger than its weakest link, but a cable whose fibers may be ever so slender, provided they are sufficiently numerous and intimately connected." The pragmatists argued not only that fallibilism is characteristic of the experimental habit of mind but that philosophy itself is intrinsically fallibilistic. Philosophy is interpretive, tentative, always subject to correction.

(3)   It is this fallibilism that brings me to the next theme that is so vital for the pragmatists – the social character of the self and the need to nurture a critical

community of inquirers. If we are fallible and always limited in our perspectives then "we individually cannot reasonably hope to attain the ultimate philosophy which we pursue; we can only seek it, therefore, for the community of philosophers. Hence, if disciplined and candid minds carefully examine a theory and refuse to accept it, this ought to create doubts in the mind of the author of the theory himself." The theme of the social character of the self and of community is played out in many variations by the pragmatic thinkers. The very idea of an individual consciousness that is independent of shared social practices is criticized. In this respect, the pragmatists sought to dismantle and deconstruct the philosophy of consciousness and the philosophy of subjectivity. What has come to be called the decentering of the subject is integral to the pragmatic project. Peirce appeals to the regulative ideal of a critical community of inquirers. Royce sought to extend this ideal to a universal community of interpreters. Dewey explored the social and political consequences of the idea of community for understanding the moral ideal of democracy. Mead was a pioneer in developing a theory of the social-psychological genesis of the social self – a theory of "practical intersubjectivity."

Today there are many who have raised doubts about the Peircian conviction that – in the long run – there will be a convergence of inquiry. But doubts about all ideal convergence do not undermine the necessity of always appealing to a critical community. On the contrary, they heighten its importance. For it is only by submitting our hypotheses to public critical discussion that we become aware of what is valid in our claims and what fails to withstand critical scrutiny. It is only by the serious encounter with what is other, different, and alien that we call hope to determine what is idiosyncratic, limited, and partial.

(4) Anti-foundationalism, fallibilism, and the nurturing of critical communities leads to the fourth theme running through the pragmatic tradition – the awareness and sensitivity to radical contingency and chance that mark the universe, our inquiries, our lives. Contingency and chance have always been problematic for philosophy. In the concern with universality and necessity, there has been a deep desire to master, contain and repress contingency – to assign it to its "proper" restricted place. For the pragmatists, contingency and chance are not merely signs of human ignorance, they are ineradicable and pervasive features of the universe. Long before the rise of quantum physics, Peirce developed a variety of arguments against the doctrine of mechanical necessity. He speculatively advanced the theory of cosmic evolution where there is a continuous interplay between evolving laws – habits of nature – and chance. But the insistence on the inescapability of chance and contingency – on what Dewey called "the precariousness of existence" where the world is a scene of risk and is "uncannily unstable" – conditioned their understanding of experience and philosophy itself. We can never hope to "master" unforeseen and unexpected contingencies. We live in an "open universe" which is always at once threatening and a source of tragedy and opportunity. This is why the pragmatists placed so much emphasis on how we are to respond to contingencies – on developing the complex of dispositions and critical habits that Dewey called "reflective intelligence."

(5) I come finally to the theme of plurality. We can see how it pervades the other

themes that I have sketched. There can be no escape from plurality – a plurality of traditions, perspectives, philosophic orientations . . . The type of pragmatism that represents what is best in our pragmatic tradition is an engaged fallibilistic pluralism. Such a pluralistic ethos places new responsibilities on each of us. For it means taking our own fallibility seriously – resolving that however much we are committed to our own styles of thinking, we are willing to listen to others without denying or suppressing the otherness of the other. It means being vigilant against the dual temptations of simply dismissing what others are saying by falling back on one of those standard defensive ploys where we condemn it as obscure, woolly, or trivial, or thinking we can always easily translate what is alien into our own entrenched vocabularies.

52

PIERRE BOURDIEU
Radical doubt* (1992)

The construction of a scientific object requires first and foremost a break with common sense, that is, with the repesentations shared by all, whether they be the mere commonplaces of ordinary existence or official representations, often inscribed in institutions and thus present both in the objectivity of social organizations and in the minds of their participants. The preconstructed is everywhere. The sociologist is literally beleaguered by it, as everybody else is. The sociologist is thus saddled with the task of knowing an object – the social world – of which he is the product, in a way such that the problems that he raises about it and the concepts he uses have every chance of being the product of this object itself. (This is particularly true of the classificatory notions he employs in order to know it, common notions such as names of occupations or scholarly notions such as those handed down by the tradition of the discipline.) Their self-evident character arises from the fit between objective structures and subjective structures which shields them from questioning.

How can the sociologist effect in practice this radical doubting which is indispensable for bracketing all the presuppositions inherent in the fact that she is a social being, that she is therefore socialized and led to feel 'like a fish in water' within that social world whose structures she has internalized? How can she prevent the social world itself from carrying out the construction of the object, in a sense, through her, through these unselfconscious operations or operations unaware of themselves of which she is the apparent subject? To not construct, as positivist hyperempiricism does when it accepts without critical examination the concepts that offer themselves to it ('achievement' and 'ascription,' 'profession,' 'actor,' 'role,' etc.) is still to construct, because it amounts to recording – and thus to ratifying – something already constructed. Ordinary sociology, which bypasses the radical questioning of its own operations and of its own instruments of thinking, and which would no doubt consider such a reflexive intention the relic of a philosophic mentality, and thus a survival from a prescientific age, is thoroughly suffused with the object it claims to know, and

* From 'Radical Doubt' in *An Invitation to Reflexive Sociology* by Pierre Bourdieu and Loïc Wacquant, University of Chicago Press, 1992. Reproduced by permission of the publisher and author.

which it cannot really know, because it does not know itself. A scientific practice that fails to question itself does not, properly speaking, know what it does. Embedded in, or taken by, the object that it takes as its object, it reveals something of the object, but something which is not really objectivized since it consists of the very principles of apprehension of the object.

It would be easy to show that this half-scholarly science borrows its problems, its concepts, and its instruments of knowledge from the social world, and that it often records as a datum, as an empirical given independent of the act of knowledge and of the science which performs it, facts, representations or institutions which are the product of a prior stage of science. In short, it records itself without recognizing itself . . .

Let me dwell on each of these points for a moment. Social science is always prone to receive from the social world it studies the issues that it poses about that world. Each society, at each moment, elaborates a body of social problems taken to be legitimate, worthy of being debated, of being made public and sometimes officialized and, in a sense, guaranteed by the state. These are for instance the problems assigned to the high-level commissions officially mandated to study them, or assigned also, more or less directly, to sociologists themselves via all the forms of bureaucratic demand, research and funding programs, contracts, grants, subsidies, etc. A good number of objects recognized by official social science and a good many titles of studies are nothing other than social problems that have been smuggled into sociology – poverty, delinquency, youth, high school dropouts, leisure, drunken driving, and so on – and which vary with the fluctuations of the social or scholarly consciousness of the time, as an analysis of the evolution over time of the main realist divisions of sociology would testify (these can be grasped through the subheadings used in main-stream journals or in the names of research groups or sections convening periodically at the World Congress of Sociology). Here is one of the mediations through which the social world constructs its own representation, by using sociology and the sociologist for this purpose. For a sociologist more than any other thinker, to leave one's thought in a state of unthought (*impensé*) is to condemn oneself to be nothing more than the instrument of that which one claims to think.

How are we to effect this rupture? How can the sociologist escape the under-handed persuasion which is exercised on her every time she reads the newspapers or watches television or even when she reads the work of her colleagues? The mere fact of being on the alert is important but hardly suffices. One of the most powerful instruments of rupture lies in the social history of problems, objects, and instruments of thought, that is, with the history of the work of social construction of reality (enshrined in such common notions as role, culture, youth, etc., or in taxonomies) which is carried out within the social world itself as a whole or in this or that special-ized field and, especially, in the field of the social sciences. (This would lead us to assign to the teaching of the social history of the social sciences – a history which, for the most part, remains to be written – a purpose entirely different from the one it presently serves.) A good part of the collective work that finds an outlet in *Actes de la recherche en sciences sociales* deals with the social history of the most ordinary objects of ordinary existence. I think for instance of all those things that have become so com-mon, so taken for granted, that nobody pays any attention to them, such as the structure of a court of law, the space of a museum, a voting booth, the notion of 'occupational injury' or of 'cadre,' a two-by-two table or, quite simply, the act of writing or taping. History thus conceived is inspired not by an antiquarian interest but by a will to understand why and how one understands.

To avoid becoming the object of the problems that you take as your object, you must retrace the history of the emergence of these problems, of their progressive constitution, i.e., of the collective work, oftentimes accomplished though competition and struggle, that proved necessary to make such and such issues to be known and recognized (*faire connaître et reconnaître*) as legitimate problems, problems that are avowable, publishable, public, official. One thinks here of the problem of 'work accidents' or occupational hazards studied by Rémi Lenoir or of the invention of the 'elderly' (troisième âge) scrutinized by Patrick Champagne and, more generally, to such staples of the sociology of 'social problems' as family, divorce, delinquency, drugs, and female labor force participation. In all these cases we will discover that the problem that ordinary positivism (which is the first inclination of every researcher) takes for granted has been socially produced, in and by a collective work of construction of social reality; and that it took meetings and committees, associations and leagues, caucuses and movements, demonstrations and petition drives, demands and deliberations, votes and stands, projects, programs, and resolutions to cause what was and could have remained a private, particular, singular problem to turn into a social problem, a public issue that can be publicly addressed (think of the fate of abortion or homosexuality) or even an official problem that becomes the object of official decisions and policies, of laws and decrees.

Here one would need to analyze the particular role of the political field and especially of the bureaucratic field. Through the very peculiar logic of the administrative commission, a logic that I am currently investigating in the case of the elaboration of the public policy of individual housing assistance in France around 1975, the bureaucratic field contributes decisively to the constitution, and to the consecration, of 'universal' social problems. The imposition of *problématique* that the sociologist – as every other social agent – suffers and of which he becomes a relay and support every time he takes up on his own account questions which are an expression of the socio-political mood of the times (for instance by including them in his survey questionnaires or, worse, by designing his survey around them) is all the more likely when the problems that are taken for granted in a given social universe are those that have the greatest chances of being allocated grants, material or symbolic, of being, as we say in French, *bien vus*, in high favor with the managers of scientific bureaucracies and with bureaucratic authorities such as research foundations, private firms, or governmental agencies. (This explains why public opinion polls, the 'science without scientist,' always beget the approval of those who have the means of commissioning them and who otherwise prove so critical of sociology whenever the latter breaks with their demands and commands.)

I will only add, to complicate things still a bit more, and to make you see how difficult, indeed well-nigh desperate, the predicament of the sociologist is, that the work of production of official problems, that is, those problems endowed with the sort of universality that is granted by the fact of being guaranteed by the state, almost always leaves room for what are today called experts. Among those so-called experts are sociologists who use the authority of science to endorse the universality, the objectivity, and the disinterestedness of the bureaucratic representation of problems. This is to say that any sociologist worthy of the name, i.e., who does what, according to me, is required to have some chance of being the subject of the problems she can pose about the social world, must include in her object the contribution that sociology and sociologists (that is, her own peers) make, in all candor, to the production of official problems – even if this is very likely to appear as an unbearable mark of arrogance or as a betrayal of professional solidarity and corporatist interests.

In the social sciences, as we well know, epistemological breaks are often social breaks, breaks with the fundamental beliefs of a group and, sometimes, with the core beliefs of the body of professionals, with the body of shared certainties that found the *communis doctorum opinio*. To practice radical doubt, in sociology, is akin to becoming an outlaw. This was no doubt acutely felt by Descartes, who, to the dismay of his commentators, never extended the mode of thinking that he so intrepidly inaugurated in the realm of knowledge to politics (see the prudence with which he talks of Machiavelli).

I now come to the concepts, the words, and the methods that the 'profession' employs to speak about, and to think, the social world. Language poses a particularly dramatic problem for the sociologist: it is in effect an immense repository of natural-ized preconstructions, and thus of preconstructions that are ignored as such and which can function as unconscious instruments of construction. I could take here the example of occupational taxonomies, whether it be the names of occupations that are in currency in daily life or the socioeconomic categories of INSEE (the French National Institute of Economic and Statistical Research), an exemplary instance of bureaucratic conceptualization, of the bureaucratic universal, and, more generally, the example of all the taxonomies (age groups, young and old, gender categories, which we know are not free from social arbitrariness) that sociologists use without thinking about them too much because they are the social categories of understanding shared by a whole society. Or, as in the case of what I called the 'categories of professorial judgment' (the system of paired adjectives used to evaluate the papers of students or the virtues of colleagues), they belong to their professional corporation (which does not exclude their being founded, in the final analysis, upon homologies between structures, i.e., upon the fundamental oppositions of social space, such as rare/banal, unique/common, etc.).

But I believe that one must go further and call into question not only classifica-tions of occupations and the concepts used to designate classes of jobs, but the very concept of occupation itself, or of profession, which has provided the basis for a whole tradition of research and which, for some, stands as a kind of methodological motto. I am well aware that the concept of 'profession' and its derivatives (professionalism, professionalization, etc.) has been severely and fruitfully questioned in the works of Magali Sarfatti Larson, Randall Collins, Elliott Friedson, and Andrew Abbott in par-ticular, who have highlighted, among other things, the conflicts endemic to the world of professions. But I believe that we must go beyond this critique, however radical, and try, as I do, to replace this concept with that of field.

The notion of profession is all the more dangerous because it has, as always in such cases, all appearance of neutrality in its favor and because its use has been an improvement over the theoretical jumble (*bouillie*) of Parsons. To speak of 'profession' is to fasten on a true reality, onto a set of people who bear the same name (they are all 'lawyers' for instance); they are endowed with a roughly equivalent economic status and, more importantly, they are organized into 'professional associations' endowed with a code of ethics, collective bodies that define rules for admission, etc. 'Profession' is a folk concept which has been uncritically smuggled into scientific language and which imports into it a whole social unconscious. It is the social product of a historical work of construction of a group and of a representation of groups that has surreptitiously slipped into the science of this very group. This is why this 'concept' works so well, or too well in a way: if you accept it to construct your object, you will find directories on hand, lists and biographies drawn up, bibliographies compiled, centers of information and data bases already constituted by 'professional' bodies, and, provided that you be a bit shrewd, funds to study it (as is very frequent in the case of lawyers for instance). The category of profession refers to realities that are, in a sense, 'too real' to be true, since it grasps at once a mental category and a social category, socially produced only by superseding or obliterating all kinds of economic, social, and ethnic differences and contradictions which make the 'profession' of 'lawyer,' for instance, a space of competition and struggle.

Everything becomes different, and much more difficult if, instead of taking the notion of 'profession' at face value, I take seriously the work of aggregation and symbolic imposition that was necessary to produce it, and if I treat it as a field, that is, as a structured space of social forces and struggles. How do you draw a sample in a field? If, following the canon dictated by orthodox methodology, you take a random sample, you mutilate the very object you have set out to construct. If, in a study of the juridical field, for instance, you do not draw the chief justice of the Supreme Court, or if, in an inquiry into the French intellectual field of the 1950s, you leave out Jean-Paul Sartre, or Princeton University in a study of American academia, your field is destroyed, insofar as these personas or institutions alone mark a crucial position. There are positions in a field that admit only one occupant but command the whole structure. With a random or representative sample of artists or intellectuals conceived as a 'profession,' however, no problem.

If you accept the notion of profession as an instrument, rather than an object, of analysis, none of this creates any difficulty. As long as you take it as it presents itself, the given (the hallowed data of positivist sociologists) gives itself to you without difficulty. Everything goes smoothly, everything is taken for granted. Doors and mouths open wide. What group would turn down the sacralizing and naturalizing recording of the social scientist? Studies of bishops or corporate leaders that (tacitly) accept the church or business problematic will enroll the support of the Episcopate and of the Business Council, and the cardinals and corporate leaders who zealously come to comment on their results never fail to grant a certificate of objectivity to the sociologist who succeeds in giving objective, i.e., public, reality to the subjective representation they have of their own social being. In short, as long as you remain within the realm of socially constituted and socially sanctioned appearances – and this is the order to which the notion of 'profession' belongs – you will have all appearances with you and for you, even the appearance of scientificity. On the contrary, as soon as you undertake to work on a genuine constructed object, everything becomes difficult:

'theoretical' progress generates added 'methodological' difficulties. 'Methodologists,' for their part, will have no difficulty finding plenty to nit-pick about in the operations that have to be carried out in order to grasp the constructed object as best one can . . .

Among those difficulties, there is the question I touched upon earlier, of the boundaries of the field. The most daring of positivists solve that question – when they do not purely and simply neglect to pose it by using preexisting lists – by what they call an 'operational definition' ('In this study, I shall call "writer" '; 'I will consider as a "semiprofession" . . .'), without seeing that the question of the definition ('So and so is not a true writer!') is at stake within the object itself. There is a struggle within the object over who is part of the game, who in fact deserves the title of writer. The very notion of writer, but also the notion of lawyer, doctor, or sociologist, despite all efforts at codification and homogenization through certification, is at stake in the field of writers (or lawyers, etc.): the struggle over the legitimate definition, whose stake – the word definition says it – is the boundary, the frontiers, the right of admission, sometimes the *numerus clausus*, is a universal property of fields.

Empiricist resignation has all appearances going for it and receives all approvals because, by avoiding self-conscious construction, it leaves the crucial operations of scientific construction – the choice of the problem, the elaboration of concepts and analytical categories – to the social world as it is, to the established order, and thus it fulfills, if only by default, a quintessentially conservative function of ratification of the doxa. Among all the obstacles that stand in the way of the development of a scientific sociology, one of the most formidable is the fact that genuine scientific discoveries come at the highest costs and with the lowest profits, not only in the ordinary markets of social existence but also, too often, in the academic market, from which greater autonomy could be expected. As I tried to argue concerning the differential social and scientific costs and benefits of the notions of profession and field, it is often necessary, in order to produce science, to forego the appearances of scientificity, even to contradict the norms in currency and to challenge ordinary criteria of scientific rigor. Appearances are always in favor of the apparent. True science, very frequently, isn't much to look at, and, to move science forward, it is often necessary to take the risk of not displaying all the outward signs of scientificity (we often forget how easy it is to simulate them). Among other reasons because the half-wits or demi-habiles, as Pascal calls them, who dwell on superficial violations of the canons of elementary 'methodology,' are led by their positivist confidence to perceive as so many 'mistakes' and as effects of incompetence or ignorance what are methodological choices founded upon a deliberate refusal to use the escape hatches of 'methodology.'

I need not say that the obsessive reflexivity which is the condition of a rigorous scientific practice has nothing in common with the false radicalism of the questioning of science that is now proliferating. (I am thinking here of those who introduce the age-old philosophical critique of science, more or less updated to fall in line with the reigning fashion in American social science, whose immune system has paradoxically been destroyed by several generations of positivist 'methodology.') Among these critiques, one must grant a special place to those of ethnomethodologists, even though, in some of their formulations, they converge with the conclusions of those who reduce scientific discourse to rhetorical strategies about a world itself reduced to the state of a text. The analysis of the logic of practice, and of the spontaneous theories with which it arms itself in order to make sense of the world, is not an end in itself – no more so than the critique of the presuppositions of ordinary (i.e., unreflexive) sociology, especially in its uses of statistical methods. It is an absolutely decisive moment, but only a moment, of the rupture with the presuppositions of lay and scholarly common sense. If one must objectivize the schemata of practical sense, it is not for the purpose of proving that sociology can offer only one point of view on the world among many, neither more nor less scientific than any other, but to wrench scientific reason from the embrace of practical reason, to prevent the latter from contaminating the former, to avoid treating as an instrument of knowledge what ought to be the object of knowledge, that is, everything that constitutes the practical sense of the social world, the presuppositions, the schemata of perception and understanding that give the lived world its structure. To take as one's object commonsense understanding and the primary experience of the social world as a nonthetic acceptance of a world which is not constituted as an object facing a subject is precisely the means of avoiding being 'trapped' within the object. It is the means of submitting to scientific scrutiny everything that makes the doxic experience of the world possible, that is, not only the preconstructed representation of this world but also the cognitive schemata that underlie the construction of this image. And those among the ethnomethodologists who rest content with the mere description of this experience without questioning the social conditions which make it possible – that is, the correspondence between social structures and mental structures, the objective structures of the world and the cognitive structures through which the latter is apprehended – do nothing more than repeat the most traditional questionings of the most traditional philosophy on the reality of reality. To assess the limitations of this semblance of radicalism that their epistemic populism imparts to them (due to their rehabilititation of ordinary thinking), we need only observe that ethnomethodologists have never seen the political implications of the doxic experience of the world which, as fundamental acceptance of the established order situated outside the reach of critique, is the most secure foundation of a conservatism more radical than that which labors to establish a political orthodoxy.

On science and politics* (1999)

On Double Truth and the Right Distance. How to avoid seeming to be complicitous with the object analyzed (notably in the eyes of those who are foreign to it) or, conversely, reductive and hostile (especially to those who are caught up in the object and who are inclined to refuse the very principle of objectivation)? How to reconcile the objectivation of belief (religious, literary, artistic, scientific, etc.) and of its social conditions of production, and the sensible and faithful evocation of the experience of belief that is inherent to being inserted and involved in a social game? Only at the cost of a very long and very difficult work – and one that is the more invisible the more successful it

* From 'Scattered Remarks' by Pierre Bourdieu, translated by Tarik Wareh and Loïc Wacquant, *European Journal of Social Theory*, 1999, 2(3): 334–340. Reprinted with permission.

is – to put oneself at a distance from the object and then to surmount this very distance, a work that bears inseparably on the object and on the relationship to the object, thus on the subject of the scientific work.

On Objectivation. Those who rebel against the very intention of objectivizing a 'subject' (who is herself capable of objectivation) could find support in the existence of a cognitive struggle over the objective representation of the social world in order to contest the pretension to escape the game of mutual objectivation that is entailed in scientific ambition. In fact, scientific objectivation arms itself with collective instruments that ordinary practices of objectivation do not have at their disposal and, above all, it is accomplished within a field capable of submitting the objectivations, which are necessarily provisional and revisable, to a collective and public testing aimed at controlling the work of 'desubjectivation' (as Bachelard says) that they presuppose, and which is perhaps never definitive.

The Epistemology of Ressentiment. Those who, like today's 'postmoderns', colourless continuators of the age-old battle of philosophy against sociology, are wont to contest social science's claims to scientificity are almost always recruited from among the philosophers who feel threatened in their anthropological monopoly; for this reason, they are not limited to the spiritualists attached to the irreducibility of the 'human person'. They find their natural allies among the failed or *déclassé* representatives of these sciences (often defrocked philosophers who have not succeeded in their conversion to history or sociology): for lack of having proven themselves on properly scientific terrain, these latter are prone to seeking the appearance of a revenge in metascientific, epistemological-looking considerations made for allowing them to convert their personal limitations into universal limits by decreeing a priori the impossibility of doing that which they were unable to do.

Symbolic Capital. To account for recognized domination and for obedience, that is, for the conditions that must be met for a command to be obeyed, one must integrate traditionally separate, nay opposing, theoretical traditions: the 'constructivist' tradition that considers symbolic schemata as the instruments of construction of the world of objects; the structuralist or hermeneutic tradition that, notably in Habermas, treats them as instruments of communication, reducing issues of power and politics to issues of meaning; finally the traditions that see in them instruments of power (or of the legitimation of power), by priority of the economic, as in Marx, or the political, as in Nietzsche. As the synthesis of the three traditions, the notion of symbolic power (or capital) enables one to account for the relations of force that are actualized in and by relations of cognition (or recognition) and of communication.

Symbolic capital exists by and for perception or, more precisely, by and for those who perceive it and who can perceive it and make it exist as such only because they are endowed with adequate categories of perception. This means that it depends, for its very existence, on those who bear its effects. These categories (or schemata) of perception are historical principles of vision and division rooted in the objective divisions of the social order (this is the case with the three 'orders' of *ancien régime* societies which, as Georges Duby has shown, are at the same time objective structures and cognitive structures) or, more precisely, in the structure of the distribution of capital. Symbolic capital is made, in the last analysis, by those who are submitted to it but if, and only if, the objective structure of its distribution is at the basis of the cognitive structures that they bring into play in order to produce it – as, for example, with such structuring oppositions as masculine/feminine, young/old, noble/common, rich/poor, white/black, etc. Nobility exists only for and by those who have at their disposal the principle of division between the noble and the common, that is to say by and for the other nobles or the commoners who have acquired the disposition to recognize it (in both senses) on account of their embeddedness in a universe objectively organized according to this principle of division.

If the claim to symbolic power that permits one to act upon the social world in its entirety or upon a particular field is universal, this capacity is very unequally accorded to the different agents according to the position they occupy in the structure of the distribution of symbolic capital within the given social space (that of noble versus commoner, of the notable versus the ordinary person, of the Nobel prizewinner versus the rank-and-file researcher, of the publisher consecrated and capable of consecrating by publication versus the newcomer in the field of publishing, etc.). Symbolic capital is the capital of recognition accumulated in the course of the whole history of prior struggles (thus very strongly correlated to seniority), that enables one to intervene effectively in current struggles for the conservation or augmentation of symbolic capital, that is, for the power of nomination and of imposition of the legitimate principle of vision and division, universally recognized in a determinate social space. These cognitive and communicative struggles which, as Goffinan has shown so well, are continually unfolding in daily existence, find their canonical form in the political struggles that use the symbolic power to cause one to see and to believe in order to impose visions of the world and, in particular, visions of the divisions of the world (principles of classification), and thereby to produce groups, families, clans, tribes, classes or nations, and to give them existence by making them visible, notably by the demonstration ('*manifestation*') or, in other universes, the procession (e.g. bridal or funeral procession), the cortège . . . etc. exhibitions of the force and form of the group, of its divisions and hierarchies.

As the logic of the symbolic is fundamentally diacritical, distinction is the specific form of profit that symbolic capital procures. Lifestyle, as the exemplary manifestation of symbolic capital, exists only by and for the gaze of the other and as diacritical deviation from the modal, ordinary, common, banal, 'average' style, a deviation that can be unwitting or obtained by a 'stylization of life'. The symbolic profit of distinction (which can be reconverted into material profits) results, apart from every intentional pursuit, from the monopolistic possession (exclusivity) of some species of capital and from the exhibition, intentional or not, of this capital and of the difference attached to its possession. This is as much as to say that the effect of distinction inherent in the unequal distribution of a good, service, or practice, contributes of itself to legitimating the structure of this distribution. The institutionalization of this effect, by customs and rules of dress, sumptuary laws, etc. tends to constitute 'status groups' ('orders', nobility, etc.) by constituting as permanent and founded in nature certain de facto differences, and by establishing mechanisms destined to assure their perpetuation (inheritance laws, matrimonial norms aimed at excluding *mésalliance*, etc.).

Symbolic capital can thus be possessed by singular agents or by collectives, especially corps, families, status groups, constituted bodies, the state. Possessor of the monopoly over legitimate symbolic violence, capable of acting as central bank of the symbolic capital accumulated by a nation, the state can exercise the power of naming, an act of consecration that confers upon a singular agent or a group its official identity, universally recognized (within the limits of its jurisdiction), its social titles of recognition (academic or occupational in particular). As the strict opposite to insult as *idios logos* (singular discourse) without consequence, and of all individual or collective strategies of defamation or degradation, aimed at eliciting discredit, the verdict (positive or negative), the solemn enunciation of the social truth of an individual or group, it places a limit, if not a term, on the struggle of all against all about the social world and about the social truth and value of those engaged in it.

One can thus understand the paradox of symbolic efficacy, revived by the reflection of philosophers (notably Austin) and linguists (Benveniste among others) on the performative. The command that makes itself obeyed, if it is an exception to the laws of physics in that it obtains an effect out of proportion to the energy expended, and thus liable to appear as a form of magic, is in perfect conformity with the law of the conservation of social energy, that is, of capital: it turns out that, to be in a position to act at a distance and without expense of energy, by virtue of an act of social magic, as with the order or the watchword (*ordre et mot d'ordre*), one must be endowed with authority, that is, authorized, in one's personal capacity or by proxy, as delegate, representative, or functionary, to set off, as by a trigger mechanism, the social energy that has been accumulated in a group or an institution by the work, often protracted and difficult, that is the condition of the acquisition and conservation of symbolic capital.

The Historical Raison d'Être of Reason. Rationalism too easily grants itself its *raison d'être*. It is perhaps on condition of radicalizing the historical critique of the supposed 'foundations' of reason, and of the social order, and of refusing all manners of transcendental *deus ex machina* which the philosophers, from Kant to Husserl to Habermas, have proposed to escape the mute confrontation with the brute fact of historical contingency, that one can discover, in history itself, how and on what conditions what we call reason was able, in certain situations and under certain conditions, to constitute itself by tearing itself away from history.

Science and Politics. One can, for heuristic purposes, oppose as two 'ideal types' arrived at by pushing to the limit, on the one hand, the most purely political form of the political field where the force of ideas would depend essentially on the force of the groups that recognize them because they recognize themselves in them, who accept them as true because they believe them to be such or, in more accurate terms, because they believe that their existence and their economic and social interests depend on them; and on the other hand, the most purely scientific form of the scientific fields where the force of ideas would depend essentially on 'their intrinsic force', as Spinoza said, that is, on the conformity of propositions or procedures to the rules of logical coherence or on compatibility with the facts. In historical reality, there is no scientific field, however 'pure', that does not entail a 'political' dimension, no political field that makes no room for some disputes over truth. That said, while in scientific fields one does not settle a debate by means of a physical confrontation or by a vote, in political fields, and in particular in those that are subjected to democratic rules, the victors are those propositions that Aristotle calls endoxic, that is those with which one is obliged to reckon because the people who matter would like them to be true and also because, partaking of the doxa, of the ordinary vision, which is also the most widespread and the most widely shared, they are liable to receive the approbation and applause of the greatest number.

It follows that the political field is in an ambiguous position: site of a competition for truth (especially about the social world), it is also the site of a competition for power (notably over the state, and the resources whose accumulation and redistribution it controls), power granted by the art of producing or mobilizing *idées-forces* that contain a force of mobilization, notably as predictions or forecasts, true or capable of making themselves come true, on account of their intrinsic force of truth or the social force that their 'bearers' have the means of mobilizing, be it by virtue of their own symbolic capital (their charisma) or through the agency of an organized group, a party. In short, things are not simple, and political struggles always make room for the logic of quasi-scientific 'verification' by argumentation and for the logic of properly political 'ratification' by plebiscite.

The social sciences are in a particularly difficult position owing to the fact that they have the social world for object and claim to produce a scientific representation of it. Each and every specialist is in this regard in competition not only with other researchers but also with the other professionals in symbolic production, and in particular journalists and politicians, and, more broadly still, with all those who work to impose their vision of the social world, with very unequal symbolic force and equally unequal success. This is the case, whether the social researcher knows it or not, wishes it or not, and even when she chooses to enclose herself in the ivory tower of a scientific practice that would be an end in and for itself, in a fantasy of purity (and equanimity) that is necessarily doomed to failure because politics is present within the field itself through the effects of temporal powers that continue to weigh on the City of science. Propositions that are inconsistent or incompatible with the facts have infinitely greater chances to perpetuate themselves there and even to prosper there than in the most autonomous scientific fields, provided that they are endowed, inside the field and also outside it, with a social authority liable to compensate for their insignificance and insufficiency by assuring them material and institutional supports (credits, grants, posts, etc.) – and conversely.

In fact, social scientists can, without contradiction, struggle, within their own sphere, to reinforce the autonomy of the scientific field and to rid it of everything political that may remain in it, and outside it in the political field itself, they can struggle to try to impose scientific truth on the social world, without being able to resort to weapons other than those of truth. And they can even, to give more force to their weak weapons, make the scientific field play the role of a realized utopia of the political field or, better, the role of a regulative idea permitting one at once to orient political practices and to submit them to a methodical questioning. The major virtue of the confrontation between the scientific field, in its different states, and the political field lies in making a very large number of questions arise regarding both fields, questions that must be converted into scientific problems liable to receiving empirical answers. And it above all prevents one from forgetting, against the typically scholastic illusion of the omnipotence of ideas, everything that separates the world of science from the world of politics, the awareness and knowledge of which must in any case orient properly scientific work and the effort to try to communicate its results in the political world.

Habitus and Freedom. If only to make things more difficult for those who would like to see in the theory of habitus a form of determinism, it will suffice to point out that the habitus offers the only durable form of freedom, that given by the mastery of an art, whatever the art. And that this freedom made nature, which is acquired, paradoxically, by the obligated or elective submission to the conditionings of training and exercise (themselves made possible by a minimal distance from necessity), is indeed, as is the freedom in regard to language and body that is called ease, a property (this is one of the senses that the Scholastics gave to the word 'habitus') or, if you wish, an acquisition and inheritance predisposed by their unequal distribution to function as capital. This then raises the question of whether there can be any liberty other than that to master one's inheritance and acquisitions. Pedagogical action can thus, because of and despite the symbolic violence it entails, open the possibility of an emancipation founded on awareness and knowledge of the conditionings undergone and on the imposition of new conditionings designed durably to counter their effects.

53

ANTHONY GIDDENS
Social science as a double hermeneutic* (1984)

It might be useful at this point to recapitulate some of the basic ideas contained in the preceding chapters. I shall summarize these as a number of points; taken together, they represent the aspects of structuration theory which impinge most generally upon problems of empirical research in the social sciences.

(1) All human beings are knowledgeable agents. That is to say, all social actors know a great deal about the conditions and consequences of what they do in their day-to-day lives. Such knowledge is not wholly propositional in character, nor is it incidental to their activities. Knowledgeability embedded in practical consciousness exhibits an extraordinary complexity – a complexity that often remains completely unexplored in orthodox sociological approaches, especially those associated with objectivism. Actors are also ordinarily able discursively to describe what they do and their reasons for doing it. However, for the most part these faculties are geared to the flow of day-to-day conduct. The rationalization of conduct becomes the discursive offering of reasons only if individuals are asked by others why they acted as they did. Such questions are normally posed, of course, only if the activity concerned is in some way puzzling – if it appears either to flout convention or to depart from the habitual modes of conduct of a particular person.

(2) The knowledgeability of human actors is always bounded on the one hand by the unconscious and on the other by unacknowledged conditions/unintended consequences of action. Some of the most important tasks of social science are to be found in the investigation of these boundaries, the signficance of unintended consequences for system reproduction and the ideological connotations which such boundaries have.

(3) The study of day-to-day life is integral to analysis of the reproduction of institutionalized practices. Day-to-day life is bound up with the repetitive character of

* From Anthony Giddens *The Constitution of Society: Outline of a Theory of Structuration*. Polity Press, 1984. Pp. 281–286.

reversible time with paths traced through time-space and associated with the constraining and enabling features of the body. However, day-to-day life should not be treated as the 'foundation' upon which the more ramified connections of social life are built. Rather, these more far-flung connections should be understood in terms of an interpretation of social and system integration.

(4) Routine, psychologically linked to the minimizing of unconscious sources of anxiety, is the predominant form of day-to-day social activity. Most daily practices are not directly motivated. Routinized practices are the prime expression of the duality of structure in respect of the continuity of social life. In the enactment of routines agents sustain a sense of ontological security.

(5) The study of context, or of the contextualities of interaction, is inherent in the investigation of social reproduction. 'Context' involves the following: (a) the time-space boundaries (usually having symbolic or physical markers) around interaction strips; (b) the co-presence of actors, making possible the visibility of a diversity of facial expressions, bodily gestures, linguistic and other media of communication; (c) awareness and use of these phenomena reflexively to influence or control the flow of interaction.

(6) Social identities, and the position-practice relations associated with them, are 'markers' in the virtual time-space of structure. They are associated with normative rights, obligations and sanctions which, within specific collectivities, form roles. The use of standardized markers, especially to do with the bodily attributes of age and gender, is fundamental in all societies, notwithstanding large cross-cultural variations which can be noted.

(7) No unitary meaning can be given to 'constraint' in social analysis. Constraints associated with the structural properties of social systems are only one type among several others characteristic of human social life.

(8) Among the structural properties of social systems, structural principles are particularly important, since they specify overall types of society. It is one of the main emphases of structuration theory that the degree of closure of societal totalities – and of social systems in general – is widely variable. There are degrees of 'systemness' in societal totalities, as in other less or more inclusive forms of social system. It is essential to avoid the assumption that what a 'society' is can be easily defined, a notion which comes from an era dominated by nation-states with clear-cut boundaries that usually conform in a very close way to the administrative purview of centralized governments. Even in nation-states, of course, there are a variety of social forms which cross-cut societal boundaries.

(9) The study of power cannot be regarded as a second-order consideration in the social sciences. Power cannot be tacked on, as it were, after the more basic concepts of social science have been formulated. There is no more elemental concept than that of power. However, this does not mean that the concept of power is more essential than

any other, as is supposed in those versions of social science which have come under a Nietzschean influence. Power is one of several primary concepts of social science, all clustered around the relations of action and structure. Power is the means of getting things done and, as such, directly implied in human action. It is a mistake to treat power as inherently divisive, but there is no doubt that some of the most bitter conflicts in social life are accurately seen as 'power struggles'. Such struggles can be regarded as to do with efforts to subdivide resources which yield modalities of control in social systems. By 'control' I mean the capability that some actors, groups or types of actors have of influencing the circumstances of action of others. In power struggles the dialectic of control always operates, although what use agents in subordinate positions can make of the resources open to them differs very substantially between different social contexts.

(10) There is no mechanism of social organization or social reproduction identified by social analysts which lay actors cannot also get to know about and actively incorporate into what they do. In very many instances the 'findings' of sociologists are such only to those not in the contexts of activity of the actors studied. Since actors do what they do for reasons, they are naturally likely to be disconcerted if told by sociological observers that what they do derives from factors that somehow act externally to them. Lay objections to such 'findings' may thus have a very sound basis. Reification is by no means purely characteristic of lay thought.

These points suggest a number of guidelines for the overall orientation of social research. First, all social research has a necessarily cultural, ethnographic or 'anthropological' aspect to it. This is an expression of what I call the double hermeneutic which characterizes social science. The sociologist has as a field of study phenomena which are already constituted as meaningful. The condition of 'entry' to this field is getting to know what actors already know, and have to know, to 'go on' in the daily activities of social life. The concepts that sociological observers invent are 'second-order' concepts in so far as they presume certain conceptual capabilities on the part of the actors to whose conduct they refer. But it is in the nature of social science that these can become 'first-order' concepts by being appropriated within social life itself. What is 'hermeneutic' about the double hermeneutic? The appropriateness of the term derives from the double process of translation or interpretation which is involved. Sociological descriptions have the task of mediating the frames of meaning within which actors orient their conduct. But such descriptions are interpretative categories which also demand an effort of translation in and out of the frames of meaning involved in sociological theories. Various considerations concerning social analysis are connected with this:

(1) Literary style is not irrelevant to the accuracy of social descriptions. This is more or less important according to how far a particular piece of social research is ethnographic, that is, is written with the aim of describing a given cultural milieu to others who are unfamiliar with it.

(2) The social scientist is a communicator, introducing frames of meaning associated

with certain contexts of social life to those in others. Thus the social sciences draw upon the same sources of description (mutual knowledge) as novelists or others who write fictional accounts of social life. Goffman is able quite easily to intersperse fictional illustrations with descriptions taken from social science research because he seeks very often to 'display' the tacit forms of mutual knowledge whereby practical activities are ordered, rather than trying to chart the actual distribution of those activities.

(3) 'Thick description' will be called for in some types of research (especially that of a more ethnographic kind) but not in others. It is usually unnecessary where the activities studied have generalized characteristics familiar to those to whom the 'findings' are made available, and where the main concern of the research is with institutional analysis, in which actors are treated in large aggregates or as 'typical' in certain respects defined as such for the purposes of the study.

Second, it is important in social research to be sensitive to the complex skills which actors have in co-ordinating the contexts of their day-to-day behaviour. In institutional analysis these skills may be more or less bracketed out, but it is essential to remember that such bracketing is wholly methodological. Those who take institutional analysis to comprise the field of sociology *in toto* mistake a methodological procedure for an ontological reality. Social life may very often be predictable in its course, as such authors are prone to emphasize. But its predictability is in many of its aspects 'made to happen' by social actors; it does not happen in spite of the reasons they have for their conduct. If the study of unintended consequences and unacknowledged conditions of action is a major part of social research, we should none the less stress that such consequences and conditions are always to be interpreted within the flow of intentional conduct. We have to include here the relation between reflexively monitored and unintended aspects of the reproduction of social systems, and the 'longitudinal' aspect of unintended consequences of contingent acts in historically significant circumstances of one kind or another.

Third, the social analyst must also be sensitive to the time-space constitution of social life. In part this is a plea for a disciplinary coming together. Social scientists have normally been content to let historians be specialists in time and geographers specialists in space, while they maintain their own distinctive disciplinary identity, which, if it is not an exclusive concern with structural constraint, is bound up with a conceptual focus upon 'society'. Historians and geographers, for their part, have been willing enough to connive at this disciplinary dissection of social science. The practitioners of a discipline, apparently, do not feel secure unless they can point to a sharp conceptual delimitation between their concerns and those of others. Thus 'history' may be seen as about sequences of events set out chronologically in time or perhaps, even more ambiguously, about 'the past'. Geography, many of its representatives like to claim, finds its distinctive character in the study of spatial forms. But if, as I have emphasized, time-space relations cannot be 'pulled out' of social analysis without undermining the whole enterprise, such disciplinary divisions actively inhibit the tackling of questions of social theory significant for the social sciences as a whole. Analysing the time-space co-ordination of social activities means studying the contextual features of locales through which actors move in their daily paths and the regionaliza-tion of locales stretching away across time-space. As I have accentuated frequently, such analysis is inherent in the explanation of time-space distanciation and hence in the examination of the heterogeneous and complex nature assumed by larger societal totalities and by intersocietal systems in general.

54

DOROTHY SMITH

The standpoint of women in the everyday world* (1987)

In previous chapters I began to define the distinctive standpoint of women and to explore the problematic yielded by that standpoint. Here I am concerned with the methods of thinking that will realize the project of a sociology for women. The chapter is built on a series of encounters between sociologist or subject, or between Two and One. One is always the subject whose subjectivity as organizer of her knowledge is imperiled by the texts Two might or does write in political or intellectual contexts. Alternative methods of thinking and methods of writing sociological texts are explored in the context of dilemmas and problems posed in these encounters.

The fulcrum of a sociology for women is the standpoint of the subject. A sociology for women preserves the presence of subjects as knowers and as actors. It does not transform subjects into the objects of study or make use of conceptual devices for eliminating the active presence of subjects. Its methods of thinking and its analytic procedures must preserve the presence of the active and experiencing subject. A sociology is a systematically developed knowledge of society and social relations. The knower who is construed in the sociological texts of a sociology for women is she whose grasp of the world from where she stands is enlarged thereby. For actual subjects situated in the actualities of their everyday worlds, a sociology for women offers an understanding of how those worlds are organized and determined by social relations immanent in and extending beyond them.

Methods of thinking could, I suppose, be described as 'theories,' but to do so is to suggest that I am concerned with formulations that will explain phenomena, when what I am primarily concerned with is how to conceptualize or how to constitute the textuality of social phenomena. I am concerned with how to write the social, to make it visible in sociological texts, in ways that will explicate a problematic, the actuality of which is immanent in the everyday world. In part what is meant by methods of thinking will emerge in the course of the chapter. This is an exploration rather than an account of a destination. We are in search of conceptual practices with which to

* From *The Everyday World as Problematic: A Feminist Sociology* by Dorothy L. Smith. Copyright 1987 by Dorothy L. Smith. Reprinted with the permission of Northeastern University Press. Pp. 105–111.

explicate the actual social relations disclosed in investigation and analysis. We are looking, in other words, for methods and principles for generating sociological texts, for selecting syntax and indexical forms preserving the presence of subjects in our accounts, in short for methods of writing sociology. Such methods must recognize that the subject of our sociological texts exists outside them, that, as Marx says, 'The real subject [matter] retains its autonomous existence outside the head just as before.' Or perhaps we go further than Marx in insisting that both subject matter and the 'head' that theorizes it as well as its theorizing are enfolded in the existence of our subject matter. A sociology for women must be conscious of its necessary indexicality and hence that its meaning remains to be completed by a reader who is situated just as she is – a particular woman reading somewhere at a particular time amid the particularities of her everyday world – and that it is the capacity of our sociological texts, as she enlivens them, to reflect upon, to expand, and to enlarge her grasp of the world she reads in, and that is the world that completes the meaning of the text as she reads.

So this chapter is concerned with how to write a sociology that will do this. It does not go so far as the practicalities of how to do it. That will be a later topic. Here the focus is on those aspects of standard methods of thinking sociologically that deny us the presence of subjects and on formulating alternatives and suggesting how we might proceed in exploring the everyday world from the standpoint of women.

To avoid potential misunderstanding, I should state first what I do not mean by the standpoint of women. A sociology for women should not be mistaken for an ideological position that represents women's oppression as having a determinate character and takes up the analysis of social forms with a view to discovering in them the lineaments of what the ideologist already supposes that she knows. The standpoint of women therefore as I am deploying it here cannot be equated with perspective or worldview. It does not universalize a particular experience. It is rather a method that, at the outset of inquiry, creates the space for an absent subject, and an absent experience that is to be filled with the presence and spoken experience of actual women speaking of and in the actualities of their everyday worlds.

In chapter 1, I explored issues for women arising from a culture and politics developed almost exclusively by men and written from the standpoint of men and not of women. This statement was as true of intellectual and scientific discourses as of TV commercials. To begin with, therefore, we had to discover how to take the standpoint of women. We did not know – there were no precedents – how to view the world from where we were. We discovered that what we had known as our history was not in fact ours at all but theirs. We discovered the same of our sociology. We had not realized what and who was not there in the texts in which we had learned to understand ourselves. Becoming a feminist in these contexts means taking this disjuncture up deliberately as an enterprise. The very forms of our oppression require a deliberate remaking of our relations with others and of these the relations of our knowledge must be key, for the dimensions of our oppression are only fully revealed in discoveries that go beyond what direct experience will teach us. But such a remaking cannot be prejudged, for in the very nature of the case we cannot know in advance what we will discover, what we will have to learn, and how it will be conceptualized. Remaking, in the context of intellectual enterprise, is itself a course of inquiry.

The exclusion of women is not the only one. The ruling apparatus is an organization of class and as such implicates dominant classes. The working class is excluded from the ruling apparatus. It also excludes the many voices of women and men of color, of native peoples, and of homosexual women and men. From different standpoints different aspects of the ruling apparatus and of class come into view. But, as I have argued in chapter 2, the standpoint of women is distinctive and has distinctive implications for the practice of sociology as a systematically developed consciousness of society.

I proposed women's standpoint as one situated outside textually mediated discourses in the actualities of our everyday lives. This is a standpoint designed in part by our exclusion from the making of cultural and intellectual discourse and the strategies of resorting to our experience as the ground of a new knowledge, a new culture. But it is also designed by an organization of work that has typically been ours, for women's work, as wives, secretaries, and in other ancillary roles, has been that which anchors the impersonal and objectified forms of action and relations to particular individuals, particular local places, particular relationships. Whatever other part women play in the social division of labor, they have been assigned and confined predominantly to work roles mediating the relation of the impersonal and objectified forms of action to the concrete local and particular worlds in which all of us necessarily exist.

The standpoint of women therefore directs us to an 'embodied' subject located in a particular actual local historical setting. Her world presents itself to her in its full particularity – the books on her shelves, the Cowichan sweaters she has bought for her sons' birthdays, the Rainforest chair she bought three years ago in a sale, the portable computer she is using to write on, the eighteenth-century chair, made of long-since-exhausted Caribbean mahogany, one of a set of four given her by her mother years ago – each is particularized by insertion into her biography and projects as well as by its immediacy in the now in which she writes. The abstracted constructions of discourse or bureaucracy are accomplishments in and of her everyday world. Her reading and writing are done in actual locations at actual times and under definite material conditions. Though discourse, bureaucracy, and the exchange of money for commodities create forms of social relations that transcend the local and particular, they are constituted, created, and practiced always within the local and particular. It is the special magic of the ubiquity of text and its capacity to manifest itself as the same in diverse multiple settings that provide for the local practices of transcendence.

A standpoint in the everyday world is the fundamental grounding of modes of knowing developed in a ruling apparatus. The ruling apparatus is that familiar complex of management, government administration, professions, and intelligentsia, as well as the textually mediated discourses that coordinate and interpenetrate it. Its special capacity is the organization of particular actual places, persons, and events into generalized and abstracted modes vested in categorial systems, rules, laws, and conceptual practices. The former thereby become subject to an abstracted and universalized system of ruling mediated by texts. A mode of ruling has been created that transcends local particularities but at the same time exists only in them. The ruling apparatus of this loosely coordinated collection of varied sites of power has been largely if not exclusively the sphere of men. From within its textual modes the embodied subject and the everyday world as its site are present only as object and never as subject's standpoint. But from the standpoint of women whose work has served to complete the invisibility of the actual as the locus of the subject, from the standpoint of she who stands at the beginning of her work, the grounding of an abstracted conceptual organization of ruling comes into view as a product in and of the everyday world.

Sociology is part of the ruling apparatus. Its relevances and subtending organization are given by the relation of the ruling apparatus to the social world it governs. The institutional forms of ruling constitute its major topics – the sociology of organizations, of education, of health, of work, of mental illness, of deviance, of law, of knowledge, and the like. The organization of sociological thinking and knowledge is articulated to this institutional structure. It pioneers methods of thinking and the systematics of articulating particular actualities to a generalized conceptual order that serves it. To a significant extent, sociology has been busy clarifying, organizing, mapping, and extending the relations of the institutional forms of ruling to the actualities of their domains.

Women's lives have been outside or subordinate to the ruling apparatus. Its conceptual practices do not work for us in the development of a sociological consciousness of our own. The grid of political sociology, the sociology of the family, of organizations, of mental illness, of education, and so forth, does not map the unknown that extends before us as what is to be discovered and explored; it does not fit when we ask how we should organize a sociology beginning from the standpoint of women. We start, as we must, with women's experience (for what other resource do we have?); the available concepts and frameworks do not work because they have already posited a subject situated outside a local and actual experience, a particularized knowledge of the world. Women are readily made the objects of sociological study precisely because they have not been its subjects. Beneath the apparent gender neutrality of the impersonal or absent subject of an objective sociology is the reality of the masculine author of the texts of its tradition and his membership in the circle of men participating in the division of the labor of ruling. The problem confronted here is how to do a sociology that is for women and that takes women as its subjects and its knowers when the methods of thinking, which we have learned as sociologists as the methods of producing recognizably sociological texts, reconstruct us as objects.

If we begin where people are actually located in that independently existing world outside texts, we begin in the particularities of an actual everyday world. As a first step in entering that standpoint into a textually mediated discourse, we constitute the everyday world as our problematic. We do so by interesting ourselves in its opacity for we cannot understand how it is organized or comes about by remaining within it. The concept of problematic transfers this opacity to the level of discourse. It directs attention to a possible set of questions that have yet to be posed or of puzzles that are not yet formulated as such but are 'latent' in the actualities of our experienced worlds. The problematic of the everyday world is an explicit discursive formulation of an actual property of the organization of the everyday world. I am talking about a reality as it arises for those who live it – the reality, for example, that effects arise that do not originate in it. Yet I am talking (or rather writing) about it. I am entering it into discourse. The term 'problematic' enters an actual aspect of the organization of the everyday world (as it is ongoingly produced by actual individuals) into a systematic inquiry. It responds to our practical ignorance of the determinations of our local worlds so long as we look for them within their limits. In this sense the puzzle or puzzles are really there. Hence an inquiry defined by such a problematic addresses a problem of how we are related to the worlds we live in. We may not experience our ignorance as such, but we are nonetheless ignorant.

The problematic, located by our ignorance of how our everyday worlds are shaped and determined by relation and forces external to them, must not be taken to imply that we are dopes or dupes. Within our everyday worlds, we are expert practitioners of their quiddity, of the way they are just the way they are. Our everyday worlds are in part our own accomplishments, and our special and expert knowledge is continually demonstrated in their ordinary familiarity and unsurprising ongoing presence. But how they are knitted into the extended social relations of a contemporary capitalist economy and society is not discoverable with them. The relations among multiple everyday worlds and the accomplishment of those relations within them create a dynamic organization that, in the context of contemporary capitalism, continually feeds change through to our local experience. In the research context this means that so far as their everyday worlds are concerned, we rely entirely on what women tell us, what people tell us, about what they do and what happens. But we cannot rely upon them for an understanding of the relations that shape and determine the everyday. Here then is our business as social scientists for the investigation of these relations and the exploration of the ways they are present in the everyday are and must be a specialized enterprise, a work, the work of a social scientist.

The contemporary feminist critique has emphasized problems in the relationship between researcher and 'subject' and has proposed and practiced methods of interview that do not objectify the research 'other.' Important as such methods are, they are not in themselves sufficient to ground a feminist sociology. Changes in the relationship of researcher and 'subjects' do not resolve the kinds of problems we have been discussing. They are not solutions so long as the sociological methods of thinking and analysis objectify what our 'subjects' have told us about their lives. We are restricted to the descriptive, to allowing the voices of women's experience to be heard, unless we can go beyond what our respondents themselves have to tell us. Important as it has been and is to hear the authentic speaking of women, it is not sufficient to ground and guide a sociological inquiry. The development of a feminist method in sociology has to go beyond our interviewing practices and our research relationships to explore methods of thinking that will organize our inquiry and write our sociological texts so as to preserve the presence of actual subjects while exploring and explicating the relations in which our everyday worlds are embedded.

55

DONNA HARAWAY
Situated knowledges: the science question in feminism and the privilege of partial perspective* (1988)

Many currents in feminism attempt to theorize grounds for trusting especially the vantage points of the subjugated; there is good reason to believe vision is better from below the brilliant space platforms of the powerful. Building on that suspicion, this essay is an argument for situated and embodied knowledges and an argument against various forms of unlocatable, and so irresponsible, knowledge claims. Irresponsible means unable to be called into account. There is a premium on establishing the capacity to see from the peripheries and the depths. But here there also lies a serious danger of romanticizing and/or appropriating the vision of the less powerful while claiming to see from their positions. To see from below is neither easily learned nor unproblematic, even if 'we' 'naturally' inhabit the great underground terrain of subjugated knowledges. The positionings of the subjugated are not exempt from critical reexamination, decoding, deconstruction, and interpretation; that is, from both semiological and hermeneutic modes of critical inquiry. The standpoints of the subjugated are not 'innocent' positions. On the contrary, they are preferred because in principle they are least likely to allow denial of the critical and interpretive core of all knowledge. They are knowledgeable of modes of denial through repression, forgetting, and disappearing acts – ways of being nowhere while claiming to see comprehensively. The subjugated have a decent chance to be on to the god trick and all its dazzling – and, therefore, blinding – illuminations. 'Subjugated' standpoints are preferred because they seem to promise more adequate, sustained, objective, transforming accounts of the world. But how to see from below is a problem requiring at least as much skill with bodies and language, with the mediations of vision, as the 'highest' technoscientific visualizations.

Such preferred positioning is as hostile to various forms of relativism as to the most explicitly totalizing versions of claims to scientific authority. But the alternative to relativism is not totalization and single vision, which is always finally the unmarked

* This article was originally published in *Feminist Studies*, vol. 14, no. 2 (Summer, 1988), reprinted by permission of the publisher, *Feminist Studies*, Inc. Pp. 583–590.

category whose power depends on systematic narrowing and obscuring. The alternative to relativism is partial, locatable, critical knowledges sustaining the possibility of
webs of connections called solidarity in politics and shared conversations in epistemology. Relativism is a way of being nowhere while claiming to be everywhere
equally. The 'equality' of positioning is a denial of responsibility and critical inquiry.
Relativism is the perfect mirror twin of totalization in the ideologies of objectivity;
both deny the stakes in location, embodiment, and partial perspective; both make it
impossible to see well. Relativism and totalization are both 'god tricks' promising
vision from everywhere and nowhere equally and fully, common myths in rhetorics
surrounding Science. But it is precisely in the politics and epistemology of partial
perspectives that the possibility of sustained, rational, objective inquiry rests.

So, with many other feminists, I want to argue for a doctrine and practice of
objectivity that privileges contestation, deconstruction, passionate construction,
webbed connections, and hope for transformation of systems of knowledge and ways
of seeing. But not just any partial perspective will do; we must be hostile to easy
relativisms and holisms built out of summing and subsuming parts. 'Passionate
detachment' requires more than acknowledged and self-critical partiality. We are also
bound to seek perspective from those points of view, which can never be known in
advance, that promise something quite extraordinary, that is, knowledge potent for
constructing worlds less organized by axes of domination. From such a viewpoint, the
unmarked category would really disappear – quite a difference from simply repeating
a disappearing act. The imaginary and the rational – the visionary and objective vision
– hover close together. I think Harding's plea for a successor science and for postmodern sensibilities must be read as an argument for the idea that the fantastic
element of hope for transformative knowledge and the severe check and stimulus of
sustained critical inquiry are jointly the ground of any believable claim to objectivity
or rationality not riddled with breathtaking denials and repressions. It is even possible
to read the record of scientific revolutions in terms of this feminist doctrine of rationality and objectivity. Science has been utopian and visionary from the start; that is one
reason 'we' need it.

A commitment to mobile positioning and to passionate detachment is dependent
on the impossibility of entertaining innocent 'identity' politics and epistemologies as
strategies for seeing from the standpoints of the subjugated in order to see well. One
cannot 'be' either a cell or molecule – or a woman, colonized person, laborer, and so
on – if one intends to see and see from these positions critically. 'Being' is much more
problematic and contingent. Also, one cannot relocate in any possible vantage point
without being accountable for that movement. Vision is always a question of the
power to see – and perhaps of the violence implicit in our visualizing practices. With
whose blood were my eyes crafted? These points also apply to testimony from the
position of 'oneself.' We are not immediately present to ourselves. Self-knowledge
requires a semiotic-material technology to link meanings and bodies. Self-identity is a
bad visual system. Fusion is a bad strategy of positioning. The boys in the human
sciences have called this doubt about self-presence the 'death of the subject' defined
as a single ordering point of will and consciousness. That judgment seems bizarre
to me. I prefer to call this doubt the opening of nonisomorphic subjects, agents,
and territories of stories unimaginable from the vantage point of the cyclopean,

self-satiated eye of the master subject. The Western eye has fundamentally been a wandering eye, a traveling lens. These peregrinations have often been violent and insistent on having mirrors for a conquering self – but not always. Western feminists also inherit some skill in learning to participate in revisualizing worlds turned upside down in earth-transforming challenges to the views of the masters. All is not to be done from scratch.

The split and contradictory self is the one who can interrogate positionings and be accountable, the one who can construct and join rational conversations and fantastic imaginings that change history. Splitting, not being, is the privileged image for feminist epistemologies of scientific knowledge. 'Splitting' in this context should be about heterogeneous multiplicities that are simultaneously salient and incapable of being squashed into isomorphic slots or cumulative lists. This geometry pertains within and among subjects. Subjectivity is multidimensional; so, therefore, is vision. The knowing self is partial in all its guises, never finished, whole, simply there and original; it is always constructed and stitched together imperfectly, and therefore able to join with another, to see together without claiming to be another. Here is the promise of objectivity: a scientific knower seeks the subject position, not of identity, but of objectivity, that is, partial connection. There is no way to 'be' simultaneously in all, or wholly in any, of the privileged (i.e., subjugated) positions structured by gender, race, nation, and class. And that is a short list of critical positions. The search for such a 'full' and total position is the search for the fetishized perfect subject of oppositional history, sometimes appearing in feminist theory as the essentialized Third World Woman. Subjugation is not grounds for an ontology; it might be a visual clue. Vision requires instruments of vision; an optics is a politics of positioning. Instruments of vision mediate standpoints; there is no immediate vision from the standpoints of the subjugated. Identity, including self-identity, does not produce science; critical positioning does, that is, objectivity. Only those occupying the positions of the dominators are self-identical, unmarked, disembodied, unmediated, transcendent, born again. It is unfortunately possible for the subjugated to lust for and even scramble into that subject position – and then disappear from view. Knowledge from the point of view of the unmarked is truly fantastic, distorted, and irrational. The only position from which objectivity could not possibly be practiced and honored is the standpoint of the master, the Man, the One God, whose Eye produces, appropriates, and orders all difference. No one ever accused the God of monotheism of objectivity, only of indifference. The god trick is self-identical, and we have mistaken that for creativity and knowledge, omniscience even.

Positioning is, therefore, the key practice in grounding knowledge organized around the imagery of vision, and much Western scientific and philosophic discourse is organized in this way. Positioning implies responsibility for our enabling practices. It follows that politics and ethics ground struggles for and contests over what may count as rational knowledge. That is, admitted or not, politics and ethics ground struggles over knowledge projects in the exact, natural, social, and human sciences. Otherwise, rationality is simply impossible, an optical illusion projected from nowhere comprehensively. Histories of science may be powerfully told as histories of the technologies. These technologies are ways of life, social orders, practices of visualization. Technologies are skilled practices. How to see? Where to see from? What limits to vision? What to see for? Whom to see with? Who gets to have more than one point of view? Who gets blinded? Who wears blinders? Who interprets the visual field? What other sensory powers do we wish to cultivate besides vision? Moral and political discourse should be the paradigm for rational discourse about the imagery and technologies of vision. Sandra Harding's claim, or observation, that movements of social revolution have most contributed to improvements in science might be read as a claim about the knowledge consequences of new technologies of positioning. But I wish Harding had spent more time remembering that social and scientific revolutions have not always been liberatory, even if they have always been visionary. Perhaps this point could be captured in another phrase: the science question in the military. Struggles over what will count as rational accounts of the world are struggles over how to see. The terms of vision: the science question in colonialism, the science question in exterminism, the science question in feminism.

The issue in politically engaged attacks on various empiricisms, reductionisms, or other versions of scientific authority should not be relativism – but location. A dichotomous chart expressing this point might look like this:

universal rationality	ethnophilosophies
common language	heteroglossia
new organon	deconstruction
unified field theory	oppositional positioning
world system	local knowledges
master theory	webbed accounts

But a dichotomous chart misrepresents in a critical way the positions of embodied objectivity that I am trying to sketch. The primary distortion is the illusion of symmetry in the chart's dichotomy, making any position appear, first, simply alternative and, second, mutually exclusive. A map of tensions and resonances between the fixed ends of a charged dichotomy better represents the potent politics and epistemologies of embodied, therefore accountable, objectivity. For example, local knowledges have also to be in tension with the productive structurings that force unequal translations and exchanges – material and semiotic – within the webs of knowledge and power. Webs can have the property of being systematic, even of being centrally structured global systems with deep filaments and tenacious tendrils into time, space, and consciousness, which are the dimensions of world history. Feminist accountability requires a knowledge tuned to resonance, not to dichotomy. Gender is a field of structured and structuring difference, in which the tones of extreme localization, of the intimately personal and individualized body, vibrate in the same field with global high-tension emissions. Feminist embodiment, then, is not about fixed location in a reified body, female or otherwise, but about nodes in fields, inflections in orientations, and responsibility for difference in material-semiotic fields of meaning. Embodiment is significant prosthesis; objectivity cannot be about fixed vision when what counts as an object is precisely what world history turns out to be about.

How should one be positioned in order to see, in this situation of tensions, resonances, transformations, resistances, and complicities? Here, primate vision is not immediately a very powerful metaphor or technology for feminist political-epistemological clarification, because it seems to present to consciousness already processed and objectified fields; things seem already fixed and distanced. But the visual metaphor allows one to go beyond fixed appearances, which are only the end products. The metaphor invites us to investigate the varied apparatuses of visual production, including the prosthetic technologies interfaced with our biological eyes and brains. And here we find highly particular machineries for processing regions of the electromagnetic spectrum into our pictures of the world. It is in the intricacies of these visualization technologies in which we are embedded that we will find metaphors and means for understanding and intervening in the patterns of objectification in the world – that is, the patterns of reality for which we must be accountable. In these metaphors, we find means for appreciating simultaneously both the concrete, 'real' aspect and the aspect of semiosis and production in what we call scientific knowledge.

I am arguing for politics and epistemologies of location, positioning, and situating, where partiality and not universality is the condition of being heard to make rational knowledge claims. These are claims on people's lives. I am arguing for the view from a body, always a complex, contradictory, structuring, and structured body, versus the view from above, from nowhere, from simplicity. Only the god trick is forbidden. Here is a criterion for deciding the science question in militarism, that dream science/technology of perfect language, perfect communication, final order.

Feminism loves another science: the sciences and politics of interpretation, translation, stuttering, and the partly understood. Feminism is about the sciences of the multiple subject with (at least) double vision. Feminism is about a critical vision consequent upon a critical positioning in unhomogeneous gendered social space. Translation is always interpretive, critical, and partial. Here is a ground for conversation, rationality, and objectivity – which is power-sensitive, not pluralist, 'conversation.' It is not even the mythic cartoons of physics and mathematics – incorrectly caricatured in antiscience ideology as exact, hypersimple knowledges – that have come to represent the hostile other to feminist paradigmatic models of scientific knowledge, but the dreams of the perfectly known in high-technology, permanently militarized scientific productions and positionings, the god trick of a Star Wars paradigm of rational knowledge. So location is about vulnerability; location resists the politics of closure, finality, or to borrow from Althusser, feminist objectivity resists 'simplification in the last instance.' That is because feminist embodiment resists fixation and is insatiably curious about the webs of differential positioning. There is no single feminist standpoint because our maps require too many dimensions for that metaphor to ground our visions. But the feminist standpoint theorists' goal of an epistemology and politics of engaged, accountable positioning remains eminently potent. The goal is better accounts of the world, that is, 'science.'

Above all, rational knowledge does not pretend to disengagement: to be from everywhere and so nowhere, to be free from interpretation, from being represented, to by fully self-contained or fully formalizable. Rational knowledge is a process of ongoing critical interpretation among 'fields' of interpreters and decoders. Rational knowledge is power-sensitive conversation. Decoding and transcoding plus translation and criticism; all are necessary. So science becomes the paradigmatic model, not of closure, but of that which is contestable and contested. Science becomes the myth, not of what escapes human agency and responsibility in a realm above the fray, but, rather, of accountability and responsibility for translations and solidarities linking the cacophonous visions and visionary voices that characterize the knowledges of the subjugated. A splitting of senses, a confusion of voice and sight, rather than clear and distinct ideas, becomes the metaphor for the ground of the rational. We seek not the knowledges ruled by phallogocentrism (nostalgia for the presence of the one true Word) and disembodied vision. We seek those ruled by partial sight and limited voice – not partiality for its own sake but, rather, for the sake of the connections and unexpected openings situated knowledges make possible. Situated knowledges are about communities, not about isolated individuals. The only way to find a larger vision is to be somewhere in particular. The science question in feminism is about objectivity as positioned rationality. Its images are not the products of escape and transcendence of limits (the view from above) but the joining of partial views and halting voices into a collective subject position that promises a vision of the means of ongoing finite embodiment, of living within limits and contradictions – of views from somewhere.

56

PATRICIA HILL COLLINS

The sociological significance of black feminist thought* (1986)

Taken together, the three key themes in Black feminist thought – the meaning of self-definition and self-valuation, the interlocking nature of oppression, and the importance of redefining culture – have made significant contributions to the task of clarifying a Black women's standpoint of and for Black women. While this accomplishment is important in and of itself, Black feminist thought has potential contributions to make to the diverse disciplines housing its practitioners.

The sociological significance of Black feminist thought lies in two areas. First, the content of Black women's ideas has been influenced by and contributes to on-going dialogues in a variety of sociological specialties. While this area merits attention, it is not my primary concern in this section. Instead, I investigate a second area of socio-logical significance: the process by which these specific ideas were produced by this specific group of individuals. In other words, I examine the influence of Black women's outsider within status in academia on the actual thought produced. Thus far, I have proceeded on the assumption that it is impossible to separate the structure and thematic content of thought. In this section, I spell out exactly what form the relationship between the three key themes in Black feminist thought and Black women's outsider within status might take for women scholars generally, with special attention to Black female sociologists.

First, I briefly summarize the role sociological paradigms play in shaping the facts and theories used by sociologists. Second, I explain how Black women's outsider within status might encourage Black women to have a distinctive standpoint *vis-à-vis* sociology's paradigmatic facts and theories. I argue that the thematic content of Black feminist thought described above represents elements of just such a standpoint and give examples of how the combination of sociology's paradigms and Black women's outsider within status as sociologists directed their attention to specific areas of sociological inquiry.

* Pp. 24–26, 29–30 from 'Learning from the Outsider Within: The Sociological Significance of Black Feminist Thought', *Social Problems*, Vol. 33, No. 6. Issue: October, 1986, pp. S14–S32. © 1986 by The Society for the Study of Social Problems. Reprinted by permission of the publisher and author.

Two elements of sociological paradigms

Kuhn defines a paradigm as the 'entire constellation of beliefs, values, techniques, and so on shared by the members of a given community' (*The Structure of Scientific Revolutions*, Chicago, 1962: 175). As such, a paradigm consists of two fundamental elements: the thought itself and its producers and practitioners. In this sense, the discipline of sociology is itself a paradigm – it consists of a system of knowledge shared by sociologists – and simultaneously consists of a plurality of paradigms (e.g., functionalism, Marxist sociology, feminist sociology, existential sociology), each produced by its own practitioners.

Two dimensions of thought itself are of special interest to this discussion. First, systems of knowledge are never complete. Rather, they represent guidelines for 'thinking as usual.' Kuhn refers to these guidelines as 'maps,' while Schutz describes them as 'recipes.' As Schutz points out, while 'thinking as usual' is actually only partially organized and partially clear, and may contain contradictions, to its practitioners it provides sufficient coherence, clarity, and consistency. Second, while thought itself contains diverse elements, I will focus mainly on the important fact/theory relationship. As Kuhn suggests, facts or observations become meaningful in the context of theories or interpretations of those observations. Conversely, theories 'fit the facts' by transforming previously accessible observations into facts. According to Mulkay, 'observation is not separate from interpretation; rather these are two facets of a single process' (*Science and the Sociology of Knowledge*, Boston, 1979: 49).

Several dimensions of the second element of sociological paradigms – the community formed by a paradigm's practitioners – are of special interest to this discussion. First, group insiders have similar worldviews, aquired through similar educational and professional training, that separate them from everyone else. Insider worldviews may be especially alike if group members have similar social class, gender, and racial backgrounds. Schutz describes the insider worldview as the 'cultural pattern of group life' – namely, all the values and behaviors which characterize the social group at a given moment in its history. In brief, insiders have undergone similar experiences, possess a common history, and share taken-for-granted knowledge that characterizes 'thinking as usual.'

A second dimension of the community of practitioners involves the process of becoming an insider. How does one know when an individual is really an insider and not an outsider in disguise? Merton suggests that socialization into the life of a group is a lengthy process of being immersed in group life, because only then can 'one understand the fine-grained meanings of behaviour, feeling, and values . . . and decipher the unwritten grammar of conduct and nuances of cultural idiom' (1972: 15). The process is analogous to immersion in a foreign culture in order to learn its ways and its language (Merton, 1972; Schutz, 1944). One becomes an insider by translating a theory or worldview into one's own language until, one day, the individual converts to thinking and acting according to that worldview.

A final dimension of the community of practitioners concerns the process of remaining an insider. A sociologist typically does this by furthering the discipline in ways described as appropriate by sociology generally, and by areas of specialization particularly. Normal foci for scientific sociological investigation include: (1)

determining significant facts; (2) matching facts with existing theoretical interpretations to 'test' the paradigm's ability to predict facts; and (3) resolving ambiguities in the paradigm itself by articulating and clarifying theory . . .

Toward synthesis: outsiders within sociology

Black women are not the only outsiders within sociology. As an extreme case of outsiders moving into a community that historically excluded them, Black women's experiences highlight the tension experienced by any group of less powerful outsiders encountering the paradigmatic thought of a more powerful insider community. In this sense, a variety of individuals can learn from Black women's experiences as outsiders within: Black men, working-class individuals, white women, other people of color, religious and sexual minorities, and all individuals who, while from social strata that provided them with the benefits of white male insiderism, have never felt comfortable with its taken-for-granted assumptions.

Outsider within status is bound to generate tension, for people who become outsiders within are forever changed by their new status. Learning the subject matter of sociology stimulates a reexamination of one's own personal and cultural experiences; and, yet, these same experiences paradoxically help to illuminate sociology's anomalies. Outsiders within occupy a special place – they become different people, and their difference sensitizes them to patterns that may be more difficult for established sociological insiders to see. Some outsiders within try to resolve the tension generated by their new status by leaving sociology and remaining sociological outsiders. Others choose to suppress their difference by striving to become bonafide, 'thinking as usual' sociological insiders. Both choices rob sociology of diversity and ultimately weaken the discipline.

A third alternative is to conserve the creative tension of outsider within status by encouraging and institutionalizing outsider within ways of seeing. This alternative has merit not only for actual outsiders within, but also for other sociologists as well. The approach suggested by the experiences of outsiders within is one where intellectuals learn to trust their own personal and cultural biographies as significant sources of knowledge. In contrast to approaches that require submerging these dimensions of self in the process of becoming an allegedly unbiased, objective social scientist, outsiders within bring these ways of knowing back into the research process. At its best, outsider within status seems to offer its occupants a powerful balance between the strengths of their sociological training and the offerings of their personal and cultural experiences. Neither is subordinated to the other. Rather, experienced reality is used as a valid source of knowledge for critiquing sociological facts and theories, while sociological thought offers new ways of seeing that experienced reality.

What many Black feminists appear to be doing is embracing the creative potential of their outsider within status and using it wisely. In doing so, they move themselves and their disciplines closer to the humanist vision implicit in their work – namely, the freedom both to be different and part of the solidarity of humanity.

57

KARIN KNORR-CETINA
Strong constructivism* (1993)

Consider the challenges constructivism, and the sociology of scientific knowledge in general, have posed for traditional philosophical beliefs. These new approaches replace the view that observation and experiment play the dominant role in the specification of scientific facts by the view that these processes involve collective negotiations, interests and the infusion of experimental outcomes with contingent features of situations. What constructivism puts its finger on in these claims is that the social is part of the production of innovation: constructivism brings into view social processes, as opposed to the methodological and individual processes with which received views of science were concerned. Now, whether one agrees or not with some of the specific claims made in this respect is beside the point; what seems not beside the point is the need for philosophy of science systematically to think through and incorporate the role of the social into normative pictures of scientific activity. In fact, it is hardly conceivable that a phenomenon like modern science, which is so intrinsically linked to modern society as an institutional and collective arrangement, should not itself display social features which philosophy must come to grips with if it is ever going to be au courant with the world in which it lives. Equally, constructivism in particular has not stressed interests so much as features which one could roughly associate with a notion of social practice – features that are inherently linked to social situations (contingency, indexicality, opportunism, emergent outcomes), to the pliability of rules and standardized criteria, to the situational role of power and the like. Besides putting its finger on the potential relevance of the social for understanding science, constructivism has raised the question of what role one should accord, in a theory of knowledge, to the reversals practice brings about – the reversal of universal standards through local conventions and opportunities, the reversal of rules through power, and the replacement of social and other characteristics of persons through situational features. With respect to this role, philosophy is called upon to think beyond Wittgenstein and Heidegger and to notice, besides the work of great scientists and the work of

* From 'Strong Constructivism', *Social Studies of Science* 23, 1993, pp. 556–557. Copyright Karin Knorr-Cetina 1993. Reprinted with permission of Sage Publications Ltd.

methodological commandments, the work of situations. Finally, there is another issue raised by constructivism which invites philosophical thinking rather than philosophical denial of existence. This is the hoary old possibility that science, too, may be based upon circular reasoning, with conclusions shaping experimental action just as the outcome of this action shapes conclusions. Closed circuitries in science come in many shapes and variants. If we must have foundations for scientific knowledge, is it not conceivable that we might work out circular foundations? What worries me about attempts at reconciling constructivism with established doctrines is that they foreclose such possibilities. In bringing us home to the received pillars of disciplinary belief, they prefer, within the perspectives from which they criticize constructivism, disciplinary regress to disciplinary progress.

58

IAN HACKING
What is social construction? The teenage pregnancy example* (2002)

Would it make sense to say that teenage pregnancy is a social construction? Would it be useful? What would it mean? I am not asking whether teenage pregnancy is a social construct. I am asking about the meaning and use of the idea of social construction. I will use this example, and also child abuse, to illustrate some of the themes from *The Social Construction of What?* (Hacking 1999, *SCOW?* for short).

That title was meant to be puzzling: you are not quite sure how to pronounce it. One point was that authors who write about social construction should take pains to say exactly *what* is supposed to be socially constructed. When we find 'The Invention of Teenage Pregnancy' (the subtitle of Arney and Bergen 1987), we need to ask that question. This paper does not tell us how Adam and Eve invented teenage pregnancy and made Cain. It is about 1960s America. So exactly *what* was invented then?

In a much more recent paper, 'The "Making" of Teenage Pregnancy' (Wong 1997), we read that the 'discourse of "teenage pregnancy"' is a social construction. Here it is not pregnancy but talk about it that is the construction. If the discourse is a construction, how could it fail to be a social one? Is 'social' redundant? That issue is examined in Chapter 2 of *SCOW?*. Teenage pregnancy is one of innumerable topics that can be used to illustrate, and make concrete, questions about the very idea of social construction in sociological contexts. There are also questions about the natural sciences, but they will not be discussed here (see *SCOW?* Ch. 3.)

A very great many items are said to be socially constructed. The very first 'social construction' book title was *The Social Construction of Reality* by Peter Berger and Thomas Luckmann (1966). Among other titles you will find the social construction of postmodernism, emotion, the feeble mind, the eighties, child abuse and quarks. You read statements such as 'the experiences of being female or of having a disability are socially constructed'. Social construction is a kettle of many very different kinds of fish. Postmodernism, quarks, child abuse, experiences and reality are, in turn, a movement, style or epoch; the conjectured fundamental particles of recent physics; a much condemned type of behaviour; what individuals experience; and who knows

* © Copyright by Ian Hacking 2003.

what 'reality' denotes – everything that exists? In fact Berger and Luckman's book was in part about the way in which our sense of reality, and of different levels of social reality, are formed in the course of face-to-face human reactions.

Social construction has become something of a slogan. It tends to reflect an anti-establishment attitude. Think of studies of the social construction of gender. Feminists of many different allegiances have argued that present and past gender distinctions need not be the way they are, have been harmful to women and that all people, but especially women and children, would be much better off without our present gendered social arrangements. This is *strong* social constructionism. X need not have existed or be like it is; X is quite bad; and we would be much better without X, or with a very different version of X. Off with X! Not many social construction theses have such a firmly radical stance. Nevertheless they urge that some X need not have been the way it is. X, in its present form seems inevitable, but it is not. That is *weak* social constructionism. Often there is an *ironic* turn as suggested by Richard Rorty's book *Contingency, Irony, and Solidarity* (1989): we cannot even think without taking X for granted, and yet X was put in place by a rather haphazard chain of events.

There is another element of constructionism, unmasking (to take a word from Karl Mannheim in translation). It does not strive to refute an idea, but to reveal the 'extra-theoretical function' served by the idea. It may try to 'disintegrate' an idea, but not by showing that it is mistaken. One argues that it has at least its present contours in response to some social function not visible to those who take the idea for granted.

Thus talk of social construction is not merely descriptive. It is cultural history with a message. It might be nice if, for any particular X (e.g. child abuse), 'the social construction of X' referred to exactly one X, be it the behaviour of abusers, the experiences of those who are abused, their memories of abuse or the discourse about child abuse conducted by children, or parents, or teachers, or social workers, or legis-lators. We have had papers called 'The Social Construction of Child Abuse' starting in 1975. Usually constructionists use one name, X, to refer simultaneously to several different types of item – the experiences, the memories, the discourse and the behaviour itself, for example. Moreover, when they discuss the social construction of X, the most important part of their work may be a description of how the different items, all referred to as 'X', *interact*. For example, the way in which discourse about child abuse interacts with the experience of being abused. This changes how children are affected and what they remember. That in turns leads to changes in what we think of as child abuse, and how we think about perpetrators and victims (even the familiar concepts 'perpetrator' and 'victim' are astonishingly new). *Interactions* between the classification, the behaviour and the people classified are the topic of Chapter 4 of *SCOW?*, and are discussed in the context of child abuse in Chapter 5. Such inter-actions are central elements of construction-oriented analyses of kinds of people, especially of potentially stigmatized individuals such as child abusers or teenage mothers.

Attending to *what* is supposed to be socially constructed can help get rid of one confusion about social construction. One may want to say that X is socially con-structed, and yet that it is real. I myself once wrote that child abuse '*is* a real evil, and it was so before the concept was constructed. It was nevertheless constructed. Neither reality nor construction should be in question'. I should have said that the *concept* of child abuse was brought into being around 1961, as the beginning of a campaign started in Denver, Colorado. Ideas about child abuse evolved – when the concept was activated, it meant battered children, but by 1980 it meant sexual abuse. Despite this recent emergence of the idea of child abuse, there has been what we now call child abuse as far back as recorded history. Let us look more closely at the two statements: the idea is 'constructed', and the behaviour is 'real'. We should not so much ask what is the meaning of each of these two statements, but what is the point of making them.

'The idea of child abuse is socially constructed.' Any idea that is debated, assessed, applied, and developed is situated in a social setting. But it is not sensible to say that every idea is constructed. No point is served by saying that the idea of digging (a ditch, say) is constructed. But there is a point in saying that the idea of child abuse was constructed, or, as I prefer to say, made and moulded. The explicit idea emerged at a definite time (1961) at a definite place (Denver) in the discussions of some authoritative people (paediatricians). It was different from the Victorian idea of cruelty to children. It became embedded in new legislation, incorporated in practices and changed a wide range of professional activities involving social workers, police, schoolteachers, parents and busybodies. Children were trained to be aware of abuse, and abusers were stigmatized, often for acts that previously had seemed anodyne. Child abuse acquired moral weight: it became the worst possible vice. The point of saying that the idea of child abuse is socially constructed is to insist that it is not inevitable, but is the product of a very specific social history that might have been very different.

'Child abuse is real.' The point of this statement is also clear, although it was more salient in 1962, when few people believed that child abuse was at all common, than today, when authorities speak of an epidemic of child abuse. Child abuse is not something that has been imagined by activists; there are innumerable cases of children who have been physically, sexually, or emotionally abused. *That* is the point of saying that child abuse is real. Bringing that fact to the attention of the public, of parents, of teachers, of legislators and of the victims themselves was one of the most valuable pieces of consciousness-raising to take place between 1960 and 1990.

It is not prudent to summarize the last two paragraphs by saying that child abuse is both real and constructed. Instead say that the *behaviour* we now call child abuse has been a fact of most human communities at most times in our history. Say that the *idea* of child abuse, and the consequences of that idea, were constructed in the course of the years following 1960. I think that 'making and moulding' is a better term than 'constructing'. Often it is better to be still more specific. For an example in the tradition of what Joseph Gusfield called agenda-setting, see Barbara Nelson's *Making an Issue of Child Abuse: Political Agenda-Setting for Social Problems* (1984).

There are degrees and kinds of child abuse. We can readily see how the scales and boundaries between them might be affected by social judgements and policies, plus pedagogical practices and technical innovations. But teenage pregnancy must seem as 'objective' a concept as could be. There are necessary and sufficient conditions for being a pregnant teen: all and only pregnant women who conceive under the age of 18. Yet the concept is not used in that way. It is used to refer to adolescents who are neither married nor about to be married. Rape is not in question: conception has been caused by more or less consensual sex.

Notice that the concept of a teenager, with the associated lifestyles and responsibilities, is one peculiar to our culture. Even the very notion of an adolescent, let alone a 'teen', and the roles appropriate to that stage in life, may be little more than a century old. Some authors suggest that adolescence was 'discovered' by Anna Freud, while others attribute the discovery to the American psychologist G. Stanley Hall, who in 1905 published two volumes under a compendium of the telling title *Adolescence: Its Relation to Psychology, Anthropology, Sociology, Sex, Crime, Religion and Education*. Far from being an inevitable way of dividing up a lifetime, the concept of adolescence was constructed in order to relate to problematic behaviour, including premarital sex and juvenile delinquency. And yet now, we can ironically add, it seems impossible to think of young people without using the idea of adolescence.

To return to our main example, let us list some of the many items that arise in the discourse about teenage pregnancy:

1 The condition of being a teen-aged pregnant woman. That is, under 18 and pregnant.

2 The women actually covered by the use of the term 'teenage pregnancy'. Not any pregnant teenager but someone in our society who is not married nor about to be married, and who is pregnant as the result of more or less consensual sex.

3 The uses of the expression 'teenage pregnancy' and other labels such as 'unwed mother', 'illegitimate child', 'bastard' and 'single parent'. Here one wants to know when and where the labels are or were used, and by whom.

4 The idea of teenage pregnancy – an idea that goes beyond the mere existence and usage of the term, but an idea that may simply not exist in most societies and at most times and places. An idea that undergoes evolution, perhaps mutations.

5 The socioeconomic classes and circumstances in which the idea of teenage pregnancy is deployed.

6 Teenage pregnancy as a social problem.

7 Institutions associated with teenage pregnancy – once, secret clinics in which babies could be born, and then given away; now support groups for teenagers who want to keep their babies.

8 Experts on teenage pregnancy – seldom adolescent mothers but usually professional experts who include this subject as part of their expertise. This includes sociologists and moralists. In some quarters mature women who once were teenage mothers may be deemed to have a special authority.

9 The statistics of teenage pregnancy.

10 The experiences of teenage pregnant women and of teenage mothers, who live in a world where there is a discourse of teenage pregnancy.

11 Groups formed for and by teenage mothers and mothers to be, for whom a sense of identity and self-pride may be important.

12 Political bravura. Cries of horror and demand for change when we learn that 12 per cent of unmarried Canadian women under the age of 18 become pregnant. Talk-shows. Politicians orate. Pollsters investigate. Editors inveigh.

And so on. An author could refer to any one of these, and publish an article called, 'The social construction of teenage pregnancy'. The point would often be to show that this way of describing and sorting people was far from inevitable, but is the product of a specific social conjuncture.

That was what Arney and Bergen (1984) argued when they wrote 'The Invention of Teenage Pregnancy'. They did not refer to (1), the condition of being an unmarried pregnant teenager. That has been with us always, and needs no invention. (What needs 'invention', or at any rate social constraint, is teenage non-pregnancy.) Arney and Bergen point out that the name (3) 'teenage pregnancy' came into being at a quite specific time and place, namely middle class America about 1965.

This is not just a new wording but a change in social meaning. Before 1965, middle-class young unmarried pregnant women were a secret. They were sent away to relatives. They had their children in sanctuaries. There were illegal abortions. The new phrase 'teenage pregnancy' went together with coming out. The (4) connotations of the idea of teenage pregnancy changed and keep on changing. In the early days it was a middle-class affair. Of late, especially in the USA the socioeconomic venue (5) has changed to poverty and to race. The 1965 meaning was pregnancy in the suburb; now it is pregnancy in the ghetto. In both cases teenage pregnancy is deemed not to be a condition or a fact, but a (6) social problem.

Institutions (7) abound, both governmental and NGOs (non-governmental organizations). We have plenty of (8) expert knowledge. (I wrote a version of this paper for a conference of experts on single parenting.) Endless arrays of (9) statistics are collected and analysed.

All of these items interact with each other. Institutions collect statistics, which reinforce institutions. Social problems beget experts, who revise the very idea of teenage pregnancy. These items affect young unmarried mothers. More interesting than any of the items mentioned so far is the way in which, for lack of a better word, the experiences (10) of the young women have dramatically changed in the past 30 years. No longer is there automatic secrecy, shame, withdrawal. Many of these mothers experience themselves as having 'grown up', matured, become responsible, as their babies have first come to term and then been infants in their arms. Of course talk of growing up and maturing is itself the adoption of a set of values derived from, even imposed by, middle-aged, middle-class culture.

There are plenty of help and self-help institutions for young single mothers. Around the corner from where I live there is '*Jennie's*', a drop-in home for young unmarried mothers and mothers-to-be, where mutual support, topped up by day care, is a great value. These phenomena have sometimes led to self-ascription and independence of choice derived from (11) self-confidence and even pride. The most impressive feature here is the change in attitude to adoption. In the 1960s, it was the norm to put the child out for adoption, and there was an elaborate infrastructure of institutions and physical plant dedicated to just that. The western world was once full of clinics, homes, wards and private hospitals dedicated to adoption. Now there are virtually none. Apparently without any formal structure, the pregnant young women have declared as with one voice that if they give birth, they want to keep their babies.

Many proper persons would prefer that most teenage mothers gave up their infants for adoption. Why? Mature parents, biological or adoptive, are deemed to be better parents. But perhaps the only substantive fact is that they may, under current economic arrangements, have more opportunities to support themselves. Incidentally a pro-adoptive policy would solve the difficulties of all those childless middle-class parents who cannot get white babies. But the mothers themselves have resisted. By some process which should fascinate sociologists, they now find adoption to be unthinkable. None of these changes helps eliminate (12), political bravura.

Teenage + pregnant seems to be about as natural a class as there is. Yet the fact that we treat this as a significant or salient class, worthy of its own label, is a fact of thoroughly contingent social history. Revised nomenclature has been proposed: early parenting. I have already suggested the subtext here. The locale is the American black inner city. The American *Personal Responsibility and Work Opportunity Reconciliation Act of 1996* repealed entitlements to welfare assistance for poor people; it replaced them by 'workfare'. Finding 10 of 101 refers to the 'crisis' of 'out-of-wedlock pregnancy' facing the nation.

Dissidents propose that in African American culture, going back through slavery to West African roots, it was the cultural norm for young women to begin to conceive not long after puberty, and by no means consistently with a permanent, let alone life-time, partner. Thus 'early' parenting is deviant relative to a European American setting; it is or could be conceived of as the norm in other milieux. The fact that it is deviant is thus argued not to be a fact of nature but a social construction.

A final element in social constructionism is unmasking. There is a certain amount of that in connection with teenage pregnancy, of drawing attention to the ways in which the proper middle-class adult world has generated a concept to keep order among the young and the poor. Notice incidentally that talk of social construction usually has an overtone of oppression, of something being fostered from above. Yet if we were even-handed, and being merely descriptive, perhaps the most exciting thing to call 'socially constructed', in connection with teens, is the new consensus from below that adopting is unthinkable. But then the slightly self-righteous tone of social construction would disappear. Here, it seems, is the underclass deciding for itself, in the face of, and utterly against the expectations of, propriety.

Perhaps we who have ceased to be teenagers could do with some more unmasking. The people who discuss teenage pregnancy at length are primarily from the welfare or knowledge industries. They might begin sceptically to ask, what are we really doing? Those providing services, advice and welfare are serving the interests of those who need help – or are they? Someone who began to ask these questions would begin to seek out allies who use the slogan 'social construction' in other contexts, be they 'gender' or 'child abuse'.

Once alliances have been forged it does not seem to me very helpful to speak of the social construction of teenage pregnancy. The trouble is that, except as a political slogan, the very phrase 'social construction' is tired, imprecise, pretentious and self-righteous. When it is not fired with political rhetoric we are better off without it. There are so many more interesting, informative, thought-provoking things to say about that remarkable cultural phenomenon, teenage pregnancy, as a social problem, as a field of expertise, as a domain of discourse and above all as the experience of young women and their children.

I began with three questions. Would it make sense to say that teenage pregnancy is a social construction? Would it be useful? What would it mean? Here are my answers. It makes sense, but it is not very useful. What it means is that the very idea of teenage pregnancy is one that came into being, in certain historical circumstances, and the practices, institutions, and experiences are the product of those circumstances. It means that the idea of teenage pregnancy is not an inevitable one, a mere description of the state of certain young women, but rather a label used both to identify, advise and control, and also, at a later time, to work internally to create pride and self-control. But there are much better ways of saying that than by talking about social construction.

References

Arney, W.R. and Bergen, B.J. (1984) 'Power and Visibility: The Invention of Teenage Pregnancy', *Social Sciences and Medicine*, 18: 11–19.

Berger, P. and Luckmann, T. (1966) *The Social Construction of Reality*. Harmondsworth: Penguin.

Hacking, I. (1999) *The Social Construction of What?* Cambridge, MA: Harvard University Press.

Hall, G.S. (1905) *Adolescence: Its Relation to Psychology, Anthropology, Sociology, Sex, Crime, Religion and Education*. New York: Appleton.

Nelson, B. (1984) *Making an Issue of Child Abuse: Political Agenda – Setting for Social Problems*. Chicago: University of Chicago Press.

Rorty, R. (1989) *Contingency, Irony and Solidarity*. Cambridge: Cambridge University Press.

Wong, J. (1997) 'The "making" of teenage pregnancy', *International Studies in the Philosophy of Science*, 11: 273–8.

59

STEVE FULLER

The project of social epistemology and the elusive problem of knowledge in contemporary society* (2002)

Social epistemology is a naturalistic approach to the normative questions surrounding the organization of inquiry. More concretely, it is a philosophy that takes seriously the history and social studies of science as a basis for setting 'knowledge policy' in the widest possible sense (Fuller 1988). However, the very existence of a field called 'social epistemology' says a lot about its origins. Its roots are clearly anglophone. From the standpoint of the major European languages, the English words 'know' and 'knowledge' cover too much semantic ground for philosophical purposes. Bertrand Russell (1940) partly recognized this point when he distinguished between 'knowledge by acquaintance' and 'knowledge by inference'. The objects of the former are apparent and particular (e.g. sensory data), those of the latter are implied and general (e.g. theoretical entities). Unfortunately, Russell drew this distinction in the context of trying to reduce the latter to the former. (His model was a logical proof, in which a novel conclusion is drawn from a series of self-evident steps in reasoning.) This project became 'the problem of knowledge' for the English-speaking world in the second half of the twentieth century, even though it is clear that Russell's formulation of the problem had already presupposed an empiricist solution, whereby a theory refers to nothing more than the sum of its possible observations.

In retrospect, it is ironic that Russell drew rhetorical support from logical positivist strictures against the reification of natural language, since a German or French speaker could easily see that only an anglophone like Russell could be misled by the homonymous use of 'knowledge' to conclude that 'knowledge by acquaintance' and 'knowledge by inference' must have something in common that is captured by the word 'knowledge'. But what is confused in English is clearly marked in German and French – not to mention Latin and Greek. The relevant distinctions between knowledge by acquaintance and by inference are *Erkenntnis/Wissenschaft, connaissance/savoir, cognitio/scientia, nous/episteme*. In other words, the English word 'knowledge' is meant to cover the objects of both *consciousness* and *science*. Yet, the former is normally

* © Copyright by Steve Fuller 2003.

concentrated in an individual's mental space, while the latter is distributed among a community of collaborators.

Social epistemology was thus prompted by the conceptual confusion concealed in the overextended use of 'know' and 'knowledge' in English. This confusion is diagnosed in a particular way, namely, in terms of the English language's occlusion of the social dimension of knowledge production. In this spirit, the fallacies of composition and division provided the original backdrop against which social epistemology was meant to be a constructive response (Fuller 1988: Preface). Both fallacies refer to the tendency to regard a whole as exactly equal to the sum of its parts. It is therefore fallacious for epistemologists to identify social knowledge with the sum of what individuals know. 'Composition' and 'division' are, respectively, the names of the bottom-up and top-down versions of this fallacious tendency. On the one hand, anglophone epistemologists tend to aggregate the beliefs of a society's members to arrive at the state of social knowledge; on the other, they tend to take a socially sanctioned statement of knowledge as representative of what everyone in that society believes (e.g. Kitcher 1993; Goldman 1999). Both inferences are fallacious because they fail to account for the effects of social interaction on what individuals accept (often passively) as counting for knowledge in their society. For example, how can it be that our lives are dominated by Darwin's and Einstein's world-views, even though the vast majority of people neither understand nor believe the theories of these two scientists? Thus, the 'public understanding of science' becomes a key site for social epistemology research (Fuller 1997).

Not surprisingly, 'epistemology' as the name of a distinct field of philosophy turns out to be of English origin. David Ferrier, a German-trained Scot, coined the term in the third quarter of the nineteenth century for the systematic study of how we know, which, given his own interest in mind-brain relations, we would now call 'cognitive science'. Yet, the expression 'cognitive science' itself contains the original confusion as a piece of Latinate English. Reflexive consistency would seem to demand that 'knowledge of knowledge' mean either 'consciousness of consciousness' or 'science of science'. The former would proceed with the intimacy of phenomenology, the latter with the detachment of positivism. In French philosophy, the choice here is very clear. It is between, on the one hand, Descartes and Sartre and, on the other, Comte and Foucault. Yet, cognitive science aspires to a middle ground that involves occluding the social activity that enables the assignment of mental states to individuals: it is, so to speak, a science of consciousness that does not require a consciousness of science. Consider the debate over whether computers can think. Regardless of whether one answers yes or no, one generally presumes that the issue turns on the intrinsic properties of computers and humans, not the social preconditions needed for attributing thoughts to either sort of entity (Fuller 1993b: Ch. 5). Social epistemology may be seen as an attempt to redress the balance here.

However, the very expression 'social epistemology' has been itself subject to critique. French and German contributors to an understanding of *Wissenschaft* or *savoir* have found the phrase redundant. After all, isn't science always already social both in its constitution and its effects? At the same time, fellow epistemologists in the English-speaking world often treat 'social epistemology' as a contradiction in terms. As it turns out, in the anglophone context, it makes a big difference whether one regards 'the problem of knowledge' as pertaining primarily to the verb 'to know' or the noun 'knowledge'. In the former case, the problem becomes a matter of getting outside one's head (i.e. to engage in an act of knowing); in the latter, a matter of managing certain products and processes (i.e. to gain access to knowledge). Anglophone epistemology has been fixated on the former, but social epistemology is mainly concerned with the latter. The contrast may be expressed more formally in terms of two strategies for generating philosophically interesting problems of knowledge:

Strategy A

1 The thing I know best is the thing with which I have had the most direct acquaintance, namely my own mind. After all, without it, I could not have made this very observation. But my mind is possibly not all that exists.

2 How, then, do I determine whether other possible things exist, and, if they exist, how can I know them, given that they seem quite different from my own mind?

Strategy B

1 We ordinarily experience everyone (and everything) as living in the same world. Yet, as people articulate their experience, it becomes clear that there are significant differences in the aspects of the world to which we have direct access.

2 What, then, accounts for these differences in access to our common reality, and what enables us to ignore them in everyday life, as we suppose that our own access is the one shared by all 'right-minded' people?

Strategy A captures the tradition of inquiry that unites Descartes and Russell, as well as Quine's progeny in analytic epistemology, especially once translation and communication are treated as versions of the problem of 'other minds' (Fuller 1988: Part 2). Strategy B extends from Augustinian theodicy through Leibniz, Hegel and Marx – as well as Karl Mannheim, the sociology of scientific knowledge and myself. Contributors to this tradition are moved by the different fates – be they ontic, epistemic or moral – that befall people, even though everyone is supposed to be equal members of humanity. (Elster 1979 is an excellent introduction to the distinct logic of this perspective.) Whereas Strategy A sets the task of epistemology as generalizing from the individual case, Strategy B sets the task as fully realizing the universal. The former task involves adding something that is missing, such as insight into other times, places and people that cannot be inferred through either deductive or inductive inference. The latter task involves redistributing something that is already present, be it called 'knowledge' or 'power'.

Strategies A and B both operate with epistemological premises that are taken to be liabilities in advancing the search for knowledge. Historically speaking, they are epitomized by, on the one hand, the Cartesian evil demon and, on the other, the Hegelian master-servant dialectic. For Strategy A, a self-centered relativism is the initial liability that needs to be overcome: I am in my own head, but I suspect that there are other things out there different from me. How do I find out? Not surprisingly, this strategy stresses methods that are biased toward realism, such as looking for ('primary') qualities that remain invariant under a variety of observations and transformations and hence escape the tricks that an evil demon might play on our naïve minds. For Strategy B, on the other hand, a totalizing realism is the initial liability: we all live in the same world, therefore everyone must think like me, at least when they are thinking right. But why does this not seem to be the case? (Are they crazy?) The relevant corrective here is a dose of methodological relativism: precisely *because* our reality is common, it cannot explain our palpable differences. We are thus better off regarding claims to a common reality as disguised partial perspectives, 'ideologies' or 'standpoints' that may gain certain local material advantage by capitalizing on our weakness for thinking in terms of totalizing forms of realism. Thus, one engages in critique to ensure that subordinate (or 'subaltern') social groups do not adopt perspectives (also known as 'false universals' or 'hegemonies') that simply serve the interests of the superior groups.

Social epistemology may be understood as operating on two levels at once. Not only does it adopt Strategy B, but it also frames the difference between Strategies A and B from that standpoint. Herein lies social epistemology's *naturalism*, namely, the idea that knowledge cannot be *about* the world unless it is clearly situated *in* the world (Fuller 1992). Appearances to the contrary, epistemologies are not created in a vacuum from first principles but in response to what already is the case. Thus, if our understanding of the world is already burdened with certain notions that may be impeding our progress, then theories of knowledge need to be designed to counteract these inertial tendencies. In Karl Popper's memorable phrase, we are born with *a priori false ideas*, the correction of which is the project of scientific inquiry. When the logical positivists formally distinguished the contexts of 'discovery' and 'justification', they were precisely in this frame of mind. Thus, they regarded any original formulation of an idea – including its original published expression – as an alloy of blindness and insight whose decontamination must precede its evaluation (Fuller 2000b: Ch.1). The chosen form of decontamination was logical translation, to which Popper (1963) famously objected, claiming that what was required was a specific kind of epistemic community, one governed by the interplay of 'conjectures and refutations'. Social epistemology attempts to flesh out the institutional context – a 'republican' science polity – that is required for the realization of Popper's ideal (Fuller 2000a).

This general attitude is traceable to the Enlightenment wits, who paradoxically admitted a *tabula rasa* conception of the mind, only then to invoke it to dismiss the gullibility of first-hand reports, such as those of the Apostles who claimed to have witnessed Jesus' Resurrection. Here we recall that naturalism's historical opposite has been 'supernaturalism', which implies that genuine knowledge somehow manages to transcend human cognitive limitations, usually by the grace of God. This is what Kant had originally opposed in *The Critique of Pure Reason* when he excoriated 'metaphysics', a term that retained this pejorative connotation in the lexicons of such major naturalists as John Stuart Mill, Ernst Mach, William James and John Dewey. If humanity has made epistemic progress, it is not due to divine dictate or permission, but because humans have organized themselves into social wholes whose knowledge is greater than that of the sum of the individuals constituting them. From this perspective, the teleologies of Hegelian historicism, Comtean positivism and Peircean pragmatism may be seen as attempts to simulate supernaturalism naturalistically by specifying a process by which higher-order human knowledge (or 'science') has been generated from a systematic critique of lower-order human knowledge (or 'consciousness'). For all of these thinkers, progress is made by approximating standards of our own making that nevertheless enable us to exercise greater control over reality as a whole. This is neither realism nor relativism in their totalising forms because it implies a much more dynamic and open-ended vision of the relationship between humans and their environment. However, the view is compatible with both constructivism and materialism.

In short, social epistemology is indebted to naturalism for the following insight: the price of acquiring any knowledge at all is that it will be somehow distorted by the conditions of its acquisition. Therefore, criticism is the only universally reliable method. The signature scientific institution of hypothesis-testing, which combines the dialectical tradition of rhetoric with the deductive tradition of logic, should be understood in just this light (Fuller 1993b: Ch.1). Thus, a theory of knowledge – be it realism or relativism – is doomed to failure if it aspires to a universality that ignores its own contingent origins as a corrective hypothesis (Fuller 1993a: Ch. 2).

However, the path from naturalism to social epistemology has been far from straight. The history of the sociology of knowledge and, more recently, science and technology studies provides the relevant context (Fuller 2002b). Both in its French (e.g. Lucien Levy-Bruhl, Emile Durkheim) and German (e.g. Wilhelm Dilthey, Karl Mannheim) incarnations, the sociology of knowledge was defined as the study of organized resistance to 'the environment', understood broadly to include not only physical nature but also individual thought processes. In the latter case, the sociology of knowledge was officially seen as complementing research in cognitive psychology, but questions were periodically raised about whether the people constituting the objects of sociological study – religious sects, political parties and, later, scientific disciplines – were to be understood as more or less 'rational' than people not so involved. In retrospect, the very question probably presupposed a confused sense of 'rationality' analogous to the confusion that still besets 'knowledge'. Nevertheless, when science was precluded from the sociology of knowledge, there was a strong inclination to regard the sociology of knowledge as mainly concerned with forms of irrationality. However, once science – the exemplar of rationality in contemporary society – was incorporated into the sociology of knowledge, a properly 'naturalistic' stance seemed to demand that all questions surrounding rationality should be 'bracketed' and all 'epistemic cultures' treated as equally adaptive in their own worlds (Knorr-Cetina 1999).

The appeal to 'bracketing' in the sociology of knowledge was not new. Indeed, science and technology studies often alludes to the precedent of Berger and Luckmann (1967). But here it is worth recalling that when Edmund Husserl originally introduced bracketing (or *epoche*) as the cornerstone of the phenomenological method, he wanted to abstract the content of thought from its spatio-temporal moorings in acts of thinking, the stuff of experimental, historical and comparative empirical investigation. Not surprisingly, such investigations have been traditionally crucial to judgements of rationality and the value of epistemic practices more generally.

However, the one big difference between Husserl and contemporary scholars in science and technology studies is that at least he realized that he was turning away from naturalism, whereas today's scholars have redefined 'naturalism' to mean merely 'science in the here-and-now'. Besides removing the normative dimension from science and technology studies, this restricted sense of naturalism has had some peculiar conceptual consequences. On the one hand, there has been a tendency to see all of contemporary society as permeated with knowledge in an unprecedented yet undiscriminating fashion, as in promiscuous talk about ours being a 'knowledge society'; on the other, there has been a tendency to reduce knowledge to power in an undifferentiated world of 'technoscience' in which knowledge is retrospectively attributed to networks that manage to satisfy their constituent nodes (Latour 1999).

From this standpoint, social epistemology aims to reverse the 'denaturalization' of knowledge that began with the sociology of knowledge's turn to Husserl. To do this, let us return to the difference between Strategies A and B. Ultimately, Strategy A poses the problem of knowledge *inside-out*: how do we get out of our individual heads and into some common reality? Strategy B poses it *outside-in*: how do we get beyond our common reality and into the mindsets that separate people? Inside-out, knowledge is posed as a problem for each individual to solve by approximating an external standard to which the individual may or may not have conscious access. There is no sense that epistemic access may be a scarce good, with one individual's access to knowledge perhaps impeding, competing with, or making demands on the epistemic access of some other individual. Rather, knowledge is regarded as what economists call a 'public good', namely, one whose value does not diminish as access increases. In contrast, the outside-in strategy portrays the individual as having to choose between two or more alternative courses of action, in full awareness that resources are limited and that other individuals will be simultaneously making similar decisions, the consequences of which will realize certain possibilities at the expense of others. This image of the knower as a 'bounded rationalist' engaged in 'knowledge management' has been a thread running throughout my work in social epistemology (Fuller 2002a). It conceives of knowledge as a 'positional' good (Hirsch 1977). This point has significant implications both for understanding the time-honoured equation 'knowledge is power' and designing knowledge-bearing institutions.

In the slogan, 'knowledge is power' (or '*savoir est pouvoir*' or '*Wissen ist Macht*'), power involves *both* the expansion and contraction of possibilities for action. Knowledge is supposed to expand the knower's possibilities for action by contracting the possible actions of others. These 'others' may range from fellow knowers to non-knowing natural and artificial entities. This broad understanding of the slogan encompasses the interests of all who have embraced it, including Plato, Bacon, Comte and Foucault. But differences arise over the normative spin given to the slogan: should the stress be placed on the *opening* or the *closing* of possibilities for action? If the former, then the range of knowers is likely to be restricted; if the latter, then the range is likely to be extended. After all, my knowledge provides an advantage over you only if you do not already possess it; hence, knowledge is a 'positional good'. This concept also helps to explain the rather schizoid attitudes toward the production and distribution of knowledge that are epitomized in the constitution of universities. In short, we do research to expand our own capacity to act, but we teach in order to free our students from the actions that have been and could be taken by others.

By virtue of their dual role as producers and distributors of knowledge, universities are engaged in an endless cycle of creating and destroying 'social capital', that is, the comparative advantage that a group or network enjoys by virtue of its collective capacity to act on a form of knowledge (Stehr 1994). Thus, as researchers, academics create social capital because intellectual innovation necessarily begins life as an élite product available only to those on 'the cutting edge'. However, as teachers, academics destroy social capital by making the innovation publicly available, thereby diminishing whatever advantage was originally afforded to those on the cutting edge. In this respect, intellectual property is anathema to the very idea of the university (Fuller 2002a). Recalling Joseph Schumpeter's (1950) definition of the entrepreneur as the 'creative destroyer' of capitalist markets, the university may be regarded as a 'meta-entrepreneurial' institution that functions as the crucible for larger societal change (Delanty 2001).

At the simplest level, the university is significant for social epistemology because it has been cross-culturally the most successful institution dedicated to the production and distribution of knowledge (Collins 1998). And, as a form of naturalistic epistemology, social epistemology must locate the normative structure of knowledge somewhere in the material world, not simply in an abstract set of propositions. Whereas proponents of Strategy A would look to certain bio-psychological properties of individuals, social epistemology's commitment to Strategy B suggests the need for a particular institutional arrangement. But at a subtler level, the university serves social epistemology's interest in recasting Russell's so-called 'problem of knowledge'. Specifically, the institution's creative destructive capacities enable a revised understanding of the ill-fated attempt to reduce knowledge by inference to knowledge by acquaintance. 'Reduction' now would be seen as the process by which research is rendered teachable, so that what had been originally grasped only as an esoteric theory would come to be integrated into people's ordinary perception of reality. In that case, the qualitative difference between inference and acquaintance that is masked by the homonymous use of 'knowledge' in English would be explained as a function of power relations that are forever creatively destroyed by universities.

References

Berger, P. and Luckmann, T. (1967) *The Social Construction of Reality*. Garden City NY: Anchor Doubleday.

Collins, R. (1998) *The Sociology of Philosophies*. Cambridge MA: Harvard University Press.

Delanty, G. (2001) *Challenging Knowledge: The University in the Knowledge Society*. Buckingham: Open University Press.

Elster, J. (1979) *Logic and Society*. Chichester: John Wiley & Sons.

Fuller, S. (1988) *Social Epistemology*. Bloomington, IN: Indiana University Press.

Fuller, S. (1992) Epistemology radically naturalized: recovering the normative, the experimental, and the social, in R. Giere (ed.) *Cognitive Models of Science*, pp. 427–59. Minneapolis, MN: University of Minnesota Press.

Fuller, S. (1993a) *Philosophy of Science and Its Discontents*, 2nd edn. New York: Guilford Press.

Fuller, S. (1993b) *Philosophy, Rhetoric and the End of Knowledge*. Madison, WI: University of Wisconsin Press.

Fuller, S. (1997) *Science*. Buckingham: Open University Press.

Fuller, S. (2000a) *The Governance of Science: Ideology and the Future of the Open Society*. Buckingham: Open University Press.

Fuller, S. (2000b) *Thomas Kuhn: A Philosophical History for Our Times*. Chicago: University of Chicago Press.

Fuller, S. (2002a) *Knowledge Management Foundations*. Woburn, MA: Butterworth-Heinemann.

Fuller, S. (2002b) Science and technology studies and the philosophy of the social sciences, in P.A. Roth and S.P. Turner (eds) *The Blackwell Companion to Philosophy of the Social Sciences*. Oxcford: Blackwell.

Goldman, A. (1999) *Knowledge in a Social World*. Oxford: Oxford University Press.

Hirsch, F. (1977) *Social Limits to Growth*. London: Routledge & Kegan Paul.

Kitcher, P. (1993) *The Advancement of Science*. Oxford: Oxford University Press.

Knorr-Cetina, K. (1999) *Epistemic Cultures*. Cambridge, MA: Harvard University Press.

Latour, B. (1999) *Pandora's Hope*. Cambridge, MA: Harvard University Press.

Popper, K. (1963) *Conjectures and Refutations*. New York: Harper & Row.

Russell, B. (1940) *An Inquiry into Truth and Meaning*. London: Routledge & Kegan Paul.

Schumpeter, J. (1950) *Capitalism, Socialism and Democracy*. 2nd edn. New York: Harper & Row.

Stehr, N. (1994) *Knowledge Societies*. London: Sage.

60

NIKLAS LUHMANN

The cognitive program of constructivism and a reality that remains unknown* (1990)

Interest in epistemological questions is not limited to philosophy today. Numerous empirical sciences have, in the normal course of their research, been forced to proceed from the immediate object of their research to questions involving cognition. Quantum physics is perhaps the best-known example, but it is no exception. In linguistics the question is raised today of what problems arise from the fact that research into language has to make use of language. Cognitive instruments have to be aquired via the object investigated by means of these very instruments and not, for example, through reflection of consciousness upon itself. Brain research has shown that the brain is not able to maintain any contact with the outer world on the level of its own operations, but – from the perspective of information – operates closed in upon itself. This is obviously also true for the brains of those engaged in brain research. How does one come, then, from one brain to another? Or to take a further example: the sociology of knowledge had demonstrated at least the influence of social factors on all knowledge, if not their role as sole determinants. This is also true, then, for this statement itself since no justification for an exception can be found, in the sense, say, of Mannheim's 'free-floating intelligence'. What conclusion is to be drawn from this? It was thought that one would have to found all knowledge on 'convention' or that knowledge was the result of a kind of 'negotiation'. But these attempts only wound up designating an ancient problem – that of the unity of knowledge and reality – by means of a new concept. Not without reason have these attempts been criticized for epistemological naiveté, since one either learns nothing about the relationship to reality or the connection is only made over theoretically unacceptable 'both/and' concessions. There is little more to be gained by calling such 'constructivism', as has recently been done, 'radical' since what is identified here as 'constructivism' hardly at first seems unfamiliar. It might be that the theory of knowledge – at least in some of its traditional variants – will be confirmed rather than caught unaware. Science is apparently reacting here to its own power of resolution. This can already be found in Plato

* From Niklas Luhmann, 'The Cognitive Program of Constructivism and a Reality that Remains Unknown', in W. Krohn et al. eds *Self-Organization: Portrait of a Scientific Revolution*, pp. 64–85, Kluwer, 1990. Reprinted with the permission of the publisher.

who reduces everyday experience to mere opinion and raises the question of what reality lies behind it. As a result, these philosophic reflections were termed, at first, 'idealism'. As we come to modern times the emergence of modern science led more and more to the conclusion that this 'underlying' reality was knowledge itself. This altered the meaning of the concept of the subject, while it is only in our century that the name 'idealism' has been replaced by 'constructivism'. There was a shift in emphasis in the conflict between realism and idealism, but it is not easy to discover in this a new theory. There is an external world, which results from the fact that cognition, as a self-operated operation, can be carried out at all, but we have no direct contact with it. Without knowing, cognition could not reach the external world. In other words, knowing is only a self-referential process. Knowledge can only know itself, although it can – as if out of the corner of its eye – determine that this is only possible if there is more than only cognition. Cognition deals with an external world that remains unknown and has to, as a result, come to see that it cannot see what it cannot see.

So far there is nothing new here, unless it be in the definiteness and self-confidence with which all this is presented as knowledge. One has to look more closely at the theoretical distinctions with which this view of things is presented in order to discover something new. Insofar as constructivism maintains nothing more than the unapproachability of the external world 'in itself' and the closure of knowing – without yielding, at any rate, to the old skeptical or 'solipsistic' doubt that an external world exists at all – there is nothing new to be found in it. Nonetheless, the theoretical form in which this is expressed has innovative aspects – even such radical innovations – that it is possible to gain the impression that the theory of a self-referring cognition closed in upon itself has only now acquired a viable form. One can express this more precisely: it has only now acquired a form in which it can represent itself as knowledge. A problem arises here, however. With the word 'constructivism' (taken over from mathematics) premature victories have been proclaimed, and one has to accept that there will be those who step aside, with a shake of the head, denying the validity of these claims. It is important, therefore, to investigate the question of what is new and convincing here – and this will lead the discussion far afield.

For reasons that can only be clarified subsequently we begin our investigation with the question: by means of what distinction is the problem articulated? That is, we do not begin with the Kantian question: how is knowledge possible? We have avoided this form of the question because it might lead us to the premature response: in this way! At first the difference is of no great consequence. The one form of the question can be translated into the other (if one is not afraid to face problems of logical hierarchies as well as their failure). One can answer the question: 'how is knowledge possible?', with 'by the introduction of a distinction'. In contrast with the tradition involving such concepts as 'diapherein' or 'discernment' here the concept of distinction is radicalized. For in order to recognize knowing it is necessary to distinguish it from what is not knowing. As a result, the question with regard to the foundation of knowledge is transformed into a question with regard to the distinction of distinguishing, that is, into an obviously self-implicative question. The passage from the search for a founding – and therefore asymmetric – relationship with regard to some unity is transformed into a search for an operatively employed difference. It is, further, easy to recognize that circularity and paradoxes can no longer be rejected but will come to play a role.

So, once again, the question is: by means of what distinction is the problem of knowledge articulated? (And, for the sake of clarity, let it be said once again: We are aware that with this question we have taken upon ourselves the difficulty of the distinction of distinguishing.)

In any case one will not be able to approach constructivism if one proceeds from the old controversy of whether the knowing system is a subject or an object. The subjectivist problem was to state and to show how it is possible by means of introspection – that is by passage to the self-reference of one's own consciousness – to form judgments about the world of others. That 'intersubjectivity' is only a word which therefore does not solve the problem should be obvious. Objectivism, on the other hand, came up with the idea of describing knowledge as a condition or process in a particular object which was often called 'organism'.

The mistake here lies in the assumption that it is possible to describe an object completely (we won't go so far as to say 'explain') without making any reference to its relation to its environment (whether this relation be one of indifference, of selective relevance and capacity for stimulation, of disconnection, or of closure). In order to avoid these problems, which arise from the point of departure taken, both subjectivist and objectivist theories of knowledge have to be replaced by the system-environment distinction, which then makes the distinction subject-object irrelevant.

With this we have the distinction central to constructivism: it replaces the distinction transcendental/empirical by the distinction system/environment. The concept environment (as well as the corresponding one of system) was not available during Kant's day. What we call 'environment' today had to be conceived of as the state of being contained and carried (*periechon*); and what we call 'system' had to be thought of as order according to a principle. Both of these were already objects of knowledge. In order to answer the question of how knowledge is possible without falling into a self-referring circle the distinction transcendental/empirical was developed. Hardly anyone accepts this distinction today despite the labor that goes into the exegesis of historical texts. But if one drops this distinction how does one then avoid the circle of the self-founding of knowledge? Why must one avoid this circle? Can't one simply say: Knowledge is what knowledge takes to be knowledge?

The serving as medium foundation for dealing with these questions offers up the distinction system/environment and, in its context, a worked-out systems theory. This makes – virtually automatically – all the investigations and knowledge gained in systems theory of potential relevance for the theory of knowledge. In contrast to the procedure in transcendentalism, investigations bearing relevance for epistemological questions do not need to be carried out primarily with this end in mind. The relevance emerges as a side-effect of other investigations (e.g., of neurophysiological investigations or in the history of science) and one only has to take care that the transitions are smoothed over and now and then put in order, for example by adequate terminological recommendations. A good example of this is Humberto Maturana's use of the word 'cognition' ('*conocimiento*') for the extension of operations under the condition of interaction with the environment, however annoying this terminology might be for professional epistemologists afraid of a biological invasion of their domain.

It has been known for quite some time already that the brain has absolutely no qualitative and only a very slight quantitative contact with the external world. All stimuli coming from without are coded purely quantitatively (principle of undifferentiated coding); furthermore, their quantity, as compared with purely internal processing events, plays but a marginal role. Incoming stimuli are also erased in fractions of a second if they are not stored in internal storage areas with somewhat longer retention times (short-term memory) – an event which is more the exception than the rule. With this, even time is made to serve the internal economy of complex processes. Apparently it is fundamental for the functioning of the brain that selected information is enclosed and not that it is let through. As if it were already information (or data) before it motivates the brain to form a representation. Such knowledge as this was not made use of by theoretical epistemology and it is only a formulation in terms of systems theory that leads to an insight which must seem surprising to epistemologists: only closed systems can know. The sociology of science has arrived at similar conclusions (which are still, for the most part, rejected as being too shocking). Whoever still maintains that knowledge is the construction of a relation to the environment that fits things as they are is welcome to his opinion, but he is forced to begin his theoretical reflections with a paradox: it is only non-knowing systems that can know; or, one can only see because one cannot see.

Philosophical epistemology has become marginal scientifically if not completely isolated; a situation that has often been lamented. This was the case for the Neo-Kantians and is the case for the Neo-Wittgensteinians. Nonetheless, anyone familiar with both sides is aware of the numerous possibilities for contact. Systems theory or, more precisely, the distinction between system and environment, could play the role of mediator here.

The effect of the intervention of systems theory can be described as a de-ontologization of reality. This does not mean that reality is denied, for then there would be nothing that operated – nothing that observed, and nothing on which one would gain a purchase by means of distinctions. It is only the epistemological relevance of an ontological representation of reality that is being called into question. If a knowing system has no entry to its external world it can be denied that such an external world exists. But we can just as well – and more believably – claim that the external world is as it is. Neither claim can be proved; there is no way of deciding between them. This does not, however, call the external world into question but only the simple distinction being/non-being which ontology had applied to it. As a consequence, the question arises: why do we have to begin with precisely this distinction? Why do we wound the world first with this distinction and no other? Systems theory suggests instead the distinction between system and environment.

If one accepts this suggestion the answer to the question, how is knowledge possible?, is to begin with as the operation of a system separated from its environment. If one, further, takes seriously that the system always has to be operationally closed then to the initial idea of separation assumptions are added regarding self-reference and recursivity. Operations of this kind are only possible within the context of a network of operations of the same system towards which they point and on which they are founded. There is no single operation that can emerge without this recursive network. At the same time the network itself is not an operation. 'Multiplicity does not act as a relay.' The whole cannot as a whole itself become active. Every operation reproduces the unity of the system as well as its limits. Every operation reproduces closure and containment. There is nothing without an operation – no cognition either. And every operation has to fulfil the condition of being one operation among many, as it cannot exist in any other form, cannot otherwise possibly be an operation.

As a result, for an observer the system is a paradox, a unity which is a unity only as a multiplicity, a unitas multiplex. Even when the system observes itself one has what is true for every observation. If a system wants to know what makes it possible that it can know, it encounters this paradox. All theory of knowledge has to begin with the resolution of a paradox.

A further consequence is: No system can perform operations outside its own limits. If new operations are integrated it means that the limits of the system have been extended. Consequently, the system cannot use its own operations to connect itself with its environment since this would require that the system operate half within and half without the system. The function of the boundaries is not to pave the way out of the system but to secure discontinuity. Whatever one wants to call cognition, if it is supposed to be an operation then the operation necessarily has to be one incapable of contact with the external world, one which, in this sense, acts blindly.

These ideas can be worked out further and the foreseeable extensions of a theory of closed, self-referring systems-in-an-environment will doubtless come to have over this route an influence on the theory of knowledge. But we will leave this question aside for the moment since we are now confronted with a fundamental question: is it possible, and is it acceptable, to call what here becomes perceptible 'knowledge' at all?

In the search for an answer to this question it is advisable to introduce a second distinction between operation and observation. This distinction occupies the place that had been taken up to this point by the unity-seeking logic of reflection. (This means, therefore, a substitution of difference for unity.)

An operation that uses distinctions in order to designate something we will call 'observation'. We are caught once again, therefore, in a circle: the distinction between operation and observation appears itself as an element of observation. On the one hand, an observation is itself an operation; on the other hand, it is the employment of a distinction. An example would be that between operation and observation. A logic that would take its point of departure here could only be established as the unfolding of a circle, and it would have to make certain that the distinction can re-enter into what it has distinguished. Spencer Brown provides explicitly for this 're-entry' after deliberately ignoring it at the beginning with his instruction to an observer to 'draw a distinction'. (Among other things this means that time is employed for the resolution of self-referring circles and paradoxes.)

An observation leads to knowledge only insofar as it leads to re-usable results in the system. One can also say: Observation is cognition insofar as it uses and produces redundancies – whereby 'redundancy' here means limitations of observation that are internal to the system. In consequence, particular observations are more or less probable.

The passage to 'constructivism' follows from the insight that it is not only for negations that there are no correlates in the environment of the system but even for distinctions and designations (therefore for observations). This does not mean (to say it once again) that the reality of the external world is being called into doubt. It is also beyond doubt that an observer can observe that and how a system is influenced by its environment or deliberately and successfully acts upon its environment. Nonetheless, all distinctions and designations are purely internal recursive operations of a system (that is, operations that form or disturb redundancies). These are operations that are not able to go beyond the system and, as if at a distant remove, pull something into it. As a result, all achievements following from these operations, above all what is usually called 'information', are purely internal achievements. There is no information that moves from without to within the system. For even the difference and the horizon of possibilities on the basis of which the information can be a selection (that is, information) doesn't exist in the external world, but is a construct – i.e. internal to the system. Does this mean, however – as is claimed in a direct line from Maturana – that the cognitive system operates 'blindly'?

The metaphor of seeing and blindness can be retained as an abbreviated mode of speech, although it does not correspond to the current level of knowledge. One must also distinguish here: if every relation to the outer world is being denied in such a metaphor, too much is being called into question. On the other hand, it must be made clear that all observation (including the observing of observations) presupposes the operative deployment of a distinction which at the moment of its use must be employed 'blindly' (in the sense of 'non-observably'). If one wants to observe the distinction in its turn, one has to employ a different distinction for which the same is true.

There can be no doubt, therefore, that the external world exists or that true contact with it is possible as a necessary condition of the reality of the operations of the system itself. It is the differentiation of what exists that is contributed by the observer's imagination, since, with the support of the specification of distinctions an immensely rich structure of combinations can be obtained, which then serves the system for decisions about its own operations.

Expressed in other words, the unity of a distinction employed for observation is constituted within the system. It is only in the observing system that things distinguished are brought to the unity of being distinct. Cognition is neither the copying nor the mapping nor the representation of an external world in a system. Cognition is the realization of combinatorial gains on the basis of the differentiation of a system that is closed off from its environment (but nonetheless 'contained' in that environment). If a system is forced to cognize with the aid of distinctions and is unable to cognize in any other manner, it means further that everything that is for the system, and which therefore has reality, has to be constituted over distinctions. The 'blind spot' of each observation, the distinction it employs at the moment, is at the same time its guarantee of a world. For example, social reality is what one, in observing a majority of observers, can observe to be uniform among them despite their differences. Social reality exists only when an observer can distinguish a majority of observers (which may or may not include himself). By 'world' is meant that which has to be assumed for every system to be the unity of the system/environment distinction (self-reference and external reference), when (and only when) this distinction is employed.

In conclusion we can say that knowing systems are real (empirical – that is, observable) systems in a real world. Without a world they could neither exist nor know. It is only cognitively that the world is unapproachable for them.

61

ROY BHASKAR

Transcendental realism and the problem of naturalism* (1979)

In this book I want to situate, resolve and explain an old question that dominates philosophical discussions on the social sciences and invariably crops up, in one guise or other, in methodological controversies within them: to what extent can society be studied in the same way as nature?

Without exaggerating, I think one could call this question the primal problem of the philosophy of the social sciences. For the history of that subject has been polarized around a dispute between two traditions, affording rival answers to this conundrum. A naturalist tradition has claimed that the sciences are (actually or ideally) unified in their concordance with positivist principles, based in the last instance on the Humean notion of law. In opposition to positivism, an anti-naturalist tradition has posited a cleavage in method between the natural and social sciences, grounded in a differentiation of their subject-matters. For this tradition the subject-matter of the social sciences consists essentially of meaningful objects, and their aim is the elucidation of the meaning of these objects. While its immediate inspiration derived from the theological hermeneutics (or interpretative work) of Schleiermacher, the philosophical lineage of this tradition is traceable back through Weber and Dilthey to the transcendental idealism of Kant. But both traditions have older antecedents and wider allegiances. Positivism, in assuming the mantle of the Enlightenment, associates itself with a tradition whose Galilean roots lie in the new Platonism of the late Renaissance; while hermeneutics, finding early precursors in Herder and Vico and possessing a partially Aristotelian concept of explanation, has always flourished in the humus of romantic thought and humanist culture. Significantly, within the Marxist camp an exactly parallel dispute has occurred, with the so-called 'dialectical materialists' on one side, and Lukács, the Frankfurt School and Sartre on the other.

Now, with the partial exception of the 'dialectical materialists' (whose specificity will be considered later), the great error that unites these disputants is their acceptance of an essentially positivist account of natural science, or at least (and more

* From, *The Possibility of Naturalism* by Roy Bhaskar, Harvester Wheatsheaf, 2nd edition, 1989. Pp 1–3, 17–22, 23. Copyright by Roy Bhaskar 1979, 1989. Reprinted by permission of Pearson Education Limited.

generally) of an empiricist ontology. Consider, for example, Winch's *The Idea of a Social Science*, probably the most influential tract written within the self-styled 'analytical' school. Winch, it will be remembered [see Reading 24], wants to demonstrate an essential identity between philosophy and social science, on the one hand, and a fundamental contrast between social and natural science, on the other. When one examines his arguments for such a contrast one finds that they reduce, in essence, to just two. The first is an argument to the effect that constant conjunctions are neither sufficient nor (contrary to, for example, Weber) even necessary for social scientific explanation, which is achieved instead by the discovery of intelligible connections in its subject-matter. This may be granted. But the required contrast is only generated if one assumes that the discovery of intelligible connections in its subject-matter is not equally the goal of natural scientific explanation (or that the identification of constant conjunctions could be necessary and sufficient for this). Winch's second argument is that social things have no existence, other than a purely physical existence, that is, as social things, apart from the concepts that agents possess of them. Besides leaving the ontological status of concepts unclear, once more the desired contrast only gets off the ground if one tacitly assumes that, with the privileged exception of thought itself, only material objects can properly be said to be 'real', that is, that in natural science *esse est percipi*. Winch's anti-naturalism thus depends entirely on empiricist theories of existence and causality. Now if, as I shall argue shortly, science employs a causal criterion for ascribing reality, and causal laws are tendencies, his contrast collapses. Of course it does not follow from this that there will be no differences between the natural and the social sciences (or, for that matter, that Winch's idea of a social science is entirely incorrect). But, by effectively ceding natural science to positivism, Winch precludes himself from locating them. The anti-naturalist faction within Marxism typically makes the same mistake.

Now I think that recent developments in the philosophy of science (and in particular those that I have elsewhere systematized under the title of 'transcendental realism') permit what the current crisis in the human sciences necessitates: a reconsideration of the problem of naturalism. Naturalism may be defined as the thesis that there is (or can be) an essential unity of method between the natural and the social sciences. It must be immediately distinguished from two species of it: reductionism, which asserts that there is an actual identity of subject-matter as well; and scientism, which denies that there are any significant differences in the methods appropriate to studying social and natural objects, whether or not they are actually (as in reductionism) identified. In contrast to both these forms of naturalism, I am going to argue for a qualified anti-positivist naturalism, based on an essentially realist view of science. Such a naturalism holds that it is possible to give an account of science under which the proper and more or less specific methods of both the natural and social sciences can fall. But it does not deny that there are significant differences in these methods, grounded in real differences in their subject-matters and in the relationships in which their sciences stand to them. In particular it will be shown that ontological, epistemological and relational considerations all place limits on the possibility of naturalism (or rather, qualify the form it must take); and that these considerations all carry methodological import. However, it will transpire that it is not in spite of, but rather just in virtue of, these differences that social science is possible; that here, as elsewhere, it is the nature of the object that determines the form of its possible science. So that to investigate the limits of naturalism is *ipso facto* to investigate the conditions which make social science, whether or not it is actualized in practice, possible . . .

As already indicated, over the last hundred years or so two broad positions in the philosophy of social science have dominated the scene: the one naturalist, the other anti-naturalist. But the dominant naturalist tradition has been based on a very different conception of science (and philosophy) from that advocated in this chapter. It has seen science as consisting essentially in the registration of (or refutation of claims about) empirical invariances between discrete events, states of affairs and the like. The hermeneutical tradition has accepted this account of natural science (or at least its implicit ontology), subjecting it at best to relatively minor qualifications. But it contends that social science is (or should be) concerned with the elucidation of meaning and the tracing of conceptual connections – activities clearly lacking counterparts in the study of the inanimate world of nature. Besides this positive claim, defenders of *Verstehen* can point, with justice, to the complete absence of explanations in social science conforming to positivist prescriptions, and in particular to the absence of universal empirical regularities of a significant kind. In response to this, positivists tend to argue that the social world is much more complex than the natural world ('interactionism', already prefigured by Mill) or that the regularities that govern it can only be identified at a more basic level ('reductionism', prefigured by Comte), and that, in any event, concepts (or meanings), to the extent that they are explanatorily relevant at all, can only be identified, or hypotheses about them tested, empirically (i.e., behaviourally). Neither party doubts for a moment that empirical invariances are necessary for laws, or that the conceptual and the empirical jointly exhaust the real. The basis of the hermeneutical tradition lies in the Kantian and Hegelian dichotomies of phenomenon/noumenon and nature/spirit. Its heyday was reached in the Manichean world of late nineteenth-century German thought which drew sharp distinctions between causal explanation (*Erklären*) and interpretative understanding (*Verstehen*), the nomothetic and the ideographic, the repeatable and the unique; and an absolute contrast between the science of the physical non-human world of nature and the science of the world of mind, of culture and of history. This was at least in part a reaction to the positivism of Comte and Mill (and their German epigones), and before them to the kind of chiliastic claims made by the Enlightenment for the new science of mechanics. And it was against this Manichean dualism – or its real or imaginary effects – that the latest wave of positivism, in the form of the systems of Popper and Hempel and their followers, was very largely aimed. The epistemological ground for this reassertion of positivism in the philosophy of the social sciences was laid by the logical atomism and positivism of the 1920s and 1930s, itself traceable through the work of the early Wittgenstein, Russell and Moore, to a reaction against the same idealism that informed the intellectual milieu of Dilthey, Simmel, Weber and Rickert. It was understandable, then, that in the wake of the anti-positivist turn taken by the later Wittgenstein and the Oxford of the 1950s one should see the emergence of a reformed and analytically sophisticated hermeneutics, represented most notably perhaps by the works of Anscombe, Dray, Charles Taylor and Winch (a partial reaction to which is evident in the writings of Davidson and, for example, Mandelbaum, on reductionist and interactionist lines respectively). In Germany this development was paralleled by the critical and dialectical hermeneutics of Gadamer, Apel and Habermas, which immediately became the target of polemical attack by Popper and his school.

Much of the history of the philosophy of the social sciences can thus be seen as a kind of historical see-saw, an oscillation to-and-fro between variants of these basic positions. Now the conception of science developed here sees science, like the positivist tradition, as unified in its essential method; and, like the hermeneutical tradition, as essentially differentiated in (or specific to) its objects. But my account of scientific method is diametrically opposed to that of positivism; and partly (though not only) in virtue of this, my account of the specific differences of the social sciences also departs in fundamental respects from that of the hermeneutical tradition.

To posit an essential unity of scientific method is to posit an account which conceives the sciences as unified in the form that scientific knowledge takes, the reasoning by which it is produced and the concepts in terms of which its production can be most adequately theorized or reconstructed. (These aspects correspond roughly to the traditional fields of epistemology, logic and metaphysics respectively.) Now the transcendental analysis of science sketched above reveals that its essence consists in the movement, at any one level of inquiry, from manifest phenomena to the structures that generate them. It shows that experimental and practical activity entails an analysis of causal laws as expressing the tendencies of things, not conjunctions of events ('epistemology'); that scientific discovery and development entails that scientific inferences must be analogical and retroductive, not simply inductive and/or deductive ('logic'); and that the process of knowledge-production necessitates a conceptual system based on the notion of powers ('metaphysics'). From this perspective, then, things are viewed as individuals possessing powers (and as agents as well as patients). And actions are the realization of their potentialities. Historical things are structured and differentiated (more or less unique) ensembles of tendencies, liabilities and powers; and historical events are their transformations.

Taken together, these three shifts in standpoint imply a radically different ontology and account of science. The prima-facie plausibility of positivism may then be seen to rest largely upon the illicit generalization, and incorrect analysis, of a special case: that of an epistemically significant closure. Realism can accommodate (and what is more explain) that case too. But it is a case without application to the social sciences, and, if treated as a norm, cannot be acted upon without generating in practice the most damaging overt and covert effects.

Now the fact that, upon any serious reflection, positivist prescriptions can be seen to be so patently inapplicable to the social sciences no doubt accounts for the greater intuitive plausibility of hermeneutical positions there. Thus most writers within this tradition have not found it difficult to show that some positivist assumption or rule is inapplicable to some or other area of social life. But they characteristically draw the wrong conclusions from this. In some cases, where it is just a matter of their extracting an anti-naturalist moral from a fundamentally correct point, the error is easily undone: by showing how the point can be accommodated within the more expansive, less restrictive account of science provided by transcendental realism. But in other cases the point itself is mistaken. And, where it is, I think that this is often traceable not just to an inadequate conception of their contrast (natural science), but to their taking over of some still more fundamental positivist assumptions into their conception of social science. Indeed, upon analysis, anti-naturalist theories of social science may often be seen to consist entirely in, or at least depend essentially on, the inversion or displacement, transformation and/or condensation of characteristically positivist themes. In this sense the effects of positivism, or rather of the philosophical problem-field that underpins it, on the philosophy of social science have been hegemonic. This problem-field is defined by an ontology of experience, empirical realism, and a sociology of man, sociological individualism, and it incorporates transcendental idealist and collectivist variants. It is this couple (empiricism/ individualism) that I think must be held largely responsible, or rather that acts as the metatheoretical trustee for the practices responsible, for the social scientific malaise.

To illustrate the tacit dominance of positivist thought, consider the fact of human agency, upon which anti-positivists have quite properly wished to insist. However their acceptance of the actualist presupposition that laws fully describe, and so completely control, the everyday world of perceived things, together with their well-grounded fear that if this notion were to be applicable to social life there would be no room left for human agency, has often encouraged them into a total voluntarism. This is nothing but the simple inverse of positivism's blanket determinism. Sartre's (or Goffman's) freely chosen selves and Durkheim's (or Parsons') internalized values reflect in the last instance the same mistaken notion of law. In fact, in given circumstances and considered in relation to their own peculiar mode of operation, social structures may be just as 'coercive' as natural laws. And, conversely, just as rules can be broken, so natural tendencies may fail to be realized. Again, by and large, writers within the hermeneutical tradition have adopted the positivist view that the objects of knowledge are events (or their counterpart in the domain of the human sciences, actions). Transposed to the hermeneutical perspective, this misconception has encouraged a definition of the social by reference to the category of behaviour, albeit of a particular, for example intentional or rule-governed, sort. Now the notion 'social science' is at present enormously confused. It is very much a hotchpotch, and requires analysis. But its distinct subject-matters cannot be separated out by using the category of behaviour. Rather one will have to look to the distinct structures that mesh together in the field of social life. Substituting an ontology of structures for one of events, and recognizing that social individuals are in general both complex and changing, provides a way of avoiding at the outset the false oppositions, such as between theory and history or the universal and the unique, on which the hermeneutical dualisms turn.

According to the non-positivist naturalism developed here, the predicates that appear in the explanation of social phenomena will be different from those that appear in natural scientific explanations and the procedures used to establish them will in certain vital respects be different too (being contingent upon, and determined by, the properties of the objects under study); but the principles that govern their production will remain substantially the same. It is the argument of this book that although, because social objects are irreducible to (and really emergent from) natural objects, and so possess qualitatively different features from them, they cannot be studied in the same way as them, they can still be studied 'scientifically'. Indeed, it is only because social objects possess such a 'non-natural surplus' (as it were), differentiating them from purely natural ones, that it makes sense to suppose that they can be studied scientifically, as social objects, at all. There can be identity of essence here, only because there is difference in substantival form.

The positivist tradition is correct to stress that there are causal laws, generalities, at work in social life. It is also correct to insist (when it does) that these laws may be opaque to the agents' spontaneous understanding. Where it errs is in the reduction of these laws to empirical regularities, and in the account that it is thereby committed to giving of the process of their identification. For in the absence of spontaneously occurring, and given the impossibility of artificially creating, closed systems, the human sciences must confront the problem of the direct scientific study of phenomena that only ever manifest themselves in open systems – for which orthodox philosophy of science, with its tacit presupposition of a closure, is literally useless. In particular it follows from this condition that criteria for the rational appraisal and development of theories in the social sciences, which are denied (in principle) decisive test situations, cannot be predictive and so must be exclusively explanatory.

The hermeneutical tradition is correct to point out that the social sciences deal with a pre-interpreted reality, a reality already brought under concepts by social actors, that is, a reality already brought under the same kind of material in terms of which it is to be grasped (which is the only possible medium of its intelligibility). So that, to put it crudely, the human sciences stand, at least in part, to their subject-matter in a subject-subject (or concept-concept) relationship, rather than simply a subject-object (or concept-thing) one. It is also correct to insist upon the methodological significance of this difference. Where it errs is in a reduction of social science to the modalities of this relationship, and its consequent failure to situate, through the possibility of reference to aspects of reality at once social and inadequately conceptualized, the possibility of rationally defensible conceptual criticism and change, most fully in the development of the concept of ideology.

Now it is in their common commitment to the ontology of empirical realism, and the individualist sociology that it presupposes, that the root source of these divergent errors will be found, in Chapter 4, to lie. In rejecting this ontology and sociology, transcendental realism also situates the possibility of a new critical naturalism (which will be elaborated in Chapters 2 and 3). Such a naturalism, it will be shown, can do justice to the proto-scientific intuitions of both positivism and its hermeneutical foil. However in contrast to positivism, it can sustain the transfactuality of social structures, while insisting on their conceptuality (or concept-dependence). And in contrast to hermeneutics, it can sustain the intransitivity of both beliefs and meanings, while insisting on their susceptibility to scientific explanation and hence critique, in a spiral (rather than circle) which reflexively implicates social science as a moment in the process that it explains. It is important to stress that the upshot of the analyses of Chapters 2 and 3 will not be a substantive sociology and psychology, but formal or a priori conditions for them. However if my argument in the previous section is correct, such philosophical investigations may yet prove to be practically indispensable conditions for the emancipation and successful development of the 'human sciences'.

62

JON ELSTER
Rational choice and the explanation of social action* (2001)

Is it a policy tool?

Subjective nature

Rational choice has become an increasingly important tool in the social sciences: economics, political science and sociology, and a more marginal one in anthropology. I would like to say something about why it is, and should be, an important tool, and also something about its limitations. I shall first make a number of conceptual observations, and then run through some examples of the use and abuse of rational choice theory.

The theory rests on a very simple idea: people want to do as well as they can. More accurately, they want to do as well as they believe they can. It is a theory about subjectively optimal choice, not about objectively optimal behaviour. Even more accurately, people want to do as well as they can, on the basis of well-founded beliefs. Again, this is a subjective idea. We are not requiring that rational agents have true beliefs, only that their beliefs are well-grounded in the evidence available to them. There is just one element that has to be added: rational actors do not simply take as given the evidence they have, but try to invest an optimal amount of resources – not too much, not too little – in acquiring new information. A doctor, for instance, has to spend some time examining an injured patient before arriving at a diagnosis and deciding what treatment to apply, but not so much time that the patient could die under his/her hands.

In Figure 1, I have written a blocked arrow from 'desires' to 'beliefs', to indicate that processes such as wishful thinking and self-deception are inconsistent with rationality. Note, however, that the diagram leaves room for an indirect influence of desires on beliefs. How much evidence we collect depends on our prior beliefs about the expected costs and benefits of gathering new information. As indicated in the diagram, it also depends on our desires. To take a simple example, a person whose desires are very present-oriented, in the sense that he does not take much account of future consequences of present behaviour, would not rationally invest many resources in finding out what those consequences might be.

This remark brings out another way in which rational choice theory is radically

* © Copyright John Elster 2003.

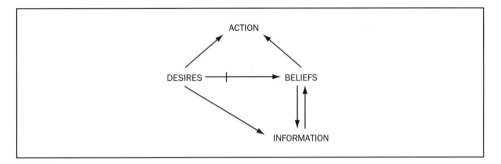

Figure 1

subjective. One might want to say that someone who pays little attention to future consequences of present behaviour is unwise, or downright stupid. Their life is likely to be nasty, brutish and short. Surely, we might want to say, drug addicts are not rational. Well, they can be. They are far from always rational, but the idea is not absurd. Imagine someone who for genetic or cultural reasons pays little attention to long-term reward and focuses almost totally on the short term. For that person, taking drugs might well be optimal. They might even anticipate that drug-taking will make them less rational in the future, but decide that this is just a cost on a par with the financial and medical consequences of drug-taking. They might well fulfil all the conditions for rationality. Their choice to become an addict could be a rational one. I do not believe this is true of most addicts, but it could be true of some.

In the light of what I have said, let us now ask: what are the kind of things that can be assessed as more or less rational? Actions, beliefs and investment in information can be rational or not, optimal or suboptimal. But desires cannot be assessed as more or less rational. In Figure 1, there are arrows going from desires, but no desires going to desires. In the machinery of action, desires are the unmoved mover. This is not strictly true. To some extent we can choose our desires. Suppose I don't get any pleasure from classical music, but I observe that my friends do. I might then decide to expose myself to a great deal of classical music, on the assumption that I will come to like it as much as they do. Although we should not say that the desire to listen to classical music is rational, the decision to develop that desire might well be. These cases are not common, but they exist.

There is a severe constraint, however, on the choice of desires. The consequences of having a new desire must be judged desirable in terms of the present desires, otherwise we would not want to develop the new desire. The classical music case satisfies that constraint. But here is a case that does not. Suppose someone suffers from an inability to defer gratification, that is, from being unable to take account of future consequences of present behaviour. And suppose scientists came up with a discounting pill, which would increase the weight of future rewards in present decisions. If the person took the pill, their life would go better. In retrospect, they would be grateful they took the pill. But if they had a choice to take the pill or not, they would refuse. Any behaviour that the pill would induce is already within their reach. They could stop smoking, start exercising or start saving right now, but they do not.

Since they do not want to do it, they would not want to take a pill that made them do it. Or to put it differently: to want to be motivated by long-term consequences of present behaviour *is* to be motivated by long-term consequences of present behaviour.

The person with a short time horizon is trapped. As the saying goes, 'The eye cannot see beyond its horizon'. A very myopic person may not be able to locate the optician that could provide them with the glasses they need. They are trapped. In a similar way, a person can be caught in a belief trap. My former student, Gerry Mackie argues that:

> women who practice infibulation [a form of female genital mutilation] are caught in a belief trap. The Bambara of Mali believe that the clitoris will kill a man if it comes in contact with the penis during intercourse. In Nigeria, some groups believe that if a baby's head touches the clitoris during delivery, the baby will die. I call these self-enforcing beliefs: a belief that cannot be revised, because *the believed costs of testing the belief are too high.*

I have insisted on the subjective nature of rationality because it is ignored by many practitioners of rational choice theory. The bad way of doing rational choice explanation is the following. One observes a certain behaviour. One notes that the behaviour has beneficial consequences for the agent. One explains the behaviour by those consequences. This completely ignores the possibility that the benefits might be entirely accidental. Let me give an example from Gary Becker's work. He observes that many people choose to take higher education. He claims, and let us assume that he is right, that higher education tends to extend the agent's time horizon, in the sense of making them pay more attention to long-term consequences of present behaviour. He observes, correctly, that this has good consequences for the agent. He then concludes that people choose higher education in order to extend their time horizon. As I have made it clear, I do not think this argument works.

Much of applied rational choice theory, therefore, repeats the functionalist fallacy that used to be common in sociology. The fallacy is that of explaining behaviour by its beneficial consequences without providing a mechanism that would show the connection. For instance, someone might point out that feuding behaviour in some societies has the socially useful effect of keeping population size at a sustainable level, and then conclude that this effect explains why people feud. This, by the way, is a real example, not an invented one. The argument has no value whatsoever as long as one doesn't specify some kind of feedback mechanism by which the consequences of feuding maintain feuding. At the level of individual action, the relevant mechanism is that of intentional and rational *choice*. If one cannot show that the agent rationally *chose* to engage in the behaviour with beneficial consequences, the existence of these consequences has no explanatory relevance.

Let me now give some examples of rational choice theory in action. I begin with a demonstration by Tom Schelling, the greatest living rational choice theorist. In his classic work *The Strategy of Conflict* he solved a puzzle that has been around for centuries or more likely millennia: why would people ever want to burn their bridges? There is no doubt that they do, but why? Some reasons are obvious enough. Commanders might burn their bridges to prevent their troops from fleeing. An individual

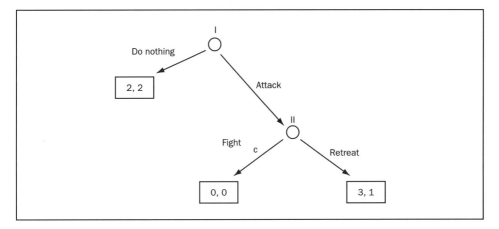

Figure 2

might burn their bridges if they fear that their courage might fail them if they have a way out. But Schelling pointed to a different mechanism, which has proved enormously useful. Consider the game shown in Figure 2. Let us assume that (I) and (II) are both rational. The numbers represent their rewards under various courses of action: the first number is the reward of (I), the second that of (II). A second's reflection shows that under these assumptions, (I) will attack and (II) will retreat. (II) might try to deter (I) from attacking, by saying that they will fight if attacked, but that threat is not credible. (I) knows that if they attack, (II) will prefer to retreat. To improve their situation, (II) can burn their bridges – eliminate the option of retreating. That will make the threat of fighting credible, and (I) will not do anything. What Schelling showed is that sometimes less is more – an agent can improve their bargaining situation by throwing away one of their options.

Here is another example which shows how rational choice theory can address and perhaps solve classic puzzles. In his work on *The Old Regime and the Revolution*, Alexis de Tocqueville made the paradoxical claim that in France before 1789, the discontent with existing conditions was greater in areas where those conditions were objectively better. The same paradox was observed in a modern classic of sociology, *The American Soldier*. In this work it was found that during the Second World War, discontent with advancement opportunities was greater in the parts of the military where these opportunities were in fact the best. Thus there was greater discontent in the Air Force than in the Military Police, although the Air Force actually had many more opportunities for advancement.

From Tocqueville to Robert Merton, social scientists have offered many explanations to account for this paradox. I think it is fair to say that none of them had the simplicity and parsimony we would expect of a good explanation. Some 25 years ago, the French sociologist Raymond Boudon offered an account which had exactly these qualities. Whether the account is correct or not, is another matter. It's a stylized model, which has yet to be confronted with the data. This being said, the model is shown in Table 1.

Table 1

	Air Force	Military Police
Number	20	20
Opportunities for promotion	5	2
Value of promotion	5	5
Cost of effort	1	1
Number who make effort	20	10
Number of disappointed	15	8

In the table, we compare two cohorts of Air Force (AF) and Military Police (MP) of 20 people each. Opportunities for promotion differ as indicated. The value of being promoted is the same. Boudon assumes, crucially, that in order to be considered for promotion an agent has to make an effort, which is costly. All agents who make an effort are equally likely to be promoted. It is easy to see that all members of the AF will make an effort. If they all do, the expected gain is $25/20 = 1.25$, which exceeds the cost. If fewer than all make the effort, the gain will be larger. It is slightly more tricky to see that only half of the MP will make an effort, perhaps by each MP making the decision by flipping a coin. If half of the MP make the effort, expected gains are $10/10 = 1$, equal to the cost. If more than half make the effort, the gains will fall short of the cost. If fewer than ten make the effort, the gains will exceed the cost, thus inducing more to make the effort. In equilibrium, each person is indifferent between making the effort and not making it.

The behaviour of the MP is known as a mixed strategy – choosing one's behaviour by some kind of randomizing mechanism. The behavioural relevance of such strategies is a controversial issue. Perhaps it's more plausible to appeal to another mechanism to explain why fewer MPs rationally decide to make the effort. It seems perfectly reasonable, however, to assume that when facing a situation with few opportunities and many competitors, some MPs will decide not to make the effort. So if we grant Boudon that only half of them will make the effort, we can deduce what we wanted to explain. Frustration and disappointment are greater in the branch with more opportunities, because more are induced to make a rational effort and fail. It makes good intuitive sense.

Let me give a further example, which illustrates the Nobel-prize winning article on 'The Market for Lemons' by George Akerlof. In the story I shall tell, a seller and a prospective buyer are negotiating the price of a piece of land on which there may or may not be oil. Both the seller and the buyer know that the value of oil to the seller, if there is oil, is between 0 and a 100 million dollars. The seller knows the exact value. The buyer assumes that the exact value is equally likely to be any number between 0 and 100 million. It is also common knowledge that the piece of land will be worth 50 per cent more to the buyer than the seller, perhaps because they have an adjoining piece of land that allows them to exploit economies of scale. What should the buyer offer?

As far as the buyer knows, the expected value of the land to the seller is 50 million dollars. If, therefore, they offer 60 million, they can expect to make a profit of 15 million. Suppose, however, that the seller accepts the offer of 50 million. That tells the buyer that the value of the land to the seller is between 0 and 50 million, with an expected value of 25 million. If the land is worth 25 million to the seller, it is worth 37.5 million to the buyer, which is less than what they offered to pay. Since this reasoning applies to any price the buyer could offer, the conclusion is that they should not bid for the land at all. There may be an opportunity for a mutually beneficial deal, but it will not be struck if the agents are rational. They are trapped in a version of the Groucho Marx paradox: I would never want to make an offer that the seller would accept.

The story is striking and may well have merited a Nobel prize, but it is false. In experiments structured like the condition I have described, 90 per cent of the subjects do make an offer. I conjecture that the reason has to do with the difficulty of looking one step ahead in situations of this kind. It is not technically difficult, but it doesn't seem to come easily to the mind. Here is another example. In June 1997, the French President Jacques Chirac called for anticipated elections to parliament. His party lost disastrously, and the Socialists came into power. I conjecture that the reason his coalition lost was that the voters understood that if he wanted early elections it was because he knew something they didn't know and he believed that he would lose if he waited. But by calling early elections, he revealed what he knew and therefore gave them a reason to vote against him. The polls told him he would win, but polls are unlike elections since holding a poll does not reveal anything to the respondents about the beliefs of the person who commissioned it. In Chirac's case, he did not anticipate that the voters would infer his beliefs from his behaviour. In the Winner's Curse, subjects fail to anticipate the beliefs which they themselves will be able to infer from the behaviour of others.

It should not surprise us that people are irrational from time to time. It is more surprising if 90 per cent of a population is irrational. It makes us suspect that irrational behaviour is more than random noise in the system. There is by now a large literature showing systematic failures of rationality in a number of situations. Many of them were first identified by the late Amos Tversky and his co-worker Daniel Kahneman. Some of them turn on people's faulty understanding of statistical infer-ence. Others turn on framing effects, as when people respond differently to a half-full glass and a half-empty one. Still others suggest that people are prone to something like magical thinking. If asked to donate to charity, they ask themselves, 'If I don't give, who will?', as if their donations could induce others to give.

Because my time is limited, I cannot enter into any detail about these findings. Instead, I shall discuss some results that indicate a more radical departure from rationality than the findings I just cited. To introduce the issue, let me cite from a comment by George Mason at the Federal Convention in Philadelphia. The discus-sion concerned whether the western lands that would accede to the Union in the future should be admitted with the same rights as the original 13 states. When Gov-ernor Morris argued that they should be admitted as second-rate states, so that they would never be able to outvote the original states, Mason argued strongly for the opposite view: 'If the Western States are to be admitted into the Union, as they arise, they must be treated as equals, and subjected to no degrading discriminations. They will have the same pride & other passions which we have, and will either not unite with or will speedily revolt from the Union, if they are not in all respects placed on an equal footing with their brethren'. Mason appeals to the pride and passions of the new states, not to their self-interest. Let us assume that it would in fact be in their interest to accede to the Union on unequal terms rather than remain outside. Why might they nevertheless refuse admission on such terms? We can perhaps understand why by considering the so-called Ultimatum Game that has been extensively studied by economists and psychologists (see Figure 3). In this game, the first player proposes a division of ten dollars between himself and the second player. Proposals can be made only in whole dollars. The second player can reject the proposal, in which case neither gets anything, or accept it, in which case the proposed division is implemented. In experiments, subjects interact anonymously, through computer terminals. Also, in the experiments I shall consider there is only 'one-shot interaction', that is, no repeated interaction between the same players.

Given these conditions, there is no reason to think that the players care about each other or that they might be concerned with building a reputation for the future. We would expect them to be concerned only with the payoffs in the experiment. If they are rational, and know each other to be rational, player (I) will propose nine dollars to himself and one dollar to player (II), who will accept the proposal. What happens in experiments is quite different. Player (I) typically offers something like seven dollars for themselves and three to player (II). Player (II) typically rejects any proposal that gives them less than three. The most plausible explanation is that if Player (II) receives a very low offer, they will reject it out of some *emotion* such as resentment or envy, and that player (I) expects them to behave in that way. Player II might be better off materially by accepting a low offer, but if their 'pride and other passions' are hurt, as Mason said, they may nevertheless refuse it.

One might ask whether player (I) might not pull their punches out of a sense of justice rather than out of an anticipation that player (II) might act on a sense of injustice. At the convention, Mason actually made both arguments. By admitting the western states on equal terms, they would do 'what we know to be right in itself'. To those who might not accept that argument, he added that the new states would in any

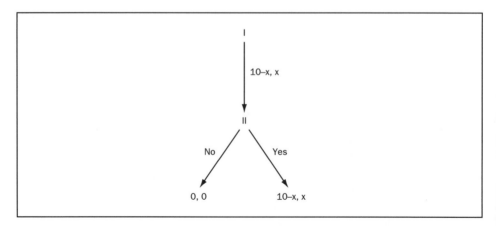

Figure 3

case be unlikely to accept a degrading proposal. He was probably wise to do so. An experiment called the Dictator Game suggests that anticipations of feelings of injustice provide a stronger motivation than feelings of justice. In the Dictator Game, Player (I) can impose a division without (II) having any choice in the matter. In that game, player I is typically much less generous.

As subjects are selected randomly to serve as player (I) or player (II), there is no reason to think they have systematically different motivations. Hence the experiments suggest that all of us are capable of being motivated by the injustice of being unfairly treated, but much less by the injustice of treating someone else unfairly. These are common-sense observations that sit badly within the rational choice framework. It might be possible to state the utility functions of the players so as to make the choices I have described appear as rational ones, but it would be a sterile and pointless exercise. One should reserve rational choice theory for cases in which the players are robustly motivated by outcomes and not by the way in which these outcomes come about or by the motivations behind them. If you buy a car that is fancier than mine, I may be envious. If I also believe that you enjoy my envy, it may turn into resentment. If I believe that you bought the car in order to make me envious, it may become murderous. These are mechanisms that cannot be harnessed by rational choice theory.

In spite of many observed deviations from rationality, rational choice theory remains privileged in the sense that it provides the only simple, parsimonious framework for explaining behaviour across the board. Many local theories have been proposed to account for the anomalous cases but they are not yet integrated into an alternative global theory. Also, the normative pull of rationality is very strong. We want to be rational. We can expect, therefore, that the more we understand deviations from irrationality, the more we will develop rational counterstrategies.

63

RANDALL COLLINS
Sociological realism* (1998)

It is often supposed that social constructivism undermines truth. If reality is socially constructed, there is no objectivity and no reality. I deny the conclusion. Social constuctivism is sociological realism; and sociological realism carries with it a wide range of realist consequences.

The philosophically strongest argument is traditionally that which is self-grounding, certain in itself, without appeal to empirical observation. The classic argument of this kind, the cogito, seeks irrefutable truths by passing statements through the acid bath of doubt. 'I am thinking' is irrefutable because 'I am not thinking' nevertheless displays oneself thinking.

The familiar conclusion from the cogito is the existence of the self. This is not the most useful path of argument. The self which is proven is ambiguous, conceivably only momentary and insubstantial. Consider what else is proven by the cogito. First of all, time exists. To doubt this ('time does not exist') is to make a statement in time. Conscious thinking occupies the saddleback of the present, merging imperceptibly with past and future.

Second, thinking exists. This thinking which is irrefutably proven takes place in language; it constitutes a kind of conversation, myself saying something to myself. The cogito reveals a speaker and an audience. Denial proves it. To think to oneself 'there is no one speaking' is uttered by a speaker; 'there is no audience for this statement' is received by an audience. Thinking has a social form.

We have not yet proved the existence of other people. This too is given by verbal thinking. Language takes place in words which carry meaning, and follows a grammar which is to a large degree inescapable if statements are to make sense. I do not invent my own language; my thinking depends on forms which have come to me ready-made, from beyond the present moment of consciousness. The constraints of language use, along with its capability for conveying meaning, imply the existence of communicative beings beyond myself. To deny that other people exist – in

* Reprinted by permission of the publisher from 'The Sociologico Cogito' in *The Sociology of Philosophies: A Global Theory of Intellectual Change* by Randall Collins, pp. 858–862. Cambridge, Mass.: Belknap Press of Harvard University Press, 1998. Copyright (1998) by the President and Fellows of Harvard College.

this specific sense – is to deny the communicability and objectivity, indeed the meaningfulness, of one's own sentences.

The reality of other people also may be derived from another aspect of the language in which we think. Words are to a large extent universals. Concepts (except for indexicals) transcend particulars; they enable one to refer to an object or a quality as appearing over again in time and in different contexts; in short, they are generalized. Apply the test of doubt: 'Universals do not exist' is a statement making use of universals. But a general concept implies a generalized viewpoint. A merely fragmentary, temporal sliver of consciousness cannot refer to an experience as 'a tree,' or even as 'that tree again'; it must be a consciousness which involves both continuity and generality. How can my particular fleeting experience give rise to the idea of universals? It must come to me from outside.

The existence of universals implies the existence of society. A concept carries with it a social stance: not merely of some one other person, but an open and universalizing viewpoint of a plurality of other persons. Just how many people this implies is not given. It is more than two; in fact it must be explicitly unspecified how many it comprises, since concepts imply meaningfulness for any and every personal stance at all. The concepts which go through one's mind are more than fleeting, having significance over and above my particular moment of thinking. Generality of perspective is at the core of our capacity to think; and this generality implies a collective, omnipresent social viewpoint.

Third, space exists. Although space is not one of the items primordially given through the sociological cogito, it may be quickly derived. If there are other people, not identical with one another in their particularity, they must exist outside one another. This existing outside cannot be merely in time, since time is a single dimension which does not itself provide room for simultaneous plurality. There must be some other dimension in which the multiplicity of selves exists; and we can call this dimension space.

We now have the existence of the time-space world as a firm reality. This is the material world of obdurate objects in ordinary experience, externally resistant to one another. One of these objects, the most certain of all, is one's body. A plurality of selves exists, outside one another in space. There are divisions between me and them; this barrier, as experienced from the inside, is my body. Another argument to the same effect (courtesy of Maine de Biran): I feel resistance to my will; this resistance is the materiality of time-space existence, which meets me first of all as the presence of my body.

The sociological cogito thus gives us assurance of several items of reality: thinking, language, other people, time and space, material bodies. This is not to say that illusions do not exist, or that mistakes cannot be made about particular things of this kind. But perceptual illusions and other mistakes can be discovered and rectified in the usual ways; particular errors occur within a framework of social language, time, and space, and do not call the reality of the framework into question. This can be demonstrated by the method of Cartesian doubt. To say 'this is not a real person but a showroom dummy (or a computer)' is nevertheless to affirm that language exists, with its social basis and so forth. The possibility that I am dreaming when I make these statements is nevertheless formulated in sentences with the same consequences;

whether I am dreaming or not at this particular moment, language and society nevertheless exist.

We seem to have drifted beyond the borders of strictly a priori argument. My arguments as to what is beyond doubt, what survives its own refutation, have led to asserting the existence of the realm of empirical experience. This seems inevitable. The distinction between purely conceptual thinking and empirical experience is not absolute, and indeed is hard to pin down precisely. Especially when one affirms a sociological view of thinking, there are regions where the empirical and the conceptual fuse; for example, this fusion takes place in every particular moment of the experience of thinking. The procedure of Cartesian doubt is a methodological game; we use it for the sake of argument, granting one's imaginary skeptical opponent the maximal possible concessions, to show what can be established at the highest level of certainty. Peirce held that Cartesian doubt is impossible, since in fact one never really doubts everything, but only focuses the beam of a targeted doubt on some specific points. Peirce meant that the Cartesian philosopher is already immersed in a stream of language. I have been drawing out the sociological realist implications of this immersion.

Let us now pass beyond the methodological cogito. A second methodological principle can guide us: we are always *in medias res*, in the middle of things. We always find ourselves in the midst of time, space, discourse, other people. *In medias res* means that our thinking is always preceded by other thinking, our own and other people's. Wherever we are is always a region from which space stretches out toward an indefinite horizon. *In medias res* is a primal experience, before we begin to probe for precision. The history of philosophy, and of mathematics, is full of deep troubles which arise in the search for precise borders and for outer limits. Difficulties arise with the infinitesimal and the infinite in time and space, and conceptually with the foundational, the first principle and the ultimate argument. Troubles appear because these formulations too arise *in medias res*.

In medias res can be taken as an empirical observation. It nevertheless is of a high order of generality, since there appear to be no exceptions. *In medias res* seems also to be part of an inescapable conceptual framework, a region in which the empirical and conceptual fuse.

Consider then from the empirical side the argument which I have been making for sociological realism. Whence did I get the ideas of the preceding paragraphs, to mount just this line of argument about a sociological cogito? Obviously, from the preceding chapters of this book, and from the empirical and theoretical work of the networks of philosophers and sociologists which have been its materials. I have not crawled into a stove, like Descartes, suddenly and inexplicably resolving to doubt everything, then spontaneously discovering that I cannot doubt that I am thinking in a social language. I have constructed this argument by assimilating the arguments of intellectual networks whose history stretches back for generations. It would be artificial to deny the existence of those historical networks, not only as ideas unfolding in time, but also as bodies of real human beings living in material space. Since I take my own argument seriously, I must agree that I am thinking an internal conversation which attempts to construct a coalition of intellectual audiences, and that the emotional energies which animate my writing come from my own experiences in intellectual networks. The immediate reality of my own activity implies the reality of a larger world of discourse, society, and bodily existence.

And there is no justification for drawing any sharp borders as to what realities are supported by this admission. I cannot deny the reality of intellectual networks; and I can find no reason for supposing that these networks alone have existed, a thin band of historical existence threading back across the centuries, without a wider social and material world surrounding them.

The social constructivist theory of intellectual life, far from being anti-realist, gives us an abundance of realities. Social networks exist; so do their material bases, the churches and schools and the audiences and patrons who have fed and clothed them; so do the economic, political, and geopolitical processes which constituted the outer sphere of causality. These successive layers of context for the minds of philosophers display no sharp borders. There is no criterion for arbitrarily stopping, for declaring that 'I concede that social reality exists; but the world of material nature does not.' It is all of a piece, all on the continuum *in medias res*.

The conclusions that we arrive at by following the empirical pathway of *in medias res* reinforce the a priori conclusions of the sociological cogito. In both directions, social constructivism leads to sociological realism.

Virtually no one actually doubts the reality of the world of ordinary experience. It is only within specialized intellectual networks that the question has arisen whether this banal reality can be proven to a high standard of argument; and even intellectuals, when they are 'off duty,' go back to assuming the reality of the ordinary time-space world. Sociological realism shows that even within intellectual contention at its most reflexive, it is possible to support banal realism. It does not follow that every kind of ontological reality is thereby supported. There are several kinds of realism and anti-realism; let us see now what sociological realism implies for some of these non-ordinary realms.

Sociological realism affirms mental and physical realities in human-sized time and space. Problems arise when statements are made about realities beyond the human-sized world. These include the objects of science, insofar as these are entities or structures which are not observed by the naked eye or acted upon by the unaided limbs; the concepts of mathematics; conceptual or abstract reality *per se*, ideas and especially universals; the mind, taken as an entity or substance. A variety of positions have been taken as to these things, either to deny their reality or to affirm that they have a higher reality than ordinary experience. These positions, denying or transcending banal reality, have been produced by intellectual networks, whose struggles for innovation in their argumentative attention space have repeatedly pushed beyond the human-sized world.

64

JÜRGEN HABERMAS
Realism after the linguistic-pragmatic turn* (1999)

The present volume brings together philosophical writings which date from the period between 1996 and 1998 and take up anew strands left in abeyance since *Knowledge and Human Interests* . . . Language-pragmatics, which I developed from the early 1970s . . . served the development of a theory of communicative action and of rationality. It provided the foundation of a critical theory of society and cleared the way for a discourse-theoretical conception of morality, law and democracy.

This explains a certain one-sidedness of theoretical strategy which the following pieces seek to correct. They centre on two basic questions in theoretical philosophy. The first concerns the ontological question of naturalism – how the normativity, unassailable from the participant's perspective, of a linguistically structured life world in which we as subjects capable of speech and action always already find ourselves, could be harmonised with the contingency of the natural-historical development of socio-cultural forms of life. The second concerns the epistemological question of realism – how the assumption of a world which is independent of our descriptions and identical for all observers could be reconciled with the linguistic-philosophical insight that we are denied direct, linguistically unmediated access to 'naked' reality. Needless to say, I deal with these themes from my earlier developed formal-pragmatic perspective . . .

Knowledge and Human Interests, indeed, had been determined by the primacy of the epistemological perspective. Therefore, the themes which shifted to the background on the way to the *Theory of Communicative Action* had still been present in it. *Knowledge and Human Interests* answered the basic questions of theoretical philosophy in terms of a weak naturalism and a transcendental-pragmatic cognitive realism (*Erkenntnisrealismus*). But these themes faded into insignificance once the demand for an epistemological justification of the critical theory of society had been rendered superfluous by the attempt to ground it directly through language-

* From Jürgen Habermas, *Wahrheit und Rechtfertigung: Philosophische Aufsätze*, Frankfurt: Suhrkamp Verlag, 1999, pp. 7–8, 13–14, 16–18, 32, 36–44, 48–51, 56–64. Translated by Piet Strydom.

pragmatics. Henceforth, I analysed the pragmatic presuppositions of action oriented towards understanding independently of the transcendental conditions of knowledge.

Under the premises of this theory of language, however, I want to take up again the neglected problems of a Kantian pragmatism . . .

Kantian pragmatism, the thrust of which I share with Hilary Putnam, bases itself on the transcendental fact that subjects capable of speech and action who allow themselves to be affected by good reasons or grounds are able to learn – in the longer term even 'not-being-able-not-to-learn'. And, indeed, they learn in both the moral-cognitive dimension of dealing with one another and the cognitive dimension of dealing with the external world. The transcendental question simultaneously expresses the post-metaphysical awareness that even the best results of such fallible learning processes in a significant sense remain *our* insights. Also true statements could only realise the epistemic possibilities which are opened for us by socio-cultural forms of life . . .

Classical pragmatism already tried to bring Kant into unison with Darwin. According to G.H. Mead and John Dewey, the detranscendentalised conditions of problem-solving behaviour are incorporated in practices which are characteristic of our natural-historically shaped socio-cultural forms of life. Then, however, the transcendental question, without losing its specificity, must be formulable in such a way that it is compatible with a naturalistic perspective.

The ontological assumption of a genetic primacy of nature necessitates also the adoption of the cognitive-realistic assumption of an independent, objective world. But in the linguistic paradigm it is no longer possible to maintain the classical form of realism which rests on the representation model of knowledge and the correspondence of statements and facts. On the other hand, realism necessitates a concept of reference also after the language-pragmatic turn which explains how we are able under different theoretical descriptions to refer to the same object (or to things of the same kind) . . .

The cognitive-realist conception in the *non-classical form* it adopted in the wake of the linguistic turn admits of being combined with a 'weak' naturalism also without surrendering the transcendental-pragmatic question.

A weak naturalism – after Kant and Darwin

Today, the opposition between Quine's strict naturalism and Heidegger's idealism of the history of Being appears in many varieties. In arguing with these dominant theoretical strategies, I want to introduce the alternative of a weak naturalism ignored by both sides . . .

From a pragmaticist perspective, the process of knowledge presents itself as intelligent behaviour which solves problems and makes learning processes possible, corrects errors and disempowers objections. The representational function of language suggests a misleading image of a thinking which pictures objects or represents facts only when it detaches itself from this context of action-related experience and discursive justifications. The 'mirror of nature' – the representation of reality – is a false model of knowledge, since the twofold relation of image and copy – and the static relation between statement and state of affairs – screens out the dynamics of the growth of knowledge through problem-solving and justification.

Cognitions result in the spatial dimension from the processing of the disillusionments in intelligent dealings with a risky environment, in the social dimension from the justification of problem solutions against the objections of other interlocutors, and in the temporal dimension from learning sequences which feed on the revision of their own errors. When one regards knowledge as a function of such a complex set of relations, then he or she appreciates how the passive moment of the experience of practical failure or success blends with the constructive moments of projection, interpretation and justification. Experiential judgements *take on form* in learning processes and *arise* from problem-solutions. It is senseless, therefore, to link the idea of the validity of judgements to the difference between being and appearance, between what is given 'as such' and 'for us' – as though knowledge of what is supposedly immediate must be cleansed of subjective ingredients and intersubjective mediations. Knowledge rather owes something to the cognitive function of these ingredients and mediations. From a pragmaticist perspective, reality is not something which is represented; it makes itself performatively felt – as the totality of resistances which we have to process and which we expect – only in the limitations to which our problem-solving and learning processes are subject.

The representational model of knowledge, which portrays 'representation' as the picturing of things or the copying of facts and 'truth' as the correspondence between picture and thing or statement and fact, fails to grasp the cognitive-operative sense of the 'overcoming' of problems and the 'success' of learning processes. What we learn from reality through active dealings with it and what we learn from objections through discursive exchange about them become sedimented in justified interpretations . . .

When one adopts this pragmatistic concept of knowledge, a naturalism presents itself which, despite detranscendentalisation, leaves intact the transcendental difference between the world and the inner-worldly. This conception rests on a single metatheoretical assumption: that 'our' learning processes, in the sense of being possible in socio-cultural forms of life alone, in a certain way only continue preceding 'evolutionary learning processes' which for their part have brought forth the structures of our forms of life. Then those structures making the learning processes of our species transcendentally possible in turn qualify as the result of less complex, natural-historical learning processes – and *thus acquire cognitive import themselves*. The 'continuation' of learning processes on a higher level, however, must be understood only in the sense of a 'weak' naturalism with which no reductionist claims are associated. A 'strict' naturalistic explanatory strategy wants to replace the conceptual analysis of lifeworldy practices by a natural scientific one, for instance a neurological or biogenetic explanation of the achievements of the human brain. A weak naturalism, by contrast, contents itself with the fundamental background assumption that the organic endowment and cultural way of life of *Homo sapiens* have a 'natural' origin and are basically accessible to an evolutionary explanation.

This proleptic presupposition of a natural-historical continuity which reaches through culture, as it were, refrains from every philosophical assumption about the relation of body and mind (e.g. in the sense of an eliminative or reductive materialism); to the contrary, it protects us from the reification of a distinction between methodological orientations which are originally ontologically neutral. As long as we retain the transcendental question, we are required to separate the hermeneutically oriented rational reconstruction of the structures of the lifeworld, which we undertake from the participant perspective, strictly from the observationally spearheaded causal analysis of the natural-historical formation of these structures. It is the idealistic fallacy of concluding from a methodological distinction that there is an ontological opposition between mind and body (or between Being and beings) which first leads to the temptation to locate the transcendental conditions of objective experience in a transmundane domain of the intelligible – or of the history of Being. On the other hand, the naturalistic fallacy according to which transcendental conditions could *without ceremony* – that is, without recourse to the problem of self-reference – be assimilated to empirical conditions and be projected into an empirically objectified realm, is but the reverse of the same medal.

Weak naturalism avoids the strategy of either taking up the 'internal perspective' of the lifeworld into the 'external view' of the objective world or of subordinating the former to the latter. It rather joins the *still separately maintained* theoretical perspectives on the metatheoretical level through the assumption of a continuity between nature and culture. This background assumption is specified in such a way, however, that the natural evolution of the species – *in analogy* to our own learning processes at the socio-cultural level of development – can be understood as a sequence of 'problem solutions' which has led to always more complex levels of development with correspondingly higher levels of learning. How this analogy is to be understood and how far the initially metaphoric expression of 'evolutionary learning' extends, is then a question which cannot be decided within the framework of any one of the two theories – theories which are for the first time related to one another through this analogy. The vocabulary of learning, which first obtains a precise sense from 'our' participant perspective (and for instance underlies the learning concepts of developmental psychology), may in turn not simply be reinterpreted in neo-Darwinstic concepts. Otherwise weak naturalism looses its point. The interpolation of a 'scale' of learning processes of different levels explains only why we could retain the transcendental difference between world and the inner-worldly without having to project the contingency of 'the for us necessary' from empirical processes on this side to the occurrence of the history of Being on the other side. For the conception of natural evolution as a process *analogous to learning* secures a cognitive import for those naturally formed structures making possible our learning processes *themselves*. This again explains why the generality and necessity of 'our' view of the objective world need not be impaired by the contingent circumstances of their genesis.

When natural evolution is regarded from the point of view of growing problem-solving capacities, the emergent properties at any given time obtain a cognitive value which from 'our' point of view counts as a growth of knowledge. This also applies to the emergent properties which characterise socio-cultural forms of life as such. Also the structures which make experiences of and statements about something in the – for us – objective world transcendentally possible, can then be understood as the outcome of a cognitively relevant process of formation. Whatever proves to be a presupposition without alternatives in 'our' epistemic situation such that every attempt to contradict or revise it seems senseless, we indeed regard in terms of the naturalistic background assumptions as one which emerged under contingent circumstances. But when these (in a weak sense) transcendental conditions have resulted from cognitively relevant adaptation, construction and selection processes (or can be conceived as having thus arisen), then the contingency of the 'for us' necessary and in any case insuperable epistemic horizon can no longer be associated with the modality of a chance process which is cognitively neutral. The analogy of learning, which we transfer to developments regulated by mutation, selection and stabilisation, qualifies the endowment of the human mind as an intelligent problem solution arrived at under the restrictive conditions of reality. This position pulls the rug from under the idea of a species-relative worldview.

Realism without representation

Kantian pragmatism is an answer to a disturbing epistemological consequence of the turn from the philosophy of consciousness to the philosophy of language. Our capacity for knowledge can no longer be analysed, as mentalism assumes, independently of our abilities to speak and act, because we find ourselves also as knowing subjects always already within the horizon of our lifeworldly practices. Language and reality interpenetrate each other in a manner that we are unable to disentangle. Every experience is linguistically impregnated, with the result that a linguistically unfiltered grasp of reality is impossible. This insight provides a strong motive for ascribing to the intersubjective conditions of linguistic interpretation and understanding the transcendental role which Kant reserved for the necessary subjective conditions of objective experience. The place of the transcendental subjectivity of consciousness is taken by the detranscendentalised intersubjectivity of the lifeworld.

So far the transcendental-philosophical sequence of explanations which enter with reflection on one's own achievements still remains untouched by the linguistic turn. Wittgenstein's language game pluralism even suggests a transcendental-idealistic interpretation. When transcendental pragmatism links with a weak naturalism, however, the genetic primacy of nature over culture already compels a cognitive-realist conception. The cognitive-realistic presupposition of an intersubjectively accessible, objective world alone can harmonise the *epistemic* priority of the linguistically articulated horizon of the lifeworld, which we cannot transgress, with the *ontological* priority of a lingustically independent reality which imposes limits on our practices. The presupposition of a world 'independent of the mind' which is 'older' than humans admits, of course, different interpretations.

The medieval controversy about universals, of which Peirce had still been very aware, has left its traces after the linguistic turn in opposing interpretations of the concept of world. When the formal-pragmatically assumed 'world' is everything that is the case, that is, 'the totality of facts, not of things' (Wittgenstein), then we have to reckon with abstract entities such as the content of statements or propositions as 'something in the world'. In opposition to this concept-realistic assumption of an 'in itself' propositionally structured world, nominalism understands the world as the totality of spatio-temporally individuated 'objects' about which we can make statements of fact . . .

(a) From an ontological point of view, the nominalistic conception is metaphysically less suspicious than concept-realism . . . The praxis of rule governed behaviour about which we 'always already' agree, however, reveals a familiarity with the 'existing generalities' of a lifeworld which is throughout normatively structured by rules. To this extent, participation in these practices freely gives rise to a concept-realistic view. This concept-realism takes on the form of Platonism only when it is projected over the horizon the linguistically structured lifeworld onto the structure of the objective world itself.

(b) Once *grammatical* concept-realism is extended to the world itself, we witness the return – in a postmentalistic Fregean version – also of the mirror model of knowledge which pragmatism for good reasons has overcome . . . Concept-realism ascribes to experience the function of sensorily picturing facts and making them present – or of intellectual contemplation. This contemplative concept of experience, however, eliminates the space for the *constructive* contribution which social subjects from within their lifeworld through intelligent dealings with a risky and disillusioning reality make to consequential problem solutions and successful learning processes. If experience is a medium in which the picturing or copying of existing states of affairs takes place, then the objectivity of knowledge demands the eradication without any trace of all constructive ingredients. By contrast, it is the linking of construction and experience which for the first time makes our fallibilism comprehensible. Only the constructive contribution of our operations to knowledge explains why the expansion of knowledge must pass through the sluice of the permanent revision of available knowledge, and why also well-grounded knowledge can be false.

Both arguments put forward under (a) and (b) speak for an 'ontological division of labour'. In the basic concepts of realism and nominalism is mirrored the methodological distinction between the hermeneutic access of the participant to the intersubjectively shared lifeworld, on the one hand, and the objectifying orientation of the hypothesis-testing observer in interaction with what confronts him in the world, on the other. Grammatical concept-realism is focused on a lifeworld in whose practices we participate and out of whose horizon we cannot step. By contrast, the nominalistic grasp of the objective world accounts for the insight that we may not reify the structure of the statement by means of which we describe something in the world into the structure of what exists itself. Simultaneously, the conceptualisation of the world as the 'totality of things, not of facts' explains how language gets in contact with the world. The concept of 'reference' must explain how the ontological priority of a nominalistically grasped objective world can be related to the epistemic priority of the linguistically articulated world. For epistemic priority may not consume ontological priority when we understand the transcendental fact of learning in a realistic sense.

Truth and justification

The reality with which we confront our statement is no 'naked' reality, but itself already linguistically impregnated . . . It seems as though the truth of a statement could only be vouched for by its coherence with other already accepted statements. A strict contextualism, however, can be reconciled neither with the cognitive-realistic presupposition, nor with the revisionary power of learning processes which change their enabling context from the inside, nor with the universalstic sense of context-transcending truth claims.

The attempt to combine the language-transcendent understanding of reference with a language-immanent understanding of truth as ideal assertability (*Behaupt-barkeit*) offers a way out of this dilemma . . . Linking up with Pierce's famous proposal, K.-O. Apel, H. Putnam and I have from time to time defended some version or another of such a discourse concept of truth . . . The epistemic formulation of the concept of truth transforms the (twofold) validity of statement >p< into the (three-fold) validity 'for us' – the ideal auditorium (Perelman) who must be able to justify a truth claim raised in respect of >p<, if there is sufficient ground to do so . . . Objections have induced me to a revision which *relates* the *retained* discourse concept of rational acceptability to a pragmatistically conceived, non-epistemic concept of truth, without assimilating 'truth' to 'ideal assertability' . . . This non-epistemic concept of truth . . . makes itself felt only operatively, thus only unthematically, in action . . .

Advances in legality

The question now arises whether the reasons which led to the surrendering of the epistemic concept of truth do not have consequences also for the concept of normative correctness.

In the present context, I do not have to go into questions concerning the grounding of discourse ethics. Of interest here is only that a cognitivist yet non-realist conception of morality as ever requires an epistemic concept of 'moral truth' or correctness. The validity of a norm consists of its discursively demonstrable recognisability; a valid norm deserves to be recognised because and to the extent that it could be accepted, that is, be recognised as valid, also under (approximate) ideal conditions of justification. Now, the revised concept of truth indeed leaves the rationalising force of a public and inclusive, violence-free and decentring form of argumentation among equals intact, but it relates the result of a successful justification to something in the objective world. Such a reference point transcending justification is lacking in the case of the correctness of moral judgements and norms. The concept of 'normative correctness' is absorbed by rational assertability under ideal conditions; its lacks the ontological connotation of a relation to objects in respect of which we assert facts.

The place of the resistance of objects on which we work in the lifeworld is here taken by the contradictions of social opponents whose value-orientations come into conflict with ours. This objectivity of another mind is made of softer matter, as it were, than the objectivity of a surprising world. However, if moral validity claims owe their obligatory force to an unconditionality *analogous to truth*, then the orientation towards the ever-widening inclusion of other claims and persons must compensate the lacking reference to the objective world. In fact, the moral point of view from which we design the ideally expanded social world of legitimately regulated interpersonal relations can provide an equivalent for the assumption of a world over which we do not freely dispose, for it is rooted in the equally unavailable pragmatic presuppositions of argumentation praxis.

Against the foil of the non-epistemic concept of truth, the epistemic concept of correctness for the first time places the constructivist thrust of discourse ethics in a proper light. Subjects capable of speech and action evaluate relevant actions and conflicts with a view to a yet to be realised universe of well-ordered interpersonal relations which they themselves *design*. To be sure, they argue from a moral point of view over which they as participants in argumentation do not dispose and which to that extent *restricts* their justificatory praxis. It is not up to them how they construct the 'realm of goals', but they design it as a universe which they themselves still have to realise. The sense of normative correctness lacks ontological connotations since moral judgements are oriented by, if not a freely chosen, then nevertheless an ideally drafted social world which cannot become real without the assistance of the morally acting subjects themselves.

Connected with this constructivism is, in any case after the detranscendentalisation of the free will of intelligible beings, that problem of self-referential moral action which Hegel unfolded in the *Phenomenology of Mind* with reference to the French Revolution . . . According to which moral standards should praxis, which is aimed at the legal institutionalisation of the presuppositions of expected moral action, orient itself? . . . Irrespective of whether with the clear conscience of the philosophy of history or without it, every morally self-referential action entangles the participants in problems . . . When one considers that constructivism replaces the static natural law assumption of eternally valid laws with the dynamics of intelligent yet morally reasonable legislation, a different view emerges which at least tones down these problems . . . A first step has already been taken in that these problems are no longer reserved for the supposed experts, but have been given over to worldwide legitimation controversies. The participants are moreover in a position to appreciate that such public controversies must be unfolded this side of the philosophy of history or worldviews in the light of publicly acceptable reasons.

Further reading

General anthologies

Brodbergen, M. (ed.) (1968) *Readings in the Philosophy of the Social Sciences*. London: Macmillan.

Brown, S.C. (ed.) (1979) *Philosophical Disputes in the Social Science*. Brighton: Harvester.

Emmett, D. and Macintyre, A. (eds) (1970) *Sociological Theory and Philosophical Analysis*. London: Macmillan.

Feigl, H. and Brodbeck, M. (eds) (1953) *The Philosophy of Science*. New York: Appelton-Century-Crofts.

Martin, M. and McIntyre, L.C. (eds) (1994) *Readings in the Philosophy of Social Science*. Cambridge, MA: MIT Press.

Natanson, M. (ed.) (1963) *Philosophy of the Social Sciences: A Reader*. New York: Random House.

General surveys

Baert, P. (1998) *Social Theory in the Twentieth Century*. Cambridge: Polity Press.

Benton, T. (1977) *The Philosophical Foundations of the Three Sociologies*. London: Routledge & Kegan Paul.

Benton, T. and Craib, I. (2001) *Philosophy of Social Science*. London: Palgrave.

Blakie, N. (1993) *Approaches to Social Inquiry*. Cambridge: Polity Press.

Braybrooke, D. (1987) *Philosophy of Social Science*. Englewood Cliffs, NJ: Prentice-Hall.

Delanty, G. (1997) *Social Science: Beyond Constructivism and Realism*. Buckingham: Open University Press.

Gordon, S. (1991) *The History and Philosophy of Social Science*. London: Routledge.

Hindess, B. (1977) *Philosophy and Methodology in the Social Sciences*. Brighton: Harvester.

Manicas, P. (1987) *A History and Philosophy of Social Sciences*. Oxford: Blackwell.

May, T. and William, M. (eds) (1998) *Knowing the Social World*. Buckingham: Open University Press.

Outhwaite, W. (1987) *New Philosophies of Social Science: Realism, Hermeneutics and Critical Theory*. London: Macmillan.

Radnitzky, G. (1970) *Contemporary Schools of Metascience*. Gotenburg: Akademieforlaget.

Ryan, A. (1970) *The Philosophy of the Social Sciences*. London: Macmillan.

Sayer, A. (1992) *Method in Social Science*. London: Routledge.

Turner, B.S. (ed.) (1999) *The Blackwell Companion to Social Theory*, 2nd edn. Oxford: Blackwell. See in particular the chapter by W. Outhwaite.

Wagner, P. (2001) *A History and Theory of the Social Sciences*. London: Sage.

Webb, K. (1995) *An Introduction to the Problems in the Philosophy of Social Science*. London: Pinter.

Part 1: Positivism, its dissolution and the emergence of post-empiricism

Alexander, J. (1982) Theoretical logic, in *Sociology, Vol. 1: Positivism, Presuppositions, and Current Controversies*. Berkeley, CA: University of California Press.

Apel, K.-O. (1967) *Analytic Philosophy of Language and the 'Geisteswissenschaften'*. Dordrecht: Reidel.

Barnes, B. (1982) *T.S. Kuhn and Social Science*. London: Macmillan.

Brown, R. (1963) *Explanation in Social Science*. London: Routledge & Kegan Paul.

Bryant, C. (1985) *Positivism in Social Theory and Research*. London: Macmillan.

Chalmers, A.F. (1999) *What is This Thing Called Science?* 3rd edn. Buckingham: Open University Press.

Fuller, S. (1993) *The Philosophy of Science and its Discontents*, 2nd edn. New York: Guilford.

Fuller, S. (2000) *Thomas Kuhn: A Philosophical History for our Times*, Chicago: Chicago University Press.

Giddens, A. (1974) *Positivism and Sociology*. London: Heinemann.

Giddens, A. (1976) *New Rules of Sociological Method*. London: Hutchinson.

Giddens, A. (1995) Comte, Popper and Positivism, in *Politics, Sociology and Social Theory*. Cambridge: Polity Press.

Giddens, A. and Turner, J. (eds) (1987) *Social Theory Today*. Cambridge: Polity Press.

Gilles, D. (1993) *Philosophy of Science in the Twentieth Century*. Oxford: Blackwell.

Gower, B. (1997) *Scientific Method: An Historical and Philosophical Introduction*. London: Routledge.

Halfpenny, P. (1982) *Positivism and Sociology*. London: Allen & Unwin.

Holmwood, J. and Steward, A. (1991) *Explanation and Social Theory*. London: Macmillan.

Laudan, L. (1996) *Beyond Positivism and Relativism*. Bouldner, CO: Westview.

Rorty, R. (1980) *Philosophy and the Mirror of Nature*. Oxford: Blackwell.

Rudner, R. (1966) *Philosophy of Social Science*. Englewood Cliffs, NJ: Prentice-Hall.

Stockman, N. (1983) *Antipositivist Theories of the Sciences*. Dordrecht: Reidel.

Part 2: The interpretative tradition

Apel, K.-O. (1980) *The Transformation of Philosophy*. London: Routledge & Kegan Paul.

Apel, K.-O. (1996) *Selected Essays*, Vol. 2. Atlantic Heights, NJ: Humanities Press.

Bauman, Z. (1987) *Hermeneutics and Social Science*. London: Hutchinson.

Bleicher, J. (ed.) (1980) *Contemporary Hermeneutics*. London: Routledge & Kegan Paul.

Dallmayr, F.R. and McCarthy, T.A. (eds) (1977) *Understanding and Social Inquiry*. Notre Dame: University of Notre Dame Press.

Fyvbjerg, B. (2001) *Making Science Matter*. Cambridge: Cambridge University Press.

Giddens, A. (1982) Hermeneutics and social theory, in *Profiles and Critiques in Social Theory*. Berkeley, CA: University of California Press.

Hollis, M. and Lukes, S. (eds) (1982) *Rationality and Relativism*. Cambridge, MA: MIT Press.

Luckmann, T. (ed.) (1978) *Phenomenology and Sociology*. Harmondsworth: Penguin.

Outhwaite, W. (1975) *Understanding Social Life: The Method Called Verstehen*. London: Allen & Unwin.

Outhwaite, W. (1983) *Concept Formation in Social Science*. London: Routledge.

Palmer, R.E. (1969) *Hermeneutics: Interpretation Theory in Schleiermacher, Dilthey, Heidegger and Gadamer*. Evanston, IL: Northwestern University Press.

Rabinow, P. and Sullivan, M. (eds) (1979) *Interpretative Social Science*. Berkeley, CA: University of California Press.

Ricoeur, P. (1970) *Freud and Philosophy: An Essay on Interpretation*. New Haven, CT: Yale University Press.

Runicman, W.G. (1972) *A Critique of Max Weber's Philosophy of Science*. Cambridge: Cambridge University Press.

Snow, A.P. (1993) *The Two Cultures*. Cambridge: Cambridge University Press.

Thompson, J.B. (1981) *Critical Hermeneutics: A Study in the Thought of Paul Ricoeur and Jürgen Habermas* Cambridge: Cambridge University Press.

Part 3: The critical tradition

Aronowitz, S. (1981) *The Crisis in Historical Materialism: Class, Politics and Culture in Marxist Theory*. South Hadley, MA: J.F. Bergin.

Connerton, P. (ed.) (1976) *Critical Sociology*. Harmondsworth: Penguin.

Dubiel, H. (1985) *Theory and Politics: Studies in the Development of Critical Theory*. London: MIT Press.

Fay, B. (1975) *Social Theory and Political Practice*. London: Allen & Unwin.

Fay, B. (1987) *Critical Social Science*. Cambridge: Polity Press.

Habermas, J. (1984) *The Theory of Communicative Action*, Vol. 1: *Reason and the Rationalization of Society*. London: Heinemann.

Habermas, J. (1987) *The Philosophical Discourse of Modernity*. Cambridge, MA: MIT Press.

Habermas, J. (1988) *On the Logic of the Social Sciences*. Cambridge, MA: MIT Press.

Held, D. (1984) *Introduction to Critical Theory*. Berkeley, CA: University of California Press.

Honneth, A. (1994) *The Critique of Power*. Cambridge, MA: MIT Press.

Jay, M. (1976) *The Dialectical Imagination: A History of the Frankfurt School and the Institute of Social Research, 1923–1950*. London: Heinemann.

Jay, M. (1984) *Marxism and Totality: The Adventures of a Concept from Lukács to Habermas*. Berkeley, CA: University of California Press.

Keat, R. (1981) *The Politics of Social Theory: Habermas, Freud and the Critique of Positivism*. Oxford: Blackwell.

Keat, R. and Urry, J. (1975) *Social Theory as Science*. London: Routledge & Kegan Paul.

O'Neill, J. (ed.) (1977) *On Critical Theory*. London: Heinemann.

Rasmussen, D.M. (ed.) (1996) *Handbook of Critical Theory*. Oxford: Blackwell.

Romm, N. (1991) *The Methodologies of Positivism and Marxism: A Sociological Debate*. New York: Macmillan.

Wiggerhaus, R. (1994) *The Frankfurt School: Its History, Theories and Political Significance.* Cambridge, MA: MIT Press.

Part 4: Pragmatism, semiotics and transcendental pragmatics

Aboulafia, M., Bookman, M. and Kamp, C. (eds) (2002) *Habermas and Pragmatism.* London: Routledge.

Apel, K.-O. (1981) *Charles S. Peirce: From Pragmatism to Pragmaticism.* Amherst, MA: University of Massachusetts Press.

Apel, K.-O. (1984) *Understanding and Explantion: A Transcendental-Pragmatic Perspective.* Cambridge, MA: MIT Press.

Apel, K.-O. (1996) *Selected Essays,* Vol. 2. Atlantic Heights, NJ: Humanities Press.

Griffith, D.R. et al. (2001) *Founders of Constructivist Postmodern Philosophy: Peirce, James, Bergon, Whithead and Hartshorne.* New York: State University of New York Press.

Joas, H. (1993) *Pragmatism and Social Theory.* Chicago: Chicago University Press.

Lewis, J.D. and Smart, R.L. (1980) *American Sociology and Pragmatism.* Chicago: Chicago University Press.

Lynd, R. (1939) *Knowledge for What? The Place of Social Science in American Culture.* Princeton, CA: Princeton University Press.

Mills, C.W. (1966) *Sociology and Pragmatism.* New York: Oxford University Press.

Mills, C.W. (1970) *The Sociological Imagination.* Harmonsworth: Penguin.

Rorty, R. (1982) *The Consequences of Pragmatism.* Minneapolis, MN: University of Minesota Press.

Part 5: The structuralist controversy: language, discourse and practice

Benton, T. (1984) *The Rise and Fall of Structural Marxism.* London: Macmillan.

DeGeorge, R. and DeGeorge, F. (eds) (1972) *The Structuralists.* New York: Anchor Books.

Dreyfus, H. and Rabinow, R. (eds) (1982) *Michel Foucault: Beyond Structuralism and Hermeneutics.* Chicago: University of Chicago Press.

Foucault, M. (1997) *Michel Foucault: The Essential Works,* Vol. 1: *Ethics.* London: Alan Lane.

Gutting, G. (ed.) (1994) *The Cambridge Companion to Foucault.* Cambridge: Cambridge University Press.

Hoy, D.C. (ed.) (1990) *The Foucault Reader.* Cambridge: Polity Press.

Kelly, M. (ed.) (1994) *Critique and Power: Recasting the Foucault/Habermas Debate.* Cambridge, MA: MIT Press.

Lecourt, D. (1995) *Marxism and Epistemology: Bachelard, Canguilhem and Foucault.* London: New Left Books.

Macksey, R. and Donato, E. (eds) (1970) *The Languages of Criticism and the Sciences of Man: The Structuralist Controversy.* London: Johns Hopkins University Press.

Swartz, P. (1997) *Culture and Power: The Sociology of Pierre Bourdieu.* Chicago: Chicago University Press.

Part 6: New directions and challenges

Abell, P. (ed.) (1991) *Rational Choice Theory*. Aldershot: Edward Elgar.

Archer, M. et al. (eds) (1998) *Critical Realism: Essential Readings*. London: Routledge.

Bateson, G. (1973) *Steps to an Ecology of Mind*. St Albans: Paladin.

Bechtel, W. and Graham, G. (eds) (1998) *A Companion to Cognitive Science*. Oxford: Blackwell.

Berger, P. and Luckmann, T. (1967) *The Social Construction of Reality*. London: Alan Lane.

Bernstein, R.J. (1976) *The Restructuring of Social and Political Theory*. Oxford: Blackwell.

Bernstein, R.J. (1983) *Beyond Objectivism and Relativism*. Oxford: Blackwell.

Bohman, J. (1991) *New Philosophies of Social Science: Problems of Indeterminacy*. Cambridge, MA: Harvard University Press.

Collier, A. (1993) *Critical Realism*. London: Verso.

Delanty, G. (2000) *Modernity and Postmodernity*. London: Sage.

de Mey, M. (1982) *The Cognitive Paradigm*. Dordrecht: Reidel.

Fuller, S. (2002) *Social Epistemology*, 2nd edn. Bloomington, IN: Indiana University Press.

Gergen, K. (2000) *Social Construction in Context*. London: Sage.

Habermas, J. (2002) *Truth and Justification: Philosophical Essays*. Cambridge, MA: MIT Press.

Hacking, I. (1999) *The Social Constructivism of What?* Cambridge, MA: Harvard University Press.

Harding, S. (1986) *The Science Question in Feminism*. Ithaca, NY: Cornell University Press.

Harding, S. (1991) *Whose Science? Whose Knowledge? Thinking from Women's Lives*. Ithaca, NY: Cornell University Press.

Harding, S. and Hintikka, M.B. (eds) (1983) *Discovering Reality: Feminist Perspectives on Epistemology, Metaphysics, Methodology and Philosophy of Science*. Dordrecht: Reidel.

Harré, R. (1986) *Varieties of Realism*. Oxford: Blackwell.

Hill Collins, P. (1990) *Black Feminist Thought, Consciousness and the Politics of Empowerment*. London: HarperCollins.

Knorr-Cetina, K. and Cicourel, A.V. (eds) (1981) *Advances in Social Theory and Methodology*. London: Routledge & Kegan Paul.

Krohn, W., Küppers, G. and Nowotny, H. (1990) *Self-Organization: Portrait of a Scientific Revolution*. Dordrecht: Kluwer.

Kukla, A. (2000) *Social Constructivism and the Philosophy of Science* London: Routledge.

Latour, B. (1987) *Science in Action*. Cambridge, MA: Harvard University Press.

Latour, B. (1993) *We Have Never Been Modern*. Hemel Hempstead: Harvester Wheatsheaf.

Maturana, H.R. and Varela, F.J. (1980) *Autopoiesis and Cognition: The Realization of the Living*. Dordrecht: Reidel.

Maturana, H.R. and Varela, F.J. (1992) *The Tree of Knowledge: The Biological Roots of Human Understanding*. Boston, MA: Shambhala.

McCarthy, D.E. (1996) *Knowledge as Culture: The New Sociology of Knowledge*. London: Routledge.

Nicholson, L. (ed.) (1990) *Feminism/Postmodernism*. London: Routledge.

O'Neill, J. (1972) *Sociology as a Skin Trade*. London: Routledge and Kegan Paul.

Putnam, H. (1975) *Mind, Language and Reality*. Cambridge: Cambridge University Press.

Sayer, A. (2000) *Realism and Social Science*. London: Sage.

Smith, D. (1987) *The Everyday World as Problematic: A Feminist Sociology*. Milton Keynes: Open University Press.

Strydom, P. (1999) Triple contingency, *Philosophy and Social Criticism*, 25(2): 1–25.

Tanesini, A. (1998) *An Introduction to Feminist Methodologies*. Oxford: Blackwell.

Turner, S. (2002) *Brains/Practices/Relativism: Social Theory After Cognitive Science*. Chicago: University of Chicago Press.

Varela, F.J., Thompson, E. and Rosch, E. (1993) *The Embodied Mind*. Dordrecht: Kluwer. Cambridge, MA: MIT Press.

von Glasersfeld, E. (1995) *Radical Constructivism: A Way of Knowing and Learning*. London: Falmer Press.

Watzlawick, P. (ed.) (1984) *Invented Reality: How Do We Know What We Believe We Know? Contributions to Constructivism*. New York: Norton.

INDEX

POSTMODERNISM AND SOCIAL RESEARCH

Mats Alvesson

- What is postmodernism?
- How can it be used to develop social research?
- How can we do social research in more creative ways?

This book integrates philosophical and theoretical ideas with fieldwork and supports the development of research methods with a sharper interpretative and self-critical edge. It provides an overview of postmodern themes, evaluates the possibilities and dangers of postmodernist thinking and develops ideas on how a selective, sceptical incorporation of postmodernism can make social research more conscious about problems and pitfalls, and more creative in working with empirical material (so called 'data'). A reflexive orientation runs throughout the book, which addresses themes such as how to understand the individual in research, how to deal with the knowledge/power connection, how to relate to language and how to unpack rather than take for granted socially dominant categories in research work. One chapter addresses the research interview in the light of postmodernist concerns about the naivety of assuming that the interviewee is simply an informant, a truth-teller authentically expressing his or her experiences and meaning. Other chapters address issues of voice, interpretation, writing and reflexivity. The book includes a range of empirical illustrations of how postmodernist ideas can inspire social research, and in all it represents an essential text for students and researchers alike.

Contents

Series editor's foreword – Preface – Introduction – Postmodernism: a sceptical overview – Key themes in postmodernism – Taking language seriously – Unpacking categories – Postmodernism and interviews – Interpreting and writing – Selectively applying pomo thinking: an illustration – Conclusions – Suggested further readings – Glossary – References – Index.

224pp   0 335 20631 X (Paperback)   0 335 20632 8 (Hardback)

SOCIAL RESEARCH
ISSUES, METHODS AND PROCESS

Tim May

The third edition of this tried and tested book works very well and should be extremely successful . . . its strength is that it covers all the principal areas of research in an accessible and lively style, treating each approach in relation to the philosophical and methodological debates that underpin them. It is logically organized and each chapter is well-structured . . . complex topics are clearly explained for the inexperienced reader, at the same time it contains enough of substance and food for thought for more advanced students.

John Scott, University of Essex

Praise for the previous edition:

This is the finest introduction to social research I have ever read . . . Methods are meticulously worked through from official statistics to comparative research via surveys, interviews, observation and documentary analysis . . . The writing is clear, concise and scholarly with the bibliography a delightful A to Z compendium of the best in sociology.

British Sociological Association Network

The fully revised and updated third edition of this hugely popular text incorporates the latest developments in the interdisciplinary field of social research, while retaining the style and structure that appealed to so many in the first two editions. Tim May successfully bridges the gap between theory and methods in social research, clearly illuminating these essential components for understanding the dynamics of social relations.

The book is divided into two parts, with Part I examining the issues and perspectives in social research and Part II setting out the methods and processes. Revisions and additions have been made to Part I to take account of new ways of thinking about the relationship between theory and research, and values and ethics in the research process. These take on board advances in post-empiricist thinking, as well as the relations between values, objectivity and data collection. Where necessary, recommended readings and references to studies that form the bases of discussions throughout the book have been updated. In Part II, additions have been made to the chapter on questionnaires, and elsewhere, new discussions have been introduced, for example, on research on the Internet, narratives, case studies and new technologies. The reader will detect many other changes, the intention of which is to aid understanding by staying up-to-date with the latest innovations in social research. The chapters follow a common structure to enable a clear appreciation of the place, process and analysis of each method, and to allow the comparison of their strengths and weaknesses in the context of discussions in Part I.

The clear writing style, chapter summaries, questions for reflection and signposts to further readings continue to make this book the ideal companion to social research for students across the social sciences. In addition, it will be recognized as an invaluable source of reference for those practising and teaching social research who wish to keep abreast of key developments in the field.

Contents
Acknowledgements – Preface to the second edition – Preface to the third edition – Introduction – Part one: Issues in social research – Perspectives on social scientific research – Social theory and social research – Values and ethics in the research process – Part two: Methods of social research – Official statistics: topic and resource – Social surveys: design to analysis – Interviewing: methods and process – Participant observation: perspectives and practice – Documentary research: excavations and evidence – Comparative research: potential and problems – Bibliography – Author index – Subject index.

272pp   0 335 20612 3 (Paperback)   0 335 20613 1 (Hardback)

openup

ideas and understanding
in social science

www.**openup**.co.uk

 **Browse, search and
order online**

 **Download detailed
title information and
sample chapters***

*for selected titles

www.**openup**.co.uk